# The Information Society Reader

Edited by

## Frank Webster

with the assistance of

## Raimo Blom, Erkki Karvonen, Harri Melin, Kaarle Nordenstreng and Ensio Puoskari

 Routledge
Taylor & Francis Group

LONDON AND NEW YORK

First published 2004
by Routledge
11 New Fetter Lane, London EC4P 4EE

Simultaneously published in the USA and Canada
by Routledge
29 West 35th Street, New York, NY 10001

*Routledge is an imprint of the Taylor & Francis Group*

Typeset in Perpetua and Bell Gothic by
Florence Production Ltd, Stoodleigh, Devon
Printed and bound in Great Britain by
TJ International Ltd, Padstow, Cornwall

*British Library Cataloguing in Publication Data*
A catalogue record for this book is available from the British Library

*Library of Congress Cataloging in Publication Data*
The information society reader / edited by Frank Webster; with the assistance
of Raimo Blom . . . [*et al.*].
p. cm. – (Routledge student readers)
Includes bibliographical references and index.
1. Information society. 2. Information technology – Social aspects.
I. Webster, Frank. II. Blom, Raimo. III. Title. IV. Series.
HM851.I545 2004
303.48′33–dc21                                    2003012385

ISBN 0–415–31927–7 (hbk)
ISBN 0–415–31928–5 (pbk)

# The Information Society Reader

There has been much debate over the idea of 'the information society'. Some thinkers have argued that information is becoming the key ordering principle in society, whereas others suggest that the rise of information has been overstated. Whatever the case, though, it cannot be denied that 'informatization' has produced vast changes in advanced societies. *The Information Society Reader* pulls together the main contributions to this debate from some of the key figures in the field. Major topics addressed include:

- Post-industrialism and Globalization
- Surveillance
- Transformations
- The Network Society
- Democracy
- Digital Divisions
- Virtual Relations.

With a comprehensive introduction from Frank Webster, and section introductions contextualizing the readings, *The Information Society Reader* will be an invaluable resource for students and academics studying contemporary society and all things cyber.

**Frank Webster** is Professor of Sociology at City University, London. He is author of *Theories of the Information Society*, 2nd edition (Routledge, 2002).

# Routledge Student Readers

Series Editor: Chris Jenks, Professor of Sociology,
Goldsmiths College, University of London

Already in this series:

## Theories of Race and Racism: A Reader
Edited by Les Back and John Solomos

## Gender: A Sociological Reader
Edited by Stevi Jackson and Sue Scott

## The Sociology of Health and Illness: A Reader
Edited by Mike Bury and Jonathan Gabe

## Social Research Methods: A Reader
Edited by Clive Seale

# Contents

# Series editor's preface

WELCOME TO THIS, the fifth in our series of *Routledge Student Readers* and one that is very much concerned with both the condition and signs of our times. Sociology has always been centrally concerned with describing, analysing and accounting for social change at the level of face-to-face interaction and through to the level of social structures. Although there are often disjunctions between these different levels what is most significant is the way that, over time, they stabilize and fit. For most of the last century social theory has been able to recognize major differences between societies or stages of development within the same society according to the organization of the division of labour and, to a large extent, the mode of economy that gave rise to such an organization. So dominant notions like pre-industrial and industrial, pre-capitalist and capitalist have served us well. However, towards the end of the twentieth century social change appeared to accelerate more than we had previously acknowledged and the social orders that we cling to became far more fragile, tenuous and liable to fragmentation. One of the main reasons for this transformation occurs in relation to both the product of our labour but also in our ability to communicate that product to one another. This is the age of 'information'.

Of course people still make things, though increasingly machines do such work for them, but the major currency in the contemporary market place is ideas. Whole industries have become established in the production of ideas, images and processes all in the form of information. Alongside this development and having an elective affinity with its progress is the growth of information technology.

Although it could not be argued that this is yet a global phenomenon, in as much as people still die of starvation in Ethiopia despite, or some might say because of, the information explosion its influence is extensive and growing. Within the nations that previously comprised the Western world information and IT permeate social relations. Explanation and, to some degree, knowledge has become formulaic, packaged and systemic, and people expect it to be so. Means of communication are legion and personalized and instant. The handcrafted letter and the large black Bakelite telephone *per* family now recede as distant memories. Now everyone of a certain age (and above) seems to sport an earphone and/or a microphone. People in public as well as private places speak into objects the size of their palms or tap maniacally at them in order to 'text' an absent friend in abbreviated code. I begin to sound disapproving yet inevitably admit to the possession of such gadgetry and confess to the inability to begin the day, let alone regularly punctuate the day, without visits to my omnipresent screens and keyboards to reply with absolute priority to the endless accumulation of email traffic.

This all-pervading presence, use and expectation of information makes up the 'information society'. But this is not just a way of describing contemporary accessories, styles, patterns of consumption or fashion. This sense of information describes the manner and the texture of social relations both face-to-face and at the level of the social structure. Wars on television, political 'spin', public relations, air traffic control, international money markets, banking, new forms of educational delivery, entertainment, interior design, eating, personal relationships, talk – all of this, and more, is part of the information society. So, now, are you and I.

Frank Webster is the ideal person to provide us with a guide and a critical appraisal of these overwhelming developments in modern society. He has been researching and publishing in this area of work for the last decade and has a reputation, both national and international, based on his seminal contributions to this field. I believe that this reader will soon establish itself as an important and well-regarded landmark in this area of sociological thinking.

The way this work is organized will surely provoke the reader's critical awareness. It is most important that those of us who are living through or perhaps inheriting the 'information society' as a way of life and a future, should be able to appreciate its possibilities for liberation and creativity but also that we should never be forgetful of the constraints, the surveillance, the differential exercise of power and the reconfigurations that it places on our day-to-day activities and relationships.

*Chris Jenks*
Professor of Sociology
Goldsmiths College, University of London

# Acknowledgements

IN PUTTING TOGETHER THIS READER we have been compelled to reduce the length of most of our selections for reasons of limited space. We wanted to offer a large range of work within the covers of an affordable student text, and this we have done, but a price is that many contributions have had to be severely edited. We thank our authors for their forbearance in this and would warn our readers of the attendant dangers. We recommend advanced readers especially to return to the originals wherever feasible in order to gain the fullest appreciation of the authors' intentions. Full details of our selections are given on the first page of each chapter.

The publishers would like to thank the following for permission to reprint their material:

Blackwell Publishing, Oxford, for permission to reprint from Yoneji Masuda (1990) *Managing in the Information Society: Releasing Synergy Japanese Style*; and Krishan Kumar (1995) *From Post-Industrial to Post-Modern Society*.

Cambridge University Press, New York, for permission to reprint from Pippa Norris (2001) 'The digital divide', in *Digital Divide: Civic Engagement, Information Poverty, and the Internet Worldwide*.

Georges Borchardt Inc. for Editions Gallimard for permission to reprint from *Discipline and Punish* by Michel Foucault, New York: Pantheon, 1977. Originally published in French as *Surveiller et Punir* © 1975 by Editions Gallimard.

Loisir et Société for permission to reprint from Nicholas Garnham (1998) 'Information society theory as ideology: a critique', *Loisir et Société*, 21 (1).

The Lutterworth Press, Cambridge for permission to reprint from Theodore Roszak (1986) *The Cult of Information*.

The Open University Press, Buckingham, for permission to reprint from David Lyon (2001) *Surveillance Society: Monitoring Everyday Life*.

Palmenia Publishing, Helsinki, for permission to reprint from Manuel Castells (2001) 'The information city, the new economy, and the network society', in Antti Kasvio *et al.* (eds) *People, Cities and the New Information Economy*.

Penguin Books Ltd for permission to reprint from Charles Leadbeater (1999) *Living on Thin Air: The New Economy* and Michel Foucault (1979) *Discipline and Punish: The Birth of the Prison*.

The Perseus Press for permission to reprint from Shoshana Zuboff (1988) *In the Age of Smart Machines*.

Random House Inc., New York, for permission to reprint from Robert B. Reich (1992) *The Work of Nations: Preparing Ourselves for 21st Century Capitalism*.

The Sagalyn Agency for permission to reprint from Robert B. Reich (1992) *The Work of Nations: Preparing Ourselves for 21st Century Capitalism*.

Sage Publications Ltd for permission to reprint from Nico Stehr (1994) *Knowledge Societies*; Anne Balsamo (1995) 'Forms of technological enchantment: reading the body in contemporary culture', in *Cyberspace, Cyberbodies, Cyberpunk*, eds M. Featherstone and R. Burrows; Nicholas Garnham (1990) 'The media and public sphere', in *Capitalism and Communication*; Zizi Papacharissi (2002) 'The virtual sphere: the internet as a public sphere', *New Media and Society*, 4 (1); and Sadie Plant (1995) 'The future looms: weaving women and cybernetics', in *Cyberspace, Cyberbodies, Cyberpunk*, eds M. Featherstone and R. Burrows.

Southern Illinois University Press for permission to reprint from Christopher Lasch (1987) 'Technology and its critics: the degradation of the practical arts', in S. E. Goldberg and C. R. Strain (eds) *Technological Change and the Transformation of America*.

Taylor & Francis Inc., http://www.routledge-ny.com, for permission to reprint from John Keane (1995) 'Structural transformation of the public sphere', *Communication Review*, 1 (1); and Langdon Winner (1996) 'Who will we be in Cyberspace?', *Information Society*, 12.

The University of California Press for permission to reprint from Theodore Roszak (1986) *The Cult of Information*.

Every effort has been made to contact authors and copyright holders of works reprinted in *The Information Society Reader*, but this has not been possible in every case. Please contact the publisher if you have information regarding the copyright position of such material and this will be remedied in future editions.

A special thankyou to Howard, who reached out:
*He is as full of valour as of kindness, Princely in both.*

# Introduction:
# Information Society Studies

■   Frank Webster

T HERE  IS  WITHIN  CURRENT  social  science  a  view,  frequently
    advanced, that information is now more central to our way of life, so much so
that many scholars conceive of the emergence of a new entity, the Information
Society. From this perspective the Information Society is seen to be as different
from Industrialism as the Industrial Society was from its predecessor, the
Agricultural Society. In the industrial era people made their livings by the sweat of
their brow and dexterity of their hands, working in factories to manufacture products. In contrast, in the Information Society livelihoods are increasingly made by
the appliance and manipulation of information, be it in software design, branding
or financial services, and the output is not so much a tangible thing as a change in
image, relationship or perception. This being so, Information Society Studies are
set to become a central component of contemporary social analysis. And of course
the emergence of such Information Society Studies is a reason why we have put
together this Reader.

Though the concept developed inside academic circles, the idea of an Information Society has taken an even stronger hold outside higher education. Nowadays
businessmen, media pundits and politicians evoke the Information Society as a
matter of routine. This resonance has been amplified by countless feature articles
and paperback books with punchy titles and an assured vision of the future, such
as *The Wealth of Information* (1983), *Being Digital* (1995) and – from the leading
American popularizer Alvin Toffler – *The Third Wave* (1980) and *Powershift*
(1990).

So prevalent is this belief that we are entering a new Information Society that
many may be surprised to encounter those who challenge the validity of the term,
though in the scholarly realm many consider it inappropriate and misleading
(Webster 2002). Nonetheless, though many academics reject the idea that a novel

Information Society is emerging, no one denies that what might be called informatization is of major significance for advanced (and other) societies. This is a clumsy word, but informatization points to the heightened importance of information, and its insinuation into all that we do nowadays, though this of itself may not signal a systemic change. Whichever interpretation one takes of what it all amounts to, information, and its movement (communication), are undeniably of enormous import nowadays (Duff 2000). Indeed, any serious effort to understand the character of contemporary societies must come to grips with information. Whether it be the mediation of so much of modern life (notably through mass media, but also the telephone and internet), or electronic dealing in currencies and investment funds which raise profound questions of national sovereignty, or even the signs with which people decorate and display themselves in this postmodern epoch (hairstyle, clothes, even body shape), then informational matters are to the fore. Such is the context and reasoning that lie behind this Reader.

In the wider society the idea that we are entering a new Information or Knowledge Society is commonplace (those who adopt the word knowledge generally do so in order to associate their vision with still grander notions). For example, take a recent book by Charles Leadbeater (1999) called *Living on Thin Air: The New Economy*. Mr Leadbeater, who worked for the influential British think tank Demos (with which he remains associated) and who reputedly developed the government White Paper, *Building the Knowledge Driven Economy* (December 1998), argues that 'knowledge capital' is the key ingredient for the 'new economy'. The flyleaf of his book quotes Premier Tony Blair to the effect that this 'book raises critical questions for Britain's future'. It also cites the opinion of an architect of the 'third way', former Minister of State Peter Mandelson, which is that 'this book sets out the agenda for the next Blair revolution'. The notion that we are entering an Age of Information can scarcely reach higher than the Prime Minister, though it extends up to the Presidency of the USA – it was Vice-President Al Gore who claimed to have coined the term the 'information superhighway' in the early 1990s. The European Union and Commission have been committed to building a European Information Society for well over a decade, to which end heavy investment has been made in research programmes, educational initiatives and numerous policy papers (the Commission's Information Society website is at http://europa.cu.int/ISPO/basics/1_basics.html).

People who are sceptical about all this talk of the new may prefer to speak of a Neo-Liberal Consensus that has engulfed the world, leading to the dominance of market criteria in everything that we do, something which subordinates informational developments to very long-established pressures. However, even these critics concede that information has become prioritized in social, economic and political affairs over recent decades. Hence whichever position one adopts, whether one is persuaded we are entering an Information Society or rather that we inhabit a much more informationally intensive environment, there can be no doubt that the issues matter enormously, both intellectually and practically.

Moreover, as readers will see more clearly as they make their way through this text, the theoretical ideas developed in academe over the last thirty years have had important influences on contemporary politics, so this isn't just a matter of academics trailing behind 'real-world' changes. Anthony Giddens (1984), a recent Director of the London School of Economics, reminds us that how we talk and think about phenomena shapes how we act (to use his sort of language, theory and concepts, and abstract knowledge more generally, are *constitutive* of the way we live). Consider, for example, how we discuss, feel and act upon theoretical ideas about 'national identity', 'race' or 'postmodernity' in this respect. Or reflect how much we are influenced, even in our most intimate relationships, by knowledge we have gleaned from abstract data (often academic, though probably mediated through television, radio and magazines) about, for instance, divorce rates, cohabitation, child rearing and romantic ideals.

In this Reader we want to engage with popular and practically influential ways that people talk about, and act on, the sort of society in which we find ourselves. The selections cover a lot of social theorists (by which we mean a range of sociologists, economists, political scientists, geographers, even a few philosophers), for two main reasons. One is to demonstrate that some theory is a very *practical* tool to help us better understand the real world. The idea that 'theory' is impractical is a caricature. Though appropriate enough to describe some writing, usually that excessively concerned with epistemology (how we know what we know), theory of a sort is crucial to how we see and think about the world around us. Theory helps us better comprehend how we live by scrutinizing evidence, and by involving itself with substantive developments. There is some theory in sociology which is armchair in the negative sense, but this is often of a sort which confuses that discipline with philosophy. The sort of theory from which this Reader draws its inspiration, that represented by the likes of Anthony Giddens, Ralph Dahrendorf and Zygmunt Bauman, has long been concerned with applying theory to illuminate the real world, as equally it has been concerned with the ways in which empirical trends feed into and reshape theoretical positions.

The second reason is because much recent social thought is, in very large part, focusing around informational issues – not surprisingly given its centrality to contemporary life (even philosophers use word processors, sociologists are on the World Wide Web, information work is expanding enormously, the explosive growth of media, new and old, is of enormous significance to how we live today . . .). In recent years, for example, arguably the single most significant piece of social analysis to have emerged is Manuel Castells' *The Information Age* (1996–98, in three volumes), a sustained account of the importance of *information networks* to how we live today. John Urry (2000), one of Britain's leading sociologists, draws on and extends this notion to emphasize the centrality of *mobilities* (of symbols, ideas, capital, images as well as people) to our present ways of life, something in which *information flows* are critical. Moreover, Daniel Bell, probably the most influential post-war American sociologist, reissued in 1999 his *Coming of Post-industrial Society* (first published 1973), a book which presaged a great deal of current thought and action as regards the Information Society (e.g. the role of higher education, the significance of service sector employment). Again, Anthony Giddens, arguably the world's leading social theorist and probably Britain's major public intellectual, places a premium on the capacity for 'heightened reflexivity' – i.e. on greater use of information/knowledge to make choices about things great and small (Lash 2002).

The mention of these thinkers leads us to an important point. Castells, Bell and Giddens are, by any standards, major social thinkers, but they share something else. This is that they are all deeply engaged with both understanding how the world is changing and in suggesting how it might change for the better. Giddens is well known today as Prime Minister Tony Blair's leading intellectual, as the codifier of the 'radical centre', also known as the 'third way' (Giddens published his book, *The Third Way,* in 1998). Daniel Bell was a political activist from the age of thirteen, and a major 'cold war intellectual' in the 1950s. Manuel Castells, born in 1942, fled Franco's Spain in the 1960s because of his political activism as a teenager, was a radical in Paris during 1968, and is now a 'post-Marxist' and adviser to the European Union and the Russian government.

Another way of putting that is to say that they all are politically committed. No one should take this to be a simplistic thing, as if we can understand them by 'reading off' their arguments from some political affiliation. By commitment we mean that these people are deeply concerned about the ways of the world, that they are involved in 'theory' because this is a requisite of knowing better the world so that its direction may be better comprehended, and its redirection influenced. We think this engagement gives an urgency and 'edge' to their work, something evident in all compelling intellectual ideas. But one should not presume that they then 'sign up' to political manifestos, or that their intellectual integrity is compromised. There is a necessary tension between their intellectual thought and political convictions, as there is in most significant social analysis. One might think here, for instance, of Max Weber's tortured essay, 'Politics as a vocation' (1918), in which Weber contrasted an 'ethic of responsibility' with an 'ethic of ultimate ends' in political matters, admiring and despising both simultaneously. Or think of Emile Durkheim's anguish about the spread of 'anomie' in modern societies, or of Ralph Dahrendorf's passionate commitment to 'liberty', instilled during his teenage experiences of Nazi Germany, or of C. Wright Mills' American populism so evident in *The Power Elite,* or of Ann Oakley's feminism which informs her academic research on the position of women as housewives or recipients of medical treatment.

It seems that among the best social thought there is found almost always a commitment to influence the world. But this isn't something that can be reduced to a straightforward political programme (though we can readily imagine ways in which a political commitment has compromised good scholarship). At the same time, it lets one better appreciate that political activity, in the more orthodox sense, is not sharply divorced from intellectual activity. When it comes to the Information Society, we find politicians have a big stake in shaping the development of this 'new' order, and intellectuals who construct the term also bring with them their own – usually more nuanced and qualified – agendas (that shouldn't be regarded as necessarily superior – politicians must act on the world, academics usually enjoy the luxury of not having to take full responsibility for their ideas which can be developed away from the pressures politicians must respond to).

All of which is to say that, while this text takes students to academic sources to study the significance of information today, they will quickly appreciate how central the matters are to contemporary commerce, work, politics and everyday life.

## Organization of the Reader

The structure of this book reflects these interests and concerns. Part One considers the popular notion of the Information Society. It offers three statements from advocates of the view that we now inhabit an Information Society. This concept is frequently presented as being self-evidently accurate, but articles by three critics who reject the term give reasons to suggest that the Information Society concept is partial. Indeed, to evoke the term may be to misunderstand profoundly the character of the world that we inhabit. At the least, any serious student of contemporary society will take information very seriously, but will also need to ask hard questions regarding the value of ascribing this an Information Society.

Part Two takes us to the father of contemporary thinking on the Information Society. Daniel Bell coined the concept of 'post-industrialism' almost forty years ago now. Over the years this transmuted into a synonym for the Information Society. In all major respects it highlights features of post-industrialism which recur in most descriptions of the Information Society. Bell's major critic is Krishan Kumar whose demolition is instanced here, though – as John Urry's essay reveals – even those who accept the criticisms of Bell can find something about 'post-industrialism' appealing as a means of understanding the present.

Part Three highlights the work of Manuel Castells (born 1942) which has been so influential in shaping the way we think about the 'information age'. Castells' trilogy, produced in the late 1990s, has had a huge effect, notably on scholarship concerned with informational developments. Its encyclopaedic knowledge and impressive powers of synthesis, combined with theoretical nous, make *The Information Age* a towering achievement and an indispensable source for students of information. However, Castells does not go unchallenged, and here a vigorous and oppositional contribution from Nicholas Garnham is included which suggests an ongoing critical engagement with Castells' terms of reference.

Part Four comes to grips with the undoubted centrality of information to the deep and rapid sets of changes we have been experiencing over recent decades. Call it globalization, de-industrialization or post-Fordism, the scale and scope of these transformations is hard to deny. The articles in this part range from those which attempt to recast the way we imagine societies in John Urry's suggestion of 'mobilities' (of ideas, people, images and products), proposals to prioritize higher education to cope with and adapt to change, analysis of the centrality of information to present-day work, production and consumption, to an insistence that gender relations be given due attention amidst all the upheaval of transformations.

Part Five highlights the brute fact that informational developments occur in an unequal society and accordingly reflect and influence those social divisions. There has been much concern in recent years of the emergence of a 'digital divide', a fear that the more privileged groups will race ahead with access to new technologies and high-grade information sources, while the poor will be left further behind. Some commentators dismiss this anxiety, convinced that, at least in the longer term, 'trickle down' will ensure that all get access to information and its associated technologies. Broadly speaking, most commentators in this sphere ally themselves with scepticism (and even hostility) towards pronouncements of the novelty and beneficence of the information explosion. Some elements of this strain of thought are present in Part One's criticisms of the Information Society concept. Here the insistence is on the power of corporate capital especially, and long-term historical trends more generally, to shape the 'information revolution' in directions which deepen entrenched interests of class, nation and capital.

Part Six provides a focus on surveillance, since information gathering and analysis is so much at the heart of the growth of information. This is evident all around, from company records, closed circuit television cameras (CCTV) in high streets, to computerized tills in supermarkets. However, surveillance, as the readings extracted here make clear, is not necessarily sinister or even a threat to liberties. Indeed, it may be an essential element of modernity itself, as well as necessary to the delivery of personal freedoms and civil rights.

Part Seven acknowledges the centrality to information's expansion of the media in all its forms. Whether it is television, cable, satellite, video or the combination of PC terminal with the tv monitor to surf the internet, media are a major expression of the 'information age'. As such, electronic media merit very close attention. Part Seven investigates this by paying attention to Jürgen Habermas' influential thinking on the 'public sphere' as a core ingredient of the democratic process which, argues Habermas, requires a space in which information may be freely developed, discussed and disseminated so that the public may make decisions on confident grounds. Some argue that this came through 'public service broadcasting' systems such as the BBC, but where might it be found in the era of the internet? And is it worth striving for, or even feasible, in the present era of digital television? From proponents to critics of the public sphere included here, readers will be able to assess the pertinence of the concept today.

Finally, Part Eight places information in a context of discussions of the arrival of 'virtualities'. This can be a weasel word, yet conceiving of the Information Society as one in which 'virtuality' predominates lends itself to thinking of a postmodern era in which the artificial (the image, the simulation) substitutes for notions of the 'real'. Our knowledge of what takes place beyond direct personal experience is phenomenal, but all of it is mediated and – for ourselves – the symbols and signs are the only reality that we may know, so perhaps the Information Society is also postmodern? And beyond the mediated, what of the ways in which reproduction itself is an artifice in an era of genetic engineering? If so much is 'unreal', shaped by media or interventions from sophisticated technologies, then might we announce postmodernity's arrival?

The Reader is designed for students, with an eye to going beyond simplistic approaches to the Information Society which presuppose that everything is happening because of a wave of technological developments. The serious student will soon appreciate that examining change is very much more complicated than that. We may all agree that information is central to the word today, but how and why and with what significance is much harder to gauge (Karvonen 2001). This Reader invites students to become engaged in these questions.

## References

Duff, Alistair S. (2000) *Information Society Studies.* London: Routledge.

Giddens, Anthony (1984) *The Constitution of Society: Outline of the Theory of Structuration.* Cambridge: Polity.

Karvonen, Erkki (ed.) (2001) *Informational Societies: Understanding the Third Industrial Revolution.* Tampere: Tampere University Press.

Lash, Scott (2002) *Critique of Information.* London: Sage.

Leadbeater, Charles (1999) *Living on Thin Air: The New Economy.* London: Hodder and Stoughton.

Urry, John (2000) *Sociology Beyond Societies.* London: Routledge.

Webster, Frank (2002) *Theories of the Information Society,* 2nd edn. London: Routledge.

# PART ONE

# The Information Society

## INTRODUCTION

■ Frank Webster

IT IS COMMONPLACE TO SAY THAT nowadays we live in an Information Society. What is meant by this concept is indistinct, yet still it has some resonance for most of us. The term *feels right* about how we live today. It conjures so many different things, each of them of the moment – a world of media saturation, of extended education for the vast majority of us in advanced locations, of generally cleverer and better informed people, of large numbers of occupations concerned with 'think work', of instantaneous movement of information across time and space and of an array of new technologies and especially the internet, but including also cable and satellite television, DVD systems and so on. . . . All of these appear to be distinguishing features our world, so, not surprisingly, when we hear the words Information Society we readily consider them to be reasonable as a description of what we are.

And yet it is remarkable that Information Society should evoke so many different associations in our minds – new technologies, higher education, symbolic work and round the clock entertainment . . . It cannot be long after reflecting on these different images that one begins to ask what fundamentally distinguishes the Information Society? For instance, is the Information Society's most important characteristic the increasing tradeability, and hence economic significance, of information? Or is it that the Information Society heralds a huge increase in cultural phenomena (television, video, movies, web sites, plus a heightened emphasis on style)? Or is it that nowadays educational attainment is so much greater and more widespread than ever before, making our society more learned and theoretically aware? Or, again, is it that communication today allows instantaneous movement of information across the globe, such that affairs can be managed in real time on a planetary scale?

It seems clear that, once one begins to ask questions such as these, then the concept 'Information Society' comes to be regarded somewhat dubiously. It certainly is evocative, but it is simultaneously fuzzy and evasive. The ambiguities surrounding the term are excusable among lay people, but what is especially surprising is that so many professional commentators evoke an Information Society without being at all clear about what they mean by the term. If social scientists do not clarify what they mean by the term, then how might the general public be expected to cope? It can seem that the word is used with abandon, yet as such it is capable of accommodating all manner of definitions. Readers should look carefully for the definitional terms used, often tacitly, by commentators in what follows. Are they, for instance, emphasizing the economic, educational or cultural dimensions when they discuss the Information Society, or is it technology which is given the greatest weight in their accounts? One might then ask, if the conceptions are so very varied and even promiscuous, then what validity remains for the Information Society concept (Webster 2002)?

Part One is divided between advocates and critics of the Information Society. In the former camp are those who argue that we do indeed inhabit such a new type of society (or are at least set to enter into one such), while against them are a number of opposing thinkers who either or both attack the particular suggestions of the advocates and jettison the idea that the notion of an Information Society has any explanatory value. The advocates characteristically are positive, even enthusiastic, about the Information Society, which is always regarded as an improvement on the Industrial era which it allegedly supersedes.

The readings in this section begin with one of the earliest statements of the arrival of the Information Society, **Yoneji Masuda** (Chapter 1), whose writings in the early 1980s were pioneering in this regard. Indeed, while we in the West tend to think that it is writers from North America especially who have led commentary on the Information Society, there is a long tradition of Information Society analysis coming from Japan, of which Masuda is a leading light (Duff 2000). It is the enthusiasm for the new that is most prominent in Masuda's account.

As with most enthusiasts, great claims are made for technology as the driver of change. In this focus Masuda is at one with most other futurists. It is typical of Information Society advocates to regard technology (whether telecommunications, computers, or new media, notably the internet, or indeed all new technologies) as both the major expression of and the primary force bringing into being the new Information Society. Masuda was an early instance with regard to emphasis being placed on computer and communications technologies, but there are many contemporaries and successors whose work might be usefully compared to his book, *Managing in the Information Society*. At base all prioritize technology as the most important feature of the new epoch, as well as being the key causal factor in bringing it into being – each is distinguishable from the other by concern with the latest technological innovations. It is the same story, but a different technology. Christopher Evans (1979) enthused about the 'mighty micro' in the late 1970s, and by the 1990s Nicholas Negroponte (1995) stressed the impact of digitalization. Currently the top concerns are with genetic manipulation and the internet.

Charles Leadbeater (Chapter 2) takes us on from Masuda almost twenty years, to a much more contemporary account of the Information Society. This approach is equally enthusiastic about change, but now there is a switch in emphasis towards highlighting the role of 'knowledge' in the new order. Technology in Leadbeater's book takes a back seat to 'thinking smart', to being an intelligent, enterprising and adaptable person in a fast-moving world in which 'living on thin air' (ideas) supersedes the old ways. Leadbeater's conception turns attention from the hardware (the range of ICTs – information and communications technologies – that are the usual bases of Information Society speculation) towards software, the 'brain work' dimensions of the information age. In this perspective 'human capital' is to the fore, and education the privileged means of ensuring it is maximized. To Leadbeater – and his theme is popular with leading politicians and business figures – the new age is one in which entrepreneurs who are 'savvy' and inventive will prosper. The old days of a 'job for life' in manufacturing or mining are long gone, and the only recipe for success is constant innovation, new ideas and enterprise.

If Leadbeater is distinctly positive about the Information Society, then Bill Gates (1995) – who surely epitomizes Leadbeater's self-starting knowledge entrepreneur – goes even further to conceive of the Information Society bringing about 'friction free capitalism', in which Adam Smith's market system is brought close to perfection because people will be better informed, companies more responsive, and activities more personalized, due to the spread of interactive technologies. This paean to capitalism is taken to further heights in the call for a 'Magna Carta for the Knowledge Age' from Esther Dyson, George Gilder, George Keyworth and Alvin Toffler (Chapter 3). What this amounts to is an insistence that the Information Society is a demassified and individualistic era, in sharp contrast to the 'Second Wave' civilization of mass production and standardization. The authors contend that only the free market, and not government, can bring this new age into healthy being.

Not surprisingly, these positive endorsements of the Information Society have induced responses from critics. Langdon Winner (Chapter 4) argues that, while we are currently undergoing major change, this is not an entirely novel experience. Thereby he suggests that announcements of a new era might better be premature. Moreover, his historical account puts people rather than technology at the core of change, observing that very often technologies are used by some people to get their way over others. This is something he shares with the lucid and uncompromising critic of technology David Noble (1977, 1984, 2001) whose analyses of the false promises of technology are essential counterweights to the techno-enthusiasts.

Theodore Roszak (Chapter 5) presents a forceful critique of enthusiasts for the Information Society, insisting that the term 'information' has been mystified during the twentieth century. In Roszak's view the Information Society idea is full of hype, something usefully resisted by close analysis of what we mean when we use a word such as 'information'. Applying the close attention to the vocabulary adopted by many commentators characteristic of the literary scholar, Roszak makes several provocative observations. Not the least of these is that today's society is based, not on information as so many Information Society advocates assert, but rather on ideas that are profound if often inchoately considered – for instance 'all men are equal', 'do unto others as you would be done by' and 'stand by your friends'.

Finally, **Kevin Robins** and **Frank Webster** (Chapter 6) present an historical review of the 'information revolution' which locates it back in time. They suggest that today's Information Society continues and deepens long-established patterns rather than announces a new age (Beniger 1986). Their account is one which refuses to start with new technologies and what they are doing to us today, but which instead suggests that a wider context is essential to fully appreciate informational trends (May 2002). In doing this they ask, not what sort of society the 'information revolution' is bringing into being, but what established social relationships are doing to information itself.

## REFERENCES

Beniger, James R. (1986) *The Control Revolution: Technological and Economic Origins of the Information Society*. Cambridge, MA: Harvard University Press.

Duff, Alistair S. (2000) *Information Society Studies*. London: Routledge.

Evans, Christopher (1979) *The Mighty Micro: The Impact of the Computer Revolution*. London: Gollancz.

Gates, Bill (1995) *The Road Ahead*. Harmondsworth: Penguin.

May, Christopher (2002) *The Information Society: A Sceptical View*. Cambridge: Polity.

Negroponte, Nicholas (1995) *Being Digital*. London: Hodder and Stoughton.

Noble, David F. (1977) *America by Design: Science, Technology, and the Rise of Corporate America*. New York: Oxford University Press.

Noble, David F. (1984) *Forces of Production: A Social History of Industrial Automation*. New York: Oxford University Press.

Noble, David F. (2001) *Digital Diploma Mills: The Automation of Higher Education*. New York: Monthly Review Press.

Webster, Frank (2002) *Theories of the Information Society*, 2nd edn. London: Routledge.

# Advocates

# Chapter 1

# Yoneji Masuda

## IMAGE OF THE FUTURE
## INFORMATION SOCIETY

From *Managing in the Information Society: Releasing Synergy Japanese Style*, Oxford: Blackwell (1990), pp. 3–10.

WHAT IS THE IMAGE OF THE information society? The concept will be built on the following two premises:

1   The information society will be a new type of human society, completely different from the present industrial society. [. . .] The basis for this assertion is that *the production of information values and not material values will be the driving force* behind the formation and development of society. Past systems of innovational technology have always been concerned with material productive power, but the future information society must be built within a completely new framework, with a thorough analysis of the system of computer-communications technology that determines the fundamental nature of the information society.
2   The developmental pattern of industrial society is the societal model from which we can predict the overall composition of the information society. Here is another bold 'historical hypothesis': *the past developmental pattern of human society can be used as a historical analogical model for future society*.

Putting the components of the information society together piece by piece by using this historical analogy is an extremely effective way of building the fundamental framework of the information society.

## The overall composition of the information society

Table 1 displays the overall framework of the information society based upon these two premises. It presents the overall composition of the information society based on a historical analogy from industrial society. Let me explain each of the major items. Of course the entire picture of the future information society cannot be given at this stage, but at least Table 1 will help the reader understand the composition of and overall relations between chapters that unfold later in the book.

1   The prime innovative technology at the core of development in industrial society was the steam engine, and its major function was to substitute for and amplify the physical labour of man. In the information society, 'computer technology' will be the innovational technology that will constitute the developmental core, and its fundamental function will be to *substitute and amplify the mental labour of man*.

2   In industrial society, the motive power revolution resulting from the invention of the steam engine rapidly increased material productive power, and made possible the mass production of goods and services and the rapid transportation of goods. In the information society, 'an information revolution' resulting from development of the computer will rapidly expand information productive power, and make possible *the mass production of cognitive, systematized information, technology and knowledge*.

3   In industrial society, the modern factory, consisting of machines and equipment, became the societal symbol and was the production centre for goods. In the information society *the information utility* (a computer-based public infrastructure), consisting of information networks and data banks, will replace the factory as *the societal symbol*, and become the production and distribution centre for information goods.

4   Markets in industrial society expanded as a result of the discovery of new continents and the acquisition of colonies. The increase in consumption purchasing power was the main factor in expansion of the market. In the information society, 'the knowledge frontier' *will become the potential market*, and the increase in the possibilities of problem solving and the development of opportunities in a society that is constantly and dynamically developing will be the primary factor behind the expansion of the information market.

5   In industrial society, the leading industries in economic development are machinery and chemicals, and the total structure comprises primary, secondary and tertiary industries. In the information society the leading industries will be *the intellectual industries*, the core of which will be the knowledge industries. *Information-related industries* will be added as *the quaternary group* to the industrial structure of primary, secondary and tertiary. This structure will consist of a matrix of information-related industries on the vertical axis, and health, housing and similar industries on the horizontal axis.

6   The economic structure of industrial society is characterized by (1) a sales-oriented commodity economy, (2) specialization of production utilizing divisions of labour, (3) complete division of production and consumption between enterprise and household. In the information society, (1) information, the axis

of socioeconomic development, will be produced by the information utility, (2) self-production of information by users will increase; information will accumulate, (3) this accumulated information will expand through synergetic production and shared utilization and (4) the economy will change structurally from an exchange economy to *a synergetic economy*.

7    In industrial society the law of price, the universal socio-economic principle, is the Invisible Hand that maintains the equilibrium of supply and demand, and the economy and society as a whole develop within this economic order. In the information society *the goal-principle* (a goal and means principle) will be the fundamental principle of society, and the synergetic feedforward, which apportions functions in order to achieve a common goal, will work to maintain the order of society.

8    In industrial society, the most important subject of social activity is the enterprise, the economic group. There are three areas: private enterprise, public enterprise and a third sector of government ownership and private management. In the information society the most important subject of social activity will be *the voluntary community*, a socio-economic group that can be broadly divided into local communities and informational communities.

9    In industrial society the socio-economic system is a system of private enterprise characterized by private ownership of capital, free competition and the maximization of profits. In the information society, the socio-economic system will be a voluntary civil society characterized by the superiority of its infrastructure, as a type of both public capital, and knowledge-oriented human capital, and by a fundamental framework that embodies *the principle of synergy and social benefit*.

10   Industrial society is a society of centralized power and hierarchical classes. The information society, however, will be a multi-centred and complementary voluntary society. It will be horizontally functional, maintaining social order by *autonomous and complementary functions of a voluntary civil society*.

11   The goal of industrial society is to establish a Gross National Welfare Society, aiming to become a cradle-to-grave high welfare society. The information society will aim for *the realization of time-value* (value that designs and actualizes future time), for each human being. The goal of society will be for everyone to enjoy a worthwhile life in the pursuit of greater future possibilities.

12   The political system of industrial society is a parliamentary system and majority rule. In the information society the political system will become a *participatory democracy*. It will be the politics of participation by citizens; the politics of autonomous management by citizens, based on agreement, participation and synergy that take in the opinions of minorities.

13   In industrial society, labour unions exist as a force for social change, and labour movements expand by the use of labour disputes as their weapon. In the information society, *citizen movements* will be the force behind the social change; their weapons will be litigation and participatory movements.

14   In industrial society there are three main types of social problems: recession-induced unemployment, wars resulting from international conflict, and the dictatorships of fascism. The problems of the information society will be future shocks caused by the inability of people to respond smoothly to rapid societal

Table 1 Pattern comparison of industrial society and the information society

| | Industrial society | Information society |
|---|---|---|
| **Innovational technology** | | |
| Core | Steam engine (power) | Computer (memory, computation, control) |
| Basic function | Replacement, amplification of physical labour | Replacement, amplification of mental labour |
| Productive power | Material productive power (increase in per capita production) | Information productive power (increase in optimal action-selection capabilities) |
| **Socio-economic structure** | | |
| Products | Useful goods and services | Information, technology, knowledge |
| Production centre | Modern factory (machinery, equipment) | Information utility (information networks, data banks) |
| Market | New world, colonies, consumer purchasing power | Increase in knowledge frontiers, information space |
| Leading industries | Manufacturing industries (machinery industry, chemical industry) | Intellectual industries (information industry, knowledge industry) |
| Industrial structure | Primary, secondary, tertiary industries | Matrix industrial structure (primary, secondary, tertiary, quaternary/systems industries) |
| Economic structure | Commodity economy (division of labour, separation of production and consumption) | Synergetic economy (joint production and shared utilization) |
| Socio-economic principle | Law of price (equilibrium of supply and demand) | Law of goals (principle of synergetic feedforward) |
| Socio-economic subject | Enterprise (private enterprise, public enterprise, third sector) | Voluntary communities (local and informational communities) |
| Socio-economic system | Private ownership of capital, free competition, profit maximization | Infrastructure, principle of synergy, precedence of social benefit |
| Form of society | Class society (centralized power, classes, control) | Functional society (multi-centre, function, autonomy) |
| National goal | GNW (gross national welfare) | GNS (gross national satisfaction) |
| Form of government | Parliamentary democracy | Participatory democracy |
| Force of social change | Labour movements, strikes | Citizens' movements, litigation |
| Social problems | Unemployment, war, fascism | Future shock, terror, invasion of privacy |
| Most advanced stage | High mass consumption | High mass knowledge creation |
| **Values** | | |
| Value standards | Material values (satisfaction of physiological needs) | Time-value (satisfaction of goal achievement needs) |
| Ethical standards | Fundamental human rights, humanity | Self-discipline, social contribution |
| Spirit of the times | Renaissance (human liberation) | Globalism (symbiosis of man and nature) |

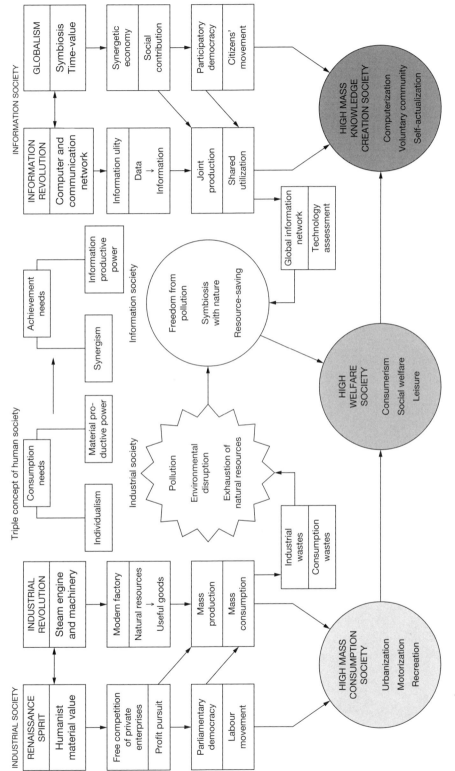

*Figure 1* Transformation process from industrial society to information society

transformation, acts of individual and group terrorists such as hijackings, *invasions of individual privacy* and the crisis of *a controlled society*.

15    The most advanced stage of industrial society is a high mass consumption stage, centring on durable goods, as evidenced by motorization (the diffusion of the automobile). The most advanced stage of the information society will be *the high mass knowledge creation society*, in which computerization will make it possible for each person to create knowledge and to go on to self-fulfilment.

16    In industrial society, the materialistic values of satisfying physiological and physical needs are the universal standards of social values; but in the information society, seeking *the satisfaction of achieved goals* will become the universal standard of values.

17    Finally, the spirit of industrial society has been the Renaissance spirit of human liberation, which ethically means respect for fundamental human rights and emphasis on the dignity of the individual, and a spirit of brotherly love to rectify inequalities. The spirit of the information society will be *the spirit of globalism, a symbiosis in which man and nature* can live together in harmony, consisting ethically of *strict self-discipline and social contribution*.

[. . .]

# Chapter 2

# Charles Leadbeater

## LIVING ON THIN AIR

From *Living on Thin Air: The New Economy,* London: Hodder and Stoughton (1999), pp. 1–17.

[. . .]

**A**LLOW ME, BRIEFLY, TO DESCRIBE where I am coming from. I do not work for a company or a university. I am neither a business consultant nor a civil servant. I have no job title nor job description, no office or expense account and I do not belong to a clearly defined occupational group. When people ask me, 'What do you do?', I find it hard to come up with a clear, concise answer. I work from home, writing mainly, sometimes books, sometimes reports, often for a think-tank, sometimes for the government or a company. The kids are perplexed by my lifestyle. They like my being around, but part of them would quite like it if I had a proper, dependable job to go to, in an office, like other people's dads. Yet my life is far more comfortable than my father's was at a similar age. As a young man he had to fight in a world war and he did not have the chance to go to university. My family goes on foreign holidays, has several computers, cable television, a microwave, two mobile phones, uses the Internet daily and drives around in a vast 'people carrier'. There are two much more significant differences: the kind of jobs we do. My wife has a job; my mother toiled for her family but not for an employer. My father had a steady, predictable, dependable career, which carried him through to a well earned, properly funded and enjoyable retirement. In contrast, although I am not yet forty, I have already had several mini-careers. For three or four years after university I worked in television. Then I had an eleven-year career as a newspaper journalist, which I brought to an end after I became exhausted by corporate upheaval and disillusioned by working sixty-five hours a week as an executive. Now

I am self-employed, independent, working from home. I am one of Charles Handy's portfolio workers, armed with a laptop, a modem and some contacts. Peter Drucker anointed people like me 'knowledge workers'. Put it another way: I live on my wits.

As I sit at my desk at home I sometimes marvel at the risk I am taking. I have commitments to my family, which mean I will need to work for another thirty years, to pay for the education of our offspring, our weakness for holidays and a retirement pension. In the last ten years I have managed, by the skin of my teeth, to keep pace with the technological changes sweeping the 'media' industries. But how will I manage to keep up in fifteen or twenty years' time, when my reflexes will be even slower and presumably I will be on my fifth or sixth career? Occasionally, usually when the cash dispenser has done something unpleasant, it seems too daunting and implausible that I should be able to make my way in such a competitive world on my own, without protection from some larger organiza- tion. At times like that I fondly imagine joining a newspaper perhaps or a television production company or an investment bank even: something solid, dependable, with a recognized brand name.

That fantasy of acquiring safety in numbers never lasts more than a minute. Most large organizations seem pretty soulless, increasingly focused, driven, lean machines, designed to deliver shareholder value. The lights never go out these days in modern companies; no sooner have you found a cosy corner of the organization to settle down in than some ambitious manager points the spotlight at you, ques- tioning your contribution to profitability. Life within such organizations is forever clouded by the threat of downsizing, reorganization or merger. Such a life seems to me to be no more secure and certainly less interesting than the slightly perilous independence I have plumped for. I have decided I will organize my work around myself and my family, and earn my living by finding people who will pay me to do things I am interested in. It's skating on thin ice, but the ice is getting thinner wherever you go these days.

Of course I am lucky. I have a good degree. Through my career as a journalist I made a lot of contacts, in business and politics. I live in London. I have marketable skills. Yet the dilemma I face — how best to provide myself with a degree of secu- rity in a more competitive, unsentimental, relentless world — faces most people. To go it alone is risky, demanding and stressful. Yet to rely upon larger organiza- tions and institutions, companies and trade unions, isn't much of an improvement, because they seem either too cumbersome or too callous. Where can we turn to find greater security in an environment as hostile as the modern global economy?

The unlikely starting point for an answer is *We're Going on a Bear Hunt*, one of our family's favourite children's books, in which a family sets out to find a bear, only to meet a series of daunting obstacles: deep mud, a cold river, a dark forest, a vio- lent storm. At each of these the family chants: 'We can't go under it. We can't go over it. We'll have to go *through* it.' That is the challenge most of us face in the pre- carious economy on which our livings now depend. We have to steel ourselves to press on, not really sure what lies ahead, but knowing that retreat is no alternative.

We have to go forward because if we retreat we end up with gridlock. Our societies and governments often seem paralysed, or at best enfeebled, in the face of economic and technological change that outstrips their capacity to respond. We are weighed down by institutions, laws and cultures largely inherited from the industrial nineteenth century; yet we confront a global economy driven by an accelerating flow of new ideas and technologies which are creating the industries and products of the twenty-first century. We have welfare systems which are impervious to reform, parliamentary systems which are recognizably Victorian and schools which still resemble their nineteenth-century forebears. Imagine fighting a modern war using cavalry: that is the position we are in.

Yet as soon as our institutions become unblocked, everything threatens to spiral out of control. As soon as outmoded old institutions are shunted out of the way, nothing stable replaces them. Nowhere is this more evident than in the world's highly strung financial markets. The Bretton Woods system of fixed exchange rates has long had its day. We cannot go back to that system. But we seem to have unleashed in its place a monster that no one can control, even that small minority which profits from it. Few people feel their lives, particularly their work lives, are more secure and under control. Instead, most people feel ensnared by the impersonal forces sweeping the global economy. It is difficult to be convinced that this is progress.

This book's first aim is to explain the swirling forces which are shaping our economic lives. These forces are partly malign but potentially very beneficial. The second is to explain why we need to reconstitute many of our institutions – social, political and economic – to enable them to withstand the gale around them and exploit the benefits on offer to the full. People feel less in control of their lives not because they suffer a lack of confidence. We will not overcome our anxiety by going into collective therapy, willing ourselves to become more entrepreneurial and flexible. Nor will we get very far by reining in the dynamic and creative forces which are driving the global economy, in particular the creation and spread of new ideas and technologies which are the well-springs of higher productivity and improved well-being. Our problem is that the institutions to which we turn to protect us from volatility and to shape our world – large companies, trade unions, welfare states, national governments – seem incapable or uninterested. Public, collective institutions seem enfeebled and overrun. Private-sector institutions seem too self-interested to be fully trusted. Piecemeal reform of old institutions will not be enough. We need to embark on a wave of radical institutional innovation and invention, to create new kinds of companies, banks, welfare organizations, governments, schools, universities which can gather our resources more effectively and so put people more in control of their lives.

Although technology has moved on in leaps and bounds in this century, we are largely living with an institutional inheritance from the Victorians. Most of our modern institutions can trace their roots to the nineteenth century. In the UK, the joint-stock company reached legal maturity with the 1862 Companies Act and became the dominant form of capitalist organization in the 1880s. Consumer co-operatives and burial associations became the basis for the modern building societies, given legal form in the friendly society and building societies law of 1874. The local authority emerged from the consolidation of the poor laws of 1834, the public-health legislation of 1848, the highways act of 1862 and the education act of 1870. Trade unions gave voice to organized labour. Institutions of higher education, incorporating scientific research, were created as the century progressed. The nineteenth century was so revolutionary because technological innovation went hand in hand with institutional innovation, itself the product of political and social change. By contrast with the Victorians we are scientific radicals but institutional conservatives. The Victorians had a grand political and social imagination to match their achievements in science and industry. Our era, thus far, has failed that test of imagination.

To understand the scale of the renewal we need, we must first understand the three forces driving change in the economies of modern societies: finance capitalism, knowledge capitalism and social capitalism.

## Finance capitalism

The most obvious and maligned force, which sends a shiver down most people's spines, is the disruptive power of deregulated, interconnected global financial markets, which swill around the world in pursuit of shareholder value. Imagine a boat that combined the scale and mass of a super-tanker with the speed and instability of a speedboat. That is the world's financial system; the force that sanctifies downsizing, restructuring and re-engineering.

[. . .]

This rolling crisis had a simple cause. The world's financial system is able to switch vast resources around the globe in an instant. A dealer in London can buy stocks in the Lebanon, government bonds in Thailand, futures in Brazil, and take a punt on the Indonesian currency, while sipping a *café latte*. Combine these powerful and volatile financial flows with attractive but fragile emerging economies, equipped with feeble, sometimes corrupt and poorly regulated financial systems, and you have a recipe for disaster. The flood of capital into emerging economies in the early 1990s was like a seriously overweight adult trying to sleep in a baby's cot. The costs are still being counted.

[. . .]

The rolling financial collapse of 1998 was waiting to happen. Banks and brokerages can hire the brightest people money can buy and equip them with the most sophisticated computers. Yet, as global financial markets have liberalized since the 1970s, this system has become prone to ever larger accidents, from the obscure Latin American debt crisis in the 1980s, through the property bubble in the US, the UK and Japan of the early 1990s, to the Asian financial crisis of 1997–98. Since the collapse in 1973 of the Bretton Woods system, which was set up after the Second World War to regulate world financial markets, there have been banking crises in sixty-nine countries. These have been combined with recessions, massive tax-funded bail-outs for bankrupt banks and currency crises, of which there have been eighty-seven since 1975, according to the World Bank. As Martin Wolf, the chief economic commentator at the *Financial Times* put it: 'Financial systems are not so much an accident waiting to happen, as one that is constantly happening.'

[. . .]

Despite all that, the argument of this book is that globalization is good. A retreat into defensive, inward-looking, nationalistic economic policies would not be progress. One of the few good things to come out of the crisis of 1998 may be a *more* integrated global financial system, strengthened by the creation of steering mechanisms to prevent it careering out of control: stricter and more transparent regulation of banks and stock markets in emerging economies; a world financial authority; an International Monetary Fund, with the resources to prevent crises snowballing; the creation of stronger regional currency blocs such as the European Single Currency, to provide greater stability; and, possibly, punitive taxes to deter short-term speculative capital movements in and out of vulnerable countries. [. . .]

This would be a turn away from the pure market, but not from the global economy. On the contrary, these measures would be designed to make global financial markets more effective by making them more transparent. The task is to maintain beneficial long-term global investment flows to emerging markets and innovative economies while taming hot money and speculative excess. The creation of a globally integrated and interconnected economy, for finance and trade, is a huge achievement. Flows of trade and investment carry ideas and people which bring with them innovation and creativity, the well-springs of economic growth and productivity. Trade encourages creativity and breeds relationships which cross borders and cultures. Global trade and investment, in the long run, will make the world stronger and more peaceful than nationalism and protectionism.

Global finance is just one force driving the modern economy. The second force, with which this book is mainly concerned, is just as persuasive and powerful as financial capitalism but less well recognized. This is 'knowledge capitalism': the drive to generate new ideas and turn them into commercial products and services which consumers want. This process of creating, disseminating and exploiting new knowledge is the dynamo behind rising living standards and economic growth. It reaches deep into our lives and implicates all of us as consumers and workers. If we were to turn our backs on the global economy, we would also leave behind the huge creative power of the knowledge economy.

## Knowledge capitalism

The modern economy's most impressive feature is its ability to create streams of new products and services. The spectacular growth of organized science, the consequent acceleration of technological change and the speed at which new ideas are translated into commercial products distinguish our era from previous ones. To list the changes in this century, particularly in its second half, in travel, communications, medicine, pharmaceuticals, robotics, information-processing and genetic engineering – to take just a few examples – is to chronicle a resolution in what we make and consume, largely enabled by the commercial application of human intelligence.

Across a wide range of products, intelligence embedded in software and technology has become more important than materials. Radios got smaller as transistors replaced vacuum tubes. Thin-fibre optic cable has replaced tonnes of copper wire. New architectural, engineering and materials technologies have allowed us to construct buildings enclosing the same space but with far less physical material than required fifty or 100 years ago. [. . .] The keys to economic advance are the recipes we use to combine physical ingredients in more intelligent and creative ways. Better recipes drive economic growth.

We are developing new recipes more quickly than ever before. More scientists are at work today than in the rest of human history. Scientific research is far more productive than in the past and its results are being translated into commercial products more quickly. As a result, we are in the early stages of the development of families of entirely new products and industries: materials that mimic biology; genetic treatments for major diseases; drugs that can target specific parts of the brain that produce emotions; and miniature robots that could work inside the human body. [. . .]

The knowledge-driven economy is not made up of a set of knowledge-intensive industries fed by science. This new economy is driven by new factors of production and sources of competitive advantage – innovation, design, branding, know-how – which are at work in all industries from retailing and agriculture to banking and software.

There are downsides to this relentless flow of new ideas. Innovation threatens familiar routines, institutions and occupations. Technology, particularly information technology, is full of false promise. New knowledge – for instance the power to manipulate our genes – creates dilemmas over its acceptable use. Yet despite these drawbacks, knowledge capitalism is the most powerful creative force we have yet developed to make people better off – something it does by generating and spreading intelligence in the usable form of products and services. Modern consumers can call on the intelligence of thousands of people embedded in the intelligent tools that they use every day: computers, cars, telephones, microwaves. Modern economies are a system for distributing intelligence. The potential of the knowledge economy will not be unlocked by defensive measures to regulate financial capitalism. Instead, we need to redesign our economies to release their potential for creating and spreading knowledge throughout our populations.

## Social capitalism

Collaboration is the driving force behind creativity. That is why social capital, to promote collaboration, is the third motive force of the new economy. At root the idea of social capital is very simple. Making your living in a market economy involves risk. When you buy a product in a shop you run the risk that it may not work. When you invest in a company you take a risk that it may go belly-up. When you agree to partner someone in a venture, you run the risk that they may let you down. Unless you are prepared to take risks, you cannot get much done, as a consumer, investor or producer. The more you can depend on people you can trust, the less risk you take. So it's easier to take risks when you have relationships with a range of people you can depend upon or if you can rely upon rules, institutions and procedures to provide you with guarantees. The more an economy promotes this capacity for sharing risks, information and rewards, the more able it will be to bring people together to back investment in new products or enter new markets. Successful economies are underpinned by social relationships which help people to collaborate, whether those are the dense web of relationships between banks and business in Japan and Germany, the co-operative relationships among craft producers in northern Italy or the social networks which thread through Silicon

Valley in California. Networks of social relationships create social capital, which is absolutely critical in this new economy. An ethic of trust and collaboration is as important in the new economy as individualism and self-interest.

We rely on institutions of welfare, insurance, education and mutual self-help to withstand the turbulence of the global economy. The welfare state was designed for a world of male full-employment and stable nuclear families which has gone for good. That is why we need to reinvigorate and revive organizations capable of creating social solidarity. This is critical for an economy that seeks to trade on its know-how and ideas. Any society that writes off 30 per cent of its people through poor schooling, family breakdown, poverty and unemployment is throwing away precious assets: brainpower, intelligence and creativity. Our tolerance of this social failure is akin to the Victorians choosing to dump millions of tonnes of coal at sea, or Henry Ford leaving tonnes of machinery out in the rain to rust. An innovative economy must be socially inclusive to realize its full potential.

[. . .]

The knowledge economy threatens to amplify existing sources of inequality while also creating distinctive divisions. Imagine we lived in a world where, due to genetic mutation, income translated directly into height. The richer you were, the taller you would be. Then imagine that the entire population of the UK were to march past you, in an hour, ranked in order of their income. After three minutes the walkers would be 2 ft tall. After a quarter of an hour the marchers would still be dwarfs of about 3 ft and they would only reach 4 ft after 24 minutes. You would have to wait until 37 minutes before a person of average height, about 5 ft 8 ins, walked by. In the final quarter of an hour, abnormally large people, more than 7 ft tall would start to appear. With three minutes left, people twice average height, 12 ft 3 ins, would pass by. It would only be in the final minute that the real giants appeared, people 30 yards high. Yet that would still not be the top. In the final seconds single men earning more than £1 million a year – top barristers, superstar city analysts, some chief executives – would lope by: they would be 235 yards tall.

These giants are the winners in a society that is increasingly organized so that the winners take all, or if not all, then a disproportionately high share of the rewards. The same dynamics are at work in television, entertainment, films, pop music and book-writing. John Grisham and Danielle Steel get multi-million dollar advances for their books, while authors whose writing is better write for nothing (an inversion of the economic law that the more you pay the better the product you get). Confined to these celebrity markets, extreme inequalities might be overlooked. Yet the cult of celebrity is spreading. In virtually every profession, an elite is pulling away from the middle and leaving the bottom trailing. Markets for many goods, whether they are computer games, books, films or legal services, are becoming more international. Larger markets mean larger rewards for the people that win. Being the winner in a local market – a school sports day – might bring you a small cup; winning in a global market – the Olympics – brings you vast rewards. As more markets internationalize, there will be a few very big winners. Success will breed success, celebrity will beget celebrity.

A trend towards inequality is deeply ingrained in modern society. Poorer people are less able than rich people to cope with the risks inherent in the global economy.

To reverse this trend we need to invest in new institutions of social solidarity. That is the defensive case for social capital. There is a creative case as well. An ethic of collaboration is central to knowledge-creating societies. To create we must collaborate.

Ideas for new products usually emerge from teams of people drawing together different expertise. Few companies have the resources to make global products that combine several different technologies. That is why joint-ventures, partnerships and alliances are proliferating. Cities such as London and Los Angeles will be at the heart of the knowledge economy because these are places where ideas and people circulate at great velocity. Collaboration is driving progress in science. In the 1890s Sir J. J. Thomson, a professor of physics at the Cavendish Laboratory in Cambridge, and a handful of co-workers discovered the electron, using simple equipment. In the early years of the twentieth century Lee de Forest and Irving Langmuir, two US scientists, developed the vacuum valve, working in small, isolated groups. Thereafter developments in this basic technology, which is at the heart of electronics, involved progressively larger teams working with the support of large organizations and wide networks of research contacts. The development of the transistor at AT&T's Bell Telephone Laboratories, by a group led by John Bardeen, Walter Brattain and William Shockley, stemmed from a project to replace the vacuum valve. The result emerged from the co-ordination of many scientists, not an isolated stroke of inventive genius. The development of the microprocessor and computer chip, the modern equivalent to the vacuum valve, took the combined work of hundreds of researchers. Biotechnology is even more collaborative: a recent research paper on yeast had 135 authors from eighty-five institutions.

[. . .]

Collaborative networks, not companies are fast becoming the basic units of innovation and production in the new economy.

## Welcome to the knowledge society

Three forces are driving modern economies – finance, knowledge and social capital. It is no coincidence that all are intangible: they cannot be weighed or touched, they do not travel in railway wagons and cannot be stockpiled in poets. The critical factors of production of this new economy are not oil, raw materials, armies of cheap labour or physical plant and equipment. These traditional assets still matter, but they are a source of competitive advantage only when they are vehicles for ideas and intelligence which give them value.

When the three forces of modern economic growth work together the economy hums, and society seems strong and creative. When they are at odds, as they have seemed to be for much of the last twenty years, society seems in danger of fragmenting and becoming more volatile. The task is to combine finance, knowledge and social capital in a virtuous circle of innovation, growth and social progress. There are three ways this could be done: by organizing society around the leadership of the market, the community or knowledge and creativity.

Those who believe that self-interest and the search for profit are the main motive force for economic growth argue that the market and private companies should primarily organize the economy. That was the argument of the new right for much of the 1980s and 1990s: that society should be rationalized, restructured and ultimately revitalized by unleashing self-interest and extending the market. The more people looked after their income, housing welfare, education, health, the better-off we would all be. This free-market argument is still influential but has run its course. A free-market society would put us at the mercy of the impersonal and capricious forces of the financial markets, widen inequalities and under-invest in the long term and the public goods on which we all rely. The rise of the know-ledge economy will force us to revise many of the claims of the new right which have passed into conventional wisdom, for example that something's value can be read from its price, as set by an open market.

In the 1990s, most critics of free markets have chosen to prioritize social capital, often with the ambiguous but superficially appealing rallying cry that we should strengthen our sense of 'community'. The argument that society should be organ-ized to maximize a sense of community comes in many guises. Stakeholder economists, such as Will Hutton, argue that we need to regulate market capitalism by enforcing upon companies obligations to communities and employees as well as shareholders. Communitarians, such as John Gray and Amitai Etzioni, argue that individuals can only realize themselves within a strong, supportive community. They share the belief that global capitalism is the enemy of community and that we need to make our societies more caring and compassionate. The communitarian critique of market capitalism is superficially appealing but eventually disappointing. Strong communities can be pockets of intolerance and prejudice. Settled, stable commun-ities are the enemies of innovation, talent, creativity, diversity and experimentation. They are often hostile to outsiders, dissenters, young upstarts and immigrants. Community can too quickly become a rallying cry for nostalgia; that kind of community is the enemy of knowledge creation, which is the well-spring of economic growth.

This battle between market and community has been central to the politics of the 1990s. The clash between market and community encouraged a string of attempts, none entirely convincing, to reconcile them: Tony Blair's and Bill Clinton's Third Way, Gerhard Schroeder's radical centre in Germany, Lionel Jospin's hope to create a market economy but not a market society in France, George Bush Jnr's compassionate conservatism, were all attempts to marry the market and community, efficiency and social justice. Governments of the right and the left have continued with broadly pro-market policies, while also strengthening social institutions. This middle way is better than the market extremism which went before. But too often this course, tacking between the demands of market and community, is reduced to a balancing act. Politics with a compromise built into its core unsurprisingly leads to piecemeal, cautious reform: one step forward, half a step back. It does not produce a new vision of how society should be organized, nor a radically new kind of politics, with a new uplifting, inspirational goal and new means to achieve it.

The emergence of the Third Way and its continental variants marked the end of free market dominance. But the way ahead is not to navigate a middle course between the old left and the new right, the community and the market. The way ahead is to adopt a different destination altogether. The goal of politics in the twenty-first century should be to create societies which maximize knowledge, the well-spring of economic growth and democratic self-governance. Markets and communities, companies and social institutions should be devoted to that larger goal. Finance and social capital should be harnessed to the goal of advancing and spreading knowledge. That will make us better off, put us more in charge of our lives and make us better able to look after ourselves. The free-market agenda has run out of steam. Communitarianism is fraught with difficulty: when it is not vague it sounds authoritarian. The goal of becoming a knowledge-driven society, however, is radical and emancipatory. It has far-reaching implications for how companies are owned, organized and managed; the ways in which rewards are distributed to match talent, creativity and contribution; how education, learning and research are organized; the constitution of the welfare state and the political system. Knowledge is our most precious resource: we should organize society to maximize its creation and use. Our aim should not be a Third Way to balance the demands of the market against those of the community. Our aim should be to harness the power of markets and community to the more fundamental goal of creating and spreading knowledge. [. . .]

# Chapter 3

# Esther Dyson, George Gilder, George Keyworth and Alvin Toffler

## CYBERSPACE AND THE AMERICAN DREAM

From *The Information Society*, 12 (1996): 295–308.

[. . .]

## Preamble

**T**HE CENTRAL EVENT OF THE 20TH CENTURY is the overthrow of matter. In technology, economics, and the politics of nations, wealth – in the form of physical resources – has been losing value and significance. The powers of mind are everywhere ascendant over the brute force of things.

In a First Wave economy, land and farm labor are the main 'factors of production.' In a Second Wave economy, the land remains valuable while the 'labor' becomes massified around machines and larger industries. In a Third Wave economy, the central resource – a single word broadly encompassing data, information, images, symbols, culture, ideology and values – is *actionable* knowledge.

The industrial age is not fully over. In fact, classic Second Wave sectors (oil, steel, auto-production) have learned how to benefit from Third Wave technological breakthroughs – just as the First Wave's agricultural productivity benefited exponentially from the Second Wave's farm-mechanization.

But the Third Wave, and the *Knowledge Age* it has opened, will not deliver on its potential unless it adds social and political dominance to its accelerating technological and economic strength. This means repealing Second Wave laws and retiring Second Wave attitudes. It also gives to leaders of the advanced democracies a special responsibility – to facilitate, hasten and explain the transition.

As humankind explores this new 'electronic frontier' of knowledge, it must confront again the most profound questions of how to organize itself for the common good. The meaning of freedom, structures of self-government, definition of property, nature of competition, conditions for cooperation, sense of community and nature of progress will each be redefined for the Knowledge Age – just as they were redefined for a new age of industry some 250 years ago.

What our 20th-century countrymen came to think of as the 'American Dream,' and what resonant thinkers referred to as 'the promise of American life' or 'the American Idea,' emerged from the turmoil of 19th-century industrialization. Now it's our turn: The knowledge revolution, and the Third Wave of historical change it powers, summon us to renew the dream and enhance the promise.

## The nature of cyberspace

The Internet [. . .] is only a tiny part of cyberspace. So just what is cyberspace?

More ecosystem than machine, cyberspace is a bioelectronic environment that is literally universal: It exists everywhere there are telephone wires, coaxial cables, fiber-optic lines or electromagnetic waves.

This environment is 'inhabited' by knowledge, including incorrect ideas, existing in electronic form. It is connected to the physical environment by portals which allow people to see what's inside, to put knowledge in, to alter it, and to take knowledge out. Some of these portals are one-way (e.g. television receivers and television transmitters); others are two-way (e.g. telephones, computer modems).

Most of the knowledge in cyberspace lives the most temporary (or so we think) existence: Your voice, on a telephone wire or microwave, travels through space at the speed of light, reaches the ear of your listener, and is gone forever.

But people are increasingly building cyberspatial 'warehouses' of data, knowledge, information and misinformation in digital form, the ones and zeros of binary computer code. The storehouses themselves display a physical form (discs, tapes, CD-ROMs) – but what they contain is accessible only to those with the right kind of portal and the right kind of key.

The key is software, a special form of electronic knowledge that allows people to navigate through the cyberspace environment and make its contents understandable to the human senses in the form of written language, pictures and sound.

People are adding to cyberspace – creating it, defining it, expanding it – at a rate that is already explosive and getting faster. Faster computers, cheaper means of electronic storage, improved software and more capable communications channels (satellites, fiber-optic lines) – each of these factors independently add to cyberspace. But the real explosion comes from the combination of all of them, working together in ways we still do not understand.

The bioelectronic *frontier* is an appropriate metaphor for what is happening in cyberspace, calling to mind as it does the spirit of invention and discovery that led ancient mariners to explore the world, generations of pioneers to tame the American continent and, more recently, to man's first exploration of outer space.

But the exploration of cyberspace brings both greater opportunity, and in some ways more difficult challenges, than any previous human adventure.

Cyberspace is the land of knowledge, and the exploration of that land can be a civilizations truest, highest calling. The opportunity is now before us to empower every person to pursue that calling in his or her own way.

The challenge is as daunting as the opportunity is great. The Third Wave has profound implications for the nature and meaning of property, of the marketplace, of community and of individual freedom. As it emerges, it shapes new codes of behavior that move each organism and institution – family, neighborhood, church group, company, government, nation – inexorably beyond standardization and centralization, as well as beyond the materialist's obsession with energy, money and control.

Turning the economics of mass-production inside out, new information technologies are driving the financial costs of diversity – both product and personal – down toward zero, 'demassifying' our institutions and our culture. Accelerating demassification creates the potential for vastly increased human freedom.

It also spells the death of the central institutional paradigm of modern life, the bureaucratic organization. (Governments, including the American government, are the last great redoubt of bureaucratic power on the face of the planet, and for them the coming change will be profound and probably traumatic.)

[. . .]


## The nature and ownership of property

Clear and enforceable property rights are essential for markets to work. Defining them is a central function of government. Most of us have known that for a long time. But to create the new cyberspace environment is to create *new* property – that is, new means of creating goods (including ideas) that serve people.

The property that makes up cyberspace comes in several forms: Wires, coaxial cable, computers and other 'hardware'; the electromagnetic spectrum; and 'intellectual property' – the knowledge that dwells in and defines cyberspace.

In each of these areas, two questions must be answered. First, what does 'ownership' *mean*? What is the nature of the property itself, and what does it mean to own it? Second, once we understand what ownership means, *who* is the owner? At the level of first principles, should ownership be public (i.e. government) or private (i.e. individuals)?

The answers to these two questions will set the basic terms upon which America and the world will enter the Third Wave. For the most part, however, these questions are not yet even being asked. Instead, at least in America, governments are attempting to take Second Wave concepts of property and ownership and apply them to the Third Wave. Or they are ignoring the problem altogether.

For example, a great deal of attention has been focused recently on the nature of 'intellectual property' – i.e. the fact that knowledge is what economists call a 'public good,' and thus requires special treatment in the form of copyright and patent protection.

Major changes in US copyright and patent law during the past two decades have broadened these protections to incorporate 'electronic property.' In essence, these reforms have attempted to take a body of law that originated in the 15th century, with Gutenberg's invention of the printing press, and apply it to the electronically stored and transmitted knowledge of the Third Wave.

A more sophisticated approach starts with recognizing how the Third Wave has fundamentally altered the nature of knowledge as a 'good,' and that the operative effect is not technology per se (the shift from printed books to electronic storage and retrieval systems), but rather the shift from a mass production, mass-media, mass-culture civilization to a demassified civilization.

The big change, in other words, is the demassification of actionable knowledge.

The dominant form of new knowledge in the Third Wave is perishable, transient, *customized* knowledge: The right information, combined with the right software and presentation, at precisely the right time. Unlike the mass knowledge of the Second Wave – 'public good' knowledge that was useful to everyone because most people's information needs were standardized – Third Wave customized knowledge is by nature a private good.

If this analysis is correct, copyright and patent protection of knowledge (or at least many forms of it) may no longer be unnecessary. In fact, the marketplace may already be creating vehicles to compensate creators of customized knowledge outside the cumbersome copyright/patent process [. . .].

[. . .]

Who will define the nature of cyberspace property rights, and how? How can we strike a balance between interoperable open systems and protection of property?

## The nature of the marketplace

Inexpensive knowledge destroys economies-of-scale. Customized knowledge permits 'just in time' production for an ever rising number of goods. Technological progress creates new means of serving old markets, turning one-time monopolies into competitive battlegrounds.

These phenomena are altering the nature of the marketplace, not just for information technology but for all goods and materials, shipping and services. In cyberspace itself, market after market is being transformed by technological progress from a 'natural monopoly' to one in which competition is the rule. [. . .]

[. . .]

The advent of new technology and new products creates the potential for *dynamic competition* – competition between and among technologies and industries, each seeking to find the best way of serving customers' needs. Dynamic competition is different from static competition, in which many providers compete to sell essentially similar products at the lowest price.

Static competition is good, because it forces costs and prices to the lowest levels possible for a given product. Dynamic competition is better, because it allows competing technologies and new products to challenge the old ones and, if they really are better, to replace them. Static competition might lead to faster and stronger horses. Dynamic competition gives us the automobile.

Such dynamic competition – the essence of what Austrian economist Joseph Schumpeter called 'creative destruction' – creates winners and losers on a massive scale. New technologies can render instantly obsolete billions of dollars of embedded infrastructure, accumulated over decades. The transformation of the US computer industry since 1980 is a case in point.

[. . .]

[. . .] In the transition from mainframes to PCs, a vast new market was created. This market was characterized by dynamic competition consisting of easy access and low barriers to entry. Start-ups by the dozens took on the larger established companies – and won.

After a decade of angst, the surprising outcome is that America is not only competitive internationally, but, by any measurable standard, America dominates the growth sectors in world economics – telecommunications, microelectronics, computer networking (or 'connected computing') and software systems and applications.

The reason for America's victory in the computer wars of the 1980s is that dynamic competition was allowed to occur, in an area so breakneck and pell-mell that government would've had a hard time controlling it even had it been paying attention. The challenge for policy [. . .] is to permit, even encourage, dynamic competition in every aspect of the cyberspace marketplace.

## The nature of freedom

Overseas friends of America sometimes point out that the US Constitution is unique – because it states explicitly that power resides with the people, who delegate it to the government, rather than the other way around.

This idea – central to our free society – was the result of more than 150 years of intellectual and political ferment, from the Mayflower Compact to the US Constitution, as explorers struggled to establish the terms under which they would tame a new frontier.

And as America continued to explore new frontiers – from the Northwest Territory to the Oklahoma land-rush – it consistently returned to this fundamental principle of rights, reaffirming, time after time, that power resides with the people.

Cyberspace is the latest American frontier. As this and other societies make ever deeper forays into it, the proposition that ownership of this frontier resides first *with the people* is central to achieving its true potential.

To some people, that statement will seem melodramatic. America, after all, remains a land of individual freedom, and this freedom clearly extends to cyberspace. How else to explain the uniquely American phenomenon of the hacker, who ignored every social pressure and violated every rule to develop a set of skills through an early and intense exposure to low-cost, ubiquitous computing.

Those skills eventually made him or her highly marketable, whether in developing applications software or implementing networks. The hacker became a technician, an inventor and, in case after case, a creator of new wealth in the form of the baby businesses that have given America the lead in cyberspatial exploration and settlement.

It is hard to imagine hackers surviving, let alone thriving, in the more formalized and regulated democracies of Europe and Japan. In America, they've become vital for economic growth and trade leadership. Why? Because Americans still celebrate individuality over conformity, reward achievement over consensus and militantly protect the right to be different.

But the need to affirm the basic principles of freedom is real. Such an affirmation is needed in part because we are entering new territory, where there are as yet no rules – just as there were no rules on the American continent in 1620, or in the Northwest Territory in 1787.

Centuries later, an affirmation of freedom – by this document and similar efforts – is needed for a second reason: We are at the end of a century dominated by the mass institutions of the industrial age. The industrial age encouraged *conformity* and relied on *standardization*. And the institutions of the day – corporate and government bureaucracies, huge civilian and military administrations, schools of all types – reflected these priorities. Individual liberty suffered – sometimes only a little, sometimes a lot.

[. . .]

All of these interventions might have made sense in a Second Wave world, where standardization dominated and where it was assumed that the scarcity of knowledge (plus a scarcity of telecommunications capacity) made bureaucracies and other elites better able to make decisions than the average person.

But, whether they made sense before or not, these and literally thousands of other infringements on individual rights now taken for granted make no sense at all in the Third Wave.

For a century, those who lean ideologically in favor of freedom have found themselves at war not only with their ideological opponents, but with a time in history when the value of conformity was at its peak. However desirable as an ideal, individual freedom often seemed impractical. The mass institutions of the Second Wave required us to give up freedom in order for the system to 'work.'

The coming of the Third Wave turns that equation inside-out. The complexity of Third Wave society is too great for any centrally planned bureaucracy to manage. Demassification, customization, individuality, freedom – these are the keys to success for Third Wave civilization.

## The essence of community

If the transition to the Third Wave is so positive, why are we experiencing so much anxiety? Why are the statistics of social decay at or near all-time highs? Why does cyberspatial 'rapture' strike millions of prosperous Westerners as lifestyle *rupture*? Why do the principles that have held us together as a nation seem no longer sufficient – or even wrong?

The incoherence of political life is mirrored in disintegrating personalities. Whether 100 percent covered by health plans or not, psychotherapists and gurus do a land-office business, as people wander aimlessly amid competing therapies. People slip into cults and covens or, alternatively, into a pathological privatism, convinced that reality is absurd, insane or meaningless. 'If things are so good,' Forbes magazine asked recently, 'why do we feel so bad?'

In part, this is why: Because we constitute the final generation of an old civilization and, at the very same time, the first generation of a new one. Much of our personal confusion and social disorientation is traceable to conflict *within us* and within our political institutions – between the dying Second Wave civilization and the emergent Third Wave civilization thundering in to take its place.

Second Wave ideologues routinely lament the breakup of mass society. Rather than seeing this enriched diversity as an opportunity for human development, they attach it as 'fragmentation' and 'balkanization.' But to reconstitute democracy in Third Wave terms, we need to jettison the frightening but false assumption that more diversity automatically brings more tension and conflict in society.

Indeed, the exact reverse can be true: If 100 people all desperately want the same brass ring, they may be forced to fight for it. On the other hand, if each of the 100 has a different objective, it is far more rewarding for them to trade, cooperate, and form symbiotic relationships. Given appropriate social arrangements, diversity can make for a secure and stable civilization.

No one knows what the Third Wave communities of the future will look like, or where 'demassification' will ultimately lead. It is clear, however, that cyberspace will play an important role knitting together in the diverse communities of tomorrow, facilitating the creation of 'electronic neighborhoods' bound together not by geography but by shared interests.

Socially, putting advanced computing power in the hands of entire populations will alleviate pressure on highways, reduce air pollution, allow people to live further away from crowded or dangerous urban areas, and expand family time.

[. . .]

'Cyberspaces' is a wonderful *pluralistic* word to open more minds to the Third Wave's civilizing potential. Rather than being a centrifugal force helping to tear society apart, cyberspace can be one of the main forms of glue holding together an increasingly free and diverse society.

## The role of government

[. . .]

Eventually, the Third Wave will affect virtually everything government does. The most pressing need, however, is to revamp the policies and programs that are slowing the creation of cyberspace. Second Wave programs for Second Wave industries – the status quo for the status quo – will do little damage in the short run. It is the government's efforts to apply its Second Wave modus operandi to the fast-moving, decentralized creatures of the Third Wave that is the real threat to progress. Indeed, if there is to be an 'industrial policy for the knowledge age,' it should focus on removing barriers to competition and massively deregulating the fast-growing telecommunications and computing industries.

One further point should be made at the outset: Government should be as strong and as big as it needs to be to accomplish its central functions effectively and efficiently. The reality is that a Third Wave government will be vastly smaller (perhaps by 50 percent or more) than the current one – this is an inevitable implication of the transition from the centralized power structures of the industrial age to the dispersed, decentralized institutions of the Third. But smaller government does not imply weak government; nor does arguing for smaller government require being 'against' government for narrowly ideological reasons.

Indeed, the transition from the Second Wave to the Third Wave will require a level of government *activity* not seen since the New Deal. Here are five proposals to back up the point.

## 1. The path to interactive multimedia access

The 'Jeffersonian Vision' offered by Mitch Kapor and Jerry Berman has propelled the Electronic Frontier Foundation's campaign for an 'open platform' telecom architecture:

> The amount of electronic material the superhighway can carry is dizzying, compared to the relatively narrow range of broadcast TV and the limited number of cable channels. Properly constructed and regulated, it could be open to all who wish to speak, publish and communicate. None of the interactive services will be possible, however, if we have an eight-lane data superhighway rushing into every home and only a narrow footpath coming back out. Instead of settling for a multimedia version of the same entertainment that is increasingly dissatisfying on today's TV, we need a superhighway that encourages the production and distribution of a broader, more diverse range of programming.
>
> (*New York Times* 11/24/93, p. A25)

The question is: What role should government play in bringing this vision to reality? But also: Will incentives for the openly-accessible, 'many to many,' national multimedia network envisioned by EFF harm the rights of those now constructing thousands of non-open local area networks?

These days, interactive multimedia is the daily servant only of avant-garde firms and other elites. But the same thing could have been said about word-processors 12 years ago, or phone-line networks six years ago. Today we have, in effect, universal access to personal computing – which no political coalition ever subsidized or 'planned.' And America's *networking* menu is in a hyper-growth phase. Whereas the accessing software cost $50 two years ago, today the same companies hand it out free – to get more people on-line.

This egalitarian explosion has occurred in large measure because government has stayed out of these markets, letting personal computing take over while mainframes rot (almost literally) in warehouses, and allowing (no doubt more by omission than commission) computer networks to grow, free of the kinds of regulatory restraints that affect phones, broadcast and cable.

[. . .]

## 2. Promoting dynamic competition

Technological progress is turning the telecommunications marketplace from one characterized by 'economies of scale' and 'natural monopolies' into a prototypical competitive market. The challenge for government is to encourage this shift – to create the circumstances under which new competitors and new technologies will challenge the natural monopolies of the past.

Price-and-entry regulation makes sense for natural monopolies. The tradeoff is a straightforward one: The monopolist submits to price regulation by the state, in return for an exclusive franchise on the market.

But what happens when it becomes economically desirable to have more than one provider in a market? The continuation of regulation under these circumstances stops progress in its tracks. It prevents new entrants from introducing new technologies and new products, while depriving the regulated monopolist of any incentive to do so on its own.

Price-and-entry regulation, in short, is the antithesis of dynamic competition.

The alternative to regulation is antitrust. Antitrust law is designed to prevent the acts and practices that can lead to the creation of new monopolies, or harm consumers by forcing up prices, limiting access to competing products or reducing service quality. Antitrust law is the means by which America has, for over 120 years, fostered competition in markets where many providers can and should compete.

The market for telecommunications services – telephone, cable, satellite, wireless – is now such a market. The implication of this simple fact is also simple, and price/entry regulation of telecommunications services – by state and local governments as well as the Federal government – should therefore be replaced by antitrust law as rapidly as possible.

This transition will not be simple, and it should not be instantaneous. If antitrust is to be seriously applied to telecommunications, some government agencies [. . .] will need new types of expertise. And investors in regulated monopolies should be permitted time to reevaluate their investments given the changing nature of the legal conditions in which these firms will operate – a luxury not afforded the cable industry in recent years.

This said, two additional points are important. First, delaying implementation is different from delaying enactment. The latter should be immediate, even if the former is not. Secondly, there should be no half steps. Moving from a regulated environment to a competitive one is – to borrow a cliche – like changing from driving on the left side of the road to driving on the right: You can't do it gradually.

## 3. Defining and assigning property rights

[. . .]

Defining property rights in cyberspace is perhaps the single most urgent and important task for government information policy. Doing so will be a complex task, and each key area – the electromagnetic spectrum, intellectual property, cyberspace itself (including the right to privacy) – involves unique challenges. The important points here are:

First, this is a 'central' task of government. A Third Wave government will understand the importance and urgency of this undertaking and begin seriously to address it; to fail to do so is to perpetuate the politics and policy of the Second Wave.

Secondly, the key principle of ownership by the people – private ownership – should
govern every deliberation. Government does not own cyberspace, the people
do.

Thirdly, clarity is essential. Ambiguous property rights are an invitation to litigation,
channeling energy into courtrooms that serve no customers and create no
wealth. From patent and copyright systems for software, to challenges over
the ownership and use of spectrum, the present system is failing in this simple
regard.

The difference between America's historic economic success can, in case after
case, be traced to our wisdom in creating and allocating clear, enforceable property rights. The creation and exploration of cyberspace requires that wisdom to be
recalled and reaffirmed.

## 4. Creating pro-Third Wave tax and accounting rules

We need a whole set of new ways of accounting, both at the level of the enterprise,
and of the economy.

'GDP' and other popular numbers do nothing to clarify the magic and muscle
of information technology. The government has not been very good at measuring
service-sector output, and almost all institutions are incredibly bad at measuring the
productivity of *information*. Economists are stuck with a set of tools designed during,
or as a result of, the 1930s. So they have been measuring less and less important
variables with greater and greater precision.

At the level of the enterprise, obsolete accounting procedures cause us to
systematically *overvalue* physical sets (i.e. property) and *undervalue* human-resource
assets and intellectual assets. [. . .]

On the tax side, the same thing is true. The tax code always reflects the varying
lobbying pressures brought to bear on government. And the existing tax code was
brought into being by traditional manufacturing enterprises and the allied forces that
arose during the assembly line's heyday.

The computer industry correctly complains that half their product is depreci-
ated in six months or less – yet they can't depreciate it for tax purposes. The US
semiconductor industry faces five-year depreciation timetables for products that
have three-year lives [. . .]. Overall, the tax advantage remains with the long, rather
than the short, product life-cycle, even though the latter is where all design and
manufacturing are trending.

It is vital that accounting and tax policies [. . .] start to reflect the shortened
capital life-cycles of the Knowledge Age, and the increasing role of *intangible* capital
as 'wealth.'

## 5. Creating a Third Wave government

Going beyond cyberspace policy per se, government must remake itself and rede-
fine its relationship to the society at large. No single set of policy changes can create
a future-friendly government. But there are some yardsticks we can apply to policy
proposals. Among them:

- **Is it based on the factory model, i.e. on standardization, routine and mass-production?** If so, it is a Second Wave policy. Third Wave policies encourage uniqueness.
- **Does it centralize control?** Second Wave policies centralize power in bureaucratic institutions; Third Wave policies work to spread power – to empower those closest to the decision.
- **Does it encourage geographic concentration?** Second Wave policies encourage people to congregate physically; Third Wave policies permit people to work at home, and to live wherever they choose.
- **Is it based on the idea of mass culture – of everyone watching the same sitcoms on television – or does it permit, even encourage, diversity within a broad framework of shared values?** Third Wave policies will help transform diversity from a threat into an array of opportunities.

A serious effort to apply these tests to every area of government activity – from the defense and intelligence community to health care and education – would ultimately produce a complete transformation of government as we know it. Since that is what's needed, let's start applying.

## Grasping the future

The conflict between Second Wave and Third Wave groupings is the central political tension cutting through our society today. The more basic political question is not who controls the last days of industrial society, but who shapes the new civilization rapidly rising to replace it. Who, in other words, will shape the nature of cyberspace and its impact on our lives and institutions?

Living on the edge of the Third Wave, we are witnessing a battle not so much over the nature of the future – for the Third Wave will arrive – but over the nature of the transition. On one side of this battle are the partisans of the industrial past. On the other are growing millions who recognize that the world's most urgent problems can no longer be resolved within the massified frameworks we have inherited.

The Third Wave sector includes not only high-flying computer and electronics firms and biotech start-ups. It embraces advanced, information-driven manufacturing in every industry. It includes the increasingly data-drenched services – finance, software, entertainment, the media, advanced communications, medical services, consulting, training and learning. The people in this sector will soon be the dominant constituency in American politics.

[. . .]

It is time to embrace these challenges, to grasp the future and pull ourselves forward. If we do so, we will indeed renew the American Dream and enhance the promise of American life.

# Critics

# Chapter 4

# Langdon Winner

## WHO WILL WE BE IN CYBERSPACE?

From *The Information Society*, 12 (1996): 63–72.

T O  T H O S E  W H O  V I E W  A M E R I C A  from other parts of the world, it must sometimes seem that we are a compulsively restless people, continually reinventing ourselves, renovating our ways of living at the drop of a hat. There seems to be no idea too extravagant, no project too far fetched that some sizable segment of the populace won't take it up, try it out, see how it works. Birthplace of new ideas, discoveries, practices, styles, gadgets, and institutions, the United States has gained renown as a laboratory for the exploration of human identities and relationships that later spread to other parts of the globe.

The propensity to personal and social reinvention goes back to the earliest days of our national experience. In the middle 18th century, it seemed likely that the British monarchs and a stable monarchical way of life in the American colonies would endure forever. Rooted in notions of hierarchy, inequality, patriarchy, and highly structured relations between patrons and clients, monarchy gave people's lives meaning and coherence. But efforts to sustain this pattern sparked discontent and eventual revolt. The colonists' successful war against King George III was also a revolution in political culture, one that overthrew monarchy as a tightly woven fabric of human relations.

During their turn at the helm, leaders of the uprising, the founding fathers, did their best to create a new society, building political, legal, and economic institutions based on models adapted from the ancient republics. Individual liberty and consent of the governed became the guiding principles. But the political institutions of the republican system were to depend on the guidance of a small group of enlightened, virtuous men, people with great souls and abilities, an arrangement that many Americans found disagreeable. It did not take long, therefore, for the republican conception of social and political relations to itself be challenged by the proliferation of rules, roles, and relations far more democratic in character. By the early 19th century, Americans were again busily self-transforming, affirming that the promise of the country was for the mass of common working people to achieve material prosperity and genuine self-government (Wood 1992).

In sum, a lifetime that stretched from 1750 to 1820 would have undergone a sequence of three radically different ways of defining what society was about, three ways of defining who a person was and where a person stood in the larger order of things. I call attention to this segment of American history to recall the fact that times of rapid transformation are not new to us. Today's zealots for the information age and cyberspace often insist that we are confronted with circumstances totally unprecedented, circumstances that require rapid transformation of society. That may be true in some respects. But it is also true that we Americans are past masters in reinventing ourselves and sometimes proceed thoughtfully to good effect.

Since the middle 19th century, episodes of person and social transformation have focused as much upon people's relationship to technological systems as they have to political institutions. By now it is a familiar story: To invent a new technology requires that (in some way or another) society also invents the kinds of people who will use it; older practices, relationships, and ways of defining people's identities fall by the wayside; new practices, relationships, and identities take root. From that standpoint, as technological devices and systems are being introduced, it is important that those who care about the future of society go beyond questions about the utility of new devices and systems, beyond even questions about economic consequences. One must also ask:

1    Around these instruments, what kinds of bonds, attachments, and obligations are in the making?
2    To whom or to what are people connected or dependent upon?
3    Do ordinary people see themselves as having a crucial role in what is taking shape?
4    Do people see themselves as competent, able to make decisions?
5    Do they feel that their voices matter in making decisions that will affect family workplace, community, nation?
6    Do they feel themselves to be fairly treated?

These are issues about conditions that sustain selfhood and civic culture, issues that should always be addressed as technological innovations emerge. If we limit our attention to powerful technical applications, their uses and market prospects, we tend to ignore what may be the single most consequential feature of technological change, the shaping of the conditions that affect people's sense of who they are and why they live together.

In our time the most important occasion for addressing such questions is the digital transformation of an astonishingly wide range of material artifacts interwoven with social practices. In one location after another, people are saying in effect: Let us take what exists now and restructure or replace it in digital format. Let's take the bank teller, the person sitting behind the counter with little scraps of paper and an adding machine, and replace it with an ATM accessible 24 hours a day. Let's take analog recording and the vinyl LP and replace it with the compact disc in which music is encoded as a stream of digital bits. Or let's take the classroom with the teacher, blackboard, books, and verbal interchange and replace it with materials presented in computer hardware and software and call it 'interactive learning' (as if earlier classrooms lacked an interactive quality). In case after case, the move to computerize and digitize means that many preexisting cultural forms have suddenly gone liquid, losing their former shape as they are retailored for computerized expression. As new patterns solidify, both useful artifacts and the texture of human relations that surround them are often much different from what existed previously. This process amounts to a vast, ongoing experiment whose long-term ramifications no one fully comprehends.

The opportunities and challenges presented by digital liquification have generated great waves of enthusiasm. Entrepreneurs are busily at work creating new products and services. Organizational innovators are experimenting with all kinds of computer-mediated collaborative work. Artists, even ones highly skeptical of information technology's overall effects, are exhilarated by the new varieties of aesthetic expression that have become available in computing and telecommunications. It is no surprise that the widespread rupture about computing has achieved ideological expression as well. The old bromides of Alvin Toffler's simplistic wave theory of history, barely fizzing a couple of years ago, have received a new injection of seltzer in the right-wing manifesto, 'Cyberspace and the American Dream: A Magna Carta for the Knowledge Age' (Dyson *et al.* 1994). In this and similar paeans to the digital age, there is a rekindling of the millennial expectations that often arise during times of technological and social change, accompanied by the ill-founded hopes of 'mythinformation,' for example, the expectation that the spread of information machines is somehow inherently democratic and that no one needs to lift a finger to achieve democratization and create a good society (Winner 1986).

But along with the excitement and sense of limitless possibilities arise some serious misgivings. As the sweeping digital liquification of social practices and institutions proceeds, one sees closely associated processes of economic liquidation that erode the former livelihoods of many working class and middle-class people. As jobs and activities and organizational structures undergo digital transformation, structures that were formerly funded are now defunded, liquidated as capital takes the opportunity to move elsewhere. In businesses, universities, government agencies, and other organizations, the connection between the introduction of new computing systems and widespread announcements of layoffs and downsizing seems obvious. Digital liquification has become the cultural solvent that enables financial and organization liquidation. [. . .] [W]hole vocations – secretaries, phone operators, bank tellers, postal clerks – have been eliminated or abolished or drastically reduced. [. . .]

Gurus on the business seminar circuit – Tom Peters, Daniel Burrus, Michael Hammar, James Champy, and the like – prefer to see these upheavals as an exhilarating challenge. [. . .] Other observers describe these developments as potentially cataclysmic for much of the population, as the 'end of work' and 'end of career' present society with conditions for which it is ill prepared (Bridges 1994; Rifkin 1995; Glassner 1994). Whatever one's anticipations on that score may be it is certainly trite that in our time some basic conditions of human identity and association are being powerfully redefined. Who will we become as such developments run their course? What kind of society and political order will emerge?

Rather than seek guidance on these matters from today's giddy manifestoes of cyberspace, perhaps we should consider relevant chapters in our own history, chapters in which technological transformation involved profound alterations in self and society, periods in which momentous choices about the future were up for grabs. Of particular relevance, in my view, are several recent studies by historians and social scientists that have tried to identify what is distinctive about human self-hood in what came to be called modern, industrial society. A number of scholars in widely different fields – David Hounshell (1984), Terry Smith (1993), Jeffrey Meikle (1979), David Noble (1977), Adrian Forty (1986), Ruth Schwarz Cowan (1983), Dolores Hayden (1981), Roland Marchand (1985), David Nye (1990), David Harvey (1989), and others – have looked at the first half of 20th century America, noticing such developments as the creation of the Ford assembly line, the spread of scientific management, the development of large, long linked systems in electricity, water supply, transit, telephone, radio, and television, seeking to explain how they achieved the form they did, how they were received by the populace as a whole, how the rise of the consumer economy with its appliances and other goods came to be defined as necessary for the good life, and how associated developments in advertising, industrial design, public relations, education, and other methods fields helped shape public opinion and channel social development.

What emerges from these studies that might be useful today? What can we take from them that might help us think about contemporary developments, that link computing with society's future? I briefly underscore several issues that seem especially important.

One consistent finding in histories of the modern period is that power over the most important decisions about how technologies were introduced was far from evenly distributed. Those who had the financial and technical wherewithal to create new technologies in earlier decades of our century often found it feasible and desirable to mold society to match the needs of emerging technological systems and organizational plans. Many leaders in the corporate sector regarded society as mere putty that could be shaped with minimal resistance from the populace affected.

Greatest latitude for overt social control was present in the workplaces where employees were often seen as malleable, subject to the routines and disciplines of work. This attitude was clearly displayed in the paternalism of F. W. Taylor's *Principles of Scientific Management* and the practices it advanced. 'In the past the man has been first,' Taylor explained. 'In the future the system must be first' (Taylor 1911, p. 7). In Taylor's vision and in similar approaches to modern American management, the authority relations of modern industry were perfectly clear. When a worker accepted employment at a particular firm, the worker was required to follow an intricate schedule specifying what to do and how to do it. The employer named the job, specified its content, and determined the extent to which the work required any knowledge or competence. Thus, as the workplaces of industrial society were organized, people were mobilized not only for productive tasks, but for fairly stable, predictable, reproducible identities as well. Such efforts carried a strong moral component. Cultural historians note that during the middle decades of the 20th century, virtues appropriate to the development of machines – productive order, efficiency, control, forward-looking dynamism – became prevailing social virtues as well (Smith 1993).

For industrial leaders like Henry Ford, Henry Luce, and Alfred Sloan, men able to achieve an overview of unfolding developments, a key realization was that continuing economic growth required the mobilization of great numbers of people not merely as producers but as consumers as well. By the 1920s it was common for corporate planners to aspire to reach deeply into people's lives, offering items and opportunities for consumption along with carefully tailored images and slogans that helped depict identities, attitudes, and life-styles that could guide people's inclinations in home life and leisure. Industrial design, advertising, and corporate-sponsored journalism and public education combined with industrial planning to promote a series of strongly endorsed social role identities that were depicted in photos, newspaper and magazine articles, and school text books (Marchand 1985). [. . .]

In this light, historians Roland Marchand and Terry Smith note the widely displayed tableaux vivants of modern life, combinations of advertising text and photography that from the 1920s to 1950s depicted:

The executive in the office tower
The worker in the clean, well-organized factory
The housewife in her appliance-filled kitchen
Children surrounded with goods for the little ones
The automobile driver speeding along a wide open highway.

The purpose of these images was to project possibilities for living in modern society at a time in which many of those possibilities were still novel. Crucial to the effect of these projections was a story about the world, a story in which people's orderly role in production was to be rewarded with an equally orderly, rational, modern role in consumption. Within well-managed corporate strategies that linked the shape of consumer goods to advertising slogans, photographs, magazine stories, and other widely promulgated inducements, people were encouraged to seek meaning and fulfillment within prescribed channels. It would be absurd to suggest that these efforts succeeded in determining the content of people's lives completely. But I think it is true to say that there were deliberate and effective moves to frame and to guide how ordinary people understood life's possibilities. One has only to live for a while in societies in which these accomplishments have not taken root – for example, prosperous societies in contemporary Europe in which consumerism as a way of life does not yet dominate the ways people understand self, family, and society – to appreciate the artificiality and pungency of modern American strategies of social control.

Histories of these developments clearly suggest that the basic terms of this social contract were nonnegotiable. The ideas and plans of everyday citizens were not regarded as crucial for corporate planning. In the advertisements and tableaux vivants, the future was always depicted as something whole and inevitable. People were to be propelled forward by forces larger than themselves into a world that was rational, dynamic, prosperous, and harmonious. One visited spectacles like the 1939 World's Fair in New York to be swept up in the excitement of it all. There were no pavilions to solicit the public's suggestions about emerging devices, systems, or role definitions. As millions of visitors strolled through the fair, they learned how to orient themselves to changes in living that seemed to have their own undeniable trajectory.

Presenting the future in this way served an important purpose. Those making choices about the direction of social priorities and investments – for example, Robert Moses and other organizers of the New York World's Fair – had no desire to open the planning of sociotechnical innovations to make the process more inclusive. Spreading the broad umbrella of 'progress' over the details of policy, economic and political elites were able to defuse public criticism. The well-managed social consensus that unfolding developments were basically nonnegotiable was reflected in the silence of public discourse about alternatives, for example, the almost complete absence of popular forums in print or elsewhere from the 1920s through the 1950s where the meaning of the new technologies and their consequences could be discussed, criticized, or debated.

Held out to the American populace as the ultimate promise of modern society was individual, material satisfaction. The modern world was to be a place in which personal desires would be fulfilled through the consumption of industrially produced commodities. So glorious was the expected bounty, that any request to negotiate its terms would have seemed positively impudent. Missing from the picture was any attention to collective goods and collective problems. Long-term social commitments and the social costs of 'progress' were obscured by the belief that individual fulfillment was all that mattered. Thus, buying and driving this automobile would give the driver and family members a sense of thrill and belonging. Then as now, the automobile was always shown on highways miraculously free of other vehicles, well-paved roads that seemed to extend infinitely, wherever happy drivers turned the steering wheel. As an ad for ethyl gasoline in the 1930s proclaimed: 'There's always room out front' (Marchand 1985, p. 362).

Another key finding from social and cultural studies of modernism takes note of the design of artifacts. Those in a position to make decisions were aware that as everyday folks looked at the novelties that bombarded them, they were apt to find these transformations complex and confusing. In that light, a commonly chosen design strategy was to conceal the complexity of devices, systems, and social arrangements and to make them appear simple and manageable. Thus, for example, streamlining and other varieties of shiny metal styling were adopted to complex, technical mechanisms within soothing, attractive surfaces. As people became comfortable with these forms, the workings of the artificial world that surrounded people seemed less and less intelligible. The same is true of the texts and pictures of advertising. Extremely simple solutions – often ones involving personal uplift with the aid of consumer purchases – were proposed for complicated, real-world problems. Eventually some of those complex problems – congestion, pollution, urban and environmental decay – emerged as difficult issues, made even more vexing by the fact that they festered for decades.

As we ponder horizons of computing and society today – for example, choices in the creation and use of computer networks on a widespread scale – it seems likely that American society will reproduce some of the basic tendencies of modernism:

- Unequal power over key decisions about what is built and why.
- Concerted attempts to enframe and direct people's lives in both work and consumption.
- The presentation of the future society as something nonnegotiable.
- The stress on individual gratification rather than collective problems and responsibilities.
- Design strategies that conceal and obfuscate important realms of social complexity.

Patterns of this kind persist because the institutions of planning, finance, management, advertising, education, and design that shaped modernity earlier this century are still extremely powerful. Occasional calls for resistance and reform by labor unions, environmentalists, consumer groups, feminists, and others have, for the most part, been neutralized or absorbed. [. . .] Possibilities for self-conscious social choice and deliberate social action are often sidetracked to become obsessions focused on the purchasing and possessing of commodities.

As strong as these basic tendencies remain, however, it is doubtful that the world taking shape within and around today's information systems will simply reproduce the terms of previous decades. In fact, many of the forms of selfhood and social organization carefully nurtured for modern society seem ill-suited for conditions that increasingly confront Americans in the workplace and elsewhere. For example, the focus of personal identity based upon holding a lasting enduring job seems destined to become a relic of the industrial past (Glassner 1994). Within the context of the global communications, global enterprise, lean production, organizational flexibility, the idea that one might become a permanent employee of one organization or even one industry is less and less sensible. Much blue collar and clerical work is now temporary. To an increasing extent even well-educated technical professionals are required to define themselves as contractors able to move from project to project, task to task, place to place among many organizations. The assumption in computer-centered enterprises is no longer that of belonging to and being crucial to any enduring framework of social relations. To an increasing extent our organizations assume perpetual expendability. How people will respond to that, how they will recreate selfhood in an era in which everyone is expendable, could well become a far more serious issue in coming decades than even the often lamented decline of real wages.

Another crisis brewing in the information society has to do with where and how people will experience membership. For modernism the prescribed frame for social relations was that of city and suburb. People were situated geographically and expected to find meaningful relationships close to home. But today it is increasingly obvious that for sizeable, economically important segments of our society, attachment is no longer defined geographically at all. Many activities of work and leisure take place in global, electronic settings and that is how people define their attachments. Robert Reich, among others, worries that the symbolic analysts of today's global webs of enterprise are now shedding traditional loyalties to their fellow citizens, leaving the less well-to-do, the less well wired to suffer in decaying cities (Reich 1991). Indeed, attitudes of this sort can be found in the sociopathic cyberlibertarianism of the 1990s as represented, for example, in the 'Cyberspace and the American Dream' of the Progress and Freedom Foundation (Dyson *et al.* 1994) and in much of the hyperventilated prose of *Wired* magazine. What is affirmed in such thinking is a fierce desire for market freedom and unfettered self-expression with no expectation that inflated cyber-egos owe anything to geographically situated others. Increasingly prevalent conditions of work and communication seem to encourage the development of ways of being human that correspond to hypertextual movements on the World Wide Web. 'Don't count on me for anything; I'm out of here with the click of a mouse.' [. . .]

There are many, of course, who expect that desirable new forms of community will emerge, that people will use their computers and the Internet to forge new social relationships and identities, including ones that might bolster local community life. Time will tell whether those lovely hopes pan out. It's anyone's guess what sorts of personalities, styles of discourse, and social norms will ultimately flourish in these new settings. [. . .]

One feature of early 20th century modernism that American society seems likely to reproduce in years to come is the habit of excluding ordinary citizens from key choices about the design and development of new technologies, including information systems. Industrial leaders still indulge the old habit of presenting as faits accomplis what otherwise might have been choices open for diverse public imaginings, investigations, and debates. In magazine cover stories, corporate advertising campaigns, and political speeches, announcements of the arrival of the Information Superhighway and similar metaphors are still pitched in the language of inevitability. Get ready for it folks, here it comes: the set-top box!

[. . .]

These are matters in which people doing research on computing and the future could have a positive influence. If we're asking people to change their lives to adapt to the introduction of new information systems, it seems responsible to solicit very broad participation in deliberation, planning, decision making, prototyping, testing, evaluation, and the like. Some of the best models, in my view, come from the Scandinavian social democracies where a variety of social and political circumstances makes close consultation with ordinary workers and citizens a much more common practice than it is in the United States (Sandberg *et al.* 1992). Broad participation of this kind is warranted by principles of democracy and social justice, but it also makes sense because it is likely to produce better systems, ones that have a better fit with genuine human needs. Unfortunately, models for innovation of this kind have been seldom tried in the United States, perhaps because they are too democratic for those who oversee our intensely inegalitarian 'market' system.

[. . .]

How reassuring; evidently the 'right design' is headed our way and again we have not had to lift a finger. Developments of this kind echo the first words of Jean-Jacques Rousseau's *Social Contract* written two centuries ago: 'Men are born free but everywhere they are in chains.' An equivalent maxim today might be: 'People are not born with brass rings in their noses, but much technological development quietly supposes that they are.'

But why should we settle for effrontery so blatant? Rather than exclude the energy and ideas of the American populace, rather than try to predetermine what the horizons of computing and society will be, research and developments in computing ought to involve the public – ordinary people from all walks of life – in activities of inquiry, exploration, dialogue, and debate. Here computer professionals could, if they so chose, exercise much-needed leadership. While it is sometimes tempting to conclude that we are merely going 'where the technology is taking us,' or that social outcomes are and should be 'determined by market forces,' the fact of the matter is that deliberate choices about the relationship between people and new technology are made by someone, somehow, every day of the year. Persons whose professional work gives them insight into the choices that matter must be diligent in expressing their knowledge and judgments to a broad public. Otherwise they may find themselves employed as mere ranch hands, helping to fit the citizenry with digital brass rings.

As the 20th century draws to a close, it is evident that, for better or worse, the future of computing and the future of human relations – indeed, of human being itself – are now thoroughly intertwined. Foremost among the obligations this situation presents is the need to seek alternatives, social policies that might undo the dreary legacy of modernism: pervasive systems of one-way communication, preemption of democratic social choice, corporate manipulation, and the presentation of sweeping changes in living conditions as something justified by a univocal, irresistible 'progress.' True, the habits of technological somnambulism cultivated over many decades will not be easily overcome. But as waves of overhyped innovation confront increasingly obvious signs of social disorder, opportunities for lively conversation sometimes fall into our laps. Choices about computer technology involve not only obvious questions about 'what to do,' but also less obvious ones about 'who to be.' By virtue of their vocation, computer professionals are well situated to initiate public debates on this matter, helping a democratic populace explore new identities and the horizons of a good society.

## References

Bridges, W. (1994) *Jobshift: How to Prosper in a Workplace Without Jobs*. New York: Addison-Wesley.

Cowan, R. S. (1983) *More Work for Mother: The Ironies of Household Technology from the Open Hearth to the Microwave*. New York: Basic Books.

Dyson, E., Gilder, G., Keyworth, G. and Toffler, A. (1994) Cyberspace and the American Dream: A Magna Carta for the Knowledge Age, Release 1.2. August 22. Washington, DC: Progress and Freedom Foundation.

Forty, A. (1986) *Objects of Desire*. New York: Pantheon.

Glassner, B. (1994) *Career Crash: America's New Crisis and Who Survives*. New York: Simon and Schuster.

Harvey, D. (1989) *The Condition of Postmodernity: An Enquiry into the Origins of Cultural Change*. Cambridge, MA: Blackwell.

Hayden, D. (1981) *The Grand Domestic Revolution: A History of Feminist Designs for American Homes, Neighborhoods, and Cities*. Cambridge, MA: MIT Press.

Hounshell, D. A. (1984) *From the American System to Mass Production, 1800–1932: The Development of Manufacturing Technology in the United States*. Baltimore, MD: Johns Hopkins University Press.

Marchand, R. (1985) *Advertising the American Dream: Making Way for Modernity, 1920–1940*. Berkeley: University of California Press.

Meikle, J. L. (1979) *Twentieth Century Limited: Industrial Design in America, 1925–1939*, Philadelphia: Temple University Press.

Noble, D. F. (1977) *America by Design: Science, Technology and the Rise of Corporate Capitalism*. New York: Knopf.

Nye, D. E. (1990) *Electrifying America: Social Meanings of a New Technology, 1880–1940*. Cambridge, MA: MIT Press.

Reich, R. B. (1991) *The Work of Nations: Preparing Ourselves for 21st-century Capitalism*. New York: Knopf.

Rifkin, J. (1995) *The End of Work: The Decline of the Global Labor Force and the Dawn of the Post-market Era*. New York: G. P. Putnam's Sons.

Sandberg, A., Broms, G., Grip, A., Sundstrom, L., Steen, J. and Ullmark, P. (1992) *Technological Change and Co-determination in Sweden*. Philadelphia: Temple University Press.

Smith, T. (1993) *Making the Modern: Industry Art and Design in America*. Chicago: University of Chicago Press.

Taylor, F. W. (1911) *The Principles of Scientific Management*. New York: Harper and Brothers.

Winner, L. (1986) Mythinformation, in *The Whale and the Reactor*. Chicago: University of Chicago Press, pp. 98–117.

Wood, G. S. (1992) *The Radicalism of the American Revolution*. New York: Knopf.

# Chapter 5

# Theodore Roszak

## THE CULT OF INFORMATION

From *The Cult of Information*, Cambridge: Lutterworth (1986), pp. 3–45.

[. . .]

### Information old-style

WHEN I WAS GROWING UP in the years just before World War II, information was nothing to get excited about. As an intellectual category, it held a humble and marginal status. Few people would have conceived of it as the subject of a 'theory' or a 'science'; it was not associated with an advanced technology that lent it glamour as well as extravagant financial value. Probably the most common public use of the word was as part of the phrase 'Information, please.' That was how you asked the operator for telephone numbers before we had 411 to dial. There was also, through the 1930s and 1940s, a popular radio program by that name which challenged listeners to stump a panel of experts by sending in unlikely questions about assorted trivia. Who was the shortest president of the United States? What grand opera contains the longest duet? What mammal reproduces by laying eggs?

That was the way most people thought about information in those days: disjointed matters of fact that came in discrete little bundles. Sometimes what was in the bundles was surprising, sometimes amusing, sometimes helpful. Most often it took the form of a number, name, date, place, event, or measurement that answered a specific question beginning with who, what, when, where, how much. Such matters got talked about in ordinary words; they did not require esoteric mathematical formulations or a special technical vocabulary. Occasionally information might be urgently important – like knowing where to press to stop the bleeding – but it was not regarded as something for which there was an insatiable public need. Certainly nobody would have credited it with the status it has acquired in our day – that of a billion-dollar industrial commodity that we should want to see produced in limitless quantities.

Of course, everybody knew there were certain businesses and professions which needed to keep lots of files filled with information. There were the accountants, the lawyers, the engineers. The standard white collar occupations – banking, insurance, brokerage houses, real estate – were characterized by rooms filled with olive-drab filing cabinets and patrolled by busy platoons of file clerks. Above all, there was the government, which, as census taker, tax collector, law enforcer, had always been the record keeper par excellence since the earliest days of civilization. [. . .]

By and large, the data processing responsibility of all these professions, public and private, was more bemoaned than celebrated. It was seen as a dispiriting necessity that could be left to low-status, usually poorly skilled office help. The familiar image of the office worker that we find in the stories of Dickens and Gogol is that of pale, pinch-faced scribes shuffling through overflowing ledgers, soulless statisticians and actuarials totaling up endless columns of figures, undernourished office clerks digging through dusty files to find an elusive memo. [. . .]

The image of data keepers got no brighter even when their occupation passed beyond the pen and pencil stage and finally entered the machine age. It was in order to save time and office space for the government and the white collar industries that business machines came into existence during the early years of this century. The key punch, the comptometer, the collator, the addressograph – all these were information processors. But nobody would have seen them as anything more than ingenious sorting and counting contraptions, of about as much intellectual interest as the air brake or the dry cell battery. Their inventors are hardly remembered; the companies that manufactured them were of no great weight in our industrial economy; those who operated them remained low-level clerical help. For the most part, the data minders of the economy were 'office girls' who might have been trained in high school or at business college and who toiled at their monotonous jobs without hope of promotion. If anything, the work they did was still usually seen by more humanistic sensibilities as a sorry example of the ongoing massification of modern life.

[. . .]


## Enter UNIVAC

[. . .]

[. . .] At the hands of innovative firms like Sperry-Rand, Control Data, and Digital Equipment Corporation (IBM was actually quite laggardly in the field until the early 1960s), the business machine was undergoing an unexpected and rapid evolution. Spurred along by military necessity during World War II and afterward by the needs of the Census Bureau, it was maturing in the direction of becoming an electrical filing device that assigned a numerical address to the data it held and could then perform a variety of rapid calculations and transformations with those data. And that, in its most rudimentary form, is a computer: a device that remembers what it counts, counts what it remembers, and retrieves whatever it has filed away at the touch of a button. The woeful young women who once tended the cumbersome key punch in the back office would surely have been amazed to know that someday there would be 'information scientists' who regarded their clanking and clacking machines as the distant ancestors of a form of mechanized intelligence possibly superior to the human mind.

The word *computer* entered the public vocabulary in the 1950s, when the most advanced models of the device were still room-sized mechanical dinosaurs that burned enough electricity to present a serious cooling problem. The first computer to enjoy a significant reputation was UNIVAC, the brainchild of John Mauchly and J. P. Eckery, with important contributions from the famous mathematician John von Neumann. [. . .] UNIVAC was the first stored-program computer; it was based on military research done at the University of Pennsylvania during the war. Its later development was helped along by contracts from the National Bureau of Standards and Prudential Insurance; finally it was bought by Remington Rand in the 1950s for a variety of data services. But UNIVAC's public debut was little more than a media gimmick. The machine was loaned to CBS television to make polling predictions in the 1952 elections. This number-crunching behemoth (it contained 5,000 vacuum tubes, but used a new, compact magnetic tape system rather than punchcards to store data) was programmed to analyze voting statistics for CBS in key districts and to compare them with early returns on election night. By doing so, UNIVAC gave a projection that quickly calculated which candidate would most likely win.

[. . .]

White collar work was one of the last occupations to enter the machine age. Well after the mines, the factories, the farms had been mechanized, office workers were still scribbling away with pen and pencil, hand-filing their papers in cabinets and loose-leaf binders. Even the typewriter (which appeared in the 1880s and did so much to bring a new generation of women workers into the offices) was a low-level manual tool, the technological equivalent of the long-defunct hand loom. Until well into the twentieth century, one looks in vain in magazines for advertisements that feature any sort of data processing equipment, let alone for books and articles celebrating their inventors and manufacturers. Compare this with the situation today, when the slickest, most futuristic ads in print and on television are those touting computers for the office, and you have a striking measure of how information has risen in status. The technology of the humble data keepers has finally outmatched the rolling mills, the dynamos, the railroads.

'Today,' a leading telecommunications firm announces in an imposing full-page advertisement, 'information is the most valuable commodity in business. *Any* business.' In times past, one would have thought of information as more of a lubricant that helped get commodities produced, or perhaps the upshot of a service like a doctor's diagnosis or a lawyer's legal opinion. And its value would not be constant (let alone universally or invariably supreme) but would vary with its accuracy and applications. But these days information is freely called product, resource, capital, currency. [. . .]

[. . .]

## Messages without meanings

In the same year Wiener produced his study *Cybernetics*, Claude Shannon of Bell Laboratories published his ground-breaking paper, 'A mathematical theory of communication,' which established the discipline of information theory, the science of messages. Shannon's work is universally honored as one of the major intellectual achievements of the century. It is also the work most responsible for revolutionizing the way scientists and technicians have come to wield the word *information* in our time. In the past, the word has always denoted a sensible statement that conveyed a recognizable, verbal meaning, usually what we would call a fact. But now, Shannon gave the word a special technical definition that divorced it from its common-sense usage. In his theory, information is no longer connected with the semantic content of statements. Rather, information comes to be a purely quantitative measure of communicative exchanges, especially as these take place through some mechanical channel which requires that message to be encoded and then decoded, say, into electronic impulses. Most people would have assumed that information had to do with what happened in the understanding of a speaker and a listener in the course of a conversation. Shannon, working out of Bell Labs, was much more interested in what might be happening in the telephone wire that ran between speaker and listener. In his paper, the fundamental concepts of information theory – noise, redundancy, entropy – are rounded up into a systematic mathematical presentation. Here, too, the 'bit,' the binary digit basic to all data processing, first appears to take its place as the quantum of information, a neatly measurable unit by which the transmitting capacity of all communications technology can be evaluated.

One can see how useful such a calculus of communications traffic is for electrical engineers dealing with the problem of channeling signals over phone wires or from space satellites, and wanting to do so with the greatest possible economy and clarity. But from the outset, Shannon was beset by the understandable confusion that arose between his restricted use of 'information' and the conventional meaning of the word. From his point of view, even gibberish might be 'information' if somebody cared to transmit it. After all a message translated into a secret code would appear to be gibberish to anyone who did not know the code; but it would be well worth sending by anyone who did. The early information scientists easily fell into thinking this way about messages and their transmissions; many of them had served as cryptographers during the war. Still this was an odd and jarring way to employ the word, and Shannon had to admit as much. Once, when he was explaining his work to a group of prominent scientists who challenged his eccentric definition, he replied, 'I think perhaps the word "information" is causing more trouble . . . than it is worth, except that it is difficult to find another word that is anywhere near right. It should be kept solidly in mind that [information] is only a measure of the difficulty in transmitting the sequences produced by some information source.' [. . .]

For a time, Shannon considered dropping the word and using another – like communications theory. With a name like that, the new field would have had more distance from the need for meaningful content which we associate with information. For example, a disease can be 'communicated' – a transmission of great consequence but without intelligent content. At one point, John von Neumann suggested – not very helpfully – that Shannon use the word *entropy*. But information became the word, a choice which Fritz Machlup has called 'infelicitous, misleading, and disserviceable' – the beginning of the term's history as 'an all-purpose weasel-word.' [. . .]

What we have here is an example of something that has happened many times before in the history of science. A word that has a long-standing, common-sense meaning is lifted from the public vocabulary and then skewed toward a new, perhaps highly esoteric definition by the scientists. The result can be a great deal of unfortunate confusion, even among the scientists themselves, who may then forget what the word meant before they appropriated it. The way physicists use the words *motion*, *time*, *gravity*, *simultaneity* has only a tenuous connection with commonplace, everyday experience. The word *order* in thermodynamics has a specialized application that at certain points diverges markedly from its normal meaning. [. . .]

In much the same way, in its new technical sense, *information* has come to denote whatever can he coded for transmission through a channel that connects a source with a receiver, regardless of semantic content. For Shannon's purposes, all the following are 'information':

$E = mc^2$
Jesus saves
Thou shalt not kill
I think, therefore I am
Phillies 8, Dodgers 5
'Twas brillig and the slithy toves did gyre and gimble in the wabe.

[. . .]

One might expect that anyone reading through the list of items above would immediately note that each stands on a markedly different intellectual level. One statement is a moral injunction; one is a mathematical formulation; one is a minor point of fact; one is a theological teaching; and the last is deliberate (though charming) nonsense. But once they have all been transformed into electrical bits, and once the technicians have got us into the habit of labeling them all information, these vital differences – which it would, for example, be rather important to draw out for children as part of their education – cannot help but be obscured.

To be sure, Shannon's work is highly technical and therefore largely inaccessible to the general public; nevertheless, its influence has been enormous. As information theory has come to be widely applied in our high tech economy, it has had a twofold impact upon our popular culture.

First of all, once 'information' had been divorced from its conventional meaning, the word was up for grabs. Following the lead of the information theorists, scientists and technicians felt licensed to make ever broader and looser use of the word. It could soon be applied to any transmitted signal that could be metaphorically construed as a 'message' – for example, the firing of a nerve impulse. To use the term so liberally is to lay aside all concern for the quality or character of what is being communicated. The result has been a progressive blurring of intellectual distinctions. Just as it is irrelevant to a physicist (from the viewpoint of the purely physical phenomenon) whether we are measuring the fall of a stone or the fall of a human body, so, for the information theorist, it does not matter whether we are transmitting a fact, a judgment, a shallow cliché, a deep teaching, a sublime truth, or a nasty obscenity. All are 'information.' The word comes to have vast generality, but at a price; the *meaning* of things communicated comes to be leveled, and so too the value.

[. . .]

Secondly, information theory *worked*. In its own field of application, it provided the electrical engineers with a powerful tool that contributed significantly to rapid innovation. With UNIVAC, the original vacuum tube computer had reached the limit of its development, and still the machines were too big and slow to carry out truly sophisticated programs. In the course of the 1950s and 1960s, however, these limitations were overcome by the development of the transistor and integrated circuit. These highly miniaturized conductors allowed the computer to be compacted and its processing functions to be vastly accelerated. At the same time, thanks again to Shannon's work, the computer was finding its way into the world's burgeoning telecommunications network so that it could extend its power beyond local, on-site use. This permitted computers to communicate with one another over great distances, and eventually, with the deployment of space satellites, to remain instantaneously in touch around the world. While the computer was shrinking physically to desk-top size, it was taking on a new, disembodied, electronic 'size' that dwarfed all previous technology in the scope of its power. In our own day, these two developments – miniaturization and telecommunications outreach – have allowed even the most modest personal computer to link into information networks that span the planet, giving them, in the view of some enthusiasts, the dimensions of a global brain.

Achievements of this astonishing order were bound to shift our understanding of information away from people (as sources or receivers) toward the exciting new techniques of communication. This is because the main concern of those who use information theory is with apparatus, not content. For that matter, the theory does not even require a human source or receiver on either side of the apparatus. The source might just as well be a ballistic missile registering its trajectory on radar; the receiver might just as well be a computer programmed to trigger a retaliatory strike. Such a situation fulfills all the mathematical requirements of the theory.

Thanks to the high success of information theory, we live in a time when the technology of human communications has advanced at blinding speed; but what people have to say to one another by way of that technology shows no comparable development. Still, in the presence of so ingenious a technology, it is easy to conclude that because we have the ability to transmit more electronic bits more rapidly to more people than ever before, we are making real cultural progress – and that the essence of that progress is information technology.

[. . .]


## Technophilia

To some degree, the ideas we have reviewed here, zany and extravagant as they may be, are part of a tradition that is as old as industrial society. They may be seen as extreme expressions of technophilia, our love affair with the machines in our lives. This is not the first time people have projected their hope for happiness and their image of perfection upon the latest magic gadget to come along. The steam engine, the electric dynamo, the automobile, the airplane – each in its time held a similar position as the reigning emblem of progress. Such technological infatuations come and go as each new wave of invention and investment makes a place for itself in our dynamic industrial economy. A century and a half ago, a Victorian futurologist filed this bit of doggerel with the *Illustrated London News*:

> Lay down your rails, ye nations near and far –
> Yoke your full trains to Steam's triumphal car.
> Link town to town; unite in iron bands
> The long-estranged and oft-embattled lands.
> Peace, mild-eyed seraph – Knowledge, light divine,
> Shall send their messengers by every line. . . .
> Blessings on Science, and her handmaid Steam!
> They make Utopia only half a dream.

What was the object of his utopian aspirations: The railway. With the benefit of hindsight, it is easy to see how naive and overwrought such expectations can be. Still, for the most part, we might be willing to bear with the salvational longings that entwine themselves around new technology. I think, however, the current fascination with the computer and its principal product, information, deserves a more critical response. This is because the computer does so ingeniously mimic human intelligence that it may significantly shake our confidence in the uses of the mind. And it is the mind that must think about all things, including the computer.

In our popular culture today, the discussion of computers and information is awash with commercially motivated exaggerations and the opportunistic mystifications of the computer science establishment. The hucksters and the hackers have polluted our understanding of information technology with loose metaphors, facile comparisons, and a good deal of out-and-out obfuscation. There are billions of dollars in profit and a windfall of social power to account for why they should wish to do this. Already there may be a large public that believes it not only cannot make judgments about computers, but has no *right* to do so because computers are superior to its own intelligence – a position of absolute deference which human beings have never assumed with respect to any technology of the past.

As it penetrates more deeply into the fabric of our daily life, enjoying at every step along the way the exuberant celebration of its enthusiasts and promoters, the computer holds the possibility of shaping our thought, or rather our very conception of thought itself, in far-reaching ways. This is all the more likely to happen within the near future because of the massive scale on which the computer is entering the schools at all levels and there forming an entire generation of students.

# Chapter 6

# Kevin Robins and Frank Webster

## THE LONG HISTORY OF THE INFORMATION REVOLUTION

From *Times of Technoculture*, London: Routledge (1999), pp. 89–110.

WHAT IS THE INFORMATION REVOLUTION? The answer to this question may seem to be self-evident. A united host of industrialists, politicians, and academics is engaged in making sure that we know that recent developments in information and communications technologies (ICTs) are laying the foundations for a new era of wealth and abundance. [. . .]

In this cocktail of scientific aspiration and commercial hype, there are a number of implicit but significant assumptions. First, it is assumed that the decisive shift has been brought about by recent technological innovations: the association of information revolution and ICTs seems self-evident. Thus, discussion of the Information Revolution is located within the history of technological development and the discourse of technological 'progress'. Second, the assumption is made that this technological revolution, like the earlier Industrial Revolution, marks the opening of a new historical era. The terms 'industrial' and 'post-industrial' society – which, through a process of ideological elision, often translate into 'capitalist' and 'post-capitalist' – mark this transition from a period of constraint and limits, to one of freedom, democracy, and abundance. A third assumption is that of the novelty of the Information Revolution. For the first time, as a consequence of the development and convergence of telecommunications and data-processing, it has become possible to harness human intelligence and reason in a systematic and scientific way. Associated with this, of course, is the unquestioned assumption that organised knowledge and information are socially beneficial. Information is the major asset and resource of a post-industrial society: 'it is . . . the raw material of truth, beauty, creativity, innovation, productivity, competitiveness, and freedom'.[1] Information in all places and at all times – that is the utopian recipe. [. . .]

In this chapter we confront and challenge these assumptions and their compla-
cent promise of technological progress, economic growth, and human betterment.
Thus, our own attempt to explore the significance of the new communications
and information technologies in terms of their genealogy, leads us to be sceptical
of the idea that they constitute a technological revolution. Whilst we would, of
course, accept the scale of innovation in this area, and the degree of its exploitation, we believe that these new technologies are revolutionary only in a rather
trivial sense.

Of course, we do not want to imply that there are not important and ongoing
transformations in the character of capitalist societies, and for sure the new information and communications technologies are implicated in these transformative
processes. [. . .]

The key issue here is that of change and continuity, and understanding this
relation is clearly a matter of disentangling different historical temporalities. In what
follows, we would like to shift attention away from the immediacy of developments
in the information domain, however compelling these may be, in favour of a longer-
term perspective. We urge this especially because, although most scholars have
focused on recent transformations, particularly as regards work processes and forms
of organisation,[2] it is our view that the mobilisation of information and communications resources may be seen to operate in terms of a much longer periodicity
than it is usually accorded.

Moreover, against those accounts that see the information society in terms of
technological revolution, it is also important to emphasise that the appropriation
of information and information resources has always been a constitutive aspect of
capitalist societies quite outside of any technological context. The appropriation
of knowledge (skill) in the factory, for example, may operate solely through hierarchical control. Similarly, nation states functioned effectively for generations
without benefit of computer technologies. Both here, and in wider contexts, organisational structures – culminating in bureaucratic institutions – may establish
effective mechanisms for the control and management of information resources. The
gathering, recording, aggregation, and exploitation of information can be – and has
been – achieved on the basis of minimal technological support.

Our point is that the 'Information Revolution' is inadequately conceived, as it
is conventionally, as a question of technology and technological innovation. Rather,
it is better understood as a matter of differential (and unequal) access to, and control
over, information resources. That is, far from being a technological issue, what
should concern us is the management and control of information within and between
groups. Raising this widens unavoidably the scope of discussions of social change,
taking it far from 'technology effects' considerations, at the same time as it, necessarily, politicises the process of technological development itself by framing it as a
matter of shifts in the availability of and access to information. Conversely, attempts
to divert analysis and debate into technical and technocratic channels serve to repress
these substantial political questions.

In a similar way, the prevailing tendency to consider information and information technology chiefly in terms of economic growth, productivity, and planning,
again puts it in a strongly technical, calculative, and instrumental context (with the
major issues being those of competitive position and the allocation of wages and

profits). Against this orthodoxy, our own approach focuses upon information and information technologies in terms of their political and cultural dimensions. In both these aspects what are raised are the complex relations between technology, information, and power. In the case of the former, what is on the agenda, in the workplace and in society as a whole, is the relationship between management and control. And in the case or the cultural dimension, what is of concern is the micro-politics of power, what Foucault calls the capillary forms of power's exist-ence. What this raises is the shaping influence of information and communication technologies on the texture, pattern, organisation, and routines of everyday life. [. . .] What is apparent, at both levels, we believe, is the indissociable relation between information/knowledge and power.

In tracing the cultural and political contexts in which information and commun-ications technologies have taken shape, we suggest that they have performed two distinct but related functions, both of which are absolutely central to the cohesion and reproduction of capitalist societies. On the one hand, they have been the mech-anism for social management, planning, and administration; and, on the other, they have been at the heart of surveillance and control strategies. Our argument is that these two functions are closely interrelated and mutually reinforcing. [. . .]

## Planning and control

Some of Anthony Giddens' work throws light on this relationship between plan-ning and control. He argues that the state must maintain an effective hold on both 'allocative resources' (planning, administration) and 'authoritative resources' (power, control). Crucial to this project, argues Giddens, is information gathering and storage, which

> is central to the role of 'authoritative resources' in the structuring or social systems spanning larger ranges of space and time than tribal cultures. Surveillance – control of information and superintendence of the activities of some groups by others – is in turn the key to the expan-sion of such resources.[3]

If information gathering, documentation and surveillance are vital to this end, it is also the case, Giddens argues, that the regularised gathering, storage, and control of information is crucial for administrative efficiency and maintenance of power.[4]

In the modern nation state allocative and authoritative control converge insofar as each comes to depend on the continuous, normalised, and increasingly centralised surveillance and monitoring of subject populations. Tendentially, moreover, alloca-tive control comes to prevail through its ability to combine (and legitimate) both administrative and authoritative functions: 'surveillance as the mobilising of admin-istrative power – through the storage and control of information – is the primary means of the concentration of authoritative resources involved in the formation of the nation-state'.[5] In advanced capitalist societies it is this administrative-techno-cratic machinery of surveillance that expresses the prevailing relations of power and designates the inherently totalitarian nature of the modern state.

> The possibilities of totalitarian rule [Giddens writes] depend upon the
> existence of societies in which the state can successfully penetrate the
> day-to-day activities of most of its subject population. This, in turn,
> presumes a high level of surveillance . . . the coding of information
> about and the supervision of the conduct of significant segments of the
> population.[6]

It is, we shall go on to argue, precisely these possibilities that are developed by the
new information technologies.

   [. . .]

   We are especially suspicious of the 'information society' scenarios sketched by
the likes of Daniel Bell,[7] where information/knowledge is represented as a beneficial and progressive social force. Information, we suggest, has long been a key
component of regulation in the modern nation state and in capitalist economies.
And the history of information management suggests that technocratic and economic
exploitation should be understood within the wider context of its disciplinary and
political deployment.[8] Particularly significant in this context has been the process
whereby authoritative control has become subsumed within the machinery of allocative control: power expresses itself through the discipline of calculative and rational
social management and administration. Historically, this process has occurred
without significant technological mediation. Increasingly, however, new technologies are drawn upon: because, as Lewis Mumford has argued, 'mechanisation,
automation, cybernetic direction' overcome the system's weakness, 'its original
dependence upon resistant, sometimes actively disobedient servo-mechanisms, still
human enough to harbour purposes that do not always coincide with those of the
system'.[9] Whether bureaucratic or technological, however, the thrust of administrative control is toward extensive and intensive documentation and surveillance of
internal populations. 'With the mechanisms of information processing (the bureaucracy using people; the computer using machines), the ability to monitor behaviour
is extended considerably', Mark Poster argues: 'The mode of information enormously extends the reach of normalising surveillance, constituting new modes of
domination that have yet to be studied'.[10] This disciplinary and calculative management of existence in advanced capitalist societies transforms itself into their culture,
their way of life, their prevailing social relations.

## The dark side of the Information Revolution

We would stress that the logic of planning and control has always been contested.
In an environment of increasing complexity and uncertainty, the urge to control
may become more intensive and more neurotic, but it does not, for that, become
more cohesive.[11] Moreover, the logic of control may invoke that of resistance.
Populations are never simply and absolutely fixed and compartmentalised; they
remain obdurately fluid and mobile. The power of resistance is an integral and
dynamic aspect of the control system, and it would be quite wrong to regard it as
only a residual force. Nonetheless, if we do not underestimate the significance of
this counter-force, then any balanced consideration should encourage us also not

to underestimate the tenacity and resourcefulness of diverse control agencies. Thus, in the present context of a historical transition beyond Fordism, it seems to us that there are also important transformations in the modalities of surveillance and control. While control is often understood as an external and directly repressive force, its real dynamics are more complex and insidious, and, in fact, ideally exploit the compliance and even the creativity of its subjects. There are signs that, after a period of 'de-subordination'[12] and destabilisation, the present period is very much about the reassertion, and the streamlining, of control strategies. This is apparent in the image of the new model worker (the flexible, compliant, self-motivated, and self-controlling worker); and also in the new model student (again self-directed, flexible, enthusiastic, and docile).[13] As cognitive intrusion and surveillance become increasingly normalised, pervasive, and insidious, so does the logic of control – of power through visibility or 'knowability' – become internalised.

The following sections aim to explore this dark underside of the Information Revolution, and to do this on the basis that serious, rather than just well-meaning, responses are only possible if we confront, not just the repressive potential of information and knowledge, but more significantly the integral and necessary relation between repressive and possible emancipatory dimensions. In the following discussion we draw attention to the administrative and disciplinary exploitation of information resources and technologies, first in a discussion of the role of information in the economic contexts of production, markets, and consumption, and then through an account of the relation between information technologies, communications, and the political system. Such discussion remains selective and incomplete. Our ambition here is to provide an overview, a cartography of the information society, to trace the cohesion in what might seem to be quite disparate developments. Whilst the exploitation of information/knowledge has a considerable history, our argument here is that the really significant moment occurs early in the twentieth century. It is at this time, and particularly in the complex matrix of forces surrounding the Scientific Management of Frederick Winslow Taylor, that the information society may be said to have been truly inaugurated.[14]

## Scientific Management and consumer capitalism

Though the image of the Industrial Revolution is one of vast, impersonal mills in which multitudinous 'hands' were ruthlessly exploited by distant capitalists, the reality was that most work – arduous though it undeniably was – took place in small units of perhaps a dozen or so employees overseen by a master.[15] It was only in the later years in the century that size became an issue when the logic of competition and cartels brought into being the corporate capitalism,[16] typically headed by oligopolistic conglomerates, that has characterised the economic and social landscape ever since. With direct supervision of labour now increasingly untenable, what became necessary were mechanisms for co-ordinating and integrating the complex and fragmented processes of production.

This requirement conjoined with the developing suspicion of an out-and-out free market and the Social Darwinist ideology that had accompanied *laissez-faire* economics.[17] Martin Sklar has traced, in the history of the United States, a growing discontent (amongst business leaders especially) with the 'wastes of competition' between the years 1890 and 1916, something which paralleled the transformation of the economy from 'property-competitive' to 'corporate-administered' capitalism.[18] More generally, as Eric Hobsbawm observes, throughout the capitalist world between 1880 and 1914 '[t]he "visible hand" of modern corporate organization and management now replaced the "invisible hand" of Adam Smith's anonymous market [and] executives, engineers and accountants therefore began to take over'.[19]

It was here that the philosophy and practice of F. W. Taylor was so crucial, with its advocacy of Scientific Management throughout society in general and its application to production especially. Scientific Management meant expert direction by engineers, factory planning, time and motion study, standardisation, and the intensive division of labour. The key word in the application of engineering principles to the industrial system of production was efficiency. Taylor 'proposed a neat, understandable world in the factory, an organisation of men whose acts would be planned, co-ordinated, and controlled under continuous expert direction. His system had some of the inevitableness and objectivity of science and technology'.[20] Factory production was to become a matter of efficient and scientific management: the planning and administration of workers and machines alike as components of one big machine.[21]

Two observations here relate to our broader argument. First, within the Taylor system, efficient production and administration (planning) is indissociably related to control over the workforce. Although these two aspects are often treated as distinct (and emphasis is often placed on the disciplinary function), we would argue that planning and control are each an integral part of the other: efficiency translates into domination and the engineering of people becomes subsumed within the engineering of things. The second point is that administration and control are a function of managerial appropriation of skills, knowledge, and information within the workplace. According to Taylor, wherever possible workers should be relieved of the work of planning, and all 'brain work' should be centred in the factory's planning department. In Anthony Giddens' terms, the collation and integration of information manifests itself in terms of both administration and surveillance. It is this dual articulation of information/knowledge for 'efficient' planning and for control that is at the heart of Scientific Management, and which, in our view, characterises it as the original Information Revolution.

Importantly, Taylorism as a system of factory control does not depend on technological support: information gathering and surveillance do not depend to any large extent upon information technologies. Its capacity to 'reduce the labour of the ordinary employee to an automatic perfection of routine'[22] is a consequence of organisational forms and of direct managerial intervention, of technique rather than technology. As such it may be inscribed within Mumford's history of the non-technological megamachine – the military is a paramount example – which is 'an invisible structure composed of living, but rigid, human parts, each assigned to his special office, role, and task, to make possible the immense work-output and grand design of this great collective organisation'.[23] If, however, this form of megatechnics replaces interpersonal modes of control with more rational and calculative procedures and establishes a certain degree of automaticity, it is the case that machinery can implement this principle more effectively. Insofar as it subordinates unreliable human components to the precise routines of machinery, technology enhances both efficiency and control. It is this realisation that constitutes Henry Ford's major contribution to the Scientific Management of production. Not only did Ford appropriate information/knowledge within the production process, but he also incorporated it into the technology of his production lines to achieve technical control over the labour process.[24]

The subsequent history of capitalist industry, we would argue, has been a matter of the deepening and extension of information gathering and surveillance to the combined end of planning and controlling the production process, and it is into this context that the new information and communications technologies are now inserting themselves. Thus, computer numerical control, advanced automation, robotics, and so on intensify this principle of technical control. The new technologies now spreading through office and service work threaten even to 'Taylorise' intellectual labour itself. Managements have carefully analysed the information routines and requirements and are aiming to introduce information technologies that will make information flows more effective, efficient, and cost-effective,[25] such that, while employees may have an enhanced degree of autonomy in their day-to-day operations, they are subject to ready and sophisticated surveillance at any time. The new technologies are also crucial in managing and co-ordinating ever more complex organisational and productive structures. The establishment and maintenance of a system of transnational corporations depends upon effective computer communications systems to handle financial transactions, corporate directives, and organisational co-ordination.

Yet Taylorism is more than just a doctrine of factory management. It became, in our view, a new social philosophy, a new principle of social revolution, and a new imaginary institution in society. Outside the factory gates, Scientific Management became a new form of social control, not just in the dominative sense of this term, but also in the more neutral sense of the 'capacity of a social organisation to regulate itself'.[26] Taylor and his various epigones believed that the idea of rational, scientific, and efficient management and regulation could be extended beyond the workplace to other social activities. They spoke of 'social efficiency', by which they meant 'social harmony' under the leadership of 'competent' experts.[27]

In 1916, Henry L. Gantt took a 'dramatic step from the planning room of the factory to the work at large', with the formation of the 'New Machine', an organisation of engineers and sympathetic reformers under Gantt's leadership, which announced its intention to acquire political as well as economic power.[28] The association is made between society and the machine; society is to be regulated and maintained by social engineers. Experts and technocrats are to be the orchestrators of a programmed society.[29] As in the factory, this calculative and instrumental regime entails a combined process of administration/planning and surveillance, and depends upon the centralised appropriation and disposal of information resources. It implies 'the intelligence of the whole', and this in the form of instrumental, theoretical, quantified data. The legitimacy of technocratic rule is justified by the command of knowledge/information: it assumes 'an objective and universal rationality based on superior knowledge'.[30]

A further legitimating aspect of Scientific Management was its undoubted capacity to increase productivity, economic growth, and, consequently, social wealth. As Charles Maier argues, it promised 'an escape from zero-sum conflict' between labour and capital: what Taylorism 'offered – certainly within the plant, and ultimately, according to its author, in all spheres of government and social life – was the elimination of scarcity and constraint'.[31] Inherent in mass production was the system of mass consumption and the promise of the consumer utopia. In Scientific Management was a broad social philosophy, a promise of reform through growth and expansion, which had great appeal to social theorists and politicians of the Progressive era (and coincided, in Britain, with Fabian principles and beliefs).

This complex and expanding system of mass production and mass consumption could only be co-ordinated and regulated if the criteria of efficiency and optimality were extended from the factory to the society as a whole. The system of consumption, particularly, must be brought under the practices of Scientific Management. It became increasingly apparent that both economic and social stability depended upon continuous and regular consumption, and upon the matching of demand to cycles and patterns of production. Ultimately what was required was the Scientific Management of need, desire, and fantasy, and their reconstruction in terms of the commodity form.[32] Thus, Taylorist principles of calculation must extend into the marketing sphere.[33] The steady movement of such commodities as clothing, cigarettes, household furnishings and appliances, toiletries or processed foods, required the creation of ways of reaching customers, taking heed of their needs, wants, and dispositions, and responding by persuasion and even redesign of products to make them more or newly attractive.[34]

In this project of systematising the management of consumption, it was Henry Ford's counterpart at General Motors, Alfred P. Sloan, who played an important and formative role. It was Sloan who, in the 1920s, introduced instalment selling, used-car trade-ins, annual model changes, styling, and brand image, to the automobile industry.[35] The objective was both to integrate production and demand, and also to intensify and 'speed up' consumption. As such, 'Sloanism' exemplified the principle of modern marketing, with its ambitions towards the Scientific Management of commodity markets and consumer behaviour.

The system of mass consumption (and the consumer society) is dependent upon the collection, aggregation, and dissemination of information. One consequence of this imperative to accumulate data on patterns of consumption was the rise of market research organisations, specialising in the aggregation of demographic and socio-economic information, and in the detailed recording of trends and patterns in sales. [. . .]

[. . .]

It is also vital, of course, to convey information to the consumer, and this informational task gave rise most obviously and pre-eminently to advertising (though it was also evident in packaging and branding commodities and in their display). In a paean to America productivism, David Potter suggests that 'advertising [is] an instrument of social control'; it is, he continues, 'the only institution which we have for instilling new needs, for training people to act as consumers, for altering men's values, and thus for hastening their adjustment to potential abundance'.[36] Through their exploitation of information resources and channels, the early advertising corporations were searching 'for a means of translating Frederick W. Taylor's ideal Scientific Management into the selling and distribution processes'.[37] What became apparent was that information resources (and information and communications technologies in their early incarnations) were the lifeblood of modern corporations and of the national and international business system.

During the second and third decades of the century, these developments were coming together to constitute a more systematic, calculative, and rationalised management of economic life. There was a concern with information management, with an emphasis on quantification and on professional and scientific procedures. Thus, in advertising, concepts from psychological research were introduced and campaigns more thoroughly prepared by pre-testing and careful analysis of advertising copy and presentation; broadcast ratings were promoted and refined to differentiate types of audience, patterns of behaviour, and preferences;[38] market research flourished and increasingly drew upon survey literature, census data, and social science techniques, feeding back into commercial strategies; public relations developed as 'the attempt, by information, persuasion, and adjustment, to engineer public support', and quite self-consciously proclaimed that 'engineering methods can be applied in tackling our problems'.[39] Informing these trends towards more effective control and planning was the faith that innovations were motivated, not by vulgar self-interest, but by the search for efficiency, expertise, and rationality in the administration of both things and people.

It is in the context of this historical outline that we can begin to understand some aspects of the current 'Information Revolution'. Our argument is that what is commonly taken as innovation and 'revolution' is in fact no more – and no less – than the extension and intensification of processes set under way some seventy or so years ago. It was the exponents of Scientific Management, in its broadest sense, who unleashed an Information Revolution.[40] Particularly important here were the strategies of the 'consumption engineers'[41] to regulate economic transactions and consumer behaviour. It was these advocates of big business who first turned to the 'rational' and 'scientific' exploitation of information in the wider society, and it is their descendants – the multinational advertisers, market researchers, opinion pollers, data brokers, and so on – who are at the heart of information politics today. It is they who are promoting and annexing cable systems, communications satellites, telecommunications links, computer resources, and so on. Their objective is the elaboration of what has been termed a global 'network market place'[42] in which ever more social functions and activities come 'on-line' (education, shopping, entertainment, etc.). What is new in their enterprise is its scale, and also its greater reliance on advanced information and communications technologies to render the Scientific Management of consumer life more efficient and automatic. The objective of a cybernetic market place, and the fantasy of society as a producing and consuming machine, goes back, however, to Taylor, Gantt, and the rest.

World marketing in the era of transnational capital demands global market research and advertising, the ability to undertake surveillance and monitoring of markets, and to launch persuasive propaganda on behalf of a particular product or corporation. The information and intelligence agencies that undertake these tasks of 'mind management' are themselves transnational enterprises and increasingly integrated across the range of information business concerns. [. . .]

The spread of global marketing is manifest, not only in new information politics, but also in its impact on communications media. The press, radio, and television have long been shaped, often in decisive ways, by the pressures of advertising, and it seems likely that the new information and communications technologies will be harnessed to the same consumerist ends.[43] The possibilities exist now both for global advertising and for more targeted advertising reaching particular segments of the audience ('narrowcasting'). Cable television is particularly important here in that its two-way communication facility allows (and, indeed, requires) the recording and surveillance of precise viewing habits. This routine logging of consumer preferences can also be enhanced by the use of such devices as 'people meters', through which each member of a monitored family is assigned a personal code which they 'tap in' when viewing and 'tap out' when leaving the set. Yet a further extension of this surveillance and information gathering is the recording of data from supermarket check-out scanners in order to establish a basis for designing specifically 'addressed' commercials to particular consumer groups. Similarly, the growth in credit cards permits the monitoring of purchasers and gives access to information about what people buy, at what price, how regularly, where, and how readily they foot the bill.

[. . .]

What new technologies enhance, we would suggest, is the Scientific Management of marketing. 'Teleshopping', global and targeted advertising, and electronic market research surveillance, all combine to establish a more rationalised and 'efficient' network marketplace.[44] Information, surveillance, efficiency: the very principles of Taylorism become intensified, extended and automated through the application of new communications and information technologies. One fundamental aspect of the 'communications revolution' has been to refine that planning and control of consumer behaviour that was already inherent in the early philosophy of Scientific Management.

## From public sphere to cybernetic state

The growth of a 'programmed' market, of a regulated and coded consumer society, is a fundamentally cultural phenomenon. The stimulation of needs, the recording of tastes, the surveillance of consumption, all reflect a more rationalised and regulated way of life. (This does not, of course, imply the necessary success of such strategies, nor does it deny the ability of individuals to derive pleasure and creativity from consumer goods.) We want now to turn to a second set of forces that have been central to the historical development of the 'information society'. We are referring to the role of information and communications resources in the political process. Here too we can trace the tendency towards combined planning and control, and here too this has been of profound significance for the cultural life of modernity.[45]

We have referred to Anthony Giddens' argument that the state, and particularly the nation state, has always been propelled into the business of surveillance and information gathering. Giddens suggests that 'storage of authoritative resources is the basis of the surveillance activities of the state', and such surveillance, he argues, entails 'the collation of information relevant to state control of the conduct of its subject population, and the direct supervision of that conduct'. The storage of authoritative resources and control depends upon 'the retention and control of information or knowledge'.[46] Information and communications capabilities have been fundamental to the state and the political sphere in a number of respects. First, they have been indispensable prerequisites for administrating and co-ordinating – maintaining the cohesion and integrity – of complex social structures. Second, they have played an important part in policing and controlling 'deviant' members of the internal population, and in the surveillance of external (potential enemy) populations. And, third, they have been central to the democratic process of political debate in the public sphere. In the following discussion we want to outline the specific shape and force that these various information functions have assumed in political life during this century.

Our historical account of the relation between information and the political system gives rise to a number of observations that can usefully be detailed at the outset. First, we should emphasise again that neither planning nor surveillance depends upon technological support. Thus, Theodore Roszak notes what the English Utilitarians recognised early in the nineteenth century, 'the persuasive force of facts and figures in the modern world': 'All the essential elements of the cult of information are there – the facade of ethical neutrality, the air of scientific rigor, the passion for technocratic control. Only one thing is missing: the computer'.[47] And the principles of disciplinary surveillance, too, have non-technological and Benthamite origins in the architecture of the Panopticon. The issue we are addressing is fundamentally about relations of power – though, having said that, we must emphasise that technologies have increasingly been deployed in the twentieth century to render the exercise of power more efficient and automatic. Our second point is that the functions of administration and control have increasingly coalesced, and regulatory and disciplinary tendencies have increasingly expressed themselves through the calculative and rational machinery of administration. Third, we argue that the idea of a democratic 'conversation' in the public sphere has given way to that of the instrumental and 'efficient' Scientific Management of political life. Along with this, surveillance has become associated with a transformation of the political identity and rights of the internal population, and comes to be directed against the 'enemy within'. Finally, we argue that, although there has always been an information politics, a particularly important moment in these processes occurred early in the twentieth century and was associated with the project of Taylorism.

To clarify these arguments, let us begin with the ideal role of information and communications in democratic political theory. In his classic account of the emergence of the bourgeois public sphere, Habermas describes the historical convergence of democratic principles, the new channels of communication and publicity, and the Enlightenment faith in Reason.[48] The public sphere is the forum, open equally to all citizens, in which matters of general and political interest are debated and ideas exchanged. It remains distinct and separate from the state, and, indeed, insofar as it is the focus of critical reasoning, it operates as a curb on state power. The fundamental principles are that 'opinions on matters of concern to the nation and publicly expressed by men outside the government . . . should influence or determine the actions, personnel, or structure of their government', and that 'the government will reveal and explain its decisions in order to enable people outside the government to think and talk about those decisions'.[49] Such democratic discussion within the frontiers of the extended nation state depends necessarily upon an infrastructure of communication and publicity. Indeed, it is only on this basis that the idea of a public can have any meaning. It is through these media that channels of communication and discourse, and access to information resources, are assured. On this basis the public use of reasoning could be assured. Gouldner describes the bourgeois public sphere as 'one of the great historical advances in rationality'.[50]

That was the aspiration, though many critics of Habermas have doubted whether the bourgeois public sphere – and the 'ideal speech situation' that it presupposes – were ever significant historical realities. For the present argument, however, these objections are not important. What concern us now are the subsequent transformations of the public sphere, which do have manifest historical palpability. One process that occurs is the intrusion of market and commodity relations into the public sphere, and this results in the transformation of reasoning into consumption.[51] But perhaps even more important has been that process through which political debate has come to be regulated by large corporate bodies and by the state ('refeudalisation' is Habermas's term for it). The 'public' is then 'superseded, managed and manipulated by large organisations which arrange things among themselves on the basis of technical information and their relative power positions', and what results is 'the dominance of corporative forms within which discussion is not public but is increasingly limited to technicians and bureaucrats', with the public now becoming 'a condition of organisational action, to be instrumentally managed – i.e. manipulated'.[52] What Habermas and Gouldner both discern is the technocratic and administrative rationalisation of political life, the Scientific Management of the public sphere and of public information and communication. Gouldner goes further, however, in recognising that this rationalising tendency is, ironically, already present in the very foundations of the public sphere. He demonstrates that

> the means to bring about the communicative competence that Habermas requires for rational discourse presuppose precisely the centralisation and strengthening of that state apparatus which increasingly tends to stifle rather than facilitate the universalisation of the rational, uninhibited discourse necessary for any democratic society.[53]

The most important cultural change with regard to the public sphere is the historical shift from a principle of political and public rationality, to one of 'scientific' and administrative rationalisation. As Anthony Giddens argues, there are problems in the very scale and complexity of the modern nation state. Social integration depends upon a strengthening and centralisation of the state, and one aspect of this is the development and regulation of communication and information resources. The rationale and justification of such tendencies become a 'technical' matter of 'efficient' management and administration over the extended territory of the nation state. On this basis, political debate, exchange and disagreement in the public sphere can come to seem 'inefficient', an inhibiting and disturbing obstacle to the rational management of society. Rational and informed discourse in the public sphere gives way to rational Scientific Management of society by technicians and bureaucrats. In this process, the very nature and criteria of rationality have been transformed. In the first case, appeal is made to the reason and judgement of the individual citizen. In the second, it is made to the scientific rationality of the expert, and to the rationality of the social system. The more 'objective' rationality of Scientific Management seems to promise a more 'efficient' democratic order than the often inarticulate and irrational citizen. Reason thus becomes instrumental, the mechanism for administrating, and thereby effectively controlling, the complex social totality. The Enlightenment ideal of Reason gives birth to what Castoriadis calls the 'rationalist ideology': the illusion of omnipotence, the supremacy of economic 'calculus', the belief in the 'rational' organisation of society, the new religion of 'science' and technology.[54]

This technocratic tendency is, of course, reflected in the positivist philosophy of Saint-Simon and Comte, which, as Gouldner persuasively argues, was inimical to the ideal of a politics open to all and conducted in public, and which maintained that public affairs were in fact scientific and technological problems, to be resolved by professionals and experts.[55] But it is with a later form of practical sociology, that associated with the extension of the principles of Scientific Management to the wider society, that such social engineering assumed its most sustained form and that the systematic exploitation of information and communications resources was taken up in earnest. And an emblematic figure here was Walter Lippmann. Scientific Management, especially when placed within the conditions of industrial democracy, embodied in the factory regime what progressive thinkers such as Walter Lippmann envisioned within society at large.[56]

Lippmann points to two dilemmas of the modern mass society. The first refers to the political competence of citizens in democratic society: 'The ideal of the omnicompetent, sovereign citizen is, in my opinion, such a false ideal. It is unattainable. The pursuit of it is misleading. The failure to produce it has produced the current disenchantment'.[57] The second dilemma is that society has attained 'a complexity now so great as to be humanly unmanageable'.[58] The implication is that central government has been compelled to assume responsibility for the control and co-ordination of this increasingly diffuse social structure. And this entails 'the need for interposing some form of expertness between the private citizen and the vast environment in which he is entangled'.[59] As in the Taylorist factory, this depends on 'systematic intelligence and information control'; the gathering of social knowledge, Lippmann argues, must necessarily become 'the normal accompaniment of action'.[60] If social control is to be effective, the control of information and communication channels is imperative. With the Scientific Management of social and political life through the centralisation of communications and intelligence activities, 'persuasion . . . become[s] a self-conscious art and a regular organ of popular government' and the 'manufacture of consent improve[s] enormously in technique, because it is now based on analysis rather than rule of thumb'.[61]

What is especially important here, we believe, is the association of public opinion theory with the study of propaganda in contemporary political discourse. Propaganda has commonly, and common-sensibly, been seen as inimical to rational political debate, as a force that obstructs public reasoning. In the context, however, of the social complexity and citizen 'incompetence' observed by Lippmann, propaganda assumed the guise of a more positive social force in the eyes of many social and political thinkers in the early decades of the century. An increasingly pragmatic and 'realistic' appraisal of the political process suggested that 'in a world of competing political doctrines, the partisans of democratic government cannot depend solely upon appeal to reason or abstract liberalism'.[62] It became clear that 'propaganda, as the advocacy of ideas and doctrines, has a legitimate and desirable part to play in our democratic system'.[63] The very complexity of the modern nation state is such that a 'free market' of ideas and debate must be superseded by the management and orchestration of public opinion. [. . .]

[. . .]

Propaganda is understood here in terms of the regulation and control of channels of communication and information in democratic societies. At one level, this is a matter of disseminating and broadcasting certain categories of information.[64] At another level, it is a matter of restricting access to specific categories of information. As Walter Lippmann makes clear, 'without some form of censorship, propaganda in the strict sense of the word is impossible. In order to conduct a propaganda there must be some barrier between the public and the event'.[65] For Lippmann, propaganda and censorship are complementary, as forms of persuasion and public opinion management. There has been a shift from the idea of an informed and reasoning public, to an acceptance of the massage and manipulation of public opinion by the technicians of public relations. The state function has increasingly come to subsume and regulate the democratic principle; and this to the point that it now seems indissociable from that principle.[66]

We have spent some time in outlining the development of rationalised political management and information control because we feel, again, that this is an important historical context for the development of new information and communications technologies. Through the impetus of Scientific Management, and the development of propaganda and public opinion research, it became clear that social planning and control depended upon the exploitation of information resources and technologies. This was the historical moment of the Information Revolution. The most recent technological developments – in space and satellite technologies, data processing, and in telecommunications – extend what was in reality a fundamentally political 'revolution' in information (and communication) management. It was this historical conjuncture that spawned the 'modern' industries and bureaucracies of public relations, propaganda, public (and private) opinion polling, news management, image production and advocacy, political advertising, censorship and 'official' secrecy, think tanks, and so on. More recent innovations have come with the increase in scale and the exploitation of technological resources.

[. . .]

## Conclusion

'Is closer and closer social control the inevitable price of "progress", a necessary concomitant of the continued development of modern social forms?'[67] We believe that this is indeed the case. Against those who see the new communications technologies as the basis for a coming 'communications era',[68] and the new information technologies as the panacea for our present 'Age of Ignorance',[69] our own argument is that their development has, in fact, been closely associated with processes of social management and control. The scale and complexity of the modern nation state has made communications and information resources (and technologies) central to the maintenance of political and administrative cohesion.

The 'Information Revolution' is, then, not simply and straightforwardly a matter of technological 'progress', of a new technological or industrial revolution. It is significant, rather, for the new matrix of political and cultural forces that it supports. And a crucial dimension here is that of organisational form and structure. Communication and information resources (and technologies) set the conditions and limits to the scale and nature of organisational possibilities. What they permit is the development of complex and large-scale bureaucratic organisations, and also of extended corporate structures that transcend the apparent limits of space and time (transnational corporations). They also constitute the nervous system of the modern state and guarantee its cohesion as an expansive organisational form. Insofar as they guarantee and consolidate these essential power structures in modern society, information and communication are fundamental to political administrative regulation, and consequently to the social and cultural experience of modernity.

The exploitation of information resources and technologies has expressed itself, politically and culturally, through the dual tendency towards social planning and management, on the one hand, and surveillance and control on the other. In historical terms, this can be seen as the apotheosis of Lewis Mumford's megamachine: technology now increasingly fulfils what previously depended upon bureaucratic organisation and structure. But the central historical reference point is the emergence, early in the twentieth century, of Scientific Management (as a philosophy both of industrial production and of social reproduction). It was at this moment that 'scientific' planning and management moved beyond the factory to regulate the whole way of life. At this time, the 'gathering of social knowledge' became 'the normal accompaniment of action', and the manufacture of consent, through propaganda and opinion management, was increasingly 'based on analysis rather than on rule of thumb'.[70] If, through Scientific Management, the planning and administration of everyday life became pervasive, it also became the pre-eminent form and expression of social control. Planning and management were, necessarily and indissociably, a process of surveillance and of manipulation and persuasion. To the extent that these administrative and dominative information strategies were first developed on a systematic basis, it was at this historical moment, we believe, that the 'Information Revolution' was unleashed. New information and communications technologies have most certainly advanced, and automated, these combined information and intelligence activities, but they remain essentially refinements of what was fundamentally a political-administrative 'revolution'.

Recent innovations in information and communications technologies have generally been discussed from a narrow technological or economic perspective. It has been a matter of technology assessment or of the exploitation of new technologies to promote industrial competitiveness and economic growth. This, in the light of our discussion, seems a partial and blinkered vision. The central question to be raised in the context of the 'Information Revolution' today, is, we believe, the relation between knowledge/information and the system of political and corporate power. For some, knowledge is inherently and self-evidently a benevolent force, and improvements in the utilisation of knowledge are demonstrably the way to ensure social progress.[71] Information is treated as an instrumental and technical resource that will ensure the rational and efficient management of society. It is a matter of social engineering by knowledge professionals and information specialists and technocrats. For us, the problems of the 'information society' are more substantial, complex, and oblique.

[. . .]

Among the significant issues to be raised by the new information technologies are their relation to social forms of organisation, their centrality to structures of political power, and their role in the cultural logic of consumer capitalism. Sociological analysis is naïve, we believe, when it treats the new telecommunications, space, video, and computing technologies as innocent technical conceptions and looks hopefully to a coming, post-industrial utopia. Better to look back to the past, to the entwined histories of reason, knowledge, and technology, and to their relation to the economic development of capitalism and the political and administrative system of the modern nation state.

[. . .]

## Notes

1    Jacques Maisonrouge, 'Putting Information to Work for People', *Intermedia*, 1984, vol. 12, no. 2, March.

2    There is a voluminous literature available. Amongst the most significant works are: Michael Piore and Charles Sabel, *The Second Industrial Divide*, New York, Basic Books, 1984; Fred Block, *Postindustrial Possibilities: A Critique of Economic Discourse*, Berkeley, University of California Press, 1990; Manuel Castells, *The Rise of the Network Society*, Oxford, Blackwell, 1996.

3    Anthony Giddens, *The Nation State and Violence: Volume 2 of A Contemporary Critique of Historical Materialism*, Cambridge, Polity Press, 1985, p. 2.

4    Thomas Richards has written vividly about this with regard to the British Empire, demonstrating an obsession with information collection on colonies and colonial subjects (maps, censuses, surveys). See Thomas Richards, *The Imperial Archive: Knowledge and the Fantasy of Empire*, London, Verso, 1993; cf. Benedict Anderson, *Imagined Communities: Reflections on the Origin and Spread of Nationalism*, revised edn, London, Verso, 1991, ch. 10.

5    Anthony Giddens, *The Nation State and Violence Volume 2 of A Contemporary Critique of Historical Materialism*, Cambridge: Polity Press, 1985, p. 181.

6    Ibid., p. 302.

7    See Krishan Kumar, *From Post-Industrial to Post-Modern Society: New Theories of the Contemporary World*, Oxford, Blackwell, 1995, ch. 2; Kevin Robins and Frank Webster, 'Information as Capital: A Critique of Daniel Bell', in J. D. Slack and F. Fejes (eds), *The Ideology of the Information Age*, Norwood, New Jersey, Ablex, 1987, pp. 95–117.

8    This is not, of course, to imply the necessary effectiveness of technocratic rule. Technocracy probably always approximates more to what S. M. Miller calls 'pseudo-technocratic society'. See S. M. Miller, 'The Coming of Pseudo-Technocratic Society', *Sociological Inquiry*, 1976, vol. 46, no. 3–4. And the 'human components' always remain recalcitrant and resistant in the face of attempted social engineering.

9    Lewis Mumford, 'Authoritarian and Democratic Technics', *Technology and Culture*, 1964, vol. 5, p. 5.

10   Mark Poster, *Foucault, Marxism and History*, Cambridge, Polity Press, 1984, pp. 103, 115.

11   Scott Lash and John Urry, *The End of Organised Capitalism*, Cambridge, Polity Press, 1987.

12   De-subordination 'means that people who find themselves in subordinate positions . . . do what they can to mitigate, resist and transform the conditions of their sub-ordination' (p. 402). Ralph Miliband, 'A State of De-subordination', *British Journal of Sociology*, 1978, vol. XXIX, no. 4, December, pp. 399–409.

13   John Holloway, 'The Red Rose of Nissan', *Capital and Class*, 1987, no. 32, Summer, pp. 142–164; [. . .].

14   See Frank Webster and Kevin Robins, *Information Technology: A Luddite Analysis*, Norwood, NJ, Ablex, 1986, pt. 3.

15   Raphael Samuel, 'Workshop of the World: Steam Power and Hand Technology in Mid-Victorian Britain', *History Workshop Journal*, 1977, no. 3, pp. 6–72.

16   This important concept was coined by William Appleman Williams, *The Contours of American History*, Cleveland, World, 1961.

17   Richard Hofstader, *Social Darwinism in American Thought*, revised edn, Boston, Beacon, 1955.

18   Martin J. Sklar, *The Corporate Reconstruction of American Capitalism, 1890–1916*, Cambridge, Cambridge University Press, 1988.

19   Eric J. Hobsbawm, *The Age of Empire, 1875–1914*, London, Weidenfeld and Nicolson, 1987, p. 45.

20   Samuel Haber, *Efficiency and Uplift: Scientific Management in the Progressive Era, 1890–1920*, Chicago: University of Chicago Press, 1964, p. xi.

21   Something of the change that took place may be gauged by comparing Taylor's emphasis on Scientific Management as the way to run businesses with Andrew Carnegie's (1903) influential primer, *The Empire of Business*, which had been published at the turn of the century (London and New York, Harper and Brothers). In this latter the route to success is mapped in terms of personality traits – character, alertness, keenness, etc. – rather than in terms of Taylor's efficiency measures.

22   J. A. Hobson, 'Scientific Management', *Sociological Review*, vol. 6, no. 3, July, p. 198.

23   Lewis Mumford, *The Myth of the Machine: Technics and Human Development*, London, Secker and Warburg, 1967, p. 189.

24   Richard Edwards, *Contested Terrain: The Transformations of the Workplace in the Twentieth Century*, London, Heinemann, 1979.

25   Mike Cooley, 'The Taylorization of Intellectual Work', in L. Levidow and B. Young (eds), *Science, Technology and the Labour Process, vol. 1*, London, CSE Books, 1981.

26   Morris Janowitz, 'Sociological Theory and Social Control', *American Journal of Sociology*, 1975, vol. 81, no. 1, July, p. 84; cf. David A. Hounshell, *From the American System to Mass Production 1800–1932: The Development of Manufacturing Technology in the United States*, Baltimore, The Johns Hopkins University Press, 1987, ch. 8.

27   Samuel Haber, *Efficiency and Uplift: Scientific Management in the Progressive Era, 1890–1920*, Chicago, University of Chicago Press, 1964, p. x.

28   Ibid., 44.

29   Edwin Layton, 'Veblen and the Engineers,' *American Quarterly*, 1962, Spring.

30   Magali Sarfatti-Larson, 'Notes on Technocracy: Some Problems of Theory, Ideology and Power', *Berkeley Journal of Sociology*, 1972, no. 17, p. 19.

31   Charles S. Maier, 'Between Taylorism and Technocracy: European Ideologies and the Vision of Industrial Productivity in the 1920s', *Journal of Contemporary History*, 1970, vol. 5, no. 2, pp. 31–32.

32   See, for example, Stuart and Elizabeth Ewen, *Channels of Desire*, New York, McGraw-Hill, 1982.

33    Herbert Casson realised early on that 'what has worked so well in the acquisition of knowledge and in the production of commodities may work just as well in the distribution of those commodities'. Herbert N. Casson, *Ads and Sales: A Study of Advertising and Selling from the Standpoint of the New Principles of Scientific Management*, Chicago, A. C. McClurg and Co., 1911, p. 71.

34    Daniel Pope, *The Making of Modern Advertising*, New York, Basic Books, 1983; Raymond Williams, 'Advertising: the Magic System', in Raymond Williams, *Problems in Materialism and Culture*, London, Verso, 1980, pp. 170–195.

35    Alfred P. Sloan, *My Years with General Motors*, London, Sidgwick and Jackson, 1965, ch. 9.

36    David M. Potter, *People of Plenty: Economic Abundance and the American Character*, Chicago, University of Chicago Press, 1954, pp. 168, 175.

37    Quentin J. Schultze, *Advertising, Science, and Professionalism*, University of Illinois at Urbana-Champaign, 1978, unpublished Ph.D. thesis, p. 116; cf. Susan Strasser, *Satisfaction Guaranteed: The Making of the American Mass Market*, Washington, Smithsonian Institute Press, 1989.

38    Donald L. Hurwitz, *Broadcast Ratings: The Rise and Development of Commercial Audience Research and Measurement in American Broadcasting*, University of Illinois at Urbana-Champaign, 1983, unpublished Ph.D. thesis.

39    Edward L. Bernays, *The Engineering of Consent*, Norman, University of Oklahoma Press, 1955, pp. 3–4, 9; cf. Abram Lipsky, *Man the Puppet: The Art of Controlling Minds*, New York, Frank-Maurice Inc., 1925.

40    This is a judgement we share with management guru Peter Drucker who describes Taylorism as 'the most powerful as well as the most lasting contribution America has made to Western thought'. Peter Drucker, *The Practice of Management*, London, Heinemann, 1955, p. 248; cf. Peter Drucker, *Post-Capitalist Society*, Oxford, Butterworth Heinemann, 1993.

41    Roland Marchand, *Advertising the American Dream: Making Way for Modernity, 1920–1940*, Berkeley, University of California Press, 1985, p. 25.

42    Herbert S. Dordick, H. B. Bradley and B. Nanus, *The Emerging Network Marketplace*, Norwood, New Jersey, Ablex, 1981.

43    Kevin Robins and Frank Webster, 'The Revolution of the Fixed Wheel: Television and Social Taylorism', in P. Drummond and R. Paterson (eds), *Television in Transition*, London, British Film Institute, 1985, pp. 36–63; Kevin Robins and Frank Webster, 'Broadcasting Politics: Communications and Consumption', *Screen*, 1986, vol. 27, nos. 3–4, May–August, pp. 30–44.

44    Dominic Cadbury, 'The Impact of Technology on Marketing', *International Journal of Advertising*, 1983, vol. 2, no. 1, pp. 72, 70.

45    Philip Corrigan and Derek Sayer, *The Great Arch: English State Formation as Cultural Revolution*, Oxford, Blackwell, 1985.

46    Anthony Giddens, *A Contemporary Critique of Historical Materialism, vol. 1, Power, Property and the State*, London, Macmillan, 1981, p. 94.

47    Theodore Roszak, *The Cult of Information*, Cambridge, Butterworth Press, 1986, p. 156.

48    Jürgen Habermas, *Strukturwandel der Öffentlichkeit*, Darmstadt, Luchterhand, 1962.

49    Hans Speier, 'Historical Development of Public Opinion', *American Journal of Sociology*, 1950, vol. 55, January, p. 376.

50    Alvin Gouldner, *The Dialectic of Ideology and Technology*, London, Macmillan, 1976; cf. Nicholas Garnham, 'The Media and the Public Sphere', in Peter Golding, Graham Murdock, and Philip Schlesinger (eds), *Communicating Politics: Mass Communications and the Political Process*, Leicester, Leicester University Press, 1986, pp. 37–53.

51    Jürgen Habermas, *Strukturwandel der Öffentlichkeit*, Darmstadt, Luchterhand, 1962, p. 194.

52    Alvin Gouldner, *Dialectic of Ideology and Technology*, London, Macmillan, 1976, pp. 139–140.

53    Paul Piccone, 'Paradoxes of Reflexive Sociology', *New German Critique*, 1976, no. 8, Spring, p. 173.

54    Cornelius Castoriadis, 'Reflections on Rationality and "Development"', *Thesis Eleven*, 1984/85, nos. 10/11.

55    Alvin Gouldner, *Dialectic of Ideology and Technology*, London, Macmillan, 1976, pp. 36–37.

56    Samuel Haber, *Efficiency and Uplift: Scientific Management in the Progressive Era, 1890–1920*, Chicago, University of Chicago Press, 1964, pp. 90, 93, 97–98.

57    Walter Lippmann, *The Phantom Public*, New York, Harcourt, Brace and Co., 1925, p. 39.

58    Walter Lippmann, *Public Opinion*, London, Allen and Unwin, 1922, p. 394.

59    Ibid., p. 378.

60    Ibid., p. 408.

61    Ibid., p. 248.

62    William Albig, *Public Opinion*, New York, McGraw-Hill, 1939, p. 301.

63    Harwood L. Childs, *Public Opinion: Nature, Formation and Role*, Princeton, Van Nostrand, 1965, p. 282.

64    Edward Bernays refers to this as 'special pleading' and Harold Lasswell writes of 'the function of advocacy', suggesting that 'as an advocate the propagandist can think of himself as having much in common with the lawyer'. Indeed, according to Lasswell, society 'cannot act intelligently' without its 'specialists on truth'; 'unless these specialists are properly trained and articulated with one another and the public, we cannot reasonably hope for public interests'. Edward L. Bernays, *Crystallising Public Opinion*, New York, Boni and Liveright, 1923; Harold D. Lasswell, *Democracy Through Public Opinion*, Menasha, WI, George Banta Publishing Company The Eleusis of Chi Omega, 1941, vol. 43, no. 1, pt. 2, pp. 75–76, 63.

65    Walter Lippmann, *Public Opinion*, London, Allen and Unwin, 1922, p. 43.

66    As Francis Rourke observes, 'public opinion (has) become the servant rather than the master of government, reversing the relationship which democratic theory assumes and narrowing the gap between democratic and totalitarian societies'. Francis E. Rourke, *Secrecy and Publicity: Dilemmas of Democracy*, Baltimore, Johns Hopkins Press, 1961, p. xi.

67    James B. Rule, *Private Lives and Public Surveillance*, London, Allen Lane, 1973, p. 43.

68    Tom Stonier, 'Intelligence Networks, Overview, Purpose and Policies in the Context of Global Social Change', *Aslib Proceedings*, 1986, vol. 38, no. 9, September.

69    Michael Marien, 'Some Questions for the Information Society', *The Information Society*, 1984, vol. 3, no. 2.

70    Walter Lippmann, *Public Opinion*, London, Allen and Unwin, 1922, pp. 408, 248 [. . .].

71    Kenneth E. Boulding and Lawrence Senesh, *The Optimum Utilisation of Knowledge: Making Knowledge Serve Human Betterment*, Boulder, CO, Westview Press, 1983.

# PART TWO

# Post-Industrial Society

## INTRODUCTION

■ Harri Melin

TODAY MANY COMMENTATORS TALK about Post-Industrial Society as if it were a self-evident fact. Yet when **Daniel Bell** (Chapter 7) first published his book *The Coming of Post-Industrial Society* in 1973 (though essays on the theme were appearing from him as early as the mid-1960s), the concept was far from being widely accepted. However, the term then quickly entered the language of social thought around the world. Today Bell's book is acknowledged as one of the most important – if contested – contributions to what is now called the Information Society. He himself took to substituting the term for Post-Industrial Society during the late 1970s, and since there are no major differences in what they describe, then this is appropriate.

*The Coming of Post-Industrial Society* is a systematic analysis of the changes in the structure of the American society from the Second World War to around 1970. It is unarguably a seminal contribution to discussions concerned with social change. Today's readers should bear in mind that Bell wrote this book over thirty years ago, well before the outbreak of interest in computers and communications, the internet, or considerations of an Information Society. In view of this it is especially salutary to reflect on just how prescient were Bell's forecasts (and the sub-title of the book, *A Venture in Social Forecasting,* signalled that Bell was indeed endeavouring to foresee the future). It is characteristic of Bell's writing that he moves from analysis of society as it is now towards consideration of its most likely future direction. Indeed, his is an insistence that Sociology should be engaged with discerning the future (which is not the same as prediction), and that this must be on the basis of identifiable trends. Thus, for instance, tracking occupational changes throughout the twentieth century allows Bell to project the continuation of trends into the future. One might object that there is something determinist about such an approach. However, it should be added that it is an inexact and contingent exercise, and that, moreover, it is necessary if politicians and policy-makers are to exercise informed influence when they make their recommendations and interventions (even though these may redirect social relationships).

Here we publish extracts from a chapter which is analysing primarily changes in *social structure*, one which in its title – *From Goods to Services: The Changing Shape of the Economy* – reveals much of its argument and focus. Throughout his work Bell insists that change may be examined on separate levels, one being social structure (largely the economy and work), another culture, and a third politics. *The Coming of Post-Industrial Society* restricts itself to the first level, though changes there do 'pose questions' for the realms of culture and politics. Bell starts his discussion with a description of the development of Industrial Society from the times of the *Communist Manifesto* (1848) to the 1960s. In the Industrial Society energy and machines have transformed the character of work. Pre-Industrial Society was agricultural, people compelled to work with nature and the elements to make a living. Industrialism is a world of semi-skilled workers and engineers engaged in fabricating 'things'. As well as this concern for 'goods', it is also a world of co-ordination, scheduling and programming. It is a world of hierarchy and bureaucracy where organizations deal with the requirements of roles, not persons (cf. Clegg 1990).

The shift from the Industrial to the Post-Industrial Society entails deep changes in the occupational structure. Here Bell evokes the work of Fritz Machlup (1962), who analysed the increasing role of knowledge to the occupational structure. A Post-Industrial Society is one based on services. Industrial occupations will decline, while the number of variegated professional occupations – united by their reliance on information/knowledge which is certified by accredited educational institutions – will continue to increase. According to Bell the Industrial Society was defined by the quantity of goods as marking the standard of living, driven by an ethic of least cost for maximum return on investment. Conversely, 'the post-industrial society is defined by the quality of life as measured by the services and amenities – health, education, recreation and the arts' (p. 87). The emphasis is less on economic efficiency and more on the value of relationships.

Bell also discussed changes in class and power structures. In his view the major class of the emerging new society is professional, and the power of the professional class is based on knowledge rather than on property. Yet the control system of the society is lodged not in any occupational class, but in the political order and, according to Bell, the question of who manages the political order remains open. Writing in the late 1960s, against a backcloth of resurgent political and intellectual radicalism, Bell judged the role of the working class to be on the wane. Though Bell was convinced that labour conflicts would remain, such struggles were no longer germane to Post-Industrialism in ways they had been during the Industrial era, when class-based politics were a fact of life and organized labour played a major part in social affairs. The coming of Post-Industrialism signals the decline of the proletariat and its replacement as a key agent of politics by professional groups. This was not a popular argument to make at the time, and it has contributed, somewhat unfairly, to depictions of Bell as a 'neo-conservative' (Steinfels 1979; cf. Waters 1996), though ironically it was been recalled in the more recent work of Manuel Castells, himself a leading 'Sixty-Eighter' (see pp. 133–64). In the extract below Daniel Bell goes even further to dismiss then contemporary talk of an emerging 'new working class' of educated labour which was allegedly alienated and rebellious (and thereby a potential catalyst of left-wing change) as nothing more than a 'radical conceit'. To be sure, white-collar employees were joining unions, and on occasion they were involved in disputes, but to Bell they shared little with the working class and were most likely to act militantly to protect their particular privileges and status above the declining working class. Further, Bell argues that politics profoundly changes in Post-Industrialism since, with the professionals predominating, key issues will become welfare, health and educational matters, and associated questions of the provision and sources of funding for these services are set to become more central. Rereading Daniel Bell from the perspective of the twenty-first century, one will wish to assess the accuracy of his projections. Was he correct to envisage the centrality to politics of professionals and their diverse concerns, the increased importance of funding and provision of welfare services, and the priority of controlling inflation?

After Bell, others have written extensively about the coming of the Information Society. However, we may say that Bell's contribution has been the main starting point for the contemporary analysis. The strength of his book lies both in his concepts and in his empirical analysis. He has been criticised for over-generalizing from conditions he found in the United States, suggesting that its expression of Post-Industrialism is the path that others must follow (is this realistic for a Zaire or Vietnam?). A related question is whether the contemporary US is really Post-Industrial in ways that Bell forecast? Do professions really predominate? Is the quality of life as opposed to quantities of material goods really a defining characteristic?

*From Post-Industrial to Post-Modern Society* (1995) by **Krishan Kumar** (Chapter 8) is also an important contribution to thinking about social change, though this book involves more a critical engagement with existing theories. Kumar's detailed examination of three contested theories of contemporary change is enormously helpful in appreciating how we live today and where we may be moving. These theories, independent yet sharing themes, are those of Information Society, Post-Fordism (cf. Amin 1994) and Postmodernity (cf. Lyotard 1984).

Our selection from Kumar centres on discussion of Daniel Bell, whom he uses as the archetypical formulator of the Information Society thesis, observing that it amounts to much the same thing as Post-Industrialism, as well as being popularized by such as Alvin Toffler (1981) and John Naisbitt (1984). According to Kumar all the writers suggest that in the Information Society the structure of the economy, the nature of work and the power structures will be radically different from those found in the Industrial Society. Further, all these see the future as being an improvement on conditions that went before.

Against this Kumar insists that the technological development and diffusion have introduced no fundamentally new principle or direction in society. On the contrary, 'Work and leisure are further industrialized, further subjected to Fordist and Taylorist strategies of mechanization, routinization and rationalization. Existing social inequalities are maintained and magnified' (p. 116). Thus in principle the capitalist industrial societies remain the same as before, and thereby talk of a novel Information Society is premature.

In a similar manner he is critical of the notion of Post-Fordism which he finds has much in common with Post-Industrialism, though it stems from Marxist traditions. According to Kumar theories of Post-Fordism look too narrowly at economic and organizational developments. He contends that Post-Fordist theory is an attempt to salvage Marxist analysis in an era when Marxist projects have largely failed. Finally, the author is also critical of Postmodernity. However, Kumar has more sympathy towards the theories of Postmodernism than he does towards Information Society and Post-Fordism. While he argues that capitalism persists in the Information Age, he reminds us that it is a huge word which too readily disguises important differences, leading to insensitivity towards real changes that have taken place. Laissez-faire capitalism is quite distinct form corporate capitalism, which in turn is not the same thing as state-directed capitalist enterprise. Accordingly, Kumar (1995) concludes that 'Post-modern capitalism shows sufficient distinctiveness to warrant an analysis that respects the radical changes of form at all levels – cultural and political as well as economic – that modern society has undergone in the last third of the twentieth century' (p. 195).

In his book *Consuming Places* (1995) **John Urry** (Chapter 9) asks the question: is Britain the first 'post-industrial society'? The author sets five tasks for the chapter we reproduce here. First, he summarizes the thesis of the Post-Industrial Society. Second, he shows how this thesis is overly 'economistic' in how it accounts for social and political life, and how it fails to address complex transformations in the ways in which people experience such changes. Third, Urry discusses people's experiences by analysing how they have been transformed by the development of industrial and urban life. Key to this are changes in the ways in which time and space are now organized and structured. Fourth, he returns to the future and considers whether time and space may change so that they establish the ground for postmodern experiences. Finally, the author argues that in Britain no new form of society is coming into being, but rather that there has been the systematic breakdown of 'organized capitalism' (Lash and Urry 1987).

Urry claims that Post-Industrial Society has not emerged, but that 'organized capitalism' is transforming into 'disorganized capitalism'. There are several points which speak in favour for this. First, the role of national societies is decreasing. Economic and cultural globalization is dramatically changing our understanding concerning society, space and geography. The second point is that mass production of standardized products in manufacturing plants employing thousands of industrial workers is becoming outmoded. Spatial organization of production has changed, the major transnational corporations operating on a global scale. Employers nowadays are the active and innovative players, while it is workers who are often reactionary, fighting – if fighting at all – to defend the benefits from the past. Furthermore, the meaning of social class is changing, and class may no longer be the important determinant of social life, culture and politics, as it was the case even thirty years ago. Finally, culture has changed in a dramatic ways, with movies, TV and internet providing new forms of culture and entertainment.

Together with Scott Lash, John Urry discusses these themes in more systematic way in their books *The End of Organized Capitalism* (1987; see also Urry 2000) and *Economies of Signs and Space* (1994). Disorganized capitalism means the development of world economy and new and transient international division of labours. It also signals a decline of distinct national economies and industrial cities. New information and communications technologies reduce the time–space distances between people and increase the powers of surveillance. A 'service class' will be the most salient new class force, while the power of the working class will decrease. These same themes are discussed also in the most prominent contemporary analysis of the Information Society, Manuel Castells, and debated by his critics (e.g. Sklair 2001). They are significantly different to the arguments presented by Daniel Bell, though it is undeniable that they occupy a similar terrain.

## REFERENCES

Amin, A. (ed.) (1994) *Post-Fordism*. Oxford: Blackwell.

Castells, M. (1996) *The Rise of Network Society*. Oxford: Blackwell.

Clegg, S. (1990) *The Modern Organizations: Organization Studies in the Postmodern World*. London: Sage.

Kumar, K. (1995) *From Post-Industrial to Post-Modern Society*. Oxford: Blackwell.

Lash, S. and Urry, J. (1987) *The End of Organized Capitalism*. Cambridge: Polity Press.

Lash, S. and Urry, J. (1994) *Economies of Signs and Space*. London: Sage.

Lyotard, J.-F. (1984) *The Postmodern Condition*. Manchester University Press.

Machlup, F. (1962) *The Production and Distribution of Knowledge in the United States*. Princeton University Press.

Naisbitt, J. (1984) *Megatrends: Ten New Directions Transforming Our Lives*. New York: Warner Books.

Sklair, L. (2001) *The Transnational Capitalist Class*. Oxford: Blackwell.

Steinfels, P. (1979) *The Neo-conservatives*. New York: Simon and Schuster.

Toffler, A. (1981) *The Third Wave*. New York: Bantam Books.

Urry, J. (2000) *Sociology Beyond Societies: Mobilities for the Twenty-first Century*. London: Routledge.

Waters, M. (1996) *Daniel Bell*. London: Routledge.

# Daniel Bell

## POST-INDUSTRIAL SOCIETY

From *The Coming of Post-Industrial Society*, Harmondsworth: Penguin (1973), pp. 126–64.

[. . .]

THE CONCEPT OF A POST-INDUSTRIAL society gains meaning by comparing its attributes with those of an industrial society and pre-industrial society.

In pre-industrial societies – still the condition of most of the world today – the labor force is engaged overwhelmingly in the extractive industries: mining, fishing, forestry, agriculture. Life is primarily a game against nature. One works with raw muscle power, in inherited ways, and one's sense of the world is conditioned by dependence on the elements – the seasons, the nature of the soil, the amount of water. The rhythm of life is shaped by these contingencies. The sense of time is one of *durée*, of long and short moments, and the pace of work varies with the seasons and the storms. Because it is a game against nature, productivity is low, and the economy subject to the vicissitudes of tangible nature and to capricious fluctuations of raw-material prices in the world economy. The unit of social life is the extended household. Welfare consists of taking in the extra mouths when necessary – which is almost always. Because of low productivity and large population, there is a high percentage of underemployment, which is usually distributed throughout the agri-cultural and domestic-service sectors. Thus there is a high service component, but of the personal or household sort. Since individuals often seek only enough to feed themselves, domestic service is cheap and plentiful. (In England, up to the mid-Victorian period, the single largest occupational class in the society was the domestic servant. In *Vanity Fair*, Becky Sharp and Captain Rawdon Crawley are penniless, but they have a servant; Karl Marx and his large family lived in two rooms in Soho in the 1850s and were sometimes evicted for failing to pay rent, but they had a faithful servant, Lenchen, sometimes two.) Pre-industrial societies are agrarian societies structured in traditional ways of routine and authority.

Industrial societies – principally those around the North Atlantic littoral plus the Soviet Union and Japan – are goods-producing societies. Life is a game against fabricated nature. The world has become technical and rationalized. The machine predominates, and the rhythms of life are mechanically paced: time is chronological, methodical, evenly spaced. Energy has replaced raw muscle and provides the power that is the basis of productivity – the art of making more with less – and is responsible for the mass output of goods which characterizes industrial society. Energy and machines transform the nature of work. Skills are broken down into simpler components, and the artisan of the past is replaced by two new figures – the engineer, who is responsible for the layout and flow of work, and the semi-skilled worker, the human cog between machines – until the technical ingenuity of the engineer creates a new machine which replaces him as well. It is a world of coordination in which men, materials, and markets are dovetailed for the production and distribution of goods. It is a world of scheduling and programming in which the components of goods are brought together at the right time and in the right proportions so as to speed the flow of goods. It is a world of organization – of hierarchy and bureaucracy – in which men are treated as 'things' because one can more easily coordinate things than men. Thus a necessary distinction is introduced between the role and the person, and this is formalized on the organization chart of the enterprise. Organizations deal with the requirements of roles, not persons. The criterion of *techne* is efficiency, and the mode of life is modeled on economics: how does one extract the greatest amount of energy from a given unit of embedded nature (coal, oil, gas, water power) with the best machine at what comparative price? The watchwords are maximization and optimization in a cosmology derived from utility and the felicific calculus of Jeremy Bentham. The unit is the individual, and the free society is the sum total of individual decisions as aggregated by the demands registered, eventually, in a market. In actual fact, life is never as 'one-dimensional' as those who convert every tendency into an ontological absolute make it out to be. Traditional elements remain. Work groups intervene to impose their own rhythms and 'bogeys' (or output restrictions) when they can. Waste runs high. Particularism and politics abound. These soften the unrelenting quality of industrial life. Yet the essential, technical features remain.

A post-industrial society is based on services. Hence, it is a game between persons. What counts is not raw muscle power, or energy, but information. The central person is the professional, for he is equipped, by his education and training, to provide the kinds of skill which are increasingly demanded in the post-industrial society. If an industrial society is defined by the quantity of goods as marking a standard of living, the post-industrial society is defined by the quality of life as measured by the services and amenities – health, education, recreation, and the arts – which are now deemed desirable and possible for everyone. The word 'services' disguises different things, and in the transformation of industrial to post-industrial society there are several different stages. First, in the very development of industry there is a necessary expansion of transportation and of public utilities as auxiliary services in the movement of goods and the increasing use of energy, and an increase in the non-manufacturing but still blue-collar force. Second, in the mass consumption of goods and the growth of populations there is an increase in distribution (wholesale and retail), and finance, real estate, and insurance, the traditional centers of white-collar employment. Third, as national incomes rise, one finds, as in the theorem of Christian Engel, German statistician of the latter half of the nineteenth century, that the proportion of money devoted to food at home begins to drop, and the marginal increments are used first for durables (clothing, housing, automobiles) and then for luxury items, recreation, and the like. Thus, a third sector, that of personal services, begins to grow: restaurants, hotels, auto services, travel, entertainment, sports, as people's horizons expand and new wants and tastes develop. But here a new consciousness begins to intervene. The claims to the good life which the society has promised become centered on the two areas that are fundamental to that life – health and education. The elimination of disease and the increasing numbers of people who can live out a full life, plus the efforts to expand the span of life, make health services a crucial feature of modern society; and the growth of technical requirements and professional skills makes education, and access to higher education, the condition of entry into the post-industrial society itself. So we have here the growth of a new intelligentsia, particularly of teachers. Finally, the claims for more services and the inadequacy of the market in meeting people's needs for a decent environment as well as better health and education lead to the growth of government, particularly at the state and local level, where such needs have to be met.

The post-industrial society, thus, is also a 'communal' society in which the social unit is the community rather than the individual, and one has to achieve a 'social decision' as against, simply, the sum total of individual decisions which, when aggregated, end up as nightmares, on the model of the individual automobile and collective traffic congestion. But cooperation between men is more difficult than the management of things. Participation becomes a condition of community, but when many different groups want too many different things and are not prepared for bargaining or trade-off, then increased conflict or deadlocks result. Either there is a politics of consensus or a politics of stymie.

As a game between persons, social life becomes more difficult because political claims and social rights multiply, the rapidity of social change and shifting cultural fashion bewilders the old, and the orientation to the future erodes the traditional guides and moralities of the past. Information becomes a central resource, and within organizations a source of power. Professionalism thus becomes a criterion of position, but it clashes, too, with the populism which is generated by the claims for more rights and greater participation in the society. If the struggle between capitalist and worker, in the locus of the factory, was the hallmark of industrial society, the clash between the professional and the populace, in the organization and in the community, is the hallmark of conflict in the post-industrial society.

This, then, is the sociological canvas of the scheme of social development leading to the post-industrial society. To identify its structural lineaments and trend lines more directly, let me turn now to the distribution of jobs by economic sector and the changing profile of occupations in the American economy.

## The sectors of work and occupations

Shortly after the turn of the century, only three in every ten workers in the country were employed in service industries and seven out of ten were engaged in the production of goods. By 1950, these proportions were more evenly balanced. By 1968, the proportions had shifted so that six out of every ten were in services. By 1980, with the rising predominance of services, close to seven in every ten workers will be in the service industries. Between 1900 and 1980, in exact reversal of the proportions between the sectors, there occurred two structural changes in the American economy: one, the shift to services, and two, the rise of the public sector as a major area of employment.

In historic fact, the shift of employment to services does not represent any sudden departure from previous long-run trends. As Victor Fuchs points out, 'For as long as we have records on the industrial distribution of the labor force, we find a secular tendency for the percentage accounted for by the Service sector to rise.' From 1870 to 1920, the shift to services could be explained almost entirely by the movement from agricultural to industrial pursuits; employment in services rose as rapidly as industry and the major increases in services were in the *auxiliary* areas of transportation, utilities, and distribution. This was the historic period of industrialization in American life. After 1920, however, the rates of growth in the non-agricultural sector began to diverge. Industrial employment still increased numerically, but already its *share* of total employment tended to decline, as employment in services began to grow at a faster rate, and from 1968 to 1980, if we take manufacturing as the key to the industrial sector, the growth rate will be less than half of the labor force as a whole.

[. . .]

The great divide began in 1947, after World War II. At that time the employment was evenly balanced. But from then on the growth rates began to diverge in new, accelerated fashion. From 1947 to 1968 there was a growth of about 60 percent in employment in services, while employment in the goods-producing industries increased less than 10 percent. Despite a steadily rising total output of goods through the 1970s, this tendency will persist. Altogether, the goods-producing industries employed 29 million workers in 1968, and the number is expected to increase to 31.6 million by 1980. However, their share in total employment will drop to less than 32 percent in 1980, from about 36 percent in 1968.

Within the goods-producing sector, employment in agriculture and mining will continue to decline in absolute terms. The major change – and the impetus to new jobs in that sector – will come in construction. The national housing goals for the 1968–1978 decade call for the building of 20 million new housing units in the private market and 6 million new and rehabilitated units through public subsidy. These goals are now finally being met, and it is expected that employment in construction will rise by 35 percent in this decade.

Manufacturing is still the single largest source of jobs in the economy. It grew at 0.9 percent a year during the 1960s largely because of increased employment in defense industries – aircraft, missiles, ordnance, communications equipment, and the like – which have higher labor components because the work is more 'custom-

crafted' than in mass production industries. But the shift away from defense spending
– with its consequent unemployment in aircraft, missiles, and communications –
means a slower rate of growth for manufacturing in the future. Any increase will
appear largely in the manufacture of building materials for housing construction.

To return to the larger picture, the most important growth area in employment since 1947 has been government. One out of every six American workers
today is employed by one of the 80,000 or so entities which make up the government of the United States today. In 1929, three million persons worked for the
government, or about 6.4 percent of the labor force. Today, twelve million persons
work for the government – about 16 percent of the labor force. By 1980 that figure
will rise to seventeen million, or 17 percent of the labor force.

Government to most people signifies the federal government. But state and
local agencies actually account for eight out of every ten workers employed by the
government. The major reason has been the expansion of schooling both in numbers
of children and in the amount of schooling and thus of the number of teachers
employed. Today about 85 percent of all pupils complete high school as against 33
percent in 1947. Educational services have been the area of fastest growth in the
country and comprised 50 percent of state and local governmental activities in 1968
(as measured by employment).

General services were the second fastest growth area for employment between
1947 and 1968, and about 10 percent of employment in general services is in private
educational institutions. Thus education as a whole, both public and private, represented 8 percent of total employment in the United States. Within general services,
the largest category is medical services, where employment rose from 1.4 million
in 1958 to 2.6 million a decade later.

➤ The spread of services, particularly in trade, finance, education, health, and
government, conjures up the picture of a white-collar society. But all services are
not white collar, since they include transportation workers and auto repairmen.
But then, not all manufacturing is blue-collar work. In 1970 the white-collar
component *within* manufacturing – professional, managerial, clerical, and sales –
came to almost 31 percent of that work force, while 69 percent were blue-collar
workers (6,055,000 white-collar and 13,400,000 blue-collar). By 1975 the white-
collar component will reach 34.5 percent. Within the blue-collar force itself
there has been a steady and distinct shift from direct production to non-production
jobs as more and more work becomes automated and, in the factory, workers
increasingly are employed in machine-tending, repair, and maintenance, rather than
on the assembly line.

In 1980 the total manufacturing labor force will number about 22 million, or
22 percent of the labor force at that time. But with the continuing spread of major
technological developments such as numerical-control machine tools, electronic
computers, instrumentation, and automatic controls, the proportion of direct
production workers is expected to go down steadily. Richard Bellmann, the Rand
mathematician, has often been quoted as predicting that by the year 2000 only
2 percent of the labor force will be required to turn out all necessary manufactured
goods, but the figure is fanciful and inherently unprovable. Automation is a real
fact, but the bogey of an accelerated pace has not materialized. But even a steady
advance of 2 to 3 percent in productivity a year, manageable though it may be

economically and socially (people are usually not fired, but jobs are eliminated through attrition), inevitably takes its toll. What is clear is that if an industrial society is defined as a goods-producing society – if manufacture is central in shaping the character of its labor force – then the United States is no longer an industrial society.

The changeover to a post-industrial society is signified not only by the change in sector distribution – the places *where* people work – but in the pattern of occupations, the *kind* of work they do. And here the story is a familiar one. The United States has become a white-collar society. From a total of about 5.5 million persons in 1900 (making up about 17.6 percent of the labor force), the white-collar group by 1968 came to 35.6 million (46.7 percent) and will rise to 48.3 million in 1980, when it will account for *half* (50.8 percent) of all employed workers.

[. . .]

Since 1920, the white-collar group has been the fastest-growing occupational group in the society, and this will continue. In 1956, for the first time, this group surpassed the employment of blue-collar workers. By 1980 the ratio will be about 5:3 in favor of the white-collar workers.

Stated in these terms, the change is dramatic, yet somewhat deceptive, for until recently the overwhelming number of white-collar workers have been women, in minor clerical or sales jobs; and in American society, as in most others, family status is still evaluated on the basis of the man's job. But it is at this point – in the changing nature of the male labor force – that a status upheaval has been taking place. In 1900 only 15 percent of American men wore white collars (and most of these were independent small businessmen). By 1940 the figure had gone up to 25 percent (and these were largely in administrative jobs). In 1970 almost 42 percent of the male labor force – some twenty million men – held white-collar jobs (as against twenty-three million who wore blue collars), and of these, almost fourteen million were managerial, professional, or technical – the heart of the upper middle class in the United States.

The total blue-collar occupations, which numbered about 12 million in 1900, rose to 27.5 million in 1968 and will rise at a slower rate to 31.1 million in 1980. In 1900, the blue-collar workers formed about 35 percent of the total labor force, a figure which reached 40 percent in 1920 and again, after World War II, in 1950, but by 1968 it was down to about 36.3 percent of the total labor force and by 1980 will reach an historic low of 32.7 percent.

The most striking change, of course, has been in the farm population. In 1900 farming was still the single largest occupation in the United States, comprising 12.5 million workers and about 37.5 percent of the labor force. Until about 1930, the absolute number of farmers and farm workers continued to rise though their share of employment began to decline. In 1940, because of the extraordinary agricultural revolution, which shot productivity to spectacular heights, the number of farm laborers began its rapid decline. In 1968, employment on the farms numbered 3.5 million, and this will decline to 2.6 million in 1980; from 4.6 percent of the work force in 1968 it will fall to 2.7 percent in 1980.

The service occupations continue to expand steadily. In 1900 there were about three million persons in services, more than half of whom were domestics. In 1968, there were almost 9.5 million persons in services, only a fourth of whom were domestics. The major rises were in such occupations as garage workers, hotel and restaurant workers, and the like. Through the 1970s, service occupations will increase by two-fifths or a rate one and one-half times the expansion for all occupations combined.

The category of semi-skilled worker (called operatives in the census classification) from 1920 on was the single largest occupational category in the economy, comprising more workers than any other group. Semi-skilled work is the occupational counterpart of mass production, and it rose with the increased output of goods. But the introduction of sophisticated new technologies has slowed the growth of this group drastically. Total employment will rise from 14 million in 1968 to 15.4 million in 1980, but the rate of increase is half the increase projected for all employment.

As a share of total employment, the percentage of semi-skilled will slide downward from 18.4 percent in 1968 to 16.2 percent in 1980 and will at that time be *third* in size ranking, outpaced by clerical, which will be the largest, and by professional and technical workers. Equally, the proportion of factory workers among the semi-skilled will probably drop. In 1968, six out of every ten semi-skilled workers were employed as factory operatives. Large numbers of them now work as inspectors, maintenance men, operators of material-moving equipment such as powered forklift trucks, and the like. Among the non-factory operatives, drivers of trucks, buses, and taxi-cabs make up the largest group.

The central occupational category in the society today is the professional and technical. Growth in this category has outdistanced all other major occupational groups in recent decades. From less than a million in 1890, the number of these workers has grown to 10.3 million in 1968. Within this category, the largest group was teachers (more than 2 million), the second largest professional health workers (about 2 million), scientists and engineers (about 1.4 million), and engineering and science technicians (about 900,000). Despite the momentary slowdown in the demand for education, and the immediate unemployment in engineering because of the shift away from defense work in 1970–1971, requirements in this category continue to lead all others, increasing half again in size (about twice the employment increase among all occupations combined) between 1968 and 1980. With 15.5 million workers in 1980, this will comprise 16.3 percent of total employment as against 13.6 percent in 1968.

[. . .]

[. . .] The classical proletariat consisted of factory workers whose class-consciousness was created by the conditions of their work. But even at its most comprehensive definition, the blue-collar group is in an increasing minority in advanced or post-industrial society. Is the proletariat, or the working class, *all* those who work for wages and salaries? But that so expands the concept as to distort it beyond recognition. (Are all managers workers? Are supervisors and administrators workers? Are highly paid professors and engineers workers?)

For a long time, Marxist sociologists simply ignored the issue, and argued that the 'inevitable' economic crises of capitalism would force a revolutionary conflict in which 'the working class' would win. In Germany in the 1920s, where the phenomenon of the new technical and administrative class was first noticed, it was categorized as 'the new middle class,' and it was in this sense that C. Wright Mills also used the idea in his 1951 book, *White Collar*. For the German sociologists, particularly Emil Lederer and Jacob Marschak, who first analyzed the phenomenon in detail, the 'new middle class' could not be an autonomous independent class, but would eventually have to support either the working class or the business community. This was also Mills's argument: 'Insofar as political strength rests upon organized economic power, the white-collar workers can only derive their strength from "business" or from "labor." Within the whole structure of power, they are dependent variables. Estimates of their political tendencies, therefore, must rest upon larger predictions of the manner and outcomes of the struggles of business and labor.'

The German sociologists, and Mills, had been writing principally about managerial, administrative, and clerical personnel. But when it became evident, particularly in the 1950s, that there was a large-scale transformation in the character of skilled work itself, with the expansion of engineering and technicians in the advanced technological fields – aerospace, computers, oil refining, electronics, optics, polymers – and that this new stratum was becoming occupationally more important as well as replacing the skilled workers as the crucial group in the industrial process, the problem of sociological definition became crucial.

The first Marxist to seek a theoretical formulation was the independent French radical Serge Mallet, who, in a series of articles in *Les Temps Modernes* and the magazine *La Nef* in 1959, wrote an analysis of the new industrial processes in France's petit counterpart to IBM, La Compagnie des machines Bull, and in the heavily automated oil refinery, Caltex. These studies, plus a long essay, 'Trade Unionism and Industrial Society,' were published in France in 1963 under the title *La Nouvelle Classe Ouvrière* (*The New Working Class*). Though untranslated, the book had a definite influence on some young American radicals. [. . .]

The Mallet thesis is quite simple. The engineers and technicians are a 'new' working class, in part replacing the old, with a potential for revolutionary leadership and the ability to play a role far beyond their numbers. They are a 'new' working class, even though well paid, because their skills are inevitably broken down, compartmentalized, and routinized, and they are unable to realize the professional skills for which they were educated. Thus they are 'reduced' to the role of a highly trained working class. The fact that they are better paid does not make them a new 'aristocracy of labor.' [. . .]

[. . .]

In principle, the idea is not new. It is central, of course, to the writing of Thorstein Veblen (little known to the French), who, in *The Theory of Business Enterprises* (1903), made a fundamental distinction between industry and business – between the engineer, devoted largely to improving the practices of production, and the finance capitalist or manager, who restricts production in order to maintain process and profit. In *The Engineers and the Price System* (1920), Veblen wrote 'A Memorandum on a Practicable Soviet of Technicians' which laid out the argument of the revolutionary potential of the production engineer as the indispensable 'General Staff of the industrial system.' [. . .]

[. . .]

Veblen wrote in the first flush of excitement after the Russian Revolution, and he felt that a syndicalist overturn of society was possible – in fact, he thought it could be the only one, since political revolutions in advanced industrial society were passé. For half a century that idea has seemed strange indeed, but its revival by the French writers has been possible because the idea of a professional new class has meshed with the idea of alienation.

Where Mallet, like Veblen, restricted his analysis largely to the technicians, the French social critic André Gorz, an editor of *Les Temps Modernes*, has extended his thesis to the 'alienated situation' of the entire professional class. Until now, he argues, the trade union movement has taken the necessary stand of fighting for 'quantitative gains,' but this continuing strategy has become increasingly dysfunctional because it has tied the workers into the productivity of the economic system and the consumption society. The new strategy for labor, as well as for all professionals, should be to fight for 'qualitative' changes, and in particular for control of production. [. . .]

[. . .]

The most serious efforts to apply Gorz's ideas to the American scene have been made by some radical young economists at Harvard, notably Herbert Gintis. Gintis sees a 'new emergent social class in modern capitalism,' a new working class which he broadly labels 'educated labor.' Drawing upon the standard work of Edward Denison, and of his Harvard colleague Samuel Bowles, Gintis emphasizes the importance of 'educated labor,' because if one compares the relative contribution of physical capital (machines and technology) with 'human capital' in the economic growth of the United States between 1929 and 1957, labor is between five and eight times more important than physical capital. But Gintis sees educated labor as pressed into a mold by the requirements of the capitalist system. A revolutionary outlook emerges because of the alienated desire of educated persons for a full life as producers, as against the fragmentation and specialization which is their lot in the workaday world. For Gintis, the student rebellion against the university foreshadows the possible revolt of all 'educated labor' against capitalism.

The weakness of this abstract analysis lies, first, in seeing the students as the model for the revolution of the future. The university, even with required courses, is not the prototype of the corporate world, and it is highly unlikely that even 'raised student consciousness' was a consciousness of 'oppression.' Universities are a 'hot house' in which a student lives in a world apart, free largely, especially today, from the sanctions and reprisals of adult authority for almost any escapades. After graduation students enter a different, highly differentiated society and begin to take on responsibilities for themselves and their new families. It is not so surprising, therefore, that whatever the initial benchmark of radicalism, the college generation, as it grows older, becomes more conservative.

A second weakness is the monolithic rhetoric about the requirements of 'the system.' Paradoxically (and perhaps tongue-in-cheek) Gintis drew his analysis not from Marcuse but from the functionalist school of sociology, particularly Talcott Parsons, which Marxists have attacked as too simple a view of the 'integration' of society. In any event, both the functionalist and the Marcusian views are too constricted in their understanding of the diversity and multiplicity of the society and the culture. There is no 'system' which 'reproduces' the existing division of labor in the next generation, but many different trends deriving from the diverse sources of occupational trends in the United States.

And third, Gintis sees bureaucratization as identical with capitalism ('The bureaucratization of work is a result of the capitalist control of the work process, as bureaucracy seems to be the sole organizational form compatible with capitalist hegemony'), rather than as a pervasive feature of the historic development of all technological and hierarchical societies, capitalist and communist. And what he misses, in his abstract conception of bureaucracy, are the large number of changes taking place in organizations which are modifying the classic hierarchical structures of bureaucracy by encouraging committees and participation. While such changes, it is true, do not alter the fundamental character of authority, the modifications often serve to provide the individual with a greater degree of participation than before.

The sources of these critiques are the moral impulses of socialist humanism, but though one can sympathize with their values, it is folly to confuse normative with analytical categories and convert social tendencies into rhetorical wish fulfillment, as Gorz and Gintis do. The engineers, for example, fit many of the attributes of the alienated 'educated worker.' Few of them are allowed to decide how their skills and knowledge will be used; the transition from a defense economy, combined with the drastic slash in research-and-development spending, has made many of them aware, for the first time, of the precariousness of a 'career.' Yet they do not in the least identify themselves with the 'working class.' (As *Fortune* found in a recent study of engineers, in June 1971, 'Many have moved up into engineering from blue-collar union families and don't want to slip back.') What counts for the engineer is the maintenance of a 'professional status.' They complain that the word engineer is now used to describe everyone from a salesman (a systems engineer at IBM) to a garbage collector (a sanitary engineer, in the Chicago euphemism). The effort to reassert their professional status – through membership in high-prestige associations, through stiffer requirements for professional certification, through changes in school curricula – is an effort at differentiation, not identification.

This effort to maintain professional status – one aspect of a society in which individual social mobility is still a positive value – comes into conflict, however, with the New Left populism, which derogates professionalism as 'elitism.' In the schools, in the hospitals, in the community, the New Left political impulse is to deplore professionalism and hieratic standing as means of excluding the people from decisions. Thus one finds today the paradox that 'educated labor' is caught between the extremes of bureaucratization and populism. If it is to resist the 'alienation' which threatens its achievement, it is more likely to assert the traditional professionalism (certainly on the ideological level) than go in either direction. To this extent, the phrase 'new working class' is simply a radical conceit, and little more.

## The constraints on change

There is little question, I believe, that in the next few decades we shall see some striking changes in the structure of occupations and professional work. Within the factories there will be new demands for control over the decisions of work as the new, younger and more educated labor force faces the prospect of long years in a mechanical harness and finds the monetary rewards (which their forebears struggled to achieve) less important. Within the professions there will be more social-mindedness as a newer generation comes to the fore and the structure of professional relationships changes. Within medicine, for example, one of the central occupations of a post-industrial society, the inevitable end of the 'fee-for-service' relationship, replaced by some kind of insurance-cum-government payment scheme, means the end of the doctor as an individual entrepreneur and the increasing centrality of the hospital and group practice. A whole new range of issues opens up: who is to run the hospitals – the old philanthropic trustees, the municipal political nominees, the doctors, the 'constituencies,' or the 'community'? How does one balance research and patient care in the distribution of resources? Should there be more big teaching hospitals with greater sophisticated facilities or more simple community medical services? Similarly, within the law, the greater role of government in welfare, services for the poor, education, consumer standards, and health provides a whole new area of public-interest law for the lawyer alongside the older areas of business, real estate, labor law, wills, and trusts. The multiplication of junior and community colleges and the break-up of the standard curricula in most universities provide an arena for experiment and change.

And yet, ironically, at a time when many needed reforms seem about to be made in the area of work and in the professions – in part out of the upheavals of the 1960s, in greater part because of the deeper forces of structural changes of a post-industrial society – there will be stronger objective constraints on such changes (apart from the vested and established interests which are always present) than in the previous several decades of American economic and social development.

There is, first, the constraint of productivity. The simple and obvious fact is that productivity and output grow much faster in goods than in services. (This is crucial in the shift in the shares of employment: men can be displaced by machines more readily in goods-production than in services.) Productivity in services because it is a relation between persons, rather than between man and machine, will inevitably be lower than it is in industry. This is true in almost all services. In retailing, despite self-service, supermarkets, and pre-packaging, the rising proportion of the labor force engaged in marketing reaches a ceiling of productivity. In personal services, from barbering to travel arrangements, the nature of the personal relations is fixed by time components. In education, despite programmed learning and television instruction and large lecture classes (which students resent), the costs of education have been increasing at 5 to 7 percent a year, while productivity for all services (including education) has shuffled upward at 1.9 percent a year. In health, despite multiphasic screens and similar mechanized diagnostic devices – a gain in numbers examined, but a loss in personal care – there is only so much of a physician's time to be distributed among patients. And, at the extreme, the example of live musical performances, where, as William J. Baumol is fond of pointing out, a half-hour quintet calls for the expenditure of 2½ man hours in its performance, and there can be no increase in productivity when the musician's wage goes up.

This problem comes to a head in the cities whose budgets have doubled and tripled in the last decades (apart from welfare) because the bulk of municipal expenditures – education, hospitals, police, social services – falls into the non-progressive sector of the economy, and there are few real economies or gains that can halt these rises. Yet it is productivity which allows the social pie to expand.

The second constraint is an inflation which has been built into the structure of the economy itself by the *secondary* effects of bilateral actions of strong unions and oligopolistic industries. The inflation which has wracked the American economy since 1968 has [. . .] become a structural problem for the economy. The major alarums and noise of collective bargaining in such major industries as steel and auto, electric products and rubber, have been, in reality, mimetic combats in that an unstated but nonetheless real accommodation has been worked out between the contending parties. The unions receive substantial wage increases, and these increases become the occasion for even more substantial price increases which the industries, with their ability to 'administer' prices, are able (until recently) to pass on to the public without protest either from the unions or from government.

As a result of this system, the unions have been able to force wages up at an average rate of 7 percent annually for the past four years. [. . .] Meanwhile productivity has been growing at only 3 percent a year. If the economy were only a manufacturing economy, this would be manageable. The labor costs in goods manufacturing are about 30 percent of the total costs. A 10 percent wage increase means, then, only a 3 percent increase in the cost of production, which can be offset by productivity. But in the services sectors, the wage proportion may run 70 percent or more of the total costs of the services, so a parallel 10 percent increase in wages adds 7 percent to the cost of services; productivity in the services sector, however, averages between 1.2 and 1.9 percent. The gap between these rates is a rough measure of the secondary effects of the cost-push factor of inflation that is being built into the system.

It is the changed nature of the service economy which is responsible for the structural elements of inflation that have become built into the economy. According to John Kenneth Galbraith's view of the 'new industrial state,' inflation is maintained by negotiated wages and ever rising administered prices in the corporate sectors of the economy. But the experience of 1965 to 1970 showed a different pattern. In those years, the price index rose 30 percent. The price of automobiles, one of the most highly concentrated industries, rose 15 percent. Durable goods – television, appliances, furniture – rose 18 percent. But the price of services – medical care, schooling, recreation, insurance – had gone up 42.5 percent. Some of that price rise was due to strong demand; yet in greater measure it was due to the increases in wages and prices in those areas with little corresponding gains in productivity.

When the pattern of steadily rising wages becomes so fixed, one finds an exacerbation in the governmental or communal services sector, for the higher 'prices' become, necessarily, higher 'taxes' – and more political grumbling. One can extend the urban problem to the society as a whole. As a larger portion of the labor force shifts into services, there is inevitably a greater drag on productivity and growth, and the costs of services, private and governmental, increase sharply. And yet there is, also inevitably, a greater demand for government activities and government goods to meet the social needs of the populace. But one then faces a painful contradiction, for if the wages in the service sectors, especially government, rise without compensating gains in productivity, they become additional claimants on social resources, competing for money needed for hospitals, schools, libraries, houses, clean water, clean air, etc.

In the nature of post-industrial society, the government has become the single largest employer in the society. But winning wage increases from the government is a far different problem from winning increases from private industry. Increasingly there looms what James O'Connor has called 'the fiscal crisis of the state.' The multiplication of government functions creates a need for new revenues. The concomitant expansion of the government bureaucracy increases costs. But government budgets are subject to constraints far different from those of private corporations, which can try to pass on their costs through price increases. Government revenues can increase in three ways. One is to step up the rate of economic growth and use the resulting gains in GNP for government purposes rather than private consumption. (This was how the government social programs were financed in the early 1960s.) But such acceleration risks inflation, and at the moment no Western society seems to know how to bring inflation under control. The second is to increase productivity in the government and service sectors, but while some gains are possible, intrinsically these will always lag behind the 'progressive' industrial sectors. A third way is to raise taxes. But there is an increasing public outcry against rising taxes. The alternative is to cut government programs and hold down spending, but given the multiple pressures from different groups – business wants to cut social programs but maintain subsidies; labor wants higher budgets in all areas; reform groups want to cut the defense budget but expand social programs – this is not easy. And in all likelihood the fiscal problems will increase. This may well be an intractable problem of post-industrial society.

A third constraint, more peculiar to the United States, is the evident fact that (from a businessman's point of view) American manufactured goods are pricing themselves out of the world market. From the view of theoretical economics, in the inevitable 'product cycle' of goods production a more advanced industrial society finds itself at a price disadvantage when a product becomes standardized, inputs are predictable, price elasticity of demand is higher, and labor costs make a difference, so that less advanced but competing nations can now make the product more cheaply. And this is now happening in American manufacture. In the world economy the United States is now a 'mature' nation and in a position to be pushed off the top of the hill by more aggressive countries, as happened to England at the end of the first quarter of this century.

If one looks at the position of the United States today in the world economy, three facts are evident:

1    Only in technology-intensive products does the United States have a favorable commercial balance in its trade with the rest of the world. In agricultural products, in minerals, fuels, and other non-manufactured and non-agricultural products, and in non-technology-intensive manufactured products, the balance is heavily the other way. In textiles, in such technological products as transistor radios, typewriters, and expensive cameras, which have now become standardized, the United States market has been swept by foreign goods. [. . .]
2    The reduction in costs of transport, and the differential in wages, has made it increasingly possible for American multi-national corporations to manufacture significant proportions of components abroad and bring them back here for assembly. [. . .]

3    Increasingly the United States is becoming a *rentier* society, in which a substantial and increasing proportion of the balance of trade consists of the return on investments abroad by American corporations, rather than exports.

All of this poses a very serious problem for American labor. The area where it is best organized, manufacture, faces a serious erosion of jobs. In response, American labor, which has traditionally been committed to free trade, is now heavily protectionist. [. . .]

[. . .]

The largest constraint is the very multiplicity of competing demands in the polity itself. A post-industrial society, as I pointed out earlier, is increasingly a communal society wherein public mechanisms rather than the market become the allocators of goods, as public choice, rather than individual demand, becomes the arbiter of services. A communal society by its very nature multiplies the definition of rights – the rights of children, of students, of the poor, of minorities – and translates them into claims of the community. The rise of externalities – the effects of private actions on the commonweal – turns clean air, clean water, and mass transit into public issues and increases the need for social regulations and controls. The demand for higher education and better health necessarily expands greatly the role of government as funder and setter of standards. The need for amenities, the cry for a better quality of life, brings government into the arena of environment, recreation, and culture.

But all this involves two problems: we don't really know, given our lack of social-science knowledge, how to do many of these things effectively; equally important, since there may not be enough money to satisfy all or even most of the claims, how do we decide what to do first? In 1960 the Eisenhower Commission on National Goals formulated a set of minimum standards for the quality of life – standards which already seem primitive a decade later – and when the National Planning Association projected these goals to 1975 and sought to cost them out (assuming a 4 percent growth rate, which we have not maintained), it found that we would be $150 billion dollars short in trying to achieve all those goals. So the problem is one of priorities and choice.

But how to achieve this? One of the facts of a communal society is the increased participation of individuals and groups in communal life. In fact, there is probably more participation today, at the city level, than at any other time in American history. But the very increase in participation leads to a paradox: the greater the number of groups, each seeking diverse or competing ends, the more likelihood that these groups will veto one another's interests, with the consequent sense of frustration and powerlessness as such stalemates incur. This is true not only locally but nationally, where, in the last twenty years, new constituencies have multiplied. The standard entities of interest-group politics used to be corporate, labor, and farm, with the ethnic groups playing a role largely in state and city politics. But in the last two decades we have seen the rise of scientists, educators, the intelligentsia, blacks, youth, and poor, all playing a role in the game of influence and resource allocation. And the old coalitions are no longer decisive. What we have been witnessing in the last decade, in fact, is the rise of an independent component, committed to neither of the two parties, whose swing vote becomes increasingly important. Thus the problem of how to achieve consensus on political questions will become more difficult. Without consensus there is only conflict, and persistent conflict simply tears a society apart, leaving the way open to repression by one sizeable force or another.

Industrial society in the West was marked by three distinctive features: the growth of the large corporation as the prototype of all business enterprise; the imprint of the machine and its rhythms on the character of work; and labor conflict, as the form of polarized class conflict, which threatened to tear society apart. All three of these elements are markedly changed in the post-industrial society.

The modern business corporation was a social invention, fashioned at the turn of the century, to implement the 'economizing mode' which had become the engine of social change in the society. It was a device which differed markedly from the army and the church (the two historic forms of large-scale organization) in its ability to coordinate men, materials, and markets for the mass production of goods. In the first half of this century, beginning symbolically with the formation of the first billion-dollar corporation, United States Steel Company in 1901 by J. P. Morgan, the role of the corporation grew steadily and the economy came to be dominated by such familiar giants as General Motors, General Electric, Standard Oil, and the other monoliths that make up the banner listing of *Fortune*'s 500 industrials. Yet by 1956 the corporation seemed to reach a plateau in the economy, when incorporated businesses accounted for over 57 percent of the total national income, and since then the proportion has remained stable.

The modern business corporation is marked by large size: of assets, sales, and the number of employees. (General Motors, the largest corporation in the United States, in 1970 had 695,790 employees; Arvin Industries, the five-hundredth-largest, had 7,850.) But the distinctive character of the services sector is the small size of unit enterprise. Though one finds giant corporations in the services fields as large as any industrial corporation – in utilities (American Telephone and Telegraph), banking (Chase Manhattan), insurance (Metropolitan Life), retail trade (Sears Roebuck) – most of the firms in retail trade, personal and professional services, finance and real estate, and hospitals employ fewer than a thousand persons. The word government conjures up a picture of huge bureaucracy, but employment at the local level of government exceeds that of state and federal, and half of this local employment is in governmental units with fewer than 500 employees.

Even where unit size is larger, in hospitals and in schools, what is different about these enterprises is the larger degree of autonomy of smaller units (the departments in the hospitals and colleges) and the greater degree of professional control. Surely this is an 'organizational society' in that the organization rather than the small town is the locus of one's life, but to make this observation, as many sociologists do, is to miss the fact that what has been appearing is a multiplicity of diverse types of organization and that the received model we have, that of the large business corporation, while still pre-eminent, is not pervasive. New forms of small professional firms, research institutes, diverse kinds of government agencies, plus schools and hospitals, which are subject to professional and community control, become the locus of life for more and more persons in the society.

The change has come not only in place, but also in character of work. In an essay I published in 1956, *Work and Its Discontents*, I wrote: 'The image of tens of thousands of workers streaming from the sprawling factories marks indelibly the picture of industrial America, as much as the fringed buckskin and rifle marked the nineteenth-century frontier, or the peruke and lace that of Colonial Virginia. The majority of Americans may not work in factories, as the majority of Americans never were on the frontier, or never lived in Georgian houses; yet the distinctive ethos of each time lies in these archetypes.' I argued, further, that while a large variety of occupations and jobs were far removed from the factory, 'the factory is archetypal because its rhythms, in subtle fashion, affect the general character of work the way a dye suffuses a cloth.'

The rhythms of mechanization are still pervasive in the United States. The nature of materials handling has been revolutionized by the introduction of mechanized devices. Office work, particularly in large insurance companies, banks, utilities, and industrial corporations has the same mechanical and drone-like quality, for routing procedures serve the same pacing functions as assembly lines. And yet, the distinctive archetype has gone. Charlie Chaplin's *Modern Times* at one time symbolized industrial civilization, but today it is a period piece. The rhythms are no longer that pervasive. The beat has been broken.

Does a new archetype exist today? The fact that in services relations are between persons led C. Wright Mills twenty years ago to declare that the white-collar world had become a 'personality market,' in which each person 'sold himself' in order to impress another and get ahead. Mills's prototype was the salesman and the setting was 'the big store.' But even at that time his argument was not entirely convincing (especially to those who tried to get service in some of these stores), and it is even less so today. New stereotypes abound. An important one – to judge from some of the television commercials – is the researcher or the laboratory technician in a white coat, carrying out an experiment (usually to prove that the sponsor's product is better than the rival's). But this is more an effort to catch the reflected authority of science than the mimesis of a new civilization.

If there are no primary images of work, what is central to the new relationship is encounter or communication, and the response of ego to alter, and back – from the irritation of a customer at an airline-ticket office to the sympathetic or harassed response of teacher to student. But the fact that individuals now talk to other individuals, rather than interact with a machine, is the fundamental fact about work in the post-industrial society.

Finally, for more than a hundred years, the 'labor issue' dominated Western society. The conflict between worker and boss (whether capitalist or corporate manager) overshadowed all other conflicts and was the axis around which the major social divisions of the society rotated. Marx had assumed, in the logic of commodity production, that in the end both bourgeoisie and worker would be reduced to the abstract economic relation in which all other social attributes would be eliminated so that the two would face each other nakedly – as would all society – in their class roles. Two things, however, have gone awry with this prediction. The first has been the persistent strength of what Max Weber called 'segregated status groups' – race, ethnic, linguistic, religious – whose loyalties, ties, and emotional identifications have been more powerful and compelling than class at most times, and whose own divisions have overridden class lines. In advanced industrial countries such as Belgium or Canada, no less than in tribal societies such as Africa or communal societies such as India, the 'status groups' have generated conflicts that have torn the society apart more sharply, often, than class issues. Second, the labor problem has become 'encapsulated.' An interest conflict and a labor issue – in the sense of disproportionate power between manager and worker over the conditions of work – remain, but the disproportions have shifted and the methods of negotiation have become institutionalized. Not only has the political tension become encapsulated, there is even the question whether the occupational psychology which Veblen and Dewey made so central to their sociology carries over into other aspects of a man's behavior as well. (A bourgeois was a bourgeois by day and a bourgeois by night; it would be hard to say this about some of the managers who are executives by day and swingers at night.) The crucial fact is that the 'labor issue' *qua* labor is no longer central, nor does it have the sociological and cultural weight to polarize all other issues along that axis.

In the next decade, the possible demands for the reorganization of work, the decline in productivity, and the persistent threat of inflation because of the disproportionate productivity in the goods and services sectors, the threats of foreign competition, and other issues such as the recalcitrance of some unions on race, or the bilateral monopolies of unions and builders in the construction trades, all may make labor issues increasingly salient and even rancorous. The fact that some unions may even turn from concern with income and consumption to problems of production and the character of work is all to the good. But it is highly unlikely that these will become ideological or 'class' issues, although they may become politicized.

The politics of the next decade is more likely to concern itself, on the national level, with such public-interest issues as health, education, and the environment, and, on the local level, crime, municipal services, and costs. These are all communal issues, and on these matters labor may find itself, on the national level, largely liberal, yet, on the local level, divided by the factious issues that split community life.

But all this is a far cry from the vision of *The Communist Manifesto* of 1848 and the student revolutionaries of 1968. In the economy, a labor issue remains. But not in the sociology and culture. To that extent, the changes which are summed up in the post-industrial society may represent a historic metamorphosis in Western society.

# Chapter 8

# Krishan Kumar

## FROM POST-INDUSTRIAL TO POST-MODERN SOCIETY

From *From Post-Industrial to Post-Modern Society*, Oxford: Blackwell (1995), pp. 6–35.

[. . .]

### The computer and the coming of information

INFORMATION, AS A CONCEPT, COMES into the world trailing clouds of glory. It is nothing less, its most eminent popularizer Norbert Wiener has said, than the main part of life's counter-offensive against the entropic impulse that will eventually cause the universe to run down. 'In control and communication' – the heart of information – 'we are always fighting nature's tendency to degrade the organized and to destroy the meaningful; the tendency . . . for entropy to increase.' Information is a requirement of our survival. It permits the necessary exchanges between us and our environment. 'To live effectively is to live with adequate information. Thus, communication and control belong to the essence of man's inner life, even as they belong to his life in society' (Wiener 1968: 19).

Wiener, the inventor of 'cybernetics', the 'theory of messages', was writing in the late 1940s and early 1950s. The timing is significant. The grand claim for information sprang from certain revolutionary developments in these years in the technology of control and communication – 'information technology', or IT, as it came to be called. The birth of information, not merely as a concept but also as an ideology, is inextricably linked to the development of the computer. This was an accomplishment of the war years and the immediate post-war period.

The timing as well as the tempo of growth indicate the computer's close relationship to the evolving military requirements of the west, principally as interpreted by the United States. Such key components of the computer as miniaturized electrical circuits were developed by the Americans for specific military uses during the Second World War – in this case proximity fuses for bombs. The electronic digital computer itself was created primarily for ballistics calculations and atomic bomb analysis. The civilian research centres where most of these developments took place, such as the Bell Laboratories of AT&T, were heavily funded by the wartime American government and supervised by such government agencies as Vannevar Bush's Office of Scientific Research and Development. As the American trade magazine *Electronics* put it in 1980, electronics 'has held an integral place in national defense since World War Two' (Noble 1986: 8, 47–56).

Just as America's world-wide military role provided both the motive and the opportunity for the development of more and more sophisticated systems of information technology, so too did the world-wide expansion of the American corporation in the years following the Second World War. 'The American corporation was faced with a "command and control" problem similar to that confronting its military counterpart. . . . Like the Pentagon, it was increasingly diversified and internationalized' (Weizenbaum 1976: 27). The multinational corporation lives by communication. It is what gives it its identity as an enterprise spanning the world. Computers and satellites are as essential to its operation as the workers and plant that produce its goods and services.

Origins do not determine destinations The atom was split as a direct result of military planning but nuclear energy has a multitude of uses. Similarly the military origins of the information revolution do not limit its effects in a vast range of non-military spheres. But origins tell us something about motivating force and shaping influences. The emergence, in the 1950s, of a military-industrial-scientific complex is not the whole story of the information society. But it is a central part of that story.


## The Third Industrial Revolution

[. . .]

It is the computer [. . .] as the 'central symbol' and 'analytical engine' of change that Daniel Bell puts at heart of his account of the coming of the Information Society. [. . .] As early as *The Coming of Post-Industrial Society* Bell had stated that 'the post-industrial society is an information society' (Bell 1973: 467) [. . .].

But the basic idea of the post-industrial society was the movement to a service society and the rapid growth of professional and technical employment (Kumar 1978: 185–240). The idea of information itself remained relatively undeveloped. Now, fortified perhaps by the rush of new technical developments in computers and communications, Bell is more confident. Information now names the post-industrial society. It is what produces and sustains it.

> My basic premise has been that knowledge and information are becoming
> the strategic resource and transforming agent of the post-industrial

society . . . just as the combination of energy, resources and machine technology were the transforming agencies of industrial society.

(Bell 1980a: 531, 545; see also Bell 1980b)

John Naisbitt's popular account in *Megatrends* snappily summarizes this: 'Computer technology is to the information age what mechanization was to the industrial revolution' (Naisbitt 1984: 22).

It has been one of the notable features of the idea of the information society that, just as with the idea of post-industrial society, its exposition and explication in the scholarly literature and at academic conferences have been accompanied by extensive popularization in the mass media and through journalistic best-sellers. Alvin Toffler, who popularized the post-industrial idea in *Future Shock*, has had an even greater success with his popularization of the idea of the information society in *The Third Wave* (1981). Almost equally successful has been John Naisbitt's bite-size rendering of the idea in *Megatrends* (1984). These popular works make helpfully explicit what are often understated or over-qualified positions in the writings of more cautiously-minded academics. In what follows I shall use Daniel Bell for the main statement of the thesis of the information society; Toffler, Naisbitt and other popularizers can supply, where necessary, the clarifying chorus.

The computer by itself would transform many of the operations of industrial society. But what has brought the Information Society into being, argues Bell, is the explosive convergence of the computer with telecommunications (a marriage some have blessed with the unlovely name 'compunications'). This has broken down the long-standing distinction between the processing of knowledge and its communication (Bell 1980a: 513). Marshall McLuhan had looked to television to bring into being the 'global village'; far more effective in linking the world has been the communications satellite. 'The real importance of Sputnik is not that it began the space age, but that it introduced the era of global satellite communications' (Naisbitt 1984: 2). The combination of satellites, television, telephone, fibre optic cable and microelectronic computers has meshed the world together into a unified knowledge grid. It has 'collapsed the information float. Now, for the first time, we are a truly global economy, because for the first time we have on the planet instantaneously shared information' (Naisbitt 1984: 57) [. . .].

The increase in knowledge is qualitative, not just quantitative. The old mass media transmitted standardized messages to uniform mass audiences. The new media of communication allow 'narrowcasting' as well as broadcasting. Linked to the computer, cable and satellite permit the segmentation and splitting of both senders and receivers into discrete and discontinuous units. Information can be processed, selected and retrieved to suit the most specialized, the most individualized requirements. 'The Third Wave thus begins a new era – the age of the de-massified media. A new info-sphere is emerging alongside the new technosphere' (Toffler 1981: 165; cf. Bell 1980a: 529).

The new info-sphere operates in a global context. No need to move; the information can be brought to your home or local office. A world-wide electronic network of libraries, archives and data banks comes into being, accessible in principle to anyone, anywhere, at any time. 'All the books in the Library of Congress can be stored in a computer no larger than a home refrigerator' (Sussman 1989:

61). The information technology revolution compresses space and time into a new 'world *oikoumene*' orientated towards the future. Past societies, says Bell, were primarily space-bound or time-bound. They were held together by territorially based political and bureaucratic authorities and/or by history and tradition. Industrialism confirmed space in the nation state while replacing the rhythms and tempo of nature with the pacing of the machine. The clock and the railway timetable are the symbols of the industrial age. They express time in hours, minutes, seconds. The computer, the symbol of the information age, thinks in nanoseconds, in thousandths of microseconds. Its conjunction with the new communications technology thus brings in a radically new space–time framework for modern society.

[. . .]

As with his earlier exposition of the post-industrial idea, Bell is meticulous in giving statistical flesh to the structural bones of the information society. Knowledge does not simply govern, to an unprecedented extent, technical innovation and economic growth; it is itself fast becoming the principal activity of the economy and the principal determinant of occupational change.

In his earlier account Bell had relied for his assessment of the 'knowledge factor' in the economy on the celebrated calculations of Fritz Machlup (1962). Latterly he has come to rely on the more sophisticated and widely reported calculations by Marc Porat (1977) of the extent of the US 'information economy'. Bell combines Porat's calculations, centred on the year 1967, of the 'primary information sector' (industries which directly produce marketable information goods and services) with his calculations of the 'secondary information sector' (information activities in the 'technostructure' of both public and private organizations, which contribute indirectly – through planning, marketing, etc. – to output, but which are not formally counted as information services in the national accounts). Together these suggest that the information economy in the United States amounts to about 46 per cent of GNP and more than 50 per cent of all wages and salaries earned, that is, more than half of the national income. 'It is in that sense that we have become an information economy' (Bell 1980a: 521; see also Stonier 1983: 24).

This remarkable degree of information activity – and Bell assumes it to have grown considerably since 1967 – is matched by the rapid growth of information workers in the occupational structure. Separating out an 'information sector' from the more general tertiary category of services, Bell shows that by the mid-1970s information workers in the United States had come to constitute the largest group of workers – almost 47 per cent – in the civilian work-force (industrial workers accounted for a further 28 per cent, service workers for 22 per cent and agricultural workers for 3 per cent). Using what he calls a more 'inclusive definition' Bell claims that already 'by 1975 the information workers had surpassed the non-information groups as a whole' (Bell 1980a: 523–4).

Naisbitt goes even further. [. . .] 'We now mass-produce information the way we used to mass-produce cars . . . this knowledge is the driving force of the economy' (Naisbitt 1984: 7). The information society, according to its proponents, brings about change at the most fundamental level of society. It initiates a new mode of production. it changes the very source of wealth-creation and the governing factors in production. Labour and capital, the central variables of the industrial society, are replaced by information and knowledge as the central variables. The labour theory of value, as classically formulated by a succession of thinkers from Locke and Smith to Ricardo and Marx, most give way to a 'knowledge theory of value'. Now 'knowledge, not labour, is the source of value' (Bell 1980a: 506) [. . .]

It is clear [. . .] that what Masuda calls 'the past developmental pattern of human society' is used as 'an historical analogical model for future society' (Masuda 1985: 620). This is in fact no more than the familiar evolutionary typology to be found in sociology since the eighteenth century. Current changes are seen according to a model derived from (assumed) past changes, and future developments are projected following the logic of the model. So just as industrial society replaced agrarian society, the information society is replacing industrial society, more or less in the same revolutionary way. Bell, using a three-fold evolutionary schema based on the movement from 'pre-industrial extractive' to 'industrial-fabrication' to 'post-industrial-information' activities, produces an elaborate and systematic comparison of all three types of society. The three are seen as distinct but equivalent modes of production, analysable according to the same principles of structure and function (Bell 1980a: 504–5; see also Stonier 1983: 23; Jones 1982: 11).

Bell, more cautious than most of his disciples, does not 'read off' from his predominantly economic model all the features of cultural and political life in the information society. As before, and with something of the same vexing stubbornness, he insists on the principle of 'the disjunction of realms'. Economy, polity and culture are distinct realms which 'respond to different norms, have different rhythms of change, and are regulated by different, even contrary, axial principles' (Bell 1976: 10; see also Turner 1989). Others, perhaps wisely, are less inhibited. If the coming of the information society is, as all claim, as revolutionary a change as the coming of industrial society, then one would surely expect profound changes to occur throughout society, and not simply – as Bell would have it – in the 'techno-economic structure'.

Such is the view of the majority of information society advocates. Toffler, for instance, connects as a systematic pattern changes in the 'info-sphere' with changes in the 'techno-sphere', the 'socio-sphere', the 'power-sphere', the 'bio-sphere' and the 'psycho-sphere' (Toffler 1981: 5). Moreover it is clear that for most of these thinkers the new information society, for all its stresses and problems, is to be welcomed and celebrated not simply as a new mode of production but as a whole way of life. Toffler speaks of 'the death of industrialism and the rise of a new civilization'. He seeks to counter the 'chic pessimism that is so prevalent today'. The emergent civilization of the Third Wave can be made 'more sane, sensible, and sustainable, more decent and more democratic than any we have ever known' (Toffler 1981: 2–3). Naisbitt likewise sees enormous potential for a fresh wave of initiative, individualism and democracy. [. . .]

[. . .]

## Old and new: work in the information society

It would be perverse and foolhardy to deny the reality of much of what the information society theorists assert. The common experiences of daily life alone are enough to confirm that. Automatic tellers in banks, automatic billing at supermarket check-outs, the virtual disappearance of cheques along with cash in most monetary transactions, word processors and fax machines, direct on-line hotel and airline bookings, direct broadcasting by satellite from any part of the world: all these are facts of everyday life for most sections of the population in the advanced industrial countries.

The linking of information world-wide for scholars and specialists is also fast becoming a reality. The catalogues of the major libraries and archives can be scanned from a multitude of points by means of a computer terminal. Much of the material deposited in these libraries can also be read locally on microfilm or microfiche. The principal stock markets of the world are electronically linked, allowing for instantaneous adjustment of stock prices in response to minute-by-minute information conveyed by the computer screens. Round-the-clock trading becomes for the first time a possibility and increasingly the practice.

The information revolution has most clearly invaded our homes (Miles 1988). Television is still the most obvious symbol of this, enhanced now by the additional facility of the video cassette recorder and the variety provided by cable and satellite. But 'telebanking', 'teleshopping' and 'teleworking' are also now making considerable inroads into our lives [. . .] 'Tele-education' may turn out to be an even more significant development. At the younger ages collective institutionalized provision would still seem to be desirable, for social as much as educational reasons. But the Open University in Britain already provides a model for home-based higher education. The potential for expansion into something like a World University of the Air is evident.

[. . .]

Tessa Morris-Suzuki, while arguing that the concept of the information society was an ideological weapon forged in response to the industrial crisis of the late 1960s in Japan, nevertheless insists that information activities have become critical in the current phase of capitalism. Monopoly capitalism, she argues, is now to a good extent 'information capitalism', 'the private appropriation of social knowledge'. With the spread of automation, the extraction of surplus value (profit) now turns on 'the perpetual innovation economy' whose key resource is knowledge. This is reflected in a distinct 'softening of the economy' in capitalist countries. In Japan, for instance, in 1970 more than half of all industries could be classified as 'hard', in the sense that material goods made up 80 per cent or more of the total value of inputs. By 1980, only 27 per cent of industries could be so classified; this indicates the growing share of corporate capital expended on non-material inputs such as software, data services, planning, and research and development (Morris-Suzuki 1984: 116; see also Morris-Suzuki 1986, 1988; Castells 1989: 28–32).

Still, the acceptance of the growing importance of information technology, even an information revolution, is one thing; the acceptance of the idea of a new industrial revolution, a new kind of society, a new age, is quite another. Here the criticism has been voluminous, sharp and largely persuasive. It has also been, to a somewhat wearisome degree, familiar. This is not surprising. Since the concept of the information society has evolved smoothly out of the earlier idea of a post-industrial society, since the two share many of the same analytical features, and since they are propagated in both cases by much the same people, we should expect that the objections to the thesis of the information society would substantially repeat those levelled against the earlier idea of the post-industrial society.

Such is the case. The information society theorists can be attacked, firstly, for their short-sighted historical perspective. As with the post-industrial theorists, they attribute to the present developments which are the culmination of trends deep in the past. What seem to them novel and current can be shown to have been in the making for the past hundred years. James Beniger, for instance, accepts the correctness of the designation of present-day society as the information society. But his detailed historical study shows this to be merely the current manifestation of a much more profound change in the character of industrial societies that took place over a century ago. This change he labels 'the Control Revolution'.

The Industrial Revolution, Beniger argues, so speeded up 'the material processing system' of society that it precipitated a crisis of control. Information-processing systems and communication technologies lagged behind those of energy generation and use. The application first of steam power and later of electricity forced innovations in communication and control in every sphere of society. Fast-moving steam trains had, for urgent reasons of safety, to be carefully monitored and controlled. The speeding up of commercial distribution as a result of steam trains and steam boats imposed wide-ranging changes in wholesale and retail organization. The pace of material through-put in factories called forth the moving assembly line (Fordism) and the 'scientific management' of labour (Taylorism). Overarching all these, and modelled as often as not on the centralized, systematized railway system that was the pioneering response to the control crisis, was the growth of a formal Weberian bureaucracy in business and governmental organizations. By 1939 at the latest, Beniger convincingly shows, the structural elements of the Information Society – including the basic principles of the computer – were all firmly in place. Post-war developments were largely extensions and applications of the control techniques – the Control Revolution – that were elaborated by an immensely creative group of scientists, technologists and marketing specialists in the period from the 1880s to the 1930s.

[. . .]

In response to the earlier thesis of the post-industrial 'service society', Harry Braverman (1974) had already shown that much service work is as 'Taylorized' as work in manufacturing industries. The office, it turned out, could be industrialized as readily as the workshop; much white-collar work was subjected to the same routinization, fragmentation and de-skilling as blue-collar work. Braverman concluded that the belief in the spread of some new principle of work, some new ethic of professionalism, as services grew in industrial economies, was misguided.

Braverman can help us understand the further expansion of scientific management in the information society. It is important to remember that Taylorism was not intended to apply simply to the lower levels of the work-force. It contained the explicit principle of 'functional management' that implied that standardization and simplification were to be features of managerial as well as manual work. Moreover, when Taylor enjoined that 'all possible brain work should be removed from the shop and centred in the planning or laying-out department' he explicitly included the brain work of managers as well as of humbler employees. Knowledge – the skill and judgement of all workers, at whatever level – was to be gathered from every part of the organization and concentrated exclusively in the planning department. The 'science' of scientific management was not to be the possession of the generality of managers but only of a specialized core concerned with overall planning. The de-skilling of most middle level managers, their loss, along with other workers, of overall comprehension and control of their work, was not some later refinement but central to the original principles of Taylorism (Littler 1978: 190–2). This goes some way to explaining the striking fact that the greatest resistance to Taylorism in the factories came not from the mass of shopfloor workers or their unions but from middle management and supervisors (Littler 1982: 190; Lash and Urry 1987: 170–1).

In practice Taylorism up to the mid-century was confined largely to manufacturing industry and to manual workers. Computerization has made possible its extension to spheres of activity and bodies of workers previously untouched. The suppliers of microelectronic office equipment have made this an explicit part of their sales pitch. [. . .]

[. . .]

'Taylorian organization' can of course be adapted not just to routine white-collar work but to the work of many professionals and skilled technicians, new and old. The computer has been hailed by many as an instrument of liberation. It will automate the tedious and tiring work and free workers to engage in more interesting and creative tasks. [. . .] This remains, currently at least, a hope or a promise rather than widespread practice. For many information workers, the application of the new technology has continued the 'dynamic of de-skilling' (Littler 1978: 189) intrinsic to Taylorian principles, complemented as these were by the tighter technical control made possible by the moving assembly line of the Fordist factory. Here was first made clear the extent to which control could be not only a system of managerial prerogatives, a bureaucratic pattern, but also a technical fact built into the very structure of the machine (Edwards 1979: 111–29).

Clerical work was once largely a man's job, involving considerable degrees of skill and levels of discretion. There was a 'craft' as well as a quasi-managerial element involved. The advent of office machinery in the form of adding machines and the Hollerith punched-card processor began the process of de-skilling, symbolized by the 'feminization' of the clerical work-force (women were 21 per cent of clerks in England in 1911 and 70 per cent by 1966). The office worker, once a craft worker, became increasingly a simple machine operator and form-filler.

The widespread application of the computer and other forms of electronic data-processing (EDP) in the office has continued this process. Clerical workers have become, as they often put it, 'slaves to the computer', mere machine feeders with virtually no comprehension of the overall purpose of their work or control of its pace. Little knowledge or training are required to carry out the routine tasks involved in preparing data for the computer or punching them onto disk or tape. It is the machine that is smart, not the worker. A vast gulf opens between the largely unskilled, largely female mass clerical work-force and the small elite of qualified managers and computer professionals, most of whom are male.

[. . .]

But why expect managers, professionals and technical workers to be themselves immune to Taylorism and technical control? Scientific management was, as we have seen, intended to apply to all levels and types of workers. And the very people who designed and operated the new technology were, as many recognized, thereby putting themselves at risk. [. . .]

   [. . .]

   Most notably of all, the continuing development of computers has Taylorized the computer professionals themselves. Computer work has followed the familiar pattern of the separation and splitting of tasks, leading to increasingly routinized work for the mass of workers and highly specialized work for a small group of designers and researchers. First systems analysts were separated from programmers, marking a significant distinction between those who conceived and those who executed software programmes. Later programmers were themselves distinguished from a more routine class of operators, who were concerned largely with the repetitive task of coding. The development of computer languages – Cobol, Fortran, etc. – and 'structured programming' have further polarized software production along skill lines. All the creativity goes into the design and preparation of programme 'packages' – such as those for payroll calculations – which are then capable of simple implementation by programmers. The de-skilling of computer programmers in particular, taken with the general de-skilling of white-collar work in automated offices, has led Morris-Suzuki to single out 'the semi-skilled computer worker' as the typical worker of the future (Morris-Suzuki 1988: 124). Webster and Robins agree: 'Many computer workers possess but an aura of skill: their daily work is little more than specialized clerical labor' (Webster and Robins 1986: 146). The 'feminization' of computer work, at the lower levels of programmers and operators, is a further, familiar, indication of fragmentation and de-skilling (Kraft 1987; Webster and Robins 1986: 177).

## The knowledge worker

Knowledge, according to information society theorists, is progressively supposed to affect work in two ways. One is the upgrading of the knowledge content of existing work, in the sense that the new technology adds rather than subtracts from the skill of workers. The other is the creation and expansion of new work in the knowledge sector, such that information workers come to predominate in the economy. Moreover it is assumed that it is the more skilled, more knowledgeable information workers who will come to constitute the core of the information economy. We have seen that for many existing workers the new information technology spells a decrease, not an increase, in knowledge and control. But perhaps this is the wrong way to view things. Are these workers not rather being displaced altogether? Is the future not more likely to be one where low-level routine jobs are automated out of existence and new, more creative, ones take their place?

   The impact of information technology on employment was one of the most hotly debated issues of the 1980s. Would the new technology increase or decimate jobs? And where would the effects be most felt? Optimists were naturally to be found a-plenty in the information technology industry and its governmental off-shoots [. . .]. Pessimists tended to be among academics and trade unionists, abetted by some financial journalists. But the most celebrated scare was raised in an official report by two civil servants presented in 1977 to the French President, Valéry Giscard d'Estaing (Nora and Minc 1980). [. . .]

[. . .]

But the main problem in assessing the impact of information technology on employment is that we are at too early a stage in the process. It is impossible yet to generalize about the long term. Optimists are as plausible as pessimists. It can be argued that the new technology will, or at least could, in the long run provide another of those 'gales of creative destruction' that Joseph Schumpeter believed periodically renewed capitalism. The constellation of information technology industries – computers, electronic components, telecommunications – could, like cars and domestic electrical goods in the first half of the century, be the springboard of renewed economic expansion and job creation (Miles and Gershuny 1986; Freeman 1987). Equally, though, it is easy to see the force of the argument that new jobs created by information technology are an initial, once-and-for-all time, bonanza, the product of the massive reorganization forced on companies as they absorb the impact of the new technology. Once the initial shock has been absorbed, the capacity for information technology to displace workers will be felt with a vengeance (Webster and Robins 1986: 127). There is also a third, more radical, position that combines 'pessimism' with optimism. That is, it accepts that information technology will drastically diminish paid employment. But it welcomes this, seeing in it not so much a threat as an opportunity to redirect time and energy to more fulfilling activities outside the formal economy of paid work (Gorz 1982, 1989; King 1982: 33–5; Jones 1982).

The debate about the *quantity* of jobs lost or gained through the applications of information technology is not, however, the main concern of the information society theorists. They generally assume a numerical gain, as their figures for the steady growth of 'information workers' suggest. But more important is the quality of the new work-force. Information society theorists look forward to the rise of a new service class of knowledge workers, men and women whose work is characterized by high levels of technical skill and theoretical knowledge, and which correspondingly demands long periods of education and training. In support of this they point to the fact that scientific, technical and professional workers have been the fastest growing occupational groups in all industrial societies in the last fifty years. Similarly, they argue, it is the 'knowledge factories', the universities and research institutes, that have now become the powerhouses of modern society, replacing the goods-producing factory of the industrial era (Drucker 1969: 52; Bell 1980a: 501; Simon 1980: 429; Stonier 1983: 43–4).

We have already had reason to doubt, on general grounds, that the work-force is increasing in skill and autonomy. In so far as Taylorism remains the master principle, information technology has a greater potential for proletarianization than for professionalization. This process can be quite effectively disguised by occupational statistics that suggest a more educated and better trained work-force. The growth of credentialism – that is, demanding higher qualifications for the same jobs – and the familiar process of the inflation of job labels and occupational self-advertisement, can all give a quite misleading impression of the growth of a more 'knowledgeable' society (Kumar 1978: 211–19).

The more detailed picture of recent occupational changes confirms this impression of a statistical sleight-of-hand designed to promote the idea of an increasingly professionalized society. Bell, for instance, singles out workers in health, education and social welfare, along with scientific and technical workers in information technology, as the key professionals of the information society. These, the workers in 'human services' and in 'professional services', are the mainstay of the new service class (Bell 1980a: 501). Over the century, the censuses do indeed record a striking rise in the number of professional, administrative and managerial employees. From constituting no more than 5–10 per cent of the work-force at the beginning of the century, they now in all western societies make up between 20–25 per cent of workers (Goldthorpe 1982: 172).

But many of these workers are professionals only in name – plumbers – as 'heating engineers', shop-keepers as 'managers', etc. Moreover the variety and heterogeneity of workers in the information sector make any general claim of increased skill and knowledge highly contentious (Miles and Gershuny 1986: 23). [. . .]

More problematic for information society theory is the expectation of the continued growth and expansion of the class of knowledge workers. The assumption of the continued growth of service workers in general has already been challenged on theoretical as well as empirical grounds. There is no natural or inevitable 'march through the sectors', from agriculture to manufacturing to services, as economies develop (Gershuny 1978; Singelmann 1978). It has been shown, for instance, that 'self-service' provisioning, using service goods such as washing machines and television sets, has already displaced some service workers and may displace more in the future (Gershuny and Miles 1983). The same uncertainty surrounds the future growth of knowledge workers. In the last two decades there has already been a sharp decline in the growth of professionals in the human services; and the growth of information workers generally – including those in the computer and telecommunications industry – has slackened and tailed off in most industrial countries (Jones 1982: 19; Guy 1987: 175; Kraft 1987: 101). An area that has been particularly hard hit – mainly as the result of computerization – is the area of middle management. The future organization, it has been suggested, may have an hour-glass shape: a few executives and research and development specialists on the top, and many clerks and operatives on the bottom. [. . .]

Most of the growth in jobs in the last two decades has indeed come from a quite different quarter: not from the knowledge sector, but from the lower levels of the tertiary economy, where the extent of skill and knowledge is not notably high. For instance, between 1973 and 1980 almost 13 million new jobs were created in the United States. Most of these were in the private sector, and most – over 70 per cent – in services and the retail trade. The typical new workers were in 'eating and drinking' establishments, including fast-food restaurants; in 'health services', mainly nurses and ancillary staff in private hospitals and private nursing homes; and in 'business services', mainly routine information workers concerned with data processing, copying and mailing. Many of the new workers were women, many of them part-time or temporary. Pay levels were low, job security and career prospects virtually nil. This pattern continued during the 1980s – in Britain as much as the United States. In Japan too, the growth of information workers has been skewed in the direction of lower level jobs concerned with 'information transfer' rather than the more skilled jobs concerned with 'information production'. In 1982, 'information transfer' workers accounted for 20 per cent of the Japanese workforce, but 'information production' workers only 13 per cent (Morris-Suzuki 1988: 131).

## Politics and markets

It is clear from this account of developments in the information economy that there is a distinct politics, as well as a political economy, of the information society. The growth of knowledge work, for instance, has evidently been directly affected by recent governmental policies. Knowledge workers in the public sector – specially those in human services – have declined while those in the private sector – especially those in business services – have increased. But state involvement in the information economy also operates at a far deeper structural level. Governments have taken a leading role in promoting and disseminating the idea of an information society – including vigorous attempts to encourage a 'computer culture' in schools and universities (Roszak 1978; Robins and Webster 1989). In Britain, not notably in the forefront of the information technology revolution, more than half of all research and development (R&D) in information technology (IT) is funded by the government; the government is responsible, as customer, for more than half of the total market in electronics; and it absorbs more than a third of all computer capacity (Webster and Robins 1986: 273).

Moreover, whatever their free-market propensities, it has been clear that governments have not been willing to give up a coordinating and directing role in the development of information technology. [. . .]

But it is in the military connection that we can perhaps most intimately see the link between government and the information society. From the very first development of the semiconductor industry at the Bell Laboratories in New Jersey in the 1940s, to the Star Wars and 'Strategic Computing' projects of the US Department of Defense in the 1980s, it has been obvious that military (defence, space, etc.) requirements have in nearly all societies been the main engine of growth of the IT industries (Japan and Germany are partial, and perhaps temporary, exceptions). Military R&D, on one estimate, is responsible for 40 per cent of total world expenditure on research, and absorbs the activities of 40 per cent of the world's research scientists and engineers. Since it is microelectronics that has revolutionized military technology – especially in missile and intelligence systems – in the past twenty years, it is not surprising to find that a large part of this vast military expenditure on R&D is devoted to work in information technology (Barnaby 1982: 243–4; see also Lyon 1988: 26–30).

In the United States, over half of government-financed R&D is military R&D (Roszak 1988: 40). The same is true of Britain, where the Ministry of Defence's spending on R&D amounts to a half of all government expenditure on R&D, and a quarter of all R&D spending in the nation. For Britain it is the electronics industry that is at the heart of the military-IT complex. Electronics companies get 46 per cent of all government aid to industry, and the government funds 60 per cent of the total R&D budget in electronics; 95 per cent of all government-financed R&D in electronics originates from one department, the Ministry of Defence. The whole of the British electronics industry is in fact heavily dependent on the military. [. . .]

Political and military actors, though they have their own motivations and interests, do not operate in a social vacuum. That social space is forcibly occupied, to a good extent, by large private multinational corporations that have their own pressing need for the most comprehensive development of information technology. The growth in the scale and complexity of organizations, their bursting of their national boundaries, have necessitated a degree of coordination and communication that has itself been a major force in the expansion of information technology. [. . .]

[. . .]

The big commercial organizations, like government departments, have developed an appetite for IT which other companies, old and new, have hurried to satisfy. In the process a powerful new group of IT multinationals has risen to prominence. These then not only further the growth of IT by their own organizational needs but are active in generating and pressing new services on other giants. These others, also partly out of their own necessities and partly to a share of the rich pickings, begin to move in on the act. A spiral develops whose main effect is the continuous creating of IT goods, services and workers (Webster and Robins 1986: 219–56; Douglas and Guback 1984: 234–5; Traber 1986: 3).

The names of the IT multinationals have become household: IBM in computers, AT&T and IT&T in telecommunications, Xerox and Olivetti in office equipment, Philips and Siemens in electronics. But the original bases in particular products and services are fast becoming irrelevant. All these companies, and the many others that are in or trying to enter the field, aim to become 'integrated information' concerns. The goal, substantially achieved in several cases, is to exploit economies of scale and mutual dependencies so as to offer the complete IT package: computers, telecommunications, electronic goods and components, cable, satellite and broadcast systems, TV and video goods and programming services, film and photography. The bulk of IT has so far been developed for the state or business user. This is where expansion has been easiest and the profits greatest. But the home has also already been firmly targeted, along with leisure and entertainment. From the point of view of information technology, distinctions between office and home, work and leisure, are largely unimportant. Indeed IT is in the business of making them unimportant.

Information technology is in fact making most of the standard industrial classifications meaningless. Hallowed divisions between 'secondary' and 'tertiary' activities become increasingly unreal. The electronics industry, the heart of the IT revolution, now integrates manufacturing and service activities so completely that it is impossible to tell where one ends and the other begins [. . .]. Robots, computer-aided design and computer-aided manufacturing clearly encourage manufacturers to get into IT themselves; and companies such as the giant motor manufacturer GM have been doing just that.

[. . .]

Information technology is clearly big business. It is at the heart of corporate capital in the late twentieth century. Corporate capital is both its main instigator and principal user. It has been estimated that about 90 per cent of all data flow via satellite systems is intra-corporate, and about 50 per cent of all trans-border data flow takes place within the communications networks of individual transnational corporations (Jussawalla 1985: 299–300). [. . .]

[. . .]

Taken with the military and political motives noted earlier, the clearly capitalist character of much IT activity has led to a widespread questioning of the whole theoretical underpinning of the idea of an information society. There is no new age, no new revolution comparable to the Industrial Revolution of the nineteenth century [. . .]. The information society is a myth developed to serve the interests of those who initiate and manage the 'information revolution': 'the most powerful sectors of society, its central administrative elites, the military establishment and global industrial corporations' (Hamelink 1986: 13). It is no more than the latest ideology of the capitalist state. 'Capitalism is still the name of the game' (Arriaga 1985: 294). 'If there is a revolution, then it is certainly *around* the hub of capitalism' (Douglas and Guback 1984: 236). [. . .]

Bell, Masuda, Stonier and other enthusiasts portray the information society as a hopeful and progressive development. It is leading to a future of greater prosperity, leisure and satisfaction or all. But so far at least it is a society designed, as of old, by and for the few: the rich and powerful classes, nations and regions of the world. 'The information revolution has not yet arrived and is nowhere yet in sight, except in the offices of stockbrokers, bankers, spy masters, meteorologists and the headquarters of transnational companies' (Traber 1986: 2). Its objectives and effects are strictly defined by the traditional goals of the political and economic elites: to increase the power of the state, both as against its own citizens and against other states; and to boost the productivity and profits of capitalist enterprises, largely by creating an integrated global market.

## Ideology and the information society

The main burden of the critique of the information society idea is that the development and diffusion of information technology have introduced no fundamentally new principle or direction in society. The remarkable speed of IT's diffusion is admitted; so too its potentiality for bringing about radical change in social arrangements (for example, Gill 1985: 181). But the new technology is being applied within a political and economic framework that confirms and accentuates existing patterns, rather than giving rise to new ones. Work and leisure are further industrialized, further subjected to Fordist and Taylorist strategies of mechanization, routinization and rationalization. Existing social inequalities are maintained and magnified. A new 'information gap' opens up between the producers and users of the new technology and those – ordinary citizens, semi-skilled operators, Third World countries – who are its (their) passive clients, customers and consumers (Rada 1982). Information abounds, but there is little concern with embodying it in a framework of knowledge, let alone cultivating wisdom in its use (Slack 1984: 254; Marien 1985: 657). Knowledge and information, once amongst the most public and freely available resources in society, now become privatized, commodified, appropriated for sale and profit (Morris-Suzuki 1986).

The theme of this criticism of the information society is one of fundamental continuity. The instruments and techniques may change, but the overriding goals and purposes of capitalist industrial societies remain the same as before. One of the most far-reaching critiques has gone so far as to see the whole information society idea as simply the latest expression of a long-standing tradition of thought and practice that they call 'social Taylorism'. Taylorism, argue Frank Webster and Kevin Robins, was not just a doctrine of factory management but 'a new social philosophy, a new principle of social revolution, and a new imaginary institution in society' (Webster and Robins 1989: 333).

Taylorism became the hub of a new technocratic ideology that did not stop at the factory or office but moved out to the world at large. Having conquered production it now turned its sights on consumption. 'Ultimately what was required was the Scientific Management of need, desire and fantasy, and their reconstruction in terms of the commodity form' (Webster and Robins 1989: 334). Scientific management in the 1930s and 1940s achieved new forms and techniques in the rise of mass advertising, systematic market research, and the whole science of making and manipulating consumer taste. Television, cable and satellite were later added to its armoury, as the market became increasingly global and in need of ever more careful management. Nor was the political sphere – the consumer as citizen – excluded from social Taylorism. Mass democracies too needed to be carefully monitored and managed. Surveillance, propaganda and public opinion measurement became standard tools in the government and administration of complex societies. The open public sphere of former liberal polities, the space made available for public discussion and debate, increasingly gave way to the administered sphere, dominated by technical expertise and narrow concepts of instrumental rationality.

The whole development of the twentieth-century state and society can therefore be regarded as the application of the principles of scientific management. Information, knowledge and science – including social science – are self-evidently the central requirements of this process. They provide the means necessary to coordinate and control the increasingly complex operations of the economy and the polity. Thus it can be argued that 'it was the exponents of Scientific Management, in its broadest sense, who unleashed an Information Revolution'. Particularly important were the 'consumption engineers' who took the lead in regulating business transactions and consumer behaviour. 'It was these advocates of big business who first turned to the "rational" and "scientific" exploitation of information in the wider society, and it is their descendants – the multinational advertisers, market researchers, opinion pollers, data brokers, and so on – who are the heart of information politics in the eighties' (Webster and Robins 1989: 336) [. . .].

'Taylorism' or 'scientific management' is evidently having to do a lot of work in this analysis; as, in an analogous way, is capitalism in the broader critique of which it is a part. This is not to object to the presentation of the 'dark underside of the information revolution' (Webster and Robins 1989: 330), nor to deny the fundamental truth of these accounts. The information society has not evolved in some neutral, value-free way. Information technology, like all technology, has been selected and shaped in conformity with certain determinate social and political interests. These interests may not always be able to control all its effects. Television, for instance, can disturb as much as it can soothe. Word processors can be as handy for the publishing activities of small oppositional groups as for the rationalizing strategies of office managers. But the bulk of information technology is complex and expensive. It requires massive capital investment and large teams of researchers. Only the most powerful interests in society – governments and large private corporations – have the resources to promote it. 'The automated office, the robotic factory and the electronic battle-field' account for over 80 per cent of the IT business (Webster and Robins 1986: 282). Not surprisingly, these interests have developed IT largely to serve their needs, as they perceive them. Power and profit, as in the past, dominate these calculations.

This is not however the whole story of the information society. To call the information society an ideology, and to relate that ideology to the contemporary needs of capitalism, is to begin, not to end the analysis. Capitalism has had many ideologies over the past two hundred years – *laissez-faire*, managerialism, welfarism, even, arguably, varieties of fascism and communism. Each has had its own kind of relation to capitalist society; each has contained its own distinctive contradictions. What kind of ideology is the ideology of the information society, and what are its particular contradictions? Ideologies, as many people have pointed out, are not just ideas in the head, but real practices, as real as any other social practices. They are lived realities. They constrain our thinking about ourselves and our world, and thus have practical consequences. 'The information society' may be a partial and one-sided way of expressing the contemporary social reality, but for many people in the industrial world it is now an inescapable part of that reality. [. . .]

[. . .]

## References

Arriaga, P. (1985) 'Toward a Critique of the Information Economy', *Media, Culture and Society* 7, 271–96.

Barnaby, F. (1982) 'Microelectronics in War', in Friedrichs, G. and Schaff, A. (eds) *Microelectronics and Society: For Better or For Worse*. Oxford: Pergamon, pp. 243–72.

Bell, D. (1980) 'The Social Framework of the Information Society', in Forester, T. (ed.) *The Microelectronics Revolution*. Oxford: Blackwell, pp. 500–49.

Braverman, H. (1974) *Labor and Monopoly Capital: The Degradation of Work in the Twentieth Century*. New York: Monthly Review Press.

Castells, M. (1989) *The Informational City: Information Technology, Economic Restructuring and Location*. London: Lawrence and Wishart.

Douglas, S. and Guback, T. (1984) 'Production and Technology in the Communication/ Information Revolution', *Media, Culture and Society* 6, 233–45.

Drucker, P. (1969) *The Age of Discontinuity*. London: Heinemann.

Edwards, R. (1979) *Contested Terrain: The Transformation of the Workplace in the Twentieth Century*. London: Heinemann.

Evans, J. (1982) 'The Worker and the Workplace', in Friedrichs, G. and Schaff, A. (eds) *Microelectronics and Society: For Better or For Worse*. Oxford: Pergamon, pp. 157–87.

Freeman, C. (1987) 'Information Technology and Change in the Techno-Economic Paradigm', in Freeman, C. and Soete, L. (eds) *Technical Change and Full Employment*. Oxford: Basil Blackwell, pp. 49–69.

Gershuny, J. I. (1978) *After Industrial Society? The Emerging Self-Service Economy*. London: Macmillan.

Gershuny, J. I. and Miles, I. (1983) *The New Service Economy: The Transformation of Employment in Industrial Societies*. London: Frances Pinter.

Gill, C. (1985) *Work, Unemployment and the New Technology*. Cambridge: Polity Press.

Goldthorpe, J. (1982) 'On the Service Class, Its Formation and Future', in Giddens, A. and Mackenzie, G. (eds) *Social Class and the Division of Labour*. Cambridge: Cambridge University Press, pp. 162–85.

Gorz, A. (1982) *Farewell to the Working Class: An Essay on Post-Industrial Socialism*. London: Pluto Press.

Guy, K. (1987) 'The UK Tertiary Sector', in Freeman, C. and Soete, L. (eds) *Technical Change and Full Employment*. Oxford: Blackwell, pp. 169–88.

Hamelink, C. J. (1986) 'Is There Life after the Information Society', in Traber, M. (ed.) *The Myth of the Information Revolution*. London: Sage, pp. 7–20.

Jones, B. (1982) *Sleepers, Wake! Technology and the Future of Work*. Brighton: Wheatsheaf.

Jussawalla, M. (1985) 'Constraints on Economic Analysis of Transborder Data Flows', *Media, Culture and Society* 7, 297–312.

King, A. (1982) 'A New Industrial Revolution or Just Another Technology?', in Friedrichs, G. and Schaff, A. (eds) *Microelectronics and Society: For Better or For Worse*. Oxford: Pergamon, pp. 1–36.

Kraft, P. (1987) 'Computer and the Automation of Work', in Kraft, P. (ed.) *Technology and the Transformation of White-Collar Work*. Hillside, NJ: Lawrence Erlbaum Associates, pp. 85–105.

Kumar, K. (1978) *Prophecy and Progress: The Sociology of Industrial and Post-Industrial Society*. Harmondsworth: Penguin Books.

Lash, S. and Urry, J. (1987) *The End of Organized Capitalism*. Cambridge: Polity Press.

Littler, C. R. (1978) 'Understanding Taylorism', *British Journal of Sociology* 29, 185–202.

Littler, C. R. (1982) *The Development of the Labour Process in Capitalist Societies*. London: Heinemann.

Lyon, D. (1988) *The Information Society: Issues and Illusions*. Cambridge: Polity Press.

Marien, M. (1985) 'Some Questions for the Information Society', in Forester, T. (ed.) *The Information Technology Revolution*. Oxford: Blackwell, pp. 648–60.

Miles, I. (1988) *Home Informatics Technology and the Transformation of Everyday Life*. London: Pinter Publications.

Miles, I. and Gershuny, J. (1986) 'The Social Economics of Information Technology', in Ferguson, M. (ed.) *New Communication Technologies and the Public Interest*. London: Sage, pp. 18–36.

Morris-Suzuki, T. (1984) 'Robots and Capitalism', *New Left Review* 147, 109–21.

Morris-Suzuki, T. (1986) 'Capitalism and Computer Age', *New Left Review* 160, 81–91.

Morris-Suzuki, T. (1988) *Beyond Computation: Information, Automation and Democracy in Japan*. London: Kegan Paul.

Naisbitt, J. (1984) *Megatrends: Ten New Directions Transforming Our Lives*. New York: Warner Books.

Noble, D. F. (1979) 'Social Choice in Machine Design: The Case of Automatically Controlled Machine Tools', in Zimbalist, A. (ed.) *Case Studies in the Labor Process*. New York: Monthly Review Press, pp. 36–63.

Noble, D. F. (1986) *Forces of Production: A Social History of Industrial Automation*. New York: Oxford University Press.

Nora, S. and Minc, A. (1980) *The Computerisation of Society: A Report to the President of France*. Cambridge, MA: MIT Press.

Rada, J. (1982) 'A Third World Perspective', in Friedrichs, G. and Schaff, A. (eds) *Microelectronics and Society: For Better or For Worse*. Oxford: Pergamon, pp. 213–42.

Robins, K. and Webster, F. (1988) 'Information as Capital: A Critique of Daniel Bell', in Slack, D. and Fejes, F. (eds) *The Ideology of the Information Age*. Norwood, NJ: Ablex Publishing, pp. 95–117.

Robins, K. and Webster, F. (1989) 'Athens Without Slaves . . . Or Slaves Without Athens? The Neurosis of Technology', *Science as Culture* 3, 7–52.

Roszak, T. (1988) *The Cult of Information: The Folklore of Computers and the True Art of Thinking.* London: Paladin.

Simon, H. A. (1980) 'What Computers Mean for Man and Society', in Forester, T. (ed.) *The Microelectronics Revolution.* Oxford: Blackwell, pp. 419–33.

Singelmann, J. (1978) 'The Sectoral Transformation of the Labor Force in Seven Industrialized Countries, 1920–1970', *American Journal of Sociology* 83, 1224–34.

Slack, J. D. (1984) 'The Information Revolution as Ideology', *Media, Culture and Society* 6, 247–56.

Stonier, T. (1983) *The Wealth of Information: A Profile of the Post-Industrial Economy.* London: Thames Methuen.

Sussman, L. (1989) 'The Information Revolution: Human Ideas and Electrical Impulses', *Encounter* 73, 60–5.

Toffler, A. (1981) *The Third Wave.* New York: Bantam.

Traber, M. (ed.) (1986) *The Myth of the Information Revolution.* London: Sage.

Turner, B. S. (1989) 'From Postindustrial Society to Postmodern Politics: The Political Sociology of Daniel Bell', in Gibbins, J. R. (ed.) *Contemporary Political Culture: Politics in a Postmodern Age.* London: Sage, pp. 199–217.

Webster, F. and Robins, K. (1986) *Information Technology: A Luddite Analysis* Norwood, NJ: Ablex Publishing Corporation.

Webster, F. and Robins, K. (1989) 'Plan and Control: Towards a Cultural History of the Information Society', *Theory and Society* 18, 323–51.

Weizenbaum, J. (1976) *Computer Power and Human Reason: From Judgment to Calculation.* San Francisco: W. H. Freeman.

Wiener, N. (1968) *The Human Use of Human Beings: Cybernetics and Society* [1954]. London: Sphere Books.

# Chapter 9

# John Urry

## IS BRITAIN THE FIRST POST-INDUSTRIAL SOCIETY?

From *Consuming Places*, London: Routledge (1995), pp. 112–25.

[. . .]

I WANT TO ASSESS THIS IDEA, that at least in parts of Britain there is a sea change taking place in the dominant economic, social and political structures. Once upon a time these could have been described as 'industrial' but they have now been transformed. It is argued that there has been a qualitative change so that some parts of Britain are now to be described as no longer industrial but as 'post-industrial'. I shall be concerned to analyse what is meant by the idea of a society whose structures and typical modes of experience are no longer based on manufacturing industry as providing the central motor, its inner dynamism.

I hope to *demonstrate* through example the virtues of what C. Wright Mills (1959) called a 'sociological imagination'. And I shall suggest that sociology must be concerned with these big questions of social and cultural change and that in doing so it cannot be based upon a narrow view of the social which is separated off from the historical, economic, geographic and political dimensions of social life. Sociology must therefore concern itself with many of its neighbouring social sciences. And indeed my view is that it provides a particularly favourable intellectual and social space in which the findings, arguments and theories from these various subjects can be brought together, compared, juxtaposed and on occasions synthesised. Auguste Comte, the early nineteenth century writer who 'invented' the term 'sociology', maintained that it should be the 'Queen' of the sciences. By contrast I would prefer the more democratic and prosaic metaphor of sociology as the 'crossroads' of the social sciences. It is the site where the arguments, findings and theories relating to the fundamental sociality of human life can be brought together. Sociology is thus a centrally important social science in part because of the space it offers for drawing together the more 'social' aspects thrown up by, but not fully investigated by, its neighbours amongst the social sciences.

First, I shall summarise the thesis of the post-industrial (PI) society and refer to some of the evidence [. . .]. Second, I shall show that although modern Western societies are indeed changing in quite spectacular ways, the specific PI society is insufficiently precise and glosses over some exceptionally important aspects of recent change. In particular, it will be shown that the thesis is overly 'economistic', it reduces social and political life to changes in the structure of the economy and fails to address complex transformations in the ways in which people *experience* such changes. Third, I shall consider the question of people's experiences more directly by analysing briefly how this had been transformed by the development of nine-teenth century industrial and urban life, with the growth of the modern personality or of modernity. It will be suggested that such developments resulted in part from some extraordinary changes in the very way in which time and especially space were organised and structured in the emerging industrial world.

Finally, I shall return to the future, so to speak, and consider whether there may be developing some current changes of time and space which are setting the ground for supposedly postmodern experiences. Overall I shall argue that what has in fact been developing in Britain is not really the growth of some new form of *society*, that is post-industrial or postmodern or indeed as other writers have argued, post-capitalist. But rather that there has been the systematic breakdown in the existing structuring of society which I shall describe as 'organised'. There has been an extraordinary complex of changes which have begun to undermine, disrupt and disorganise the existing structures of social life – disruptions of economy, politics and culture which the notion of post-industrialism does not begin to grasp adequately. Britain is not then the first post-industrial society but it is one of the first 'former industrial countries' (what economists might I suppose call FICs) char-acterised by marked levels of *dis*-organisation.

First, then, I shall consider the PI society thesis in an absurdly truncated fashion (see Bell 1974). There are a number of points. First, there is taking place a major shift in the structure of employment in modern societies. Both primary and secondary production require decreasing labour inputs because of the exceptional possibilities for technological change and innovation. Especially in manufacturing industry there is a dramatic decline in the labour required per unit of output. Tertiary industry (services) by contrast is more labour-intensive and there are fewer chances of implementing labour-saving innovations. There has been as a result a major shift in the employment structure of modern economies with dramatically increasing numbers employed in the provision of services.

Second, there is a simultaneously marked increase in the demand for services. People's basic needs, especially for food, clothing, housing, do not rise as fast as real incomes rise: and out of such rising income there is increasing expenditure on services rather than on material goods.

Third, much labour in all forms of employment becomes increasingly based on 'theoretical knowledge' and its codification into abstract systems. The production, distribution and control of knowledge is the central characteristic of a PI society.

Establishments concerned with education, research and information-handling assume a heightened importance.

Fourth, the individual firm becomes subject to increased government regulation as the whole society comes to be much more socially planned. There is a shift from the 'economising' mode of behaviour to what Daniel Bell terms a 'sociologising' mode, to take into account values, needs and human purposes, the 'public interest' that is not necessarily well-reflected in the market.

Fifth, there is a growing technocracy as those engaged in the planning and control of knowledge will gain increased power. Birth, property and family background become less important bases of social stratification than skill and education, or what Dore calls the 'diploma disease' (1976).

Sixth, there is the development of new social classes and social groups and the reduced importance of what Alain Touraine terms the 'old social classes' which were based on the ownership and the non-ownership of property. Overlaying those forms of social conflict are the new forms structured by divisions between those possessing and those not possessing certain forms of knowledge, between those employed in large bureaucracies and those excluded, and between those who are powerful technocrats and those who are not. Manufacturing industry no longer generates the social class divisions which structure the whole of society (Touraine 1974).

There is moreover plenty of empirical evidence to support elements of this thesis in modern Britain. Thus the proportion of the employed population working in manufacturing industry has fallen from 36 per cent in 1971 to 24 per cent in 1986: while the proportion of people working in service industry has risen from 52 per cent in 1971 to 67 per cent in 1986. Or to put it another way, in 1971 there was 1 manufacturing worker to 1.4 service workers; in 1986 the ratio was 1:2.7, almost double [. . .]. There has been a marked increase in those people working in non-manual occupations, from 1 in 7 in 1911 to nearly 1 in 3 in 1981; the proportion of the employed population in professional managerial positions has risen from 1 in 7 in 1911 to over 1 in 4 in 1981. [. . .] Social conflicts as reflected in strike rates in different industries are at a markedly lower level in the service industries where only 9 per cent of such establishments recorded a strike/lockout in the previous year, compared with 27 per cent in manufacturing industry (calculated from Daniel and Milward 1983: table IX.II). There has also been the growth in the last twenty or so years of an amazing array of pressure and interest groups aiming in part to moderate the influence of the market and to ensure that 'social' criteria are partly brought to bear on matters of public policy. [. . .]

[. . .]

Thus far then I have summarised some of the main tenets of the PI thesis and briefly considered some of the empirical evidence which lends support to it. I shall now turn to consider some deficiencies of this argument. A first point to consider is that the thesis is a little dated. Thus Miller wrote of the American formulations in the 1960s that: 'the post-industrial society was a period of two or three years when GNP, social policy programme, and social research and universities were flourishing. Things have certainly changed' (1975: 25). There are two very obvious ways in which things have changed. First, there has been the growth of unemployment and of underemployment, now 20 per cent in Liverpool [. . .]. It is obviously much more sensible to talk of Liverpool and indeed many towns and cities as simply 'deindustrialised'. Second, it has clearly been part of Conservative Party policy to try fairly systematically to reverse certain aspects of the PI society. Although it has done more to encourage service industries through changes in its regional policy, it has by contrast attempted to undermine employment, funding and supposed power of the knowledge-based elite (as most of us are only too painfully aware!), and to re-emphasise the central role of the market, of 'economising' rather than 'sociologising'! As Riddell says of Thatcherism, it is an attempt to construct a society which is 'a cross between nineteenth century Birmingham and contemporary Hong Kong, located in Esher' (1983: 165).

Government policy is not the end of the matter though. One undoubted difficulty in the PI thesis is that there is considerable ambiguity in the very idea of a service itself. Two criteria are normally proposed; that the item can only be consumed at the point of production (such as a lecture, a haircut, a restaurant meal); and that the item takes a non-material form (such as consultation with a GP, live theatre, a seminar). The trouble is that not all services meet both criteria, and some, for example take-out meals from McDonald's, do not really meet either criterion.

Indeed some services really consist in part at least of material commodities and the more that this is the case then such industries may contain forms of scientifically managed and relatively less skilled labour similar to much of manufacturing industry. Indeed it may be more correct to think of modern societies as dualistic, with considerable differences maintained over time between those people who have relatively well-paid, skilled, secure jobs protected by unions or professional bodies and those who have less well-paid, relatively unskilled, part-time/temporary jobs which are not protected by either unions or professions. Jobs in the service industry consist of both of these, the division between the two often being drawn on gender, ethnic or age grounds (see discussion in Miles 1985). Three points should thus be noted about services at this point: most of us are service-producers, all of us are service-consumers, and services are an extremely heterogeneous category with few if any characteristics which unite them.

There is also only limited evidence that people do in fact increasingly wish to purchase services as such. Although there has been a dramatic increase in employment in service industry, there has been much less of an increase in spending on services *per se*. Thus while it is true that the higher a person's income, the greater the proportion of it that is spent on services, data over time show relatively little increase. Thus in Britain the proportion of the national income spent on services has risen from 9.5 per cent of total expenditure in 1954 to 12 per cent in 1985 (*Family Expenditure Survey* 1986). The categories of expenditure to increase most over this period have been on housing and cars, whose proportions have both doubled. At the same time however there have been much faster increases in the prices of services as opposed to those of manufactured goods. This means that there has been a considerable increase in real expenditure on our homes, cars and consumer goods in the post-war period (see discussion of the 1954–74 period in Gershuny 1978: ch. 5). There has thus been some growth of what Gershuny has described and analysed as the *self-service* society (Gershuny 1978; Gershuny and Miles 1983). Thus we entertain ourselves, drive ourselves, feed ourselves, do up our houses, using often highly sophisticated material goods produced within manufacturing industry. In a way then many of us are more skilled but that is the result of providing more services ourselves. At the same time, many of those working in services are in fact employed directly or indirectly in producing services *for manufacturing firms*, as accountants, lawyers, systems analysts, R.&D., etc. So while a very high proportion of the employed population are to be found in service employment, this does not at all mean that all those people are providing final services to the consumer. Perhaps up to half do not.

There are three other problems I want to discuss with the PI thesis. These might be described as the problems of history, geography and sociology. First, then, history. It is a commonplace to say that societies proceed through three economic stages, in which first primary industry, second secondary industry, and finally tertiary industry is the largest and most dynamic sector each in turn (normally called the Fisher-Clark thesis). At best however this thesis could apply to Western countries (and it does not work for Japan) but even in the case of Britain it is rather misleading. During the supposed heyday of Victorian manufacturing industry there was in fact a considerable growth of service industry, in both income and employment terms. By the beginning of the twentieth century only about 40 per cent of the national income stemmed from 'manufacture, mining, industry' and well over half was accounted for by a variety of services. *Employment* in services was also fairly high, accounting for 45 per cent of the labour force by 1911 and this was by no means all in domestic service (Deane and Coles 1962). Service employment was of course particularly important in the south-east, as a result of the exceptional influence of the City of London, whose importance lay in the near monopolisation of the commercial activities necessary for the development of world, and not merely just of British, trade (see Ingham 1984).

The geographical problem is that there is considerable variation in the degree to which a post-industrial pattern is to be found. Indeed there are really marked variations within relatively limited areas. Consider the five urban areas identified in Liverpool in 1981. The proportion of higher professionals and managers varies by a factor of almost 7 between the area with the highest and lowest proportions; while the percentages of non-manual employees varies from 17 per cent to 38 per cent of the economically active population. Furthermore, the proportion of the workforce with higher education qualifications varies by a factor of 4 for men and by a factor of 5 for women. There was also twice as high a proportion of manufacturing employees in some areas than in others.

There is of course further geographical variation *between* cities both within a country and between countries. These variations reflect at least in part an international division of labour with certain service industries and occupations concentrated in particular cities, particularly those in which the headquarters of the major world corporations tend to be based. There has been the growth of what one can loosely term 'world cities' whose power and influence stem in part from providing the location of the headquarters of the major world manufacturing and services enterprises. They are thus substantially dependent upon the locational decisions of manufacturing firms and are not simply to be viewed as PI service cities. Liverpool most definitely is not a world city (except of course for two consumer services, namely music and football).

The sociological problem is perhaps the knottiest of all and concerns the degree to which these changes in the structure of the economy actually affect the ways in which people live their day-to-day lives. Is there some distinctive 'PI' way of thinking and feeling which somehow corresponds to these current economic changes? I shall approach this issue by briefly considering some of the ways in which it was thought that the growth of industrial society in the nineteenth century actually transformed people's day-to-day experiences, that it led to a modern consciousness or modernity. I shall suggest furthermore that central to these changes in the nature of modern life were amazing changes in how people's lives were organised through time and space.

I will begin here with one of the most perceptive early attempts to describe such changes in the nature of life in industrial Britain. This is to be found in *The Manifesto of the Communist Party*, where Marx and Engels wrote . . .:

> Constant revolutionizing of production, uninterrupted disturbance of all social relations, everlasting uncertainty and agitation, distinguish the bourgeois epoch from all earlier times. All fixed, fast-frozen relationships . . . are swept away. . . . All that is solid melts into air, all that is holy is profaned.
>
> (Marx and Engels 1964: 53–4)

In other words, modern society is the first known society in which the dominant class has a vested interest in change, transformation, and in dissolving economic and social relations as fast as they come to be established. [. . .]

[. . .]

There is thus a kind of permanent revolution involved. For modern society to flourish there has to be a continuous transformation in people's very personalities. They have to be much more fluid and open, they must strive for change and renewal, they must not long nostalgically for the fast-frozen relations of the real or fantasised past, and they should actively seek out new forms of activity and belief. Social life was thus transformed, particularly with the growth of large cities in which all sorts of people were thrown together, with the concentration of workers within uncharacteristically large workplaces, and with the transformed means of communication between these new industrial cities.

Two features of nineteenth century modern life are especially worth noting. First there was the modernisation of public urban space, the quintessential form being the Parisian boulevard, brilliantly designed by the irrepressible Baron von Haussmann, the Prefect of Paris, during the Second Empire (see Berman 1983). The boulevards were envisaged as arteries in a transformed system of urban circulation. Paris was developed as a unified physical and human space through which people could move at greatly enhanced speed. Distances were transformed and people came to accept as normal the multitude of casual, superficial contacts and experiences characteristic of normal urban life, the 'passing moment' as Baudelaire terms it (cited in Berman 1983: 133). The boulevards provided the context for new kinds of urban experience, particularly that of being privately close while under public gaze. This anonymity was particularly facilitated because of the growth of *traffic* which is the setting for Baudelaire's primal modern scene where he says (in translation): 'I was crossing the boulevard, in a great hurry, in the midst of a moving chaos, with death galloping at me from every side' (cited in Berman 1983: 159).

Second, in a way even more striking was the central importance of the growth of the railway in structuring the modern consciousness (see Schivelbusch 1980). What this development did was to bring machinery into the foreground of people's everyday experience outside the workplace. An incredibly powerful, moving mechanical apparatus became a relatively familiar feature of everyday life. Unfortunately for British Rail it was the second half of the *nineteenth* century that was the age of the train. This generated one of the most distinctive experiences of the modern world, restructuring the existing relations between nature, time and space. There were a number of amazing changes: the very building of the railways flattened and subdued nature; rail travellers were propelled through space as though they were mere parcels; the landscape came to be viewed as a swiftly passing series of framed panoramas; passengers were thrown together with large numbers of strangers in an enclosed space and new ways of maintaining social distance had to be learnt; the greatly faster speed of rail traffic meant that the existing patchwork of local times had to be replaced with a standardised time based on Greenwich; and the extraordinary mechanical power of the railway created its own space. [. . .]

[. . .]

I will now return from the nineteenth century to speculate a little more about the future. What are going to be the main changes in the structure of economic, social and political life as we approach the year 2000? What are the late twentieth century ways of experiencing the world corresponding to the boulevard and the railway? Are there some characteristic PI or 'postmodern' sites in which new kinds of personality are being constructed?

I will approach the final section of this chapter by suggesting that the problem about the distinction between industrial and PI societies is that too much emphasis is placed upon one aspect of economic change minimising other aspects of the social structure of Western countries. I want instead to argue that such societies are best thought of as having once been not simply 'industrial' but 'organised' during the first half to two-thirds of this century and that what is now happening in such societies is that a mutually reinforcing set of disruptions of those organised patterns has been established. There were a number of interconnected features of such organisation: increasing dominance of large national economic, social and political institutions over people's lives; increasing average size of workplaces; rising rate of capital concentration; banks, industry and the state working together; residence and plant locations becoming more and more urbanised; collective bargaining taking place more and more on a national scale; the industrial male working class reaching its greatest size; and politics and culture reflecting the confrontation of nationally organised social classes. British politics was very much structured by such divisions of social class. People largely lived in class homogeneous neighbourhoods, people voted significantly in terms of one class or another, other forms of politics took their patterning from divisions of social class. The considerable powers of the working class and the labour movement in Britain derived from the leading role of particular groups of workers – of mainly male workers living in certain major cities, mostly employed in large plants in manufacturing industry and mining. Relations within the workplace structured social conflict and political life. Furthermore, it seemed that these processes would continue to grow in importance – that is, that plants would get bigger and bigger, that Western economies would become increasingly monopolistic, that more and more people would live in large cities, that major manufacturing industries would increasingly dominate whole regions, that male-based trade unions would continue to grow in importance and so on.

That pattern has now shifted into reverse in many advanced Western societies and in the last decade or two they have begun to 'disorganise' [. . .] (see Lash and Urry 1987, 1994). Some Western societies such as the USA began this process at an early date; others, such as Sweden, rather recently. Britain began to disorganise somewhere in between. There are a number of interdependent processes involved.

The first point to note relates to the very term 'society' which I have been using quite often in this chapter. It is in some ways the central concept of sociology. It can be loosely defined as the complex of relations between the major social institutions within a given state-determined territory. Society corresponds to the nation-state. As such, relatively well-defined national societies are a fairly recent invention of human ingenuity. Moreover within a century or two of their invention they are already past their prime. A bewildering array of developments have recently occurred which have undermined the obvious coherence, wholeness and unity of individual societies. Such developments include the growth of multinational corporations whose annual turnover dwarfs the national income of some individual nation-states; the spectacular development of electronically transmitted information which enables geographically distant units to be organisationally unified; the fragile growth of means of mass communication which can simultaneously link 20–30 per cent of the world's population in a shared cultural experience; the possibility of technological disasters that know no national boundaries and the awesome realisation that human existence itself is dependent upon the relatively unpredictable decisions of the leaders of major powers. There has thus been a marked 'globalisation' of economic and social relationships and a greatly heightened awareness of the 'simultaneity' of events and experiences occurring in geographically distant locations.

Second, mass production of standardised products in manufacturing plants employing thousands of male workers will undoubtedly become a thing of the past. What manufacturing workers there are will increasingly produce more specialised products in plants employing considerably fewer workers with higher levels of capital equipment. There have been a number of interrelated changes in Britain: sizeable increases in the number of self-employed people; the growth in the size of the secondary labour force so that it is now calculated that one-third of the labour force consists of part-time, temporary and home workers; a considerable rise in the rate at which new firms have been formed and hence in the number of small firms in both manufacturing and service industry; a very large increase in the proportion of manufacturing employment to be found in small enterprises; a sizeable decline in the numbers of people employed in the average manufacturing plant even in very large multi-plant, multinational enterprises; a tendency for large firms to be broken up into smaller decentralised units, or to develop new forms of devolved ownership such as franchising or new sub-contracting arrangements which enable much more flexible responses to new products and markets (see Hakim 1987; Shutt and Whittington 1987; and Lash and Urry 1987).

Third, there have been enormous changes in the spatial organisation of production. Companies are now able to operate on a world scale, to move in and out of countries taking advantage of different wage and strike rates, to subdivide their operations in pursuit of a global strategy, to force workers to compete with each other to gain or keep new production. As the *New York Times* put it, firms had to 'automate, emigrate, or evaporate'. [. . .] The development of new forms of electronically transmitted information and of jet transport and travel have permitted extraordinary levels of vertical disintegration and spatial relocation. Even within the UK there has been a marked tendency for whatever new industry there is to be located outside the major cities and for there to be extremely high rates of depopulation from the major conurbations and a general growth of employment and population away from the industrial heartlands of Britain. [. . .]

Furthermore, a fourth point is that employers appear to be much more mobile and innovative, the workforce seems to be increasingly reactionary – seeking to preserve or even to return to outmoded patterns of industry, technology and values. Employers increasingly appear as progressive, as being on the side of the new, as being not in favour of the *status quo* but in favour of change, breaking with tradition, and modernising for the future. Simultaneously, a number of developments have served to bring about a heightened identification of workers in the private sector with their firms. This has in turn encouraged a commitment to the career chances given by the firm's internal labour market, to becoming employee shareholders, and to collective bargaining at the level of the individual enterprise.

Fifth, social life, culture and politics are no longer predominantly organised in terms of social class. This is partly because current inequalities of income, wealth and power do not produce homogeneous social classes which share common experiences of class deprivation, or even vote the same way at elections. It is also because a much wider variety of other social groups are now willing and able to organise. Such social movements struggle around issues of gender, the environment, nuclear weapons, urban inequalities, racial discrimination, social amenities, level of rates and so on. Such groups are generally organised on a relatively decentralised basis – in the case of urban riots no real organisation at all – and the focus of their hostility is particular to the 'state' and sometimes to the labour movement itself. Indeed we may well expect increasing amounts of social conflict simply because there are more bases now of opposition in contemporary Britain. In a paradoxical sense fewer and fewer groups have a strong vested interest in the *status quo*. But that in turn means that the labour movement no longer has a monopoly on principled opposition and struggle. Social conflict has become more pluralistic, structured by a much wider variety of interests, and involving very many different enemies including the state, bureaucracies, male trade unionists, white workers, and so on.

Finally, culture too has changed. Popular music, styles of dress, new developments in film, TV and theatre have been in part structured by a strong opposition to authority and especially to the authority of 'age'. It was an undoubted consequence of the political and cultural changes in the 1960s and 1970s that personal identity and individual self-assertion became highly valued goals of human experience in the West. But this emphasis not only challenges authority structures such as the family, the school, the monarchy, the police and courts and so on: it also questions the basis of joining and participating in collective organisations such as trade unions. As Raphael Samuel says: 'Collectivity . . . is seen rather as an instrument of coercion, promoting uniformity rather than diversity, intimidating the individual, and subordinating the minority to the unthinking mass' (Samuel 1985). There has thus grown up a suspicion of the centralised organisation, whether it is a trade union, a professional association, an educational institution, a political party or a pressure group. This kind of radical individualism has profoundly contradictory effects. It leads both to challenges to authority in many spheres of social life, *and* it makes it harder and harder to sustain collectivities and collective action.

This set of developments has been generated by a number of significant processes: the growth of the electronic mass media, the disruption of class homogeneous neighbourhoods and the development of a relatively unattached middle class. It has been suggested that what results is a relatively depthless world in which people no longer pursue life-time projects or narratives and seek short-term advantage in a kind of 'calculating hedonism'. People's lives are not therefore viewed as the pursuit of ideals, or as part of a collective project. They are much more like those immortalised in the deeply cynical writings of Erving Goffman, of whose vision of human life Clifford Geertz has said: 'life is just a bowl of strategies' (1983: 25).

This is in turn connected with the growth of what postmodernist writers have described as the development of play, distance, spectacle, mobility and transgression. Some of the clearest examples of these can be found in contemporary architecture, one aspect of this being the development of some cities of consumption, as opposed to previously dominant industrial cities. To take just one example: it has been suggested that the shopping mall in West Edmonton in Canada represents the ultimate in this postmodern nirvana. The completed mall will be the ultimate temple of depthless consumerism, playfulness and hedonism. It is a mile long with over 800 shops, a 2.5-acre indoor lake with four deep-sea mini submarines, a reproduction Spanish galleon, dolphins, an eighteen-hole mini golf course, 40 restaurants, a 10-acre water park, a nineteenth century imitation Parisian boulevard (Haussmann will no doubt be turning in his grave), a New Orleans street with nightclubs, and a hotel offering a variety of theme rooms in such styles as Hollywood, Roman and Polynesian!

However, at the same time, there has been another interesting development in contemporary architecture – the development of vernacular or neo-vernacular design. Incidentally this can be seen locally in the Lancaster Plan where a distinctive Lancaster vernacular style has been identified and elaborated (Jencks 1991: 96–104; and see Bagguley *et al.* 1990). This development has become relatively widespread so that it would be fairly difficult these days to propose new shops, offices or houses in existing town centres which were not in part at least related to existing architectural style, building materials and the immediate context. As Jencks says, even large multinational developers these days adopt a form of local pastiche (1991). The main exceptions to this are to be found in residues of modernism such as Milton Keynes. While the modern movement viewed space as abstract, rational, homogeneous and the very essence of architecture, this postmodernist, neo-vernacular variant sees space as historically specific, rooted in conventions, particularistic, ambiguous and subordinate to context (see Edgar 1987, for a brief consideration of some political implications).

Such a shift is moreover part of a more general reaction against the modern and in a way against the future. It is part of a trend within post-industrial Britain – a kind of collective nostalgia not merely for the supposedly *Gemeinschaft* qualities of rural communities but for the skills, meanings and certainties of our immediate industrial past (see Turner 1987, on 'nostalgia'). As Britain becomes rapidly deindustrialised so a huge industry has grown up around the 'authentic' reconstruction of the workplaces, houses and streets of that industrial era. It is more than somewhat paradoxical that some of the least prepossessing sites of industrialisation have become transformed into some of the more successful tourist locations in contemporary Britain. Apart from the Albert Dock complex, other northern examples include Bradford, Wigan Pier, the Beamish Industrial Museum in the north-east, Black Country World, in Dudley Ironbridge Gorge and so on. It is as though once most people no longer work in industry so such industrial workplaces and streets become celebrated – they can be represented as part of our interesting past, part of our national heritage. As Patrick Wright asserts, there is something distinctive about 'living in an old country' (1985). Preservationism enables a kind of nationalisation of history but a nationalisation in which work, industry and indeed the working class become part of our national history. The PI thesis thus ignores how once industry has declined, so it can and will be celebrated and preserved. As Americans now say, all Britain is a museum. Nostalgia then for industrial times past is a widespread and permanent feature of PI Britain. It is believed that there has been a huge loss, that a plethora of skills, solidarities and meanings which were bound up with particular places, have been eroded for ever. The PI thesis is therefore far too modernist, it is based on the idea that history is future-oriented, and moves forward through time while the world of industry will be shunted to the sidings of history.

[. . .] We do live in a society which could be described as PI but that is not a very useful way of thinking about such developments. Culturally we live in a society where nostalgia, the vernacular and tradition mingle in a kind of pastiche with play, spectacle and transgression. Economically, the society is one in which the products of manufacturing industry are still absolutely central in providing us with goods that enable us to provide ourselves with services: but it is a national economy dislocated by both globalisation and fragmentation. Politically, Britain is a former industrial country and many of the certainties of politics derived from that period are dissolving before our eyes. At the same time that industrial past is endlessly available to us, to be mined and manufactured in political forms such as 'Victorian values' or the 'traditional working class'. That past will not as a consequence be evacuated from the centre stage of British culture for many decades to come.

## References

Bagguley, P. *et al.* (1990) *Restructuring: Place, Class and Gender*. London: Sage.
Bell, D. (1974) *The Coming of Post-Industrial Society*. London: Heinemann.
Berman, M. (1983) *All That is Solid Melts into Air: The Experience of Modernity*. London: Verso.

Daniel, W. and Milward, N. (1983) *Workplace Industrial Relations in Britain*. London: HEB.

Deane, P. and Coles, W. (1962) *British Economic Growth 1688–1959*. Cambridge: Cambridge University Press.

Dore, R. (1976) *The Diploma Disease*. London: Allen and Unwin.

Edgar, D. (1987) 'The new nostalgia', *Marxism Today*, March: 30–5.

Geertz, C. (1983) *Local Knowledge*. New York: Basic Books.

Gershuny, J. (1978) *After Industrial Society?* London: Macmillan.

Gershuny, J. and Miles, I. (1983) *The New Service Economy*. London: Frances Pinter.

Hakim, C. (1987) 'Homeworking in Britain', *Employment Gazette*, February: 92–104.

Ingham, G. (1984) *Capitalism Divided*. London: Macmillan.

Jencks, C. (1991) *The Language of Post-Modern Architecture*. London: Academy Editions.

Lash, S. and Urry, J. (1987) *The End of Organized Capitalism*. Cambridge: Polity Press.

Lash, S. and Urry, J. (1994) *Economies of Signs and Space*. London: Sage.

Marx, K. and Engels, F. (1964) [1848] *Manifesto of the Communist Party*. London: Modern Reader.

Miles, I. (1985) 'The new post-industrial state', *Futures*, December.

Miller, S. M. (1975) 'Notes on neo-capitalism', *Theory and Society* 2: 1–36.

Riddell, P. (1983) *The Thatcher Government*. Oxford: Martin Robertson.

Samuel, R. (1985) 'Breaking up is very hard to do', *Guardian*, 2 December.

Schivelbusch, W. (1980) *The Railway Journey: Trains and Travel in the Nineteenth Century*. Oxford: Blackwell.

Shutt, J. and Whittington, R. (1987) 'Fragmentation strategies and the rise of small units: cases from the north west', *Regional Studies* 21: 13–24.

Touraine, A. (1974) *The Post-Industrial Society*. London: Wildwood House.

Turner, B. S. (1987) 'A note on nostalgia', *Theory, Culture and Society* 4: 147–56.

Wright, P. (1985) *On Living in an Old Country*. London: Verso.

Wright Mills, C. (1959) *The Sociological Imagination*. New York: Oxford University Press.

# PART THREE

# The Network Society

## INTRODUCTION

■ Frank Webster

M ANUEL CASTELLS (Chapters 10 and 11) is the world's leading figure when it comes to delineating the Information Age. This is his own favoured term, and he has explicitly rejected the more commonly used concept of 'information society' (Castells 2000a).

Born in Barcelona in February 1942, Castells has long been a stellar thinker. A student radical, he fled from Spain to Paris in the early 1960s to escape from Franco's fascist regime, and in France quickly established a reputation as a seminal thinker with his path-breaking book, *The Urban Question: A Marxist Approach* (1972). He was a participant in the events of 1968, and in consequence was pursued by the authorities, but he then left for California in 1979. The University of California, which showed remarkable prescience in awarding Castells a position at Berkeley though he was still in his twenties, has been amply rewarded for its trust in him. Today he occupies a position as Professor of Planning and Sociology, a particularly appropriate designation since it signals the span of his interests and influences. He has been domiciled in the US since 1979, but it should be stressed that he is a quintessential cosmopolitan: he travels extensively, has doctoral students from across the globe, is married to a Russian (Emma Kiselyova) with whom he frequently writes, has a daughter and grandchildren in Amsterdam, and spends a good deal of his time in Europe (and especially in his home city of Barcelona where he retains a university chair). This biography leaves its mark on his work, which is remarkable well informed about a huge range of nations and regions, draws generously upon in-depth research of postgraduates (all of which is acknowledged) and on Castells' own studies of different places.

As the years passed by Castells has produced a series of enormously rich and influential works. Most of these were concerned with his first and abiding great love, urban life and change (he is generally regarded as an urbanist), but his publications have reached far beyond local significance, having things to say about much wider developments. His most important works, each influential and award-winning, have been *The City and the Grassroots* (1983), *The Informational City* (1989) and, most recently, *The Information Age* (1996–8). Along the way Castells re-examined and rethought his youthful Marxist commitment, though he has never rescinded his passionate engagement with real-world trends and is indubitably a man of the Left. His most recent book, co-authored with a Finn (Pekka Himanen), is a radical argument in favour of a social democratic (rather than free market) approach to informational matters (Castells and Himanen 2002). *The City and the Grassroots* marks something of a watershed in his thinking since it is here that Castells turned his attention to urban social movements (notably gays in San Francisco), and where he most radically questions the value of Marxist class categories. Since then he has consistently looked to find sources of change beyond the established political parties and the labour movement, and he is alert to emergent organisations, whether amongst feminists, ecologists, neo-fascism or chiliastic religious groups. All along Castells has kept himself close to practical affairs, indicated by his willingness to serve as an adviser to, most recently, the European Commission on Information Society issues, and his collaborations with local and national politicians – for instance, in 1993 he wrote *The New Global Economy in the Information Age* with Fernando Enrique Cardoso, who went on to be President of Brazil, and in 1997 he produced *Local and Global: Management of Cities in the Information Age* with Jordi Borja, a Spanish mayor.

However, it was the publication, between 1996 and 1998, of a trilogy titled *The Information Age* that vaulted Castells into the position of being very much more than an analyst of urban change. The trilogy led to recognition of Manuel Castells as an authoritative commentator on nothing less than contemporary civilisation itself, and it has transformed the way in which many think about our world. The three books have been translated into no less than eighteen languages and reprinted annually since they first appeared. New editions have appeared of two of the three volumes (Castells 2000b and c), and an accessible update has been published to reach a still wider audience (Castells 2001).

Castells conceives of a 'network society' as what distinguishes the 'information age', this being a society in which 'information flows' lead increasingly to decisions being made on a global scale in real time. His projection is of constantly circulating financial, technical and cultural information with an immediacy without precedent which has enormous consequences for our ways of life, shaping economic relations, politics and organisational structures.

The first reading from Castells outlines the conception of the 'information age', while the second elaborates his notion of the 'new economy' which is its accompaniment. Nothing, it should be said, can substitute for engaging with Castells' trilogy itself, where one gets a full appreciation of his encyclopaedic coverage, his empirical grasp and impressive synthesising capabilities. Castells writes with a passion and urgency, combined with an extraordinary capacity to contextualise and integrate, which makes for a compelling read.

Castells argues that there are enormous consequences of the 'network society'. These range from the promotion of 'informational cities' which occupy positions as switching centres for the global information networks and in which congregate key sorts of workers (professional, highly educated, cosmopolitan), to changes in organisations which lead to 'flat' management and which promote the fast-moving and adaptable 'informational labour', to nothing less than transformation of the entire stratification system.

Central to Castells' conception is that 'informational capitalism' is different from earlier forms of market society. It is his view that the new society emerged from the crises of the 1970s when capitalism got into trouble through declining profitability, burgeoning social costs, and the unsettling effects of a large and overnight rise in oil prices, and the post-war settlement which had provided full employment, rising standards of living and assured welfare provision began to unravel. Castells suggests that the simultaneous development of new information technologies happened amidst this crisis and provided a possible way out. Informationalism promised revitalisation, increased productivity and expansion. Information and communications technologies, combined with accompanying new ways of working and a global reach that is instantaneous, have enabled the economy to escape the doldrums and enter into a new form, informational capitalism.

Castells identifies many distinctive aspects of informational capitalism, always in contrast to what went before. Prominent in the new age is the fact that intense and unceasing change is normal, so people must get accustomed to instability as a way of life. There are no longer the steady rhythms of boom and slump; nowadays crises hit unexpectedly (the dotcom collapse, runs on currencies) and as matters of routine. Further, those incapable of adapting to hectic innovation and uncertainty will suffer the most, since anything which stands still will sooner or later fail. A business that does not introduce new products or services, or an occupation which fails to reskill, is sure to come unstuck. Those who are most likely to succeed in this information age are those equipped with the special qualities of 'informational labour' – i.e. those who are well educated and able to constantly re-educate themselves, and who are articulate, connected, analytical and alert to opportunity. Such a group will win out all round – whether in business, politics or in life generally since they are at one with the new age. Indeed, the emergence of informational labour signals the emergence of a new form of stratification which Castells sees as having a threefold divide: informational labour at the apex, generic labour in the middle (where it is always under threat) and, right at the bottom, an excluded underclass which is poorly educated and unskilled and struggling to find a place in informational capitalism.

When it comes to politics the old guard, notably organised labour, is massively weakened, being stuck in a slow and stolid track. They are replaced by those who are media-savvy and at ease with the latest network technologies, who outpace the ponderous, institution-oriented leaders of an earlier period. If you want a picture of the new, think of Greenpeace or Friends of the Earth, with their media-friendly spokespeople, their adroit information campaigns, their global networks and facility with the Web. And contrast it with an image of the old, the Trades Union Congress or Workers' Education Association, where 'due processes' must be followed, where 'official speakers' are those who do the talking, and where new technologies remain intimidating.

Manuel Castells' work has certainly set the agenda for thinking about the 'information age', but it has not been without its critics. For instance, Abigail Halcli and Frank Webster (2000) offer a sceptical analysis of the suggestion that we have experienced profound changes in stratification. They suggest that the alleged rise of 'informational labour' is overstated and that indeed this is a rather old theme in social analysis. Their account stresses the conservatism of established forms of inequality and suggests that Castells runs away with his enthusiasm for the new.

Finally, in the third extract **Nicholas Garnham** (Chapter 12) presents a systematic and rigorous critique of Castells' entire theoretical edifice. Garnham teases Castells' ambiguous use of the term information, insists that networks are nothing new, chastises Castells for his apparent embrace of postmodernism, and charges that his approach is technologically determinist and that Castells is unclear about what exactly drives capitalism. A broadside against the most influential account of social change in decades, Garnham scores a number of impressive hits on Castells. There is a comprehensive range of critical response, though chiefly in English, to Castells' *oeuvre* in Webster and Dimitriou (2004), which may be consulted by more advanced students.

## REFERENCES

Borja, Jordi and Castells, Manuel (1997) *Local and Global: Management of Cities in the Information Age*. London: Earthscan.

Carnoy, M., Castells, M., Cohen, S. S. and Cardoso, F. E. (1993) *The New Global Economy in the Information Age*. University Park, PA: Pennsylvania State University Press.

Castells, Manuel (1972) *The Urban Question: A Marxist Approach*, trans. Alan Sheridan. Cambridge, MA: MIT Press, 1977.

Castells, Manuel (1983) *The City and the Grassroots: A Cross-Cultural Theory of Urban Social Movements*. Berkeley: University of California Press.

Castells, Manuel (1989) *The Informational City: Information Technology, Economic Restructuring and the Urban-Regional Process*. Oxford: Blackwell.

Castells, Manuel (1996) *The Rise of the Network Society*, vol. 1 of *The Information Age: Economy, Society and Culture*. Oxford: Blackwell.

Castells, Manuel (1997) *The Power of Identity*, vol. 2 of *The Information Age: Economy, Society and Culture*. Oxford: Blackwell.

Castells, Manuel (1998) *End of Millennium*, vol. 3 of *The Information Age: Economy, Society and Culture*. Oxford: Blackwell.

Castells, Manuel (2000a) 'Materials for an Exploratory Theory of the Network Society', *British Journal of Sociology* 5 (1): 5–24.

Castells, Manuel (2000b) *The Rise of the Network Society*, 2nd edn. Oxford: Blackwell.

Castells, Manuel (2000c) *End of Millennium*, 2nd edn. Oxford: Blackwell.

Castells, Manuel (2001) *The Internet Galaxy: Reflections on the Internet, Business and Society*. Oxford: Oxford University Press.

Castells, Manuel and Himanen, Pekka (2002) *The Information Society and the Welfare State: The Finnish Model*. Oxford: Oxford University Press.

Halcli, Abigail and Webster, Frank (2000) 'Inequality and Mobilization in *The Information Age*', *European Journal of Social Theory* 3 (1): 67–81.

Webster, F. and Dimitriou, B. (eds) (2004) *Manuel Castells: Sage Masters of Modern Social Thought*, 3 vols. London: Sage.

Chapter 10

# Manuel Castells

## AN INTRODUCTION TO THE
## INFORMATION AGE

From *City*, 7 (1997), pp. 6–16.

**I**N THE LAST DECADE I was struck, as many have been, by a series of major historical events that have transformed our world/our lives. Just to mention the most important: the diffusion and deepening of the information technology revolution, including genetic engineering; the collapse of the Soviet Union, with the consequent demise of the international Communist movement, and the end of the Cold War that had marked everything for the last half a century; the restructuring of capitalism; the process of globalization; emergence of the Pacific as the most dynamic area of the global economy; the paradoxical combination of a surge in nationalism and the crisis of the sovereign nation-state; the crisis of democratic politics, shaken by periodic scandals and a crisis of legitimacy; the rise of feminism and the crisis of patriarchalism; the widespread diffusion of ecological consciousness; the rise of communalism as sources of resistance to globalization, taking in many contexts the form of religious fundamentalism; last, but not least, the development of a global criminal economy that is having significant impacts in international economy, national politics, and local everyday life.

I grew increasingly dissatisfied with the interpretations and theories, certainly including my own, that the social sciences were using to make sense of this new world. But I did not give up the rationalist project of understanding all this, in a coherent manner, that could be somewhat empirically grounded and as much as possible theoretically oriented. Thus, for the last 12 years I undertook the task of researching and understanding this wide array of social trends, working in and on the United States, Western Europe, Russia, Asian Pacific, and Latin America. Along the way, I found plenty of company, as researchers from all horizons are converging in this collective endeavour.

My personal contribution to this understanding is the book in three volumes that I have now completed, *The Information Age*, with the first volume already published, and the two others scheduled for publication in 1997. The first volume analyses the new social structure, the network society. The second volume studies social movements and political processes, in the framework of and in interaction with the network society. The third volume attempts an interpretation of macro-social processes, as a result of the interaction between the power of networks and the power of identity, focusing on themes such as the collapse of the Soviet Union, the emergence of the Pacific, or the ongoing process of global social exclusion and polarization. It also proposes a general theoretical synthesis.

I will take this opportunity to share with you the main lines of my argument, hoping that this will help a debate that I see emerging from all directions in the whole world. I see coming a new wave of intellectual innovation in which, by the way, British researchers are at the forefront.

Trying to summarize a considerable amount of material within one hour I will follow a schematic format. I will focus on identifying the main features of what I consider to be the emerging, dominant social structure, the network society, that I find characteristic of informational capitalism, as constituted throughout the world. I will not indulge in futurology: everything I say is based on what I have perceived, rightly or wrongly, already at work in our societies. I will organize my lecture in one disclaimer, nine hypotheses, and one conclusion.

## Disclaimer

I shall focus on the structure/dynamics of the network society, not on its historical genesis, that is how and why it came about, although in my book I propose a few hints about it. For the record: in my view, it resulted from the historical convergence of three *independent* processes, from whose interaction emerged the Network society:

- The Information Technology Revolution, constituted as a paradigm in the 1970s.
- The restructuring of capitalism and of statism in the 1980s, aimed at superseding their contradictions, with sharply different outcomes.
- The cultural social movements of the 1960s, and their 1970s aftermath (particularly feminism and ecologism).

The Information Technology Revolution DID NOT create the network society. But without information technology, the Network Society would not exist.

Rather than providing an abstract categorization in what this Network Society is, let me summarize its main features and processes, before attempting a synthesis of its embedded logic in the diversity of its cultural/institutional variations. There is no implied hierarchy in the sequence of presentation of these features. They all interact in, guess what, a network.

## 1. An informational economy

It is an economy in which sources of productivity and competitiveness for firms, regions, countries depend, more than ever, on knowledge, information, and the technology of their processing, including the technology of management, and the management of technology. This is not the same as a service economy. There is informational agriculture, informational manufacturing, and different types of informational services, while a large number of service activities, e.g. in the developing world, are not informational at all.

The informational economy opens up an extraordinary potential for solving our problems, but, because of its dynamism and creativity, it is potentially more exclusionary than the industrial economy if social controls do not check the forces of unfettered market logic.

[. . .]

## 2. A global economy

This is not the same as a world economy. That has existed, in the West, at least since the sixteenth century. The global economy is a new reality: it is an economy whose core, strategically dominant activities have the potential of working as a unit in real time on planetary scale. This is so for financial and currency markets, advanced business services, technological innovation, high technology manufacturing, media communication.

Most economic activity in the world and most employment are not only national but regional or local. But, except for subsistence economies, the fate of these activities, and of their jobs, depend ultimately on the dynamics of the global economy, to which they are connected through networks and markers. Indeed, if labour tends to be local, capital is by and large globalized – not a small detail in a capitalist economy. This globalization has developed as a fully fledged system only in the last two decades, on the basis of information/communication technologies that were previously not available.

The global economy reaches out to the whole planet, but it is not planetary, it does not include the whole planet. In fact, it excludes probably a majority of the population. It is characterized by an extremely uneven geography. It scans the whole world, and links up valuable inputs, markets, and individuals, while switching off unskilled labour and poor markets. For a significant part of people around the world, there is a shift, from the point of view of dominant systemic interests, from exploitation to structural irrelevance.

[. . .]

This is different from the traditional First World/Third World opposition, because the Third World has become increasingly diversified, internally, and the First World has generated social exclusion, albeit in lesser proportion, within its own boundaries. Thus, I propose the notion of the emergence of a Fourth World of exclusion, made up not only of most of Africa, and rural Asia, and of Latin American shanties, but also of the South Bronx, La Courneuve, Kamagasaki, or Tower Hamlets of this world. A fourth world that, as I document extensively in volume three, is predominantly populated by women and children.

## 3. The network enterprise

At the heart of the connectivity of the global economy and of the flexibility of informational capitalism, there is a new form of organization, characteristic of economic activity, but gradually extending its logic to other domains and organizations: the **network enterprise**. This is not the same as a network of enterprises. It is a network made either from firms or segments of firms, or from internal segmentation of firms. Multinational corporations, with their internal decentralization, and their links with a web of subsidiaries and suppliers throughout the world, are but one of the forms of this network enterprise. But others include strategic alliances between corporations, networks of small and medium businesses (such as in Northern Italy or Hong Kong), and link-ups between corporations and networks of small businesses through subcontracting and outsourcing.

So, the network enterprise is the specific set of linkages between different firms or segments, organized ad hoc for a specific project, and dissolving/reforming after the task is completed, e.g. IBM, Siemens, Toshiba. This ephemeral unit, The Project, around which a network of partners is built, is the actual operating unit of our economy, the one that generates profits or losses, the one that received rewards or goes bust, and the one that hires and lays off, via its member organizations.

[. . .]

## 4. The transformation of work and employment: the flexi-workers

Work is at the heart of all historical transformations. And there is no exception to this. But the coming of the Information Age is full of myths about the fate of work and employment.

With the exception, and an important one, of Western Europe, there is no major surge of unemployment in the world after two decades of diffusion in information technology. Indeed, there is much higher unemployment in technologically laggard countries, regions, and sectors.

All evidence and analysis points to the variable impact of technology on jobs depending on a much broader set of factors, mainly firms' strategies and governments' policies. Indeed, the two most technologically advanced economies, the US and Japan, both display a low rate of unemployment. In the US in the last four years there is a net balance of 10 million new jobs, and their educational content for these new jobs is significantly higher than that of the pre-existing social structure: many more information-intensive jobs than hamburger flippers' jobs have been created. Even manufacturing jobs are at an all time high on a global perspective: between 1970 and 1989, manufacturing jobs in the world increased by 72 per cent, even if OECD countries, particularly the US and the UK, have indeed de-industrialized.

There is certainly a major unemployment problem in the European Union, as a result of a combination of rigidities in the institutional environment, strategies of global redeployment by firms and, more importantly, the restrictive macro-economic policies induced by an insane obsession with fitting in the Maastricht criteria that nobody, and particularly not Germany, will be able to qualify for, in an incredible example of collective alienation in paying respect to gods of economic orthodoxy that have taken existence independently from us.

There is indeed a serious unemployment problem in the inner cities of America, England, or France, among the uneducated and switched off populations, or in low technology countries around the world, particularly in the rural areas.

For the majority of people in America, for instance, unemployment is not a problem. And yet, there is a tremendous anxiety and discontent about work. There is a real base for this concern:

(a) There is the transformation of power relationships between capital and labour in favour of capital, through the process of socio-economic restructuring that took place in the 1980s, both in a conservative environment (Reagan, Thatcher) and, to a lesser but real extent, in a less conservative environment (Spain, France). In this sense, new technologies allowed business to either automate or [undertake] offshore production or outsource supplies or to subcontract to smaller firms or to obtain concessions from labour or all the above.

(b) The development of the network enterprise translates into downsizing, subcontracting, and networking of labour, inducing flexibility of both business and labour, and individualization of contractual arrangements between management and labour. So, instead of layoffs what we often have are layoffs followed by subcontracting of services on an ad hoc, consulting basis, for the time and task to be performed, without job tenure and without social benefits provided by the firm.

[. . .]

This is indeed the general trend, exemplified by the rapid growth in all countries of self-employment, temporary work, and part-time, particularly for women. In England, between 40 and 45 per cent of the labour force seems to be already in these categories, as opposed to full-time, regularly salaried employment, and is growing. Some studies in Germany project that in 2015, about 50 per cent of the labour force would be out of stable employment. And in the most dynamic region in the world, Silicon Valley, a recent study we have just completed shows that, in the midst of a job creation explosion, in the last ten years, between 50 per cent at least and 90 per cent of new jobs, most of them highly paid, are of this kind of non-standard labour arrangement.

The most significant change in work in the Information Age is the reversal of the socialization/salarization of labour that characterized the industrial age. The 'organization man' is out, the 'flexible woman' is in. The individualization of work, and therefore of labour's bargaining power, is the major feature characterizing employment in the network society.

[. . .]

## 5. Social polarization and social exclusion

The processes of globalization, business networking, and individualization of labour weaken social organizations and institutions that represented/protected workers in the Information Age, particularly labour unions and the welfare state. Accordingly, workers are increasingly left to themselves in their differential relationship to management and to the market place.

Skills and education, in a constant redefinition of these skills, became critical in valorizing or devaluing people in their work. But even valuable workers may fall down for reasons of health, age, gender discrimination, or lack of capacity to adapt to a given task or position.

As a result of these trends, most societies in the world, and certainly OECD countries, with the US and the UK at the top of the scale, present powerful trends towards increasing inequality, social polarization, and social exclusion. There is increasing accumulation of wealth at the top, and of poverty at the bottom.

In the US inequality has regressed to the pre-1920s period. In the limit, social exclusion creates pockets of dereliction with various entry points, but hardly any exits. It may be long-term unemployment, illness, functional illiteracy, illegal status, poverty, family disruption, psychological crisis, homelessness, drugs, crime, incarceration, etc. Once in this underworld, processes of exclusion reinforce each other, requiring a heroic effort to pull out from what I call the black holes of informational capitalism, that often have a territorial expression. The proportion of people in these black holes is staggering, and rapidly growing. In the US, it may reach above 10 per cent of the population, if you consider that simply the number of adults under the control of the justice system in 1966 was 5.4 million, that is almost 3 per cent of the population, while the proportion of people below the poverty line is 15 per cent.

The Information Age does not have to be the age of stepped-up inequality, polarization and social exclusion. But for the moment it is.

## 6. The culture of real virtuality

Shifting to the cultural realm, we see the emergence of a similar pattern of networking, flexibility, and ephemeral symbolic communication, in a culture organized around electronic media, including in this communication system the computer-mediated communication networks. Cultural expressions of all kinds are increasingly enclosed in or shaped by this world of electronic media. But the new media system is not characterized by the one-way, undifferentiated messages through a limited number of channels that constituted the world of mass media. And it is not a global village.

Media are extraordinarily diverse, and send targeted messages to specific segments of audiences and to specific moods of the audiences. They are increasingly inclusive, bridging from one another, from network TV to cable or satellite TV, radio, VCR, musical video, walkman type of devices, connected throughout the globe, and yet diversified by cultures, constituting a hypertext with extraordinary inclusive capacity. Furthermore, slowly but surely, this new media system is moving towards interactivity, particularly if we include CMC [computer mediated communication] networks, and their access to text, images, and sounds, that will eventually link up with the current media system.

Instead of a global village we are moving towards mass production of customized cottages. While there is oligopolistic concentration of multimedia groups around the world, there is at the same time, market segmentation, and increasing inter-action by and among the individuals that break up the uniformity of a mass audience. These processes induce the formation of what I call *the culture of real virtuality*. It is so, and not virtual reality, because when our symbolic environment is, by and large, structured in this inclusive, flexible, diversified hypertext, in which we navigate every day, the virtuality of this text is in fact our reality, the symbols from which we live and communicate.

[. . .]

## 7. Politics

This enclosure of communication in the space of flexible media does not only concern culture. It has a fundamental effect on **politics**. In all countries, the media have become the essential space of politics. Not all politics takes place through the media, and imagemaking still needs to relate to real issues and real conflicts. But without significant presence in the space of media, actors and ideas are reduced to political marginality. This presence does not concern only, or even primarily, the moments of political campaigns, but the day-to-day messages that people receive by and from the media.

I propose the following analysis:

- To an overwhelming extent people receive their information, on the basis of which they form their political opinion, and structure their behaviour, through the media, particularly television and radio.
- Media politics needs to simplify the message/proposals.
- The simplest message is an image. The simplest image is a person.
- Political competition revolves around personalization of politics.
- The most effective political weapons are negative messages. The most effec-tive negative message is character assassination of opponents' personalities. The politics of scandal, in the US, in Europe, in Japan, in Latin America etc. is the predominant form of political struggle.

[. . .]

- Political marketing is the essential means to win political competition in democratic politics. In the Information Age it involves media adver-tising, telephone banks, targeted mailing, image making, image unmaking, image control, presence in the media staging of public appearances etc. This makes it an excessively expensive business, way beyond that of traditional party politics, so that mechanisms of political financing are obsolete, and parties use access to power as a way to generate resources to stay in power or to prepare to return to it. This is the fundamental source of political cor-ruption, to which intermediaries add a little personal twist. This is also at the source of systemic corruption, that feeds scandal politics. The use of scandal as a weapon leads to increased expense and activity in intelligence, damage control, and access to the media. Once a market is created intermediaries appear to retrieve, obtain, or fabricate information, offering it to the highest bidder. Politics becomes a horse race, and a soap opera motivated by greed, backstage manoeuvres, betrayals and, often, sex and violence, becoming hardly distinguishable from TV scripts.

- Those who survive in this world become politically successful, for a while. But what certainly does not survive, after a few rounds of these tricks, is political legitimacy, not to speak of citizens' hope.

## 8. Timeless time

As with all historical transformations, the emergence of a new social structure is necessarily linked to the redefinition of the material foundations of life, **time and space**. Time and space are related in society as in nature. Their meaning, and manifestations in social practice, evolve throughout histories and across cultures, as Giddens, Thrift, Harvey, Adams, Lash, and Urry, among others, have shown.

I propose the hypothesis that the network society, as the dominant social structure emerging in the Information Age, is organized around new forms of time and space: timeless time, the space of flows. These are the dominant forms, and not the forms in which most people live, but through their domination, they affect everybody. Let me explain, starting with time, then with some greater detail on space, given the specific interests of many in this conference.

In contrast to the rhythm of biological time of most of human existence, and to the clock time characterizing the industrial age, a new form of time characterizes the dominant logic of the network society: **timeless time**. It is defined by the use of new information/communication technologies in a relentless effort to annihilate time, to compress years in seconds, seconds in split seconds. Furthermore, the most fundamental aim is **to eliminate sequencing of time**, including past, present, and future in the same hypertext, thus eliminating the 'succession of things' that, according to Leibniz, characterizes time, so that without things and their sequential ordering there is no longer time in society. We live, as in the recurrent circuits of the computer networks in the encyclopedia of historical experience, all our tenses at the same time, being able to reorder them in a composite created by our fantasy or our interests.

David Harvey has shown the relentless tendency of capitalism to eliminate barriers of time. But I think in the network society, that is indeed a capitalist society, but something else at the same time, all dominant processes tend to be constructed around timeless time. I find such a tendency in the whole realm of human activity. I find it certainly in the split second financial transactions of global financial markets, but I also find it, for instance, in instant wars, built around the notion of a surgical strike that devastates the enemy in a few hours, or minutes, to avoid politically unpopular, costly wars. Or in the blurring of the life cycle by new reproductive techniques, allowing people a wide range of options in the age and conditions of parenting, even storing their embryos to eventually produce babies later either by themselves, or through surrogate mothers, even after their procreators are dead. I find it in the twisting of working life by the variable chronology of labour trajectories and time schedules in increasingly diverse labour markets. And I find it in the vigorous effort to use medical technology, including genetic engineering, and computer-based medical care to exile death from life, to bring a substantial proportion of the population to a high level of life expectancy, and to diffuse the belief that, after all, we are eternal, at least for some time.

As with space, timeless time characterizes dominant functions and social groups, while most people in the world are still submitted to biological time and to clock time. Thus, while instant wars characterize the technological powers, atrocious, lingering wars go on and on for years, around the planet, in a slow-motion destruction process, quasi-ignored by the world until they are discovered by some television programme.

I propose the notion that a fundamental struggle in our society is around the redefinition of time, between its annihilation or desequencing by networks, on one hand, and, on the other hand, the consciousness of glacial time, the slow-motion, inter-generational evolution of our species in our cosmological environment, a concept suggested by Lash and Urry, and a battle undertaken, in my view, by the environmental movement.

[. . .]

## 9. The Space of Flows

Many years ago (or at least it seems to me as many) I proposed the concept of Space of Flows to make sense of a body of empirical observation: dominant functions were increasingly operating on the basis of exchanges between electronic circuits linking up information systems in distant locations. Financial markets, global media, advanced business services, technology, information. In addition, electronically based, fast transportation systems reinforced this pattern of distant interaction by following up with movements of people and goods. Furthermore, new location patterns for most activities follow a simultaneous logic of territorial concentration/decentralization, reinstating the unity of their operation by electronic links, e.g. the analysis proposed in the 1980s on location patterns of high tech manufacturing; or the networked articulation of advanced services throughout the world, under the system labelled as 'global city'.

Why keep the term of space under these conditions? Reasons: (1) These electronic circuits do not operate in the territorial vacuum. They link up territorially based complexes of production, management, and information, even though the meaning and functions of these complexes depend on their connection in these networks of flows. (2) These technological linkages are material, e.g. depend on specific telecommunication/transportation facilities, and on the existence and quality of information systems, in a highly uneven geography. (3) The meaning of space evolves – as the meaning of time. Thus, instead of indulging in futurological statements such as the vanishing of space, and the end of cities, we should be able to reconceptualize new forms of spatial arrangements under the new technological paradigm.

[. . .]

To proceed with this conceptualization I build on a long intellectual tradition, from Leibniz to Harold Innis, connecting space and time, around the notion of space as a coexistence of time. Thus, my definition: space is the material support of time-sharing social practices.

What happens when the time-sharing of practices (be it synchronous or asynchronous) does not imply contiguity? 'Things' still exist together, they share time, but the material arrangements that allow this coexistence are inter-territorial or transterritorial: **the space of flows is the material organization of time-sharing social practices that work through flows**. What concretely this material organization is depends on the goals and characteristics of the networks of flows, for instance I can tell you what it is in the case of high technology manufacturing or in the case of global networks of drug traffic. However, I did propose in my analysis some elements that appear to characterize the space of flows in all kinds of networks: electronic circuits connecting information systems; territorial nodes and hubs; locales of support and social cohesion for dominant social actors in the network (e.g. the system of VIP spaces throughout the world).

Dominant functions tend to articulate themselves around the space of flows. But this is not the only space. **The space of places continues to be the predominant space of experience**, of everyday life, and of social and political control. Places root culture and transmit history. (A place is a locale whose form, function, and meaning, from the point of view of the social actor, are contained within the boundaries of physical contiguity.)

In the network society, a fundamental form of social domination is **the prevalence of the logic of the space of flows over the space of places**. The space of flows structures and shapes the space of places, as when the differential fortunes of capital accumulation in global financial markets reward or punish specific regions, or when telecom systems link up CBDs to outlying suburbs in new office development, bypassing/marginalizing poor urban neighbourhoods. The domination of the space of flows over the space of places induces intra-**metropolitan dualism** as a most important form of social/territorial exclusion, that has become as significant as regional uneven development. The simultaneous growth and decline of economies and societies within the same metropolitan area is a most fundamental trend of territorial organization, and a key challenge to urban management nowadays.

[. . .]

But there is still something else in the new spatial dynamics. Beyond the opposition between the space of flows and the space of places. As information communication networks diffuse in society, and as technology is appropriated by a variety of social actors, segments of the space of flows are penetrated by forces of resistance to domination, and by expressions of personal experience. Examples:

(a) Social movements, Zapatistas and the Internet (but from the Lacandona forest). But also American Militia.

(b) Local governments, key agents of citizen representation in our society, linking up through electronic networks, particularly in Europe (see research by Stephen Graham).

(c) Expressions of experience in the space of flows.

Thus, we do witness an increasing penetration, and subversion, of the space of flows, originally set up for the functions of power, by the power of experience, inducing a set of contradictory power relationships. Yes, it is still an elitist means of communication, but it is changing rapidly. The problem is to integrate these observations in some theory, but for this we still lack research, in spite of some insightful elaborations, such as the one by Sherry Turkle at MIT.

The new frontier of spatial research is in examining the interaction between the space of flows, the space of places, function, meaning, domination, and challenge to domination, in increasingly complex and contradictory patterns. Homesteading in this frontier is already taking place, as shown in the pioneering research by Graham and Marvin, or in the reflections of Bill Mitchell, but we are clearly at the beginning of a new field of study that should help us to understand **and to change** the currently prevailing logic in the space of flows.

## Conclusion: the Network Society

So, what is the Network Society? It is a society that is structured in its dominant functions and processes around networks. In its current manifestation it is a capitalist society. Indeed, we live more than ever in a capitalist world, and thus an analysis in terms of capitalism is necessary and complementary to the theory of the network society. But this particular form of capitalism is very different from industrial capitalism, as I have tried to show.

The Network Society is not produced by information technology. But without the Information Technology Revolution it could not be such a comprehensive, persuasive social form, able to link up, or de-link, the entire realm of human activity.

So, is that all? Just a morphological transformation? Well, historically, transformation of social forms has always been fundamental, both as expressions and sources of major social processes, e.g. standardized mass production in the large factory as characteristic of the so-called Fordism, as a major form of capitalist social organization; or the rational bureaucracy as the foundation of modern society, in the Weberian conception.

But this morphological transformation is even more significant because the network architecture is particularly dynamic, open-ended, flexible, potentially able to expand endlessly, without rupture, bypassing/disconnecting undesirable components following instructions of the networks' dominant nodes. Indeed, the February 1997 Davos meeting titled the general programme of its annual meeting 'Building the Network Society'.

This networking logic is at the roots of major effects in our societies. Using it:

- capital flows can bypass controls
- workers are individualized, outsourced, subcontracted
- communication becomes at the same time global and customized
- valuable people and territories are switched on, devalued ones are switched off.

The dynamics of networks push society towards an endless escape from its own constraints and controls, towards an endless supersession and reconstruction of its values and institutions, towards a meta-social, constant rearrangement of human institutions and organizations.

Networks transform power relationships. Power in the traditional sense still exists: capitalists over workers, men over women, state apparatuses still torture bodies and silence minds around the world.

Yet, there is some order of power: the power of flows in the networks prevails over the flows of power. Capitalists are dependent upon uncontrollable financial flows; many workers are at the same time investors (often unwillingly through their pension funds) in this whirlwind of capital; networkers are inter-related in the logic of the network enterprise, so that their jobs and income depend on their positioning rather than on their work. States are bypassed by global flows of wealth, information, and crime. Thus, to survive, they band together in multilateral ventures, such as the European Union. It follows the creation of a web of political institutions: national, supranational, international, regional, and local, that becomes the new operating unit of the information age: the network state.

[. . .]

In this complexity, the communication between networks and social actors depends increasingly on shared CULTURAL CODES. If we accept certain values, certain categories that frame the meaning of experience, then the networks will process them efficiently, and will return to each one of us the outcome of their processing, according to the rules of domination and distribution inscripted in the network.

Thus, the challenges to social domination in the Network Society revolve around the redefinition of cultural codes, proposing alternative meaning and changing the rules of the game. This is why the affirmation of IDENTITY is so essential, because it fixes meaning autonomously vis-à-vis the abstract, instrumental logic of networks. I am, thus I exist. In my empirical investigation I have found identity-based social movements aimed at changing the cultural foundations of society to be the essential sources of social change in the Information Age, albeit often in forms and with goals that we do not usually associate with positive social change. Some movements, that appear to be the most fruitful and positive, are proactive, such as feminism and environmentalism. Some are reactive, as in the communal resistances to globalization built around religion, nation, territory, or ethnicity. But in all cases they affirm the preeminence of experience over instrumentality, of meaning over function, and, I would dare to say, of use value of life over exchange value in the networks.

[. . .]

The implicit logic of the Network Society appears to end history, by enclosing it into the circularity of recurrent patterns of flows. Yet, as with any other social form, in fact it opens up a new realm of contradiction and conflict, as people around the world refuse to become shadows of global flows and project their dreams, and sometimes their nightmares, into the light of new history making.

[. . .]

Chapter 11

# Manuel Castells

# THE INFORMATION CITY,
# THE NEW ECONOMY, AND THE
# NETWORK SOCIETY

From Antti Kasvio *et al.* (eds) *People, Cities and the New Information Economy*, Helsinki: Palmenia (2001), pp. 22–37.

[. . .]

O UR TASK IN THIS CONFERENCE IS to examine interactions between the transformation of the economy and of the spatial environments – increasingly cities – in which we live. In order to understand the role of cities in the New Economy one has to understand first what is the New Economy. I really think that there is a New Economy, but which is not the Internet or dotcom economy. It is an economy in which companies – or firms or entrepreneurs – around the world are working on the basis of Internet and in which their organizational and innovation logic is embedded in the Internet or related information technologies. The New Economy is not just the Internet economy, but an economy that works through, by and with the Internet and with those things that the Internet represents. In a similar manner, the industrial economy was not simply an economy producing electricity, but an economy that worked with electricity. Internet is the electricity of the Information Age, and therefore it embodies all kinds of organizational innovation. It also embodies managerial strategies that introduce new rules of the game. The game is about the creation of wealth and the production of our lives through the production of objects.

This economy is not based on technology, rather it is based on productivity. If there is New Economy, it exists because there is the possibility and, in some cases, an actual realisation of a dramatic surge in productivity growth. This can already be observed in areas of the world in which the New Economy is in full fledge, like in California, but it can also be observed in many sectors and firms around the world in a very uneven way. This unevenness is exactly where the problem lies. We are in a new production system, which is certainly capitalist. But there are so many kinds of capitalisms that once we have said that it is capitalism, we still have to say many other things in order to understand it – and particularly if we want to transform it. One can, of course, just decide that it exists without wanting to transform it. But if one wants to transform it, then one has to understand it. So the New Economy is based essentially on productivity growth, but this productivity growth is built upon our ability to do things a new way with the new information technologies.

The new information technologies refer certainly to the Internet, but they are also about all kinds of other things – like, for example, the information technology-based systems of mobility, both personal and all other kinds of mobility: from air transportation to mobile telephony. Air transportation, of course, is an information technology. It might feel too scary if there were no pilots and just computers would be flying our planes. Actually, the computers do, however, fly planes – the computers do all kinds of things.

Now let us go step by step in trying to understand firstly what is this New Economy and secondly how it works, which are to some extent different things. Thirdly we try to understand which are the social and political challenges that arrive from this New Economy. Fourthly, we try to describe how cities play into this New Economy and into these challenges in terms of what is the structural role of the city as we are observing it today. Finally we try to examine which are the kinds of policy debates and policy implications at the level of cities that will allow cities to play a more dynamic and positive role in this New Economy. I won't be prescriptive – I am never prescriptive – but I will rather emphasize which are the choices and challenges that arise for cities in this new environment.

## The basis of the New Economy

The New Economy is based fundamentally on three major features. The first concerns productivity. Productivity is derived from the application of knowledge and from the practice of innovation; productivity growth is the actual source of wealth. Knowledge-based productivity means that everything that enhances knowledge determines the ability to generate greater wealth. This certainly does not solve the problem of distribution, but it is related to the creation of wealth. Knowledge leads, however, to increased productivity only as far as it promotes the productive application of knowledge, which is innovation. Innovation and knowledge are not the same thing, but they go necessarily together in the generation of productivity. You must find new ways to generate knowledge and to apply knowledge to useful things if you want to make innovations.

The New Economy is thus based upon the growth of productivity through knowledge and innovation as well as in the ability to increase our capacity of knowledge-creation, which is directly supported by new information technologies. This happens because new information technologies allow the development of what we call positive feedback between the process of knowledge and the application of knowledge. Let us, for instance, look at electricity: what electricity did was not important as long as the electrical engine was not able to process energy and to implement energy everywhere in all conditions. What information technology and particularly the Internet are doing these days is that we cannot only generate knowledge through the process of innovation but we can also make this knowledge specific and applied to any context, to any task anywhere. In other words, knowledge becomes portable and applicable and knowledge becomes specific to the task and the orientation of the problem that you have to solve at every level.

This capacity of distributing knowledge, learning from what you do with this knowledge and fitting it back into the system in a self-expanding process, is really an essential feature of the New Economy. This is so because information itself has always been the base of the economy everywhere and throughout history. But nowadays we have the technological capacity to constantly feed back knowledge and information into the processes of production, management and distribution, which gives a possibility for constant learning. People and processes learn to learn. This constant process of interaction is what the new kinds of micro-electronic-based information technologies allow. But I leave this observation simply as a footnote that I will not develop further, because for the moment I do not know enough about it. Similar kinds of things are starting to happen in the biological-based information technology, especially in genetic engineering, which is the next information technology revolution with extraordinary consequences and challenges for humankind. So the first feature of the New Economy is the ability to develop through information and communication technology knowledge-based, innovation-based productivity growth.

The second essential feature of the New Economy is connected to the fact that competitiveness operates in a global environment. That is what we call a global economy. By competitiveness I simply mean increasing market share. In other words, competition between economic actors, be it individuals or firms, regions or countries, takes place in a globally interdependent system. This global interdependent system is also new because of its new technological basis. We do not have a world economy starting in the 1990s. World economy as such is an old concept, an old historical reality, and many historians are right in showing this. But what actually is globalization is a different matter. It is the ability to have the core activities of the economy – which is not everything, but rather such things as capital markets, major multi-national corporations, key management processes, science and technology and highly skilled labor – working today as a unit in real time on a planetary scale. This is new simply because of the new technological basis. We have the telecommunications and information system and air transportation and sea transportation capability to make the system work as a unit in real time on a planetary scale. Closely interacting with this, we have also the new institutional environment for this to happen, which means liberalization and deregulation on a global scale. In that sense, governments are as responsible for globalization as for the development of information technology. Governments created globalization. The problem is that now they cannot control it. They have unleashed a process in which now they have to do something else. They can play into the global process, but they cannot control it. So, competitiveness is global, and this is actually relatively new in historical terms. Therefore it is the second major structural feature of the New Economy.

Thirdly performance in the New Economy is dependent upon a new organizational form, which is networking. Networking is the equivalent for the information age in the same sense as the large corporation, the large factory, the mass-standardized production process, the assembly-line production and distribution process were for the industrial age. Some people have called the latter Fordism, but I don't know whether the expression makes too much honor to Henry Ford. I call it Leninism, because Lenin in fact adored Henry Ford and tried to implement Fordism in the Soviet Union. But whatever you call it, it has been a system based on large-scale standardization and vertical organizations that require a strict division of labor and an extreme rationalization of each process. The key for performance in the New Economy is, on the other hand, networking. Networking is the capacity to assemble resources in a very flexible, adaptable way around projects and then to do these projects. After that you dissolve the elements of the network that have performed the project and you re-organize it in some other project. So, the project becomes the unit. This does not mean that corporations cease to exist, but corporations exist and are sustainable only as long as there are internal networks, connected to other networks, both of large corporations and small and medium-sized firms organized in networks.

The networking form of social organization, which is the most adaptable and the best performing one is nowadays eliminating the other organizational forms simply through competition. You have a large, vertical bureaucracy competing with these networks that proliferate and organize themselves throughout the world – and you know what's going to happen. It has happened, in fact, to many of these large corporations. Either they become networks or they disappear. I'm not saying that the old corporations are dying. Only those that are not able to transform themselves into networks are dying. The networks are not necessarily the instruments of freedom, you can have very oppressive networks. Networks are flexible, adaptable, much more competitive and more able to process resources and to follow signals effectively. Networks are not, however, a recent form of organization. Networks have existed throughout history. Why then is the whole economy suddenly organized around networks? Society, too, is finding the New Economy. Networks have always had great advantages and great problems. The great advantage has been their flexibility, their adaptability. Their great problem has been the difficulty to exercise coordination functions beyond a certain size and level of complexity. That's why throughout history – armies, churches, states – all big machines that have been the basis to mobilize people, to oppress or to control them, have been the winners against networks. Networks were the refuge of solidarity, interpersonal support, families, friends, survival – the private life, the survival life. The official life has been large-scale organizations and big machines, because networks have not been able to master resources. They could not develop a focus on one particular point and concentrate large-scale resources on it. They could not handle complexity.

Now technology, new information technology, allows the decentralization of execution, the variable geometry of the components of the network and, yet, an effective coordination of its tasks and control on the unity of the purpose of a particular network. So, coordination, decentralized execution and the ability to process constant change by adapting to new nodes by combining new networks has become possible because of technology. Now, I think, you could see a little bit of my empirically based conception about the role of technology. Technology is not what changes society. Society and the economy are changed by all kinds of other things like new sources of competitiveness, new values, new strategy, new objectives. But without this kind of technology all these attempts to, for instance, network would not happen. So, technology is a necessary, but not sufficient condition for the change into the New Economy and into the new society.

The New Economy is consequently based around new sources of productivity that are, on their part, based upon information technology-based knowledge and innovation, new forms of competition characterized by the global environment, by the global economy, and new forms of performance characterized by information technology-based networking and networking capabilities. But in what sense is this New Economy new? How does it work? And why is it so new? I would say that the simplest way to try to understand how it works is by focusing on three processes, which are critical in all economies. What changes for capital? What changes for labor? What changes for the source of creativity, and the source of productivity as well, which is innovation? Capital in the New Economy changes in its function and in its workings. First of all, what changes is the formation of a global financial market, which is fully integrated and fully interdependent. Even if all savings are not in this market, all savings and all capital are conditioned by what happens in this globally interdependent financial market. Again, this financial market has become global and has become interdependent on the basis of institutional changes, deregulation, liberalization and privatization and, at the same time, technological transformation. The development of computer networks, the development of telecommunications that allow the integration of this market, all this is absolutely critical in the functioning of the New Economy because, ultimately, the value of a firm, but also the value of a country as measured by the currency, depends on the judgements of this global financial market.

## The workings of the New Economy

Firms are valued at what the financial market states their value as. The value of currencies is determined by this global financial market. As for countries, it is important to remember that currently the global currency market exchanges every day 2.2 *trillion* dollars, which is substantially over the GDP of the United Kingdom. It's even more than the GDP of France. Therefore, what happens in this financial market determines everything you do regardless of how innovative you are or how good your products or ideas are. The only thing that counts, ultimately, is what this global financial market thinks of you.

But how does this global financial market operate? A critical matter, besides interdependence, is the increasing development of ECNs (Electronic Communication Networks), through which you trade directly. The whole process of disintermediation illustrated by all telephone companies these days – or mobile telephone companies – are contributing very much to this, because you are going to be able to trade your stocks on-line, to bet your savings and the savings of your children and do that everywhere in the world. Let us take as an illustration: South

Korea, one of the countries with the most advanced Internet development in terms of the use of the Internet. Thirty per cent of stock investments in South Korea are done on-line and with a large proportion coming to mobile betting, but there are 30% already on-line. So this is disintermediation. In the United States currently about 20% of investors' trading is done directly on-line, bypassing investing companies.

The technology of transaction is important first, because it lowers transaction costs considerably – by about 50%. By lowering transaction costs, technology opens up much greater possibilities to the market. Many more people go directly into the market. Second, because it broadens the possibility of financial trading directly from individual investors to the market, it extraordinarily increases the sources of complexity and reaction to the market. If you are investing directly on-line, you have all kinds of information. You have to process this information and react to it immediately. Therefore, instead of having a number of big investors that can, more or less, understand the overall situation of the market and adjust to long-term strategies [you have a] [. . .] mass of small investors betting on-line [that] is a mass of people who are playing with their lives each minute. So, the development of electronic transactions is transforming the logic of global financial markets in terms of increasing complexity and therefore increasing volatility, besides increase in size.

This is being related to an institutional technological transformation of the markets, the development of electronic stock exchanges. As you know, the current tendency is for the world to become closer and closer to what Nasdaq is. Nasdaq is an electronic market, and there is no Wall Street for Nasdaq. You may perhaps look at the Nasdaq index every morning, but nevertheless it is only an electronic entity. In other areas, like future trades, the largest networks are not American anymore. Eurex, which is a German-Swiss electronic network, is the largest futures market in the world. Chicago, which invented futures, is being eaten alive by the electronic network these days. Wall Street is actually considering going partially into electronic mode. The (at least temporarily) failed connection between the London and Frankfurt stock exchange included an agreement with Nasdaq to create a Tokyo–London–Frankfurt American Nasdaq-style of electronic exchange. We are thus moving towards an electronic exchange market place for the moment. This technology is the result of globalization of the financial markets, but at the same time, technology is not indifferent. This technology means that you have much greater possibilities to move savings from anywhere in the world to any other place at speed – electronic speed – and generate the ability, supposedly, to mobilize extraordinary masses of capital at extraordinary speeds. But in addition you have to manage this. You have to be able to make judgements on this stock market, or on this securities market in general terms, because this is where the value – not only of your companies, but also of your savings – is determined. This is a very personal problem and thus not only a technical matter. It is about your money and about the money of your children.

How, then, for instance, is the value of your Nokia stock decided? Well, as you know, this is a matter of deep debate in the economic field these days. The short version of the matter is that it is not determined by profits. It is not just about calculating the profits of a company. Yes, in the long term, as any good micro-economist will tell you, profits have to coincide with the other criteria, with investment at least in the long term. But, what is the long term? What matters today is the nanosecond in terms of the speed of the realization of capital. And in the very short term, markets do not process only profit information, they process all kinds of information. They process political stability or instability, the personal problems of Alan Greenspan or of Duisenberg in the morning, at breakfast, at home. If Alan Greenspan looks good, the markets go up and if he looks bad, the markets go down. That is not profit, that's information. Because of the Internet, financial gossip is nowadays a cottage industry. You have tens and tens of on-line companies, for example Whisper.com, that gives you the latest gossip about everything. You have securities evaluation companies, Moody's and others, which give you an evaluation on everything in short.

What actually determines the value of stocks, which determines the value of firms and consequently also the value of economies, is a process of information turbulences. Profit is one element in it, but only one. When Nokia stock collapsed in summer 2000, Nokia was doing very well. No-one doubts about the performance of the company: it has a great product, an expanding market, good technology, people at the company were managing alright. But it just happened that profits were not going to be earned exactly as well as suspected. This occurred in a context where people were getting nervous for all kinds of other reasons. And then Nokia went down. As another example we can take Intel: has it a future? The company slogan is 'Intel inside', and Intel is nowadays inside right about everything. Nevertheless, in autumn 2000 the stock of Intel took a tremendous beating. Certainly, many companies are nowadays over-valued and other companies may be under-valued. But why are companies either over-valued or under-valued and then just jump from one place to another, from one value to another? And depending on the period of time you look at, you can say that, oh – it has collapsed or has not collapsed. We have been collapsing since April 2000 in the technology stocks, but then it might happen that, for instance, the supreme court decides something and the stocks may be zooming upwards again. Anyhow, we cannot know whether some really great economic decision has been made in between. On the other hand, we can take the last 5 years – and not the last 5 months. In this period the technology stocks have, for most companies, multiplied their value by between 3 and 10. So if you take 5 years it is a story. If you take 5 months it is another. Take the next 5 months, and it may be again quite different.

So, are we in a bubble economy? No, because a bubble economy refers implicitly to the notion of a market in which there is an equilibrium line, a natural order of things that then is disturbed by irrational exuberance, as Mr Schiller would put it, but in which ultimately things go back. That is, however, the old world, whereas now we are in a New Economy. The New Economy is an economy in which valuation is decided in the global financial market through information turbulences, of which traditional economic calculation is only one of the criteria. We published this year a little book in London with Anthony Giddens, George Soros, Paul Volcker and others on the logic of global capitalism. Paul Volcker, as you know, is the former chairman of the Federal Reserve Board in the United States, and he has a little chapter there, which is the best description I have seen of global financial markets. He has, for instance, a sentence which says that well, in fact today's global financial markets don't work on objective reality. They work on the basis of perception. Or, better said, perception is reality. And we are not dealing with a post-modern anthropologist, but with Mr Paul Volcker.

Often we do not discuss these kinds of matters in meetings on municipal policies and cities. But nowadays the world is being determined by information turbulences, which has all kind of implications. That is the New Economy. Therefore we are not in a bubble economy that is going to be re-established, because if we have bubbles forming and disappearing, I don't call this a bubble economy. Rather, I would call it sparkling water. And that is one of the key dimensions of the New Economy.


## Labor in the New Economy

I will discuss the second item more shortly, because it a technically less complex. Labor has also changed extraordinarily, the most important thing being the key role of flexibility in labor markets and in employment. The constant re-allocation of resources to networks is the critical matter. Unemployment in itself is not an issue in the New Economy. Some economists fear unemployment, others don't, but it has nothing to do with the New Economy. Some New Economies actually could produce unemployment, but not all. The empirical evidence is there, and according to it no relationship exists between information technology and unemployment. We could perhaps discuss it in more detail later. Anyhow, flexibility is the key. Flexibility means, in fact, the end of stable employment in the same company, of a predictable career pattern for the rest of your life, which has been the prevailing mode of employment during the industrial age. It doesn't mean necessarily that people are going to be worse [off]. Some may be, whereas some won't. This depends on the society rather than on the labor market. The norm is flexibility. And companies will not be able to keep inflexible labor on their payroll, because others won't.

Talent, highly skilled labor becomes the key resource for productivity growth and the key resource for any company. How to produce highly skilled labor, how to attract such labor, how to keep it in a network or in the firm becomes the number one issue for any major or small company. People talk about the intelligent corporation, but the small companies need intelligence even more, because the only thing you have is your brain. This is closely connected to an increasing multiculturalism, because multiculturalism of the labor market is another major structural change of the New Economy. You cannot have a New Economy without global mobility of labor and without the ability of people to move from one place to another. Silicon Valley would not exist today as a leading technological center without immigrant labor. During the 1990s a colleague of mine, Annalee Saxenian, has produced a wonderful study on the matter. Thirty per cent of the new companies created in the Silicon Valley in the 1990s are headed either by an Indian or Chinese CEO. If we would add the Brazilians, Israelis, Russians, etc., perhaps also some West Europeans from time to time, they would be close to 40 %. This is an absolutely critical issue, because countries that will be closed to the immigration of labor in the level of menial jobs won't have anyone to do basic jobs, because of the changing demographic structure of the population. At the level of productivity such countries will not have enough labor to fulfill the highly skilled tasks in any company. One notion is to solve this with education, but if you start reforming your education system today, you get the yields in twenty years.

One essential characteristic of the New Economy is that labor is highly divided and highly segmented in terms of its ability to contribute to productivity growth. My fundamental distinction here is between skilled and non-skilled labor. This is an old, industrial society division. But now we perceive it as a division between self-programmable and generic labor. Self-programmable labor is one that has the installed cultural, educational capacity to re-program itself throughout its life. Generic labor is one that executes. It does not have any other capacity, but to understand some instructions and to execute them. Generic labor co-exists with generic jobs and with machines throughout the world. The combination between the three components changes depending upon firms' strategies and countries.

## Innovation – the fuel of the New Economy

The third key transformation in the process of the New Economy besides the transformation of capital and labor is the transformation of innovation. Innovation is the ability to create new products and processes and to think about new relationships between the economy and society. I want to emphasize three matters again mainly just in headlines. Here I have built upon the work by two outstanding Finnish researchers. You know, Finland does not produce only Linus Torvalds, Nokias and engineers. It produces also outstanding social researchers, and two of them have happened to be around in Berkeley. [Pekka Himanen's 2001 book, *The Hacker Ethic and the Spirit of the Information Age* about the open-source culture is critical.] Ilkka Tuomi has just finished a book on innovation and on the relationships between organizations, innovation and society. In my opinion it is the most important work produced on what is innovation now. From their analyses, which coincide with some of the things I know from other contexts, we could say two things. The culture of innovation is a culture of sharing information, not of hiding innovation. The open-source culture that Linus Torvalds and then Linux exemplifies is not limited to software or to Linux. It is characteristic of the new forms of productivity growth in the New Economy. This changes everything in terms of property rights, intellectual property, everything. It is a whole field – if you want, we can discuss it, but this is absolutely critical. The culture of innovation is based on open source at every level. It is about the sharing of information and about win-win strategies. You win, I shall win, and together we will win even more. Already the speed of innovation is such that if you simply base your strategy in keeping information to yourself, in 6 months it will be obsolete. Moore's law used to be 18 months, now it's 6 months. The information will be obsolete and since you have not shared it with anybody, nobody has shared anything with you, and in the end you have nothing but your old technology and your old ideas.

A second important aspect of modern cultures of innovation is organizational learning, which happens mainly through networking and internal synergy in organizations. What one needs is the ability to share within the organizations, which is connected to the notion of open organizations rather than to closed organizations.

The first element is cultural and only after it comes the organizational. Organizations must be open to the innovation process, learn from the innovation process and be ready to change themselves. In other words, you may have great technology, but if you do not have the ability to innovate in your organization, the technology collapses. This has a lot to do with cities, but I will come to this a little later.

The third aspect of the innovation process is that innovation is increasingly produced by territorial concentrations of production and innovation, which create innovation through synergy. Synergy, remember, is two plus two is five. Synergy happens in territorially concentrated areas, such as Silicon Valley, for instance. Silicon Valley is entirely based on the ability to have your ideas from other people and from other companies operating there. This has, as a matter of fact, always been the case. If you wanted to paint in the 1920s, you had to go to Paris. Now you go to Paris to see what they painted in the 1920s but, fundamentally, synergy has always been related to territorially concentrated milieus of innovation. With Peter Hall we did a world survey of these matters a few years ago, published as *Technopoles of the World*, which shows the notion of 'milieu of innovation'. The milieu of innovation is the territorial concentration of the ability to innovate in certain clusters. Concerning these clusters, again here, Annalee Saxenian has demonstrated how Silicon Valley is not a mysterious thing – it is based on networks. This cluster does not consist simply of people landing together, it is about people working together and companies networking with each other. The author demonstrated, for instance, why the area around Boston that was much more advanced than in Silicon Valley could not follow the level of technological innovation and business excellence that Silicon Valley did. Boston was based on large, vertically organized companies that did not cooperate, did not create territorial networks, whereas Silicon Valley is all based upon territorially based networks. You may be told that people want to go to Silicon Valley because it has such a nice climate. Actually they cannot see the climate, because they spend their time in traffic-jams and work 70 hours a week. They need to just because the housing costs are about five times those of in Helsinki for the same space. So, they don't go there for that. They go there because if they are not there, they don't know what's going on. And this cannot be done over the Internet. Once you know, then you can go over the Internet, but first you have to be there to know.

These kinds of territorial networks have expanded through global networks between territories. The most recent work by Annalee Saxenian, not published yet, is about the expansion of global networks on the base of what she calls entrepreneurial networks. People who graduate from Stanford create a company in Silicon Valley then, if they are Chinese, go back to China to create a company in China, come back to Silicon Valley and go around the world. That's why airlines are doing such a great business. But these global networks are not based simply on individuals or on firms. They are based on territorially concentrated complexes. This is important for city development. If you want an empirical demonstration of this we can look at the geography of the Internet. The Internet has a very definite geography. One of my students, Matthew Zook in Berkeley, is finishing his dissertation, which is the first systematic mapping of Internet content domains, Internet content providers' domains worldwide. It is a rigorous study, it works and the results are stunning. Internet that is supposed to be the spaceless, free-floating industry and activity of futurologists, is the most concentrated industry in the world. I am talking here about content provision. It's even more so if you do the analysis in terms of some other technological criteria. But just in terms of content provision we can see first, that it's concentrated in countries. Certainly in the United States, but the United States is losing its relative share vis-à-vis other countries. The United States still has over 50% of total Internet domains, but it's declining. The share used to be 80% two years ago (Zook 1998).

In a few countries in the world and within countries content production is mainly concentrated in major metropolitan areas. In terms of the world, the hierarchy is: first New York, second Los Angeles, third San Francisco Bay Area, fourth London in terms of the actual proportion of Internet domains. But, in every country it's the same: Internet content providers are concentrated in a few areas and particularly in the largest metropolitan areas. Even more interesting, within each city – Matthew Zook's mapping has gone down to the intra-city level – it's concentrated in certain neighborhoods. Like in a staggering proportion in the Bay Area, it's concentrated in one small area in San Francisco, which is called the South of Market area and in New York it's all in Manhattan, certainly, but within Manhattan there are three main points of concentration, mainly at what is called Silicon Alley, which is what is called south of Houston in New York. Anyway, it is about the concentration of concentration of concentration of the Internet, which theoretically you could do from a mountain-top just as well! But you just don't do it for two reasons. First of all, the Internet processes information, and the major centers of production of information are the major metropolitan centers. Therefore, they are also the major centers of Internet users and content producers. Internet industry, more than anything else, works on synergy. On people knowing someone else, knowing what's going on, being there as an artistic, creative milieu. And this happens in neighborhoods.

## The challenges of the New Economy for cities

Now I think that we have talked enough about the New Economy. Let's move into cities. But, before doing that let us state quickly that this economy has extraordinary challenges at the social level. [. . .] Fundamentally, I see four major challenges: one is the individualization and fragmentation of society. Networks are great, but they are usually networks of individuals. The social fabric of society is being transformed into networks, which is good for the individuals who feel great, but it's not so good for those who cannot afford being individuals. They are too weak for that in whatever you decide the concept of weakness is.

Second, there is an increasing divide between people with vastly different cultural and educational resources. The digital divide is not important in terms of access. With probable universal access of Internet in developed countries within five years that is not any longer the issue. The issue is what you do with your cultural and educational resources once you are connected. If you know what to do with the Internet you are great. If you don't, you are much worse than before the Internet because other people know. So, the digital divide is a cultural and educational divide.

The third major challenge is multiculturalism. The New Economy is based on the notion of multiculturalism. Some societies can manage, while others have great difficulty and will have to live with it. Fourth is the notion of what I call the territorial divide between places that are connected throughout the world in dynamic networks. The space of flows is a world consisting of space that is connected through these flows of networks. But there are also places, which are disconnected from these global networks. This tendency is, in fact, also facilitated by the new technological infrastructures.

There is another wonderful book about to be published by Steve Graham and Simon Marvin from Newcastle University called 'Splinter Urbanism' in which they empirically show how the telecommunications and Internet and transportation infrastructure are being set up around the world in a way which is splintering not only the world, but also cities. This doesn't happen simply in terms of having or not having the Internet, but rather in terms of who has broadband and who hasn't. The current technological infrastructure is creating new electronic spaces, which leave aside territorial spaces in conditions of isolation and ultimate marginality in the Information Age. So, these are very big challenges.

## How can cities face these challenges?

How do cities deal with both the opportunities and the challenges? First of all, let me remind you that in this age of telecommunications in which locality was supposed to disappear through communication over the Internet we are about to become, for the first time, 50% urban on the planet. The projection for twenty-five years is that over two-thirds of the population will be concentrated in cities and metropolitan areas, and most likely with the current trends, by the end of the century we will be overwhelmingly urban. Urban, but in addition metropolitan, which means that an increasing proportion of this urban population is in large, vast metropolitan areas formed by connections between metropolitan areas. There are gigantic cities throughout the world. Some people don't realize it, because they still consider that London and Paris are different. Yes, they are different, but they are two hours away by train from center to center. So, the Brits still think that they are isolated by the Channel, but they are not. They are going to be swallowed by this uncontrollable Europe. In other words, seriously speaking, what we do have is an urban world. At the time where we could theoretically decentralize, we are in fact spatially concentrating.

You don't have to be very sophisticated in order to understand why this is so. It is enough to just read the available studies on the matter. It is always the same: people move to cities not because they love it, but because that's where the best jobs are and the opportunities for everything are, particularly education for their children. And if they don't have children? Well, to find someone to take the preliminary step. As well as the opportunities and the services in every aspect, from cultural amenities to education to technology to everything. Metropolitan areas are the magnets of our world. Why do these opportunities arise in cities? Well, remember the conclusions of perhaps the most important urban book in the last ten years, Peter Hall's book, *Cities in Civilization*, his magnum opus, which analyzes the evolution of urban civilization and particularly the relationship between creativity, innovation, productivity and urban culture. It is clear that cities have throughout history been the seedbeds of innovation in cultural, economic and technological terms in every possible aspect and ultimately, the seedbeds of information. So, it's not so surprising that in the Information Age, an age based on information, knowledge, processing of symbols, generation of ideas, etc., cities are the centers of this New Economy and of this new cultural capacity. But cities are, at the same time, different today because they are based on a new spatial architecture. They are based on global networks of cities connecting to each other. Innovation does not happen, let's say in financial terms, in Wall Street or Tokyo, but *between* Wall Street, Tokyo, London and so on. In other words, you have the concentration of cultural innovation in cities and major metropolitan areas. At the same time you have the connection through electronic and transportation networks between these nodes, which form a global architecture of networked cities. This is our urban world, which is not a world of competing cities, but a world of cooperating cities.

In this particular world how could cities both foster the role in innovation and how can they help to cope with the challenges that I mentioned? In terms of innovation a number of studies show that innovation depends, fundamentally, on people being innovative; that is, being culturally sophisticated, well educated, and entrepreneurial. It looks like these people are increasingly attracted to vibrant, urban cultures. A book [. . .] published [. . .] in the United States by Joel Kotkin, called *The New Geography*, which relates the new trends in the United States, the new professional managerial class, the creators of new ideas and new wealth, states that the first thing people decide when they want to find a job is what is the nicest city in terms of having fun there. People are very weird, so the notion of where to have fun may vary. I would think, normally, that everybody would like to go to Barcelona, but some people don't, so, in that sense, I would say the development of cities as cultural centers is the best information technology strategy for a city. Technoparks are finished. They are alright for megalomania like in Malaysia, but technoparks, at this point, can be good, useful industrial areas, but are not the elements that create value in a city. This is the 1980s strategy, not the current strategy. The current strategy is to have good educational facilities, good nightclubs, good ideas, good places to live, and then attract young entrepreneurs who actually will be the creators of wealth and opportunity.

Cities are also being key in the development of technological markets and in innovative uses of new technologies. The public services' use of new technology is the new frontier of the New Economy. Until now the New Economy has been technology-driven. But there is only so much you can do with the current technology, even with a mobile phone. The young people have invented every possible thing, and I mean every possible thing to do with a mobile phone, but there is a limit. So, on the other hand social services, educational services, health services – all kinds of basic items – are still very much underdeveloped in terms of new technologies, in spite of good experiences with experiments here and there. This is something that city governments and city-based public institutions could develop (and in many cases are developing) and this in fact is very good feedback in terms of new innovation and business policy. You create a market because public services pay for it and then you have companies, which go into this market niche and on the basis of this they can export to other urban markets. So, this is something that is really happening.

Now, in terms of the social challenges, we are fundamentally inducing, for the moment, a society of non-sharing in terms of material wealth and a shared cultural meaning. A society of individualism is a society which is extraordinarily dynamic, but at the same time a society of potential isolation in terms of the cultural meaning that could be shared by society. The restoration of meaning has a very important material dimension in which cities both in terms of the actual activities in the city, the shared activities in the city, from local celebrations to cultural activities to physical activities, the restoration of monumentality, the restoration of meaning and the ability to share symbols in the city have a key element in building local identity and sharing in increasingly multicultural societies. Also the reconstruction of political legitimacy through citizen participation including community computer networks is an experience that has been developed in a number of cities around the world, and we badly need this reconstruction of political legitimacy because, remember, we are in a major crisis.

Kofi Annan recently commissioned a global survey of people's opinions vis-à-vis their governments, and according to the results of this survey two-thirds of the people in the world think they are not governed by the will of the people. I know through my UN contacts that the only ones that fare relatively well are the Scandinavian democracies, but the United States does not fare well at all. So, in other words, there is a major problem with political legitimacy. It looks like local governments are better placed than national governments for the rebuilding of this legitimacy and ultimately of the trust between people and their governments. So, in conclusion, we are in a creative world, in an extraordinarily productive world, but at the same time we have major problems and potential dangers of social exclusion, personal isolation and loss of shared meaning. Public policy is essential, more than ever, to rebuild meaning and legitimacy, but because of the crisis of legitimacy and because of the complexity of managing a global problem from the global level, local society and local institutions could be key elements and key instruments in the rebuilding of both meaning and legitimacy. Not as isolated entities, but as networks of local governments. The experiences in Europe in particular of building networks of cities, the experiences throughout the world of building networks of cities could be the development of a networked institutional system, which could actually re-establish the relationship between a networked economy and the network society through networks of local institutions. In the network society, cities are at the same time the source of value and the source of meaning, but they will only be sustainable if people value this value and share the meaning.

# References

Castells, M., Hall, P. (1994) *Technopoles of the World: The Makings of 21st Century Industrial Complexes.* Routledge.
Graham, S. and Marvin, S. (forthcoming) *Splintering Urbanism.* Routledge.
Hall, P. (2001) *Cities in Civilization.* Fromm International.

Himanen, P. (2001) *The Hacker Ethic and the Spirit of the Information Age*. London: Vintage.

Hutton, W. and Giddens, A. (eds) (2000) *On the Edge: Living with Global Capitalism*. Blackwell.

Kotkin, J. (2000) *The New Geography How the Digital Revolution Is Reshaping the American Landscape*. Random House.

Saxenian, A. (1996) *Regional Advantage Culture and Competition in Silicon Valley and Route 128*. Harvard University Press.

Saxenian, A. (1999) *Silicon Valley's New Immigrant Entrepreneurs*. Public Policy Institute of California.

Tuomi, I. (2002) *Networks of Innovation: Change and Meaning in the Age of the Internet*. Oxford University Press.

Zook, M. A. (1998) 'The Web of Consumption: The Spatial Organization of the Internet Industry in the United States'. Paper presented at the Association of Collegiate Schools of Planning 1998 Conference, Pasadena, CA, November 5–8.

# Chapter 12

# Nicholas Garnham

## INFORMATION SOCIETY THEORY AS IDEOLOGY

From *Loisir et Société,* 21 (1) (1998): 97–120.

[. . .]

CONFRONTATION WITH THE THEORY of the Information Society, both as science and ideology, is now unavoidable. Here is a theory of communication massively presenting itself as both a way of understanding the present historical moment and the dominant development trends in society and at the same time as the favoured legitimating ideology for the dominant economic and political powerholders.

The term Information Society is now used in the policy arena – for instance in European Commission documents (for example European Council 1994) – more as a mantra to justify whatever policy is proposed than as a substantive analysis. However lying behind the term is a real theoretical construct. For the purpose of both exposition and critique I will focus on the version of this theory laid out by Manuel Castells in his recent magnum opus *The Rise of Network Society* (Castells 1996) and *The Power of Identity* (Castells 1997). I do this because Castells' is the most sophisticated version available and it is always most productive to critique a theory in its strongest version. Tilting at straw men may occasionally be fun but it is not ultimately very productive. Based upon a wide range of research and empirical evidence from around the world it far outdistances the juvenile aperçu of the Negropontes (Negroponte 1996) and Tofflers (Toffler 1980) of this world. Furthermore Castells firmly situates his theoretical project within the Enlightenment tradition of critical emancipatory social science.

## Communication theory and emancipatory social science

Since we all have limited endowments of time and energy the exercise of human curiosity alone is, in my view, insufficient to justify the choice of a field of study or the questions to be pursued within it. We cannot justify the effort of communication theory merely in terms of the pervasiveness, even less the modishness, of some of the epiphenomena we study – such as television or the Internet. The study of communication [. . .] has to be seen as part of the Enlightenment project of the human sciences – to understand our social world in order – in so far as possible – to free humans from oppression, by nature or their fellow human beings, experienced as fate.

This project has insistently raised and attempted to answer a number of key questions. The most important of these is the question of social order. What is it that enables social formations characterized by increasing complexity and specialization of social functions – especially the division of labour – and spatial extension to be co-ordinated to the extent that we can talk about a society or a culture at all? The second key question is the obverse of that of order, namely that of social reproduction, development or change; the attempt to specify the conditions and the forces that lead either to the reproduction of such social forms or to their replacement by new social forms. The third key question is what, within this process of social co-ordination and reproduction, is the relationship between structure and agency and, as a related question, how does agency work? Given that we are culture creating animals – that we inescapably endow our actions with meaning – what weight are we to place respectively on coercion, the rational calculation of self interest or on legitimizing cultural norms in our explanation of social co-ordination and reproduction?

It is clear that human social development has been, from a very early stage, in part dependent upon the development of technologies and institutions of social communication which break out spatially and temporally from face-to-face interpersonal communication based upon speech and gesture. How we choose to explain that relationship between communication and other social structures and practices is precisely a key matter for theoretical dispute. But we do not necessarily need to follow those theorists who make communications the primary explanatory variable [. . .] to draw three important lessons for current theory. First that social communication becomes dependent upon the mobilization of and access to scarce resources – including human capital resources. For instance all humans are equally endowed with the capacity for speech, but literacy requires training and thus has been historically, and is still, differentially distributed. This leads inexorably to the need to understand how a given mode of production structures control over these resources and with what effect on what is communicated by whom to whom and for what purpose. Second all social communication depends upon and is shaped by technology from iconic representation and above all the invention of writing onwards. We thus need to see the development of these technologies within the wider history and sociology of technology – its genesis, deployment and use. Again this is a crucial element in the assessment of the validity of Information Society theory. Third that the development of systems of mediated social communication was accompanied by – it can be argued produced – a class of communication specialists. Most social theories in effect have embedded within them – and Information Society theory is no exception – a theory of the role of these specialists, whether identified as priests, intellectuals or knowledge workers. Certainly no theory of social communication can by-pass analysis of the formation and social function of this group.

## Castells' Information Society: the argument in outline

How then does Information Society theory address these issues? What kind of explanation for social structure and dynamics is being offered?

Although Castells attempts to retain a notion of human agency and is careful to point to the importance and possibility of differing national policy responses and to the growing importance of social movements and local forms of cultural resistance, in the end the Information Society, as he presents it, is technologically determined. The source of the dynamic of social change and what are seen as epochal and global transformations in the structure of the economy, in social stratification, politics and culture is a technological paradigm based upon a cluster of innovation in information and communication technology largely stemming from Silicon Valley in the 1970s. Drawing on Innis, McLuhan and Bell, while acknowledging the influence of Schumpeter and Weber, the argument is that a small group of innovators responded to capitalism's crisis of profitability by introducing a set of new technologies that massively raised productivity. This then had three major impacts on the economy: a) It led to the creation of the so-called network firm as a response to increased levels of competition induced by accelerated innovation and thus product cycles (through a process of what he calls 'knowledge working upon knowledge'); b) An increased level of globalization – particularly for finance capital – made possible by the ability to operate globally in real-time computerized telecommunication networks; and c) A new division of labour polarized between knowledge workers who have the skills and adaptability to operate in networks (what he calls the interactors) and the increasingly fragmented, insecure industrial and service workers who are fixed in location and at the margins of the networks and at the mercy of network flexibility (what he calls the interacted).

These developments in turn work their effects, as we shall, in culture and politics with the end of class struggle and the national politics based upon it, the rise of social movements and the creation of a 'culture of real virtuality'.

While I would not wish to deny the reality of some of these developments in economic structure, the labour market, politics and culture to which Castells points, there are serious problems with the theoretical explanation of them which has, as always, implications for political action.

In analysing Castells' theory of the network society we need to pose three questions.

a)   What kind of explanation is being offered of social restructuring?
b)   Does the evidence support such explanations or, alternatively, can we draw different analytical conclusions from the same evidence?
c)   Whether the processes identified are sufficiently novel to justify the claim that we are entering a new era of informational capitalism, the network society and the information age?

## A new mode of production

The general structure of Castells' argument is clear. It derives from the classic tradition of political economy and deploys both an expressive totality and base/superstructure model to explain the relationship between changes in the mode of production and changes in society at large, particularly culture and politics. Castells claims that we are entering a new information age characterized by a new mode of production, informational capitalism, and a new global social structure, the network society. This transformation is driven, or determined, at the base by a change in the mode of production from industrial to informational capitalism which, in its turn, is technologically determined by developments in information and communication technology, which exercises its effect primarily by raising productivity. That this process is technologically determined is made clear when Castells defines Informational as 'a specific form of social organisation in which information generation, processing and transmission become the fundamental sources of production and power because of new technological conditions emerging in this historical period' (Castells 1996, p. 21, f. 33). This process of dynamic change produces changes in the organization of production and the structure of the market on a global scale, creating the network enterprise and the network society within which domination is exercised via information flows through global communication networks.

There are then two alternative, although not necessarily incompatible, explanations of the effect of these developments on the superstructure of culture and politics. On the one hand informational capitalism restructures the labour process and the labour market, and by so doing restructures class relations. At the same time it is spatially rearranging global power relations, in what Castells calls a space of flows, such that the power of territorially based and politically accountable entities, especially nation states, are undermined. On the other hand the development of information and communications technologies in the form of the multimedia potential of the Information Superhighway have a direct impact on culture and thus on our understanding of the world and thus on politics by creating a 'culture of real virtuality'.

Huge epochal and totalizing claims are being made here and a technologically determinist theory of communication has become THE theory of society with a vengeance. Not only is it technologically determinist but it is also structuralist. For all Castells' attempts to keep the flame of political hope and action alive and his attachment to social movement theory, in the end it is the logic of the structure that determines because the network constitutes a new social morphology and 'the network society [is] characterized by the preeminence of social morphology over social action'.

## Castells' argument in detail

Let me now turn to look in more detail at the structure of Castells' argument and the evidence adduced to support it.

Following Daniel Bell, Castells argues that societies are characterized by what he calls modes of production (what would more usually he called relations of production), which determine the distribution of the surplus, and by modes of development (what would more normally be called forces of production), which determine the level and quality of the surplus. The primum mobile of the system is productivity the level of which is technologically determined.

[. . .]

Thus the shift from industrial to informational capitalism is driven and explained by the new sources of productivity growth, 'the technology of knowledge generation, information processing and symbol communication'. There are a number of problems with the way Castells conceptualizes the informational mode of development and its relation to the mode of production which produces a serious fault line at the very heart of his theoretical argument.

## Productivity

The first, and this is common to the whole post-industrial, Information Society tradition stemming from Bell, relates to the concept of surplus which in turn affects the meaning of the concept productivity. The issue is first whether we define surplus in technical terms as a relation between inputs and outputs within the production process or in social terms as a relation between consumption and investment. And second, what numerator we use to measure differences and thus the level of productivity. This is a problem that the rather outmoded concept of the labour theory of value and the related concept of surplus value was designed to address. This is particularly important because, as Castells and others who think like him are forced to admit (Castells 1996, p. 74), the available statistics on productivity do not support the revolutionary claims being made for the impact of information and communication technology (Madrick 1998 and Sichel 1998). As productivity is currently measured, in input/output terms, the productivity of the system is independent of distributional relations – that is to say labour has to be seen as homogeneous and measurable, however crudely, in terms of hours worked aggregated over the economy as a whole. If one thinks of an economy as a producer of human material welfare in conditions of material scarcity and in the context of the non-expandable real biological time of human producers and consumers, then measuring productivity in terms of human time inputs makes crude sense, since what is at issue is what level of goods and services, including non-work time, we can consume during a given real life time. For both individuals and society as a whole, hours worked (accepting the problem of measuring non-paid work hours) compared with levels of consumption, whether measured in monetary terms or in terms of a consumption bundle, remains the best available measure of our standard of living and the extent of our freedom from the realm of necessity. The problem here for the information society thesis is that the model is essentially thermodynamic. The labour theory of value works as a model for the process so long as labour time is largely a matter of energy expended and consumption largely a matter of energy reconstituted or saved. This model has worked because historically the major rises in productivity have come directly or indirectly through the technological harnessing and application of energy, and rises in welfare have been rises in energy consumed and a decline in hours worked. The problem with the productivity as driver model is the question of whether this can meaningfully he applied to nonmaterial production, to a non-entropic economy of bits as opposed to an entropic economy of atoms. This may indeed be why we cannot measure the claimed productivity growth derived from the information and communication technology revolution, but then the proposed technologically determined explanation doesn't work either.

If we look, on the other hand, at surplus as a relation between consumption and investment, then it is determined historically not by the forces but by the relations of production. This failure to adequately conceptualize the relations of production flows through as we shall see into a failure, crucially damaging to the structure of the theory, to understand the relation between technology, the labour process and labour market restructuring, the relation between technological innovation and competition and the relation between production and circulation, in particular finance capital.

## The impact of ICTs

In fact hidden within Castells's definition of the new informational mode of development lie three quite different explanations for its impact, each of which will have different consequences for social structure and process.

a) The impact of ICTs directly, as both product and process innovation, on material production. If there are productivity improvements there should be no problem of capturing them in existing measures and they do not show up.

b) The impact on productivity through the impact on the organization of production. Here the network enterprise is seen as the driver of productivity growth. The problems here are threefold. First the need to separate out organizational structures and costs, which are overheads and may indeed lower productivity, from those which do raise productivity. The second is to distinguish the contribution of productivity enhancing organizational change which depends upon ICTs from that which doesn't. A major problem for Castells' argument, as he himself admits, is that two of the most successful world economies in terms of productivity growth, Japan and Germany, have a relatively low level of ICT uptake in production.

c) The impact of the informational mode of development lies in 'knowledge working upon knowledge', what Bell called theoretical knowledge which he placed at the heart of his explanatory framework (Bell 1973).

## The role of theoretical knowledge

This important confusion then works its way into the next stage of the argument. The confusion surrounds, first, the definition of the informational mode and the nature of the determinations at work. There is here, as in Bell and other Information Society theorists, an ambivalent shifting between explanation in terms of information and communication technology and its impact on the organization and output of material production on the one hand, and an explanation in terms of the information, where the key source of increased productivity and added value (these are often confused) is what is described as 'knowledge working on knowledge'. Here an important distinction needs to be made between:

a)   Knowledge production processes that raise productivity by feeding into the material production process – developments in computer aided design or robotics for instance;
b)   Knowledge production processes which improve the quality of the product or service. These will have a differential impact on productivity and welfare in products and service – for instance innovation in medical science may raise either some or all people's welfare by improving the quality of the medical services they receive without raising the productivity of health workers;
c)   Knowledge production as a source of competitive advantage via product or service innovation.

While knowledge working on knowledge, or theoretical or specialized knowledge as it is sometimes called, has clearly contributed over a long historical period to increasing productivity, it is not clear either that the trend has been raised by the development of ICTs or that the productivity of knowledge production itself has been increased.

In fact Castells, and others who argue like him within a Schumpeterian paradigm, place great stress on innovation. Indeed one of the major political arguments he draws from his analysis is that the major remaining role for the nation state is the creation of innovation clusters in order to enhance national competitiveness. In so doing, he fails to distinguish the role of innovation within inter-firm competition and its role in enhancing system-wide productivity. Here we come to a major problem with the technological determinism of the system.

## Informationalism

Castells writes that

> [e]ach mode of development has also a structurally determined performance principle around which technological processes are organised: industrialism is oriented towards maximising output; informationalism is oriented towards technological development, that is towards the accumulation of knowledge and towards higher levels of complexity in information processing. While higher levels of knowledge may result in higher levels of output per unit of input, it is the pursuit of knowledge and information that characterises the technological production function under informationalism.
>
> (Castells 1996, pp. 17–18)

This is a tautology which not only doesn't explain anything, it in fact abandons the previous explanation in terms of productivity growth. It stems from a misunderstanding of the so-called performance principle of capitalism, which in its turn stems from the original mischaracterization of the relation between forces and relations of production. Capitalism's performance principle is NOT maximization of output – this may or may not be the end result. It has been a system oriented to and producing economic growth because its performance principle is accumulation through competition. It is competition that drives innovation and productivity growth across the economy as a whole. Indeed for both Schumpeter and Hayek, the case for capitalist competitive markets rests upon their efficiency as search mechanisms and creators of innovation rather than upon their efficiency creating characteristics in the sense of minimizing the ratio of inputs to outputs. But at the level of the firm, innovation may not raise productivity at all. Its profits may derive from capturing market share and the rent that derives from a temporary monopoly of unique product or service characteristics. Castells claims without producing any evidence that the network economy has become more competitive on a global scale and that the mobilization of the informational paradigm has both caused and is a response to this growth in competitiveness. While the increased openness of national markets will induce a temporary rise in the level of competition, the resulting competition for global market share is likely to create oligopoly at a higher level, i.e. the system as a whole does not become more competitive. The problem is that there is much evidence of increased concentration, and an accompanying rise in levels of corporate profitability, which does not usually mean an increase in competitiveness. This increasing concentration is in part attributable, not to increased competitiveness, but to the increasing returns to scale and resulting rent capture in high tech innovation. Thus developments in organizational and market structure may have more to do with innovation as a barrier to market entry in technology markets than they have to do with raising productivity.

But this misunderstanding of the role of competition as a driver of the capitalist accumulation process also undermines Castells' explanation of the structure of the new network society and the labour market restructuring that accompanies it. At issue here is not only the nature but also the novelty of these processes since a claim is being advanced, as we should remember, that we are entering a new age.

## The role of networks

As I have explained, the concept of the network lies at the heart of Castells' theory. The argument is that it is the growth in the speed, reach and functionality of communication networks that is driving economic and social development. This leads to:

a)   Organizational change – the rise to dominance of the network enterprise.
b)   Changes in market structure – globalization and the dominance of finance capital.
c)   Changes in the nature of labour and the structure of labour market on a global scale.
d)   Resulting changes in the nature of class power and class conflict.
e)   A changing role for the nation state and other geographically situated centres of political power.

The concept of the network is used to mobilize three quite different arguments. The first, in some ways the most important for Castells, and at the same time the weakest, relates to globalization and finance capital. But all of them exaggerate the novelty of networks as forms of social and economic organization within which power is exercised, and thus at the same time exaggerate both the extent and the novelty of the impact of ICTs.

'The network society is, for the time being, a capitalist society. . . . But this kind of capitalism is profoundly different from its historical predecessors. It has two fundamental distinctive features: it is global and it is structured to a large extent around a network of financial flows' (Castells 1996, p. 471). Leaving aside what is meant by 'for the time being', we need to ask what is meant by this and is it novel enough to be described as a new form of capitalism?

Castells argues that the capitalist mode of production and the informational mode of development are articulated by finance capital's need for the knowledge and information generated and enhanced by information technology. Note that we are a long way here from productivity in the process of labour working on matter as the primum mobile. Now there is no question that a major driver of the global development of information and communication networks has been finance capital. Nor can it sensibly be argued that the rise of a global financial market based upon high-speed communication networks should raise productivity by accelerating the turnover time of capital. Nor is it in question that these developments have both increased the instability of the financial system and caused problems for the exercise of economic power by nation states and other politically accountable instances of power. The question is the extent of its novelty and the wider determining power Castells attributes to it.

Let us start with the concept of networks. The capitalist mode of production and its organizational forms have been underpinned by communication networks of remarkable extension and speed since at least Rowland Hill's hub and spoke reorganization of the British postal service in the early 19th century. The system of monetary market exchange is itself such a network, in Castells' terms, a space of information flows. In neglecting this, Castells is forced to argue that the capitalist class no longer exists because the network has created 'a faceless collective capitalist made up of financial flows operated by electronic networks'. But wasn't this precisely Marx's concept of the nature of capital? Castells' failure to understand the long term nature of the capitalist market system is underlined when he argues that this faceless collective capitalist 'is not simply the expression of the abstract logic of the market, because it does not truly follow the law of supply and demand: it responds to the turbulence and unpredictable movements of non calculable anticipation induced by psychology and society as much as by economic processes'. But have any serious analysts of the political economy of capitalism ever seen markets simply following the laws of supply and demand? Ever since finance capital broke free of industrial and mercantile capital through a long historical process of the creation of faceless collective capital through a banking and credit system, joint stock companies, stock, futures and insurance markets, capital flows have been subject to speculative turbulence and rent taking on the part of financial intermediaries. Keynes, among others, wrote of the impact of social psychology on this process. More damagingly Castells seems to think that capital can induce production (whatever exactly that means) and that value can be created within the autonomous flows of capital on a global network without passing through a process of real production and consumption.

'Capital accumulation proceeds, and its value making is generated, increasingly, in the global financial markets enacted by information networks in the timeless space of financial flows' (Castells 1996, p. 472).

But of course capital has to invest if value is to be appropriated. In words of Saskia Sassens (Sassens 1991) global capitalism has always to come down to earth.

Castells turns the relation between finance capital and the rest of the economy on its head: 'What is sometimes called the "real economy" and what I would be tempted to call the "unreal economy" since in the age of network capitalism the fundamental reality where money is made and lost, invested and saved, is in the financial sphere.' Even a swift glance at the list of the world's richest men would soon disabuse him of this fact.

This failure to see that markets have always been networks also leads him to overestimate, in my view, the significance of the network enterprise and the role of circulation in relation to production.

## The network enterprise

But the concept of the network enterprise represents an important step in Castells' causal chain of determination between technology and culture.

'It is the convergence and interaction between a new technological paradigm and a new organizational logic that constitutes the historical foundation of the information economy' (Castells 1996, p. 152).

The thrust of the argument is a familiar post-Fordist one – the move from mass production to flexible production and an accompanying shift from 'vertical bureaucracies to the horizontal corporation' (p. 164). This new organizational form is structured around networks and appears to involve the dissolution of the firm or corporate unit as we have known it in favour of a constantly 'varying geometry' of horizontal relationships and alliances which go beyond and escape the managerial control of the firm. However it is at this point that the argument becomes most problematic. Here we need to distinguish between the organization of the firm as a set of property relations and control over income flows, a set of principle/agent relations directed at accumulation through profit on the one hand, and the organization of a specific production or labour process on the other. The relationship between the two has always been variable, both as between firms and sectors and historically. But its dialectic is contained, and has to be so contained for a capitalist mode of production to continue, within the bounds of property relations. Thus whatever the flexibility of the network enterprise, the flexibility and porosity of organizational boundaries must always be limited. Once again it is not the technical but the social relations of production that are determinant. That is to say the informational mode of development is developed for and put at the service of a set of property relations and the goal of accumulation, not vice versa. Indeed this is why networks have always presented a problem within a competitive market-based economic system as we can see now with Internet. Networks are essentially collaborative rather than competitive systems. They operate as a shared resource rather than a system of resource exchange. Because of network externalities they operate optimally as a monopoly, i.e. everyone is connected, and without internal barriers to the interactive flows within them. Markets on the other hand need barriers because it is only at barriers, where exchange can be stopped or diverted, that prices can he charged and a share of value captured. As the future development of the Internet will undoubtedly demonstrate, using a network for the mutual exchange of information with seamless interconnection of all with all is inherently incompatible with using the network as a technical infrastructure for competitive market relations.

The same dilemma is illustrated by intellectual property. Studies show that knowledge production is highest with free exchange. The problem is that in a society where the incentive structure is based upon extracting differential rents or profits on a market, it is necessary to create artificial intellectual property rights and thus barriers to the free exchange of knowledge. Thus Castells' dismissal of the classic theories of the modern corporation, whether Chandler's economies of scale and scope model (Chandler 1977) or Williamson's transaction costs model (Williamson 1975), are misplaced. It is true that new technologies of production and organizational co-ordination will (have?) change the trade-offs involved in maximizing economies of scale and scope and minimizing transaction costs. This may indeed affect the optimum size of the firm, the benefits to be derived from horizontal or vertical integration, the desirability of outsourcing, etc. However, Castells' own statistics show an increase in multinational corporate concentration on a global scale which, for property ownership reasons outlined above, must be vertical hierarchies, even if the production and circulation processes they control and from which they derive the necessary profits are more horizontal, i.e. the pyramid of power and control is flatter.

## The end of class struggle

This thesis of the rise of the network enterprise is then used as one of the bases for the argument of the end of class struggle between capital and labour. As we have seen, the first argument is that global financial networks have created 'a faceless collective capital' and thus there are no longer any capitalists. The problem with this argument is that it neglects the problem of human agency. Even if we accept a structural argument concerning the determining effect of the logic of capital, we are left with the problem of how this is operationalized in the actions of individual human agents. Class theory, in both its Marxist and Weberian forms, proposes a theory of interests as the motivating relay between structure and agency. It is assumed that there is struggle over scarce resources even if, in the Weberian version, this is not just confined to material resources, but includes the social and cultural resources covered by the term status. Thus the logic of capital only works its invisible magic as a social logic so long as individual capitalists, or the institutional agents of capital, are driven to accumulate through the search for profit on competitive markets. Similarly the Schumpeterian model of 'creative destruction', that in part underlies Castells' vision, depends upon the figure of the entrepreneur as its deus in machina, and we are left with the problem of what drives the entrepreneur.

Because Castells, in common with many Information Society theorists, is forced to dispense with competitive property relations as the main driver, since it is technological change that is the explanatory variable, he is also forced to descend into mysticism to explain the power and actions of his new ruling class – the networkers. They are the carriers of a 'spirit of informationalism'. [. . .]

[. . .]

[. . .] It is not clear that new forms of economic organization need – there is certainly no evidence that they now have – a new form of ethical justification. But Castells argues that the network is underpinned by the 'spirit of informationalism' which is 'the culture of "creative destruction" accelerated to the speed of optoelectronic circuits that process its signals. Schumpeter meets Weber in the cyberspace of the cultural enterprise' (Castells 1996, p. 199). Descent into this kind of hyperbolic language, a form of rhetorical bullying, is a sure sign that the writer is on shaky theoretical and empirical ground. In describing the nature of this culture, the link between Information Society theory and postmodernism becomes clear. 'It is a culture, indeed, but a culture of the ephemeral, a culture of each strategic decision, a patchwork of experience and interests rather than a charter of rights and obligations. It is a multi-faceted, virtual culture' (p. 199). As we shall see, this spirit of informationalism then acts as an important determinant at the cultural level. But, perhaps most interesting of all, by drawing upon Weber, Castells is in fact proposing a different explanatory model of social development. When he argues that Weber's work 'still remains the methodological cornerstone of any theoretical attempt at grasping the essence of cultural/institutional transformations that in history usher in a new paradigm of economic organisation', now it is cultural/institutional transformation – the spirit of informationalism – that is the driver rather than technological change or productivity.

## Labour

Leaving that question to one side Castells moves from Network to Labour as the next step in the explanatory chain.

> The technological and managerial transformation of labour, and of production relationships, in and around the emerging network enterprise is the *main lever* by which the informational paradigm and the process of globalisation affect society at large.
>
> (p. 201)

> Down in the deep of the nascent social structure a more fundamental process has been triggered by informational work, the desegregation of labour, ushering in the network society.
>
> (p. 279)

This is a classic argument from Marxist political economy and none the worse for that. The question we need to ask, however, is whether the picture of the restructuring of labour relations is realistic, and if so, is it a new phenomenon and are the conclusions drawn in terms of the changing nature of global power relations justified?

In the description of labour restructuring are embedded two different arguments. First that there is a new global division of labour that decisively shifts power away from labour. Where it shifts power to – whether to capital or to the network – is precisely a matter of dispute. But labour loses power because it is individualized and desegregated.

[. . .]

## The networker

At the same time the labour market is dualized and characterized at the top by the rise, familiar from Information Society theory generally, of what are variously described as networkers, interactors, deciders, what are often called knowledge workers or symbolic analysts. Castells is ambivalent as to whether these developments express an inescapable structural logic and whether this logic is or is not capitalist.

> Notwithstanding the formidable obstacles of authoritarian management and exploitative capitalism, information technologies call for greater freedom for better informed workers to deliver the full promise of its productive potential. The networker is the necessary agent of the network enterprise made possible by new information technologies.
>
> (p. 223)

Here the networker is seen as a technologically determined social role, but at the same time the potential hero of a new, freer and more flexible social order, which would or will supersede capitalism. This is a familiar argument from Bell and chimes well with the argument that a de-massified culture is the superstructural effect of the creation of this new type of worker. Perhaps most interesting it is a reworking of Marx's argument for the proletariat as the vanguard of history, but born this time round from technology and the network, not the contradictions of the relations of production.

On the other hand he argues that these trends do not stem from 'the structural logic of the informational paradigm, but are the result of the current restructuring of capital–labour relations, helped by the powerful tools provided by new information technologies and facilitated by a new organisational form, the network enterprise' (p. 273). Precisely, but this is not an argument for a new era but for a continuation of a long struggle between capital and labour within the labour process, of the separation of mental and manual labour, and of what Beninger has called The Control Revolution (Beniger 1986). That global capitalist organization and the resulting international division of labour poses problems for the organizational co-ordination of labour and for the development of a common class consciousness would hardly have been news to 19th-century socialists.

But there is also an argument about a shift of power from capital to information labour because it is argued 'the deployment of information technology increases dramatically the importance of human brain input into the work process'.

The crucial points to be made here are:

a)   The need to distinguish between the growth of forms of mental labour and the shift from energy to brainpower as the dominant form of labour's human capital input into the production process as a long term process, and its impact on the capital–labour relation. In short the shift from energy to brainpower does not necessarily change the subordination of labour to capital.

b)   The need to distinguish between types of mental labour – for instance between mental labour employed within the material production process, within circulation, within services, each with different effects on the overall economic system and in its turn different from mental labour within public bureaucracies such as education, which have a socially mediated relationship to the production process.

c)   The need to distinguish between the indispensability of a certain factor of production – in this case information workers – and the exercise of strategic power.

In short the argument about the changing nature of work, the structure of the labour market and their impact on culture and politics need to be integrated into a wider ranging sociology of what I will call intellectuals – for instance the work of Bourdieu, or Perkins' historical analysis *The Rise of Professional Society* (Perkins 1989), which interpret the rise of information work and its place within the structure of stratification and power in a non-technologically determined and more fruitful way, but which do not invest the present moment with the weight of epochal revolutionary change nor invest the information workers with power they evidently don't exercise.

## The superstructure

Let me now turn finally to the effect of this supposed transformation in the economic base to its effect at the level of the superstructure. I make no apology for using this old-fashioned terminology precisely because, as I have already argued, Castells himself is working within just such a framework.

The superstructural effects of the new informational mode of development are explained in two different ways. These are by no means necessarily mutually incompatible, but they do need to be distinguished for the purposes of analysis and critique.

The first argues that the effect comes via the labour process and the resulting restructuring of the global division of labour, and of the relationship between geographical territories or places that results. Here the explanation for a changing cultural and political process is sought in a polarization between a cosmopolitan global elite on the one hand and locally, grounded, but trapped labour, and its experiences on the other, between the spaces of flows and places. 'Labour loses its collective identity, becomes increasingly individualised in its capacities, in its working conditions and in its interests and projects' ([Castells 1996,] p. 475). The old struggle between capital and labour is replaced by 'a more fundamental

opposition between the bare logic of capital and the cultural values of human experience'. We see here a close relationship between Information Society theory and the
postmodernist stress on the culture of difference, the politics of identity and social
movements.

Common to much current information society theorizing is a failure to distinguish between the effects of new ICTs on the economy in general, which then may
or may not have significant effects in the spheres of politics and culture, and the
effects directly on politics and culture themselves – for instance the claims made
for the Internet as an agent of democratic renewal and the 'reinvention' of government or the supposed de-massification and globalization of the media. Crucially, for
example, statistics purporting to demonstrate the growth of the media and its
importance as a source of employment creation fail to distinguish between producer
services, the use of ICTs within the process of production, and circulation in general
which have shown dynamic growth, and final demand, the domestic consumption
of media products and services. These last have certainly grown, but not spectacularly, and, as recent broadband trials have shown, the willingness to consume new
services is highly constrained by disposable income.

Within Castells' theory there are three distinct types of explanation of the effect
of the informational mode of development on politics and culture. The first, as we
have already seen, is, in effect a classic class-consciousness effect. Changes in the
labour process and the division of labour produce a 'spirit of informationalism'
which favours a culture of the ephemeral – what Castells calls 'timeless time'. Here
we can see quite clear relations with certain versions of postmodern theorizing,
which celebrate the pleasures derived from a constantly shifting play of unanchored
signifiers. Apart from the key question of whether we can empirically demonstrate
the existence of this 'spirit of informationalism' and if so, whether culture really
is dominated by the cultural forms hypothesized as its effect, we then need to go
on to ask whether this cultural form is liberating, as is often implicitly assumed, or
ideological in the sense of distracting attention from underlying, more deeply
rooted, structures of interest and whether one of the ways in which this ideological process works is by favouring the entertainment over the pedagogic mode of
media function to the detriment of social learning processes and social cohesion. It
is to this question, for instance, that critics such as Neil Postman have addressed
themselves (Postman 1986). Here we also need to make a connection with the post-
Habermasian debate on the Public Sphere. Does democracy itself require a rational
mode of discourse to which the very ephemerality of this new culture is inimical?
This line of reasoning also shares some points in common with Bourdieu's arguments concerning the new media culture as the culture of a new *petite bourgeoisie*
which, far from possessing the high levels of cultural capital possessed by the
networking knowledge workers lacks cultural capital and therefore requires a high
turnover culture, which does not require a long apprenticeship for either its appreciation or production. These are all-important questions for current communication
theory. But in terms of the claims for epochal change, we need also to ask whether
these characteristics are new or whether on the contrary they are the product of
the problems of creating value with information commodities, which drives a
constant search for novelty and new cycles of cultural consumption of commodities, which are not destroyed in use. The pursuit of the ephemeral and the pleasures

of the fashionable in the sphere of consumption among all classes was noted at least as early as Voltaire's observations on 18th-century Britain. It would appear to be just as much the spirit of capitalism as Weber's celebrated Puritan abnegation.

## De-massification

The second claimed impact on culture and politics within Castells' theory is that of de-massification – what he describes as 'the present and future of television's decentralisation, diversification and customisation' (p. 340). On the one hand, it is argued that the restructuring of work has created individualized workers who then demand a more individualized cultural product and reject mass political parties in favour of a range of issue-based social move merits. On the other hand, the revolution in information and communication technology, by lowering the cost and extending the range of alternative distribution networks, has massively extended the range of choice open to cultural consumers and, at the same time and as a consequence, fragmented the audience. This extended choice and fragmentation is then seen as liberating.

There are a number of problems with this de-massification thesis. The first is empirical. Is it in fact taking place, and if so to what extent? The second is causal – is technological change in the system of distribution a cause or necessary condition of the restructuring of the audience? Looked at empirically, de-massification trends can be exaggerated. In cinema and recorded music a small number of titles continue to capture a high proportion of revenues, both nationally and globally. The audience share of network TV has declined in the face of competition from cable, satellite and video, but this decline has not been dramatic, and the number of channels watched on a regular basis has only modestly expanded. There is a general and continuing trend towards concentration in the newspaper market. If one factors in globalization, one of the supposed effects of the technological revolution, then the situation is more complicated. At one level the spread of global media products, services and producing conglomerates is a deepening of massification. After all one of the logics driving globalization is economies of scale. Secondly increased choice at a local level may coincide with, even be bought at the expense of, massification at the global level. The problem remains not primarily distribution costs and bottlenecks, but the relation between the costs of production and potential revenues, and between hits and flops. Neither is significantly affected by the technological revolution. Indeed it is significant that the new audio-visual distribution technologies of cable and satellite are not diversifying production but fighting to obtain, and thus pushing up the price of, the major global mass audience pullers, feature films and selected high profile sporting events. However the countervailing trends also need to be borne in mind, and again they have little to do with technology. Rising standards of living enable consumers to afford a greater choice and the exercise of this choice may take the form of a realizable demand for local material, thus counteracting globalizing trends. Indeed we can hypothesize that the reason the more lurid versions of the US cultural imperialism thesis have not come to pass is that this thesis was based upon the empirical observation of a period before locally generated revenues reached a level at which local production could be supported. Rather than point to a technological process of de-massification, historical evidence supports the idea of a continual dialectic within cultural production and consumption between massification and fragmentation, between the general and the particular, as there is more generally between the individual and society, the citizen and the state, the agent and the structure, a dialectic inflected by technological change certainly, but not determined by it.

## A culture of real virtuality

Finally, most ambitiously, but also most problematically, Castells proposes an alternative explanation of the effect of the informational mode of development on culture and politics that is both more systemic and more direct.

'The convergence of social evolution and information technologies has created a material basis for the performance of activities throughout the social structure' (p. 471).

Here the relation of technology to culture is seen as acting directly within the field of culture itself. Current developments in Information and Communication Technology (ICTs) are compared in their revolutionary cultural impact to the invention of the alphabet.

'Because culture is mediated and enacted through communication systems, cultures themselves, that is our historically produced system of beliefs and codes, become fundamentally transformed and will be more so over time, by the new technological system' (p. 328).

As a result he argues, drawing upon McLuhan and theories of de-massification, 'we can hardly underestimate the significance of the Information Superhighway' (p. 328). Why? Because 'the potential integration of text, images and sounds in the same system, interacting from multiple points, in chosen time (real or delayed) along a global network in conditions of open and affordable access does fundamentally change the character of culture' (p. 328).

It is, he argues, creating a 'Culture of Real Virtuality'. This is an argument familiar from Baudrillard and other post modernists.

> Cultures are made up of communication processes. And all forms of communication, as Roland Barthes and Jean Baudrillard taught us many years ago, are based on the production and consumption of signs. Thus there is no separation between 'reality' and symbolic representation.
>
> (p. 372)

This tired nominalism, derived from semiology's misreading of the nature of language, elides a number of distinct issues:

a)   The relation between communication systems and communication media, i.e. the same audio-visual text can be distributed on networks with different structures and technical characteristics.

b)   Between media and language. A range of audio-visual texts can employ a range of languages or codes of representation.

c)   Between language and culture. Communication takes place in and through symbols, but it is neither exclusively nor even mainly about symbols. This is the great deconstructionist fallacy of infinite interpretative regress. A large part of any life is involved in engagement with non-symbolic realities, including other human beings, and symbols are used to communicate about, to represent, to reflect those realities. Of course there is always a disjuncture between symbol and represented reality, but while human users are aware of this, the functional fit has been good enough over evolutionary time for humans to act on the correct assumption that, while communicated reality and symbols are distinct, one can communicate accurately about the other. This in its turn is a different issue from the relation of concepts or cultural meanings, also communicated through symbol systems, to any underlying 'truth', universal or otherwise.

In conclusion, what I have attempted to argue here is that the serious, concentrated analysis and critique of Information Society theory has been placed unavoidably at the centre of the concerns of scholars of communication by history itself. It is the dominant ideology of the current historical period. It raises questions which are unavoidable for anyone who wishes to understand the relationship between the structures and processes of social communication, and social structure and processes more generally; in short if we wish to understand and intelligently act upon the world in which we actually live.

These questions concern:

a)   Impacts at the general level of the mode of production, in particular the relation between forces and relations of production.
b)   Impacts at the level of the organization of production itself and thus on the structure and consciousness of labour and on social stratification. This in particular will include an analysis of the social position and function of information workers.
c)   Impacts on the spheres of politics and culture.

No relation between these levels, and thus no theory of the totality, can be assumed, but must be empirically demonstrated. The answers to these questions, both theoretical and empirical, offered by Information Society theory are inadequate and unconvincing. In particular the claim of novelty, and thus of revolutionary change, is made for what in fact are long-term structures and processes. In particular, as Braudel has reminded us in relation to the flexibility of capital within a space of flows, the answers are more likely to be inscribed in the *longue durée* of capitalist development than on the Information Superhighway.

> Capitalism alone has relative freedom of movement . . . faced with inflexible structures (those of material and, no less, of ordinary economic life), it is able to choose the area where it wants and is able to meddle, and the areas it will leave to their fate, incessantly reconstructing its own structures from these components, and thereby little by little transforming those of others. The choice may be limited, but what an immense privilege to be able to choose.
>
> (Braudel 1975, p. 405)

## References

Bell, D. (1973) *The Coming of Post Industrial Society*. Harmondsworth: Penguin.

Beniger, J. (1986) *The Control Revolution*. Cambridge, MA: Harvard University Press.

Braudel, F. (1975) *Capitalism and Material Life 1400–1800*. London: Weidenfeld and Nicolson.

Castells, M. (1996) *The Rise of Network Society*. Oxford: Blackwell.

Castells, M. (1997) *The Power of Identity*. Oxford: Blackwell.

Chandler, A. (1977) *The Visible Hand*. Cambridge, MA: Harvard University Press.

European Council (1994) *Europe and the Global Information Society*.

Madrick, J. (1998) 'Computers: Waiting for the Revolution', in *New York Review of Books*, vol. XLV, no. 5.

Negroponte, N. (1996) *Being Digital*.

Perkins, H. (1989) *The Rise of Professional Society*. London: Routledge.

Postman, N. (1986) *Amusing Ourselves to Death*.

Sassens, S. (1991) *The Global City*. Princeton, NJ: Princeton University Press.

Sichel, D. (1998) *The Computer Revolution: An Economic Perspective*. New York: Brookings Institute Press.

Toffler, A. (1980) *The Third Wave*. London: Collins.

Williamson, O. (1975) *Markets and Hierarchies*. New York: Free Press.

# PART FOUR

# Transformations

INTRODUC

ı L  acknowledgement that we are
sustained changes in our ways of life.
ırs has witnessed the most sustained
arresting thought to realize that, for
much as before. To be sure, plagues
as never far away, but for thousands
ırs had. Subsistence farming, a peas-
forty years (with frightening levels of

ıounced the end of this, as factory
ansformed the land and higher stan-
longevity. Contemporary accounts of
ı mill made much of the magnitude
being struck by the awesome power
cter of the new factory work being
ınds of milking, sowing and reaping

ng this new world, still its coming
even slow. The steam engine, for
ıland during the nineteenth century
the towns and factories took several
ınge that is concentrated into very

much shorter time spans – for instance, computer communications technologies pervaded the office within a decade, while the internet's spread since the mid–1990s is remarkable. More important even than this acceleration in the diffusion of technical innovations, we have in addition the routinization of change itself – the normality that things are impermanent. Today no one expects things to be the same even in ten years' time. We can see this in the spread of technologies especially – in the rapid uptake of microelectronic technologies, in the spread of personal computers, in genetic engineering. But it is also evident in the rapid destruction of old industries such as coal mining and steel making and the emergence of new ones such as systems engineering and web site design. It is also present in the increased uncertainties of life today – from where one might find employment, to how durable are one's intimate relations. Everyone reading this will be aware of talk about the 'end of a job for life', of the 'collapse of tenure', of the need to retrain as a matter of course, of the instabilities of private life (Sennett 1998). For some, and perhaps for most in the right circumstances, the constancy of change is invigorating and positive, but elsewhere it gives rise to deep anxiety and apprehension. One might hope that one's marriage will survive, but divorce statistics must give rise to doubt; one's religious convictions may be sincere, but will they be able to withstand assault from alternative religions?; the order book of one's employer may be full today, but who is to tell whether a global challenge will come from cheaper labour costs across the ocean or a new and better product from across the way?

The pace of change has quickened and has continued to accelerate in recent decades, so much so that it is anticipated that even the next decade will see major changes in how we live (this frequently starts with being associated with the latest technologies – the genome project as well as with the internet, but accounts quickly move on to discuss issues such as religion, ethnicity and migration as key factors precipitating change). Whether this represents the continuation and even deepening of established patterns and trends or heralds the arrival of a radically new social and economic order is a contentious matter, but the scale and pace of change is beyond dispute.

Not surprisingly, then, sociologists endeavour to chart where we are going and why we might be moving in particular directions, driven by the desire to get greater understanding that we might better control the direction of change. Buzz words such as 'globalization' (Held *et al.* 1999), 'reflexive modernization' (Giddens 1990) and 'postmodernity' (Lyon 1999) are attempts to name what is taking place. Part Two has already presented thinking on the coming of 'Post-industrial Society', and this too is an effort to comprehend major social, economic and political change. Other important thinkers refer to the growth of a 'risk society' (Beck 1992), the emergence of 'disorganized capitalism' (Lash and Urry 1987), or the triumph of the market system which marks the 'end of history' (Fukuyama 1992). Significantly, almost all commentators focus upon information (and, closely connected, information and communications technologies) as having an especially important role to play in contemporary social change. Not surprisingly, then, the conception of an Information Society has an especial appeal to many seeking to identify the new era into which we are moving.

One of the most ambitious and persuasive attempts to explain the present has been that it marks a transition from Fordism to Post-Fordism (Webster 2002, ch. 4). This is an encompassing effort to characterize what we once were and what are the distinguishing features of the present. The suggestion is that Fordism (which was pre-eminent from about 1945 to the mid–1970s) was characterized by standardization and uniformity, the prominence of nation states, welfare provision for national citizens, mass production, which fitted with increasing mass consumption, and the centrality to life of class (as a distinguisher of lifestyle, politics, education and more). Post-Fordism signals a break with this, evidencing global connectivity, more intense competition which spans national borders, free market orthodoxy, customization of products and services, and the replacement of class with more individuated lifestyle choices, instanced in involvement in 'issue politics' such as save the whales or feminism (Harvey 1989; Amin 1994). Themes developed here, notably during the 1990s, find echoes in the extracts we have selected for Part Four.

**John Urry** (Chapter 13) offers us a way of understanding the present by suggesting that we might think in terms of 'mobilities' – of peoples, products, images, information and wastes – to better appreciate our age. Evoking Manuel Castells (prioritized in Part Three), Urry suggests that 'networks' of relationships, in which new 'scapes' and 'flows' now predominate, enable us to conceive of a world that has moved beyond former ways of thinking and acting that were bounded and secured by notions such as 'society' being synonymous with the 'nation state', and technology as being an autonomous force in society. The days when the word 'society' could unproblematically evoke 'Britain' or 'France', and when commentators could describe epochs as 'the Railway Age' since the train impacted so forcefully, are surely gone. Our globalized world, one in which electronic flows of currency, news and entertainment unceasingly move across and within national borders, where migration is an everyday event for many working in business, where airplane travel has become cheap in less than a generation, such that an annual holiday abroad is an ordinary affair, is one which makes outdated earlier frames of reference. Where does 'society' begin and end at a time when one's everyday shopping provides a full range of cosmopolitan experiences (food stuffs from just about anywhere in the world, at any time), when for many at work it is a routine part of the job to communicate with others from around the globe (and where many co-workers in the office are migrants)? The metaphor 'mobility' helps us think more clearly and imaginatively about the constant movements of ideas, goods and people across and through territories, as well as perceiving ways in which social values permeate technological designs, uses and applications. 'Mobilities' lead us to conceive ways of life which are fluid and permeable, rarely if ever settled (and then only temporarily) to a quite unprecedented extent (Urry 2000).

**Robert Reich** (Chapter 14), a member of President Bill Clinton's Cabinet in the 1990s, draws attention to new forms of stratification that are becoming evident in the transformations through which we are living. In Reich's view 'symbolic analysts' will soon predominate, since it is these well-educated deal-makers, managers, innovators and organizers who play the key roles in this fast-changing and borderless epoch. The symbolic analysts are connected across time and space in intricate 'webs' of relationships, capable thereby of keeping up with the competitive pressures and innovative breakthroughs. Their greatest asset is high-level education which equips them to be comfortable with change, able to adapt, analyse and move on. They live in, and fit well with, the 'mobilities' of the new century.

Nico Stehr (Chapter 15) provides a closely-argued and nuanced analysis of the part played by knowledge in the current transformations. Echoing themes from Daniel Bell's Post-Industrial Society thesis, Stehr traces the central role of knowledge in manufacturing processes, the importance of symbols in today's economy, changing forms of work which promote knowledge, and the heightened significance of consumption. Arguing for the value of the term 'knowledge society', Stehr goes further to suggest that once-discernible distinctions between social and economic spheres of life are breaking down, contributing to what he terms, provocatively, 'fragile societies' that are made – and unmade and remade – much more readily than hitherto (Stehr 2001). This makes for societies which are full of possibility, but also ones which are inherently chaotic (Stehr 2003).

Finally, **Anne Balsamo** (Chapter 16) places gender at the heart of developments. We are reminded here especially of women's presence in information technology, cyberspace, as well as in technologies developed in previous periods. Balsamo insists on an *embodied* notion of information, and provides an imaginative and exploratory account of changes as they relate to gender and 'racial' divisions. Balsamo argues that it is necessary to understand that technologies now, and increasingly, assume organic characteristics as they become integrated into the body (pacemakers, hip replacements, cosmetic surgery, foetal monitors, a host of drug regimes, from beta blockers to contraceptive pills . . .), and that this use of 'new technologies of corporality' must not be overlooked, not least because it means that the divides between the organic and the cultural, the natural and the technological, have become more blurred than ever. A crucial consequence of such blurring is that apparently once-fixed gender relations are increasingly open to challenge and reformulation, while these relations yet remain material (they are not reducible to mere 'discourses' as so many postmodern commentators imply). Presenting a 'matrix of forms of technological embodiment' in women, Balsamo distinguishes various types of such bodies: the 'marked', the 'repressed', the 'labouring', and the 'disappearing'. Doing so she at once challenges presentations of gender which offer a culturally homogeneous picture of gender (there is in truth a range of representations) and, at the same time, reveals something of the variety of forces that contribute to the reality of 'material bodies'.

## REFERENCES

Amin, Ash (ed.) (1994) *Post-Fordism*. Oxford: Blackwell.
Beck, Ulrich (1992) *Risk Society: Towards a New Modernity*. London: Sage.
Fukuyama, Francis (1992) *The End of History and the Last Man*. London: Hamish Hamilton.
Giddens, Anthony (1990) *The Consequences of Modernity*. Cambridge: Polity.
Harvey, D. (1989) *The Condition of Postmodernity: An Enquiry into the Origins of Cultural Change*. Oxford: Blackwell.

Held, David, McGrew, A., Goldblatt, D. and Perraton, J. (1999) *Global Transformations: Politics, Economics and Culture*. Cambridge: Polity.

Landes, David (1969) *The Unbound Prometheus: Technological Change and Industrial Development from 1750 to the Present*. Cambridge University Press.

Lash, Scott and Urry, John (1987) *The End of Organised Capitalism*. Cambridge: Polity.

Lyon, David (1999) *Postmodernity*, 2nd edn. Buckingham: Open University Press.

Sennett, R. (1998) *The Corrosion of Character: The Personal Consequences of Work in the New Capitalism*. New York: Norton.

Stehr, Nico (2001) *The Fragility of Modern Societies: Knowledge and Risk in the Information Age*. London: Sage.

Stehr, Nico (2003) *The Governance of Knowledge*. London: Routledge.

Thompson, E. P. (1967) 'Time, Work-Discipline and Industrial Capitalism', *Past and Present* 38, December: 56–97.

Urry, J. (2000) *Sociology Beyond Societies: Mobilities for the Twenty-first Century*. London: Routledge.

Webster, Frank (2002) *Theories of the Information Society*, 2nd edn. London: Routledge.

# Chapter 13

# John Urry

## MOBILE SOCIOLOGY[1]

From *British Journal of Sociology*, 51 (1) (2000): 185–203.

[. . .]

## Introduction

I N  T H I S  A R T I C L E  I  O U T L I N E  some categories relevant for developing sociology as a 'discipline' as we enter the next century. I argue for a sociology concerned with the diverse mobilities of peoples, objects, images, information and wastes; and of the complex interdependencies between, and social consequences of, these diverse mobilities.

Elsewhere I have shown how mobilities are transforming the historic subject-matter of sociology which within the 'west' has focused upon individual societies and their generic characteristics (Urry 2000). In *Sociology Beyond Societies* I develop a 'post-societal' agenda for sociology elaborating how various global 'networks and flows' undermine endogenous social structures that possess the power to reproduce themselves. New rules of sociological method are necessitated by the apparently declining powers of national societies since it is they that have historically provided the intellectual and organizational context for sociology. Some of the diverse mobilities that are materially transforming the 'social as society' into the 'social as mobility' include imaginative travel, movements of images and information, virtual travel, object travel and corporeal travel (see Urry 2000: ch. 3). The consequence of such diverse mobilities is to produce what Beck terms the growth of 'inner mobility' for which coming and going, being both here and there at the same time, has become much more globally normal (1999: 75–6).

In this article I show how mobilities criss-crossing societal borders in new temporal-spatial patterns constitutes a novel agenda for sociology, of mobility. Much twentieth-century sociology has been based upon the study of occupational, income, educational and social mobility. This literature regarded society as a uniform surface and failed to register the geographical intersections of region, city and place, with the social categories of class, gender and ethnicity. Further, there are crucial flows of people within, but especially beyond, the territory of each society, and these flows relate to many different desires, for work, housing, leisure, religion, family relationships, criminal gain, asylum seeking and so on. Moreover, not only people are mobile, but so too are many 'objects', 'images', 'informations' and 'wastes'. Mobility is thus to be understood in a horizontal rather than a vertical sense, and it applies to a variety of actants and not just to humans.

Bauman's vertical metaphor of 'gardening' to characterize modern societies is pertinent here (1987). He suggests that a gardening state has replaced earlier 'game-keeper' states that were not involved in giving society an overall shape and were uninterested in detail. By contrast the gardening state presumes exceptional concern with pattern, regularity and ordering, with what is growing and with what should be weeded out. Legislators have been central to careful tendering by the gardening state, with using their reason to determine what is, and is not, productive of order. The social sciences have been part of that application of reason to society through facilitating the husbandry of societal resources, identifying what is and what is not to be cultivated and determining what are the exact conditions of growth of particular plants.

However, the new global order appears to involve a return to the gamekeeper state and away from that of the gardener. The gamekeeper was concerned with reg-ulating mobilities, with ensuring that there was sufficient stock for hunting in a par-ticular site but not with the detailed cultivation of each animal in each particular place. Animals roamed around and beyond the estate, like the roaming hybrids that currently wander in and especially across national borders. States are increasingly unable or unwilling to garden their society, only to regulate the conditions of their stock so that on the day of the hunt there is appropriate stock available for the hunter. As Beck has recently argued: 'capital, culture, technology and politics merrily come together to roam *beyond* the regulatory power of the national state' (1999: 107).

The former East European societies were 'gardening' societies. Following the Second World War, the individual societies of Central and Eastern Europe constructed exceptionally strong frontiers both from the 'West' and especially from each other. Cultural communication into and out of such societies was exception-ally difficult. The Cold War chilled culture as well as politics. So although such societies were internationally linked via the hegemony of the USSR, there was a parallel emphasis upon cultural involution and the reinforcement of strongly rein-forced national networks. It constituted an interesting social laboratory based upon the concept of 'society'.

But what happened was that regional frontiers of each society were transgressed, they were got around through various fluid-like movements. The attempt to freeze the peoples and cultures of 'Eastern Europe' could not be sustained. The Berlin Wall was of course the most dramatic example of this attempted gardening the people of a society. But through the 1960s, forms of communication and later of leisure travel noticeably increased. Both peoples and objects especially began to flow across the carefully constructed borders, often involving what has been termed the 'invisible hand of the smuggler' (Braun *et al.* 1996: 1). Objects of the 'West' became used and talked about in multiple informal ways, helping the citizens of such societies to form new bases of personal identity, new ways of collectively remembering and new images of self and society. Many citizens went to inordinate lengths to learn about and to acquire objects that were immutable in their western-ness. Thus these societies became surrounded by hordes of 'animals' (consumer goods, images, western ideas and so on) which increasingly crossed into and over the land that had been so carefully husbanded. Their populations chased after the animals and trampled underfoot the carefully tended plants. [. . .]

In the next section I consider 'sociology' and 'society' in more detail, before turning briefly to global networks and fluids. I consider how notions of complexity can analyse intensely mobile hybrids that roam across the globe and help to create a self-reproducing global order. I conclude with some observations about the implications of this mobile order for 'sociology', the science of 'society'.

## 'There is no such thing as society'

When former British Prime Minister Margaret Thatcher famously declared that 'there is no such thing as society', sociologists led the charge to critique her claim. They declared that there are obviously societies and that Thatcher's claim indicated the wrongness of her policies based upon trying to reduce the societal to the interests of 'individual men and women and their families'. However, the riposte to Thatcher from the sociological community was not fully justified since it is actually unclear just what is meant by 'society'. Although there is something 'more' in social life than 'individual men and women and their families', exactly what this surplus amounts to is not so obvious. [. . .]

Sociological discourse has indeed been premised upon 'society' as its object of study (Billig 1995: 52–3; Hewitt 1997; Urry 2000: ch. 1). This was especially so from the 1920s onwards as sociology was institutionalized, especially within the American academy. [. . .] This construction of the discourse of sociology around the concept of society in part stemmed from the apparent autonomy of American society throughout the twentieth century and is thus to universalize the American societal experience.

However, what most of these formulations neglect to specify is how 'society' connects to the system of nations and nation-states. Billig argues that: 'the "society" which lies at the heart of sociology's self definition is created in the image of the nation-state' (1995: 53). Interestingly American-based theories of society have frequently ignored the 'nationalist' basis of American and indeed of all western societies. They have typically viewed nationalism as surplus to society that only needs deployment in situations of 'hot' extremism, situations which supposedly do not describe societies of the 'West' (Billig 1995: 52–4).

In theorizing society, sovereignty, national citizenship and social governmentality lie at its core. Each 'society' is a sovereign social entity with a nation-state that organizes the rights and duties of each societal member or citizen. Most major sets of social relationships flow within the territorial boundaries of the society. The state possesses a monopoly of jurisdiction or governmentality over members living within the territory or region of the society. Economy, politics, culture, classes, gender and so on, are societally structured. In combination they constitute a clustering or a 'social structure'. Such a structure organizes and regulates the life-chances of each member of the society in question.

This societal structure is not only material but also cultural, so that its members believe they share some common identity that is bound up in part with the territory that the society occupies or lays claim to. And *contra* the argument of much sociology, central to most such societies is a vernacular nationalism that articulates the identities of each society through its mundane differences from the other. These include the waving of celebratory flags, singing national anthems, flying flags on public buildings, identifying with one's own sports heroes, being addressed in the media as a member of a given society, celebrating Independence Day and so on (Billig 1995).

However, societies are never entirely self-reproducing entities. Sociology has a tendency to treat what is 'outside' the society as an unexamined environment. But no society, even in the heyday of the nation-state earlier this century, has been separate from the very system of such states and from the notion of national identity that mobilizes sovereign societies. [. . .] It is through this interdependence that societies are constituted as partially self-regulating entities, significantly defined by their banal or vernacular differences from each other.

Over the past two centuries this conception of society has been central to North American and West European notions of what it is to possess the rights and duties of social citizenship. To be human meant that one is a member or citizen of a particular society. Historically and conceptually there has been a strong connection between the idea of humanness and of membership of a society. Society here means that ordered through a nation-state, with clear territorial and citizenship boundaries and a system of governance over its particular citizens. [. . .]

In this account 'society' and its characteristic social divisions of especially social class are strongly interconnected with the 'nation-state'. Mann shows that societies, nations and states have been historically intertwined (1993: 737). They developed together and should not be conceptualized as billiard balls existing only in external relations with one another. Mann evocatively talks of the sheer patterned messiness of the social world and of the mutually reinforcing intersections of class and nation, as societies developed their 'collective powers' especially over nature.

Sociology as a specific academic practice was the product of this particular historical moment, of an emergent industrial capitalism in Western Europe and North America. It took for granted the success of modern societies in their spectacular overcoming of nature. Sociology specialized in describing and explaining the character of these modern societies based upon industries that enabled and utilized dramatic new forms of energy and resulting patterns of social life. As such sociology adopted one or other versions of a tradition–modernity divide that implied that a revolutionary change had occurred in North Atlantic rim societies between 1700–1900. [. . .]

Each society was sovereign, based upon a social governmentality. The concerns of each society were to be dealt with through national policies, especially from the

1930s onwards through a Keynesian welfare state that could identify and respond to the risks of organized capitalism (Lash and Urry 1987, 1994). These risks were seen as principally located *within* the geographical borders and temporal frames of each society. And solutions were devised and implemented within such societal frontiers. National societies were based upon a concept of the citizen who owed duties to, and received rights from, their society through the core institutions of the nation-state. This 'societal' model applied to the dozen or so societies of the North Atlantic rim. Most of the rest of the world was subject to domination by these societies of the North Atlantic rim.

In the next section I consider further this system which contemporary changes have put into question and which suggest that Thatcher was right when she said there is no such thing as society. But that there may not be such a thing as society is not because of the power of individual human subjects, but because of their weakness in the face of 'inhuman' fluid and mobile processes of globalization. Wallerstein points out that: 'What is fundamentally wrong with the concept of society is that it reifies and therefore crystallizes social phenomena whose real significance lies not in their solidity but precisely in their fluidity and malleability' (1991: 71).

## Global networks and fluids

A useful starting point here is Mann's description of the contemporary world

> Today, we live in a global society. It is not a unitary society, nor is it an ideological community or a state, but it is a single power network. Shock waves reverberate around it, casting down empires, transporting massive quantities of people, materials and messages, and finally, threatening the ecosystem and atmosphere of the planet.
>
> (1993: 11)

He makes a number of points here: there is no unified global society but there are exceptional levels of global interdependence; unpredictable shock waves spill out 'chaotically' from one part to the system as a whole; there are not just 'societies' but massively powerful 'empires' roaming the globe; and there is mass mobility of peoples, objects and dangerous human wastes.

What then are appropriate metaphors to make sense of these transformations? Mol and Law argue that there are three distinct metaphors of space or social topologies, regions, networks and fluids (1994; Urry 2000: ch. 2). First, there are *regions* in which objects are clustered together and boundaries are drawn around each particular regional cluster. Second, there are *networks* in which relative distance is a function of the relations between the components comprising the network – the invariant outcome is delivered across the entire network that often crosses regional boundaries. And third, there is the metaphor of the *fluid* that flows: 'neither boundaries nor relations mark the difference between one place and another. Instead, sometimes boundaries come and go, allow leakage or disappear altogether, while relations transform themselves without fracture. Sometimes, then, social space behaves like a fluid' (Mol and Law 1994: 643).

The sociological concept of society is based upon the metaphor of a region, namely that 'objects are clustered together and boundaries are drawn around each particular cluster' (Mol and Law 1994: 643). And one way to study globalization is through seeing it involved in inter-regional competition with 'society'. Globalization could be viewed as the replacing of one region, the bounded nation-state society of the 'West', with another, that of global economy and culture. And as both economy and culture are increasingly globalized, so the old dominant region of society appears to become relatively less powerful. In the fight between these two regions it looks as though the global region will win out and defeat the societal region (see Robertson 1992).

But this is only one way of understanding globalization. Globalization can also be viewed not as one larger region replacing the smaller region of each society, but as involving alternative metaphors of *network* and *fluid* (Mol and Law 1994; Waters 1995; Albrow 1996; Castells 1996, 1997; Eade 1997; Held *et al.* 1999; Beck 1999). The globalization literature has described the wide variety of new *machines and technologies* that dramatically compress or shrink time–space. These technologies carry people, information, money, images and risks, and flow within and across national societies in increasingly brief moments of time. Such technologies do not derive directly and uniquely from human intentions and actions. They are intricately interconnected with machines, texts, objects and other technologies. The appropriate metaphor to capture these intersections of peoples and objects is not that of a vertical structure that typically involves a centre, a concentration of power, vertical hierarchy and a formal or informal constitution. Castells argues, by contrast, that we should employ the metaphor of network. [. . .]

[. . .]

Castells defines a network as a set of interconnected nodes – the distance between social positions are shorter where such positions constitute nodes within a network as opposed to those which lie outside the particular network. Networks are to be viewed as dynamic open structures, so long as they are able to effect communication with new nodes and to innovate (Castells 1996: 470–1). [. . .]

Network here does not mean purely social networks since the 'convergence of social evolution and information technologies has created a new material basis for the performance of activities throughout the social structure. This material basis, built in networks, earmarks dominant social processes, thus shaping social structure itself' (Castells 1996: 471). Networks thus produce complex and enduring connections across space and through time between peoples and things (see Murdoch 1995: 745). They spread across time and space which is hugely important, since according to Law, if 'left to their own devices *human actions and words do not spread very far at all*' (1994: 24). Different networks possess different reaches or abilities to bring home distant events, places or people, to overcome the friction of regional space within appropriate periods of time (Emirbayer and Sheller 1999: 748). This requires mobilizing, stabilizing and combining peoples, actions or events elsewhere into a stable network, an immutable mobile (Latour 1987). [. . .]

[. . .]

There are two further speets of networks to distinguish here, namely, scapes and flows. *Scapes* are the networks of machines, technologies, organizations, texts and actors that constitute various interconnected nodes along which *flows* can be relayed. Such scapes reconfigure the dimensions of time and space. Once particular scapes have been established, then individuals and especially corporations within each society will normally try to become connected to them through being constituted as nodes within that particular network. They will seek to develop their own hub airport or at least have regular flights to such airports; they will wish their local schools to be plugged into the internet; they will try to attract satellite broadcasting; they may even seek to reprocess nuclear waste products and so on. Between certain nodes along some scapes extraordinary amounts of information may flow, of financial, economic, scientific and news data and images, into which some groups are extremely well plugged-in while others are effectively excluded. What becomes significant is what Brunn and Leinbach term 'relative' as opposed to 'absolute' location (1991: xvii). This creates novel inequalities of flow as opposed to the inequalities of stasis. Graham and Marvin maintain that what is involved here is a rewarping of time and space by advanced telecommunication and transportation structures, as scapes pass by some areas and connect other areas along information and transport rich 'tunnels' (1996: 60). Social and spatial distances are no longer homologous (Beck 1999: 104).

So far I have talked rather generally of global networks criss-crossing the regional borders of society, thus bringing out some aspects of contemporary 'deterritorialization' (Lefebvre 1991: 346–8). These notions will now be made more precise by distinguishing between two different kinds of such networks, *global networks* and what I will call *global fluids*.

Numerous 'global' enterprises, such as American Express, McDonald's, Coca Cola, Disney, Sony, BA and so on, are organized on the basis of a *global network* (see Ritzer 1992, 1995, 1997). Such a network of technologies, skills, texts and brands ensures that more or less the same product is delivered in more or less the same way in every country in which the enterprise operates. Such products are produced in predictable, calculable, routinized and standardized environments. These companies have produced enormously effective networks based upon immutable mobiles with few 'failings'. Such networks depend upon allocating a very large proportion of resources to branding, advertising, quality control, staff training and the internalization of the corporate image, all of which cross societal boundaries in standardized patterns so maintaining constancy. Distance is measured in terms of the time taken to get to the next McDonald's, the next Disney park, the next BA hub airport and so on, that is, from one node in this global network to the next. Such global networks can also be found within oppositional organizations such as Greenpeace. Like other global players it devotes much attention to developing and sustaining its brand identity throughout the world. Greenpeace's brand identity has 'such an iconic status that it is a world-wide symbol of ecological virtue quite above and beyond the actual practical successes of the organization' within particular societies (Szerszynski 1997: 46).

Second, there are *global fluids*, the heterogeneous, uneven and unpredictable mobilities of people, information, objects, money, images and risks, that move chaotically across regions in strikingly faster and unpredictable shapes. Such global fluids (as opposed to networks) demonstrate (see Deleuze and Guattari 1986, 1988; Lefebvre 1991; Mol and Law 1994; Augé 1995; Kaplan 1996; Shields 1997) no clear point of departure or arrival, just de-territorialized movement or mobility (rhizomatic rather than arboreal). They are relational in that they productively effect relations between the spatially varying features of a scape that would otherwise remain functionless. Fluids move in particular directions at certain speeds but with no necessary end-state or purpose. They possess different properties of viscosity and, as with blood, can be thicker or thinner and hence move in different shapes at different speeds. They move according to certain temporalities, over each minute, day, week, year and so on. Most importantly, fluids do not always keep within the scape – they may move outside or escape like white blood corpuscles through the 'wall' of the blood vessel into tinier and tinier capillaries; hence their power is diffused through these various fluids into very many often minute capillary-like relations of domination/subordination. Different fluids spatially intersect in the 'empty meeting grounds' of the non-places of modernity, such as motels, airports, service stations, the internet, international hotels, cable television, expense account restaurants and so on.

I have thus set out some characteristics of global networks and fluids. Because these are inhuman hybrids, conceptions of agency that specifically focus upon the capacities of humans to attribute meaning or sense or to follow a social rule are inappropriate. This is not to suggest that humans do not do such things, not to suggest that human do not exert agency. But they only do so in circumstances which are not of their own making; and it is those circumstances – the enduring and increasingly intimate relations of subjects *and* objects – that are of paramount significance. This means that the human and physical worlds are elaborately intertwined and cannot be analysed separately from each other, as society and as nature, or humans and objects. Also agency is not a question of humans acting independently of objects in terms of their unique capacities to attribute meaning or to follow rules. If then there is no autonomous realm of human agency, so there should not be thought of as being a distinct level of *social* reality that is the unique outcome of humans acting in and through their specific powers. Various writers have tried to develop the thesis of the dialectic of individuals making society and society making individuals (Berger and Luckmann 1967). But such a dialectic would only be plausible if we mean by society something trivial, that is pure social interactions abstracted from the networks of intricate relationships with the inhuman. Since almost all social entities do involve networks of connections between humans and these other components, so there are no uniquely *human* societies as such. Societies are necessarily hybrids.

More generally, Laclau and Mouffe show the impossibility of society as a valid object of discourse (1985). What we can ask stitches a 'society' together when inhuman networks criss-cross it in strikingly new ways at ever-faster speeds? The classic philosophical–sociological debates as to the respective virtues of methodological individualism versus holism, or in their later manifestations, structurationism versus the dualism of structure, are unhelpful here. They do not deal with the complex consequences of diverse mobilities; the intersecting sensuous relations of humans with diverse objects; the timed and spaced quality of relations stretching across societal borders; and the complex and unpredictable intersections of many 'regions, networks and flows'. To describe these as either 'structure' or as 'agency' does injustice to the complexity of such relations. [. . .]

In the next section I consider whether notions of 'complexity' can illuminate such inhuman, mobile intersecting hybrids – is complexity the basis of post-social' knowledge?

## Complex mobilities

The 'complex' nature of both physical and social systems means that they are characterized by a very large number of elements that interact physically and informationally over time and result in positive and negative feedback loops (see Byrne 1998; Cilliers 1998; Wallerstein 1998; Thrift 1999, on recent social science applications of chaos/complexity theory). Such systems interact dissipatively with their environment and have a history that evolves irreversibly through time. Emergent, unintended and non-linear consequences are generated within such systems, consequences that are patterned but unpredictable, distant in time and/or space from where they originate and involving potential system bifurcation.

In the physical sciences complexity theory uses mathematical formulae and computer algorithms to characterize the enormously large number of iterative events. In certain experiments, the analysis of increases in the reproduction patterns of gypsy moths showed, through resulting changes in population size, dramatic non-linear changes in the quality of the system. Changes in the parameter resulted in transformations in the system; in certain contexts, order generates chaos. The more complex the system the more likely it is that small fluctuations will be critical (see Prigogine and Stengers 1984).

This iterative character of systems has been insufficiently interrogated within sociology. [. . .] Partly this is because of the presumed a-temporal character of the social world, rather than the seeing of all social hybrids as necessarily historical. [. . .] But it has also stemmed from the baleful consequences of the divide between structure and agency. In sociological thought the millions of individual iterative actions are largely subsumed under the notion of 'structure' (such as the class structure, or the structure of gender relations or social structure) which is seen as 'ordered' and reproduced through continuous iteration. The concept of structure solves the problem of iteration for sociology. However, social systems do change and sociology then draws upon the concept of agency to argue that some sets of agents can on occasions manage to escape such a structure and effect change in it. If social systems change then this is seen to result from agency.

Certain authors have however seen the limitations of this formulation. [. . .]
[. . .]
Capitalism, we now know, has indeed broken down many Chinese walls and has gone global. Can complexity provide some illumination into such a global capitalism? Is an emergent level of the 'global' developing that is recursively self-producing, where its outputs constitute inputs into an autopoietic circular system of 'global' objects, identities, institutions and social practices. And if there is, what are its complex properties, how are chaos and order combined in the global? First, we can note that billions of individual actions occur, each of which is based upon exceptionally localized forms of information. Most people most of the time act iteratively in terms of local information, knowing almost nothing about the

global connections or implications of what they are doing. However, these local actions do not remain simply local since they are captured, represented, marketed, circulated and generalized elsewhere. They are carried along the scapes and flows of the emerging global world, transporting ideas, people, images, monies and technologies to potentially everywhere. Indeed such actions may jump the scapes, since they are fluid-like and difficult to keep within particular channels (such as the internet jumping from military to road protester communications).

The consequences for the global level are non-linear, large-scale, unpredictable and partially ungovernable (baroque rather than romantic: see Kwa 1998). Small causes at certain places produce massive consequences elsewhere. Consider a pile of sand; if an extra grain of sand is placed on top it may stay there or it may cause a small avalanche. The system is self-organized but the effects of local changes can vary enormously (Cilliers 1998: 97). The heap will maintain itself at the critical height and we cannot know in advance what will happen to any individual action or what its consequence will be for the pile of sand.

The emergent global order is one of constant disorder and disequilibrium. The following are some recent examples of where millions of actions based upon local knowledge have, through iteration, resulted in unpredictable and non-linear consequences at the emergent global level (see Urry 2000: ch. 2 on each of these). For US military communications in the event of a nuclear war there developed the arpanet/internet, but which has then provided a scape which has generated extraordinary flows of image, information and non-military communications throughout the world (internet use has grown faster than any previous new technology). In 1989 there was the almost instantaneous collapse of all of 'communist' Eastern Europe, once it was seen that the particular local centre of the Kremlin was unable and unwilling to prevent such an occurrence. The apparently 'rational' decision of millions of individual people to exercise their right to drive has resulted in carbon gas discharges that threaten the long-term survival of the planet (even where most motorists are aware of such consequences). And omnipotent consumerism has almost everywhere generated religious fundamentalism. Barber apocalyptically describes the emergent global order as being locked in a major conflict between the consumerist 'McWorld' on the one hand, and the identity politics of the 'Jihad', on the other (1996). There is a 'new world disorder' in which McWorld and Jihad depend upon, and globally reinforce, each other.

There is a kind of spiralling global disequilibrium that threatens existing public spheres, civil society and democratic forms. There are of course forms of global governance designed to dampen down some of these forms of disequilibrium, but mostly they are based upon national governments acting within particular *local* contexts. Baker has elaborated on how the relationship between the centre and the periphery, or what he calls the 'centriphery', functions to create both order and turbulence in social life (1993). He suggests that the centriphery functions as an attractor, which is defined as the space to which the trajectory of any particular system is over time attracted (Byrne 1998: 26–9; Cilliers 1998: 96–7). In this case the centriphery is a dynamic pattern that is repeated at many different levels, involving flows of energy, information and ideas that simultaneously create both centres and peripheries. The trajectory of social systems is irreversibly attracted to the centriphery.

Baker further argues that

> [t]oday, particular multinational industries center vast amounts of
> human activity, locating specific aspects of their enterprise in different
> continents. In each of these cases, the exchange of goods and services
> binds and lubricates a dynamic relationship between the center and
> the periphery. As centering progresses, it deepens the periphery. . . .
> Because centering and peripheralizing involve the transformation of
> energy and information and, thus, the creation of entropy, the process
> is irreversible.
>
> (1993: 140)

A specific form taken by the strange attractor of the centriphery is that of
'globalization', whereby there is a parallel irreversible process of globalization-
deepening-localization-deepening-globalization and so on. Both are bound together
through a dynamic relationship, as huge flows of resources move backwards and
forwards between the global and the local. Neither the global nor the local can
exist without the other. They develop in a symbiotic, irreversible and unstable set
of relationships, in which each gets transformed through billions of world-wide iter-
ations. Small perturbations in the system can result in unpredictable and chaotic
branching of such a system, as has happened with what Imken terms the 'non-linear,
asymmetrical, chaotically-assembled . . . new artificial life-form of the global
telecommunications *Matrix*' (Imken 1999: 92).

## Conclusion

I have thus illustrated how 'complexity' systems can assist in the analysis of mobile
hybrids. How though does this leave 'sociology' which would seem to be cast adrift
once we leave the relatively safe boundaries of bounded societies? Most of the tentative certainties that sociology has cautiously erected would appear to dissolve with
the structure of feeling entailed by complexity. These developments seem to imply
a post-disciplinary social/cultural/political science with no particular space or role
for individual disciplines (see Sayer 1999). Why should 'sociology' analyse these
intersecting complex mobilities that have travelled onto the intellectual stage in such
a powerful fashion? [. . .]

First, most other disciplines are subject to extensive forms of discursive normalization, monitoring and policing that make them poor candidates for post-
disciplinary reconfiguration. Indeed theories, methods and data may be literally
expelled from such disciplines since they are viewed as too 'social' and outside the
concerns of that particular policed discipline (see Urry 1995: ch. 2). There are many
examples of how sociology provides a place of temporary intellectual dwelling for
those marginalized by discursive normalization in adjacent disciplines. Moreover,
sociology's discursive formation has often demonstrated a relative lack of hierarchy,
a somewhat unpoliced character, an inability to resist intellectual invasions, an
awareness that all human practice is socially organized, a potential to identify the
social powers of objects and nature, and an increasing awareness of spatial and

temporal processes. While all these wreak havoc with any remaining notion of society *tout court*, sociology could develop a new agenda for a discipline that is losing its central concept of human 'society'. It is a discipline organized around networks, mobility and horizontal fluidities. More generally, Diken advocates the 'more "mobile" theorizing' that will be necessary to deal with emerging hybrid entities, as well as with so-called societies (1998: 248).

Dogan and Pahre show the importance of 'intellectual mobility' for innovation in the social sciences (1990). Their extensive research demonstrates that innovation does not principally result from those scholars who are firmly entrenched within disciplines, nor from those practising a rather general 'interdisciplinary' or 'post-disciplinary' studies. Rather innovation results from academic mobility across clear disciplinary borders, a mobility that generates 'creative marginality'. It is this marginality, resulting from scholars moving from the centre to the periphery of their discipline and then crossing its frontiers that produces new productive hybridities in the social sciences. [. . .] Sociology has often been the beneficiary of the 'creative marginality' of such creative 'in-migrants'.

Further, most important developments in sociology have at least indirectly stemmed from social movements with 'emancipatory interests' fuelling a new or reconfigured social analysis. Examples of such mobilized groupings which at different historical moments have included the working class, farmers, the professions, urban protest movements, the student's movement, the women's movement, immigrant groups, environmental NGOs, the gay and lesbian movement, 'disabled' groups and so on. The emancipatory interests of these groupings are not always directly reflected within sociology; more they have had a complex and refracted impact. But in that sense, sociology has been 'parasitic' upon these movements, thus demonstrating how the 'cognitive practices' of such movements have helped to constitute public spaces for thinking new thoughts, activating new actors, generating new ideas within societies (Eyerman and Jamison 1991: 161; Urry 1995: ch. 2). Societies were organized through debate occurring within a relatively delimited national, public sphere. The information and knowledge produced by its universities centrally formed those debates and delimited possible outcomes. Disciplines were particularly implicated in contributing knowledge to such a public sphere, and indeed in constituting that sphere as part of a national civil society (Cohen and Arato 1992; Emirbayer and Sheller 1999).

However, the increasingly mediatized nature of contemporary civil societies transforms all of this. It is not so much that the mass media reflects what goes on elsewhere, so much as what happens in and through the media is what happens elsewhere. The sphere of public life that provided the context for knowledge produced within the academy is now increasingly mediatized (see Dahlgren 1995). Thrift describes the cosmopolitan mediatization of complexity science, especially as organized in and through the Sante Fe Institute (Thrift 1999). Debate is concerned as much with image, meaning and emotion, as it is with written texts, cognition and science. The global economy of signs, of globally circulating information and images, is transforming the public sphere into an increasingly denationalized, visual and emotional public stage (Urry 2000: ch. 7; Knorr Cetina 1997).

And on that mediated public stage, many social groupings are appearing, developing partially, imperfectly and contingently, a kind of globalizing civil society. This is summarized within the World Order Models Project. Falk documents the wide-spread growth of trans-national citizens' associations, world-wide shifts towards democratization and non-violence, huge difficulties for national states in maintaining popularity and legitimacy, and the more general growth of diverse global trends (1995; and see Archibugi *et al.* 1998). Falk concludes that: 'Such cumulative developments are facilitating the birth and growth of global civil society' (Falk 1995: 35). And it is this set of social transformations that could constitute the social base for the sociology of mobilities I have elaborated in this article. The social basis of a 'global civil society' and its emancipatory interests may result in a 'sociology of mobilities' of the sort I have outlined here, as we move chaotically into the next century.

[. . .]

## Note

1    I am grateful for the discussions on 'networks' in the discussion group Team Theory in the Lancaster University Sociology Dept. I am also grateful for the comments of John Law, Will Medds, Mimi Sheller and Sylvia Walby.

## References

Albrow, M. (1996) *The Global Age*, Cambridge: Polity.
Archibugi, D., Held, D. and Köhler, M. (eds) (1998) *Re-imagining Political Community*, Cambridge: Polity.
Augé, M. (1995) *Non-places*, London: Verso.
Baker, P. (1993) 'Chaos, order, and sociological theory', *Sociological Inquiry* 63: 123–49.
Barber, B. (1996) *Jihad vs McWorld*, New York: Ballantine.
Bauman, Z. (1987) *Legislators and Interpreters*, Cambridge: Polity.
Beck, U. (1999) *What is Globalization?* Cambridge: Polity.
Berger, P. and Luckmann, T. (1967) *The Social Construction of Reality*, London: Allen Lane.
Billig, M. (1995) *Banal Nationalism*, London: Sage.
Braun, R., Dessewfly, T., Scheppele, K., Smejkalova, J., Wessely, A. and Zentai, V. (1996) *Culture Without Frontiers*, Internationales Forschungszentrum Kulturwissenschaften, Vienna: Research Grant Proposal.
Brunn, S. and Leinbach, R. (eds) (1991) *Collapsing Space and Time: Geographic Aspects of Communications and Information*, London: Harper Collins.
Byrne, D. (1998) *Complexity Theory and the Social Sciences*, London: Routledge.
Castells, M. (1996) *The Rise of the Network Society*, Oxford: Blackwell.
Castells, M. (1997) *The Power of Identity*, Oxford: Blackwell.
Cilliers, P. (1998) *Complexity and Post-modernism*, London: Routledge.
Cohen, J. and Arato, A. (1992) *Civil Society and Political Theory*, Cambridge, MA: MIT Press.
Dalhgren, P. (1995) *Television and the Public Sphere*, London: Sage.
Deleuze, G. and Guattari, F. (1986) *Nomadology*, New York: Semiotext(e).
Deleuze, G. and Guattari, F. (1988) *A Thousand Plateaus: Capitalism and Schizophrenia*, London: Athlone Press.
Diken, B. (1998) *Strangers, Ambivalence and Social Theory*, Aldershot: Ashgate.
Dogan, M. and Pahre, R. (1990) *Creative Marginality*, Boulder, CO: Westview Press.
Eade, J. (ed.) (1997) *Living the Global City*, London: Routledge.
Emirbayer, M. and Sheller, M. (1999) 'Publics in history', *Theory and Society* 28: 145–97.

Eyerman, R. and Jamison, A. (1991) *Social Movements: A Cognitive Approach*, Cambridge: Polity.

Falk, R. (1995) *On Human Governance*, Cambridge: Polity.

Graham, S. and Marvin, S. (1996) *Telecommunications and the City*, London: Routledge.

Held, D., McGrew, A., Goldblatt, D. and Perraton, J. (1999) *Global Transformations*, Cambridge: Polity.

Hewitt, R. (1997) *The Possibilities of Society*, Albany, NY: SUNY Press.

Imken, O. (1999) 'The convergence of virtual and actual in the Global Matrix', in M. Crang, P. Crang and J. May (eds) *Virtual Geographies*, London: Routledge.

Kaplan, C. (1996) *Questions of Travel*, Durham, NC: Duke University Press.

Knorr Cetina, K. (1997) 'Sociality with objects', *Theory, Culture and Society* 14: 1–30.

Kwa, C. (1998) 'Romantic and baroque conceptions of complex wholes in the sciences', mimeo, University of Amsterdam.

Laclau, E. and Mouffe, C. (1985) *Hegemony and Socialist Strategy*, London: Verso.

Lash, S. and Urry, J. (1987) *The End of Organized Capitalism*, Cambridge: Polity.

Lash, S. and Urry, J. (1994) *Economies of Signs and Space*, London: Sage.

Latour, B. (1987) *Science in Action*, Milton Keynes: Open University Press.

Law, J. (1994) *Organizing Modernity*, Oxford: Basil Blackwell.

Lefebvre, H. (1991) *The Production of Space*, Oxford: Blackwell.

Mann, M. (1993) *The Sources of Social Power, vol. 2*, Cambridge: Cambridge University Press.

Mol, A and Law, J. (1994) 'Regions, networks and fluids: anaemia and social topology', *Social Studies of Science* 24: 641–71.

Murdoch, J. (1995) 'Actor-networks and the evolution of economic forms: combining description and explanation in theories of regulation, flexible specialization, and networks', *Environment and Planning A* 27: 731–57.

Prigogine, I. and Stengers, I. (1984) *Order out of Chaos*, New York: Bantam.

Ritzer, G. (1992) *The McDonaldization of Society*, London: Pine Forge.

Ritzer, G. (1995) *Expressing America*, London: Pine Forge.

Ritzer, G. (1997) '"McDisneyization" and "post-tourism": complementary perspectives on contemporary tourism', in C. Rojek and J. Urry (eds) *Touring Cultures*, London: Routledge.

Robertson, R. (1992) *Globalization*, London: Sage.

Sayer, A. (1999) 'Long live postdisciplinary studies! Sociology and the curse of disciplinary parochialism/imperialism', *British Sociological Association Conference*, Glasgow, April.

Shields, R. (1997) 'Flow as a new paradigm', *Space and Culture* 1: 1–4.

Szerszynski, B. (1997) 'The varieties of ecological piety', *Worldviews: Environment, Culture, Religion* 1: 37–55.

Thrift, N. (1999) 'The place of complexity', *Theory, Culture and Society* 16: 31–70.

Urry, J. (1995) *Consuming Places*, London: Routledge.

Urry, J. (2000) *Sociology Beyond Societies*, London: Sage.

Wallerstein, I. (1991) *Unthinking Social Science*, Cambridge: Polity.

Wallerstein, I. (1998) 'The heritage of sociology, the promise of social science', *Presidential Address, 14th World Congress of Sociology*, Montreal, July.

Waters, M. (1995) *Globalization*, London: Routledge.

# Chapter 14

# Robert Reich

## THE THREE JOBS OF
## THE FUTURE

From *The Work of Nations: Preparing Ourselves for 21st Century Capitalism*, New York: Vintage (1992), pp. 171–84.

THE USUAL DISCUSSION ABOUT the future of the American economy focuses on topics like the competitiveness of General Motors, or of the American automobile industry, or, more broadly, of American manufacturing, or, more broadly still, of the American economy. But, as has been observed, these categories are becoming irrelevant. They assume the continued existence of an American economy in which jobs associated with a particular firm, industry, or sector are somehow connected within the borders of the nation, so that American workers face a common fate; and a common enemy as well: The battlefields of world trade pit our corporations and our workers unambiguously against theirs.

No longer. In the emerging international economy, few American companies and American industries compete against foreign companies and industries – if by *American* we mean where the work is done and the value is added. Becoming more typical is the global web, perhaps headquartered in and receiving much of its financial capital from the United States, but with research, design, and production facilities spread over Japan, Europe, and North America; additional production facilities in Southeast Asia and Latin America; marketing and distribution centers on every continent; and lenders and investors in Taiwan, Japan, and West Germany as well as the United States. This ecumenical company competes with similarly ecumenical companies headquartered in other nations. Battle lines no longer correspond with national borders.

[. . .]

The point is that Americans are becoming part of an international labor market, encompassing Asia, Africa, Latin America, Western Europe, and, increasingly,

Eastern Europe, and the Soviet Union. The competitiveness of Americans in this global market is coming to depend, not on the fortunes of any American corporation or on American industry, but on the functions that Americans perform – the value they add – within the global economy. Other nations are undergoing precisely the same transformation, some more slowly than the United States, but all participating in essentially the same transnational trend. Barriers to cross-border flows of knowledge, money, and tangible products are crumbling; groups of people in every nation are joining global webs. [. . .]

Americans thus confront global competition ever more directly, unmediated by national institutions. As we discard vestigial notions of the competitiveness of American corporations, American industry, and the American economy, and recast them in terms of the competitiveness of the American work force, it becomes apparent that successes or failures will not be shared equally by all our citizens.

Some Americans, whose contributions to the global economy are more highly valued in world markets, will succeed, while others, whose contributions are deemed far less valuable, fail. GM's American executives may become more competitive even as GM's American production workers become less so, because the functions performed by the former group are more highly valued in the world market than those of the latter. So when we speak of the 'competitiveness' of Americans in general, we are talking only about how much the world is prepared to spend, *on average*, for services performed by Americans. Some Americans may command much higher rewards; others, far lower. No longer are Americans rising or falling together, as if in one large national boat. We are, increasingly, in different, smaller boats.

2

In order to see in greater detail what is happening to American jobs and to understand why the economic fates of Americans are beginning to diverge, it is first necessary to view the work that Americans do in terms of categories that reflect their competitive positions in the global economy.

[. . .]

Essentially, three broad categories of work are emerging, corresponding to the three different competitive positions in which Americans find themselves. The same three categories are taking shape in other nations. Call them *routine production services*, *in-person services*, and *symbolic-analytic services*.

*Routine production services* entail the kinds of repetitive task performed by the old foot soldiers of American capitalism in the high-volume enterprise. They are done over and over – one step in a sequence of steps for producing finished products tradeable in world commerce. Although often thought of as traditional blue-collar jobs, they also include routine supervisory jobs performed by low- and mid-level managers – foremen, line managers, clerical supervisors, and section chiefs – involving repetitive checks on subordinates' work and the enforcement of standard operating procedures.

Routine production services are found in many places within a modern economy apart from older, heavy industries (which, like elderly citizens, have been given the more delicate, and less terminal, appellation: 'mature'). They are found even amid the glitter and glitz of high technology. Few tasks are more tedious and repetitive, for example, than stuffing computer circuit boards or devising routine coding for computer software programs.

Indeed, contrary to prophets of the 'information age' who buoyantly predicted an abundance of high-paying jobs even for people with the most basic of skills, the sobering truth is that many information-processing jobs fit easily into this category. The foot soldiers of the information economy are hordes of data processors stationed in 'back offices' at computer terminals linked to worldwide information banks. They routinely enter data into computers or take it out again – records of credit card purchases and payments, credit reports, checks that have cleared, customer accounts, customer correspondence, payroll, hospital billings, patient records, medical claims, court decisions, subscriber lists, personnel, library catalogues, and so forth. The 'information revolution' may have rendered some of us more productive, but it has also produced huge piles of raw data which must be processed in much the same monotonous way that assembly-line workers and, before them, textile workers processed piles of other raw materials.

Routine producers typically work in the company of many other people who do the same thing, usually within large enclosed spaces. They are guided on the job by standard procedures and codified rules, and even their overseers are overseen, in turn, by people who routinely monitor – often with the aid of computers –how much they do and how accurately they do it. Their wages are based either on the amount of time they put in or on the amount of work they do.

Routine producers usually must be able to read and to perform simple computations. But their cardinal virtues are reliability, loyalty, and the capacity to take direction. Thus does a standard American education, based on the traditional premises of American education, normally suffice.

[. . .]

*In-person services*, the second kind of work that Americans do, also entail simple and repetitive tasks. And like routine production services, the pay of in-person servers is a function of hours worked or amount of work performed; they are closely supervised (as are their supervisors), and they need not have acquired much education (at most, a high school diploma, or its equivalent, and some vocational training).

The big difference between in-person servers and routine producers is that *these* services must be provided person-to-person and thus are not sold worldwide. [. . .] In-person servers are in direct contact with the ultimate beneficiaries of their work; their immediate objects are specific customers rather than streams of metal, fabric, or data. In-person servers work alone or in small teams. Included in this category are retail sales workers, waiters and waitresses, hotel workers, janitors, cashiers, hospital attendants and orderlies, nursing-home aides, child-care workers, house cleaners, home health-care aides, taxi drivers, secretaries, hairdressers, auto mechanics, sellers of residential real estate, flight attendants, physical therapists, and – among the fastest-growing of all – security guards.

In-person servers are supposed to be as punctual, reliable, and tractable as routine production workers. But many in-person servers share one additional requirement: They must also have a pleasant demeanor. They must smile and exude confidence and good cheer, even when they feel morose. They must be courteous and helpful, even to the most obnoxious of patrons. Above all, they must make others feel happy and at ease. It should come as no surprise that, traditionally, most in-person servers have been women. The cultural stereotype of women as nurturers – as mommies – has opened countless in-person service jobs to them.[1]

By 1990, in-person services accounted for about 30 percent of the jobs performed by Americans, and their numbers were growing rapidly. [. . .] In the United States during the 1980s, well over 3 million *new* in-person service jobs were created in fast-food outlets, bars, and restaurants. This was more than the total number of routine production jobs still existing in America by the end of the decade in the automobile, steelmaking, and textile industries combined.[2]

*Symbolic-analytic services*, the third job category, include all the problem-solving, problem-identifying, and strategic-brokering activities we have examined in previous chapters. Like routine production services (but *unlike* in-person services), symbolic-analytic services can be traded worldwide and thus must compete with foreign providers even in the American market. But they do not enter world commerce as standardized things. Traded instead are the manipulations of symbols – data, words, oral and visual representations.

Included in this category are the problem-solving, -identifying and brokering of many people who call themselves research scientists, design engineers, software engineers, civil engineers, biotechnology engineers, sound engineers, public relations executives, investment bankers, lawyers, real estate developers, and even a few creative accountants. Also included is much of the work done by management consultants, financial consultants, tax consultants, energy consultants, agricultural consultants, armaments consultants, architectural consultants, management information specialists, organization development specialists, strategic planners, corporate headhunters, and systems analysts. Also: advertising executives and marketing strategists, art directors, architects, cinematographers, film editors, production designers, publishers, writers and editors, journalists, musicians, television and film producers, and even university professors.

Symbolic analysts solve, identify, and broker problems by manipulating symbols. They simplify reality into abstract images that can be rearranged, juggled, experimented with, communicated to other specialists, and then, eventually, transformed back into reality. The manipulations are done with analytic tools, sharpened by experience. The tools may be mathematical algorithms, legal arguments, financial gimmicks, scientific principles, psychological insights about how to persuade or to amuse, systems of induction or deduction, or any other set of techniques for doing conceptual puzzles.

Some of these manipulations reveal how to more efficiently deploy resources or shift financial assets, or otherwise save time and energy. Other manipulations yield new inventions – technological marvels, innovative legal arguments, new advertising ploys for convincing people that certain amusements have become life necessities. Still other manipulations – of sounds, words, pictures – serve to entertain their recipients, or cause them to reflect more deeply on their lives or on the human condition. Others grab money from people too slow or naïve to protect themselves by manipulating in response.

Like routine producers, symbolic analysts rarely come into direct contact with the ultimate beneficiaries of their work. But other aspects of their work life are quite different from that experienced by routine producers. Symbolic analysts often have partners or associates rather than bosses or supervisors. Their incomes may vary from time to time, but are not directly related to how much time they put in or the quantity of work they put out. Income depends, rather, on the quality, originality, cleverness, and, occasionally, speed with which they solve, identify, or broker new problems. Their careers are not linear or hierarchical; they rarely proceed along well-defined paths to progressively higher levels of responsibility and income. In fact, symbolic analysts may take on vast responsibilities and command inordinate wealth at rather young ages. Correspondingly, they may lose authority and income if they are no longer able to innovate by building on their cumulative experience, even if they are quite senior.

Symbolic analysts often work alone or in small teams, which may be connected to larger organizations, including worldwide webs. Teamwork is often critical. Since neither problems nor solutions can be defined in advance, frequent and informal conversations help ensure that insights and discoveries are put to their best uses and subjected to quick, critical evaluation.[3]

When not conversing with their teammates, symbolic analysts sit before computer terminals – examining words and numbers, moving them, altering them, trying out new words and numbers, formulating and testing hypotheses, designing or strategizing. They also spend long hours in meetings or on the telephone, and even longer hours in jet planes and hotels – advising, making presentations, giving briefings, doing deals. Periodically, they issue reports, plans, designs, drafts, memoranda, layouts, renderings, scripts, or projections – which, in turn, precipitate more meetings to clarify what has been proposed and to get agreement on how it will be implemented, by whom, and for how much money. Final production is often the easiest part. The bulk of the time and cost (and, thus, real value) comes in conceptualizing the problem, devising a solution, and planning its execution.

Most symbolic analysts have graduated from four-year colleges or universities; many have graduate degrees as well. The vast majority are white males, but the proportion of white females is growing, and there is a small, but slowly increasing, number of blacks and Hispanics among them. All told, symbolic analysis currently accounts for no more than 20 percent of American jobs. The proportion of American workers who fit this category has increased substantially since the 1950s (by my calculation, no more than 8 percent of American workers could be classified as symbolic analysts at midcentury), but the pace slowed considerably in the 1980s – even though certain symbolic-analytic jobs, like law and investment banking, mushroomed. [. . .]

## 3

These three functional categories cover more than three out of four American jobs. Among the remainder are farmers, miners, and other extractors of natural resources, who together comprise less than 5 percent of American workers. The rest are mainly government employees (including public school teachers), employees in regulated industries (like utility workers), and government-financed workers (American engineers working on defense weapons systems and physicians working off Medicaid and Medicare), almost all of whom are also sheltered from global competition.

Some traditional job categories – managerial, secretarial, sales, and so on – overlap with more than one of these functional categories. The traditional categories, it should be emphasized, date from an era in which most jobs were as standardized as the products they helped create. Such categories are no longer very helpful for determining what a person actually does on the job and how much that person is likely to earn for doing it. [. . .]

[. . .]

That a job category is officially classified 'professional' or 'managerial' likewise has little bearing upon the function its occupant actually performs in the world economy. Not all professionals, that is, are symbolic analysts. Some lawyers spend their entire working lives doing things that normal people would find unbearably monotonous – cranking out the same old wills, contracts, and divorces, over and over, with only the names changed. Some accountants do routine audits without the active involvement of their cerebral cortices. Some managers take no more responsibility than noting who shows up for work in the morning, making sure they stay put, and locking the place up at night. (I have even heard tell of university professors who deliver the same lectures for thirty years, long after their brains have atrophied, but I do not believe such stories.) None of these professionals is a symbolic analyst.[4]

Nor are all symbolic analysts professionals. In the older, high-volume economy, a 'professional' was one who had mastered a particular domain of knowledge. The knowledge existed in advance, ready to be mastered. It had been recorded in dusty tomes or codified in precise rules and formulae. Once the novitiate had dutifully absorbed the knowledge and had passed an examination attesting to its absorption, professional status was automatically conferred – usually through a ceremony of appropriately medieval pageantry and costume. The professional was then authorized to place a few extra letters after his or her name, mount a diploma on the office wall, join the professional association and attend its yearly tax-deductible meeting in Palm Springs, and pursue clients with a minimum of overt avarice.

But in the new economy – replete with unidentified problems, unknown solutions, and untried means of putting them together – mastery of old domains of knowledge isn't nearly enough to guarantee a good income. Nor, importantly, is it even necessary. Symbolic analysts often can draw upon established bodies of knowledge with the flick of a computer key. Facts, codes, formulae, and rules are easily accessible. What is much more valuable is the capacity to effectively and creatively *use* the knowledge. Possessing a professional credential is no guarantee of such capacity. Indeed, a professional education which has emphasized the rote acquisition of such knowledge over original thought may retard such capacity in later life.

## 4

How, then, do symbolic analysts describe what they do? With difficulty. Because a symbolic analyst's status, influence, and income have little to do with formal rank or title, the job may seem mysterious to people working outside the enterprise web, who are unfamiliar with the symbolic analyst's actual function within it. And because symbolic analysis involves processes of thought and communication, rather than tangible production, the content of the job may be difficult to convey simply. In answering the question 'What did you do today, Mommy (or Daddy)?' it is not always instructive, or particularly edifying, to say that one spent three hours on the telephone, four hours in meetings, and the remainder of the time gazing at a computer screen trying to work out a puzzle.

Some symbolic analysts have taken refuge in job titles that communicate no more clearly than this, but at least sound as if they confer independent authority nonetheless. The old hierarchies are breaking down, but new linguistic idioms have arisen to perpetuate the time-honored custom of title-as-status.

Herewith a sample. Add any term from the first column to any from the second, and then add both terms to any from the third column, and you will have a job that is likely (but not necessarily) to be inhabited by a symbolic analyst.

| Communications | Management | Engineer |
| Systems | Planning | Director |
| Financial | Process | Designer |
| Creative | Development | Coordinate |
| Project | Strategy | Consultant |
| Business | Policy | Manager |
| Resource | Applications | Adviser |
| Product | Research | Planner |

The 'flat' organization of high-value enterprise notwithstanding, there are subtle distinctions of symbolic-analytic rank. Real status is inversely related to length of job title. Two terms signify a degree of authority. (The first or second column's appellation is dropped, leaving a simpler and more elegant combination, such as 'Project Engineer' or 'Creative Director.') Upon the most valued of symbolic analysts, who have moved beyond mere technical proficiency to exert substantial influence on their peers within the web, is bestowed the highest honor – a title comprising a term from the last column preceded by a dignified adjective like Senior, Managing, Chief, or Principal. One becomes a 'Senior Producer' or a 'Principal Designer' not because of time loyally served or routines impeccably followed, but because of special deftness in solving, identifying, or brokering new problems.

Years ago, fortunate and ambitious young people ascended career ladders with comfortable predictability. If they entered a core corporation, they began as, say, a second assistant vice president for marketing. After five years or so they rose to the rank of first assistant vice president, and thence onward and upward. Had they joined a law firm, consulting group, or investment bank, they would have started as an associate, after five to eight years ascended to junior partner, and thence to senior partner, managing partner, and finally heaven.

None of these predictable steps necessitated original thought. Indeed, a particularly creative or critical imagination might even be hazardous to career development, especially if it elicited questions of a subversive sort, like 'Aren't we working on the wrong problem?' or 'Why are we doing this?' or, most dangerous of all, 'Why does this organization exist?' The safest career path was the surest career path, and the surest path was sufficiently well worn by previous travelers so that it could not be missed.

Of course, there still exist organizational backwaters in which career advancement is sequential and predictable. But fewer fortunate and ambitious young people dive into them, or even enter upon careers marked by well-worn paths. They dare not. In the emerging global economy, even the most impressive of positions in the most prestigious of organizations is vulnerable to worldwide competition if it entails easily replicated routines. The only true competitive advantage lies in skill in solving, identifying, and brokering new problems.

## Notes

1   On this point, see Arlie Russell Hochschild, *The Managed Heart: The Commercialization of Human Feeling* (Berkeley: University of California Press, 1983).
2   US Department of Commerce, Bureau of Labor Statistics, various issues.
3   The physical environments in which symbolic analysts work are substantially different from those in which routine producers or in-person servers work. Symbolic analysts usually labor within spaces that are quiet and tastefully decorated. Soft lights, wall-to-wall carpeting, beige and puce colors are preferred. Such calm surroundings typically are encased within tall steel-and-glass buildings or within long, low, postmodernist structures carved into hillsides and encircled by expanses of well-manicured lawn.
4   In the remainder of this [chapter], when discussing symbolic analysts, I shall, on occasion, illustrate my point by referring to lawyers, management consultants, software engineers, and other professionals, but the reader should understand that this is a shorthand method of describing only the symbolic and analytic work undertaken by such professionals.

# Chapter 15

# Nico Stehr

# THE ECONOMIC STRUCTURE OF KNOWLEDGE SOCIETIES

From *Knowledge Societies,* London: Sage (1994), pp. 121–59.

**T**HERE ARE [. . .] SEVERAL IMPORTANT reasons for addressing the nature of the changing economic structure of modern society. First, development of knowledge societies is connected to basic transformations in the structure of economic activity. The engine of much of the dynamics of economic activity and the source of much of the growth of added economic value can be attributed to knowledge. Paradoxically perhaps, the self-transformation of the economy diminishes the importance of the economy to individuals and society. Of course, it does not eliminate it. But from the point of view of the individual, for example, the economy of knowledge societies has the enabling quality of allowing central-life interests to progressively drift away from purely economic ones or, from a macro-perspective of social conflicts, for instance, a shift toward more generalized struggles not primarily driven by material clashes can be discerned. The conditions which allow for such displacements also render traditional economic discourse (and policy derived from such premises) less powerful. At the same time, natural, social and cultural conditions, namely scientific-technical, environmental and institutional change, often treated as exogenous factors by neo-classical economics, become increasingly important to economic activity.

Secondly, the emergence of a primarily knowledge-based labor force cannot be understood apart from a profound transformation in the economic system; and, thirdly, public debate and political discourse on modern society is still captivated and impoverished, perhaps dominated but certainly often limited, by reference to economic considerations. Prevalent popular orientation and a frequent basis for political judgments are references to economic imperatives and therefore how policies and conduct generally fit with 'free' market forms; that is, political realities are frequently defined in a most restrictive fashion.

A fourth reason is the quality of the link between the economic system and other societal sectors, for example the private world, which is changing and justifies a re-examination of the assumption of a self-propelled development of economic change, on the one hand, and the firm separation between the economy and other sectors of society, on the other. In addition, the extent to which situational and contingent rather than transcontextual and universal effects play a role in economic relations justifies a theoretical approach to economic relations informed by sociological considerations.

Fifthly, sociological discourse, in the past few decades, has been increasingly separated from economic discourse. It is possible to conceive of this distancing as a matter of the increasing differentiation of social science discourse. Economics lost interest in the analysis of social institutions, while sociology conceded the study of socio-economic phenomena to economics (cf. Swedberg 1987; Granovetter 1990). Finally, both economic analysis and sociology lost interest in the study of the societal and socio-economic act of science and technology. However, it is now, in the light of existing economic conditions, less certain that such a state of affairs represents a proper cognitive priority and intellectual division of labor. The sociological contribution to the analysis of economic relations should not merely be peripheral nor should the treatment of scientific and technical change be considered exogenous to economic analysis (cf. Dosi *et al.* 1988).

Central to my analysis is the thesis that the origin, social structure and development of knowledge societies is linked first and foremost to a radical transformation in the *structure of the economy*, including a set of novel and largely unintended consequences, for example in the area of terms of trade, inflation, productivity, competitiveness and employment. Moreover, the ways in which society is affected and co-ordinates its economic activities and agents are changing. Although the central thesis will be that we are witnessing the emergence of a new structure and organization of economic activity on the basis of a new combination of the forces of production, Emile Durkheim's specification of the general status of economic factors within a primarily sociological analysis, first introduced at the end of the nineteenth century for his own central theoretical category of the division of labor in society, remains valid. That is, Durkheim ([1893] 1964: 275) draws a distinction in the use of the category of division of labor by sociologists and economists; for the latter, 'it essentially consists in greater production. For us, this greater productivity is only a necessary consequence, a repercussion of the phenomenon. If we specialize, it is not to produce more, but it is to enable us to live in new conditions of existence that have been made for us.' Attention in this instance indeed centers only secondarily on outcomes. The primary focus is on how outcomes become possible, are sustained, organized and perhaps even continue to grow.

Productive processes in *industrial society* are governed by a number of factors all of which appear to be on the decline in their relative significance as conditions for the possibility of a changing, particularly *growing* economy: the dynamics of the supply and demand for primary products or raw materials; the dependence of employment on production; the importance of the manufacturing sector which processes primary products; the role of labor (in the sense of manual labor); the close relation between physical distance and cost and the social organization of work; the role of international trade in goods and services; and the nature of the limits to economic growth. The most common denominator of the changes in the structure of the economy seems to be a shift from an economy driven and governed, in large measure, by 'material' inputs into the productive process and its organization to an economy in which transformations in productive and distributive processes are determined much more by 'symbolic' or knowledge-based inputs and outputs. However, social science discourse and official data collection still tend to think of economic activity primarily in terms of the production of commodities.

The economy of industrial society is initially and primarily a material economy and then changes gradually to a monetary economy. Keynes' economic theory, particularly as outlined in his *General Theory* (1936), reflects this transformation; it becomes, as evident recently, a symbolic economy. The changes in the structure of the economy and its dynamics are increasingly a reflection of the fact that knowledge becomes the leading dimension in the productive process, the primary condition for its expansion and for a change in the limits to economic growth in the developed world. In short, the point is that for the production of goods and services, with the exception of the most standardized commodities and services, factors other than 'the amount of labor time or the amount of physical capital become increasingly central' (Block 1985: 95) to the economy of advanced societies.

A close examination of the literature in economics indicates, however, that the function of knowledge and information in economic activity is, for the most part, ignored by economists. Either that, or they introduce knowledge as an exogenous variable, as an expense and generally treat it as a black box.[1] There are significant exceptions of course, and I will refer to them.[2] But the general and disparaging observation by Stigler (1961: 213) is still close to the mark: 'One should hardly have to tell academicians that information is a valuable resource: knowledge *is* power. And yet it occupies a slum dwelling in the town of economics.' Knowledge is a residual, even invisible component of production and assets. Knowledge has many 'qualitative' components and quality has not yet prospered within economic discourse. Despite its apparent ascent as a source of added economic value, for example, knowledge remains elusive.

The specific changes in the economic *structure* may be described briefly as follows. The important changes in the relations of production, the nature of work and the composition of the labor force will be dealt with in greater detail below.

## The diminishing role of primary materials

The striking change here is the 'uncoupling' of the raw material economy from the industrial economy. The uncoupling has been accompanied in recent decades, perhaps slowed, by a secular decline in the price of commodities when compared to the price of manufactured goods. The decline of commodity prices has been uneven. It has been particularly strong in the case of metals. [. . .] In general these developments imply that the recent 'collapse in the raw materials economy seems to have had almost no impact on the world of industrial economy' (Drucker 1986: 770). The traditional assumption of economists has of course been that changes in the price structure, most surely dramatic changes, ought to have a profound impact on the cycle of economies.

However, the significant decline in the price of most raw materials has not brought about an economic slump, except perhaps in those countries which rely to a large degree on trade with raw materials. On the contrary, production has grown. [. . .]

The demand for raw materials in manufacturing diminishes 'not only because of miniaturization (e.g. chips) and the reduction of energy requirements, but also because of the revolution in material science. One asks less for specific materials . . . and more for the properties needed (e.g. tensility, conductivity) and the material combinations that can provide those properties' (Bell 1987: 9). [. . .]

[. . .]

[. . .] These shifts in the input of raw materials result from a combination of factors, including of course technological changes, but also from the relative price changes of factors, environmental regulations, market pressures and consumer preferences. It is, of course, very difficult to factor out the contribution of each of these influences and possibly others to the use of raw materials in production. However, it is evident that the thesis that growing production and consumption invariably entails increasing natural resource use has to be re-examined in light of these developments.

## The changing manufacturing sector

It is by no means unusual to encounter assertions even today which treat work in the manufacturing sector of the economy as relatively homogeneous. That is, work found in the manufacturing sector continues to be understood as one of the few remaining examples of the kind of work which classic economic and sociological theory had in mind when it spoke of labor, namely work carried out by dependent and exploited laborers in industrialized settings. This type of work in the manu-facturing sector is also often perceived as one of the last bastions against the increasing trend toward greater differentiation, new rationality, more extensive flexibility, self-determination and increased reflexivity of work in the service sector of the economy (cf. Offe 1984: 24–25). The upshot is, of course, that the worlds of work and economic sectors are seen as operating according to different rationalities, one technical, or perhaps better, 'functional' rationality and the other a kind of 'substantial' rationality (cf. Mannheim [1935] 1940: 51–56). Consistent with some of the traditional general assumptions of contemporary theories of society, especially the notion of functional differentiation, the governing theme in understanding the modern economy becomes a reference to the normative and material *differentiation* among economic sectors rather than *linkage* and comple-mentarity.

Assuming that the differentiation of the modern economy into three sectors remains plausible, what is less contentious is that the character of labor in modern society is changing. The central questions for analysis become whether the changes in work are mainly confined to a specific sector of the economy or whether the transformation occurs in all sectors, perhaps driven by similar forces and constraints and whether the pattern of labor found in one sector increasingly extends into other sectors of the economy?

By the same token, it is widely postulated that the overall economic importance of, or the capacity to add value to, the manufacturing sector is declining and
that the primary significance of economic activity has shifted to the service sector.
These conjunctures at times have been discussed under the heading of 'de-
industrialization' (for example, Bluestone and Harrison 1982). It is worth noting that
Daniel Bell does not, as far as I can tell, ever expressly advance, in the context of
his extensive comments on the nature of the post-industrial economic structure of
society, the thesis that the manufacturing sector actually *shrinks* in economic importance. Bell (1979a: 163) explicitly contends that post-industrial society involves
a 'change from a goods producing to a service society'. As a result perhaps, the
frequent reading of his theory that the aggregate importance of the manufacturing
sector diminishes under post-industrial conditions acquires a certain credibility. As
a matter of fact, the designation 'post-industrial' itself supports such an image. And
the almost 'logical' inference of that kind of interpretation is that the industrial
sector of the economy becomes largely dispensable in an affluent economy.

But exactly the opposite is the case. Contrary to many assumptions, the manufacturing sector and industrial production are not declining in importance in
contemporary society. [. . .]
     [. . .]
As the distribution of the contribution of the manufacturing sector (at *constant
prices*)[3] to the GDP of selected economies in Table 2 indicates, the share of the
manufacturing sector between 1978 and 1990 has declined somewhat in some of
the countries, remained stable in others and increased in the case of the Japanese
economy. In other words, the repeated observation that the 'shift to services' represents a change toward an increased consumption of services *at the expense* of
manufactured (or agricultural) products is mistaken. The data indicate that there
has not been a significant shift in the relative contribution of the different sectors
of the economy to the total output (see also Baumol *et al.* 1985).

However, within the manufacturing sector rather significant transformations are
taking place. First and foremost, production is switching away from commodities
which are material intensive. Although Peter Drucker (1986: 773) does not offer
a precise source for his estimate, he relates that the raw materials in a semiconductor microchip account for 1–3 percent of total production cost; in an
automobile their share is 40 percent, and in pots and pans it is 60 percent. But also
in older industries the same scaling down of raw material needs goes on, and with
respect to old products as well.[4] The result is, for the time being, that two forms
of manufacturing are emerging:

> one is material based, represented by the industries that provided
> economic growth in the first three quarters of this century. The other
> is information- and knowledge-based: pharmaceuticals, telecommunica-
> tions, analytical instruments and information processing such as
> computers.
>
> (Drucker 1986: 779)

And, most of the economic growth in the manufacturing sector, in terms of value
added, occurs in the knowledge-based industries.

*Table 2* Percentage of gross domestic product (at 1985 prices) generated by manufacturing activity,[1] 1978–1990

|      | Canada | US   | Japan | Australia | Austria | France | Germany (FRG) | UK   |
|------|--------|------|-------|-----------|---------|--------|---------------|------|
| 1978 | 19.0   | 22.7 | 25.6  | 19.6      | 26.4    | 24.9   | 33.2          | 26.1 |
| 1979 | 19.0   | 22.7 | 26.3  | 19.8      | 26.8    | 24.8   | 33.5          | 25.0 |
| 1980 | 17.8   | 21.8 | 25.9  | 19.7      | 26.7    | 24.2   | 32.5          | 23.2 |
| 1981 | 17.8   | 21.7 | 27.3  | 19.4      | 26.4    | 23.7   | 32.1          | 21.4 |
| 1982 | 16.0   | 20.9 | 27.4  | 18.4      | 26.3    | 23.3   | 31.3          | 21.1 |
| 1983 | 16.6   | 21.3 | 27.9  | 17.9      | 26.1    | 23.3   | 31.2          | 20.4 |
| 1984 | 17.6   | 22.3 | 30.0  | 17.6      | 26.5    | 22.6   | 31.8          | 20.5 |
| 1985 | 17.7   | 22.4 | 29.5  | 17.3      | 26.9    | 22.1   | 31.4          | 20.7 |
| 1986 | 17.3   | 22.3 | 28.0  | 17.8      | 26.7    | 21.5   | 31.4          | 20.7 |
| 1987 | 17.4   | 22.4 | 28.9  | 17.5      | 26.0    | 20.8   | 30.4          | 19.8 |
| 1988 | 17.5   | –    | 29.7  | 17.6      | 27.0    | 21.0   | 30.3          | –    |
| 1989 | 17.5   | –    | 30.6  | 17.4      | 27.4    | 21.1   | 30.4          | –    |
| 1990 | 16.1   | –    | 31.3  | 16.7      | 27.9    | 20.9   | 30.4          | –    |

Note

1  The manufacturing activities include: (1) food, beverages and tobacco; (2) textile, wearing apparel and leather industries; (3) wood, and wood products, including furniture; (4) paper and paper products, printing and publishing; (5) chemicals and chemical petroleum, coal, rubber and plastic products; (6) non-metallic mineral products; (7) basic metal industries; (8) fabricated metal products, machinery and equipment; and (9) other manufacturing industries.

*Source*: OECD, *National Accounts: Detailed Tables, 1978–1990*, volume 2 (1992)

Secondly, connected with these changes is a persistent modification in the kind of employment activity typical of the manufacturing sector. Most available official statistics on employment reflect only insufficiently continuing changes in predominant occupational skills and employment patterns in manufacturing. However, information on the percentage of 'administrative, technical and clerical workers' in the manufacturing industries, for example in Great Britain between 1959 and 1982, indicate an appreciable shift in the balance of occupations within the manufacturing sector (cf. Cutler *et al.* 1986: 77). In the case of other countries for which the same type of information is available, consistent shifts toward a larger proportion of 'administrative, technical and clerical' employees as a proportion of all employees in manufacturing can be observed. [. . .] None the less, these figures should only be considered as representing a crude quantitative approximation and likely significant underestimation of a trend toward knowledge-based manufacturing and therefore a demand for skills very much unlike those traditionally expected and practiced in industry. Most importantly, these figures do not show the transformation of job skills and tasks faced by employees in manufacturing who are not, based on conventional typologies, classified as 'white-collar workers' or as 'administrative, technical and clerical workers'. A disaggregation of the information for the manufacturing sector as a whole would, in addition, show that the scale of the shift toward a greater proportion of 'administrative, technical and clerical' personnel and the extent of the substitution of knowledge-based occupations depends on the type

*Table 3* Aggregate hours of work by sector in Germany (FRG), 1960–1991 (millions of hours)

|      | Agriculture | | Manufacturing | | Service | | State | |
|------|--------|-------|--------|------|--------|-------|--------|-------|
|      | Total  | %     | Total  | %    | Total  | %     | Total  | %     |
| 1960 | 8,478  | (100) | 26,101 | (100)| 17,032 | (100) | 4,259  | (100) |
| 1965 | 7,027  | (84)  | 25,868 | (99) | 16,894 | (99)  | 5,172  | (121) |
| 1970 | 5,141  | (61)  | 24,632 | (95) | 16,343 | (96)  | 4,468  | (105) |
| 1975 | 3,909  | (46)  | 20,438 | (79) | 15,869 | (93)  | 6,105  | (143) |
| 1980 | 3,084  | (37)  | 19,922 | (77) | 16,355 | (96)  | 6,553  | (154) |
| 1985 | 2,943  | (34)  | 17,379 | (67) | 16,226 | (95)  | 6,735  | (159) |
| 1990 | 1,973  | (23)  | 18,186 | (70) | 17,148 | (101) | 6,754  | (159) |
| 1991 | 1,898  | (22)  | 18,359 | (70) | 17,728 | (104) | 6,711  | (158) |

*Source*: Kalmbach (1988: 174) and private communication

of industry. But what is needed even more urgently, independent of conventional occupational labels, is a detailed examination of the actual work tasks carried out by employees in industry.

Moreover, the proportion of the production cost in the industrial sector which accrues to knowledge grows and assumes remarkable proportions. In other words, the major source of revenue increasingly comes from software rather than the production of hardware [. . .]

[. . .]

A distinction which becomes quite central in this respect, therefore, is between technical means of production characteristic of industrial society which were, for the most part, experience-based or craft-based technologies and the means of production of the knowledge society which are based, also for the most part, on a 'scientification' of skills. New industries within the manufacturing sector will be derivative of knowledge rather than experience. The skills most valued in manufacturing will not be (practical) experience but systematic knowledge.

[. . .]

These changes, characteristic of the change from industrial society to knowledge society, and the different systems of production in each, are differences in the wake of growing mutual dependence and integration during the twentieth century of scientific knowledge and technical practices and objects (Böhme *et al.* 1978). Production becomes increasingly an extension and specification of laboratory knowledge and leads to the construction of 'idealized' technical objects, which makes it possible to transcend, to some extent at least, more technical and craft-based knowledge in production [. . .]. The greater the comprehensiveness of scientific models and idealized technical objects, the 'more scope they offer for rationalizing technical expertise and practices since they provide a measure of efficiency for machines, and hence designs, which are not derived from current practices' (Whitley 1988: 394). Estimates about the impact of these developments on the production process, changes within sectors of the economy or employment patterns which utilize rather conventional statistical data, for example, the relative presence of 'white-collar' occupations within the manufacturing or service sector of the economy, likely tend to seriously underestimate the transformations because these categories themselves, inherited from industrial society, become obsolete.

Moreover, and also contrary to many conventional assumptions, the normative and material differentiation of economic sectors in modern society is by no means the most significant or important observation one is forced to advance on the basis of the evidence about the pattern of interrelations among economic sectors. For in this instance too, linkage, complementarity or interdependence among sectors is the more incisive observation. For example, service-type inputs are needed at every stage of the production process in the manufacturing sector, or the delivery of most service-type jobs directly or indirectly requires products which originate in the industrial sector of the economy.

In many respects, therefore, the well-established conceptual distinction between the economic sectors, especially between the service and the manufacturing sectors is misleading, at least under contemporary conditions. More specifically, most *goods* purchased are intended to provide a service or a function and there are few 'pure' *services* unconnected to certain commodities. The distinction between goods and services becomes even more ambivalent when one takes into consideration the option of the consumer to purchase, lease or rent (and thereby enjoy the service of) a commodity. In short, 'the output of economic activity may range from that of pure goods to pure services. However, most – and indeed an increasing proportion of – goods embody some non-factor intermediate services, and most services embody some intermediate goods' (Dunning 1989: 4).

## Production against employment

The future of work has been a central concern of social theorists for centuries ever since employment in the sense of a commitment to paid work, in eighteenth-century Europe, became not only an existential imperative but an emblem of civilization. In the eighteenth and nineteenth centuries, the notion of the future of work for most social theorists meant an emancipation *from* the worst physical drudgery and toils associated with work at the time, namely a reduction in work time, greater autonomy and generally more challenging work tasks, whereby liberation from work was thought to be more likely than emancipation *within* the work context. Indeed, the emancipatory potential of industrialization has been fulfilled in the sense that the average work week has been reduced dramatically from more than 80 to less than 40 hours. But in this century too, skeptics remained convinced that workers would find self-fulfillment outside work. That is to say, the standard account of the (inherent) constraints of production and the implicit coercive if not exploitative consequences of a concentration of ownership continued to provide the apparently persuasive background for the thesis that labor in the end is really only another *means of production*.

In the context of the theory of post-industrial society (Bell 1976: 148–149), however, new hopes seem to be raised about the chances of an emancipation of workers within the context of work because post-industrial society is a *communal* society in which the social unit is the community organization rather than the individual, a world in which the modalities are 'cooperation and reciprocity rather than coordination and hierarchy'. In the salient experience of work, 'men live more and more outside nature, and less and less with machinery and things; they live with, and encounter one another.' The question and the reality of any changes in the *quality* of the work context and the demands placed on workers, for example in terms of skill requirements, will be briefly discussed in the next section and at greater length once I analyze the fastest growing segment of the labor force in modern society, namely the group of knowledge-based occupations or 'experts, counselors and advisers.'

The issue which should be taken up first concerns the question of the future of work in a different sense, though not new to discussions about labor in this century, namely the relative *scarcity of work*, the threat of persistent secular unemployment and therefore the much strained relation between economic growth and full employment. The grim question becomes whether, in a knowledge-intensive economy, technology and knowledge not merely eliminate jobs but also work since not so long ago the much more positive conclusion reached after intensive study was that technology destroys jobs but not work. [. . .]

The specific change I have in mind concerns the extent to which employment, especially but not only in the manufacturing sector of the economy, ceases to be a (positive) function of output in this sector; that is, 'increased manufacturing production in developing countries has actually come to mean *decreasing* blue-collar employment. As a consequence, labor costs are becoming less and less important as a "comparative cost" and as a factor in competition' (Drucker 1986: 775). In traditional terms, this development is of course a reflection of increased productivity in the manufacturing sector and therefore of a decrease in the labor/output ratio. The output of the manufacturing sector in advanced economies increases and retains its relative economic importance while its contribution to employment declines. Drucker (1986: 776) predicts, therefore, that developed countries will in twenty-five years 'employ no larger a proportion of the labor force in manufacturing than developed countries now employ in farming – at most, ten percent'.

But the uncoupling of production from labor is more general since the overall increase in the number of unemployed persons has been soaring in the past two decades. The traditional close link between output and employment ceases to accompany shifts in the economy and creates the 'paradox' of growth and unemployment (cf. Therborn 1986). While the evidence in this regard for the manufacturing sector is clear and can draw on a heritage of information dating back a number of decades, there is no comparable experience for the service sector and its growing efforts to search for efficiencies. [. . .] However, it is very likely that the search for efficiencies will be concentrated in the service sector in the future.

Between 1970 and 1989, the number of unemployed increased from 10 million to more than 25 million in the Organization for Economic Cooperation and Development (OECD) countries. [. . .]

One might of course, in the light of these figures, be prompted to offer the entirely correct observation that, despite the increase in unemployment in the past three decades in OECD countries, both the *total labor force* (that is, the number of people registered as working or available for work) and the number of individuals employed or *total employment* has increased substantially. The dramatic increase in unemployment rates, it could be noted further, might therefore at least also be the result of a rapid growth in the supply of labor. However, a growing supply of labor must not invariably, as least as far as relevant historical precedents in the United States, Japan and Germany are concerned, go hand in hand with rising unemployment. A rapid growth in the labor force has been associated with sustained rates of low unemployment. Yet, given the now widely institutionalized expectation in advanced industrial societies that the state and the economy must find ways to guarantee their citizens acceptable and perhaps steadily improving standards of living [. . .], growing and significant rates of unemployment constitute a serious political challenge to governments. Moreover, sustained and consequential unemployment represents a critical challenge to the maintenance of social citizenship rights. In short, it is possible that we are confronted with a new and sustained volume as well as a new structure of unemployment and novel political consequences.

The nature of unemployment has definitely changed in the past two decades. [. . .] The rise and the persistence of long-term unemployment is both related to, but also independent of, the overall unemployment rate. During the 1980s, long-term unemployment grew despite economic recovery and expansion during the later part of the decade. Obviously, the personal and social costs of long-term unemployment are enormous. In the case of many countries of the European Union, high levels of unemployment are now often associated with declining chances of finding a job at all [. . .]. Thus, if the experience of the 1980s is any indication of future patterns of unemployment, the incidence of long-term unemployment will continue at a high level, or even increase in times of more significant economic downturn *and* growth. The rise and the persistence of long-term unemployment is likely due to a number of factors, such as the increase in nonstandard work (part-time and short-term employment), and produces different patterns of exposure to long-term unemployment depending, for example, on the age, education, gender or regional residence of workers. In the long run, however, the most significant factor may well be reduced requirement for labor as a result of fundamental transformations in the economy preventing entry into the workforce in the first place, changing skill requirements displacing workers for extensive periods of time and a mismatch between competencies in demand and those available among unemployed persons.

[. . .]

The data on which most of these observations are based are aggregate unemployment rates. The structural composition of unemployed individuals according to different criteria and on reasons for unemployment are not easy to obtain; nor is the comparative analysis of unemployment rates without serious problems since unemployment is conceptualized and politically managed in very different ways across OECD countries. Aside from national unemployment regimes, for example, the *links* between the welfare state and the labor market, the result is that both the level and the development of unemployment rates will be structured differently. However, this does not mean that observers are completely immobilized in discerning certain fundamental employment changes.

[. . .]

There is serious reason, I believe, to assume that restoring full employment [. . .] is no longer feasible in knowledge societies. Economic processes which in the past may have compensated for severe dislocations of the labor market cannot be counted on anymore. Because the technological changes under way will ultimately impact with special force in the private and public service sector, this sector is no longer capable or can no longer be expected to absorb displaced employees from the other economic sectors, but will itself contribute to a decline in the quantity of available work.[5] Governments and companies in almost every field of economic activity are forced and determined to do more with fewer employees. The repercussions of such a development are considerable. They are significant because full-time paid labor in industrial society was not merely a matter of existential necessity but basic to citizenship rights of individuals and because the volume of the compensatory fiscal activities of the welfare state is dependent on the employment performance of the economy.[6]

## The social anatomy of work

A discussion of the relevant changes of labor and of the workplace in the economy of knowledge societies may be separated into two more or less distinct considerations. First, there is the question of the *quantity* of labor which likely obtains in knowledge societies, and associated with specific structural trends in available work, changes in the meaning of the social construct of 'work'. I have already discussed this issue briefly. Secondly, there is the question of the *quality* of work activities, particularly the required qualifications, typical work activities and the social organization of production. But in each instance, the most significant common issue is whether labor in knowledge societies primarily consists of an extension of trends established in industrial societies, though some of the conditions which justify speaking of a continuation of entrenched patterns may not be the same anymore. In the case of the quality of work activities, for example, one might conclude, although low-skilled manual labor may not be the typical work activity in knowledge societies anymore, that so-called 'intellectual labor' is subject to the same processes of rationalization, coercion and control that affected manual labor in industrial society. In this section, I will concentrate on the second set of issues although a few observations of the social construct of labor are in order.

The meaning associated with the term 'work' today is a product of industrial society. What constitutes work in industrial society is much more narrowly defined than was the case in pre-industrial society. In a number of ways, work activities in industrial society became more clearly separated from non-work activities. The emergent boundaries between the economic and social spheres correspond to the distinction between work and non-work activities: the *spatial* division between the place of work and the location for other types of conduct is among the most important distinction in industrial society. Equally self-evident is the differentiation of work *time* and leisure. Finally, the use of the term 'work' is often restricted to work associated with *employment*, or self-employment.

One of the potentially contentious but also crucial questions of contemporary society is whether the primary meanings associated with the term 'work', especially its narrowness, will or can persist in a world in which work, in the traditional sense of the term, will likely become much more scarce.[7] In knowledge societies, individuals who never join the 'regular' workforce, who are forced out of work, or decide to be unemployed, do not simply drop out of society. They are integrated into society by knowledge as the new principle of sociality. However, they are likely to be mainly *objects* of knowledge and not subjects of knowledge.

It is by no means a novel observation that the social organization of work is changing and that the nature of the change has to do with what originally constituted, at least according to Marx and Engels, the condition for the possibility of the division of labor in society, namely, the separation of labor into manual and intellectual labor (cf. Marx and Engels [1932] 1960: 28). The shift is away from manual to intellectual labor, and therefore to a corresponding increase in the role knowledge and learning play in shaping work and the ability to work.

Within this set of issues, at least two distinct questions may be identified. First, the extent to which, in the course of these changes, the nature of work *activities*, of work organization and experience with work undergoes changes; secondly, the changing conditions of production raise questions about the relation between work and other social arrangements, for example, social inequality, education, culture, leisure, the family, and their respective boundaries. [. . .]

[. . .]

In a more general sense, in recent years the focus of the sociology of work, the sociology of organizations and industrial sociology has been on the extent to which the work environment and the social organization of work activities have been transformed enough to justify the conclusion that work in advanced industrial society justifies either the label of a perpetuation of trends already in place in industrial society (perhaps even a worsening of some attributes of work activities), or whether, as a result of the changing working conditions, work and its environment changes dramatically and constitutes a break with the kind of work typical of industrial society.

In the case of the dominant perspective of industrial society in which a certain kind of technological progress or regime is closely linked to mass production systems, intensive productivity gains and the capacity to produce an abundance of goods as well as hierarchical forms of work organization and control, the answer is almost self-evident. In the end, the (capitalist) logic at work always contributes, as emphasized at one time, to a massive alienation of workers, or as argued more recently, to an extensive de-skilling of the work force (e.g. Braverman 1974).[8] The ability of management to preserve and exercise domination is assured by virtue of holding on to or monopolizing *knowledge* about the conceptions on which production is based. That is, the successful separation of execution and conception is the key to the control and persistent degradation of the worker. The new version of the oppression thesis also generalizes about the workplace without any credit to the imagination of the worker and specific conditions of work. The thesis minimizes, consistent with Marx's portrait of the labor process in capitalist society, the ability of the worker to affect his or her working conditions. Technological developments simply reproduce the domination of capital over labor, often on a more repressive scale and contribute, as Merton (1947: 80) already expresses it, to an 'enforced obsolescence of skills'.[9] These observations tend to make inferences about processes from outcome. In general, therefore, the much discussed Braverman thesis, developed decades later, about the irreversible de-skilling process of labor treats the change in the nature of technological paradigms, the specificity of the workforce, the dynamics of work and local conditions as a black box. But one might also ask whether it is something inherent in the process of material production which requires the detachment of planning and execution, or whether the disconnection stems rather from the desire of management to control and exploit labor?[10]

Today, fascination with the constraining features of the conditions which give rise to more hierarchy and control have been replaced by equally strong convictions about a new technology and a logic of organizing production which is essentially permissive (cf. Hirst and Zeitlin 1991; [. . .]). These views are linked in turn to the distinction between the declining regime of mass manufacturing ('Fordism') and the growing system of 'flexible specialization' in production (cf. Piore and Sabel 1984). As a result, technology is no longer seen as a dehumanizing force but as one which enables or at least holds the promise of participation in the affairs of work. In the sphere of work, the profound anxiety about the destructive ways of technology are now replaced by animated discussions about the freedoms from control. The vocabulary of intentionality and agency, thought to be obsolete, reappears in discussions of work, production and the social organization of work (e.g. Cavestro 1989). Paradoxically, the technology once feared to have become self-regulating now regulates itself in the sense of negating regulation. None the less, perspectives which emphasize the enabling features of new technology should not commit the same fallacy associated with assertions about the inherently repressive nature of production technologies, namely, to declare, as Karl Marx for example did, that technology invariably reproduces domination. Even if new technologies allow for greater flexibility and require it for greater efficiency, they do not thereby automatically also foreclose the possibility, depending on local circumstances and the nature of (economic and political) 'partnerships' that technology happens to find itself lodged in, that versatility and innovative capacity is restricted in the interest of sustaining hierarchical control of owners and managers.[11] There is not a natural role for technology as such in all of this.

[. . .]

## From the employment society to the consumption society

Compared to virtually all other prior historical societies, the modern capitalist societies that emerged in North America and Europe during the eighteenth and nineteenth centuries have been most concerned with the conditions of employment. The extraordinary and consistent preoccupation with paid work and the emergence of paid labor as a social activity separate from the household justify the label of 'employment societies' (Keane 1988). Not surprisingly, economic discourse, too, is preoccupied with concerns directly linked to the worlds of production (of goods and services), work and incomes (in the form of rents, interest and wages). In other words, economic discourse today continues to be linked to the eighteenth-century definition of the *major* factors of production, namely, capital and labor, its mix and consequences measured in monetary units. The world of work finds its mirror image in the sphere of consumption. Society produces in order to consume and it consumes in order to produce. For many purposes, such a focus indeed may still be quite appropriate. For example, if one is concerned with the productivity of capital or labor, such an arithmetic is sufficient. Even though in modern societies 'less than one sixth of the total time of the average fit adult' (Gershuny 1988: 6) is devoted to paid work, paid labor as a separately institutionalized activity continues to constitute the major social activity of large segments of the population and much of the energies of modern society are still geared toward efforts to constantly expand the production of goods and services.

However, if the focus and the implied equivalence as well as equilibrium between production and consumption shift, both in the case of those who are still part of the realm of labor and those who are not, namely, from work in the narrow sense of the term, to *forms of life* of employees and households in modern society, then an analysis, as Niklas Luhmann (1988: 164–166) for example has emphasized, of the *consumption* side – especially in relation to the total wealth (*Besitzstand*) – is more pertinent than is the mere income of individuals or households.[12] Consumption acquires greater independence from production. Undoubtedly, work provides meaning to consumption. As the aggregate of work shrinks and as the relative amount of time individuals devote in their lifetime to work for which they are compensated is reduced and as consumption is less immediately tied to labor, the meaning of consumption changes as well.

The growth in the total wealth and entitlements of individuals and households has accelerated enormously. Many individuals and households become, through pension funds for example, indirect owners of the means of production as well, though such ownership of course has lost much of its traditional attributes. What is meant here, therefore, is not related to the shift, although quite real, in the quantity of time spent outside the work environment and therefore a shift in central-life interests (Dubin 1956) to leisure activities. The focus still remains with the material or economic well-being of individuals and households; however, forms of life, in as much as they are dependent on material well-being, are not driven any more by considerations directly linked to the value of income but consumption patterns and their determinants, namely the *Besitzstand* of the actor(s). The determinants of the consumption patterns are related to the specific circumstances of the individual and the household unit. Structures of social inequality resonate with such circumstances as well.[13]

Among the outcomes of such a change in the circumstances which affect forms of life and material well-being is a closer link between the economic and social spheres, or a shift in the economic dependency relations of individuals and households. But even more importantly, the specificity of social conflicts in knowledge societies changes dramatically. The displacement of concerns and struggles which primarily revolve around the satisfaction of economic needs, the allocation of monetary income, interests and rents, shifts the locus of major societal conflicts to more generalized and global needs. The primary role in terms of which social struggles take place no longer involves *workers as workers* and the owners of the means of production as capitalists. The locus of the conflicts shifts to the individual as a configuration of roles, or as Alain Touraine ([1984] 1988: 11) puts it, to the *social actor* in any one of his or her roles: 'One could almost say that it is the human being as living being.' One of the principal axes of conflicts pits the consumer against production regimes of all sorts.[14] The generalization of issues contested in societal conflicts deprives knowledge societies of a central locus and arena in which these struggles take place.

## The emergence of the symbolic economy

A further major change in the structure of the economy of post-industrial societies is the emergence of an (internationalized) symbolic economy which 'deals' in monetary and non-monetary symbolic commodities. Peter Drucker (1989: 127) assumes that the symbolic economy, in the form of money flows, already shapes and rivals the transnational material economy.[15]

Initially, the term 'symbolic commodities' should be put into quotation marks, lest one simply assumes that the full range of symbolic commodities has *economic*, *legal* and *practical* qualities not unlike any other commodity, for example durable goods which have a certain utility independent of the specific context in which the product is produced, exchanged or consumed, and a legal status, especially property rights attached to it. None of these attributes applies, at least in the strict sense, to a number of the symbolic commodities. Most importantly perhaps, the identity and utility of the symbolic items are often highly context sensitive and cannot be 'understood' or estimated separate from the context in which they originated and were 'consumed'. The proximity of the context of production and utilization of symbolic commodities is often quite close; the life expectancy of symbolic commodities is fairly limited. Property rights to symbolic commodities are virtually absent. The regulative principles which govern market exchanges and intervention into the market do not apply in full force to exchange processes involving symbolic commodities.

Symbolic 'commodities' of a monetary nature, in particular capital movements, cross-rates, exchange rates, interest-rate differentials and credit flows, are to a considerable extent 'unconnected to trade – and indeed largely independent of it' and 'greatly exceed trade finance' (Drucker 1986: 782); they are more important now for the world economy than the traditional flow of goods and services.[16] The gold exchange standard which operated for much of the life span of industrial society has been replaced by the electronic information system of today.

Symbolic commodities of a non-monetary nature are, for example, data ('sets of numbers'), technological trajectories, statistics, fashion regimes, programs, product marketing and organizational 'knowledge' as well as the growing flow of information within and across national boundaries. The acceleration of the flow of information increases uncertainty; more precisely, it reduces the length of those moments in which certainty appears to prevail. The rapid dissemination of symbolic goods accelerates their obsolescence. In the manufacturing industry, for example, the growing importance of symbolic commodities for the provision of products and their production raises costs and demands larger markets to absorb these expenditures. Commodities and services, to a growing extent, embody knowledge.

Developments of the monetary symbolic economy, changes in its trends and abrupt shifts occur often in response to anticipated political events or are driven by unanticipated crises in different parts of the world. Indeed, not only trade in goods and services is very much affected by the symbolic economy, the dynamics of the symbolic economy often have political repercussions. In addition, in the traditional realm of international trade and services, the movement of *symbolic commodities*, that is, knowledge, has become a more salient factor in the world economy (cf. Dickson 1984: 163–216).

## The eclipse of time, distance and place

One further significant effect of the production of goods and services more dependent on knowledge is the growing irrelevance of time and place (and therefore
distance) as a constraint for production; that is, competitive advantages increasingly
are expressed in symbolic terms and such capital is much more mobile within and
across national boundaries. The potential for spatial reorganization and the re-
disposition of time in production, distribution and consumption activities arises from
the ability of information technology to 'overcome' time and distance constraints.
However, the uneven mosaic of existing spatial divisions of firms and enterprises,
that is, the existing high geographical concentration of industries within and among
nations, will not suddenly give way to a less structured and unequal location of
economic activities. Nor does the increasing emancipation of the productive process
from time and place mean that production is no longer taking place within country
or region-specific social and political contexts and constraints or that only decentralization effects will be observable. While constraints on place do not disappear
altogether, changing spatial and time constraints allow for *many more locational configurations* than was the case under previous regimes with much more restrictive
constraints [. . .]. As a matter of fact, new constraints including the compression
of time are added as production becomes knowledge-based manufacturing, and
others, such as the existing services and the infrastructure generally in a particular
location, remain significant in decisions to abandon or position enterprises.

None the less, contemporary 'locational capacities' of firms and enterprises,
although not equally distributed across the range of manufacturing and service industries, have multiplied considerably. Companies have more choice as to where they
decide to combine mobile and relatively immobile, i.e. country or region-specific,
endowments. Specific decisions of course will depend on a host of factors, for
example, the reasons for investing in the first place, the product characteristics,
the behavior of competitors, the regulations and policies of host countries and social
and cultural factors [. . .]. Most importantly, however, the relative eclipse in the
importance of scarce locational features, distance and time for productive processes,
and in many instances, services, represents a radical inversion of the governing
calculus compared to the importance of locational configurations which count
for economic production processes in industrial societies. In industrial societies
production is in principle still tied closely to location (region) and/or time by virtue
of the weight and cost of moving crucial productive ingredients, factors which
allow for manufacture of commodities in the first place. In contrast, knowledge, in
principle, is highly mobile and travels well. Under the proper conditions, especially
in the presence of economic incentives, knowledge not only travels well but
fast. This also means that an efficient communication infrastructure will be quite
important for the economy in the knowledge society (cf. Nicol 1985: 192;
Henderson and Castells 1987). The choices of potential contexts for production
have multiplied immeasurably and have become, as some economists begin to name
it, 'global'. It also means that the kinds of considerations which enter into the determination of the location of production extend beyond those crucial in the past,
namely a calculus primarily, though rarely only, driven by considerations of
economic efficiency.

Historically, location theories which tried to explain the distribution of employment in manufacturing, for example, have emphasized the constraints related to the costs of transportation, access to the means of production, especially labor and the relative rigidity of production methods. At the same time, the relevant boundaries within contemporary economic discourse still presume that the decisive boundaries are those of the (sovereign) nation-state. The growing irrelevance of location and time for production, distribution and consumption also means that the link between what were once thought to be norms or 'rationalities' of *different* social systems, for example leisure and economics, converge or are confronted in decisions about production facilities. Location is more than merely an allocation problem [. . .].

In knowledge societies, production and enterprises are, or will be, largely emancipated from the geographical features of a location. The redefinition and rearrangement in the location of enterprises or production are related, on the one hand, to the 'enabling developments in the service components of goods production, and information handling and communication technologies' (Britton 1990: 536) and, on the other hand, dramatic changes in the production regimes themselves. Important consequences follow from this. In many instances, the specific location for production, while independent of a certain *natural* geographical location, as was often the case in the past, in fact has to exist or be created in the first place. In that respect at least, the choice of location remains rather closely tied to the idea of a specific context and particular locations, constraints which then account for the spatial division of labor. In the United States, 'high-tech industries are likely to be found in states with traditions of innovative manufacturing, and within major metropolitan areas where business services and other urban amenities are ample' (Glasmeier 1990: 73). It is a (socially) constructed context in which these firms decide to locate, a context which can be provided for production, in principle, almost anywhere, especially if one assumes that the calculations which lead to a particular location of economic activities are not based exclusively on economic dimensions.

The efficiency of economic activities that are functionally interdependent will, in the future, not decrease despite increasing physical distance between parts of production activities (cf. Nicol 1985: 198). Similarly, a decentralization of organizational activities should not seriously interfere with the ability to communicate and co-ordinate tasks. The ability to more freely divide activities spatially actually turns into an asset for economic activities. As long as the determination of location can emancipate itself from the now dominant close relationship between costs and distance, other factors such as the availability of skills and composition of the labor force will influence locational decisions. As a result, it is probably safe to assume that urban concentration, for example, will not decline; on the contrary, it may continue to increase despite the diminishing importance of the cost of transportation for goods and services.

The growing irrelevance of time to production does not mean that time becomes unimportant altogether either, but rather takes on a very different kind of importance. For example, the possibility of a closer co-ordination of production schedules, even over a great distance, means that questions of the storage of parts and the like declines, and production is closer to actual needs. It is therefore more important now to have a specific item available at a precise instant, yet to live up to that requirement becomes easier as production schedules 'communicate' with each other.

New production technologies often imply that a major economic factor is not so much the time spent producing, but the time during which equipment is idle, including 'downtime' because of malfunctions. Thus, the irrelevance of the time of year or day in production renews the issue of total time of production and of working hours. Knowledge-based production is more flexible and allows for, some would argue requires, a much greater flexibility in working hours.

The reasons for the irrelevance of time and place for production and the provision of services have to do, on the one hand, with technologies, or better technological regimes, which 'diminish' space and 'shrink' time and, on the other hand, with the qualities of the object that need to be moved in order to produce and in order to consume. Limits to the speed and ease with which the prerequisites of production and the 'products' can be moved are increasingly disappearing. The *enabling* technologies (Dicken 1992: 103) which overcome the limits to movement in industrial society (and generate different frictions of space and time in knowledge societies) are the new media of communication and transportation. For much of human history and a considerable portion of the life span of industrialized society, the speed with which materials, products and individuals were transported was identical to the speed and obstacles faced by entities which had to be communicated across distances. In addition, the costs of moving both tangible and intangible goods was quite sensitive to the distance which had to be traveled and the volume which had to be moved. Today, the mobility of 'information' and the speed with which tangible goods are moved are increasingly at odds. Much of the cost of communication is virtually independent of distance (cf. de Sola Pool 1990: 34–39) and volume, while the cost of the transport of goods is still contingent on distance and volume. Moreover, the cost of communication has fallen sharply. The gap in the time, ease and cost it takes to move information and tangible products represents one of the constraints on production or incentives to reduce the amount of tangible entities used in production. In addition, some of the same enabling technologies have altered the rigidities of production regimes and corporate organization, making both potentially more divisible and adding further to the process of emancipating production from constraints of time and place.

## New limits to growth

Ralf Dahrendorf (1988: 123) makes the point that the 1970s were a time of 'enormous exaggeration. The exaggeration of gloom and doom.' Not since José Ortega y Gasset's *The Revolt of the Masses* and Oswald Spengler's *Decline of the West* in the late 1920s and early 1930s have so many books been written about the pending descent and dissolution of a way of life. But no title better reflected and symbolized the spirit of the discussion and concerns than the study of the Club of Rome on the *Limits to Growth* (Meadows *et al.* 1972). The despairing prognosis of the 1972 Report was that present growth trends in world population, industrialization, food production, environmental decay (in particular, pollution) and the exhaustion of natural resources have to come to a halt within the next century.

The thesis that the world will reach the limits of resource availability on global scale is self-evident or a tautology. For practical purposes, what is relevant is the time scale. And in this respect at least, discussion about the limits of growth, both then and probably now, continues to suffer from simply extrapolating established trends into the future. The limits-to-growth discussion of the early 1970s was, of course, based on certain premises about the nature of the modern productive and distributive process, with trends extended into the (near) future given specific assumptions, especially about not only scarce but finite resources and a growing world population (cf. Meadows *et al.* 1972). The outcome of such reflections was the conviction that continued economic growth in industrial societies, and efforts of Third World pre-industrial economies to catch up, is not sustainable and will, in fact, soon lead to catastrophe. But these predictions were soon contradicted by competing analyses (e.g. Leontief 1977) and events. But at issue here is not whether economic growth is desirable or whether the ratio of resources to population trends and the impact of economic growth on the environment will lead to a sudden reversal in secular advances in economic well-being in the near future, but, rather, the changes in the nature of the productive process itself (not only driven by economic considerations) and the political agenda on any discussion about the limits to economic growth.

One of the crucial deficiencies of the Meadows Report is not so much the notion of constraints on economic activity and patterns of growth, or even 'limits', but concerns the determination of such limits, namely the simple extrapolation of existing trends into the future. More extrapolation ignores a whole range of dynamic economic, social and political processes which determine future outcomes, including self-fulfilling and defeating conduct.

The growing centrality of knowledge to the productive process alters the import of certain resources and accelerates the significance of others with different limits. The outcome is that new or different but not necessarily no limits to growth become relevant. One of the commendable outcomes of the *Limits to Growth* has been to affect the agenda of political discourse and policy. The issue of environmental consequences of human activity is now part of the political agenda in many countries.

The changing limits to the growth of national economies or to the global economy also raise the question of the contribution of 'knowledge' to production and increases in output. Available aggregate estimates from economists tend to be fairly imprecise as well as ambivalent; perhaps such figures will never be very precise. One estimate available for the United States credits 'knowledge', which in this instance includes advances in technological, managerial and organizational knowledge, as a source for 54 percent of the total gain in economic growth during the period of 1948–1973 (Denison 1979: 2), while knowledge accounted for only 26 percent of the growth in the years between 1929 and 1948 (Denison 1979). But as the author of these figures points out himself, these percentages are obtained as residual figures 'because there is no way to estimate it directly' (Denison 1979: 131). In fact, the economic growth due to knowledge is therefore, following the advice of Solow (1957), merely that 'percentage of the measured growth rate in output that cannot be explained by the growth rate of total factor inputs and by other adjustments made for other types of productivity increases' (Feller 1987:

240). Since the different 'variables' typically taken into consideration in these estimates tend to be interrelated, but no theory about their interdependence is available in economic discourse, decompositions of the relative contributions to economic growth only constitute mere illustrations of the growth process (cf. Nelson 1981). For the most part, estimates of the contribution of knowledge (or technology) to economic growth in the long term are just beginning to be researched more comprehensively (e.g. Fagerberg 1988, 1991). For the time being, many dimensions of the use and change produced by knowledge in the economy are not taken into consideration in these estimates. It is, therefore, quite possible that the contribution of knowledge is systematically under-represented to date. And since the estimates are aggregate figures, it is far from clear which sectors and what commodities are knowledge-intensive and which are not; at least these numbers do not allow for any inferences about such questions. In addition, the increased importance of the knowledge factor does not imply that the 'welfare' of society benefits, assuming one has a definite notion of what constitutes a contribution to the welfare of society. But it is entirely possible that much of the growth attributed to knowledge occurs as a result of the production of weapons, other destructive means, commodities which have detrimental environmental impact, nuclear energy or reflect work done in the area of space exploration, all with dubious social utility. In short, the figures need to be much more carefully dissected, although the question of the social utility of economic growth raises difficult, contentious questions (cf. Heilbroner 1973).

## The fragility of the future

Although much effort has been invested in the reduction of the contingencies of economic affairs and in the improvement of the possibilities of planning and forecasting, the economy of the knowledge society is, as much as the rest of global society, increasingly subjected to a rise in indeterminacy. While success may at times justify the high hopes of many that techniques and technologies will be developed to reduce if not eliminate much of the uncertainty from economic conduct, sudden and unexpected events almost invariably disconfirm, almost cruelly, such optimistic forecasts about the possibility of anticipating and therefore controlling future events. As a matter of fact, and paradoxically, one of the sources of the growing indeterminacy can be linked directly to the nature of the technological developments designed to achieve greater certainty. The new technology contributes to and accelerates the malleability of specific contexts because of its lower dedication (limitation) to particular functions. Technological developments add to the fragility of economic markets and the need of organizations operating in such a context to become more flexible in order to respond to greater mutability in demand and supply. In the sphere of production, as a result, a new utopian vision arises, a vision which Charles Sabel (1991: 24)[17] sketches in the following and deliberately enabling terms:

> Universal materializing machines replace product-specific capital goods;
> small and effortlessly re-combinable units of production replace the

hierarchies of the mass-production corporation; and the exercise of autonomy required by both the machines and the new organizations produces a new model producer which view of life confounds the distinction between the entrepreneurial manager and the socialist worker-owner.

Much of the standard discussion of these matters, at least until recently, has been animated by opposite expectations. Bell (1973a: 26), for example, confidently asserts that the 'development of new forecasting and "mapping" techniques makes possible a novel phase in economic history – the conscious, planned advance of technological change, and therefore the *reduction of indeterminacy* about the economic future' (emphasis added).

But the factor of greater fragility, malleability and volatility is not confined to the economy, the labor market and the social organization of work and management, nor does it merely have 'positive' effects on social relations and individual psyches. Greater vulnerability corresponds to greater fragility and greater flexibility is linked to new regimes of exclusion.

## Notes

1   The economic concept of *capital* is narrowly defined and refers to fixed, physical capital equipment in plant and organizations. Such capital is recognized as *investment*, that is, as objects which must be purchased. However, the acquisition of knowledge, for example, in the sense of research and development, creating of organizational structures, educational programs or the development of skills are treated as *expenses* and not as contributing to the capital formation of organizations.

2   One of the significant exceptions among economic theorists is Friedrich von Hayek (e.g. [1945] 1948) for whom the central problem of economic theory is the problem of knowledge and who, despite his methodological individualism, views social institutions such as economic markets as knowledge-bearing phenomena. Markets are not allocative mechanisms but rather epistemological devices 'in which knowledge that could not be collected by a single mind is yet rendered accessible and usable for human purposes' (Gray 1988: 55). Markets embody tacit knowledge.

3   Using constant rather than current prices and therefore focusing on quantity rather than both volume changes and price changes generates a somewhat more accurate picture of the relative position of the manufacturing sector. When measured in current prices, the share of manufacturing in the US has constantly *fallen* since 1978; at constant prices, however, its contribution remains stable as Table 2 demonstrates. The difference in the two trends reflects the higher productivity in the manufacturing sector relative to other sectors and therefore a relative decline in its prices, for example, compared to prices in services. By the same token, the decline in the contribution of the manufacturing sector to the GDP in the United Kingdom, measured in *current prices*, could be a consequence of the same factors. But in the case of the United Kingdom, constant prices were not available.

4   Peter Drucker and Daniel Bell refer almost in unison, though without citing a source for their information, to the following relations for illustrative purposes: (a) Drucker (1986: 773) contends that 'fifty to 100 pounds of fiberglass cable transmits as many telephone messages as does one ton of copper wire'; and (b) Bell (1987: 8) recounts that 'one hundred pounds of optical fibers in a cable can transmit as many messages as one ton of copper wire'. I assume that both authors found their information in a newspaper or magazine.

5    The image of the dilemma of the laboring society increasingly losing work but also of being emancipated from the burden of work may be found in Hannah Arendt ([1960] 1981).

6    Karl Hinrichs and his colleagues (1988) offer a number of resolutions and options to this dilemma which do not simply either reduce the legal claims individuals are allowed to make on the income-maintenance programs of the state or increase the contributions of employers and those still employed to the welfare state. The option which assumes particular significance in the context of their considerations is the working time and the possibility of devising ways to reduce it across the board in order to generate additional employment.

7    One social theorist who has reflected on the appropriateness of the narrow, employment-centered term of work and offered suggestions for a broader understanding of work is Enzo Mingione. For example, he proposes that work should include 'all types of formal employment, but also a variety of irregular, temporary or occasional activities undertaken to raise cash and various activities that produce use values, goods and services for direct consumption either by the individual and his/her household or other individuals or households, which are more or less necessary for the survival' of the individuals and households (Mingione 1991: 73). One of the purposes of the new broader definition of work is to join conceptually more closely what already has been joined in practice, namely the social and economic spheres of activity. Another consequence of the broader conception, then, is to offer an analysis of the importance of the 'informal' economy. [. . .]

8    Although the de-skilling thesis is often associated with the work of Harry Braverman, there are numerous predecessors, reviewing developments in production processes of industrial society, that conclude, as Helmut Schelsky (1954: 20), for example does: 'The closer we approach automation, though without ever fully reaching it, the greater the degree to which work becomes spiritless and stressful and the lesser the extent to which it requires interest in technical matters and skills or even initiative of any sort.' However, Schelsky anticipates a further state in the evolution of work in which, after automation has been achieved, the worker will be required to perform highly skilled tasks, for example, in the course of supervising and controlling highly complex production equipment.

9    Merton assumes, as do the proponents of the later de-skilling thesis, that the obsolescence of skills is irreversible. In the light of the kind of production technology used, a compensation process is presumably not considered likely. The increasing employment of labor-saving technology produces the enforced obsolescence of skills among the workers. The social and psychological consequences of discarding acquired skills are mainly connected to the demotion of status (including the possible loss of the public identity of the job) and the destruction of the positive self-image of the worker, stemming from the once confident use of those skills. In short, as Merton (1947: 80) anticipates as well, 'alienation of workers from their job and the importance of wages as the chief symbol of social status are both furthered by the absence of a social meaning attributable to the task. Increased specialization of production leads inescapably to a greater need for predictability of work behavior and, therefore, for *increased discipline in the workplace*.'

10   For Theodor Adorno (1969) and André Gorz ([1971] 1976: 170), for example, the answer can only be, at least as long as one examines the issue from the (interested) point of view of the owner of the means of production, that it is not technical progress 'in the true sense' which requires hierarchy and a fragmented division of labor in industry but the effort and determination of the class of owners for maximum exploitation. In addition, such aims are not necessarily compatible with the most efficient use of production techniques and work organization. The relations of production still dominate the forces of production.

11   Summing up a number of case studies in this area of research, Jones (1990: 306) arrives at such a cautionary note when he observes that 'in general the prospect of using these systems [flexible specialization] to tighten hierarchical control over final operations may prove more appealing to many managers than the surrender of detailed powers to the shop floor *that is necessary* for versatile and innovative productive capability.'

12   Among sociologists who emphasized rather early the growing importance of the consumer position of individuals in modern society, at the expense of the importance of the occupational position, for their consciousness and status, are Helmut Schelsky (1956: 65) and Ralf Dahrendorf ([1957] 1959: 273).

13   Niklas Luhmann (1988: 165) illustrates this proposition as follows, 'whether one is married or not and whether one has children or not, whether the spouse works or not and whether, as the case may be, one may have to support divorced spouses, whether one lives in an inherited home or has to rent – all these factors contribute more significantly to the economic life chances than collectively agreed upon wage rates or, as the ease may be, insurance or pension payments.'

14   More concretely, the new social conflicts have involved consumers in quite a spectacular and many-faceted way. They have spoken out against 'schools or against the university in the name of education, against the scientific-political complex in the name of public good, against hospitals in the name of health, against urban planning in the name of interpersonal relations, against the nuclear industry in the name of ecology' (Touraine [1984] 1988: 110).

15   Following the 'currency crisis' in the third week of September 1992, the *New York Times* (September 23, 1992, Section C1) was prompted to observe that 'on a dull day, hundreds of billions of dollars' worth of marks, yen, dollars and other currencies change hands, as speculators bet on the direction of currency markets and money managers seek opportunities overseas. On a busy day, volume can top a trillion dollars. That is a lot of money. And as last week proved, the combined power of all these traders can overwhelm the power of governments, even when all of Europe is trying to act in concert. The events provided a bitter reminder to central bankers and finance ministers around the world that the power of governments to control economies and currencies has eroded.'

16   Drucker (1986: 782) provides the following figures to illustrate the claim: 'World trade in goods is larger, much larger, than it has ever been before. And so is the "invisible trade", the trade in services. Together, the two amount to around $2.5 trillion to $3.0 trillion a year. But the London Eurodollar market, in which the world's financial institutions borrow and lend to each other, turns over $300 billion each working day, or $75 trillion a year, a volume at least 25 times that of world trade.'

17   Sabel acknowledges that he has been seen as the major author and therefore responsible for this utopian vision; however, he prefers to subscribe to a more 'prudent version of these caricatures'. This is a perspective which accounts for the 'diversity and similarity of efforts to adjust to the new competitive environment' (Sabel 1991: 24–25).

# References

Adorno, Theodor (1969) 'Spätkapitalismus oder Industriegesellschaft', in T. Adorno (ed.) *Spätkapitalismus oder Industriegesellschaft*, Verhandlungen des 16. Deutschen Soziologentages. Stuttgart: Ferdinand Enke, pp. 12–26.

Arendt, Hannah [1960] (1981) *Vita activa, oder vom tätigen Leben*. Munich: Piper.

Baumol, W. J. *et al.* (eds) (1985) 'Unbalanced Growth Revisited: Asymptotic Stagnancy and New Evidence', *American Economic Review* 75: 806–817.

Bell, Daniel (1976) *The Cultural Contradictions of Capitalism*. New York: Basic Books.

Bell, Daniel (1979) 'The Social Framework of the Information Society', in Michael L. Dertouzos and Joel Moses (eds) *The Computer Age: Twenty-Year View*. Cambridge, MA: MIT Press, pp. 163–211.

Bell, Daniel (1987) 'The World and the United States in 2013', *Daedalus* 116: 1–31.

Block, Fred (1985) 'Post-industrial Development and the Obsolence of Economic Categories', *Politics and Society* 14: 71–104, 416–441.

Bluestone, Barry and Harrison, Bennett (1982) *The Deindustrialization of America*. New York: Basic Books.

Braverman, Harry (1974) *Labor and Monopoly Capital: The Degradation of Work in the Twentieth Century*. New York: Monthly Review Press.

Britton, Stephen (1990) 'The Role of the Production', *Progress in Human Geography* 14: 529–546.

Cavestro, William (1989) 'Automation, New Technology and Work Content', in Stephen Wood (ed.) *The Transformation of Work?* London: Unwin Hyman, pp. 219–234.

Cutler, T., Williams, K. and Williams, J. (1986) *Keynes, Beveridge and Beyond*. London: Routledge and Kegan Paul.

Dahrenforf, Ralf [1957] (1959) *Class and Class Conflict in Industrial Society*. Stanford, CA: Stanford University Press.

Dahrenforf, Ralf (1988) *The Modern Social Conflict: An Essay on the Politics of Liberty*. Berkeley: University of California Press.

Denison, E. (1979) *Accounting for Slower Economic Growth*. Washington, DC: Brookings Institute.

Dicken, P. (1992) *Global Shift: The Internationalization of Economic Activity*, 2nd edn. New York: Guilford Press.

Dickson, David (1984) *The New Politics of Science*. New York: Pantheon Books.

Dosi, Giovanni *et al.* (1988) (eds) *Technical Change and Economic Theory*. London: Pinter.

Drucker, Peter (1986) 'The Changed World Economy', *Foreign Affairs* 64: 768–791.

Drucker, Peter (1989) *The Age of Discontinuity: Guidelines to Our Changing Society*. New York: Harper and Row.

Dubin, Robert (1956) 'Industrial Workers' Worlds: A Study of the "Central Life Interests" of Industrial Workers', *Social Problems* 3: 131–142.

Dunning, John H. (1989) 'Transnational Corporations and the Growth of Services: Some Conceptual and Theoretical Issues', *United Centre on Transnational Corporations Current Studies Series A*, no. 9. New York: United Nations.

Durkheim, Emile [1893] (1964) *The Division of Labor in Society*. New York: Free Press.

Fagerberg, J. (1988) 'Why Growth Rates Differ', in G. Dosi *et al.* (eds), op. cit., pp. 432–457.

Fagerberg, J. (1991) 'Innovation, Catching Up and Growth', in OECD (eds) *Technology and Productivity: the Challenge for Economic Policy*. Paris: OECD, pp. 37–46.

Feller, I. (1987) 'The Economics of Technological Change Filtered Through a Social Knowledge System Framework', *Knowledge* 9: 233–253.

Gershuny, Jonathan I. (1988) *The Social Economics of Post-Industrial Societies* A Report to the Joseph Rowntree Memorial Trust. Bath: University of Bath.

Glasmeier, Amy (1990) 'High-Tech Policy, High-Tech Realities: The Spatial Distribution of High-Tech Industry in America', in Jurgen Schmandt and Robert Wilson (eds) *Growth Policy in the Age of High Technology: The Role of Regions and States*. Boston: Unwin Hyman.

Gorz, Andre [1971] (1976) 'Technology, Technicians and Class Struggle', in Andre Gorz (ed) *The Division of Labour: The Labour Process and Class Struggle in Modern Capitalism*. Hassock: Harvester, pp. 160–189.

Hayek, F. von [1945] (1948) 'The Use of Knowledge in Society', in *Individualism and Economic Order*. Chicago: University of Chicago Press, pp. 77–91.

Heilbroner, R. (1973) 'Economic Problems of a Post-Industrial Society', *Dissent* 20: 163–176.

Henderson, Jeffrey and Castells, Manuel (eds) (1987) *Global Restructuring and Territorial Development*. London: Sage.

Hinrichs, K., Offe, C. and Wiesenthal, H. (1988) 'Time, Money and Welfare-State Capitalism' in John Keane (ed.) *Civil Society and the State: New European Perspectives*. London: Verso, pp. 221–243.

Hirst, P. and Zeitlin, J. (1991) 'Flexible Specialization Versus Post-Fordism: Theory, Evidence and Policy Implications', *Economy and Society* 20: 1–56.

Jones, B. (1990) 'New Production Technology and Work Roles: A Paradox of Flexibility Versus Strategic Control', in R. Loveridge and M. Pitt (eds) *The Strategic Management of Technological Innovation*. New York: Wiley, pp. 293–309.

Keane, John (1988) *Democracy and Civil Society*. London: Verso.

Keynes, John M. (1936) *The General Theory of Employment, Interest and Money*. London: Macmillan.

Leontief, W. (1977) *The Future of the World Economy*. New York: Oxford University Press.

Luhmann, Niklas (1988) *Die Wirtschaft der Gesellschaft*. Frankfurt am Main: Suhrkamp.

Mannheim, Karl [1935] (1940) *Man and Society in an Age of Reconstruction: Studies in Modern Social Structure*. London: Routledge and Kegan Paul.

Meadows, D. *et al.* (1972) *The Limits to Growth*. New York: Universe Books.

Merton, Robert K. (1947) 'The Machine, the Worker and the Engineer', *Science* 105: 79–84.

Mingione, Enzo (1991) *Fragmented Societies: A Sociology of Economic Life Beyond the Market Paradigm*. Oxford: Blackwell University Press.

Nelson, R. (1981) 'Research on Productivity Growth and Productivity Differentials: Dead Ends and New Departures', *Journal of Economic Literature* 19: 1029–1064.

Nicol, Lionel (1985) 'Communication Technology: Economic and Spatial Impacts', in Manuel Castells (ed.) *High Technology, Space and Society*. Beverly Hills, CA: Sage, pp. 191–209.

Offe, Klaus (1984) *Arbeitsgesellschaft: Strukturprobleme und Zukunftsperspektiven*. Frankfurt am Main: Campus Verlag.

Piore, Michael J. and Sabel, Charles F. (1984) *The Second Industrial Divide*. New York: Basic Books.

Sabel, Charles F. (1991) 'Moebius-strip Organisations and Open Labor Markets: Some Consequences of the Reintegration of Conception and Execution in a Volatile Economy', in P. Bourdieu and J. S. Coleman (eds) *Social Theory for a Changing Society*. Boulder, CO: Westview Press, pp. 23–54.

Schelsky, Helmut (1954) 'Zukunftsaspekte der industriellen Gesellschaft', *Merkur* 8: 13–28.

Schelsky, Helmut (1956) 'Gesellschaftlicher Wandel', *Offene Welt* 41.

Sola Pool, Ithiel de (1990) *Technologies without Boundaries: On Telecommunications in a Global Age*. Cambridge: Harvard University Press.

Solow, R. (1957) 'Technical Change and the Aggregate Production Function', *Review of Economics and Statistics* 39: 312–320.

Stigler, George J. (1961) 'The Economics of Information', *Journal of Political Economy* 69: 213–225.

Swedberg, Richard (1987) 'Economic Sociology: Past and Present', *Current Sociology* 35: 175–221.

Therborn, Göran (1986) *Why Some People Are More Unemployed Than Others: The Strange Paradox of Growth and Unemployment*. London: Verso.

Touraine, Alain [1984] (1988) *Return of the Actor: Social Theory in Postindustrial Society*. Minneapolis: University of Minnesota Press.

Whitley, Richard (1988) 'The Transformation of Expertise by New Knowledge: Contingencies and Limits to Skill Scientification', *Social Science Information* 27: 391–420.

# Chapter 16

# Anne Balsamo

## FORMS OF TECHNOLOGICAL EMBODIMENT

From M. Featherstone and R. Burrows (eds) *Cyberspace, Cyberbodies, Cyberpunk*, London: Sage (1995), pp. 215–37.

## Introduction

**T**HIS ESSAY ADDRESSES the contemporary cultural conjuncture in which the body and technology are co-joined in a literal sense, where machines assume organic functions and the body is materially redesigned through the use of new technologies of corporeality. Broadly, the examples I consider, taken from the media of everyday life, [. . .] signal ways in which the 'natural' body has been dramatically refashioned through the application of new technologies of corporeality. By the end of the 1980s, the idea of the merger of the 'biological' with the 'technological' had infiltrated the imagination of Western culture such that the cyborg – the 'technological-human' – has become a familiar figuration of the subject of postmodernity. For whatever else it might imply, this merger relies on a reconceptualization of the human body as a boundary figure belonging simultaneously to at least two previously incompatible systems of meaning – 'the organic/natural' and 'the technological/cultural'. At the point at which the body is reconceptualized not as a fixed part of nature, but as a boundary concept, we witness an ideological tug-of-war between competing systems of meaning which include and in part define the material struggles of physical bodies.

[. . .]

My intent for this project is to contribute to the development of a 'thick perception' of the body in contemporary culture from a feminist standpoint. For Michel Feher (1987), 'thick perception' involves an analysis of the 'different modes of construction of the human body'. [. . .]

[. . .]

Accordingly, 'thick perception' is a Foucauldian technique for understanding the ways in which the body is conceptualized and articulated within different cultural discourses. To think of the body as a social construction and not as a natural object provokes a deceptively simple question: how is the body, as a 'thing of nature', transformed into a 'sign of culture'? The work I examine in this project begins with the assumption that 'the body' is a social, cultural and historical production: 'production' here means both product and process. As a product it is the material embodiment of ethnic, racial and gender identities, as well as a staged performance of personal identity, of beauty, of health (among other things). As a process it is a way of knowing and marking the world, as well as a way of knowing and marking a 'self'. The process of elaborating an informed 'perception' of the body in contemporary culture must simultaneously abstract a discourse of the body and construct an interpretation of it. 'Reading' as a culture and interpretive practice is the central mechanism of my discursive production. But what I read are not simply textual or media representations of the gendered body, but more specifically social practices of 'making the body gendered'. The act of reading as 'making a discourse' apparent is meant to suggest an active practice of perception that has been determined in specific ways: I have been unconsciously trained, more consciously taught, cajoled and ambushed in my efforts to decipher the cultural construction of the gendered body in various textual forms. This is to say that, although this project is thoroughly grounded in contemporary body scholarship, it is not a reading that springs fully formed from the current moment, as if there existed a singularly unified discourse to read or, relatedly, a singular body to write. Rather I focus on a continuum of discourses which includes the popular cultures of the body as well as scholarly works of body theory. The point is to annotate a taxonomy of the ways in which the techno-body is constructed in contemporary culture. In contrast to those who would argue that there is a dominant – singular – form of the postmodern techno-body, I argue that when starting with the assumption that bodies are always gendered and marked by race it becomes clear that there are multiple forms of technological embodiment that must be attended to in order to make sense of the status of the body in contemporary culture.

## Seeing things differently

The story Arthur Kroker relates (Kroker and Kroker 1987) about the body in postmodernity, or hyper-modernity in his terms, is that it has been 'unplugged from the planet'; accordingly, the signal form of the postmodern body is the disappearing body – a notion that the natural body has no ontological status separate from the proliferation of rhetorics that now invest the body with simulated meaning. In his brilliant, although somewhat convoluted reading of the body in contemporary culture, Kroker argues that in its dissolution, the body is subordinated to various apparatuses of power; in the process the body is transformed in historically specific ways. For example, in explaining how the body is ideologically subordinated he points to the way in which bodies are: 'inscribed by the mutating signs of the fashion industry as skin itself is transformed into a screen effect for a last, decadent and desperate search for desire after desire' (Kroker and Kroker 1987: 21). [. . .]

[. . .]

When Kroker reads the signs of the times of the postmodern body in the art of various visual and performance artists, he finds ample evidence to develop his theses on the disappearing body. The gendered identity of this body is noticed obliquely. [. . .] The insight he offers about gender is that women's bodies have always been postmodern because they have always known the invasion of cultural rhetorics that would define them according to broader systems of power. According to Kroker, women's bodies have always served as an inscribed text upon which are written the dominant myths of masculinist culture – myths that would define those bodies as that which is the 'other' of man, interpellated by ideology, and discursively constructed as unruly, threatening, uncontrollable. But if women's bodies have been always invaded by various rhetorics of power, how then is the disappearance of the body (the invaded body) a new condition endemic to postmodernity? The only possible response is that the disappearing body actually marks the historically specific identity of the male body as it experiences this corporeal invasion for the first time.

The feminist story of the postmodern body begins with the assumption that bodies are always gendered and marked by race. In attending to the way that Kroker builds his body theory, it is clear that for him 'the body' is an idealist abstraction. As far as it goes, this is a provocative story. But it is only a partial story of postmodern corporeality. What is missing is a material dimension that takes into account the embodied markers of cultural identity. The polemic in this paper argues that the body can never be constructed as a purely discursive entity. In a related sense, it can never be reduced to a pure materialist object. Better to think of the dual 'natures' of the body in terms of its 'structural integrity' to use Evelyn Fox Keller's (1992) term. This is to assert that the material and the discursive are mutually determining and non-exclusive. Kroker's theory of the 'disappearing' body notwithstanding, the material body remains a constant factor of the postmodern, post-human condition. It has certain undeniable material qualities that are, in turn, culturally determined and discursively managed; qualities that are tied to its physiology and to the cultural contexts within which it makes sense, such as its gender and race identities.

## Cyberpunk techno-bodies

Here then is a different story about the postmodern body that is abstracted from contemporary science fiction. As a work of the feminist imaginary, this narrative extracted from Pat Cadigan's (1991) cyberpunk novel, *Synners*, explicitly discusses an often-repressed dimension of the information age: the material identity of the techno-body. True to its genre determinations, *Synners* concerns a loosely identified 'community' of computer users, each of whom is differently, albeit thoroughly, engaged with the technologies of cyberspace – simulation machines, global communication networks, corporate databases and multi-media production systems. What we encounter in the Cadigan novel is the narrativization of four different versions of postmodern embodiment: the laboring body, the marked body, the repressed body and the disappearing body. In this sense, the four central characters symbolize the different embodied relations one can have, in fiction and in practice, to a technological formation. The following figure roughly illustrates how Sam, Gabe, Gina and Visual Mark (the four main characters) represent four corners of an identity matrix constructed in and around cyberspace.

*Sam*
(the body that labors)

*Gina*
(the marked body)

*Gabe*
(the repressed body)

*Visual Mark*
(the disappearing body)

*Figure 1*

Where Sam hacks the net through a terminal powered by her own body, Visual Mark actually inhabits the network as he mutates into a disembodied, sentient artificial intelligence (AI). Although both Gina and Gabe travel through cyberspace on their way to someplace else, Gabe is addicted to cyberspace simulations and Gina merely endures them. Each character plays a significant role in the novel's climactic confrontation in cyberspace: a role determined, in part, by their individual relationships to Diversifications (the genre-required evil multinational corporation) and, in part, by their bodily identities. What follows is a brief synopsis of the body biography of each character.

In the course of the novel, Visual Mark, in true cyberpunk fashion, spends less and less time off-line and more and more time plugged in to the global network known as 'the System'. This leads him to reflect on the metaphysical nature of his physical body: 'he lost all awareness of the meat that had been his prison for close to fifty years, and the relief he felt at having laid his burden down was as great as himself' (1991: 232). After suffering a small stroke while jacked in, Visual Mark prepares for 'the big one' – a stroke that will release his consciousness into the system and allow him to leave his meat behind.

> He was already accustomed to the idea of having multiple awareness and a single concentrated core that were both the essence of self. The old meat organ would not have been able to cope with that kind of reality, but out here he appropriated more capacity the way he once might have exchanged a smaller shirt for a larger one.
>
> (1991: 325)

And sure enough, while his body is jacked in, Mark strokes out. As his meat dies, both his consciousness and his stroke enter 'the System'. In the process, his stroke is transformed into a deadly virus (or spike) that initiates a world-wide network crash.

Sam, Gabe's daughter and the only real hacker among the four, is a virtuoso at gaining access to 'the System'. She is the character who best describes the labor of computer hacking and the virtual acrobatics of cyberspace travel: '[i]f you couldn't walk on the floor, you walked on the ceiling. If you couldn't walk on the ceiling, you walked on the walls, and if you couldn't walk on the walls, you walked in them, encrypted. Pure hacking' (1991: 351). As competent as she is in negotiating the cyberspatial landscape of the net, Sam tries to live her embodied life outside of any institutional structure. Her only affiliations are to other punks and hackers who form a community of sorts and who live out on 'the Manhattan–Hermosa strip, what the kids called the Mimosa, part of the old postquake land of the lost' (1991: 7). Sam trades encrypted data and hacking talents for stray pieces of equipment and living necessities. In what proves to be a critically important 'information commodity' acquisition, Sam hacks the specifications for an insulin-pump chip reader that runs off body energy. When every terminal connected to 'the System' is infected by Visual Mark's stroke/virus, Sam's insulin-pump chip reader is the only noninfected access point to the net. Connected by thin needles inserted into her abdomen, the chip reader draws its power from Sam's body. Seventeen-year-old Sam is a cyberspace hacker of considerable talent who shuns the heroic cowboy role. And for the most part, she is content to provide the power while others, namely Gina and Gabe, go in for the final showdown.

Gabe spends most of his working time, when he should be designing advertising campaigns, playing the role (Hotwire) of a *noir* leading man in a computer simulation built from pieces of an old movie thriller (1991: 41). Where Visual Mark cleaves to cyberspace because the world isn't big enough for his expansive visual mind, Gabe becomes addicted to cyberspace because the world is just too big for him. He retreats to the simulation pit for the safety and familiarity it offers. 'He'd been running around in simulation for so long, he'd forgotten how to run a realife, real-time routine; he'd forgotten that if he made mistakes, there was no safety-net program to jump in and correct for him' (1991: 239). Throughout the novel, Gabe moves in and out of a real-time life and his simulated fantasy world. In real-time his body is continually brought to life, through pain, intoxication and desire caused by Gina, first when she punches him in the face with a misplaced stab intended for Visual Mark, then later when he gets toxed after she feeds him two LotusLands (a 'mildly hallucinogenic beverage'). After they make love for the first time, Gina wonders if Gabe has ever felt desire before: 'She didn't think Gabe Ludovic had ever jumped the fast train in his life. Standing at the end of fifteen years of marriage, he'd wanted a lot more than sex. The wanting had been all but tangible, a heat that surprised both of them' (1991: 243). After a climactic cyberspace struggle, his repressed body reawakens; Gabe learns to feel his body again (or for the first time) with Gina's help.

Like Visual Mark, Gina is a 'synner' who synthesizes images, sound and special effects to produce virtual reality music videos. For all her disdain and outright hostility toward other people and institutions, 'Badass Gina Aiesi' has an intense emotional connection to Visual Mark, her partner of 20 years, that she romanticizes in an odd way:

> They weren't smooch-faces, it didn't work that way, for her or for him.
> . . . One time, though . . . one time, three–four–five years into the
> madness, there'd been a place where they had come together one night,

and it had been different. . . . He'd been reaching, and she'd been reaching, and for a little while there, they'd gotten through. Maybe that had been the night when the little overlapping space called their life had come into existence.

(1991: 213)

Gina's body, marked by its color, 'wild forest hardwood', and her dreadlocks, figures prominently in the narrative description of her sexual encounters, first with Visual Mark and then with Gabe. After both she and Visual Mark have brain sockets implanted, they jack in together and experience a visual replay of shared memories: 'The pov was excruciatingly slow as it moved across Mark's face to her own, lingering on the texture of her dreadlocks next to his pale, drawn flesh, finally moving on to the contrast of her deep brown skin' (1991: 216). The characteristics that mark Gina are her anger, her exasperated love for Mark and the color of her skin.

Like the dramatic climax in recent cyberpunk films such as *Circuitry Man* (1989), *Lawnmower Man* (1991) and *Mindwarp* (1991), the final showdown in *Synners* takes place in cyberspace. Working together, the small Mimosa community assembles a work-station (powered by Sam's insulin-pump chip reader) that enables Gina and Gabe to go on-line to fight the virus/stroke – an intelligent entity of some dubious ontological status that now threatens the integrity of the entire networked world. Like a cyberspace Terminator, the virus/stroke is hyper-rationally determined to infect/destroy whomever or whatever comes looking for it. In the course of their cyberspace brawl, Gabe and Gina confront the virus's simulation of their individual worst fears. A 'reluctant hero' till the very end, Gabe's cyberspace enemy is a simple construct: the fear of embodiment. 'I can't remember what it feels like to have a body', he repeats obsessively during his final confrontation in cyberspace. What he learns through the encounter is that his whole body is a hot-suit; that is, he learns to feel the body that he has technologically repressed.

In one sense, Cadigan writes fiction implicitly informed by Donna Haraway's cyborg politics: the gendered distinctions among characters hold true to a cyborgian figuration of gender differences whereby the female body is coded as body-in-connection and the male body as a body-in-isolation. It illuminates the gendered differences in the way that the characters relate to the technological space of information. Sam and Gina, the two female hackers, actively manipulate the dimensions of cybernetic space in order to communicate with other people. Gabe and Visual Mark, on the other hand, are addicted to cyberspace for the release it offers from the perceived limitations of their material bodies. Even as the novel's characters illuminate the gendered distinctions among computer network users, its racial characterizations are less developed. The racial distinctions between characters are revealed through the representation of sexual desire. Gina is the only character to be identified by skin color. She is also the focal object and subject of heterosexual desire, for a moment by Mark, and more frequently by Gabe; and, we know both men's racial identities by their marked difference from Gina's. The unmarked characters are marked by the absence of identifying marks. In different ways then and with different political inflections, the novel reasserts that gender and race are critical elements of post-human identity.

Throughout the book, the characters' material bodies are invoked through descriptions of sexual encounters, bathroom breaks, food consumption, intoxication effects and physical death. The key insight to emerge from the novel is that the denatured techno-body remains a material entity. Although it may be culturally coded and semiotically marked, it is never merely discursive. This is to say that even as *Synners* discursively represents different forms of technological embodiment, it also reasserts the critical importance of the materiality of bodies in any analysis of the information age.

Expanding upon this delimited reading of *Synners* as both cultural landmark and cognitive map yields another version of the matrix above that offers a taxonomy of forms of technological embodiment. The ground upon which this matrix is constructed is the shifting table of body theory: each quadrant is a multidimensional space for filing body snapshots, art installations, performances, readings, enactments and corporeal forms. The qualities that mark each form of embodiment are illustrated by various incarnations of the techno-body. This taxonomy shares characteristics with those constructed by other body scholars, notably Bryan Turner (1984, 1991) and Arthur Frank (1991). Frank's schema most closely resembles the matrix developed in this essay. For example, his notion of the 'disciplined' body shares qualities with my notion of the repressed body. In other cases, our categories do not simply match up, although there are strong resonances. In his account of the 'communicative body', he identifies elements that I assign to both the 'laboring body' and the 'marked body'. The communicative body, for Frank, is an expressive realization of itself, 'no longer appropriated by institutions and discourses, but by the body's own' life (1991: 80). This quality of expression is a key characteristic of the marked body in my matrix; the subtle difference between Frank's account of the communicative body and mine of the marked body is tied to a notion of agency. I see the marked body as bearing the signs of culture, even when these signs are appropriated by the body in question. The quality of corporeal expression that Frank rightly emphasizes is one that I assign to the laboring body – both as it is based in the facticity of reproduction and, reflecting a Marxist influence, in the conditions of productive labor. Both Turner and Frank recognize, to different degrees, the gendered nature of forms of embodiment; they are less specific about the racial aspects of those forms though. In the following sections, I consider the gendered and racial dimensions of a range of new bio-technological forms of embodiment. The aim is to illustrate how material bodies are both discursively constructed and culturally disciplined at a particular historical moment.

| | |
|---|---|
| *The LABORING Body* | *The DISAPPEARING Body* |
| Mothers as Wombs | Bio-engineering |
| Microelectronics Workers | Bodies and Databases |
| | |
| *The REPRESSED Body* | *The MARKED Body* |
| Virtual Reality | Multi-cultural Mannequins |
| Computer Communication | Cosmetic Surgery |

*Figure 2* Postmodern forms of technological embodiment

## The marked body

The marked body signals the fact that bodies are eminently cultural signs, bearing the traces of ritual and mythic identities. In similar ways, both the fashion industry and the cosmetic surgery profession have capitalized on the role of the body in the process of 'identity semiosis' – where identities become signs and signs become commodities. The consequence is the technological production of identities for sale and rent. Material bodies shop the global marketplace for cultural identities that come in different forms, the least permanent as clothes and accessories worn once and discarded with each new fashion season, the most dramatic as the physical transformation of the corporeal body accomplished though surgical methods. Thus the natural body is technologically transformed into a sign of culture.

High fashion – as one technology of urban corporeal identity – is preoccupied with multiculturalism. One of the consequences is that in reading the body displayed on the glossy pages of American fashion magazines, it is evident that the politics of representation are very confused. For example, from its very first US issue in January 1957, *Elle* magazine regularly included photography layouts that featured black and other non-white models wearing various 'deconstructed' fashions. The May 1988 cover of *Elle* that showcased the faces of two models, one white in the background, made-up in conventional fashion, the other black in the foreground, wearing no discernible make-up, betrays the cultural politics at the center of the worldview of the high fashion industry where 'black bodies' serve as mannequins for designer messages intended for affluent white readers. The narrative constructed around *Elle*'s black bodies and white bodies concerns the fashion industry's appropriation of the trope of primitivism as a seasonal fashion look. In this case, the fashion apparatus deploys signs of the 'primitive' in the service of constructing an antifashion high fashion look. While another *Elle* article explained that the American 'love of the exotic' has translated into career success for several new multicultural supermodels it was rarely mentioned that they were few of the women who could actually afford the clothes featured as items in the new primitivism line that cost upwards of $1000. Thus an interesting paradox takes shape: the black bodies of supermodels are used as billboards for designer messages about the fetishization of black identity as the cultural sign of the ethnic primitive. Just as they are admitted to the elite club of well-paid supermodels, black models are coopted to a cultural myth of racial subordination.

This appropriation of the signs of cultural primitivism for the visual consumption of mostly white readers illuminates the mass-mediated rehearsal of the construction of cultural identity, where what is reviled and despised is projected onto the body of the 'other' such that the identity of the 'One' is established as that which is good and pure and sacred. At the same time, the body of the 'other' is fetishized and eroticized in its object form. In this way, the proper hierarchy of white bodies over black bodies is subtly, and compulsively, reinscribed in each season's look. The recuperative power of corporate culture and its premier technology, mass media advertising, extends far beyond the appropriation of black identity and tropes of primitivism. As the recent trend of deconstructionism as high fashion look attests, even the markers of poverty are able to be rearticulated to a different economic logic. The focal figure and preferred mannequin of these fashion campaigns is the eroticized dark brown female body, but the valorized subject is the white, Western woman, whose white body can be liberated, temporarily, from the debasement of everyday life through her consumption and mimicry of anti-fashion style.

Much like those physicians who use sonograms and laparoscopes to look through the material body, cosmetic surgeons also make use of new visualization technologies to exercise a high-tech version of Foucault's scientific bio-power that effects, first, the objectification of the material body and, second, the subjection of that body to the discipline of a normative gaze. In the past five years, several cosmetic surgeons have begun using a new high-tech video imaging program as a patient consultation device. In the process, the medical gaze of the cosmetic surgeon is transformed into the technological perspective of the video camera. Using computer rendering tools, such as erasers, pencils and 'agenic cursors', the cosmetic surgeon manipulates the digitized image of the prospective patient in order to visually illustrate possible surgical transformations. One of the consequences is that the material body is reconfigured as an electronic image that can be technologically manipulated on the screen before it is surgically manipulated in the operating room. In this way, the video consultation enables the codification of surgical 'goals' – goals which effect, in short, the inscription of cultural ideals of Western beauty.[1] Where visualization technologies bring into focus isolated body parts and pieces, surgical procedures carve into the flesh to isolate parts to be manipulated and resculpted. In this way, cosmetic surgery literally transforms the material body into a sign of culture. The discourse of cosmetic surgery offers provocative material for a discussion of the cultural construction of the gendered body because, on the one hand, women are often the intended and preferred subjects of such discourse, and on the other, men are often the bodies doing the surgery. Cosmetic surgery is not then simply a discursive site for the 'construction of images of women', but, in actuality, a material site at which the physical female body is technologically dissected, stretched, carved and reconstructed according to cultural and eminently ideological standards of physical appearance.

## The laboring body

Bodies that labor include a full range of working bodies as well as maternal bodies. In the broadest sense these are all reproductive bodies involved in the continuation of the human race in its multiple material incarnations. Such bodies are often invisible in postmodern discourse. But, because they are centrally involved in the reproduction of various technological formations, including now the 'natural' family unit, they must be counted as key postmodern cultural forms.

Perhaps the most obvious form of the laboring body is the maternal body which is increasingly treated as a technological body – both in its science fictional and science factual form as 'container' for the fetus, and in its role as the object of technological manipulation in the service of human reproduction. How, specifically, are the material bodies of pregnant women affected by cultural discourses?

In a discussion of the politics of new reproductive technologies, Jennifer Terry (1989) examines how these technologies are deployed in the service of institution-alized practice of surveillance, whereby pregnant women are watched in the name of 'public health' to determine whether they are taking drugs or alcohol while pregnant. In 1989, newspapers across the USA reported on the spectacle of 'cocaine mothers' – the mediated identity of women who deliver babies who show traces of cocaine in their systems at birth. Since 1990, several women, branded thus by the media, have been charged with criminal child neglect for the delivery of a controlled substance to a minor. One of the consequences is that maternal rights of body privacy are set against the rights of a fetus to the state's protec-tion. The personification of the fetus as an entity with 'rights' is made possible, in part, because of the use of visualization technologies such as sonograms and laparo-scopes. In the application of these technologies, the material integrity of the maternal body is technologically deconstructed, only to be reconstructed as a visual medium to look through to see the developing fetus who is now, according to some media campaigns, 'the most important obstetrics patient'. In short, the use of these technologies of visualization creates new cultural identities and enables new agents of power that, in turn, create new possibilities for the discipline of maternal bodies. In this way, cultural discourses not only establish the meaning of material bodies, but also significantly delimit the range of freedom of some of those bodies.

Attending to laboring bodies also suggests the need to investigate the material conditions of the production of the cheap, high-tech devices purchased in bulk by US consumers of electronic commodities. For example, silicon chips are relatively inexpensive to manufacture and assemble because of the use of cheap labor in south-east Asia. In the course of his investigation of Malaysia's labor contribution to the microelectronics industry, Les Levidow (1991) discovered that women workers were the preferred employees for electronic firms because it is believed that 'they are naturally suited to the routinized work of the electronics assembly line: nimble fingers, acute eyesight, greater patience' (1991: 106). Although these women are compensated monetarily, daughters contribute a significant percent-age of their earnings to their families. Other forms of compensation are more intangible, and double-edged. Women factory workers experience a measure of independence from 'village elders', who would have bound them to traditional Islamic practices and values but, at the same time, they risk significant health prob-lems in the form of blindness, respiratory disease and psychological and sexual manipulation. The point is not to argue that these are the only laboring bodies that bear the brunt of technologically assisted disciplinary actions, but rather to assert that women are far more likely to be the targets of such discipline. This is in part due to their historically designated position within labor networks tied to their physiology, that is, as possessing nimble fingers suited for detailed handwork. It is also a consequence of the gendered division of labor whereby women occupy the lowest paying positions because of active discrimination, beliefs about women's inferiority, their socialization to service roles, and the social and cultural pressures to marry, bear children and forego compensated employment in favor of unpaid domestic labor.

## The repressed body

Repression is a pain management technique. The technological repression of the material body functions to curtail pain by blocking channels of sensory awareness. In the development of virtual reality [VR] applications and hardware, the body is redefined as a machine interface. In the efforts to colonize the electronic frontier – called cyberspace or the information matrix – the material body is divorced from the locus of knowledge. The point of contact with the interior spaces of a virtual environment – the way that the computer-generated scene makes sense – is through an eye-level perspective that shifts as the user turns her head; the changes in the scene projected on the small screens roughly correspond with the real-time perspectival changes one would expect as one normally turns the head. This highly controlled gaze mimes the movement of a disembodied camera 'eye' – a familiar aspect of a filmic phenomenology where the camera simulates the movement of perspective that rarely includes a self-referential visual inspection of the body as the vehicle of that perspective. Although some VR users report a noticeable lag time in the change of scene as the head turns, that produces a low-level nauseous feeling, for the most part the material body is visually and technologically repressed. This repression of the body is technologically naturalized in part because we have internalized the technological gaze to such an extent that 'perspective' is a naturalized organizing locus of sense knowledge. As a consequence, 'the body', as a sense apparatus, is nothing more than excess baggage for the cyberspace traveler.

In short, what these VR encounters really provide is an illusion of control over reality, nature and, especially, over the unruly, gender and race-marked, essentially mortal body. There is little coincidence that VR emerged in the 1980s, during a decade when the body was understood to be increasingly vulnerable (literally, as well as discursively) to infection, as well as to gender, race, ethnicity and ability critiques. At the heart of the media promotions of virtual reality is a vision of body-free universe. In this sense, these new technologies are implicated in the reproduction of at least one very traditional cultural narrative: the possibility of transcendence whereby the physical body and its social meanings can be technologically neutralized. In the speculative discourse of VR, we are promised whatever body we want, which doesn't say anything about the body that I already have and the economy of meanings I already embody. What forms of embodiment would people choose if they could design their virtual bodies without the pain or cost of physical restructuring? If we look to those who are already participating in body reconstruction programs, for instance, cosmetic surgery and bodybuilding, we would find that their reconstructed bodies display very traditional gender and race markers of beauty, strength and sexuality. There is plenty of evidence to suggest that a reconstructed body does not guarantee a reconstructed cultural identity. Nor does 'freedom from a body' imply that people will exercise the 'freedom to be' any other kind of body than the one they already enjoy or desire. This is to argue that, although the body may disappear representationally in the virtual worlds of cyberspace and, indeed, we may go to great lengths to repress it and erase its referential traces, it does not disappear materially in the interface with the VR apparatus, or in its engagement with other high-tech communication systems.

In the Jargon File,[2] the entry on 'Gender and ethnicity' claims that although 'hackerdom is still predominantly male', hackers are gender and color-blind in their interactions with other hackers due to the fact that they communicate (primarily) through text-based network channels. This assertion rests on the assumption that 'text-based channels' represent a gender-neutral medium of exchange, and that language itself is free from any form of gender, race or ethnic determinations. Both of these assumptions are called into question not only by feminist research on electronic communication and interpretive theory, but also by female network users who participate in the virtual subcultures of cyberspace.[3] Studies of the new modes of electronic communication indicate that the anonymity offered by the computer screen empowers antisocial behaviors such as 'flaming' and borderline illegal behaviors such a trespassing, e-mail snooping and MUD-rape.[4] And yet, for all the anonymity they offer, many computer communications reproduce stereotypically gendered patterns of conversation.[5] Hoai-An Truong, a member of the Bay Area Women in Telecommunications (BAWIT) writes:

> Despite the fact that computer networking systems obscure physical characteristics, many women find that gender follows them into the on-line community, and sets a tone for their public and private interactions there – to such an extent that some women purposefully choose gender neutral identities, or refrain from expressing their opinions.[6]

This is a case where the false denial of the body requires the defensive denial of the body in order to communicate. For some women, it is simply not worth the effort. Most men never notice. The development of and popular engagement with cybernetic networks allow us the opportunity to investigate how myths about identity, nature and the body are rearticulated with new technologies such that traditional narratives about the gendered, race-marked body are socially and technologically reproduced.

## The disappearing body

Of all the forms of technological embodiment, the disappearing body is the one that promises most insistently the final erasure of gender and race as culturally organized systems of differentiation. Bio-engineered body components are designed to duplicate the function of material body parts; bit by bit the 'natural' body is literally reconstructed through the use of technological replacement parts. But even as the material body is systematically replaced piece by piece, system by system, gender identity does not entirely disappear. 'Sexy Robots' and war machines still bear the traces of conventional gender codings. In the case of bodies that more literally disappear into cyberspace – here I'm talking about the technological coding of bodies as part of electronic databases – racial identity functions as a submerged system of logic to organize body information, even as it is coded in bits and bytes.

As part of a special preview of the year 2000 and beyond, the 1988 February issue of *Life* magazine featured an article called 'Visions of tomorrow' that included a report on the replaceable body parts that were already 'on the market' . . . elbow and wrist joints, and tendons and ligaments. We are told how succeeding genera-tions of artificial 'devices' will be even more complex than the ones we have today, aided by research in microelectronics and tissue engineering. For example, glass eyes will be replaced with electronic retinas, pacemakers with bionic hearts, and use of the already high-tech insulin dispenser will soon become obsolete in favor of an organically grown biohybrid system that could serve as an artificial pancreas. The availability of manufactured body parts has subtly altered the cultural understanding of what counts as a natural body. Even as these technologies provide the realistic possibility of replacement body parts, they also enable a fantastic dream of immor-tality and control over life and death.

Images, such as the *Life* magazine illustration of the 'future body', show how male and female bodies are constructed differently with respect to their reproduc-tive and sexual functions. The replaceable body featured in the *Life* article is gendered through the inclusion of photographs of plastic penile implants and the plastic non-functional testicle. It is certainly ironic that although the article specu-lates about a future when 'a Sears catalogue of body options' will be widely available, the one body prosthesis currently available through the Sears Catalogue is not pictured – the female breast form. Although its symbolic and ultimately hegemonic function has been sharply criticized, this non-functional prosthesis is widely used by women who have had radical mastectomies. Since the *Life* photograph includes other body prostheses that are neither implanted (an arm-hand device, for example) nor functional (the plastic testicle), the exclusion of the artificial breast form, which is also not implanted and non-functional, subtly reveals the intended gender of the future body. Obliquely referred to in the article, but not pictured in the *Life* photo-graph, the female body is signified through a reference to the development of an artificial uterus. This association between the female body and the uterus or the womb signals the dominant cultural definition of the female body as primarily a reproductive body. Such a metonymic relationship is far from innocent, though. In this future vision, the male body is marked by the signs of a fully able, embodied person, whereas the female body is marked only by a textual reference to the arti-ficial uterus. This rendition of the 'future' female techno-body recalls the construction of the female techno-body in the discourse of reproductive technolo-gies – as a container for the fetus.

The relationship between material bodies and the information collected about those bodies is of central concern to people who ask the question, 'Who counts?' This leads to the investigation of both those who determine who counts as instances of what identities, and also those who are treated as numbers or cases in the construction of databases. The politics of databases will be a critical agenda item for the 1990s as an increasing number of businesses, services and state agencies go 'on-line'. Determining who has access to data, and how to get access to data that is supposedly available to the 'public', is a multidimensional project that involves the use of computers, skill at network access and education in locating and negoti-ating government-regulated databases. Even a chief data coordinator with the US Geological Survey asserts that 'data markets, data access, and data dissemination are complicated, fuzzy, emotional topics right now'. She 'predicts that they likely will be the major issues of the decade'.[7] Questions of public access and of the status of information collected on individuals are just now attracting public attention.

For those who monitor the insurance industry's interest in database development, there are already several warning signs about the material consequences of digitizing bodies. The Human Genome Project (HGP) is a big-science enterprise that promises to deliver an electronically accessible map of all 100,000 genes found on human chromosomes. This electronic map could be used for diagnostic screening; all that is needed is a sample of genetic material collected as part of the application process for life insurance. One insurance company in the US has already petitioned for the right to require a sample of saliva with each new client's application. The ethics of constructing electronic maps of the human genetic code is a critical concern for those involved in the HGP; in fact, in 1994, 5 percent of the Project's budget was set aside for ethical research. This concern with ethics has not deterred the development of related projects whose ethical implications are more directly contested, and whose methods of gene recording are less digital and more biological. For example, the aim of the Human Genome Diversity project (a project related to the HGP) is to record 'the dwindling genetic diversity of Homo sapiens by taking DNA samples from several hundred distinct human populations and storing them in gene banks' (Gutin 1994).

Researchers could then examine the DNA for clues to the evolutionary histories of the populations and to their resistance or susceptibility to particular diseases. Even though this seems like an entirely benevolent project on the surface, members of the populations targeted to be archived think otherwise. In a letter dated 18 November 1993, Chief Leon Shenandoah and the Onondaga Council of Chiefs demanded that the Project's directors 'cease and desist immediately all activities regarding DNA structures (genetic fingerprints) of the people of Onondaga and Cayuga Nations and other indigenous nations and people'.

> Your process is unethical, invasive and may even be criminal. It violates the group rights and human rights of our peoples and indigenous peoples around the world. Your project involves the very genetic structures of our beings.[8]

The issue at stake is the creation of a 'bank' of information about a certain population whose members have no official right to assess the accuracy of the information collected about them, let alone to monitor the intended or potential use of such information. This raises questions about intellectual property rights, informed consent and rights of privacy. Members of populations whose genetic material is 'banked' at various laboratories are not alone in their vulnerability to the misuse of collected information. Any consumer who uses credit cards or other forms of digital funds transfer is equally disempowered in terms of the right of ownership of the information collected. Such widely distributed research programs as the Human Genome Project and the Human Genome Diversity Project are in fact re-tooling notions of privacy and corporeal identity. They demonstrate how the reality of the material body is very much tied to its discursive construction and institutional situation. Digitized representations of corporeal identity impact material bodies. The politics of representation in these cases are doubly complex in that it is difficult not only to determine how the body is being represented, but also who is the agent of representation. Given the 'truth status' of scientific discourse, it is difficult to assert that a representation has been constructed.

## Conclusion

Postmodern embodiment is not a singularly discursive condition. Failure to consider the multiple ways in which bodies are technologically engaged is to perpetuate a serious misreading of postmodernity as structured by a uniformly dominant cultural logic. Although, if pressed, most critics would probably assert that they don't believe in a 'uniformly' dominant culture logic, such claims implicitly inform both Arthur Kroker's work on 'Body invaders' and Fredric Jameson's elaboration of the cultural logic of postmodernity. Such a reading obscures the consideration of the diverse range of political forces that determine the reality of material bodies. In offering the matrix of forms of technological embodiment, I argue that the material body cannot be bracketed or 'factored out' of postmodern body theory. This is not an argument for the assertion of a material body that is defined in an essentialist way – as having unchanging, trans-historical gender or race characteristics. Rather, it is to argue that the gender and race identity of the material body structures the way that body is subsequently culturally reproduced and technologically disciplined. What becomes obvious through the study of new reproductive technologies that enable the visualization of the fetus in the womb, there is no blank page of gender identity. That unsigned moment before the birth certificate is marked with an 'F' or an 'M' is an artifact of a mythic era; we are born always already inscribed.

In Pat Cadigan's narrative *Synners*, the female body is symbolically represented as a material body and as a body that labors. The male body, in contrast, is repressed or disappearing. This suggests two points of disagreement with Kroker's theory of 'the disappearing body': that there is no singular form of postmodern embodiment, and that 'disappearing body' is not a post-human body-without-gender. In contrast, I argue that the 'disappearing body' is a gendered response to cultural anxieties about body invasion. Masculinist dreams of body transcendence and, relatedly, masculinist attempts at body repression, signal a desire to return to the 'neutrality' of the body, to be rid of the culturally marked body.

The technological fragmentation of the body functions in a similar way to its medical fragmentation: body parts are objectified and invested with cultural significance. In turn, this fragmentation is articulated to a culturally determined 'system of differences' that not only attributes value to different bodies, but 'processes' these bodies according to traditional, dualistic gendered 'natures'. This system of differentiation determines the status and position of material bodies which results in the reification of dualistic codes of gender identity. So, despite the technological possibilities of body reconstruction, in the discourses of bio-technology the female body is persistently coded as the cultural sign of the 'natural', the 'sexual' and the 'reproductive', so that the 'womb', for example, continues to signify female gender in a way that reinforces an essentialist identity for the female body as the 'maternal body'. In this sense, an apparatus of gender organizes the power relations manifest in the various engagements between bodies and technologies. I offer the phrase 'technologies of the gendered body' as a way of describing such interactions between bodies and technologies.[9] Gender, in this schema, is both a determining cultural condition and a social consequence of technological deployment. My intent is to illuminate the ways that contemporary discourses of technology rely on a logic of binary gender identity as an underlying organizational framework to structure the possibilities of technological engagement, and ultimately to limit the revisionary potential of such technologies.

## Notes

1   For an extended discussion of the way in which cosmetic surgeons rely on Western ideals of feminine beauty see Balsamo (1992).
2   The Jargon File, version 2.0.10, 01 July 1992. Available on-line from ftp.uu.net. Also published as *The Hacker's Dictionary*.
3   See especially: Sherry Turkle and Seymour Papert (1992) and Dannielle Bernstein (1991).
4   For a discussion of the ethical policy dimensions of computer communication see Jeffrey Bairstow (1990), Bob Brown (1990), Pamela Varley (1991), Laurence H. Tribe (1991) and Willard Uncapher (1991).
5   For a discussion of the gendered nature of communication technologies see especially Lana Rakow (1988). For other studies of the gendered nature of computer use see: Sara Kiesler *et al.* (1985) and Sherry Turkle and Seymour Papert (1990).
6   Hoai-An Truong, *Gender Issues in Online Communication*, CFP93 (version 4.1). Available on-line from ftp.eff.org. No date given.
7   The quotation is from Nancy Tosta, chief of the Branch of Geographic Data Coordination of the National Mapping Division, US Geological Survey in Reston, Virginia ('Who's got the data?', *Geo Info Systems*, September 1992: 24–7). Tosta's prediction is supported by other statements about the US government's efforts to build a Geographic Information System (GIS): a database system whereby 'all public information can be referenced by location'. See Lisa Warnecke (1992). Managing data, acquiring new data and guarding data integrity are issues of concern for GIS managers. Because of the cost of acquiring new data and guarding data integrity, GIS managers sometimes charge a fee for providing information. This process of charging 'has thrown [them] into a morass of issues about public records and freedom of information; the value of data, privacy, copyrights, and liability and the roles of public and private sectors in disseminating information' (see Tosta 1991).
8   From the letter to the National Science Foundation Division Director, Jonathan Friedlaender. The letter, and Friedlaender's response, circulated on several electronic discussion lists: one copy was posted to sci-tech-studies on 21 December 1993.
9   Here I implicitly draw on Teresa deLauretis's transformation of Foucault's notion of the 'technology of sex' into the 'technologies of gender'. She uses this phrase to name the process by which gender is 'both a representation and a self-representation produced by various social technologies, such as cinema, as well as institutional discourses, epistemologies, and critical practices' (deLauretis 1987: ix).

## References

Bairstow, Jeffrey (1990) 'Who Reads Your Electronic Mail?', *Electronic Business* 16 (11): 92.
Balsamo, Anne (1992) 'On the Cutting Edge: Cosmetic Surgery and the Technological Production of the Gendered Body', *Camera Obscura* 28: 207–37.
Bernstein, Dannielle (1991) 'Comfort and Experience with Computing: Are They the Same for Women and Men?', *SIGGSE Bulletin* 23 (3): 57–60.
Brown, Bob (1990) 'EMA Urges Users to Adopt Policy on E-mail Privacy', *Network World*, 29 Oct.: 7.44.2.

Cadigan, Pat (1991) *Synners*. New York: Bantam.

deLauretis, Teresa (1987) *Technologies of Gender: Essays on Theory, Film, and Fiction*. Bloomington: Indiana University Press.

Feher, Michel (1987) 'Of Bodies and Technologies', in Hal Foster (ed.) *Discussions in Contemporary Culture*, DIA Art Foundation, Seattle, WA: Bay Press, pp. 159–65.

Frank, Arthur W. (1991) 'For a Sociology of the Body: An Analytical Review', in Mike Featherstone, Mike Hepworth and Bryan S. Turner (eds) *The Body: Social Process and Cultural Theory*. London: Sage, pp. 36–102.

Gutin, Joann C. (1994) 'End of the Rainbow', *Discover*, November: 71–5.

Kiesler, Sara, Lee Sproull and Eccles, Jacquelynne (1985) 'Poolhalls, Chips and War Games: Women in the Culture of Computing', *Psychology of Women Quarterly* 9 (4): 451–62.

Kroker, Arthur and Kroker, Marilouise (eds) (1987) *Body Invaders: Panic Sex in America*. New York: St Martin Press.

Levidow, Les (1991) 'Women who Make the Chips', *Science as Culture* 2 (10): 103–24.

Rakow, Lana (1988) 'Women and the Telephone: The Gendering of a Communications Technology', in Cheris Kramarae (ed.) *Technology and Women's Voices: Keeping in Touch*. Boston: Routledge, pp. 207–8.

Terry, Jennifer (1989) 'The Body Invaded: Medical Surveillance of Women as Reproducers', *Socialist Review* 39: 13–44.

Tosta, Nancy (1991) 'Public Access: Right or Privilege?', *Geo Info Systems*, Nov./Dec.: 20–5.

Tosta, Nancy (1992) 'Who's Got the Data?', *Geo Info Systems*, Sept.: 24–7.

Tribe, Laurence H. (1991) 'The Constitution in Cyberspace', *The Humanist* 51 (5): 15–21.

Turkle, Sherry and Papert, Seymour (1990) 'Epistemological Pluralism: Styles and Voices within the Computer Culture', *Signs* 16 (11): 128–57.

Turner, Bryan S. (1984) *The Body and Society: Explorations in Social Theory*. Oxford: Basil Blackwell.

Turner, Bryan S. (1991) 'Recent Developments in the Theory of the Body', in Mike Featherstone, Mike Hepworth and Bryan S. Turner (eds) *The Body: Social Process and Cultural Theory*. London: Sage, pp. 1–35.

Uncapher, Willard (1991) 'Trouble in Cyberspace', *The Humanist* 51 (5): 5–14.

Varley, Pamela (1991) 'Electronic Democracy', *Technology Review*, Nov./Dec.: 40–3.

Warnecke, Lisa (1992) 'Building the National GI/GIS Partnership', *Geo Info Systems*, April: 16–23.

# PART FIVE

# **Divisions**

## INTRODUCTION

■ Kaarle Nordenstreng

**A**CCOUNTS OF THE INFORMATION SOCIETY introduce two conflicting perspectives. The first promises a prosperous global community where
people live peacefully together as an 'interconnected human family', with technology
improving 'the well-being of all people on this planet', to quote then Vice-President
Al Gore's vision of the Global Information Infrastructure (GII) espoused towards the
middle of the 1990s (Mansell 2001, p. 420). The second perspective opens an opposite view with information and communication technologies serving predominantly
as new means of maintaining, and even worsening, inequality between people and
nations, whereby haves and have-nots are separated from each other, not only by the
traditional socio-economic factors, but also by a 'digital divide' – a concept launched
by the same Clinton administration that promoted GII. So, while the two perspectives are fundamentally opposed, one foreseeing an end to divisions and the other
their exacerbation, they originate from the same political and intellectual realm.
As in the Bible, so here the ideas of paradise and hell hang together.

The intellectual history of these perspectives takes us back to the 1960s–70s
and to the story of the New World Information and Communication Order (NWICO).
The growth of television, with new cable and satellite transmission potentialities,
gave rise both to hopes for a 'global village' (in the spirit of Marshall McLuhan
[1911–80], then, as now, a much quoted seer), and to anxieties about worsening
international relations by television broadcasting across national borders. National
sovereignty became a strategic issue in East–West and North–South relations, and

simultaneously the blessings of modernization in the developing countries were questioned as economic and technological advances did not automatically lead to improved general welfare (Nordenstreng and Schiller 1979). Equality and harmony in the world appeared to be threatened not only by the cold war division, but increasingly by socio-economic structures seen as legacies of old colonialism and new capitalism. An unholy alliance of developing countries led by the Non-aligned Movement, socialist countries led by the Soviet Union, and dissident pockets in western countries launched the concept of a 'new international order' where socio-economic equality was to the fore. In this spirit the United Nations produced declarations in the 1970s in support of a New International Economic Order (NIEO) as well as a NWICO.

Accordingly, the NWICO was an early attempt to promote equity and to counter divisions in the global field of information and media. But the attempt was soon aborted, mainly because the administration led by Ronald Reagan (1981–9) withdrew the United States from multilateral arenas, notably UNESCO, followed by Margaret Thatcher's government (1979–91) leaving in support. This left the idealist programmes largely in the hands of non-governmental organizations, while the slogan of a 'new world order' took on a new meaning after the collapse of Soviet societies and US-led commercial forces came to dominate debates and their favouring of free market capitalism appeared supreme (Nordenstreng and Schiller 1993).

However, by the turn of the millennium international communication had become a central element of the debates around globalization, and in this development the concept of Information Society occupied a strategic place (Vincent *et al.* 1999). It became fashionable again to speak in favour of global equality, boosted by the new information and communication technologies (ICTs). A good deal of this enthusiasm may have been window dressing for ICT industries and a far cry from the approach of those forces which originally fought for equality and against divisions. All the same, the idea of a global Information Society inspired the United Nations Development Programme (UNDP) to focus its *Human Development Report 2001* on how new technologies might be made to work for human development and how particularly ICTs were 'creating networks with growing reach, falling costs'. Also the International Labour Organization (ILO) issued its yearbook *World Employment Report 2001* with the subtitle 'Life at work in the information economy'. For its part the World Bank established a 'Global Information and Communication Technologies Department' to support developing countries to bridge divides by means of economic growth and ICTs. Meanwhile, the Organization for Economic Co-operation and Development (OECD) published *Understanding the Digital Divide* with a focus on the advanced industrialized countries and the divides both between and within them, while the European Union introduced a whole programme promoting an egalitarian Information Society within its own area. This international activity will culminate with the World Summit on the Information Society (WSIS) in Geneva, December 2003, and in Tunis, 2005.

It seems likely that these high profile exercises will promote the first of the above-mentioned two perspectives, emphasizing steady progress towards paradise.

But they also admit the second perspective which is concerned about maintaining equality and eliminating divisions. Actually, the Information Society is frequently presented as a way to bridge gaps caused by social inequalities – ironically just the opposite to what is often suggested by the digital divide thesis where the Information Society figures rather as a cause of the problem.

There is a broad consensus that ICTs are highly relevant to socio-economic welfare and that the concept of the Information Society is an integral part of the strategic concern about global development. Moreover, it is widely understood that the crux of the matter is not just technical infrastructure but ultimately knowledge-based 'social capabilities' (Mansell and Wehn 1998; Mansell 2001). This is demonstrated by pockets of ICT centres in developing countries such as India, with open source software practices challenging the Microsoft hegemony (see http://www.bytesforall.org/). Part of this movement of empowerment for 'the majority of the world' is even hardware innovation known as 'Simputer' (see http://www.simputer.org/). Paradoxically, the developing world turns here from an object requiring assistance to an admirable subject providing leadership – in line with the universal 'spirit of the Information Age' (Himanen 2001).

While these developments may be taken as blessings of free market-led global-ization, they can also suggest a need for interventionist governance, both in national and international levels. Actually governance, or 'eGovernance', is one of the emerging concepts inspired by more critical perspectives towards the Information Society, both in industrialized and developing countries. So it is not only 'deregulation' that has happened in the media and telecommunications fields, since there has been a simultaneous shift of understanding whereby the Information Society is perceived to require judicious government (and supra-government) intervention. This system of governance, however global by its dimensions, sees a continuing role for the state (Morris and Waisbord 2001; Raboy 2002).

These perspectives should be kept in mind when reading the selections. Common in all these debates is the issue of equality, something foundational to consideration of divisions in its variable expressions. One of these is the 'knowledge gap' which became popular among social scientists in the progressive atmosphere of the 1970s, but which was sidelined by the postmodern turn of the 1980s. It is symptomatic that it is now back on the agenda – boosted by critical approaches to the Information Society (see e.g. http://www.sit.wisc.edu/~ichungcheng/knowledgegap1.htm).

**Herbert Schiller** (1919–2000) (Chapter 17) was a tireless critic of the corporate-dominated communication world since his classic *Mass Communications and American Empire* (1969). His work is an essential resource for students concerned to appreciate divisions – between nations and classes especially – perpet-uated and perhaps even worsened by the 'information revolution'. The text repro-duced here is taken from one of his anthologies with the telling title *Information Inequality: The Deepening Social Crisis in America* (1996). Schiller does not feel a need to elaborate the concept of inequality as such – any more than he used to elaborate the concepts of sovereignty, or democracy. He takes for granted their positive meanings, and commits his energies to exposing how private corporations work against their full expression. Schiller's paradigm highlights a division under which people live in an information-saturated society, yet private corporate power deprives them of reliable and high quality information. In such a society there is a surfeit of 'information garbage' for the mass (escapist entertainment, soaps, sports, chat shows and the like), while prime information (that which empowers and gives leverage over economic and social matters) goes to those with the deepest pockets and occupying the most powerful positions. Schiller sees such information deprivation occurring across the board of US society in the mid-1990s: from media to education and science, from health and environment to national security. For him there is no doubt that the internet also becomes consumed by this 'phenomenal growth of corporate power'. Schiller would surely applaud the emancipatory use of the internet by the anti-globalization movement, but he would still warn against misplaced naivety towards corporate forces. If Herbert Schiller appears to some an outdated doom monger, one should note that the dangers of excessive corporate power appear in his painting against the background of a positive landscape of a more humane and democratic condition. In this respect he continues in the tradition of the Frankfurt School during the Information Age (Webster 2002, ch. 6).

**Pippa Norris** (Chapter 18) was one of the first to write a book on the digital divide – with a question mark. The extract chosen here lays down three distinct aspects of the divide: the *global divide* meaning inequalities of the internet access between countries, the *social divide* between groups within societies, and the *democratic divide* between those who do and those do not use the political potential of the internet. Based on not only United States, but also OECD and EU data, Norris argues that the role of the internet reflects and reinforces, rather than transforms, the structural features of each country's political system.

Finally, and in a sweeping survey, **Christopher Lasch** (1932–94) (Chapter 19) attacks as illusory the view that technology is neutral. He argues instead that its development has been driven by the search to extend greater control in the transformation of work amid changing class structures. Lasch, a historian and social critic who combined radicalism and conservatism in equal measure (Lasch 1991, 1995), presents a review of technological innovation which insists on the primacy of divisions of power in its design and development. It is the view of Lasch that the present so-called Second Industrial Revolution is guided by a search for heightened control over work processes since this bolsters the power of the managerial and technical elites which decide upon technological implementation. Lasch ends gloomily with the still stronger suggestion that, even more than the profit motive, modern technological innovation expresses a desire to eliminate the human factor in search of total control. To Lasch this is a pathology which threatens our very humanity – a profound division indeed.

## REFERENCES

Himanen, Pekka (2001) *The Hacker Ethic and the Spirit of the Information Age*, with Prologue by Linus Tordvalds and Epilogue by Manuel Castells. New York: Random House.

ILO (2001) *World Employment Report 2001: Life at Work in the Information Economy.* Geneva: ILO. Available on-line at: http://www.ilo.org/public/english/support/publ/wer/overview.htm.

Lasch, Christopher (1991) *The True and Only Heaven: Progress and Its Critics.* New York: Norton.

Lasch, Christopher (1995) *The Revolt of the Elites and the Betrayal of Democracy.* New York: Norton.

Mansell, Robin (2001) 'Regenerating Information and Communication Inequalities?', in Srinivas Melkote and Sandra Rao (eds) *Critical Issues in Communication: Looking Inward for Answers.* New Delhi: Sage, pp. 420–42.

Mansell, Robin and Wehn, Uta (eds) (1998) *Knowledge Societies: Information Technology for Sustainable Development.* Oxford: Oxford University Press.

Morris, Nancy and Waisbord, Silvio (eds) (2001) *Media and Globalization: Why the State Matters.* Lanham, MD: Rowman and Littlefield.

Nordenstreng, Kaarle and Schiller, Herbert (eds) (1979) *National Sovereignty and International Communication.* Norwood, NJ: Ablex.

Nordenstreng, Kaarle and Schiller, Herbert (eds) (1993) *Beyond Sovereignty: International Communication in the 1990s.* Norwood, NJ: Ablex.

OECD (2001) *Understanding the Digital Divide.* Paris: OECD. Available on-line at: http://www1.oecd.org/dsti/sti/prod/Digital_divide.pdf.

Raboy, Marc (ed.) (2002) *Global Media Policy in the New Millenium.* Luton: Luton University Press.

Schiller, Herbert (1969) *Mass Communications and American Empire.* New York: Augustus M. Kelley.

UNDP (2001) *Human Development Report 2001. Making New Technologies Work for Human Development.* New York: UNDP and Oxford University Press. Available on-line at: http://www.undp.org/hdr2001/.

Vincent, Richard, Nordenstreng, Kaarle and Traber, Michael (eds) (1999) *Towards Equity in Global Communication: MacBride Update.* Cresskill, NJ: Hampton Press.

Webster, Frank (2002) *Theories of the Information Society.* London: Routledge.

# Chapter 17

# Herbert Schiller

## DATA DEPRIVATION

From *Information Inequality*, New York: Routledge (1996), pp. 43–57.

### Data deprivation

**A**N ALL-EMBRACING STRUCTURAL transformation of the last fifty years has been the ascendance of corporate power and the corresponding decline of government authority over key areas of national economic, political, and social life. This has occurred in all industrialized as well as less developed economies, though with considerable variability from one country to another.

In the United States, where this change is most fully developed, it is also less evident because of the continuing, though declining, global hegemonic role of the American state. This requires a huge military, intelligence, and police apparatus to monitor and discipline the far-flung territories as well as a potentially disaffected domestic public. This vast apparatus, now being reluctantly downsized, still confers great power on the state. The trend, however, has been to extend private decision making at the expense of governmental authority.

In the increasingly central spheres of communication and information, the shift from state to private power is especially marked and observable. Here, too, exceptional conditions conceal the full dimensions of the transfer of authority. Not least is the capability of the private informational machine to withhold the evidence of its own primacy and activity. Additionally, there is the continuing barrage, issuing from the same source, of an 'information glut,' and the burdens of living in an 'information society.' This clamor serves to divert attention from the very real, but largely invisible, deficit of socially necessary information.

What are the effects of the enormous extension of private power in the informational sphere? They can be appreciated best, perhaps, by considering what has been happening to individual expression, and how this is explained. Historically, the threat to individual expression has been seen to come from an arbitrary state. This view is embodied in the US Constitution where free speech is explicitly protected against governmental power and its potential for abuse. And so it has been for centuries; states limiting and suppressing individual expression, and individuals and social movements struggling to reduce and overcome censorial power.

A new condition now exists, though it is one that is barely acknowledged! What distinguishes this era is that the main threat to free expression has shifted from government to private corporate power. This does not imply that the state has lost its taste for controlling individual expression. It means instead that a more pervasive force has emerged that now constitutes a stronger and more active threat to such expression.

Today, the power of huge, private, economic enterprises is extended across national and international boundaries, influencing and directing economic resource decisions, political choices, and the production and dissemination of messages and images. The American economy is now hostage to a relatively small number of giant private companies, with interlocking connections, that set the national agenda. This power is particularly characteristic of the communication and information sector where the national cultural-media agenda is provided by a very small (and declining) number of integrated private combines.[1] This development has deeply eroded free individual expression, a vital element of a democratic society.

At the same time, the new private information power centers strive actively and, to date, successfully to persuade the public that their corporate message- and image-making activity is a daily exercise in individual free expression. This effort relies heavily on a century-old Supreme Court ruling that the corporation is an individual. It follows from this extravagant interpretation that the threat to individual expression can come only from the state.

How this logic works is exemplified in a full-page advertisement in the *New York Times* in which the Freedom Forum Foundation approvingly quotes the view of Supreme Court Justice, Thurgood Marshall: 'If the First Amendment means anything, it means that a state has no business telling a man, sitting alone in his own house, what books he may read or what films he may watch. Our whole constitutional heritage rebels at the thought of giving government the power to control men's minds.'[2] And so it does! Readers of the ad might not know that the Freedom Forum is the creation of the Gannett Corporation, one of the nation's largest media combines, owner of a country-wide chain of local papers and the national newspaper, *USA Today*. The Gannett enterprise precisely fits the definition of a media conglomerate, heavily dependent on corporate advertising revenues, disseminating carefully processed material to millions of readers and viewers.

In quoting Justice Marshall's cautionary words, the Gannett Corporation is identifying its powerful, nationally expressed voice as individual expression. At the same time it is deflecting attention from its oversized influence on popular opinion and shifting the nation's focus to the older and familiar concern, state control of expression. Where once there was justified fear of government control and censorship of speech, today there is a new form of censorship, structurally pervasive, grounded in private concentrated control of the media, and generally undetectable in a direct and personal sense.

Marshall's words, were they to include the new reality, could well be recast: If the First Amendment means anything, it means that a media combine has no business telling an individual, sitting alone in that person's own house, what books to read or what films to watch. Our whole constitutional heritage rebels at the thought of giving giant information corporations the power to control people's minds.

There is more than enough justification for this reformulation of traditional free speech doctrine. What American voices, other than corporate ones, can afford to pay half a million dollars or more for a thirty-second TV commercial on national television? Elder statesman George Kennan recently reflected: 'As things stand today, without advertising presumably very little of the communications industry would survive.'[3] Given these economic realities, much of the space in the American cultural house has been appropriated for corporate messages. This has become literally so. Atlanta, for example, is seriously considering renaming some of its streets and parks with corporate logos, 'Coca-Cola Boulevard' and 'Georgia Pacific Park' to raise funds.[4]

Corporate speech has become a dominant discourse, nationally and internationally. It has also dramatically changed the context in which the concepts of freedom of speech, a free press, and democratic expression have to be considered. While the corporate voice booms across the land, individual expression, at best, trickles through tiny constricted public circuits. This has allowed the effective right to free speech to be transferred from individuals to billion dollar companies which, in effect, monopolize public communication.[5]

Corporate influence now penetrates almost every social space. One of its earliest and continuing efforts has been to shake off, or at least greatly reduce, the relatively modest restraints imposed on its economic and social decision making. These limitations derived from the populist and reform movements of the late nineteenth century and the devastating impact of the Great Depression in the 1930s. The rapacious behavior of the industrial monopolies that emerged after the Civil War, and the social misery that accompanied the economic crisis of sixty years ago, compelled the political leadership of those times to produce a variety of protective social measures. These included Social Security, bank and financial regulations, communication and transport rules, and labor's right to organize. The upsurge of the civil rights, feminist, and anti-Vietnam War movements in the 1960s introduced additional social protections. Undeniably, these also interfered with the freedom of corporations to ignore such matters.

Since the end of World War II, and especially the last twenty-five years, corporate power has countered these developments with intensive and largely successful efforts. It has pressed to remove the machinery of socially responsible supervision. This goes under the name of deregulation. It has led the campaign to privatize a variety of activities and functions that had been under public administration. And it has sought to extend market relationships to new spheres of rapidly growing economic activity, e.g. information management.

Deregulation, privatization, and the expansion of market relationships have affected all corners of the economy. Here, only the impact on the national information condition – no peripheral area – will be considered. The generation and provision of information and entertainment, and the technology that makes it possible, are among the most dynamic elements in the economy. How these are put together profoundly affects the character of the national information condition. The hope is always that they will constitute the basis for an informed population and a democratic social order. In fact, when the effects of privatization, deregulation, and expanded market relationships are added to the corporate near-monopoly on public communication channels, a deep, though not generally visible, erosion in the national information infrastructure can be detected.

Bill McKibben, in *The Age of Missing Information*, reflects on the loss of understanding of nature and its ways.

> I've tried to describe some of the information that the modern world
> – the TV world – is missing. Information about the physical limits of a
> finite world. About sufficiency and need, about proper scale and real
> time, about the sensual pleasure of exertion and exposure to the ele-
> ments, about the human need for community and for solid, real skills.[6]

McKibben is calling attention to a real loss. But here, I am examining another kind of missing information. It is a consequence of a warped social institutional environment.

The spectacularly improved means of producing, organizing, and disseminating information has transformed industrial, political, and cultural practices and processes. Manufacturing, elections, and creative efforts are increasingly dependent on informational inputs. This has conferred great value on some categories of information. The production and sale of information have become major sites of profit making. What had been in large measure a social good has been transformed into a commodity for sale.

Wherever potentially profitable information is produced, the drive for its commercialization rapidly follows. In the scientific sector, for example, research findings have become a source of intense effort to gain competitive advantage. Profit-seeking ventures now penetrate the core of many major universities and threaten to undermine the openness of the scholarly community.

*Science*, the publication of the American Association for the Advancement of Science (AAAS), increasingly publishes accounts of distinguished scientists engaged in deal making, organizing their own companies, or selling their findings to existing enterprises. A more and more typical report observes: 'In many areas of biology these days it's hard to find a researcher who doesn't hold biotech equity (in a for-profit company).'[7] The University of Miami's vice president for research voiced concern over this condition:

> As money becomes less and less available, more people are going to be
> compromising their principles, compromising their time. . . . We can
> get to the point at some stage in this process where we're not research
> universities any longer but fee-for-service corporations – hired guns.[8]

No less emphatic in his disapproval of these developments, Derek Bok, as reported in the *Chronicle of Higher Education*, in his final 'President's Report' to Harvard's Board of Overseers, found 'the commercialization of universities as (perhaps) the most severe threat facing higher education.' Harvard's former president said: '[Universities] appear less and less as a charitable institution seeking truth and serving students and more and more as a huge commercial operation that differs from corporations only because there are no shareholders and no dividends.'[9]

This distinction, too, may be rapidly disappearing. In mid-1993, Harvard Medical School announced its intention to invite the Healthcare Investment Corporation, 'the largest venture capital firm in the biotechnology field,' to 'share facilities in a new building.' More than this, the site will be filled 'with companies that intend to turn Harvard science into health care products by working closely with the research teams and even financing some of them, with Harvard holding the patents and the companies paying licensing fees . . ..'[10]

The ties between university researchers and private corporations have grown so close that the Director of the Food and Drug Administration felt compelled to issue a statement in 1994: 'There is a growing recognition in the academic and scientific communities that certain financial arrangements between clinical investigators and product sponsors, or the personal financial interests of clinical investigators and product sponsors, can potentially bias the outcome of clinical trials.'[11] In brief, research itself may be contaminated by these increasingly institutionalized arrangements.

The commercial incursion is not limited to universities. The single largest generator of new information, produced in pursuit of its public functions, is the United States Government. Not surprisingly, the rich informational pool derived from governmentally undertaken and financed activity has been an early target for corporate takeover. In the last fifteen years it has been enveloped in market relationships, its contents commercialized, and its disposition privatized. Its widespread general availability, formerly underwritten by public taxation, has been progressively narrowed and subjected to the criterion of ability to pay.

Government information has been steadily siphoned off into commercial products, where it has not been eliminated entirely. The American Library Association called attention to this phenomenon early on and has continued to voice its concern. In the most recent edition of its fourteen-year old chronology, 'Less access to less information by and about the US Government,' it continues to document the multiplying efforts to restrict and commercialize government information. At the same time, some government holdings have been made more accessible by electronic distribution. How long this will endure without fees and charges being introduced is an open question.[12] The practice of selling governmental (or any) information, serves the corporate user well. Ordinary individual users go to the end of the dissemination queue. Profoundly antidemocratic in its effect, privatizing and/or selling information, which at one time was considered public property, has become a standard practice in recent years.

A subset of the wider phenomenon has been the behavior of political leaders who leave office. US District Court Judge Charles A. Richey ruled in a 1975 decision 'that [documents and other informational matter] produced or kept by a public official in the administration and performance of the powers and duties of a public office belong to the government and may not be considered the property of the official.' But his ruling to date has been mostly ignored.[13]

Nearly twenty years after the Richey ruling, the *New York Times* editorialized after the November 1992 elections: 'Over the years, Presidents have managed to establish legal claim to their papers chiefly because they possessed them when they left office. Rather than fight with departing Presidents, Federal officials negotiated for limited access.'[14] Under this perverse procedure, former President Richard Nixon sued, and was upheld by a US District Court of Appeals for compensation for the White House tapes and papers that were seized when he was the subject of the Watergate scandal.[15]

Withholding public documentation for private gain is not limited to former Presidents. Innumerable other former high governmental officials have taken personal possession of papers associated with their public service. Cavalierly regarding public documents as private property, the material has been used for financial gain in the sale of personal memoirs and historical studies.

There is still another factor, in addition to greed, that has limited and misshapen what should be the public record. The Bush Administration, for example, destroyed vital information to prevent it from coming into the possession of its successor. Federal archivists reported many computer tapes were missing from the White House computer record.[16] Upon assuming office, the Clinton Administration did nothing to preserve the Bush computer record. Actually, the Administration was excoriated by, once again, Judge Richey, for its dilatory behavior. 'This case has been one of avoidance of responsibility by the government bureaucracy.'[17] The Clinton Administration contested Richey's ruling, but it was upheld by the US Court of Appeals for the District of Columbia.[18] Whether the Government will appeal further or abide by the Appeals Court decision and take measures to safeguard for archival use its own electronics communications is, as this book goes to press, uncertain.

The commercialization and privatization of government and scientific information has become a paradox. Unarguably, it has been of great benefit to affluent users who now have access to kinds and amounts of data that would have been unimaginable only a few years ago. Commercialization therefore has been rewarding to private information providers and to their clients. For the rest of the population, the vast majority, the quality and the availability of information leaves a lot to be desired. In the domain of general governmental information, the supply has been curtailed severely. The American Library Association notes that 'since 1982, one of every four of the Government's 16,000 publications has been eliminated.'[19]

## The National Security State and information

While commercialization and privatization of information have been steadily encroaching on the public's information supply, the information policies of the National Security State have exacted a still heavier toll on the public's access to the vital information over most of the twentieth century, especially the last fifty years of the Cold War. As the Cold War has subsided – though not entirely disappeared – some of its effects on the national information condition have begun to be noted and tentative steps taken to change decades-old policies. The National Archives, for example, 'has estimated it has 300 million to 400 million classified documents dating from the World War I era to the mid-1950s. Countless other documents are housed at other Government agencies.'[20] The Pentagon, the CIA, and the State Department are three major storehouses of long-term and current classified information.

Another agency with an overflowing stockpile of such material is the Department of Energy, the national keeper of nuclear arms and nuclear programs. The Department of Energy, according to its Secretary, possesses 'at least thirty-two million pages of secret papers.' This still-secret hoard is given this appreciation by Mrs O'Leary, the Energy Department's Secretary: 'it's thirty-two Washington Monuments . . . it's three miles worth of data.' Its real significance – the impact of nuclear tests and released radiation, the existence and extent of toxic waste sites, unexamined government–corporate deals, and so on – can hardly be represented by physical measurements of the documentation.[21]

Beyond the withholding of vast amounts of information, much of it deserving to be known by the public but much of it of questionable value to anyone, the massive classification of data for 'national security' has had an appalling effect on American society since the end of World War II. It has served to create a general climate of secrecy and acted as a deterrent to public discussion of countless political issues that deserved widespread airing, rather than airtight suppression.

In 1994, indicative of the continuing, though unacknowledged, economic crisis, the Government acted to revise and loosen some of its classification procedures. A Pentagon–CIA study on security classification of documents estimated the costs of maintaining an extensive system of security management as 'more than $14 billion a year in the private sector alone.'[22] One unexpected benefit of the economic crunch, therefore, may be the financial inability of the Government's coercive centers to continue to put as much documentation as they would like under lock and key. But unbridled enthusiasm that the country is on its way to general information declassification is not yet warranted. Though President Clinton ordered millions of documents declassified in 1994 and extended the order in 1995 to all secret documents more than twenty-five years old, the chief defenders of secrecy, the CIA, the Pentagon, and the State Department continue to resist complying.[23]

## Varieties of privatization: contracting out

There is more to the problem of making public information widely available than the obstacles raised by its commercialization and governmental secrecy, important as these are. The advance of privatization into more and more governmental activities has taken different forms. One of the most widespread, and whose effects are still to be fully calculated, is what is called 'contracting out.' In this arrangement, government at any level – local, state, or national – makes deals to have some of its functions undertaken by private contractors. [. . .] [T]his is essentially the direction that public school management is taking.

Justified to the public as a significant money-saving strategy and as a means of reducing the role of government – a central tenet of conservative doctrine for a very long time, particularly pronounced in the Reagan years, and infused with new vigor in the 104th Congress – contracting, or 'outsourcing,' has been a flourishing field in Washington, and elsewhere around the country. It has been widely adopted for all kinds of what were once public services – fire protection, waste disposal, some elements of the judicial system, libraries, and even policing. According to a statement of the US General Accounting Office, 'civilian agencies currently spend about $55 billion per year on contracts and have become increasingly dependent on contractors to help agencies manage and carry out their missions.'[24] In some government agencies, for example, the Department of Energy, the Environmental Protection Agency, and the National Aeronautics and Space Administration, 'contractors are performing virtually all of the work.'[25]

In addition to the colossal waste found to exist in the general practice of contracting out governmental information functions (see OMB report[24]), there are related problems that seriously affect the national information supply, especially the needs of the general citizenry. The American Library Association describes one of these problems: 'The increased emergence of contractual agreements with commercial firms to disseminate information collected at taxpayer expense, [has resulted in] higher user charges for government information and the proliferation of government information in electronic format only.'[26] In each case, the individual, ordinary user is disadvantaged.

Still more problematic, when the information function is transferred from governmental oversight, criteria other than public interest may determine the formats, organization, and categories of the information produced. What may be of importance to the general user may be of little concern to largescale commercial users. When the supply function is commercialized, the priority inevitably goes to the major paying customers. When this occurs, what may be missing is not even realized. If the collection and organization process is exclusionary at the outset, data absence may not be recognized. But visible or not, deprivation exists.

The reliance on private firms to do what once was the government's work, via contracting out, has grown markedly in recent years in keeping with the conservative philosophy of abandoning the protective social role of Government. It has had especially damaging effects on the public information supply. The Office of Management and Budget (OMB) noted that despite the huge sums involved in the private contracting sphere, information about the management of the projects was sadly missing. Auditors were in short supply and as of the end of 1992, $160 billion in contracts had not been audited. In short, no one knew how the taxpayers' money had been spent, although there were enough clues to indicate that the waste was staggering.[27]

Contracting out governmental activities to private enterprise has created a vast black hole in information about the government's essential functions. Yet it is only part of the story of a growing deficiency in such information. When public business is removed from government management, under its new private managers, it is likely to become less transparent to the public. This condition has been widened and institutionalized by the wave of deregulation that has swept over the nation since the mid-1970s. Whether these practices will be reversed in the years ahead remains to be seen, though the trends are hardly reassuring. What can be safely said at this time, is that the damage to public information is already severe, its full dimensions still largely unknown, and its impact likely to be long-lasting.

## Deregulation

Actually, deregulation of industry in the United States predates the 1970s. It began to appear, in limited ways, as early as the Eisenhower era (1952–1960). The New Deal measures, initiated in the 1930s, began to be rolled back by a resurgent corporate sector, enriched and reinvigorated by the massive military outlays required for waging World War II, as well as the immediate postwar recovery expenditures. In this period, American Big Business concentrated its energies on consolidating its hold on the domestic economy and expanding into a wide-open European and global market. The regulations imposed in the Roosevelt era, though never acceptable to Big Business, were borne relatively easily while the economy grew rapidly at home and abroad. American products and services, for two decades, filled the global shelves. The US dollar was the global currency.

Relatively quickly however, the Western European and Japanese economies gained strength and the bite of their competition into American business' profitability began to be felt. The immediate corporate reaction at home was to focus on regulation as the chief source of its problem. 'By the late 1970s,' two Washington journalists reported, 'complaints of excessive regulation had become management's all-purpose cop-out. Were profits too low? Blame regulation. Were prices too high? Blame regulation. Was American industry unable to compete with foreign competition? Blame regulation.'[28]

Besides the ideological value in blaming regulation for the emerging business difficulties in the '70s, substantial material objectives also were served. In the communication sector this was particularly evident. Writer Jeremy Tunstall explained the growing pressure for deregulation as one means to hold on to the US' world hegemonic position:

> Behind the loose deregulatory consensus lie the twin assumptions that communication is becoming the number one industry in the world, and that the traditional position of the U.S. as numero uno in all aspects of electronics/telecommunications/video/entertainment/computers/ information technology is being challenged. A central purpose [of deregulation of communications] is to maintain both communications and the U.S. as number one.[29]

Tunstall also observed that 'American business had geared itself up much more systematically in the last decade [1970–1980] to influence politics,' through lobbying and the use of the mass media.[30]

Tunstall's perceptions were well grounded. With almost unlimited access to the domestic information system – actually it owned it – American Big Business moved decisively, with the communication sector in the forefront, to get rid of whatever rules they regarded as impediments to management autonomy and profit making. Primarily, aim was taken at the social functions of Government that had been strengthened in the Roosevelt period and expanded in the brief Great Society years of Lyndon Johnson, which lasted only from the mid-1960s to the early 70s. 'The prime targets,' the aforementioned Washington reporters noted, 'were those agencies that sought to protect consumers and workers and to improve the air, water, and workplace. They were the agencies, in effect, that tried to get industry off the backs of the people.'[31]

Another target was the Federal Communications Commission (FCC), with its mandate to oversee the vital and powerful communications sector. It too, had to be 'reined in,' though anyone familiar with the industry-serving commission had to regard its alleged role as a protector of the public interest, and a scourge of the broadcasters, as a fantasy.

In any case, reducing or eliminating the social regulatory function over consumer and workplace protection and corporate communication practices, also meant reducing or eliminating public information about these crucial social spheres. When industry is relieved of certain democratic obligations to pay its share of taxes, control pollution, reduce toxic wastes, cease interfering with work place rights of the labor force, provide adequate children's and public affairs TV programming, the data concerning these social undertakings either vanishes or never gets collected. In short, data vital to social well-being silently falls out of the national information supply, its absence noted, if at all, only when some later potential user finds it no longer exists or never was generated.

Indicative of what now may be a pervasive condition was the experience of the Task Force on National Health Care Reform, established in the first days of the then newly-elected Clinton Administration. In formulating its proposals, it encountered an unexpected difficulty: it could not find basic data. The *New York Times* reported that the Task Force 'discovered that the Government quit collecting state-by-state data on health spending a decade ago. The Federal Government tabulated health spending by state from 1966 through 1982, but has not compiled state data since then . . . .'[32] What this account does *not* say is that this data gap originated with the many data discontinuances ordered by the Reagan White House in its zeal to cut out the social functions of government. As this kind of data apparently was of little interest to commercial vendors and their corporate clientele, it just 'disappeared,' like critics in Argentina or Chile in the 1970s.

Another especially egregious example of withholding data has been the unconscionable suppression by knowledgable corporate tobacco management, for two decades, of research findings revealing the linkage of smoking to cancer. With no obligation to provide its internally generated information to a public regulatory authority, a generation of citizens' health has been sacrificed to the sovereign law of proprietary information.[33]

The absence of health and human welfare data as a consequence of deregulated corporate activity, directly affects the well-being of the entire population. Less vital, though hardly inconsequential, are gaps in economic information that may cause large numbers of people substantial loss. For example, a pitifully inadequate oversight staff in the Securities and Exchange Commission can hardly cope with the potential for financial malpractice in the enormous mutual funds industry. Here is an account of the current condition of oversight in this industry. 'What tools are available,' asks a reporter, 'to mutual fund regulators for monitoring America's rapidly growing . . . industry? Pitifully few.' This for an industry of 4,900 firms and more than $2 trillion of Americans' savings. The information offered investors is often bland or impenetrable legalese. It is an industry seriously undermonitored and thereby potentially waiting for a debacle.[34]

Paradoxically, accompanying the shortfall of social welfare, human care, and economic information essential to the well-being of the majority is an enormously enlarged amount of custom-tailored information priced for an upscale clientele and thereby available to commercial and corporate users, or whoever can afford to pay for it. The information needs of the corporate sector, to the most minute and refined degree, are now satisfied instantaneously. What is occurring in the information sphere is of a piece with what can be observed in the economy at large. The social order is splitting into at least a two-tiered structure, one with a full and expanding range of social and economic amenities; the other with a declining share of both, but also with a growing amount of junk food, junk entertainment, and junk information.

Finally, deregulation in the communication sphere, in addition to encouraging a more rapid concentration of facilities – radio, TV, cable, and press – in fewer and fewer hands, also enables the newer media, especially cable, to claim First Amendment rights. When and if these rights are conferred, the now heavily concentrated cable franchise owners (MCOs, multiple cable owners) will be able, among other benefits, to avoid their obligation to provide public access channels in the communities they serve. Their argument is that they are being deprived of their free speech if government insists that they make some of their channels available for public purposes. This is a development to watch for in the future.

## The current scene

In sum, the last fifty years have witnessed a phenomenal growth of corporate power deployed across the social and economic landscape. The expansion of this power has relied heavily on three far-reaching structural changes in the institutional infrastructure: deregulation of economic activity, privatization of functions once public, and commercialization of activities once social.

Taken together and applied to the now-central sector of communication and information, the impact of these processes is profoundly altering the informational condition and the democratic character of American society. The corporate voice is the loudest in the land. Immense amounts of new information are produced but are available mainly to those who can afford their costs. The collection of socially vital information has been neglected or withheld, where it has not been entirely eliminated.

All this has occurred partly as a consequence of a wilful effort to destroy as much of the social function of government as possible, and as an accompaniment of the deregulatory process whereby unsupervised corporate activity leaves few traces of its work. And, not least, public communication, for the most part, is underwritten and directed by the corporate sector. Independent voices struggle, generally unsuccessfully, to be heard. Economic activity, politics, and social well-being are either undertaken or evaluated largely by or with commercial criteria.

Though these developments have been maturing over many decades, the tempo has accelerated in the last fifteen or so years, reaching a crescendo with the election and early legislative activity of the 104th Congress in 1995. However conservative the character of this body, it is the inevitable outcome of the direction corporate power has chosen to take since the end of World War II. The unwavering and persistent objectives of the business system over this period have been to extend its authority, while at the same time narrowing that of the national government, particularly its social function. Newt Gingrich and his supporters in and outside the Congress may sound like wild men to those who grew up with New Deal or Great Society expectations. Yet their conservative credo that regards government responsibility for national welfare as a blueprint of socialism is only the most recent expression of the same message that has been financed by Big Business and disseminated through their corporate media and entertainment channels for decades.[35]

And so, despite the impressive capabilities of the new information technologies and the proliferation of electronic informational networks, there is little likelihood that the data deficit of social information will soon disappear. The new informational networks more likely will be absorbed into the commercial cocoon that has engulfed most of society's activities. The Internet itself is not exempt from the powerful commercializing and for-profit currents flowing nationally and internationally. Plans and moves to commercialize the Internet already exist and may be expected to be implemented in the time ahead. With the perspectives and approaches now in command in Washington, and throughout the country, the crisis in American information and communication can only deepen.

## Notes

1    Ben Bagdikian, *The Media Monopoly*, 4th edn (Boston: Beacon, 1993).
2    *New York Times*, February 11, 1993, sec. A, p. 11.
3    George Kennan, *Around the Cragged Hill* (New York: WW Norton, 1993), p. 167.
4    Peter Applebome, 'Adman in Atlanta Tries to Sell City,' *New York Times*, February 9, 1993, sec. A, p. 8.
5    Kennan, op. cit. p. 167.
6    Bill McKibben, *The Age of Missing Information* (New York: Random House, 1992), p. 236.
7    Marcia Barinaga, 'Confusion on the Cutting Edge,' *Science*, vol. 257, July 31, 1992, pp. 616–619. Also, 'Hughes' Tough Stand on Industry Ties,' *Science*, vol. 259, February 12, 1993, pp. 884–889.
8    Anthony De Palma, 'Universities' Reliance on Companies Raises Vexing Questions in Research,' *New York Times*, March 17, 1993, Sec. B, p. 8.
9    Liz McMillen, 'Quest for Profits May Damage Basic Values of Universities, Harvard's Bok Warns,' *Chronicle of Higher Education*, no. 32, April 24, 1991, p. 1.
10   Susan Diesenhouse, 'Harvard's New Test-Tube Business,' *New York Times*, August 22, 1993.
11   Stephen Burd, 'FDA Seeks Disclosure of Companies' Financial Ties to Researchers,' *Chronicle of Higher Education*, October 5, 1994, sec. A, p. 28.
12   'Less Access To Less Information By and About the US Government: XXII, A 1994 Chronology: January–June,' *American Library Association*, Washington, DC, bi-annual, June 1994.
13   'Richard M. Nixon v. Arthur F. Sampson, Government Records Are Public Property,' advertisement in *New York Times*, June 2, 1993, Sec. A, p. 13.
14   'Richard Nixon's Unjust Demand,' editorial, *New York Times*, November 19, 1992.
15   'Court Says Nixon Must Be Compensated for Tapes,' *New York Times*, November 18, 1982.

16    John O'Neill, 'Bush Tapes Lost, US Archivists Say,' *New York Times*, March 14, 1993, p. 16.

17    'Judge Calls Administration Lax on Predecessors' Computer Records,' *New York Times*, June 9, 1993, p. 8.

18    Neil A. Lewis, 'Government Told to Save Messages Sent by Computer,' *New York Times*, August 14, 1993, p. 1.

19    'Less Access to Less Information,' op. cit.

20    Neil A. Lewis, 'A Debate Rages Over Disclosure of US Secrets,' *New York Times*, January 14, 1994, sec. A, p. 11.

21    William J. Broad, 'US Begins Effort to Recast the Law on Atomic Secrets,' *New York Times*, January 9, 1994, p. 1.

22    Tim Weiner, 'Bills Seek to Slash the Number of US Secrets,' *New York Times*, March 3, 1994.

23    Tim Weiner, 'Some Spying Secrets Will Stay Out in the Cold,' *New York Times*, February 18, 1995, sec. 4, p. 3.

24    Statement of J. Dexter Peach before the Subcommittee on Oversight and Investigations, Committee on Energy and Commerce, House of Representatives, December 3, 1992. GAO Report, 'Federal Contracting,' GAO/T-RCED-93–2.

25    Keith Schneider, 'US Lack of Supervision Encouraged Waste in Contracts,' *New York Times*, December 2, 1992, p. 1.

26    'Less Access to Less Information,' op. cit.

27    Schneider, op. cit.

28    Susan Tolchin and Martin Tolchin, *Dismantling America* (Boston: Houghton Mifflin, 1983), pp. 4–5.

29    Jeremy Tunstall, *Communication Deregulation* (Oxford: Basil Blackwell, 1986), p. 7.

30    Ibid., p. 12.

31    Tolchin and Tolchin, op. cit. pp. 39–40.

32    Robert Pear, 'Health Data Sought by Clinton is No Longer Collected,' *New York Times*, March 1, 1993, sec. A, p. 13.

33    Philip J. Hilts, 'Cigarette Makers Debated the Risks They Denied,' and 'Tobacco Maker Studied Risk But Did Little About Results,' *New York Times*, June 16, 1994, p. 1, and June 17, 1994, p. 1.

34    Diana B. Henriques, 'Seeking Data on Funds, Investors and Regulators Find Frustration,' *New York Times*, August 9, 1994, sec. A, p. 1.

35    'Gingrich Denounces Editorial "Socialists,"' *New York Times*, March 9, 1995, sec. A, p. 9.

# Chapter 18

# Pippa Norris

## THE DIGITAL DIVIDE

From *Digital Divide: Civic Engagement, Information Poverty, and the Internet Worldwide*, New York: Cambridge University Press (2000), pp. 1–22.

[. . .]

**T**HE CONCEPT OF THE DIGITAL DIVIDE is understood as a multidimensional phenomenon encompassing three distinct aspects. The *global divide* refers to the divergence of Internet access between industrialized and developing societies. The *social divide* concerns the gap between information rich and poor in each nation. And lastly within the online community, the *democratic divide* signifies the difference between those who do, and do not, use the panoply of digital resources to engage, mobilize and participate in public life. [. . .]

### The global divide among countries

Few doubt the potential impact of digital technologies for reshaping the flow of investment, goods and services in the global marketplace. Like the Californian Gold Rush of the 1850s, dotcoms have scrambled to stake their claims in the virtual frontier. Productivity and efficiency gains from investments in ICTs remain difficult to gauge but the US Department of Commerce estimates that industries producing computer and communications hardware, software and services have had a major impact on the US economy: generating up to one third of real economic growth in America from the mid- to late 1990s, reducing inflation through falling prices for microchips and hardware, and sparking remarkable productivity gains among the workforce.[1] These developments fuelled an intense flurry of heady speculation about the emergence of a new economy breaking the traditional business rules, although, mirroring the fluctuating fortunes of the Nasdaq index and the death of hundreds of dotcom start-ups, more cautious voices have subsequently warned that beyond a few isolated sectors, such as the travel or insurance industries, 'bricks and mortar' assets still count for successful business–customer relations, along with old-fashioned notions such as profitability for investors, brand names, sales and distribution systems.[2]

In the social sphere, few question the significance of cyberculture for trans-forming leisure hours, community networks and personal lifestyles.[3] Thousands of Internet sites and over two billion web pages cater to every conceivable interest from acupuncture to zoology.[4] Within a decade of its launch, America has become all Internet, all the time. The public has also flooded online in comparable countries such as Canada, Sweden and Australia.[5] The Internet population surged from about three million worldwide users in 1994 to over 377 million in late 2000.[6] Yet the potential for this medium, currently reaching about 5% of the world's population, has only started to be exploited. Despite some indications of a possible slow-down in sales of personal computers in the saturated US market, connectivity seems likely to gain momentum in the near future: Metcalf's law suggests that the value of a network is proportional to the square number of people using it: the more people link to the Internet, the greater its utility, the more it attracts.[7]

But what has been, and what will be, the impact of digital technologies on poorer countries? Surf at random, click on this, click on that, and whose voices do you hear around the globe? There are many plausible reasons why the emerging Internet age may reinforce disparities between postindustrial economies at the core of the network and developing societies at the periphery.[8] As many warn, the basic problem is 'To them that hath shall be given'. If investment in digital technologies has the capacity to boost productivity, advanced economies like Sweden, Australia and the United States at the forefront of the technological revolution may be well placed to pull even further ahead, maintaining their edge in future decades. A few middle-level economies like Taiwan, Brazil and South Korea may manage to leverage themselves profitably into niche markets within the global marketplace, servicing international corporations based elsewhere by providing software development or manufacturing silicon chips. But most poorer societies, lagging far behind, plagued by multiple burdens of debt, disease and ignorance, may join the digital world decades later and, in the long term, may ultimately fail to catch up.[9]

International organizations have sounded the alarm. The OECD warns that affluent states at the cutting edge of technological change have reinforced their lead in the new knowledge economy but so far the benefits of the Internet have not yet trickled down far to Southern, Central and Eastern Europe, let alone to the poorest areas in Sub-Saharan Africa, Latin America and South-East Asia.[10] The UN Development Report argues that productivity gains from information technologies may widen the chasm between the most affluent nations and those that lack the skills, resources and infrastructure to invest in the information society: '*The network society is creating parallel communications systems: one for those with income, education and literally connections, giving plentiful information at low cost and high speed; the other for those without connections, blocked by high barriers of time, cost and uncertainty and dependent upon outdated information.*'[11] Echoing these concerns, UNESCO emphasizes that most of the world's population lacks basic access to a telephone, let alone a computer, producing societies increasingly marginalized at the periphery of communication networks.[12] Leaders in the World Bank, European Union, United Nations and G-8 have highlighted the problems of exclusion from the knowledge economy, where know-how replaces land and capital as the basic building blocks of growth.[13] Initiatives have been launched to address this problem but disparities in the distribution of information and communication technologies are deep-seated, suggesting that they will not easily be eradicated or ameliorated. The global flow of traditional media like news, books or scholarly research has long displayed center–periphery inequalities, with information flowing primarily from North to South, an issue generating heated debate during the 1980s centered on UNESCO's controversial New World Information Order.[14] Technology has always held promise as an engine of economic growth for transforming developing nations – including machines for printing, textiles manufacture and iron railways in the 19th Century, and automobiles, oil production and television in the 20th – but critics argue that in practice this promise has often mainly served to benefit the industrialized world.[15]

Yet at the same time *if* technological diffusion can be achieved in poorer societies, and it is a big 'if', then many observers hope that the Internet provides multiple opportunities for socioeconomic and democratic development. Digital networks have the potential to broaden and enhance access to information and communications for remote rural areas and poorer neighborhoods, to strengthen the process of democratization under transitional regimes, and to ameliorate the endemic problems of poverty in the developing world. With connectivity as the umbilical cord, enthusiasts hope that the Internet will eventually serve multiple functions as the world's favorite public library, school classroom and medical database, post office and telephone, marketplace and shopping mall, channel for entertainment, culture and music, daily news resource for headlines, stocks and weather, and heterogeneous global public sphere. In the heady words of the G-8 Okinawa Charter: '*Our vision of an information society is one that better enables people to fulfill their potential and realize their aspirations. To this end we must ensure that IT serves the mutually supportive goals of creating sustainable economic growth, enhancing the public welfare, and fostering social cohesion, and work to fully realize its potential to strengthen democracy, increase transparency and accountability in governance, promote human rights, enhance cultural diversity, and to foster international peace and stability.*'[16] The Internet may allow societies to leapfrog stages of technological and industrial development. On the production-side, if Bangalore companies can write software code for IBM or Microsoft, and if Costa Rica can manufacture chips for Intel, then potentially entrepreneurs can offer similar services from Malaysia, Brazil and South Africa. The Internet encourages market globalization: small craft industries and the tourism industry in Bali or the Maldives can deal directly with customers and holidaymakers in New York and London, irrespective of distance, the costs of advertising, and the intermediate distribution chains of travel agents and retail businesses.[17] The Internet also offers promise for the delivery of basic social services like education and health information across the globe, a function that may be particularly important for middle-level professionals serving their broader community.[18] Potentially local teachers or community officials connected to the digital world in Lagos, Beijing or Calcutta can access the same electronic journals, books and databases as students at the Sorbonne, Oxford or Harvard. Distance learning can widen access to training and education, via open universities in India, Africa and Thailand, and language websites for schools.[19] Networks of hospitals and health care professionals in the Ukraine, Mozambique and Stockholm can pool expertise and knowledge about the latest research on AIDS. Peasant farmers using village community centers can learn about storm warnings and market prices for their crops, along with employment opportunities in local towns. Where peripheral regions lack access to the traditional media, the convergence of communication technologies mean that potentially the Internet can deliver virtual local newspapers, streaming radio and television video, as well as other services.

Moreover many hope that within a few years many of the existing barriers to access will be overcome with the combination of technological breakthroughs, market competition and state initiatives. The Internet has usually been delivered via bulky desktop personal computers tethered to telephone wires, but multiple cheaper devices are rapidly facilitating wireless access including NTT's DoCoMo mobile phones using I-mode in Japan, Nokia's Communicator using WAP-enabled services in Europe, and handheld personal digital assistants like Handspring and Palm Pilots which are popular in the US.[20] Prototype disposable pre-paid cell phones and laptops are under development, along with speech-recognition software and voice-activated Internet services. The price of hardware, software and services has been plummeting, due to increased competition in telecommunications combined with computer technologies' falling costs, faster speeds and smaller microprocessors.[21] In the 1960s Intel founder Gordon Moore predicted that, for the foreseeable future, chip density, and hence computing power, would double every eighteen months while costs would remain constant. During the last thirty years 'Moore's Law' has proved remarkably prescient. Every eighteen months, you can get twice as much power for the same cost. Telecommunications bandwidth, the speed at which data can be moved through the phone network, is experiencing similarly dramatic improvements due to high-speed fiber-optic cable, satellites and wireless communication technologies, all of which can be used on the same network. There have been parallel developments with computer memory and storage devices such as rewritable CD ROMs. In 1980, a gigabyte of storage cost several hundred thousand dollars and occupied a room. It now fits on a credit-card device you carry in your pocket. As well as technological innovations, public-sector initiatives in developing countries as diverse as Estonia, Costa Rica and Bangladesh have promoted the infrastructure, skills training and knowledge necessary to widen use of digital technologies.

The implications of these developments promise to sweep well beyond the economic sphere. Observers hope that digital technologies will shift some of the global disparities in power as well as wealth, by fostering a worldwide civic society countering the role of international agencies, strengthening the voice of the developing world, dissolving some of the boundaries of the nation-state, and reinforcing the process of democratization.[22] By directly linking political activists in different countries, and reducing the costs of communication and networking, the Internet may foster new types of mobilization by transnational advocacy networks around the world.[23] By connecting disparate social movements, coalitions can be formed that mobilize a global civic society, such as protestors concerned about the World

Trade Organization meetings in Seattle and Washington DC, the anti-landmine campaign, the anti-sweatshop manufacture of Nike shoes, and opposition movements in Burma, linking indigenous groups in developing societies with a diverse mélange of Norwegian environmentalists, Australian trade unionists and European human rights organizations.[24] The Internet may facilitate the networking and mobilizing functions of NGOs working across national borders, as a countervailing force to the influence of technocratic elites and government leaders running traditional international organizations.[25] The role of the Internet may be even more important as a force for human rights, providing a global platform for opposition movements challenging autocratic regimes and military dictatorships, despite government attempts to restrict access in places like China and Cuba.[26] Therefore many observers have emphasized that the emerging years of the Internet age have generated substantial worldwide inequalities in access and use although, if this could be overcome, it is widely believed that digital technologies will provide multiple opportunities for development.

The role of technology for development has therefore fuelled a debate among cyber-optimists envisaging the positive role of the Internet for transforming poverty in developing societies, cyber-skeptics who believe that new technologies alone will make little difference one way or another, and cyber-pessimists who emphasize that digital technologies will further exacerbate the existing North–South divide. This debate generates a series of questions [. . .]. Today which nations around the globe are digital leaders and laggards? What explains variations across countries in Internet use; in particular is it levels of socioeconomic development, investments in human capital, the process of democratization, or something else? Does the Internet create new inequalities, or reinforce existing divisions evident for decades in the spread of old communication technologies? Attempts to move beyond speculative theorizing about these questions face major challenges. The World Wide Web remains in its adolescence; any examination of trends is limited to just a decade. Technology continues to evolve rapidly, along with its social uses, so that projected estimates are often rapidly overtaken by events. Yet despite the need for considerable caution in weighing the available evidence, if we can establish the main drivers behind the diffusion of the Internet, and if these prove similar to the reasons behind the adoption of older forms of information technologies, then we are in a much better position to understand and predict the probable pattern of future developments, the potential consequences of the rise of the Internet age, and also the policy initiatives most likely to overcome the global divide.

## Social stratification within countries

Equally important, many official agencies have expressed concern about the development of a widening digital divide *within* societies. Technological opportunities are often highly unevenly distributed, even in nations like Australia, the United States and Sweden at the forefront of the information society. As the Internet has become increasingly central to life, work and play – providing job opportunities, strengthening community networks, and facilitating educational advancement – it becomes even more important if certain groups are systematically excluded, such as poorer neighborhoods, working class households, or peripheral rural communities. Governments in many countries have recognized this issue and developed initiatives designed to tackle this potential problem. The EU prioritized social inclusion as one of the three key objectives when launching the Europe Action Plan in Lisbon in March 1999.[27] In the United States, a series of studies by the Department of Commerce, *Falling through the Net*, have emphasized lower rates of Internet penetration among poorer households, those with limited education, the African-American and Hispanic populations, rural communities, and among women and girls.[28] [. . .] The latest data show that notable divides in Internet penetration still exist between Americans with different levels of income and education, different racial and ethnic groups, old and young, single and dual-parent families, and those with and without disabilities.[29] Many industry leaders in the corporate sector have expressed concern that too many people are being left behind in the information age, and multiple non-profit organizations and foundations have highlighted this problem.[30] Governments in Finland, Germany, Canada and Sweden have all announced programs to address access inequalities, often blending private and public resources. The British government, for example, has established a network of city learning centers, introduced a scheme to distribute re-conditioned computers to homes in poor neighborhoods, and developed a national grid linking all public libraries to the Internet.[31]

Will digital inequalities prove a temporary problem that will gradually fade over time, as Internet connectivity spreads and 'normalizes', or will this prove an enduring pattern generating a persistent division between info-haves and have-nots? Again the debate divides cyberpessimists who emphasize deep-seated patterns of social stratification and the growth of an unskilled underclass in technological access, cyber-skeptics who believe that technologies adapt to society, not vice versa, and cyber-optimists who hope that in affluent postindustrial societies, at least, the digital divide will eventually succumb to the combined forces of technological innovations, markets and the state. Rosy scenarios suggest that inequalities in Internet access may prove a short-term phenomenon, similar to the type of households that could afford to buy television sets when services were first introduced in the early 1950s. In this perspective, the profile of the online community will probably come to reflect society as a whole given the wider availability of simpler and cheaper plug-and-play technologies and faster broadband services, facilitating delivery of popular mass entertainment including streaming video-on-demand. Robert Wright argues that high-tech companies will compete to connect the public with a speed and efficiency that no government program can match, even in the neighborhoods of the urban poor, once there is mass demand for the services.[32] For those with personal computers, free Internet services, email and web hosting services are already widely available, albeit with advertising strings attached.[33] The market may be insufficient to close the gap but the non-profit sector has also been active. Major American corporations like Microsoft, Intel, Hewlett-Packard and AT&T have foundations devoted to expanding access to local communities, most often through donating educational equipment and fostering training in deprived areas, complementing state initiatives designed to furnish the younger generation with keyboard skills and training in wired schools. Telecommunications policy may play an important role here if the Internet is treated as a public utility, so that access is made widely available through public libraries, community centers and private homes, much as telephone services were regulated to produce low-cost services and universal access to rural areas.[34]

The interesting question is not whether there will be *absolute* social inequalities in Internet access; of course there will be, as in every other dimension of life. Alexander Graham Bell's commercial telephone service was launched in the United States in 1877, nevertheless today in America, more than a century later, there remain pockets of racial inequality in access to household telephones. Cable TV started to become available in the mid-1960s but today, due to choice or necessity, only two-thirds of American households are connected, along with about half of all households in industrialized nations.[35] Given substantial inequalities in the old mass media, it would be foolishly naive to expect that the Internet will magically transcend information poverty overnight. The more intriguing series of questions [. . .] concern whether there are special barriers to digital technologies, such as their greater complexity or costs, and whether *relative* inequalities in Internet use will be similar to disparities in the penetration rates of older communication technologies.

## The democratic divide

The last challenge, and perhaps the most intractable issue, concerns the potential impact of the digital world on the distribution of power and influence in political systems. Even if we assume, for the sake of argument, that Internet penetration rates will gradually widen throughout society there is growing awareness that nevertheless a substantial *democratic divide* may still exist between those who do and do not use the multiple political resources available on the Internet for civic engagement. What will be the impact of digital technologies in the public sphere?

The Internet has generated deeply contested alternative visions about the future. Again the most positive perspective is held by *cyber-optimists* who emphasize the Panglossian possibilities of the Internet for the involvement of ordinary citizens in direct democracy. Digital technologies hold promise as a mechanism facilitating alternative channels of civic engagement such as political chat-rooms, electronic voting in general elections and for referenda issues, and the mobilization of virtual communities, revitalizing levels of mass participation in public affairs.[36] The use of the Internet by groups and social movements is often believed to exemplify digital politics. This view was certainly popular in the mid-1990s and the revolutionary potential of digital technologies continues to be expressed by many enthusiasts such as George Gilder.[37] Yet as the Internet evolved, a darker vision has been articulated among *cyber-pessimists* who regard digital technology as a Pandora's box unleashing new inequalities of power and wealth, reinforcing deeper divisions between the information rich and poor, the tuned-in and the tuned-out, the activists and the disengaged. This account stresses that the global and social divides already discussed mean that Internet politics will disproportionately benefit the elite.[38] In this perspective, despite the potential for technological innovations, traditional interests and established authorities have the capacity to reassert their control in the virtual political sphere, just as traditional multinational corporations have the ability to reestablish their predominance in the world of e-commerce.[39] Lastly, *cyber-skeptics* argue that both these visions are exaggerated, since so far the potential of the Internet has failed to have a dramatic impact on the practical reality of 'politics as usual', for good or ill, even in countries at the forefront of digital technologies'.[40] For example, during the 2000 American presidential campaign the major candidates used their web pages essentially as glossy shop-windows, as fundraising tools, and as campaign ads, rather than as interactive 'bottom up' formats for public comment and discussion.[41] Technology, in this view, is a plastic medium that flows into and adapts to pre-existing social molds.

[. . .]

[. . .] The first decade of the emerging Internet age has seen a process of restructuring and adaptation as political institutions have learnt what does, and doesn't, work using digital technologies. Yet precisely because this is a period of experimental transition and institutional change it is particularly important to draw the appropriate lessons based on the available evidence, to map the current state of play, and to consider how the Internet functions in a wide range of political systems, including but also beyond the United States and Western Europe.

The optimistic claims that the interactive capacities of digital technologies will facilitate a new era of direct democracy, characterized by widespread citizen deliberation in affairs of state, like a virtual Agora, while attractive as a normative ideal, is ultimately implausible in practice as soon as we understand who becomes involved in digital politics. As we shall see, the cross-national survey evidence indicates that those who take advantage of the opportunities for electronic civic engagement are activists most likely to participate via conventional channels. As a medium of choice par excellence, it seems improbable that digital politics will reach the disengaged, the apathetic and the uninterested, if they choose to spend their time and energies on multiple alternative sites devoted to everything from the stock market to games and music. In this regard, the Internet seems analogous to the segmented magazine market, where some subscribe to *The Atlantic Monthly*, *The Economist* and *Foreign Affairs*, but others pick *Golfing Weekly* or *Playboy*. The available studies of politically oriented discussion groups, bulletin boards and online chat rooms have found these largely fail as deliberative fora, instead serving as places to reinforce like-minded voices.[42] Claims for the potential of digital direct democracy to revitalize mass participation can find few crumbs of support from these studies. As the same time the skeptics' claim that nothing much will change in the political system, as most established political institutions will adapt digital technologies to facilitate existing functions, while admittedly more realistic and closer to the mark, overlooks the occasional indications that, here and there, now and then, like a faint sporadic seismic tremor, some disruptive threats to politics as usual are already becoming evident, similar to the dotcom survivors that manage to threaten and destabilize multinational corporations in the marketplace.

Rejecting the view that either everything will change as direct democracy comes to replace representative governance, or that nothing will change as the digital world merely replicates 'politics as usual', [I argue] that digital technologies have the capacity to strengthen the institutions of civic society mediating between citizens and the state, especially the power of insurgents. The more any agency lacks traditional organizational resources, the more open it is to using digital technologies strategically for restructuring and organizational innovation. Established 'inside-the-beltway' political actors, drawing on substantial organizational and financial resources, legal authority, time-honored practices and conventional ways of doing business, can be expected to be among the slowest to adapt to the digital challenge, including candidates and elected politicians in the major parties, ministers and civil servants administrating government departments, executives and managers employed in the public sector, advocates and lobbyists working for traditional interest groups, officials and leaders in international organizations, and journalists and broadcasters in the mainstream mass media. Established political institutions, just like major corporations, can be expected to adapt the Internet to their usual forms of communication, providing information online, but not reinventing themselves or rethinking their core strategy in the digital world, unless successfully challenged. In contrast, insurgent organizations traditionally have fewer political assets, fewer traditional advantages, but also fewer inhibitions about adapting flexibly to the opportunities for information and communication via the Internet. If this account is essentially correct, digital politics can be expected to have most impact in leveling the playing field, not completely but at least partially, for a diverse range of insurgent movements and challengers, such as transnational advocacy networks, alternative social movements, protest organizations and minor parties, such as those concerned with environmentalism, globalization, human rights, world trade, conflict resolution and single issue causes from all shades of the political spectrum, ranging from genetically modified food and anti-fuel taxes to animal rights and anti-sweat shops. The Internet does not drive these insurgent movements – these causes are triggered by deeper passions – but it facilitates their organization, mobilization and expression.[43]

Information and the mechanisms for delivering it are the life-blood and sinews of the body politic. Some power comes out of the barrel of a gun. Some power can be bought with the resources of wealth and income. Some may be inherited by sultans and princelings. But in democratic systems the primary coinage of the realm – the resource that persuades, that influences, that swings votes – is information. 'Information' comes in all shapes and forms, from the publication of official documents by government departments to brief news bulletins on the hour, from lengthy parliamentary debates to thirty-second campaign ads, and from demonstrations by new social movements to informal conversations over the water cooler. Political organizations are essentially designed as control systems for the transmission of information, binding together the activities of all members within the unit and communicating priorities to the external world. Some information exchanges are brief and transitory; others use rich and well-developed channels. What the explosive growth of connectivity via the Internet does is to alter the transmission of information among networks, shrinking costs, maximizing speed, broadening reach and eradicating distance. Potentially these changes can have profound consequences for altering the balance of resources and power between insurgent challengers and established organizations within the political system. Hierarchical communication channels, typical in bureaucratic organizations like government departments and international agencies, become less effective and slower mechanisms of information transmission than horizontal networks shared by informal coalitions of alternative social movements. National boundaries to information flows dissolve, allowing global networks to flourish.[44] Independent upstarts and multiple sources of 'news', where immediacy outweighs authority, challenge the legitimacy of traditional journalism in the newspapers and television. Formal organizations like trade unions, established interest groups and mass-branch political parties find themselves hemorrhaging members, saddled with assets like local organizations that may have become liabilities to adaptation in the digital world. Advantages like money and manpower remain valuable in the new environment; major parties, established lobbyists, government departments and corporations seeking to communicate their message can buy glitzy off-the-peg multimedia campaign websites from professional design agencies and maintain them in-house by fulltime staff. But a few volunteers working for minor parties or smaller groups can rival their efforts online at relatively low cost, if they have some basic technical skills, compared with the steep barriers to producing television commercials or buying newspaper ads. Communication costs fall, and information costs plummet even faster: with wider and easier access to official sources, opposition groups and social movements can challenge the authority and expertise of government ministers, civil servants and elected officials on their own turf.

The main democratic potential of digital information and communication technologies lies in strengthening organizational linkages and networking capacities in civic society, tipping the balance of relevant political resources from money, members and bureaucratic organizations to know-how and technical skills, providing more open and pluralistic forms of competition for insurgents among parties, interest groups, alternative social movements and the independent media, and expanding the resources of information released by government departments, official bodies and international agencies. This process alters the opportunities for the institutions of civic society, particularly insurgents, to network horizontally with each other, to challenge the authority of established institutions, and to reinforce their linkages with activists. Strengthening these bonds, it will be argued, has the capacity to produce sudden disruptions to politics as usual, especially for flash coalitions mobilizing suddenly like a guerrilla army then dissolving again, exemplified by events such as the anti-capitalism violent protest in the City of London in June 1999, direct action campaigns against the World Trade Organization on the streets of Seattle in December 1999, anti-globalization protests against the World Bank/International Monetary Fund in Prague in September 2000, and the Poujadist fuel price revolt by farmers and truckers that swept the European continent in October 2000. Such occurrences remain relatively rare, but they can have immediate impact on the policy process, and they are important as indicators of the disruptive potential of digital politics. Some flash protests are temporary phenomena. Other transnational advocacy networks manage to sustain longer-term electronic coalitions, such as the International Campaign to Ban Landmines that resulted in a treaty signed by 122 nations in 1997. Global protest movements and direct action demonstrations spreading across national borders have existed for decades, such as the anti-nuclear movement in the 1950s and the anti-Vietnam protests of the 1960s, or even further back the anti-slavery and the suffrage movements in the 19th century. The phenomenon is far from new but these movements are facilitated in an environment of minimal-cost instantaneous global communications where technology can be used by a diverse coalition to challenge the legitimacy of international organizations and the authority of national governments. Governments, like British red-coats lined up in perfect formations, seem unsure how to respond, flustered, when suddenly out-maneuvered by the ad-hoc coalitions of truck drivers and fuel tax protestors, the environmental activists and animal rights lobbies, the anti-capitalists and anti-globalist forces. It is true, as cyber-skeptics claim, that most established political institutions actively resist the disruptions caused by digital politics, in a process of dynamic organizational conservatism, preferring to co-opt the capacities of new technologies to preexisting functions, rather than being forced to reinvent themselves in the Internet age. But it is also true that the capacities of the Internet are adapted more easily by smaller, more flexible challengers, a process that strengthens the pluralism of civic society in established democracies, and one that is particularly important for the process of democratic consolidation, and for opposition movements and insurgents seeking to challenge authoritarian rule around the globe.

[. . .]

## Notes

1   US Department of Commerce. 1999. *The Emerging Digital Economy II*. US Department of Commerce, Washington, DC. http:www.ecommerce.gov/ede. For estimates of productivity gains in other postindustrial societies see OECD. 2000. *Information and Technology Outlook 2000*. Paris: OECD. Annex 1.

2   See Philip Evans and Thomas S. Wurster. 1999. *Blown to Bits: How the New Economics of Information Transforms Strategy*. Cambridge, MA: Harvard Business School; Don Tapscott, David Ticoll and Alex Lowy. 2000. *Digital Capital: Harnessing the Power of Business Webs*. Cambridge, MA: Harvard Business School; Carl Shapiro and Hal R. Varian. 1998. *Information Rules: A Strategic Guide to the Network Economy*. Cambridge, MA: Harvard Business School; Clayton M. Christensen. 2000. *The Innovator's Dilemma: When New Technologies Cause Great Firms to Fall*. New York: HarperCollins Publishers.

3   See, for example, Steven G. Jones (ed.). 1998. *Cybersociety 2.0: Revisiting Computer-mediated Communication and Community*. Thousand Oaks, CA: Sage. The estimate of the number of American users of Napster in August 2000 is from Media Metrix. www.mediametrix.com.

4   The estimate of 2.1 billion unique web pages publicly available on the Internet in July 2000 is provided by Cyveillance, a company based in Arlington, Virginia, in a report 'Sizing the Internet' which suggests that 7.3 million unique pages are added daily to the total. www.cyveillance.com/newsroom/3012.asp. Also reported in Janet Kornblum. 2000. 'The News behind the Net'. *USA Today*. 11 July 2000. http://www.usatoday.com/life/cyber/tech/jk071100.htm.

5   On the US see regular estimates from surveys conducted by the Pew Canter for the People and the Press. www.peoplepress.org. For a 20-nation study including Sweden and Australia see IriS/MORI Internet Survey Jan.–March 1999.

6   [. . .] http://www.NUA.ie. The estimate of approximately 377 million users worldwide is for Fall 2000.

7   Metcalf's law is named after Robert Metcalf, founder of 3Com Corporation. See Larry Downes and Chunka Mui. 2000. *Unleashing the Killer Apps*. Cambridge, MA: Harvard Business School Press. Pp. 24–5.

8   Tim Hayward. 1995. *Info-Rich, Info-Poor: Access and Exchange in the Global Information Society*. K. G. Saur; William Wresch. 1996. *Disconnected: Haves and Have-Nots in the Information Age*. New Brunswick, NJ: Rutgers University Press.

9    Francisco Rodriguez and Ernest J. Wilson III. 2000. 'Are poor countries losing the Information Revolution?' *The World Bank infoDev Working Paper Series*. May. www.infoDev.org/library/wilsonrodriguez.doc.

10   OECD. 1999. *Communications Outlook 1999*. Paris: OECD. Pp. 85–98. Also www. oecd.org.

11   UNDP. 1999. *Human Development Report 1999*. New York: UNDP/Oxford. P. 63.

12   UNESCO. 1998. *World Communication Report: The Media and Challenges of the New Technologies*. Paris: UNESCO.

13   See, for example, the G-8 *Okinawa Charter on Global Information Society*. 23 July 2000. http://www.g8kyushu-okinawa.go.jp/w/documents/it1.html.

14   J. Galtung and M. Ruge. 1965. 'The Structure of Foreign News'. *Journal of Peace Research*. 1: 64–90; Hamid Mowlana. 1997. *Global Information and World Communication*. 2nd edn. London: Sage.

15   For a comprehensive overview see Surendra J. Patel (general ed.). 1993–5. *Technological Transformation in the Third World*. 5 vols. Aldershot: Avebury. See also case studies in David J. Jeremy. 1992. *The Transfer of International Technology: Europe, Japan and the USA in the Twentieth Century*. Aldershot: Edward Elgar; Nathan Rosenberg and Claudio Frischtak (eds). 1985. *International Technology Transfer: Concepts, Methods and Comparisons*. New York: Praeger; David Charles and Jeremy Howells. 1992. *Technology Transfer in Europe*. London: Belhaven Press; Manas Chatterji. 1990. *Technology Transfer in the Developing Countries*. New York: St Martin's Press; S. R. Melkote. 1991. *Communication for Development in the Third World: Theory and Practice*. Newbury Park, CA: Sage Publications; Wilbur Schramm. 1964. *Mass Media and National Development*. Stanford, CA: Stanford University Press.

16   G-8 *Okinawa Charter on Global Information Society*. 23 July 2000. http://www. g8kyushu-okinawa.go.jp/w/documents/it1.html.

17   International Telecommunications Union. 1999. *Challenges to the Network: Internet for Development*. Geneva: ITU. P. 7; Celia W. Dugger. 2000. 'Connecting Rural India to the World'. *New York Times* 28 May. http://www.nytimes.com/library/tech/yr/mo/biztech/articles/28india.html.

18   Tim Hayward. 1995. *Info-Rich, Info-Poor: Access and Exchange in the Global Information Society*. K. G. Saur; William Wresch. 1996. *Disconnected: Haves and Have-Nots in the Information Age*. New Brunswick, NJ: Rutgers University Press.

19   S. Arunachalam. 1999. 'Information and Knowledge in the Age of Electronic Communication: A Developing Country Perspective'. *Journal of Information Science*. 25(6): 465–476.

20   M. Rao, S. R. Bhandari, S. M. Iqbal, A. Sinha and W. U. Siraj. 1999. 'Struggling with the Digital Divide: Internet Infrastructure, Policies and Regulations'. *Economic and Political Weekly*. 34 (46–47): 3317–3320.

21   On the deregulation and market liberalization of telecommunications see ITU. 1999. *Trends in Telecommunication Reform 1999*. Geneva: ITD. www.itu.org. On the falling costs of ICT goods and services see OECD. 2000. *Information and Technology Outlook 2000*. Paris: OECD. Chapter 2, 'Information Technology Markets.'

22   See the discussion in Jerry Everard. 2000. *Virtual States: The Internet and the Boundaries of the Nation-State*. London: Routledge.

23   Howard Frederick. 1992. 'Computer Communications in Cross-Border Coalition-Building: North American NGO Networking against NAFTA'. *Gazette* 50: 217–242.

24   See Sylvia Ostry. 2000. 'Making Sense of it All: A Post-mortem on the Meaning of Seattle'. In *Seattle, the WTO, and the Future of the Multilateral Trading System*. Eds Roger B. Porter and Pierre Sauve. Cambridge, MA: The Center for Business and Government, John F. Kennedy School of Government; Margaret B. Keck and Kathryn Sikkink. 1998. *Activists beyond Borders – Advocacy Networks in International Politics*. Ithaca, NY: Cornell University Press; Maxwell A. Cameron (ed.). 1998. *To Walk Without*

*Fear: The Global Movement to Ban Landmines.* Oxford: Oxford University Press; J. Zelwietro. 1998. 'The Politicization of Environmental Organizations through the Internet'. *Information Society* 14 (1): 45–55.

25    M. Ayres. 1999. 'From the Streets to the Internet: The Cyber-diffusion of Contention'. *Annals of the American Academy of Political and Social Science* 566: 132–143.

26    Leonard R. Sussman. 2000. 'Censor Dot Gov: The Internet and Press Freedom 2000' *Freedom House Press Freedom Survey 2000.* http://www.freedomhouse.org/pfs2000/sussman.html; Kevin A. Hill and John E. Hughes. 1998. *Cyberpolitics: Citizen Activism in the Age of the Internet.* Lanham: Rowman and Littlefield; Mamoun Fandy. 1999. 'Cyberresistance: Saudi Opposition between Globalization and Localization'. *Comparative Studies in Society and History* 41 (1): 124–147; William Drake, Shanthi Kalathil and Taylor C. Boas. 'Dictatorships in the Digital Age: Some Considerations on the Internet in China and Cuba.' *iMP: The Magazine on Information Impacts*; Jon B. Alterman. 1998. *New Media, New Politics? From Satellite Television to the Internet in the Arab World.* Washington, DC: Washington Institute for Near East Policy.

27    The Lisbon European Council. 2000. *An Agenda of Economic and Social Renewal for Europe. European Commission.* 23–24 March. http://europa.eu.int.

28    NTIA. 1999. *Falling Through the Net.* Washington, DC: Department of Commerce. www.ntia.doc.gov.ntiahome/fttn99. See also Anthony G. Wilheim. 2000. *Democracy in the Digital Age: Challenges to Political Life in Cyberspace.* New York: Routledge.

29    NTIA. 2000. *Falling Through the Net.* Washington, DC: Department of Commerce. http://www.digitaldivide.gov/reports.htm.

30    See, for example, the Benton Foundation's network, www.digitaldividenetwork.gov. See also Bill Gates. 'Statement at the White House Conference on the New Economy'. April 5 2000. www.microsoft.com/billgates/speeches/04-05wh.htm; Steve Case. 1998. '*Community Update: Election '98*', www.aol.com, keyword Steve Case. October 6 1998.

31    Department of Trade and Industry. 2000. *Closing the Digital Divide: Information and Communication Technologies in Deprived Areas.* http://www.dti.gov.uk. See also http://open.gov.uk.

32    Robert Wright. 'Our Gang: TRB from Washington'. *New Republic Online.* February 14 2000.

33    For example, K-Mart's Bluelight in the US and Dixons' Freeserve in the UK, although it should be noted that subscribers to the latter still have to pay for local telephone calls.

34    This argument is expressed by Robert Putnam. 2000. *Bowling Alone: The Collapse and Revival of American Community.* New York: Simon and Schuster. P. 175.

35    Pippa Norris. 2000. *A Virtuous Circle: Political Communications in Post-Industrial Democracies.* Cambridge: Cambridge University Press. Table 5.2. The figure represents the average percentage of households in 29 OECD nations with cable or satellite TV in 1997.

36    See Benjamin R. Barber. 1998. 'Three scenarios for the Future of Technology and Strong Democracy'. *Political Science Quarterly.* 113 (4): 573–589.

37    George Gilder. 2000. *Telecosm: How Infinite Bandwidth will Revolutionize Our World.* New York: Free Press. For earlier discussions see, for example, Edward Schwartz. 1996. *Netactivism: How Citizens Use the Internet.* Sebastapol, CA: Songline Studios; Wayne Rash, Jr. 1997. *Politics on the Net: Wiring the Political Process.* New York: W. H. Freeman; Howard Rheingold. 1993. *The Virtual Community: Homesteading on the Electronic Frontier.* Reading, MA: Addison Wesley.

38    See, for example, Peter Golding. 1996. 'World Wide Wedge: Division and Contradiction in the Global Information Infrastructure'. *Monthly Review* 48 (3): 70–85; Peter Golding. 1998. 'Global Village or Cultural Pillage? The Unequal Inheritance of the Communication Revolution'. In *Capitalism and the Information Age: The Political Economy*

*of the Global Communication Revolution*. Eds R. W. McChesney, E. Meiksins Wood and J. B. Foster. New York: Monthly Review Press; Peter Golding. 2000. 'Information and Communications Technologies and the Sociology of the Future'. *Sociology*. 34 (1): 165–184.

39  See, for example, Robert W. McChesney. 1999. *Rich Media, Poor Democracy*. [Champaigne-Urbana, IL]: University of Illinois Press. Pp. 182–185.

40  Michael Margolis and David Resnick. 2000. *Politics as Usual: The Cyberspace 'Revolution'*. Thousand Oaks, CA: Sage.

41  Media Metrix. October 2000. *Campaign 2000: Party Politics on the World Wide Web*. www.mediametrix.com.

42  See Richard David. 1999. *The Web of Politics*. Oxford: Oxford University Press. Chapters 2 and 3; Anthony Wilhelm. *Democracy in the Digital Age: Challenges to Political Life in Cyberspace*. New York: Routledge. Chapter 5.

43  For the argument that the Internet is an intervening rather than driving variable in the rise of transnational advocacy networks see Margaret E. Keck and Kathryn Sikkink. 1998. *Activists Beyond Borders – Advocacy Networks in International Politics*. Ithaca, NY: Cornell University Press.

44  For example, if 5% of the total generic top-level domains are from a particular country, then 5% of the total number of hosts surveyed under generic top level domains are reallocated to that country. For details, see OECD. 1999. *Communications Outlook 1999*. Paris: OECD. P. 87.

# Chapter 19

# Christopher Lasch

## THE DEGRADATION OF THE PRACTICAL ARTS

From S. E. Goldberg and C. R. Strain (eds) *Technological Change and the Transformation of America*, Carbonade, IL: Southern Illinois University Press (1987), pp. 79–90.

### Taylorism revisited

THE PREVAILING VIEW of the relations between technology and values can be simply stated. Technology is ethically neutral. It is a tool that can be put to good uses or bad uses. How it is used will depend on our values, not on technology itself. Instead of talking about technology, which is simply a given, a normal aspect of our everyday environment, we would do better to talk about values and about the possibility of humanizing the industrial order. We would do better to remind ourselves, in other words, that machines, after all, are merely servants of the human beings who design them.

One of the founders of a high-technology communications company expressed these opinions in a recent interview:

> Technology is absolutely neutral and the same microprocessors [can] be used for good or evil. The determination of that really comes through what the individual, what the collective group of individuals, align themselves with. What our values are, what priorities we have in life, I think that's what the real question is, not the technology.

The same ideas appear in a full-page advertisement for the international company United Technologies, entitled 'Technology's Promise': 'Ethically, technology is neutral. There is nothing inherently either good or bad about it. It is simply a tool, a servant, directed and deployed by people for whatever purpose they want fulfilled.'

It tells us something about this way of looking at the issue that it so often appears under corporate sponsorship. It is an interpretation designed to provide reassurance and to create the illusion that we all have a share in deciding how new technologies will be used. Note the vagueness of this talk about 'individuals,' 'collective groups of individuals,' and 'people,' which discourages us from asking just which people in particular design and control our technology, which people are served by it, and which people, on the other hand, stand to lose by the continuing development of this technology along its present lines.

An examination of the impact of technology on the transformation of work and the changing class structure of industrial society dispels the illusion that technology is a neutral and impersonal force. It is misleading even to speak of the impact of technology on the work process, since this formulation implies that technology originates outside the work process – in the laboratory, presumably – and has an 'impact' designed or anticipated by no one in particular. In fact, much of modern industrial technology has been deliberately designed by managers for the express purpose of reducing their dependence on skilled labor. One of the early architects of this technology, Frederick Winslow Taylor, the founder of scientific management, spoke much more candidly about technology and its implications than corporate spokesmen and their propagandists speak today. In his book, *The Principles of Scientific Management*, published in 1911, he described a struggle for control of production between management and workers. The success of scientific management, as Taylor saw it, depended not so much on the introduction of machinery as on the managers' expropriation of the craft knowledge formerly controlled by the workers – 'this mass of traditional knowledge,' as Taylor called it, 'a large part of which is not in the possession of management.' That the workers understood the implications of Taylor's reforms is shown by their resistance to them. As Taylor noted, his attempt to redesign the work process, to deprive workers of any technical initiative, and to reduce them to the position of carrying out orders issued by the planning department, 'immediately started a war, . . . which as time went on grew more and more bitter. . . . No one who has not had this experience can have an idea of the bitterness which is gradually developed in such a struggle.' In a remarkable passage, Taylor admits that the workers' resistance to scientific management was well founded. When workmen, formerly his friends, asked him, 'in a personal, friendly way, whether he would advise them, for their own best interest, to turn out more work,' he 'had to tell them,' he says, 'as a truthful man . . . that if he were in their place he would fight against turning out any more work, just as they were doing, because under the [new] system they would be allowed to earn no more wages than they had been earning, and yet they would be made to work harder' (1911, pp. 32, 49–50, 52).

The movement for fully automated industrial production in our own time, sometimes referred to as the second Industrial Revolution, originated in a struggle for control of production in the years immediately following World War II, under conditions remarkably similar to the conditions that earlier had inspired Taylor's scientific management. 'What is today called "automation" is conceptually a logical extension of Taylor's scientific management,' Peter Drucker has written (1967, p. 26). Taylor had attempted to separate the planning from the execution of tasks; but his innovations had achieved only partial success. At the end of World War II, many industries continued to depend heavily on skilled labor, notably the machine-tool industry itself, and the workers still controlled the pace of production. The rapid growth of industrial unionism under the New Deal, moreover, made workers increasingly resistant to managerial authority. In a book that appeared in 1948, *The Union Challenge and Management Control*, Neil Chamberlain noted labor's increasing interest in the effects of 'technological changes,' 'types of machinery,' and 'methods of production.' He predicted that the 'next category of managerial authority in which the unions will seek to deepen and widen their participation will be the category of production' (1948, p. 87). Managers resented union interference with their own prerogatives, as they understood them. One executive summed up the issue facing industry in a single question: 'Who runs the shop – them or us?' (Noble 1984, p. 30).

As David Noble demonstrates in his book, *Forces of Production*, automation commended itself to industrialists, after World War II, precisely because it promised to turn back this threat and to solidify their control over production. The evidence on this point is abundant and unambiguous. According to Earl Troup of General Electric, numerical control of machine production brought 'a shift of control to management, [which] is no longer dependent upon the operator.' In 1953, a group of engineers at MIT cited among the advantages of numerical control that it eliminated the need for skilled workers. 'Little judgment is required and the work is so routine that it is desirable to use a person with little technical skill who will be satisfied with repetitive, entirely prescribed work.' A report issued by the Harvard Business School in 1952 pointed out that computerized production meant the 'reduction of human attention and skill. . . . Since the control of the machine is automatic, the function of the operator is to load, unload, and start the machine. . . . A skilled machinist is no longer required to operate the machine.' *Business Week* reported in 1959 that automated machine tools 'run almost untouched by human hands.' 'The fundamental advantage of numerical control,' according to a 1976 editorial in *Iron Age*, is that 'it brings production control to the Engineering Department.' This consideration led the *American Machinist* to refer to numerical control as not just a 'strictly metalworking technique' but a 'philosophy of control.' A report on automation published by Earl Lundgren in 1969 noted that 'a prime interest in each subject company was the transfer of as much planning and control from the shop to the office as possible.' Two years later a report issued by the Small Business Administration arrived at the same conclusion. 'Much of the skill formerly expected of the machinist operator is now applied by the design engineer, the methods analyst, and the parts programmer.' An MIT study made the same finding in 1978. 'We believe we see a definite thrust toward deskilling of the N/C machine operators.' As a result, 'production output, machine downtime, and quality data were more easily obtainable, thus enhancing managerial control' (Noble 1984, pp. 232–40).

The drive for managerial control leads to a search for more and more sophisticated machinery and ultimately for the fully automated factory – the managerial paradise held up by *Fortune* magazine in 1946, at the outset of the second Industrial Revolution, as the ideal industrial environment, the 'factory of tomorrow' in which human beings have been altogether replaced by machines that 'are not subject to any human limitations,' 'do not mind working around the clock,' 'never feel hunger or fatigue,' 'are always satisfied with working conditions,' and 'never demand higher wages' (Leaver and Brown 1946, pp. 165, 204).

Experience with the trouble caused by human beings has occasionally led management in the opposite direction, of course. Instead of attempting to eliminate the 'human factor' of production, some companies have delegated managerial tasks to workers in the hope of 'motivating' them and of giving them a feeling of participation. Experiments with 'job enrichment' and 'self-management' have usually been abandoned, however, as soon as managers begin to understand that such programs make many of their own functions obsolete. In Lynn, Massachusetts, a pilot project inaugurated by General Electric in 1968, at the height of the enthusiasm for self-management and for Douglas MacGregor's 'Theory Y,' was abandoned a few years later, not because the volume or quality of production had suffered but because the union had begun to press for expansion of the program. Like many other managers, those at GE discovered that automation did not free them altogether from dependence on human labor, while its introduction created serious problems of 'morale.' ('If you treat us like button-pushers,' one operator said, 'we'll work like button-pushers.') On the other hand, efforts to improve morale by giving workers more responsibility have the unfortunate effect – unfortunate from management's point of view – of whetting the workers' appetite for responsibility and of demonstrating, moreover, that workers are quite capable of exercising it. In the end, the management of GE, according to Noble, sacrificed productivity to power. One executive observed that 'productivity may be less real an issue to management than conformity to established work rules' (Noble 1984, pp. 265–323).

The historical record, then, indicates that industrial technology has grown out of concrete struggles for control over production and takes its existing shape not because this is the shape dictated by ethically neutral considerations of technical efficiency but because it concentrates decision making in a managerial and technical elite. These considerations should make us suspicious of the rosy predictions of a 'postindustrial' society in which technological innovation will lead to an abundance of skilled jobs, eliminate disagreeable jobs, and make life easy for everyone. Everything we know about technological 'progress' indicates, on the contrary, that it promotes inequality and an unprecedented centralization of political and economic power. Whenever we hear that some new technology is inevitable, we should consult the historical record, which shows that technical innovations usually appeal to industrialists not because they are inevitable or even because they make for greater productive efficiency, but because they consolidate the industrialist's power over the work force. The triumph of industrial technology testifies not to the inexorable march of science but to the defeat of working-class resistance.

It is a muddled, ahistorical view of the Industrial Revolution that dismisses this resistance as an attempt to 'postpone the inevitable,' as J. David Bolter writes in his study of the coming 'computer age.' It is equally muddled to argue that since the 'computer age' is upon us, our best hope lies in 'reforming the age of computers from within' (Bolter 1984, p. 229). In the past, efforts to reform industrial technology from within, usually led by engineers, served merely to reinforce the lessons already driven home by workers' resistance to the introduction of new technologies: that those technologies serve the interests of capital and that even those who design and manage the machines have little to say about the uses they are put to.

Over and over again, new technologies have reduced even the engineer's work to a routine. What originates as a craft degenerates into a series of automatic operations performed more or less unthinkingly. Computer programming is no exception to this pattern. As Sherry Turkle notes, 'Today, programs are written on a kind of assembly line. The professional programmer works as part of a large team and is in touch with only a small part of the problem being worked on' (1984, p. 170). In the early days of the computer, many people hoped that electronic technology could be captured by the counterculture. But things did not turn out that way. Computers encourage centralization and bureaucracy. Instead of humanizing industry, the personal computer came to serve as an escape from industry for hobbyists and even for professional programmers seeking to achieve in the privacy of the home the control they could no longer exercise at work. Turkle reminds us that 'people will not change unresponsive government or intellectually deadening work through involvement with their machines at home.' But personal computers offer the illusion of control in 'one small domain,' if not in the larger world of work and politics (p. 175). Sold to the public as a means of access to the new world of postindustrial technology, personal computers in fact provide escape from that world. They satisfy a need for mastery and control denied outlets elsewhere.

There is nothing inherent in computers or in any other type of machinery that leads inevitably to the degradation of work instead of the enhancement of work. Automated machine tools can be used either by craftsmen to perform a variety of tasks or by unskilled operators to perform the same task over and over. In practice, however, managers become uneasy if workers assert too much control over production, and they have accordingly devoted a great deal of energy and imagination to the elimination of the 'human factor,' as they call it. The ideal machine, in their eyes, is a machine that eliminates the need for human intervention altogether. Insofar as Taylorite principles continue to govern the development of industrial technology, the growing reliance on numerically controlled machines and on computers will simply recapitulate the history of machine tools at an earlier stage in their development. The deskilling of the work force will continue, in other words, checked only by the irreducible dependence on skilled labor that even the most sophisticated machinery has not yet found a way to eliminate.

## Sabel and the thesis of democratic technology

But what if Taylorite principles have begun to lose their hold on industry? The hope that the deskilling process can be reversed rests not on the claim that new computer-based technologies will automatically create a new class of skilled workers, as Drucker and other technological optimists assume, but on the demonstration that mass production economies have reached the limit of their capacity to generate sustained growth. Charles F. Sabel, whose qualified optimism about technology distinguishes him both from mindless optimists like Alvin Toffler and John Naisbitt and, on the other hand, from critics of technology like David Noble, Harry

Braverman, and Lewis Mumford, argues that the 'breakup of mass markets' in the seventies and eighties will force American industry to abandon Taylorism and to adopt a more flexible system of production. Taylorism assumes that 'large numbers of potential customers have essentially identical and well-defined wants.' The specialized markets that are increasingly important today, on the other hand, demand 'general-purpose machines and an adaptable work force' (Sabel 1982, pp. 201–2). Where critics of technology go wrong, according to Sabel, is in ignoring the decisive influence of markets. It is the market, not some hypothetical struggle for power in the workplace, that determines the uses to which any given technology is put. In a mass market, technology is centralized and hierarchical. When diversified markets prevail, however, technology becomes diversified in its own right: flexible, decentralized, and democratic.

In *The Second Industrial Divide*, Sabel and Michael J. Piore elaborate these arguments in some detail. The saturation of industrial markets, they contend, confronts mature mass-production economies with a choice between two conflicting lines of policy. The first is a 'geographic extension of the mass-production system,' designed to create new markets for mass-produced commodities and to control the fierce competition that now prevails among the major industrial powers (Piore and Sabel 1984, p. 252). The rise of multinational corporations already foreshadows this policy, but private corporations cannot by themselves bring an integrated global economy into being. Economic integration on this scale, according to Piore and Sabel, would also require a globalization of the Keynesian economic policies that helped to stabilize the national economies of the industrial countries after World War II. An attempt to raise purchasing power would require, among other things, aid to debtor countries and a global war against poverty. Domestically, it would require some form of national economic planning, not to mention an enlargement of the welfare functions of the state. By means of such policies, the United States and other industrial nations might create new markets, in Sabel's words, 'without fundamentally shaking management's power to control, invest in, and limit changes in the organization of work' (Sabel 1982, p. 201).

The second line of development points in a different direction, one that is foreshadowed, according to Piore and Sabel, by the revival of small-scale craft production in selected industries in Italy, Germany, and Japan. The second line of development, 'flexible specialization,' points to a new 'technological paradigm' based on short production runs, a highly skilled work force, and a resurgent sense of community. A single example explains why 'flexibility depends upon cooperation,' according to Piore and Sabel. Under mass production, the training of skilled workers consists of the formal learning provided by the state-supported school system together with a highly specialized training added by the corporation, which enables workers to master particular tasks in a particular firm. Flexible production, however, requires more broadly trained workers, who 'can shift rapidly from one job to another.' Under flexible production, individual firms have little incentive to invest in training workers who may be hired away from them by competitors; but since all these firms have a collective interest in broadly skilled workers, they find ways to fuse work skills with the 'larger life of the community.' A system of flexible production thus requires the 'regeneration of resources required by the collectivity but not produced by the individual units of which it is composed.' These resources include not only the school system but the family, the institutions of local government, and voluntary associations of various kinds. More broadly, they include the tradition of 'yeoman democracy' in the United States, as Piore and Sabel call it, as opposed to the market-oriented liberalism that has dominated American politics in the age of mass production. 'In market liberalism,' they write, 'property is to be used to maximal advantage of its possessor; in yeoman democracy, property is to be held in trust for the community. . . . It is this recognition of the indispensability of *community* that makes yeoman democracy . . . the political analogue of the cooperative competition of craft production' (Piore and Sabel 1984, pp. 252, 273–5, 299–301, 305–6).

This is an appealing vision of the future, not least because it coincides with a revival of interest, among scholars in a variety of disciplines, in the indigenous tradition of American republicanism on which new forms of economic and political life might draw. The weakness of this analysis lies in its underestimation of the difficulties that lie in the way of communitarian solutions of the crisis of mass production. As one reviewer notes, Piore and Sabel 'are strangely silent on how the distribution of economic power dictates the course of technological choice' (Kuttner 1985, p. 31). The present distribution of economic power clearly militates against policies that favor localism, craftsmanship, and the subordination of property rights to local and regional needs. The present distribution of power favors the globalist solution, or even worse, a return to laissez-faire: an attempt to dismantle the regulations imposed on industry in the past, to protect American corporations from foreign competition by means of tariffs and import quotas, and to curtail the power of trade unions. Reaganism, the political face of Taylorism under pressure, amounts to an attempt to counter foreign competition without giving up the technology of mass production.

## Technology and the ideology of total control

Piore and Sabel sometimes write as if the demands of flexible, specialized production would in themselves generate a revival of the community life required to sustain it. To show the dependence of flexible production on a reinvigorated civic life is the considerable achievement of their book. But a revival of civic life surely has to be seen as a precondition, not as a consequence of new technologies. The accumulating evidence that mass production economies no longer work very efficiently adds another argument to the already impressive indictment of their dehumanizing effects. The inefficiency of mass production does not in itself guarantee its replacement by a better productive system, however. That depends on a redistribution of power and wealth, on the formation of political movements designed to achieve this, and on a profound change in our values.

Capitalism is more than a system of production for profit, it is also a worldview, an ideology. From the beginning, the technology of mass production was closely bound up with the fantasy that man can free himself from limitations imposed by nature and achieve godlike powers over nature through his own inventions. The dream antedates capitalism, but the productive capacities released by capitalism, together with the scientific revolution, the discovery of the New World, and the

Cartesian revolution in philosophy gave it a plausibility, in the modern world, that it had never had before. 'In the place of the speculative philosophy taught in the schools we can have a practical philosophy,' said Descartes, 'by means of which [we can render] ourselves the masters and possessors of nature' (Spragens 1981, p. 56). A Faustian revolt against human limitations, in particular against the human body, held out the hope that intelligence, once it freed itself from the prison of the body – the seat of human limitations – can grasp timeless truths and, through technology, conquer scarcity, sickness, and perhaps some day even death itself. 'The day will come,' wrote Condorcet in the eighteenth century, 'when death will be due only to extraordinary accidents or to the decay of the vital forces, and . . . ultimately the average span between birth and decay will have no assignable value' (Spragens 1981).

Much more than the profit motive, it is this ideology of total control that drives and perpetuates our technology. The determination to eliminate the 'human factor of production' is the heart and soul of modern technology, not an incidental by-product of Taylorism that can be discarded now that it has become necessary, we are told, to produce goods for diversified markets. Theoretically, it is possible to design machines that can be used by skilled craftsmen in a variety of ways. Theoretically, it is possible to design a technological system that embodies both a respect for human capacities and an acknowledgment of human limitations. It is theoretically possible to design a technological system, in other words, that satisfies the desire for moral wisdom instead of the desire for domination. But such a system would be completely incompatible with the delusion that underlies the present system, the delusion that we can make ourselves lords of the universe. It would consist of machines designed to enhance and develop human capabilities and to satisfy the instinct of workmanship, as Veblen called it, not to relieve mankind of the need for imagination and ingenuity by assigning these qualities to a small class of technicians. The vision behind our technology assumes that most people find little pleasure in hard work or in strenuous activity of any kind, and it proposes to free them from toil for a life of leisure. It assumes, moreover, that most people are incapable of sustained mental effort in any case, and that even the best minds, indeed, can never altogether free their thoughts from the corrupting influence of emotion and subjective 'values.'

Here is the most important reason that engineers find it so difficult to entrust their machines to the care of mere human beings. It is not simply the defense of their class privileges that makes them resist demands for worker participation, but the belief that human intervention can only distort and subjectify the beautiful objectivity of the machine. Now that scientists and engineers have devised machines that can allegedly think for themselves, contamination becomes a greater menace than ever before, since the condition of this so-called thinking is precisely that it operate at a level of abstraction where feelings play no part. The promise of the computer age, as it appears to its prophets and propagandists, is the hope that thought can divorce itself from emotion – the most intractable of the human limitations from which technology aspires to deliver us. The utopia of artificial intelligence – the final destination of our civilization, we are told, the earthly paradise that lies beyond even the fully automated factory – rests on the premise that thought can dispense with the thinking self. It can thus overcome the emotional and bodily limitations that have encumbered humanity in the past. Theorists of artificial intelligence celebrate the mind's clarity, as opposed to what one of them, Marvin Minsky, revealingly refers to as the 'bloody mess of organic matter' (Turkle 1984, p. 255).

It is often said that modern science implies an assault on human pride, for example by showing that the earth is not the center of the universe, or again by teaching that men are descended from apes. David Bolter restates this cliché when he argues that the computer fosters an awareness of our 'temporal limitations' (1984, p. 122). It is more accurate to say that the culture of modern science deplores human limitations but refuses to acknowledge that they are inherent in the human condition, insisting instead that the unaided human intellect can rise above these limitations. The scientific worldview hates the body not merely because it decays but because it is held to be the source of desire. On this view of things, it is because human beings are driven by bodily needs and desires that their understanding is so limited. Only by escaping from these appetites or by overcoming their effects on the consciousness can humans arrive at understanding. The modern faith in disembodied intelligence reaches its climax in the fascination with machines that think with perfect clarity because they have no feelings to get in the way. Here again, what looks at first like a rather disparaging view of humanity barely conceals the grandiose, narcissistic fantasy of annihilating human limitations through the use of machines – the controlling fantasy of modern times, carried here to its logical conclusion. Listen to the feverish speculations of Edward Fredkin of MIT, who once referred to artificial intelligence as the 'next step in evolution.'

> Basically, the human mind is not most like a god or most like a computer. It's most like the mind of a chimpanzee and most of what's there isn't designed for living in high society [he means advanced industrial society] but for getting along in the jungle or out in the fields. . . . The mere idea that we have to be the best in the universe is kind of far-fetched. . . . The fact is, I think we'll be enormously happier once our niche has limits to it. We won't have to worry about carrying the burden of the universe on our shoulders as we do today. We can enjoy life as human beings without worrying about it.
>
> (Turkle 1984, pp. 262–3)

The social vision implied by this kind of thinking is as regressive as the escapist psychology behind it. The psychology is the fantasy of total control, absolute transcendence of the limits imposed on mankind by its lowly origins. As for the social vision, it carries one step further the logic of industrialism, in which the centralization of decision making in an educated elite frees the rest of us from the burden of political participation.

Technology is a mirror of society, not a 'neutral' force that can 'be used for good or evil.' It shows us ourselves as we are and as we would like to be, and what it reveals, in the case of the so-called second Industrial Revolution, is an unflattering image of the American at his most incorrigibly escapist, hoping to lose himself – in every sense of the term – in the cool precision of machines that know everything except everything pertaining to that 'bloody mess of organic matter.'

## References

Bolter, J. David (1984) *Turing's Man: Western Culture in the Computer Age*. Chapel Hill: University of North Carolina Press.

Chamberlain, Neil (1948) *The Union Challenge and Management Control*. New York: Harper.

Drucker, Peter (1967) 'Technology and Society in the Twentieth Century,' in Melvin Kranzberg and Carroll W. Pursell, Jr. (eds) *Technology in Western Civilization*, vol. 2. New York: Oxford University Press.

Kuttner, Robert (1985) 'The Shape of Things to Come,' *The New Republic* 192: 29–32.

Leaver, E. W. and Brown, J. J. (1946) 'Machines Without Men,' *Fortune* 34: 165 ff.

Noble, David F. (1984) *Forces of Production: A Social History of Industrial Automation*. New York: Alfred A. Knopf.

Piore, Michael J. and Sabel, Charles F. (1984) *The Second Industrial Divide*. New York: Basic Books.

Sabel, Charles F. (1982) *Work and Politics: The Division of Labor and Industry*. New York: Cambridge University Press.

Spragens, Thomas A. (1981) *The Irony of Liberal Reason*. Chicago: University of Chicago Press.

Taylor, Frederick Winslow (1911) *The Principles of Scientific Management*. New York: Harper and Brothers.

Turkle, Sherry (1984) *The Second Self: Computers and the Human Spirit*. New York: Simon and Schuster.

# PART SIX

# Surveillance

## INTRODUCTION

■ Raimo Blom

IN RECENT HISTORY there have been periodic protests about the growth of surveillance and fears about the consequent loss of liberties this entails. George Orwell's *Nineteen Eighty-four*, published in 1949, is the archetypical expression of this apprehension, a dystopia which has come to symbolize concern about surveillance developed by the nation state in the hands of 'big brother'. Ever since then – and in truth even before – there have been civil libertarians especially who have campaigned against threats of increased surveillance (e.g. Campbell and Connor 1986; Hillyard and Percy-Smith 1988; Davies 1996). The spread of computer and communications technologies especially, and heightened sensitivity towards their apparently infinite potential for surveillance, has ensured that periodically there appears extensive documentation and attendant protests about the increased exposure of citizens to surveillance agencies. For example, in recent months there has been considerable publicity and unease concerning the Echelon software system which has been designed to co-ordinate and integrate fifty or so intelligence centres worldwide. Its 'host environment' is the United States' National Security Agency (NSA) which has the ability to store five *trillion* pages of text, a breath-taking capacity to amass files on people (Bamford 2001, pp. 404, 427). There is also anxiety expressed about the insistence of government that e-mail records be retained by server companies for at least twelve months – so that usage may be tracked as a weapon in the 'war against terrorism'.

Related, if less dramatic, is the harvesting of what has been called 'transactional information' (Burnham 1983) which is generated every time one sends an e-mail, or makes a credit card purchase or direct debit exchange. When combined and arranged such data provides a detailed and intimate portrait of individuals' habits and actions (Gandy 1993). Though much of the concern about this increased surveillance focuses upon police (Marx 1988) and military applications (spy satellites, telecommunications intercept technologies and the like), there is also anxiety expressed about the rapid development of closed circuit television cameras in towns and cities (Norris and Armstrong 1999), and in credit checking agencies which appear able to report on most adults in the population (Davies 1996), as well as the potential for abuse of computerized health or welfare records. In view of this it is perhaps not surprising that there has now emerged a sub-discipline of 'surveillance studies' (Lyon 2001; *Surveillance and Society* 2002).

Since the most common reaction to the spread of surveillance is disapproval, it might appear odd to observe that many social scientists have come to be persuaded that surveillance is an inescapable feature of modernity itself, something which is inescapable and which, indeed, may be responsible for ensuring individual freedoms. The argument here suggests that, to be treated as a unique individual, then one must be subject to surveillance in order to ascertain one's particular needs and dispositions. For example, universal suffrage requires that the name, sex, age and residence of each citizen is recorded so that his or her right to vote can be exercised. Of course, the consequence of forming an electoral register is that the entire adult population can be readily identified and located (and there is considerable disquiet about how the electoral register may be used – a moment's thought will suggest ways in which it can be analysed to reveal, for instance, family relationships), but its compilation and public availability is surely a requisite of a full democracy in which each person may have a vote and where everyone can be approached by competing political parties. Again, if organizations are to be able to deliver the extraordinarily diverse range of consumer products and services now available, then it follows that there must be high levels of surveillance to ensure that demand is met in a timely manner. Retailers need to know which goods are being sold, at what rate, in which places, to be confident that they can match supply and demand. Electronic tills facilitate this stock control, but on-line ordering and use of loyalty cards enable the store to identify individual patterns of purchase very precisely, arguably then letting the retailer be still more effective in meeting customers' needs. Thinking along lines such as this, one might begin to question the easy logic of those who argue that surveillance necessarily intrudes and thereby diminishes one's individuality (Giddens 1990). For instance, using a telephone means that every call is registered so that the company may connect callers, appropriately charge customers, and ensure the system works smoothly. This does mean that every call is monitored, which might be viewed as intrusive (imagine how revealing one's itemized phone record is), yet access to the telephone system simultaneously provides enormous benefits, such as ready connection to family and friends wherever they may be, all of which can increase one's choices and sense of autonomy. The same, only more so, goes for the internet (Ball and Webster 2003).

Michel Foucault (1926–84) (Chapter 20) is a key figure in studies of surveillance, though his influence on contemporary thought is much wider. This comes especially through his insistence that *knowledge* and *power* are always conjoined; that there is never 'innocent' knowledge, since it is always an expression of power relationships. For instance, knowledge about the body and diet has empowered experts such as dieticians, their knowledge giving such people power over others when it comes to advice as regards 'healthy eating' (consider in this context the slimming business). Foucault's general concern to connect power and knowledge by examining 'discourses' of modernity such as medicine, madness and sexuality also found an application in his influential book, *Discipline and Punish: The Birth of the Prison* (1979 [1975]). Here Foucault traced a shift from *punishment* to *discipline*, from responses to crime in terms of *spectacle* (the public execution, placing in the stocks, etc.) to *rehabilitation*, a transition which signalled a move towards calculation, precision and due weighting of crime. The move towards such discipline required new and detailed knowledge about crime and criminals (the circumstances of the crime, the condition and disposition of the criminal, the record in and outside prison), which brought new forms of recording and new forms of expertise.

Crucial to the exercise of this changed disciplinary regime of prison was continuous surveillance, and key to this was the new spatial and social organization of power. Foucault's major example for this is Jeremy Bentham's Panopticon, an architectural design for prisons which allowed many to be watched by a few who could not themselves be seen. In the Panopticon the surveyed do not know whether they are actually being surveyed at any one time, but they live with the knowledge that they can be subject to continuous observation. For Foucault the Panopticon was the architecture of power used in a wide variety of organizations, a new form of power aimed at normalizing the behaviour of individuals and harmonizing the wider society. Our extract from Foucault, though brief, clarifies an approach which has been enormously influential on recent thinking about surveillance. Some approaches have even argued that the wave of new information and communications technologies are allowing the development of an 'electronic panopticon' (Webster and Robins 1986, pt. 3) where people are monitored by unseen forces – often automated – more systematically than ever before.

It should be said that the themes of surveillance and control are not new in social sciences. Karl Marx (1818–83) drew attention to features of capitalist control of workers in the nineteenth century. From a very different position, Frederick Taylor (1947) advocated 'scientific management', at the core of which was intense monitoring of workers as the responsibility of managements. Later Harry Braverman (1974) gave a radical spin to Taylor, to suggest that tighter control – and an associated deskilling of work – was integral to the capitalist labour process. It appears that Braverman's prognosis has not come to be, since workers frequently have more autonomy now. However, though direct supervision by superiors may have declined, this may be because new technologies heighten the possibilities of monitoring workers. There is not so much need for personal supervision since it can be replaced by very detailed monitoring of working life and the regular reporting of it. Today's worker may be autonomous, but his or her every action is often followed by electronic technologies.

Anthony Giddens (1985, 1991) acknowledges the significance of heightened surveillance in the modern world, but he resists the temptation to interpret this as altogether negative. On the contrary, Giddens' influential theory of 'reflexive modernization' regards reflexivity as a defining characteristic of human action. This refers to the process of continuous examination of social practices and their reformation on the basis of this reflection. In certain circumstances reflexivity may be highly intensive, but it is never less than routine and constitutive of social actions. Thus 'reflexive monitoring of action' is always involved in human life and, indeed, is something which distinguishes humans from other animals. But it is modernity which makes surveillance the basic condition for both social control and gaining and using liberties. Consequently, surveillance is not only a threat, since it is also essential to the development of reflexivity.

**Shoshana Zuboff**'s book, *In the Age of the Smart Machine*, has been an influential analysis of work and power which is consonant with a good deal of Giddens' thinking. She demonstrates the power of technology to reorder the organizational life and the rules of the game at work. The necessities of learning and performance associated with new technology requires new kinds of social relationships and new divisions of power in work organizations. Information developments make work more abstract, being less 'hands on' than before, with the stress increasingly on software, systems and the manipulation of symbols. Zuboff (Chapter 21) calls the emerging new structures 'informated organizations' which contrast with the traditional and somewhat deterministic concept of automation. Informated organizations also require new ways of management. The focus is more on 'high commitment' approaches to handling the workforce, the emphasis being on teams, participation, empowerment and decentralization.

**David Lyon** (Chapter 22) has emerged as a leading figure in contemporary 'surveillance studies'. In this extract he offers a multifaceted picture of different perspectives on surveillance in modern societies. If the Panopticon is a central metaphor of the surveillance society, then theories of simulation and virtual organization (Baudrillard, Poster) exceed the model. This then leads to ideas of the *superpanopticon* and *hypersurveillance* where computerization and digitalization magnify surveillance functions and makes possible their extension to earlier unknown spheres of monitoring and control. Lyons' message is that we must balance our analysis of the surveillance society, taking into account classical sociological concerns for material conditions of life, action and opportunities for political engagement.

## REFERENCES

Ball, K. and Webster, F. (2003) (eds) *The Intensification of Surveillance: Crime, Terrorism and Warfare in the Information Age*. London: Pluto.

Bamford, J. (2001) *Body of Secrets: Anatomy of the Ultra-Secret National Security Agency*. New York: Doubleday.

Braverman, Harry (1974) *Labor and Monopoly Capital: The Degradation of Work in Twentieth Century*. New York: Monthly Press.

Burnham, David (1983) *The Rise of the Computer State*. London: Weidenfeld and Nicholson.

Campbell, D. and Connor, S. (1986) *On the Record: Surveillance, Computers and Privacy*. London: Michael Joseph.

Davies, S. (1996) *Big Brother: Britain's Web of Surveillance and the New Technological Order*. London: Pan.

Foucault, Michel (1979 [1975]) *Discipline and Punish: the Birth of the Prison*, trans. Alan Sheridan. Harmondsworth: Penguin.

Gandy, Oscar H. Jr (1993) *The Panoptic Sort: A Political Economy of Personal Information*. Boulder, CO: Westview Press.

Giddens, Anthony (1985) *The Nation State and Violence: Volume Two of a Contemporary Critique of Historical Materialism*. Cambridge: Polity Press.

Giddens, Anthony (1990) *The Consequences of Modernity*. Cambridge: Polity Press.

Giddens, Anthony (1991) *Modernity and Self-identity: Self and Society in the Late Modern Age*. Cambridge: Polity Press.

Hillyard, P. and Percy-Smith, J. (1988) *The Coercive State: The Decline of Democracy in Britain*. London: Fontana.

Lyon, David (2001) *Surveillance Society: Monitoring Everyday Life*. Buckingham: Open University Press.

Marx, Gary T. (1988) *Undercover: Police Surveillance in America*. Berkeley: University of California Press.

Norris, C. and Armstrong, G. (1999) *The Maximum Surveillance Society: The Rise of CCTV*. Oxford: Berg.

Orwell, George (1949) *Nineteen Eighty-four*. London: Secker & Warburg.

*Surveillance and Society* (2002) available on-line at http://www.surveillance-and-society. org/journalvlil.htm. First issue 2002.

Taylor, Frederick W. (1947) *Scientific Management*. London: Harper and Row.

Webster, F. and Robins, K. (1986) *Information Technology: A Luddite Analysis*. Norwood, NJ: Ablex.

# Chapter 20

# Michel Foucault

## PANOPTICISM

From *Discipline and Punish: The Birth of the Prison*, London: Vintage Books Edition (1979), pp. 200–3, 207–9, 216–17, 298–306.

[. . .]

**B**ENTHAM'S *PANOPTICON* **IS** the architectural figure of this compo-sition. We know the principle on which it was based: at the periphery, an annular building; at the centre, a tower; this tower is pierced with wide windows that open onto the inner side of the ring; the peripheric building is divided into cells, each of which extends the whole width of the building; they have two windows, one on the inside, corresponding to the windows of the tower; the other, on the outside, allows the light to cross the cell from one end to the other. All that is needed, then, is to place a supervisor in a central tower and to shut up in each cell a madman, a patient, a condemned man, a worker or a schoolboy. By the effect of backlighting, one can observe from the tower, standing out precisely against the light, the small captive shadows in the cells of the periphery. They are like so many cages, so many small theatres, in which each actor is alone, perfectly individualized and constantly visible. The panoptic mechanism arranges spatial unities that make it possible to see constantly and to recognize immediately. In short, it reverses the principle of the dungeon; or rather of its three functions – to enclose, to deprive of light and to hide – it preserves only the first and eliminates the other two. Full lighting and the eye of a supervisor capture better than darkness, which ultimately protected. Visibility is a trap.

To begin with, this made it possible – as a negative effect – to avoid those compact, swarming, howling masses that were to be found in places of confine-ment, those painted by Goya or described by Howard. Each individual, in his place, is securely confined to a cell from which he is seen from the front by the supervisor; but the side walls prevent him from coming into contact with his companions. He is seen, but he does not see; he is the object of information, never a subject in communication. The arrangement of his room, opposite the central tower, imposes on him an axial visibility; but the divisions of the ring, those separated cells, imply a lateral invisibility. And this invisibility is a guarantee of order. If the inmates are convicts, there is no danger of a plot, an attempt at collective escape, the planning of new crimes for the future, bad reciprocal influences; if they are patients, there is no danger of contagion; if they are madmen there is no risk of their committing violence upon one another; if they are schoolchildren, there is no copying, no noise, no chatter, no waste of time; if they are workers, there are no disorders, no theft, no coalitions, none of those distractions that slow down the rate of work, make it less perfect or cause accidents. The crowd, a compact mass, a locus of multiple exchanges, individualities merging together, a collective effect, is abolished and replaced by a collection of separated individualities. From the point of view of the guardian, it is replaced by a multiplicity that can be numbered and supervised; from the point of view of the inmates, by a sequestered and observed solitude (Bentham, 60–64).

Hence the major effect of the Panopticon: to induce in the inmate a state of conscious and permanent visibility that assures the automatic functioning of power. So to arrange things that the surveillance is permanent in its effects, even if it is discontinuous in its action; that the perfection of power should tend to render its actual exercise unnecessary; that this architectural apparatus should be a machine for creating and sustaining a power relation independent of the person who exercises it; in short, that the inmates should be caught up in a power situation of which they are themselves the bearers. To achieve this, it is at once too much and too little that the prisoner should be constantly observed by an inspector: too little, for what matters is that he knows himself to be observed; too much, because he has no need in fact of being so. In view of this, Bentham laid down the principle that power should be visible and unverifiable. Visible: the inmate will constantly have before his eyes the tall outline of the central tower from which he is spied upon. Unverifiable: the inmate must never know whether he is being looked at at any one moment; but he must be sure that he may always be so. In order to make the presence or absence of the inspector unverifiable, so that the prisoners, in their cells, cannot even see a shadow, Bentham envisaged not only venetian blinds on the windows of the central observation hall, but, on the inside, partitions that intersected the hall at right angles and, in order to pass from one quarter to the other, not doors but zig-zag openings; for the slightest noise, a gleam of light, a brightness in a half-opened door would betray the presence of the guardian. The Panopticon is a machine for dissociating the see/being seen dyad: in the peripheric ring, one is totally seen, without ever seeing; in the central tower, one sees everything without ever being seen.

It is an important mechanism, for it automatizes and disindividualizes power. Power has its principle not so much in a person as in a certain concerted distribution of bodies, surfaces, lights, gazes; in an arrangement whose internal mechanisms produce the relation in which individuals are caught up. The ceremonies, the rituals, the marks by which the sovereign's surplus power was manifested are useless. There is a machinery that assures dissymmetry, disequilibrium, difference. Consequently, it does not matter who exercises power. Any individual, taken almost at random, can operate the machine: in the absence of the director, his family, his friends, his visitors, even his servants. Similarly, it does not matter what motive animates him: the curiosity of the indiscreet, the malice of a child, the thirst for knowledge of a philosopher who wishes to visit this museum of human nature, or the perversity of those who take pleasure in spying and punishing. The more numerous those anonymous and temporary observers are, the greater the risk for the inmate of being surprised and the greater his anxious awareness of being observed. The Panopticon is a marvellous machine which, whatever use one may wish to put it to, produces homogeneous effects of power.

A real subjection is born mechanically from a fictitious relation. So it is not necessary to use force to constrain the convict to good behaviour, the madman to calm, the worker to work, the schoolboy to application, the patient to the observation of the regulations. Bentham was surprised that panoptic institutions could be so light: there were no more bars, no more chains, no more heavy locks; all that was needed was that the separations should be clear and the openings well arranged. The heaviness of the old 'houses of security', with their fortress-like architecture, could be replaced by the simple, economic geometry of a 'house of certainty'. The efficiency of power, its constraining force have, in a sense, passed over to the other side – to the side of its surface of application. He who is subjected to a field of visibility, and who knows it, assumes responsibility for the constraints of power; he makes them play spontaneously upon himself; he inscribes in himself the power relation in which he simultaneously plays both roles; he becomes the principle of his own subjection. By this very fact, the external power may throw off its physical weight; it tends to the non-corporal; and, the more it approaches this limit, the more constant, profound and permanent are its effects: it is a perpetual victory that avoids any physical confrontation and which is always decided in advance.

[. . .]

[. . .] Bentham's Preface to *Panopticon* opens with a list of the benefits to be obtained from his 'inspection-house': '*Morals reformed – health preserved – industry invigorated – instruction diffused – public burthens lightened –* Economy seated, as it were, upon a rock – the gordian knot of the Poor-Laws not cut, but untied – all by a simple idea in architecture!'

Furthermore, the arrangement of this machine is such that its enclosed nature does not preclude a permanent presence from the outside: we have seen that anyone may come and exercise in the central tower the functions of surveillance, and that, this being the case, he can gain a clear idea of the way in which the surveillance is practised. In fact, any panoptic institution, even if it is as rigorously closed as a penitentiary, may without difficulty be subjected to such irregular and constant inspections: and not only by the appointed inspectors, but also by the public; any member of society will have the right to come and see with his own eyes how the schools, hospitals, factories, prisons function. There is no risk, therefore, that the increase of power created by the panoptic machine may degenerate into tyranny; the disciplinary mechanism will be democratically controlled, since it will be constantly accessible 'to the great tribunal committee of the world'. This Panopticon, subtly arranged so that an observer may observe, at a glance, so many different individuals, also enables everyone to come and observe any of the observers. The seeing machine was once a sort of dark room into which individuals spied; it has become a transparent building in which the exercise of power may be supervised by society as a whole.

The panoptic schema, without disappearing as such or losing any of its properties, was destined to spread throughout the social body; its vocation was to become a generalized function. The plague-stricken town provided an exceptional disciplinary model: perfect but absolutely violent; to the disease that brought death, power opposed its perpetual threat of death; life inside it was reduced to its simplest expression; it was, against the power of death, the meticulous exercise of the right of the sword. The Panopticon, on the other hand, has a role of amplification; although it arranges power, although it is intended to make it more economic and more effective, it does so not for power itself, nor for the immediate salvation of a threatened society: its aim is to strengthen the social forces – to increase production, to develop the economy, spread education, raise the level of public morality; to increase and multiply.

How is power to be strengthened in such a way that, far from impeding progress, far from weighing upon it with its rules and regulations, it actually facilitates such progress? What intensificator of power will be able at the same time to be a multiplicator of production? How will power, by increasing its forces, be able to increase those of society instead of confiscating them or impeding them? The Panopticon's solution to this problem is that the productive increase of power can be assured only if, on the one hand, it can be exercised continuously in the very foundations of society, in the subtlest possible way, and if, on the other hand, it functions outside these sudden, violent, discontinuous forms that are bound up with the exercise of sovereignty. The body of the king, with its strange material and physical presence, with the force that he himself deploys or transmits to some few others, is at the opposite extreme of this new physics of power represented by panopticism; the domain of panopticism is, on the contrary, that whole lower region, that region of irregular bodies, with their details, their multiple movements, their heterogeneous forces, their spatial relations; what are required are mechanisms that analyse distributions, gaps, series, combinations, and which use instruments that render visible, record, differentiate and compare: a physics of a relational and multiple power, which has its maximum intensity not in the person of the king, but in the bodies that can be individualized by these relations. At the theoretical level, Bentham defines another way of analysing the social body and the power relations that traverse it; in terms of practice, he defines a procedure of subordination of bodies and forces that must increase the utility of power while practising the economy of the prince. Panopticism is the general principle of a new 'political anatomy' whose object and end are not the relations of sovereignty but the relations of discipline.

The celebrated, transparent, circular cage, with its high tower, powerful and knowing, may have been for Bentham a project of perfect disciplinary institution; but he also set out to show how one may 'unlock' the disciplines and get them to function in a diffused, multiple, polyvalent way throughout the whole social body. These disciplines, which the classical age had elaborated in specific, relatively enclosed places – barracks, schools, workshops – and whose total implementation had been imagined only at the limited and temporary scale of a plague-stricken town, Bentham dreamt of transforming into a network of mechanisms that would be everywhere and always alert, running through society without interruption in space or in time. The panoptic arrangement provides the formula for this generalization. It programmes, at the level of an elementary and easily transferable mechanism, the basic functioning of a society penetrated through and through with disciplinary mechanisms.

[. . .]

On the whole, therefore, one can speak of the formation of a disciplinary society in this movement that stretches from the enclosed disciplines, a sort of social 'quarantine', to an indefinitely generalizable mechanism of 'panopticism'. Not because the disciplinary modality of power has replaced all the others; but because it has infiltrated the others, sometimes undermining them, but serving as an intermediary between them, linking them together, extending them and above all making it possible to bring the effects of power to the most minute and distant elements. It assures an infinitesimal distribution of the power relations.

A few years after Bentham, Julius gave this society its birth certificate. Speaking of the panoptic principle, he said that there was much more there than architectural ingenuity: it was an event in the 'history of the human mind'. In appearance, it is merely the solution of a technical problem; but, through it, a whole type of society emerges. Antiquity had been a civilization of spectacle. 'To render accessible to a multitude of men the inspection of a small number of objects': this was the problem to which the architecture of temples, theatres and circuses responded. With spectacle, there was a predominance of public life, the intensity of festivals, sensual proximity. In these rituals in which blood flowed, society found new vigour and formed for a moment a single great body. The modern age poses the opposite problem: 'To procure for a small number, or even for a single individual, the instantaneous view of a great multitude.' In a society in which the principal elements are no longer the community and public life, but, on the one hand, private individuals and, on the other, the state, relations can be regulated only in a form that is the exact reverse of the spectacle: 'It was to the modern age, to the ever-growing influence of the state, to its ever more profound intervention in all the details and all the relations of social life, that was reserved the task of increasing and perfecting its guarantees, by using and directing towards that great aim the building and distribution of buildings intended to observe a great multitude of men at the same time.'

Julius saw as a fulfilled historical process that which Bentham had described as a technical programme. Our society is one not of spectacle, but of surveillance; under the surface of images, one invests bodies in depth; behind the great abstraction of exchange, there continues the meticulous, concrete training of useful forces; the circuits of communication are the supports of an accumulation and a centralization of knowledge; the play of signs defines the anchorages of power; it is not that the beautiful totality of the individual is amputated, repressed, altered by our social order, it is rather that the individual is carefully fabricated in it, according to a whole technique of forces and bodies. We are much less Greeks than we believe. We are neither in the amphitheatre, nor on the stage, but in the panoptic machine, invested by its effects of power, which we bring to ourselves since we are part of its mechanism. [. . .]

[. . .]

We have seen that, in penal justice, the prison transformed the punitive procedure into a penitentiary technique; the carceral archipelago transported this technique from the penal institution to the entire social body. With several important results.

1.   This vast mechanism established a slow, continuous, imperceptible gradation that made it possible to pass naturally from disorder to offence and back from a transgression of the law to a slight departure from a rule, an average, a demand, a norm. In the classical period, despite a certain common reference to offence in general, the order of the crime, the order of sin and the order of bad conduct remained separate in so far as they related to separate criteria and authorities (court, penitence, confinement). Incarceration with its mechanisms of surveillance and punishment functioned, on the contrary, according to a principle of relative continuity. The continuity of the institutions themselves, which were linked to one another (public assistance with the orphanage, the reformitory, the penitentiary, the disciplinary battalion, the prison; the school with the charitable society, the workshop, the almshouse, the penitentiary convent; the workers' estate with the hospital and the prison). A continuity of the punitive criteria and mechanisms, which on the basis of a mere deviation gradually strengthened the rules and increased the punishment. A continuous gradation of the established, specialized and competent authorities (in the order of knowledge and in the order of power) which, without resort to arbitrariness, but strictly according to the regulations, by means of observation and assessment hierarchized, differentiated, judged, punished and moved gradually from the correction of irregularities to the punishment of crime. The 'carceral' with its many diffuse or compact forms, its institutions of supervision or constraint, of discreet surveillance and insistent coercion, assured the communication of punishments according to quality and quantity; it connected in series or disposed according to subtle divisions the minor and the serious penalties, the mild and the strict forms of treatment, bad marks and light sentences. You will end up in the convict-ship, the slightest indiscipline seems to say; and the harshest of prisons says to the prisoners condemned to life: I shall note the slightest irregularity in your conduct. The generality of the punitive function that the eighteenth century sought in the 'ideological' technique of representations and signs now had as its support the extension, the material framework, complex, dispersed, but coherent, of the various carceral mechanisms. As a result, a certain significant generality moved between the least irregularity and the greatest crime; it was no longer the offence, the attack on the common interest, it was the departure from the norm, the anomaly; it was this that haunted the school, the court, the asylum or the prison. It generalized in the sphere of meaning the function that the carceral generalized in the sphere of tactics. Replacing the adversary of the sovereign, the social enemy was transformed into a deviant, who brought with him the multiple danger of disorder, crime and madness. The carceral network linked, through innumerable relations, the two long, multiple series of the punitive and the abnormal.

2.   The carceral, with its far-reaching networks, allows the recruitment of major 'delinquents'. It organizes what might be called 'disciplinary careers' in which, through various exclusions and rejections, a whole process is set in motion. In the classical period, there opened up in the confines or interstices of society the confused, tolerant and dangerous domain of the 'outlaw' or at least of that which eluded the direct hold of power: an uncertain space that was for criminality a training ground and a region of refuge; there poverty, unemployment, pursued innocence, cunning, the struggle against the powerful, the refusal of obligations and laws, and organized crime all came together as chance and fortune would dictate; it was the domain of adventure that Gil Blas, Sheppard or Mandrin, each in his own way, inhabited. Through the play of disciplinary differentiations and divisions, the nineteenth century constructed rigorous channels which, within the system, inculcated docility and produced delinquency by the same mechanisms. There was a sort of disciplinary 'training', continuous and compelling, that had something of the pedagogical curriculum and something of the professional network. Careers emerged from it, as secure, as predictable, as those of public life: assistance associations, residential apprenticeships, penal colonies, disciplinary battalions, prisons, hospitals, almshouses. These networks were already well mapped out at the beginning of the nineteenth century: 'Our benevolent establishments present an admirably coordinated whole by means of which the indigent does not remain a moment without help from the cradle to the grave. Follow the course of the unfortunate man: you will see him born among foundlings; from there he passes to the nursery, then to an orphanage; at the age of six he goes off to primary school and later to adult schools. If he cannot work, he is placed on the list of the charity offices of his district, and if he falls ill he may choose between twelve hospitals. . . . Lastly, when the poor Parisian reaches the end of his career, seven almshouses await his age and often their salubrious régime has prolonged his useless days well beyond those of the rich man' (Moreau de Jonnés, quoted in Touquet).

The carceral network does not cast the unassimilable into a confused hell; there is no outside. It takes back with one hand what it seems to exclude with the other. It saves everything, including what it punishes. It is unwilling to waste even what it has decided to disqualify. In this panoptic society of which incarceration is the omnipresent armature, the delinquent is not outside the law; he is, from the very outset, in the law, at the very heart of the law, or at least in the midst of those mechanisms that transfer the individual imperceptibly from discipline to the law, from deviation to offence. Although it is true that prison punishes delinquency, delinquency is for the most part produced in and by an incarceration which, ultimately, prison perpetuates in its turn. The prison is merely the natural consequence, no more than a higher degree, of that hierarchy laid down step by step. The delinquent is all institutional product. It is no use being surprised, therefore, that in a considerable proportion of cases the biography of convicts passes through all these mechanisms and establishments, whose purpose, it is widely believed, is to lead away from prison. That one should find in them what one might call the index of an irrepressibly delinquent 'character': the prisoner condemned to hard labour was meticulously produced by a childhood spent in a reformatory, according to the lines of force of the generalized carceral system. Conversely, the lyricism of marginality may hold inspiration in the image of the 'outlaw', the great social nomad, who prowls on the confines of a docile, frightened order. But it is not on the fringes of society and through successive exiles that criminality is born, but by means of ever more closely placed insertions, under ever more insistent surveillance, by an accumulation of disciplinary coercion. In short, the carceral archipelago assures, in the depths of the social body, the formation of delinquency on the basis of subtle illegalities, the overlapping of the latter by the former and the establishment of a specified criminality.

3.   But perhaps the most important effect of the carceral system and of its extension well beyond legal imprisonment is that it succeeds in making the power to punish natural and legitimate, in lowering at least the threshold of tolerance to penality. It tends to efface what may be exorbitant in the exercise of punishment. It does this by playing the two registers in which it is deployed – the legal register of justice and the extra-legal register of discipline – against one another. In effect, the great continuity of the carceral system throughout the law and its sentences gives a sort of legal sanction to the disciplinary mechanisms, to the decisions and judgements that they enforce. Throughout this network, which comprises so many 'regional' institutions, relatively autonomous and independent, is transmitted, with the 'prison-form', the model of justice itself. The regulations of the disciplinary establishments may reproduce the law, the punishments imitate the verdicts and penalties, the surveillance repeat the police model; and, above all these multiple establishments, the prison, which in relation to them is a pure form, unadulterated and unmitigated, gives them a sort of official sanction. The carceral, with its long gradation stretching from the convict-ship or imprisonment with hard labour to diffuse, slight limitations, communicates a type of power that the law validates and that justice uses as its favourite weapon. How could the disciplines and the power that functions in them appear arbitrary, when they merely operate the mechanisms of justice itself, even with a view to mitigating their intensity? When, by generalizing its effects and transmitting it to very level, it makes it possible to avoid its full rigour? Carceral continuity and the fusion of the prison-form make it possible to legalize, or in any case to legitimate disciplinary power, which thus avoids any element of excess or abuse it may entail.
   But, conversely, the carceral pyramid gives to the power to inflict legal punishment a context in which it appears to be free of all excess and all violence. In the subtle gradation of the apparatuses of discipline and of the successive 'embeddings' that they involve, the prison does not at all represent the unleashing of a different kind of power, but simply an additional degree in the intensity of a mechanism that has continued to operate since the earliest forms of legal punishment. Between the latest institution of 'rehabilitation', where one is taken in order to avoid prison, and the prison where one is sent after a definable offence, the difference is (and must be) scarcely perceptible. There is a strict economy that has the effect of rendering as discreet as possible the singular power to punish. There is nothing in it now that recalls the former excess of sovereign power when it revenged its authority on the tortured body of those about to be executed. Prison continues, on those who are entrusted to it, a work begun elsewhere, which the whole of society pursues on each individual through innumerable mechanisms of discipline. By means of a carceral continuum, the authority that sentences infiltrates all those other

authorities that supervise, transform, collect, improve. It might even be said that nothing really distinguishes them any more except the singularly 'dangerous' character of the delinquents, the gravity of their departures from normal behaviour and the necessary solemnity of the ritual. But, in its function, the power to punish is not essentially different from that of curing or educating. It receives from them, and from their lesser, smaller task, a sanction from below; but one that is no less important for that, since it is the sanction of technique and rationality. The carceral 'naturalizes' the legal power to punish, as it 'legalizes' the technical power to discipline. In thus homogenizing them, effacing what may be violent in one and arbitrary in the other, attenuating the effects of revolt that they may both arouse, thus depriving excess in either of any purpose, circulating the same calculated, mechanical and discreet methods from one to the other, the carceral makes it possible to carry out that great 'economy' of power whose formula the eighteenth century had sought, when the problem of the accumulation and useful administration of men first emerged.

By operating at every level of the social body and by mingling ceaselessly the art of rectifying and the right to punish, the universality of the carceral lowers the level from which it becomes natural and acceptable to be punished. The question is often posed as to how, before and after the Revolution, a new foundation was given to the right to punish. And no doubt the answer is to be found in the theory of the contract. But it is perhaps more important to ask the reverse question: how were people made to accept the power to punish, or quite simply, when punished, tolerate being so. The theory of the contract can only answer this question by the fiction of a juridical subject giving to others the power to exercise over him the right that he himself possesses over them. It is highly probable that the great carceral continuum, which provides a communication between the power of discipline and the power of the law, and extends without interruption from the smallest coercions to the longest penal detention, constituted the technical and real, immediately material counterpart of that chimerical granting of the right to punish.

4.    With this new economy of power, the carceral system, which is its basic instrument, permitted the emergence of a new form of 'law': a mixture of legality and nature, prescription and constitution, the norm. This had a whole series of effects: the internal dislocation of the judicial power or at least of its functioning; an increasing difficulty in judging, as if one were ashamed to pass sentence; a furious desire on the part of the judges to judge, assess, diagnose, recognize the normal and abnormal and claim the honour of curing or rehabilitating. In view of this, it is useless to believe in the good or bad consciences of judges, or even of their unconscious. Their immense 'appetite for medicine' which is constantly manifested – from their appeal to psychiatric experts, to their attention to the chatter of criminology – expresses the major fact that the power they exercise has been 'denatured'; that it is at a certain level governed by laws; that at another, more fundamental level it functions as a normative power; it is the economy of power that they exercise, and not that of their scruples or their humanism, that makes them pass 'therapeutic' sentences and recommend 'rehabilitating' periods of imprisonment. But, conversely, if the judges accept ever more reluctantly to condemn for the sake of condemning, the activity of judging has increased precisely to the extent that the

normalizing power has spread. Borne along by the omnipresence of the mechanisms of discipline, basing itself on all the carceral apparatuses, it has become one of the major functions of our society. The judges of normality are present everywhere. We are in the society of the teacher-judge, the doctor-judge, the educator-judge, the 'social worker'-judge; it is on them that the universal reign of the normative is based; and each individual, wherever he may find himself, subjects to it his body, his gestures, his behaviour, his aptitudes, his achievements. The carceral network, in its compact or disseminated forms, with its systems of insertion, distribution, surveillance, observation, has been the greatest support, in modern society, of the normalizing power.

5.    The carceral texture of society assures both the real capture of the body and its perpetual observation; it is, by its very nature, the apparatus of punishment that conforms most completely to the new economy of power and the instrument for the formation of knowledge that this very economy needs. Its panoptic functioning enables it to play this double role. By virtue of its methods of fixing, dividing, recording, it has been one of the simplest, crudest, also most concrete, but perhaps most indispensable conditions for the development of this immense activity of examination that has objectified human behaviour. If, after the age of 'inquisitorial' justice, we have entered the age of 'examinatory' justice, if, in an even more general way, the method of examination has been able to spread so widely throughout society, and to give rise in part to the sciences of man, one of the great instruments for this has been the multiplicity and close overlapping of the various mechanisms of incarceration. I am not saying that the human sciences emerged from the prison. But, if they have been able to be formed and to produce so many profound changes in the episteme, it is because they have been conveyed by a specific and new modality of power: a certain policy of the body, a certain way of rendering the group of men docile and useful. This policy required the involvement of definite relations of knowledge in relations of power; it called for a technique of overlapping subjection and objectification; it brought with it new procedures of individualization. The carceral network constituted one of the armatures of this power-knowledge that has made the human sciences historically possible. Knowable man (soul, individuality, consciousness, conduct, whatever it is called) is the object-effect of this analytical investment, of this domination-observation.

6.    This no doubt explains the extreme solidity of the prison, that slight invention that was nevertheless decried from the outset. If it had been no more than an instrument of rejection or repression in the service of a state apparatus, it would have been easier to alter its more overt forms or to find a more acceptable substitute for it. But, rooted as it was in mechanisms and strategies of power, it could meet any attempt to transform it with a great force of inertia. One fact is characteristic: when it is a question of altering the system of imprisonment, opposition does not come from the judicial institutions alone; resistance is to be found not in the prison as penal sanction, but in the prison with all its determinations, links and extra-judicial results; in the prison as the relay in a general network of disciplines and surveillances; in the prison as it functions in a panoptic regime. This does not mean that it cannot be altered, nor that it is once and for all indispensable to our kind of

society. One may, on the contrary, [c]ite the two processes which, in the very continuity of the processes that make the prison function, are capable of exercising considerable restraint on its use and of transforming its internal functioning. And no doubt these processes have already begun to a large degree. The first is that which reduces the utility (or increases its inconveniences) of a delinquency accommodated as a specific illegality, locked up and supervised; thus the growth of great national or international illegalities directly linked to the political and economic apparatuses (financial illegalities, information services, arms and drugs trafficking, property speculation) makes it clear that the somewhat rustic and conspicuous work force of delinquency is proving ineffective; or again, on a smaller scale, as soon as the economic levy on sexual pleasure is carried out more efficiently by the sale of contraceptives, or obliquely through publications, films or shows, the archaic hierarchy of prostitution loses much of its former usefulness. The second process is the growth of the disciplinary networks, the multiplication of their exchanges with the penal apparatus, the ever more important powers that are given them, the ever more massive transference to them of judicial functions; now, as medicine, psychology, education, public assistance, 'social work' assume an ever greater share of the powers of supervision and assessment, the penal apparatus will be able, in turn, to become medicalized, psychologized, educationalized; and by the same token that turning-point represented by the prison becomes less useful when, through the gap between its penitentiary discourse and its effect of consolidating delinquency, it articulates the penal power and the disciplinary power. In the midst of all these mechanisms of normalization, which are becoming ever more rigorous in their application, the specificity of the prison and its role as link are losing something of their purpose.

If there is an overall political issue around the prison, it is not therefore whether it is to be corrective or not; whether the judges, the psychiatrists or the sociologists are to exercise more power in it than the administrators or supervisors; it is not even whether we should have prison or something other than prison. At present, the problem lies rather in the steep rise in the use of these mechanisms of normalization and the wide-ranging powers which, through the proliferation of new disciplines, they bring with them.

[. . .]

## References

Bentham, J., *Works*, ed. Bowring, IV, 1843.
Touquet, H. du, *De la condition des classes pauvres*, 1846.

# Chapter 21

# Shoshana Zuboff

## MANAGING THE INFORMATED ORGANIZATION

From *In The Age of Smart Machines,* New York: Basic Books (1988), pp. 387–414.

[. . .]

### Technology is a place

**PUT YOUR EYE TO THE KALEIDOSCOPE** and hold it toward the light. There is a burst of color, tiny fragments in an intricate composition. Imagine a hand nudging the kaleidoscope's rim until hundreds of angles collapse, merge, and separate to form a new design. A fundamental change in an organization's technological infrastructure wields the power of the hand at the turning rim. Technological change defines the horizon of our material world as it shapes the limiting conditions of what is possible and what is barely imaginable. It erodes taken-for-granted assumptions about the nature of our reality, the 'pattern' in which we dwell, and lays open new choices. When the telephone makes it possible to pursue intimate conversations without bodies that touch or eyes that meet, or when the electric light rescues the night from darkness, the experience is more than simply an element within the pattern. Such innovations give form and definition to our worldly place and provoke a new vision of the potential for relatedness within it. It is in this sense that technology cannot be considered neutral. Technology is brimming with valence and specificity in that it both creates and forecloses avenues of experience.

History reveals the power of certain technological innovations to transform the mental life of an era – the feelings, sensibilities, perceptions, expectations, assumptions, and, above all, possibilities that define a community. From the social influence of the medieval castle,[1] to the coming of the printed book,[2] to the social and physical upheaval associated with the rise of the automobile[3] – each specific example serves to drive home a similar message. An important technological innovation is not usefully thought of as a unitary cause eliciting a series of discrete effects. Instead, it can be seen as an alteration of the material horizon of our world, with transformative implications for both the contours and the interior texture of our lives. Technology makes the world a new place – a conception expressed by Fernand Braudel when he wrote:

> It was only when things went wrong, when society came up against the ceiling of the possible, that people turned of necessity to technology, and interest was aroused for the thousand potential inventions, out of which one would be recognized as the best, the one that would break through the obstacle and open the door to a different future. . . . In this sense, technology is indeed a queen: it does change the world.[4]

Yet the metaphor of the kaleidoscope is finally a limited one. Those pretty fragments align themselves at random, but change in human societies is not quite as blind. Between the turning of the rim and the emergence of a new pattern, there is another force that infuses the final configuration of elements with meaning: the human activity of choice. Though intentions do not always predict consequences, humans do attempt to proceed by constructing meaning; assessing interests; and, with varying degrees of awareness, making choices. As the ceiling of the possible is newly defined, opportunities for choice are multiplied. Should I fly or drive or take a train? What is my destination? Should I use the telephone to maintain intimate contact with friends I rarely see? Whom should I call? How often? For how long should we speak? It is here in the realm of choice that technology reveals its indeterminacy. Though it redefines the possible, it cannot determine which choices are taken up and to what purpose.

Some theorists have attributed systematic and purposeful agency to the managerial use of technology. They argue that managers are interested exclusively in technology as a means of controlling, limiting, and ultimately weakening their work force.[5] The data I have presented suggest a more complicated reality. Even where control or deskilling has been the intent of managerial choices with respect to new information technology, managers themselves are also captive to a wide range of impulses and pressures. Only rarely is there a grand design concocted by an elite group ruthlessly grinding its way toward the fulfillment of some special and secret plan. Instead, there is a concentration of forces and consequences, which in turn develop their own momentum. Sometimes these lines of force run in predictably straight paths. At other times, they twist and spiral, turn corners, and flow to their opposite. Activities that seem to represent choices are often inert reproductions of accepted practice. In many cases, they are convenient responses to the press of local exigencies. In some instances, they may actually reflect a plan.

To fully grasp the way in which a major new technology can change the world, as described by Braudel, it is necessary to consider both the manner in which it creates intrinsically new qualities of experience and the way in which new possibilities are engaged by the often-conflicting demands of social, political, and economic interests in order to produce a 'choice.' To concentrate only on intrinsic change and the texture of an emergent mentality is to ignore the real weight of history and the diversity of interests that pervade collective behavior. However, to narrow all discussion of technological change to the play of these interests over-looks the essential power of technology to reorder the rules of the game and thus our experience as players. Moreover, these two dimensions of technological change, the intrinsic and the contingent, need to be understood, not separately, but in rela-tion to one another. The same innovation that abstracts work and increases its intellectual content, thus enhancing the learning of lower level employees [. . .], can also, within the context of the choices by which it is adapted, be experienced as a new source of divisiveness and control [. . .].

The dilemmas of transformation that have been described are embedded in the living detail of everyday life in the workplace as it undergoes computerization. They are dilemmas precisely because of the way they reveal the subtle interplay between essence and choice. Information technology essentially alters the contours of reality – work becomes more abstract, intelligence may be programmed, organizational memory and visibility are increased by an order of magnitude beyond any histor-ical capability. Individuals caught up in this newly configured reality face questions that did not need to be asked before. New possibilities arise and require new delib-erations. The duality of information technology – its capacity to automate and to informate – provides a vantage point from which to consider these choices. The relative emphasis that organizations give to these capacities will become the foun-dation for a strategic conception of technology deployment and so will shape the way the dilemmas are confronted and resolved.

The organizations described in this book have illustrated how the need to defend and reproduce the legitimacy of managerial authority can channel potential innova-tion toward a conventional emphasis on automation. In this context, managers emphasize machine intelligence and managerial control over the knowledge base at the expense of developing knowledge in the operating work force. They use the technology as a fail-safe system to increase their sense of certainty and control over both production and organizational functions. Their experiences suggest that the traditional environment of imperative control is fatally flawed in its ability to adequately exploit the informating capacity of the new technology.

In these organizations, the promise of automation seemed to exert a magnetic force, a seduction that promised to fulfill a dream of perfect control and heal egos wounded by their needs for certainty. The dream contains the image of 'people serving a smart machine,' but in the shadow of the dream, human beings have lost the experience of critical judgment that would allow them to no longer simply respond but to know better than, to question, to say no. This dream brings us closer to fulfilling Hannah Arendt's dreadful forecast of a world in which behaviorism comes true:

> The last stage of the laboring society, the society of jobholders, demands
> of its members a sheer automatic functioning, as though individual
> life had actually been submerged in the over-all life process of the species
> and the only active decision still required of the individual were to let
> go, so to speak, to abandon his individuality, the still individually sensed

pain and trouble of living, and acquiesce in a dazed, 'tranquilized,' functional type of behavior. The trouble with modern theories of behaviorism is not that they are wrong but that they could become true, that they actually are the best possible conceptualization of certain obvious trends in modern society. It is quite conceivable that the modern age – which began with such an unprecedented and promising outburst of human activity – may end in the deadliest, most sterile passivity history has ever known.[6]

That managers may give themselves over to this dream because of inertia and convenience rather than cogent analysis is all the more disturbing. Organizations that take steps toward an exclusively automating strategy can set a course that is not easily reversed. They are likely to find themselves crippled by antagonism from the work force and the depletion of knowledge that would be needed in value-adding activities. The absence of a self-conscious strategy to exploit the informating capacity of the new technology has tended to mean that managerial action flows along the path of least resistance – a path that, at least superficially, appears to serve only the interests of managerial hegemony.

Yet what would seem to be a maddeningly predictable story line has its share of surprises, false starts, dead ends, trap doors, tarnished hopes, and real failures. The seeds of an informating strategy were apparent in each of the organizations described here, especially in Cedar Bluff, Global Bank Brazil, and DrugCorp. In the absence of a comprehensive strategy, no single organization fully succeeded in exploiting the opportunity to informate.

The interdependence of the three dilemmas of transformation I have described – knowledge, authority, and technique – indicates the necessary comprehensiveness of an informating strategy. The shifting grounds of knowledge invite managers to recognize the emergent demands for intellective skills and develop a learning environment in which such skills can develop. That very recognition contains a threat to managerial authority, which depends in part upon control over the organization's knowledge base. A commitment to intellective skill development is likely to be hampered when an organization's division of labor continuously replenishes the felt necessity of imperative control. Managers who must prove and defend their own legitimacy do not easily share knowledge or engage in inquiry. Workers who feel the requirements of subordination are not enthusiastic learners. New roles cannot emerge without the structures to support them. If managers are to alter their behavior, then methods of evaluation and reward that encourage them to do so must be in place. If employees are to learn to operate in new ways and to broaden their contribution to the life of the business, then career ladders and reward systems reflecting that change must be designed. In this context, access to information is critically important; the structure of access to information expresses the organization's underlying conception of authority. Employees and managers can hardly be partners in learning if there is a one-way mirror between them. Techniques of control that are meant to safeguard authority create suspicion and animosity, which is particularly dysfunctional when an organization needs to apply its human energies to inventing an alternative form of work organization better suited to the new technological context.

The interdependence among these dilemmas means that technology alone, no matter how well designed or implemented, cannot be relied upon to carry the full weight of an informating strategy. Managers must have an awareness of the choices they face, a desire to exploit the informating capacity of the new technology, and a commitment to fundamental change in the landscape of authority if a comprehensive informating strategy is to succeed. Without this strategic commitment, the hierarchy will use technology to reproduce itself. Technological developments, in the absence of organizational innovation, will be assimilated into the status quo.

## The division of labor and the division of learning

Organizational theorists frequently have promoted a conception of organizations as 'interpretation systems.'[7] The computer mediation of an organization's productive and administrative infrastructure places an even greater premium upon an organization's interpretive capabilities, as each organizational level experiences a relatively greater preponderance of abstract cues requiring interpretation. This is as true for the plant manager as for the pulp mill worker, for the banker as well as for the clerk. In each case, oral culture and the action-centered skills upon which that culture depends are gradually eroded, and perhaps finally displaced, by the incursions of explicit information and intellective skill.

As bureaucratic coordination and communication become more dependent upon mastering the electronic text, the *acting-with* skills of the white-collar body are subordinated to the demands associated with dominating increasing quantities of abstracted information. In many cases, traditional functional distinctions no longer reflect the requirements of the business. When managers increase their engagement with the electronic text, they also risk a new kind of hyperrationalism and impersonalization, as they operate at a greater distance from employees and customers.

When the textualizing consequences of an informating technology become more comprehensive, the body's traditional role in the production process (as a source of effort and/or skill in the service of *acting-on*) is also transformed. The rigid separation of mental and material work characteristic of the industrial division of labor and vital to the preservation of a distinct managerial group (in the office as well as in the factory) becomes, not merely outmoded, but perilously dysfunctional. Earlier distinctions between white and blue 'collars' collapse. Even more significant is the increased intellectual content of work tasks across organizational levels that attenuates the conventional designations of manager and managed. This does not mean that there are no longer useful distinctions to be made among organizational members, but whatever these distinctions may be, they will no longer convey fundamentally different modes of involvement with the life of the organization represented by the division of abstract and physical labor. Instead, the total organizational skill base becomes more homogeneous.

In the highly informated organization, the data base takes on a life of its own. As organizations like Cedar Bluff develop mechanisms that allow data to be automatically generated, captured, and stored, they begin to create their own image in the form of dynamic, detailed, real-time, integrated electronic texts. These texts can provide access to internal operations as well as external business and customer data; they can be designed with enough reflexivity to be able to organize, summarize, and analyze aspects of their own content. The electronic text becomes a vast symbolic surrogate for the vital detail of an organization's daily life. Such data constitute an autonomous domain. They are a public symbolization of organizational experience, much of which was previously private, fragmented, and implicit – lodged in people's heads, in their sensual know-how, in discussions at meetings or over lunch, in file drawers, or on desktops.

The textualization process moves away from a conception of information as something that individuals collect, process, and disseminate; instead, it invites us to imagine an organization as a group of people gathered around a central core that is the electronic text. Individuals take up their relationship toward that text according to their responsibilities and their information needs. In such a scenario, work is, in large measure, the creation of meaning, and the methods of work involve the application of intellective skill to data.

Under these circumstances, work organization requires a new division of learning to support a new division of labor. The traditional system of imperative control, which was designed to maximize the relationship between commands and obedience, depended upon restricted hierarchical access to knowledge and nurtured the belief that those who were excluded from the organization's explicit knowledge base were intrinsically less capable of learning what it had to offer. In contrast, an informated organization is structured to promote the possibility of useful learning among all members and thus presupposes relations of equality. However, this does not mean that all members are assumed to be identical in their orientations, proclivities, and capacities; rather, the organization legitimates each member's right to learn as much as his or her temperament and talent will allow. In the traditional organization, the division of learning lent credibility to the legitimacy of imperative control. In an informated organization, the new division of learning produces experiences that encourage a synthesis of members' interests, and the flow of value-adding knowledge helps legitimate the organization as a learning community.

The contemporary language of work is inadequate to express these new realities. We remain [. . .] prisoners of a vocabulary in which managers require employees; superiors have subordinates; jobs are defined to be specific, detailed, narrow, and task-related; and organizations have levels that in turn make possible chains of command and spans of control. The guiding metaphors are military; relationships are thought of as contractual and often adversarial. The foundational image of work is still one of a manufacturing enterprise where raw materials are transformed by physical labor and machine power into finished goods. However, the images associated with physical labor can no longer guide our conception of work.

The informated workplace, which may no longer be a 'place' at all, is an arena through which information circulates, information to which intellective effort is applied. The quality, rather than the quantity, of effort will be the source from which added value is derived. Economists may continue to measure labor productivity as if the entire world of work could be represented adequately by the assembly line, but their measures will be systematically indifferent to what is most valuable in the informated organization. A new division of learning requires another vocabulary – one of colleagues and co-learners, of exploration, experimentation, and innovation. Jobs are comprehensive, tasks are abstractions that depend upon insight and synthesis, and power is a roving force that comes to rest as dictated by function and need. A new vocabulary cannot be invented all at once – it will emerge from the practical action of people struggling to make sense in a new 'place' and driven to sever their ties with an industrial logic that has ruled the imaginative life of our century.

The informated organization is a learning institution, and one of its principal purposes is the expansion of knowledge – not knowledge for is own sake (as in academic pursuit), but knowledge that comes to reside at the core of what it means to be productive. Learning is no longer a separate activity that occurs either before one enters the workplace or in remote classroom settings. Nor is it an activity preserved for a managerial group. The behaviors that define learning and the behaviors that define being productive are one and the same. Learning is not something that requires time out from being engaged in productive activity; learning is the heart of productive activity. To put it simply, learning is the new form of labor.

The precise contours of a new division of learning will depend upon the business, products, services, and markets that people are engaged in learning about. The empowerment, commitment, and involvement of a wide range of organizational members in self-managing activities means that organizational structures are likely to be both emergent and flexible, changing as members continually learn more about how to organize themselves for learning about their business. However, some significant conceptual issues are raised by the prospect of a new division of learning in the informated organization. The following discussion of these issues does not offer a rigid prescription for practice but suggests the kinds of concrete choices that define an informating strategy.

## Managerial activities in the informated organization

As the intellective skill base becomes the organization's most precious resource, managerial roles must function to enhance its quality. Members can be thought of as being arrayed in concentric circles around a central core, which is the electronic data base. The skills required by those at the core do not differ in kind from those required at a greater distance from the core. Instead of striking phenomenological differences in the work that people do, the distance of any given role from the center denotes the range and comprehensiveness of responsibilities, the time frame spanned by those responsibilities, and the degree of accountability for cross-functional integration attached to the role. The data base may be accessed from any ring in the circle, though data can be formatted and analyzed in ways that are most appropriate to the information needs of any particular ring of responsibility.

On the innermost ring, nearest to the core, are those who interact with information on a real-time basis. They have responsibility for daily operations, and the level of data they utilize is the most detailed and immediate. Because intellective skill is relevant to the work of each ring of responsibility, the skills of those who manage daily operations form an appropriate basis for their progression into roles with more comprehensive responsibilities.

The jobs at the data interface become increasingly similar to one another as the informating process evolves. In the advanced stages of informating, these become 'metajobs,' because the general characteristics of intellective skill become more central to performance than the particular expertise associated with specific production-related functions. Expertise either is available from on-site specialists or is built into information systems. For example, at Cedar Bluff, top managers believed that they would solve the problem of vanishing artistry by building that expertise into the information system capability. The know-how of managers with years of experience could be systematized and made available to operators who would never have the same degree of involvement in the action contexts that had developed the personal and specific knowledge associated with action-centered skill.

This relationship between general intellective skills and expertise in specific areas was also illustrated in the case of the calculator models at Cedar Bluff. Operators needed the kind of understanding that would allow them to know when and how to use a model, and when to be critical of its assumptions or outputs. That quality of understanding did not depend upon being able to match the expertise that went into the models' calculations. The operator with a conceptual approach to the process, skilled in data-based reasoning, and familiar with the theory that links elements in the production process, may not be able to reproduce the knowledge of an individual with years of hands-on experience or expert training. Nevertheless, he or she should be able to understand the conceptual underpinning of a problem well enough to select among potential analytic strategies and to access the expert knowledge that is required. Intellective skill is brought to bear in the definition of the problem for analysis, the determination of the data that is required for analysis, the consideration of the appropriateness of an analytical approach, and the application of the analysis to improved performance.

The activities arrayed on the responsibility rings at a greater distance from the core incorporate at least four domains of managerial activity: intellective skill development, technology development, strategy formulation, and social system development. For example, the crucial importance of the intellective skill base requires that a significant level of organizational resources be devoted to its expansion and refinement. This means that some organizational members will be involved in both higher-order analysis and conceptualization, as well as in promoting learning and skill development among those with operational responsibility. Their aim is to expand the knowledge base and to improve the effectiveness with which data is assimilated, interpreted, and responded to. They have a central role in creating an organizational environment that invites learning and in supporting those in other managerial domains to develop their talents as educators and as learners. In this domain, managers are responsible for task-related learning, for learning about learning, and for educating others in each of the other three domains.

A new division of learning depends upon the continued progress of informating applications. This managerial domain of technology-related activity comprises a hierarchy of responsibilities in addition to those tasks normally associated with systems engineering, development, and maintenance. It includes maintaining the reliability of the data base while improving its breadth and quality, developing approaches to system design that support an informating strategy, and scanning for technical innovations that can lead to new informating opportunities. Members with responsibility for the development of technology must be as concerned with the use of technology (Do people understand the information? Do they know how to use it?) as they are with other aspects of design and implementation. This kind of technological development can occur only in the closest possible alignment with organizational efforts to promote learning and social integration. Technology develops as a reflection of the informating strategy and provides the material infrastructure of the learning environment.

Learning increases the pace of change. For an organization to pursue an informating strategy, it must maximize its own ability to learn and explore the implications of that learning for its long-range plans with respect to markets, product development, new sources of comparative advantage, et cetera. A division of learning that supports an informating strategy results in a distribution of knowledge and authority that enables a wide range of members to contribute to these activities. Still, some members will need to guide and coordinate learning efforts in order to lead an assessment of strategic alternatives and to focus organizational intelligence in areas of strategic value. These managers lead the organization in a way that allows members to participate in defining purpose and in supporting the direction of long-term planning. The increased time horizon of their responsibilities provides the reflective distance with which they can gauge the quality of the learning environment and can guide change that would improve collective learning.

There is considerable interdependence among these four domains of managerial activity (intellective skill development, technology development, strategy formulation, and social system development). For example, activities related to intellective skill development cannot proceed without the social system management that helps to foster roles and relationships appropriate to a new division of learning. Activities in either of these domains will be frustrated without technological development that supports an informating strategy. Integration and learning are responsibilities that fall within each domain, because without a shared commitment to interdependence and the production of value-adding knowledge, the legitimacy of the learning community will suffer. Business outcomes such as cost, efficiency, quality, product development, customer service, productivity, et cetera, would result from coordinated initiatives across domains. Managerial work would thus be team-oriented and interdisciplinary, and would promote the fluid movement of members across these four domains of managerial activity.

The concentric structure depends upon and promotes both vertical and horizontal organizational integration. There are no predetermined boundaries between any rings within the organizational sphere or between the domains of managerial authority. The skills that are required at the data interface nearest to the core of daily operating responsibilities provide a coherent basis for the kind of continual learning that would prepare people for increasingly comprehensive responsibilities. The relative homogeneity of the total organizational skill base suggests a vision of organizational membership that resembles the trajectory of a professional career, rather than the two-class system marked by an insurmountable gulf between workers and managers. The interpenetration between rings provides a key source of organizational integration.

Some observers of the emerging technological environment have predicted an increasingly bifurcated distribution of skills in the workplace.[8] On the other extreme, the operators at Piney Wood [. . .] believed that in the future all factory workers would be college graduates. The concentric organizational structure suggests that the solution to future skill requirements need not be as drastic as either of these scenarios implies. While it is probable that entry-level requirements will become more demanding, the increased homogeneity of skills and the continuity between organizational rings entails an ongoing commitment to training and education in order to facilitate career progression. The shape of skill distribution thus is more likely to represent a curve than the discontinuous step function that characterizes the traditional hierarchy, with its more rigid distinction between managers and the managed.

## The body's new work: managing the intricacy of posthierarchical relationships

The vision of a concentric organization is one that seems to rely upon metaphors of wholeness – interdependency, fluidity, and homogeneity each contribute to organizational integration. What is required of managers in such a workplace, where learning and integration constitute the two most vital organizational priorities? How is the social system of such an organization to be managed?

As we have seen, the abstract precincts of the data interface heighten the need for communication. Interpretive processes depend upon creating and sharing meaning through inquiry and dialogue. New sources of personal influence are associated with the ability to learn and to engender learning in others, in contrast to an earlier emphasis upon contractual relationships or the authority derived from function and position.

What new patterns of relationships will characterize this kind of learning environment? What will replace the familiar map that the model of imperative control has provided? The answer to this question derives from one of the most significant dialetics of an informating strategy. In a conventional organization, managers' action-centered skills are geared toward the politics of interpersonal influence, principally as they pertain to maintaining reciprocities, managing superiors, and gathering or disseminating information. These skills are shaped by the demands of achieving smooth operations and personal success under conditions of hierarchical authority. People develop their expectations about how to treat one another largely in reference to rank and function. An informating strategy does place severe demands upon managers' action-centered skills in the service of *acting-with* but in a very different context. The relationships to be managed are both more dynamic and more intricate than earlier patterns. The shape and quality of relationships will vary in relation to what people know, what they feel, and what the task at hand requires. Relationships will need to be fashioned and refashioned as part of the dynamism of the social processes, like inquiry and dialogue, that mediate learning. Such relationships are more intricate because their character derives from the specifics of the situation that are always both pragmatic – what it takes to get the work done best – and psychological – what people need to sustain motivation and commitment.[9]

In the information panopticon, managers (like those at Metro Tel) frequently tried to simplify their managerial tasks by displacing face-to-face engagement with techniques of surveillance and control. As a consequence, they became isolated from the realities of their organizations as they were increasingly insulated by an electronic text that in turn was even more vulnerable to workers' antagonisms. The demands of managing intricate relationships reintroduce the importance of the sentient body and so provide a counterpoint to the threat of hyperrationalism and impersonalization that is posed by computer mediation. The body now functions as the scene of human feeling rather than as the source of physical energy or as an instrument of political influence. Human feeling operates here in two ways. First, as members engage in their work together, their feelings are an important source of data from which intricate relations are structured. Second, a manager's felt sense of the group and its learning needs is a vital source of personal knowledge that informs the development of new action-centered skills in the service of *acting-with*.

The demands of a learning environment can reduce the psychological distance between the self and the organization because active engagement in the social processes associated with interpretation requires more extensive participation of the human personality. In a traditional approach to work organization, employees could be treated as objectively measurable bodies, and in return, they could give of their labor without giving of their selves. The human being as wage earner and the human being as subjective actor could remain separate. In an environment of imperative control, managers can remain indifferent to what their subordinates feel, as long as they perform adequately. This 'is' was eventually translated to 'ought,' as incursions of private feeling into the workday came to be seen as squandering the organization's time. It was this view that ultimately triumphed over the professionals at DrugCorp who had unwittingly textualized their own playfulness. As they struggled with their notions of legitimate work behavior, DrugCorp's managers tried to define the self out of the workday. But when work involves a collective effort to create and communicate meaning, the dynamics of human feeling cannot be relegated to the periphery of an organization's concerns. How people feel about themselves, each other, and the organization's purposes is closely linked to their capacity to sustain the high levels of internal commitment and motivation that are demanded by the abstraction of work and the new division of learning.

The relationships that characterize a learning environment thus can be thought of as posthierarchical. This does not imply that differentials of knowledge, responsibility, and power no longer exist; rather, they can no longer be assumed. Instead, they shift and flow and develop their character in relation to the situation, the task, and the actors at hand. Managing intricacy calls for a new level of action-centered skill, as dialogue and inquiry place a high premium on the intuitive and imaginative sources of understanding that temper and hone the talents related to *acting-with*. The dictates of a learning environment, rather than those of imperative control, now shape the development of such interpersonal know-how.

The seeds of this new intricacy are already evident in several of the organizations I have described. The managers at Cedar Bluff who learned to join their workers in asking questions and searching for answers were already engaged in forging patterns far more intricate than the simpler prescriptions derived from faith in managerial authority. The professionals of DrugCorp, normally divided by function, professional discipline, and organizational rank, had invented new modes of relationships based upon a valued exchange of information, shared inquiry, and play. At Global Bank Brazil, bankers and operations managers were groping for new relationships that would reach beyond turf and hierarchy in order to better serve their customers. At Tiger Creek, managers and workers reached and stumbled as they attempted to shift the logic of their relationship from one based on hierarchy to one shaped by the pragmatic opportunities offered by a redistribution of knowledge. In each of these cases, organizational members were confronted with rich new possibilities engendered by an informating technology. In each case, they discovered that exploiting these new opportunities required new forms of relationships governed by the necessities of learning and performance rather than by the rules of an older faith – rules that sort, rank, and separate.

[. . .]

## The informated organization and recent trends in work organization

As the years passed at Cedar Bluff, managers began to confront more openly and honestly the challenges to their skills that had been unleashed by the informating process. It was not untypical for organizations pursuing high commitment strategies to feel the strains of participative management and to experience a good bit of conflict concerning the limits of managerial prerogatives. At Cedar Bluff, however, the demands on managers had become relentlessly insistent. The knowledge requirements of the data interface, the vulnerability of plant performance to variations in operator skill and motivation, and the broad accessibility of data had lent new urgency to questions about the skills, roles, and structures that should define the organization. This was vividly illustrated by the turmoil that surrounded the development of a new pay and promotion system for hourly workers. The operators had become increasingly proficient in operating the plant, and after several years of producing pulp at far below the equipment's true capacity, production levels began to climb. As operators' skills improved, so did their dissatisfaction with the pay and promotion system. They believed that it arbitrarily limited the amount of learning for which they could be rewarded. Amid mounting dissension, a committee consisting of operators and managers from the various areas of the plant was appointed to gather data on the problem and to recommend new policies. The plant had reached production levels of more than nine hundred tons a day, but as the committee went into session, operators were heard to say, 'That's the last nine-hundred-ton day this plant will see until the pay and promotion problems are resolved.'

In the months that followed, their predictions came true; the plant returned to earlier production levels. Cedar Bluff's managers were especially frustrated because they could not identify the causes of the downturn. Only rarely could a manager point to something that operators were doing incorrectly that might be contributing to poor production. They concluded that the disappointing performance could be attributed, not to what operators were doing, but to what they *were not* doing. The operators' errors were sins of omission – an underutilization of the data interface resulting from their refusal to notice, to think, to explore, to experiment, or to improve. In other words, the power of the new technology was going to waste. Managers felt helpless to alter the situation. It was only when the new pay and promotion system was finally developed and accepted by a majority vote that production levels began to climb once again.

There are several lessons to be learned here. First, the requirements of an informating strategy support existing work-improvement efforts, such as the high commitment approach to work force management, with its emphasis on self-managing teams, participation, and decentralization. Organizations that are already pursuing this approach are more likely to have developed both the ideological context and the social skills necessary to plan and implement an informating strategy. In this regard, Cedar Bluff provides an important contrast not only to Piney Wood but also to organizations, like Global Bank Brazil, that have minimal experience with work-system innovation. Second, the demands for a redistribution of knowledge and the consequent challenge to the managerial role that can be unleashed by the informating process are likely to exacerbate the growing pains associated with participative management and to accelerate the need for positive change. Third, organizational innovations designed to create high commitment work systems typically have focused upon the hourly work force. In most cases, and Cedar Bluff is one example, the managerial hierarchy has remained relatively intact, while team organization and pay-for-skill systems have been designed for the operational work force. In contrast, an informating strategy suggests the need for a more wholistic reconceptualization of the skills, roles, and structures that define the total organization. Partial change efforts, as at Tiger Creek, or technology-driven initiatives, as at Global Bank Brazil, are unlikely to result in the kind of learning environment necessary for an ongoing and robust approach to the informating process. Finally, managing in an informated environment is a delicate human process. The ability to use information for real business benefit is as much a function of the quality of commitment and relationships as it is a function of the quality of intellective skills.

The words of the clerk at Global Bank Brazil continue to echo: 'Will things be any different now?' In response, we can say that the opportunity is there, and we now know more about what it will take. An informating strategy requires a comprehensive vision based upon an understanding of the unique capacities of intelligent technology and the opportunity to use the organization to liberate those capacities. It means forging a new logic of technological deployment based upon that vision. A coherent rationale will be necessary, particularly when the tide of conventional thinking and familiar assumptions on this subject can submerge many important choices regarding basic technological design and management. Cedar Bluff's plant manager foresaw this danger:

> The technology is going in the direction that says one person operates the master controls. Is the technology right? We don't believe it is, and we are working hard to convince our vendors to leave the design flexible enough so that it does not preclude the uses we want to make of it.

The informated organization does move in another direction. It relies on the human capacities for teaching and learning, criticism and insight. It implies an approach to business improvement that rests upon the improvement and innovation made possible by the enhanced comprehensibility of core processes. It reflects a fertile interdependence between the human mind and some of its most sophisticated productions. As one worker from Tiger Creek mused:

> If you don't let people grow and develop and make more decisions, it's a waste of human life – a waste of human potential. If you don't use your knowledge and skill, it's a waste of life. Using the technology to its full potential means using the man to his full potential.

[. . .]

## Notes

1 Michel Bur, 'The Social Influence of the Motte-and-Bailey Castle,' *Scientific American* (May 1983): 132–40.
2 See, for example, Luciett Febvre and Henri-Jean Martin, *The Coming of the Book: The Impact of Printing 1450–1800* (London: NLB, 1976); Amanda Wood, *Knowledge Before Printing and After: The Indian Tradition in Changing Kerala* (Oxford: Oxford University Press, 1985); Elizabeth Lisenstein, *The Printing Press as an Agent of Change* (Cambridge: Cambridge University Press, 1979).
3 See, for example, James J. Flink, *The Car Culture* (Cambridge: MIT Press, 1975); and James J. Flink, *America Adopts the Automobile: 1895–1950* (Cambridge: MIT Press, 1970).
4 Fernand Braudel, *The Structures of Everyday Life: Civilization and Capitalism 15th–18th Century*, vol. I (New York: Harper and Row, 1981), 435.
5 The classic formulation of this point of view can be found in Harry Braverman's *Labor and Monopoly Capital* (New York: Monthly Review Press, 1974); see also David Noble, *The Forces of Production* (New York: Oxford University Press, 1984); Harley Shaiken, *Work Transformed* (New York: Bolt, Rinehart and Winston, 1984).
6 Hannah Arendt, *The Human Condition* (Chicago: The University of Chicago Press, 1958), 322.
7 See, for example, Richard C. Daft and Karl E. Weick, 'Toward a Model of Organizations as Interpretation Systems,' *Academy of Management Review* 9 (1984): 284–95; Aaron Wildarsky, 'Information as an Organizational Problem,' *Journal of Management Studies* 20 (1983): 29–40.
8 See for example Robert Kuttner, *The Economic Illusion: False Choices Between Prosperity and Social Justice* (Boston: Houghton Mifflin Co., 1984).
9 I refer the reader to a recent critique of ego functions and social relationships in the postmodern era written by the psychologist-philosopher Eugene T. Gendlin. He argues that contemporary relationships are more 'intricate' than can be accounted for by our nineteenth century models of authority – models upon which Freud's concept of psychic structure was based. I borrow the term *intricate* from Gendlin's usage, as his formulation provides the general context within which these alterations in workplace relations are a salient example. See Eugene T. Gendlin, 'A Philosophical Critique of the Concept of Narcissism: The Significance of the Awareness Movement,' in D. M. Levin (ed.) *Pathologies of the Modern Self: Postmodern Studies* (New York: New York University Press, 1987), 251–304.

# Chapter 22

# David Lyon

## NEW DIRECTIONS
## IN THEORY

From *Surveillance Society: Monitoring Everyday Life*, Buckingham: Open University Press (2001), pp. 107–25.

**IN THE 1994 FILM** *The Net*, Sandra Bullock finds herself without an identity. That is, she has been stripped of all her electronic coordinates, an ordinary person in extraordinary circumstances of loss. She desperately seeks the means of piecing together again the symbols of self and the tokens of trust without which she is bereft and agonizingly anonymous. Wim Wenders' 1991 picture, *Until the End of the World*, tells a different story. William Hurt, carrying a top-secret device, is on the run from industrial bounty-hunters. The breathtaking global chase is both physical and electronic and slows only in the Australian outback, where the film ends. This movie explores ways in which, despite the array of communication and information technologies that supposedly connect us, self-understanding and real human contact are elusive.[1]

The tension between the two films says something about surveillance. We rely on surveillance technologies to hold things together and to provide the acceptable currencies of identity and eligibility. Yet the same technologies fail to provide a satisfactory account of our lives let alone infuse our relationships with a sense of meaningful interaction. And as we have seen, surveillance technologies may also be used to channel our lives in directions we do not desire or to thwart us from proper participation in aspects of life. In theorizing surveillance, an understanding of new technologies can easily be out of touch with the crucial dimension of lived experience. Given the structural disappearance of bodies, with which surveillance tries to cope, what are the prospects for a return to embodied personhood as a mode of critique within a sociology of surveillance?

At the start of the twenty-first century it is clear that communication and information technologies have become central to understanding social change. Computer dependence has become a feature of both global connections and of everyday life. Indeed, globalization and daily living in the contemporary world are in part constituted by our relation with computers. No country wishes to miss out on the establishment of an information infrastructure. Few citizens or consumers wish to be excluded from the network of information flows, at least as far as having access to telephones, televisions and the Internet is concerned. But the obverse of the information society is the surveillance society. The world of electronic connectivity works both ways. It brings the global village to our doorstep. And at the same time it extracts personal data from us that are then processed, manipulated, traded and used to influence us and to affect our life chances.

Explaining how and why this happens has become a matter of controversy. The sociology of communication and information technologies started, naturally enough, by demonstrating how computerization enhances and sometimes alters social processes such as bureaucratic organization.[2] As the nation state and capitalistic enterprises were the first to engage the new technologies, questions arose of how balances of power might be disturbed, or social control might become less restrained.

Anthony Giddens warned of the increasing potentials for totalitarian government, and Gary T. Marx cautioned that 'new surveillance' technologies used in American policing may portend the coming 'maximum surveillance society'.[3] In these kinds of account, the classic concerns of sociological analysis reappear. We participate, wittingly or otherwise, in the production of social forces that may one day overwhelm us. The dream of greater control could boomerang back to demobilize us as sovereign subjects. This kind of account resonates with an equally classic narrative – the revenge of the modern machine.

But what if the computer is more than a modern machine? What if the computer is implicated in the social and cultural transformation of modernity itself?[4] And what if it thus requires novel modes of analysis appropriate to this putative transformation? This would alter the picture somewhat. Placed next to the social sifting and sorting power of today's surveillance practices and the rapid rise of risk management as a rationale for surveillance, the questions posed have a fresh mien. Does this mean that older models, such as the panopticon, require revising or rejecting? Either way, what constructive new directions for theory are needed to make sense of surveillance today?

Such questions have prompted a number of interesting and important studies showing how databases may be thought of as discourse[5] or how surveillance has slipped into simulation mode.[6] These take their cues from the work of Michel Foucault and Jean Baudrillard rather than from more classical sociological sources. They claim to show, moreover, how those older approaches are no longer adequate. For example, the rational autonomous individual, central to Max Weber's sociology of bureaucratic organization, may be viewed not so much as an 'anthropological invariant'[7] as a construct. Now, argues Mark Poster, computer databases may construct 'subjects' or, rather 'objects', whose identities are dispersed. As such they may still be subject to domination but in a new modality. Bentham's panopticon gives way to the electronic superpanopticon.

The concept of the panopticon actually straddles these different stories. The idea of an all-seeing eye, enhanced electronically, is common to both sorts of account.[8] But it is put to quite different uses. On the one hand it relates to its modern utilitarian Benthamite frame, where the prison architecture becomes an automated machine. On the other, in a more postmodern mood, the panopticon is a form of discourse whose repertoire is realized in simulation. The question is, are these two approaches incommensurate, as participants in the debate themselves maintain, or do they provide complementary accounts that together yield a fuller picture of the phenomena in question?

This is a question of some moment, for both analytical and political reasons. It raises, first, an issue of sociological concern: what theory is adequate to the present information-saturated social environment? The insights and limitations of each kind of theory may be explored with respect to a specific set of circumstances, the digitization of surveillance. But, second, much hangs on this question politically. Developing appropriate responses, particularly those involving regulation or resistance, depends crucially on understanding what kind of power is exercised in surveillance societies today.

## Computers and modern surveillance

Four strands of surveillance theory may be distinguished, each profoundly connected with classic conceptions of modernity. In the next section, I examine some postmodern strands. Surveillance may be understood in relation to the nation state, to bureaucracy, to what might be termed technological logic (or 'technologic' for short) and to political economy. In each case, the accent is on the increasingly routine, systematic and focused attention paid by organizations to individual's lives – hence, 'surveillance'[9] – as part of an overarching process. And in each case it is noted that computerization was introduced from the 1960s to enhance and expand the surveillance function.

As we shall see, however, there are limitations to these accounts, which I anticipate briefly here. The computer appeared as an adjunct, a feature added as it were from the outside. The result is that technology often tends to be viewed as external to social relations, and only internal to the discrete social sectors within which it is 'applied'. Realizing the potential for a sub-field that might be called 'surveillance studies', in which commonalities would be recognized between practices in different sectors, was to depend both on the proliferation of computerized surveillance and on the rise to prominence of Michel Foucault's studies of power-knowledge.[10]

The four strands may be characterized briefly as follows. The nation state orientation focuses on political imperatives that require surveillance, within geopolitical and military struggles. It leans, theoretically, on the work of Mosca, Pareto, Sorel and Michels, and points up the internal control achieved in a given country, even though the incentive to perfect the system is struggle between states. Christopher Dandeker rightly argues that the military origins of modern surveillance have been understated.[11] Externally, military power becomes increasingly bureaucratized in modern times, and this is paralleled by the bureaucratization of policing internally. For Dandeker, the corollary of external military organization is pacified internal situation[12] and both require a steady augmentation of surveillance. Professional and bureaucratic military power can only exist dependent an a taxation system within capitalist economies.

The extremes of nation state surveillance are clearly visible in pre-1989 eastern European societies with their notoriously intrusive and fearful secret police services, such as the KGB (USSR), Stasi (East Germany) and so on. But George Orwell, and his novel *Nineteen Eighty Four*, provided the most lasting and vivid metaphors for state surveillance. Big Brother's supposedly benign face looming down from the telescreen on the hapless Winston Smith; the bureaucratic 'doublespeak' from the Ministry of Truth. Though they could be read as commentaries on communism, they were actually warnings about the surveillance potentialities of any modern nation state. Big Brother could appear in a capitalist context. Giddens' sociological cautions about modern nation states and totalitarianism are bred in the same theoretical stable.

The second strand of surveillance theory is closely related to the first, although its key theorist is Max Weber. Its best literary exponent, however, would not be Orwell so much as Franz Kafka. The latter's novels of political control, such as *The Trial*,[13] depict the terrifying fear instilled by uncertainty. Who wants this information, what do they already know, is it correct, and what will be done with what I divulge? These novels express the experiences of those dominated by bureaucracy rather than Weber's colder description of the machinery of bureaucratic organization itself.

Weber's (equally chilling, in the end) iron cage portrays surveillance as a product not of struggle between states or of rapacious class interests, but of rationalization. Irrationalities may successfully be eliminated by bureaucratic means, producing rationally calculable administrative action. The surveillance function lies primarily in the files, those dismal dossiers that store information on each individual, the knowledge of which produces and reproduces power. For Weber, bureaucratic surveillance is a means of procuring efficiency, especially in the large scale and unwieldy tasks that confront any expanding modern nation state.

It was such Weberian approaches that inspired some classic accounts of computerization in bureaucratic contexts, notably James Rule's pioneering study of *Private Lives, Public Surveillance*.[14] Rule highlighted the ways in which the shift from paper to computer files occurs but he also showed that some features of government surveillance reappear in commercial contexts. Writing in the late 1960s, his work embraced not only the computerization of bureaucratic processes in the realm of the state but also those visible in the rapidly growing operations of credit card companies. Rule tried to assess against an ideal typical total surveillance situation how large scale bureaucratic institutions encroach steadily into new domains. A Weberian stance may also be detected in David Burnham's cautionary study, *The Rise of the Computer State*,[15] a book even more concerned about the centralizing of state power through the use of computer databases. In this book however, the motif of technologic, the third strand of modern surveillance studies, is writ large.

Although for a number of reasons Jacques Ellul's contribution to sociology has seldom been seen as mainstream,[16] it is in his work in particular that insights into the technologic of modernity appear. In contrast with many others who use 'technology' to refer both to artefacts and to processes, Ellul worked with the broader concept of *la technique*. It is *la technique* that integrates the machine into society, that constructs the social world that the machine needs. *La technique* is above all an orientation to means rather than to ends, that seeks relentlessly for the one best way to operate, and in so doing steadily seems to erode human agency. It tends to be self-augmenting, irreversible, all-embracing and progresses geometrically. One of Ellul's telling examples is policing. As it is technically augmented, policing requires increasingly that all citizens be supervised, in the interests of apprehending more efficiently those who behave criminally. The perfection of unobtrusive police technique puts all under discreet surveillance.[17]

Many sociological studies of policing in the late twentieth century start with a deferential nod towards Ellul. Gary T. Marx's well-known investigation into American undercover practices is one case in point; Richard Ericson and Kevin Haggerty's *Policing the Risk Society* is another.[18] Some of Ellul's explicit ideas also survive in the hands of others in the surveillance studies field. Langdon Winner's use of 'function creep', for example, suggests that once in place a surveillance technique such as a digitized identification number will tend to expand to cover other purposes.[19] And Oscar Gandy sees the extension of personal record-keeping systems and precision marketing in terms of Ellul's 'self-completing system' even though he warns against 'assigning it intelligence and needs or some kind of integrative reality'.[20]

Although Ellul's own work represents more of an orientation than a triumph of detailed empirical demonstration of the power of *la technique*, it is clear that at least as far as the technicization of policing is concerned his fears were more than justified. Today's high-tech methods have turned officers into information brokers, operating not only according to legal warrant, but also to the codes of insurance companies.[21] Given the rise of database marketing with its consumer group classification and social sorting strategies, one wonders what he would have made of electronic commerce.

One difficulty with the Ellulian approach, some argue, lies in its apparent determinism, and the relative lack of attention paid to the politics of resistance or what Giddens calls the dialectic of control.[22] I say 'apparent' determinism, though, because Ellul maintained throughout his work a strong sense of the ambiguity of technology. His is not, in my view, an essentialist account that can only find negative expressions of technology, although one might be forgiven for coming to this conclusion from some of his work.[23] It would also be somewhat surprising if someone celebrated for his underground resistance work during the Second World War were not also committed to questioning technology politically.

Political economy, the fourth strand in modern surveillance theory, places new technologies firmly in arenas of conflicting interests – thus, in principle at least, stressing more the contestability of surveillance. In practice, even some political economy approaches lay such heavy weight on the might of capitalist corporations and the global capitalist system that the impulse to extend surveillance appears almost as invincible as in some Ellulian accounts. Surveillance is here seen as a strategic means for the reproduction of one class and its interests over another. It is especially prevalent in capitalist productive relations, where in the early industrial period placing workers under one factory roof facilitated their central coordination and control by making them more visible to owners and managers.

Various writers, notably Harry Braverman,[24] undertook Marxian surveillance studies that were to stimulate a long-lasting debate on the nature of workplace power.[25] But by the 1970s and 1980s this was being successfully expanded to include the political economy of capitalism in its increasingly consumer phase. Frank Webster and Kevin Robins, for instance, analyse not only the surveillance aspects of Taylorism in workplaces, but also of social Taylorism or 'Sloanism' applied in consumer contexts, in the attempt to manage consumption through the collection and processing of data on consumer behaviour.[26] They see an electronic panopticon at work.

Another major study of the political economy of personal information is Gandy's *The Panoptic Sort*,[27] which draws extensively on Weberian approaches – the rationalization of marketing – and also uses Foucault's description of the panopticon as its leading metaphor and analytical tool. Gandy's approach is instructive. He sees consumer surveillance operating on panoptic principles, whereby personal data is used to sort populations into consuming types. Electronic technologies are harnessed to assign varying economic values to different groups, and thus to computerize the production of inequality. This 'discriminatory technology . . . discards at the same time as it skims off the high-quality targets of opportunity'.[28]

These four strands of surveillance theory make considerable strides in helping to explain why surveillance is so important to modernity. More particularly, they show how computerization magnifies certain surveillance functions as well as making possible their extension into other spheres. From the political imperatives of nation state power comes a reminder of the long term historical forces behind surveillance, although this perspective offers little that would prepare us for the growth of economic as well as military competition between states. The association of surveillance with bureaucracy also has deep roots in modernity, with the ongoing and relentless pursuit of rationalization. The quest of prediction and calculability redoubles with the onset of computerization. However, unless this perspective is linked with others it tends towards one-dimensionality, and to seeing technological development as an essentially rationalizing process.[29]

While determinism is even more likely to be linked with increased surveillance as a product of technologic, this third position nonetheless has some solid virtues. In particular, this strand stresses a cultural vision, the dream of perfect knowledge, to be realized by technological means, of which surveillance is a prime instance. Uncoupled from any other goals apart from the bureaucratic end of efficiency, it is easy to see how surveillance could be thought of as self-justifying as well as self-augmenting. The determined drive to perfect technologically-aided perception expresses a deep desire in contemporary culture. It has psychological and also religious dimensions, which is also part of the Ellulian argument.

It is almost uncanny to see how each new technology is never sufficient. As a colleague observed to me, commenting on closed-circuit television surveillance as an example: 'as soon as you have one camera, you want to see around the next corner . . . then you want to see in the dark as well, so you add infrared cameras. Then you want to see more detail so you add more powerful zoom lenses. And then you think, if only I could hear what they are saying as well, so you add powerful directional microphones to your cameras . . . .'[30] Ellul insists that this techno-cultural imperative has religious roots in a misplaced western faith in human capacities to solve social problems without reference to transcendent criteria. In the end, a candid acknowledgement of human finitude, frailty and dependence is the Ellulian antidote to such modernist hubris.

It comes as no surprise that political economy approaches often cast sceptical eyes on such ideas as technologic. They emphasize as ever the role of the state and the economy in shaping surveillance practices and processes. To my mind this complements rather than contradicts the technologic position. This final approach offers the timely reminder that any technological encounter – not least those involving surveillance – will display subject positions that are either dominant or subordinate. How far this perspective admits of bureaucratic imperatives or of the role of conscious agents in surveillance situations depends on which theorists are in question. Webster and Robins, and Gandy, mentioned above, allow for both in their work.

The modern strands of surveillance theory discussed here show how computerization enhances and extends familiar processes, often producing some fresh fears about centralized control, or the violability of personal life. But they often tend to view technology as a separate category from social life, that impinges upon that life, albeit in more invasive or even more carceral ways. One might be forgiven for asking if this kind of approach is adequate to the conditions that obtain at the start of the twenty-first century. Technology has become the very medium of everyday life – one has only to be intruded upon by cellphone conversations or observe bank machine transactions on any street corner to see this – such that an increasingly dominant proportion of social relations are in part constituted by technology. It is these kinds of insight that have spurred efforts to reconsider surveillance in terms of a superpanopticon and of simulation.

## Superpanopticon and hypersurveillance

It is ironic that Foucault, who had almost nothing to say about computers, should inspire some radically new approaches to digitized surveillance. Collectively, they might be thought of as postmodern perspectives. The source of the Foucaldian irony is not hard to trace, however. Foucault popularized the idea of the panoptic as the epitome of social control in modern times. What had once featured merely as an innovative and influential approach to prison architecture, produced by an eccentric social reformer, was reinvented by Foucault as a paradigmatic example of modern discipline.

Jeremy Bentham's late eighteenth-century design for a panopticon prison relied on an elaborate apparatus of blinds on the inspection tower windows to prevent inmates seeing their observer, back lighting to illuminate prisoners and a semi-circular arrangement of classified cells so that the category as well as any action of prisoners was immediately apparent. The idea was to automate the disciplinary system, to induce self-monitoring in prisoners, and to render real-life inspectors all but redundant. It has not escaped the attention of a number of commentators that electronic technologies permit the perfection of such a panopticon, but now through software architectures.

Although it was Foucault's insightful analyses that stimulated the association of the panopticon and electronic surveillance, it was, ironically, a fairly unFoucaldian version of the panopticon that first appeared.[31] The panopticon, it seemed, could be fitted into existing analyses of discipline and social control without the baggage of discourse. It was left to Mark Poster to pick up on the distinctively discursive elements of Foucault's analysis, which he does with his reminder that 'databases are configurations of language'.[32] Thus Poster deliberately deflects attention from what he argues are the action-orientated surveillance theories deriving from Marx and Weber. For Poster, the recognition that databases deal in symbols and representations opens them to poststructural analysis.[33] This undoubtedly places theory in a more postmodern frame.

Poster elaborates on discourse in order to make the connections with databases. Subjects, first, are configured as such, or are given cultural significance, through language. In modern contexts, where individual consciousness is privileged, this means that subjects tend to be fixed within binary opposites such as freedom/determinism. In everyday life, subjects are constantly reconstituted through interpellation or 'hailing'. Thus we unreflectively accept our designation in particular subject positions (student, employee, cabdriver, chairperson) as part of our daily interactions. Such interpellation – still at the level of language – is never complete or final. It is ever open to challenge, reconfiguration, resistance, even where identities appear to be fixed. The cultural construction of the subject by such means indicates how 'discourse was configured as a form of power and power was understood as operating in part through language'.[34]

As Poster observes, Foucault does not follow through with a theory of discursive power, so much as its demonstration through his famous histories of punishment and of sexuality. Discourse reveals its power by positioning 'the subject in relation to structures of domination in such a way that those structures may *then* act upon him or her'.[35] The panopticon's power does not reside simply in the (supposedly) ever-observant guard. Rather, it is manifest in the way that the whole discourse and practice of the system bears down, constituting the subject as criminal and normalizing him or her into rehabilitation, or as Bentham conceived it, moral reform.[36] For Poster, computer databases bring panoptic principles out of the jail and into mainstream society to operate as a 'superpanopticon', reconfiguring once more the constitution of the subject.[37]

The database extends writing, according to Poster, removing it further from any one 'author' than conventional, non-electronic writing does. The database also adds both a new mobility (it is transferable in space) and durability (it is preservable in time) to writing. The database 'text' is no one's and everyone's. And yet it is owned by some institution – a library, a corporation, a hospital – and thus amplifies that institution's power. People know this and from time to time admit their fears to a pollster or even refuse to divulge requested information – for instance, on a membership or warranty form. But at the same time, and apparently impervious to moments of resistance, power is extended effortlessly. This is in part because subjects constantly participate in their own surveillance by making cellphone calls, automated bank transactions, Internet bookings and so on. Thus, concludes Poster, 'Individuals are plugged into circuits of their own panoptic control, making a mockery of theories of social action, like Weber's, that privilege consciousness as the basis of self-interpretation, and liberals generally, who locate meaning in the intimate, subjective recesses behind the shield of the skin'.[38]

The personal database connects identifying symbols such as government social insurance numbers with discrete records of benefits claimed or tax paid. In the case of corporations, records of purchases and other transactions are made, such that a picture can be created of legal compliance or of buying habits. These, Poster suggests, count as instances of Foucault's 'grids of specification'. The subject is multiplied and decentred in the database, acted on by remote computers each time a record is automatically verified or checked against another, without ever referring to the individual concerned. The database as language performs certain actions. Computers become 'machines for producing retrievable identities'.[39] Electronic interpellation thus takes writing into another realm, hinting at how the subject is reconstituted. At the same time it reveals the potential for domination inherent in the databases as well as possibilities for its modification within the overall process.

The panopticon produces subjects with desires to improve their inner lives. In contrast the superpanopticon constitutes objects, individuals with dispersed identities, who may remain unaware of how those identities are construed by the computer. We are once again back with disappearing bodies. Modern surveillance has everything to do with individuation,[40] distinguishing carefully between one identifiable individual subject and the next. But postmodern surveillance takes this further, into the multiplication of identities, split off from and yet reconnectable with the individuals whose data constitutes them. The identities thus constituted are simulated as a variety of what Baudrillard calls 'hyperreality'. Individuals have new forms of presence. As Poster says, these are subject positions that define them for all those agencies and individuals who have access to the database.[41] But what are the origins and consequences of such simulation? For one answer to this we must turn to a second strand of theory.

William Bogard uses Baudrillard rather than Foucault as his theoretical springboard into the simulated world of surveillance. For Bogard, it is simulation that represents the crucial omission from contemporary modern accounts of surveillance. Again, electronic technologies are the key. Virtual replace actual processes and electronic signs and images of objects and events replace their real counterparts.[42] What began in military fields with war-gaming techniques or stealth weapons has spread via areas like ecological environment simulations, or corporate simulations of their markets, to surveillance. In contrast with Foucault, much of Baudrillard's work is precisely predicated on the development and proliferation of communication and information technologies.

For Baudrillard, simulation is the 'reproduction of the real' by means of codes and models, 'in the same way that computerized images are a function of their program'.[43] Simulation tries to achieve a reality effect while simultaneously concealing the absence of the real. The real becomes redundant as a referential ground for the image – hence, hyperreality. The hyperreal, then, is the code (the 'technologies of signalization') that precedes the 'real' and brings it into being. In Baudrillard's 'telematic societies' – information societies to others – simulation is the 'reigning scheme'.[44] This is how the code comes to prominence as the mode of domination and control.

In Baudrillard's scheme, images once represented the real, as, he suggests, in the Christian communion, where the bread is the 'body of Christ'. Then, false appearances developed, to be attacked by Karl Marx as the illusions and fetishes of a capitalist order. The information age ushers in a third stage, in which modern modes of representation break down, as the image is shown to conceal an absent presence – there is no real. Baudrillard presses on to consider a fourth moment, where social relations themselves are hyperrealized. This, he controversially claims, spells the 'end of the social', which is Bogard's entry point for considering surveillance.

In Bogard's account, 'hypersurveillant' control both intensifies surveillance and attempts to take it to its absolute limit. The speed of computing allows surveillance to overtake itself, as it were, and to operate in advance of itself. It turns into a technology of pre-exposure and pre-recording, prior to the occurrence of the behaviour or the event in real time. The Cromatica system that predicts suicide attempts on underground train stations provides a good example. [. . .] For Bogard, the panopticon is not only digitized, so that it can be understood as a form of discourse; it is seen thus as a strategy of exposure and recording, conveys it into a paradoxical realm where surveillance looks *on* the screen, rather than behind it. As in Poster's work, an impatience with modern accounts pervades this text. Bogard, too, aspires to go 'beyond Marx and Weber'.[45]

Speed is central. The idea behind surveillant simulation is to win the race to see first, to foresee. Paul Virilio dubs this principle 'dromology'.[46] It works as control by deflecting the attention to appearances, by generating uncertainty. Such appearances already occur in the physical panopticon and their intention is to create uncertainty.[47] But the panopticon generates uncertainty about what the observer might be able to see now, rather than about what might be 'seen' of what has not yet happened. The computer profile, which organizes multiple sources of information to scan for matching or exceptional cases, tries to second-guess behaviours. In what amounts to an 'informated form of stereotyping'[48] the profile is used as an advance notice of likely purchases – which in the case of electronic commerce will trigger advertising targeted at specific persons – or an advance warning of potential offences, in the case of police computer systems.

But, says Bogard, the informated stereotype is not merely a 'false image' used to justify power differences. It is more a self-fulfilling prophecy, as the reality comes to resemble the image. Verification may occur prior to identification, at least identification in the modern sense. With the right password, or code, life can continue as normal. Without it, the individual is served up as a suspect or as a marketing target. Is Bogard correct about this? I shall make further comments about his perspective below but at this point let us just note that it lacks empirical substance in an important respect. It is not necessarily wrong, but one area in which insufficient research has been done is on how 'realities come to resemble the image' in the surveillance context. A critical understanding of this process will make a considerable contribution to surveillance studies.[49]

Simulant surveillance technologies have some important features. They simulate factuality rather than documenting empirical events, thus reinforcing the uncertainty of subjects. They aim to deter and to prevent or to guide and enable certain behaviours. The more daily life is mediated by electronic technologies and the more the screen events substitute for experience, the less the working of these technologies is perceptible. For Foucault, discipline normalizes people to moral standards of behaviour or to institutional requirements. For Bogard, in 'telematic' societies, individuals are 'supernormalized' according to codes, managed as flows of data. Simulated surveillance may also be understood in relation to transparent surfaces, sterile zones, breaks and flows of images, and as technological imaginary.

Bogard comments on the paradox that whereas surveillance wishes to get beneath the surface, to see behind the world as it appears, simulation sees *across* the surface. What is visible is all that is visible. Perception itself becomes transparent, in this view, with the goal of eliminating the difference between the real and the illusion. Again, where modern surveillance aimed at creating clean, sterile environments of order, simulation aspires to take this further, towards perfect disinfection. Bogard connects this with biomedical surveillance, with its accompanying uncertainties about moments of death or the boundaries of the body.

Bogard also highlights the shift from surveillance to simulation by observing that the former is a means of recording, and, as such, it already shows signs of simulation. For in recording – an event, a word, a transaction – a copy has been made, and a break created in the flow, which in turn is the start of a fresh flow. Lastly, and this is the point towards which Bogard's other observations converge, simulation has to do with pure control, so much so that the 'imaginary annihilates the image'.[50] Simulation attempts to go beyond the limits of surveillance, to a virtual reality where the spaces and times to be controlled are manufactured ones. The environment can be perfectly controlled. Indeed, it no longer requires control, it *is* control.

The Bogardian perspective takes us unremittingly into the realm of the hyperreal. In doing so it tends to flatten the social world in ways that I try to avoid [. . .]. It is not that simulated surveillance does not occur on an increasing scale or that computer-generated identities based on data fragments do not actually circulate within surveillance databases with consequences for subjectivity and for social justice. The problem is rather that, in pursuing surveillance into the shadowy world of panoptic imagery, the real world of embodied persons itself appears to have dissolved. We are thus left with a vision that is at once playful and paranoid. It is also paralysed politically.

## New surveillance in theory

The two kinds of surveillance theory discussed here present what appear to be quite divergent accounts, especially if the exhortations are heeded to go 'beyond Marx and Weber'. At the same time, these theories have in common a desire to explain the electronic enhancement of surveillance since the late twentieth century. They also recognize that Foucault's studies, particularly those of the panopticon, are relevant to that explanation. In what follows, I argue that while going 'beyond' Marx, Weber and others may be required for an adequate theory of contemporary surveillance practices, 'going beyond' does not entail forsaking *in toto* the modes of analysis inspired by them. Indeed, important continuities exist between the different theoretical modes, and aspects of the newer theories can add nuance to the older, for their mutual benefit, and to the advantage of the quest for appropriate surveillance theory.

The classically orientated theories have in common a search for the social – and especially the institutional – roots of surveillance processes as they have developed, especially in the twentieth century. Thus military competition between nation states, the rationalization expressed in bureaucracy and the class imperatives of capitalism are viewed variously as the origins and the providers of the essential dynamics for modern surveillance. Each emphasizes aspects of surveillance that can be readily understood as magnifying the power of the institution employing the relevant practices to the relative disadvantage of individuals who are thus located, recorded, observed, monitored, classified and processed. Each also has excellent exemplars in discrete areas, such as in factory or office organization, urban planning or policing, and so on.

The shortcomings of the more conventional approaches, particularly when it comes to understanding the impact of new technologies on surveillance, may be summarized as follows. The strength of specific studies of institutional areas is a weakness when it comes to new technologies, which often have the effect of producing convergence.[51] Management functions of supervision and monitoring, for example, become blurred when electronic technologies are adopted.[52] Similarly, a focus on surveillance that seeks commonalities across institutional areas will note features such as the use of computer matching using different databases, which are found in areas such as marketing and policing. It is hard to imagine these two being uttered in the same breath in more conventional accounts.

This speaks to another concern. Technology often appears as an 'external' factor in earlier accounts rather than as a mode of mediating daily life. As such, technology may seem to exhibit some essential features – such as rationalizing, or producing efficiency – rather than ones that are flexible, malleable, constructed, contestable. Lastly, when it comes to the relevance of theory to policy, the laudable concern for disadvantaged individuals (understandable in terms of a classic society/individual dualism) sometimes means that the systematic disadvantaging of whole populations is missed (though this is not true of Marxian approaches, of course). Thus privacy appears as the complementary item – the policy antidote – in the surveillance/ privacy binary relation.

The newer theories commend themselves by focusing explicitly on the differences made by communication and information technologies. Poster's work attempts to recalibrate surveillance theory in terms of the language of computer databases and thus of discursive power. By showing what the database *does*, how its peculiar language *performs* certain functions, Poster indicates fresh avenues for surveillance inquiry, structured around the idea of the superpanopticon. How the data subject is positioned within the database's grid of specification reveals much about the domination involved as well, insists Poster, as how it might be countered. Similarly, Deleuze's isolation of the code, as discussed by Bogard, indicates further the means of power within surveillant simulation. Again, this sieve-like code is not fixed, but, as Christine Boyer says, transmutes, undulates and is constantly at work.[53] This is another insight into the specific differences made in surveillance by the use of computer-based technologies.

On their own, however, the newer theories also fail to satisfy completely. Poster's work, while highly suggestive, does not yet go far enough. While he acknowledges the interesting features of Marxian and Weberian theories, he does not return to them to say how they might still provide explanatory purchase on the problems of current surveillance. Rather, they are discarded as action-based theories, inappropriate to the world of database language and discourse. In addition, while Poster makes brief mention of 'biopower' – the concept at the heart of Foucault's *History of Sexuality* – and leans on it implicitly, he does not full incorporate it into his account of surveillance.

One could argue that Poster's superpanopticon actually depends upon biopower for its operation. For Foucault, biopower originated in the dusty-sounding statistical study of populations. But it 'made knowledge-power an agent of transformation of human life'.[54] Counting bodies, argues Ian Hacking, had the subversive effect of creating 'new categories into which people had to fall, and so to create and render rigid new conceptualizations of the human being'.[55] Translate this into computer language and its significance emerges. Note its massive expansion and automation in the contemporary surveillance and simulation of behaviours under the sign of mobility. Contrast this with the counting of relatively static bodies of earlier modernity and one can see that what began in the era of 'moral science' has precise ramifications for the codes that order social life today.

Bogard's work, on the other hand, goes too far. His extravagant prose, a trait not entirely absent from Baudrillard's output as well, serves to obscure rather than clarify. Thought important and insightful, his probing of paradox and ambiguity leaves the impression of a highly determined, inescapable web of electronic impulses, the essentialist core of which is simulation, spinning off unchecked through the post-social spheres. Seemingly aware of this, Bogard concludes with a note on 'cyborgian boredom' as a mode of resistance. This will hardly do. One doubts that electronic ennui will catch on quickly as an alternative to liberal solutions of data protection and privacy law.

It is unfortunate but unsurprising that Bogard falls prey to just the same mistakes as his mentor, Baudrillard. The metaphors that inform his work take off on their own and he seems to deny that they refer to any reality except their own.[56] Digital codes are all that is left. But even Baudrillard notes the way that in contemporary simulation 'digitality is its metaphysical principle . . . and DNA its prophet'. In the genetic code the 'genesis of simulacra' finds its archtype.[57] As we have seen, the computer-assisted coding and sorting of DNA has both its arcane aspects and its all-too-concrete effects on embodied persons and on particular social groups. It is easy to slip into surface preoccupations and self-referentiality. Simulacra do indeed challenge the 'real'. But an alternative response is to pursue a sociology that acknowledges the instability of categories with a view to participating in their value-based transformations.

[. . .]

## Returning the body

Any social theory worthy of the name will offer a mode of interpreting the processes that pattern today's world. In this case, the process in question is surveillance. We are right to expect theory to explain why some things happen in the way that they do in terms of both historical background and likely developments. Theory is constrained by empirical evidence, events and trends that can in some way be demonstrated. But theory is never produced by mere evidence. It is an argument, a process of rhetoric, that relies for its illuminatory power on metaphors and on commitments. These are the elements of theory that cannot be proved but cannot but be presupposed.

To understand surveillance today it is not enough to rely on classical sources of the sociological imagination. Marx, Weber, Simmel and others provide fascinating and essential insights but is it anachronistic to rummage in their theories for clues about emergent features of informational network societies. Equally, I have argued, some prominent social theories that take cognizance of the new technologies fail to do full justice to the problems raised by surveillance. In part, this is because they shelve the classical sociological heritage and its concerns with action, the material conditions of life, and the prospects for political engagement.

This is not just a plea for a patching together of theoretical pieces, although I do think that a disciplined eclecticism is a valid way forward. The pattern for the patchwork should be provided by a more coherent view of embodied persons, of the cultural obsession with omniperception, and of an ethic to guide the politics of surveillance. These elements are either underplayed or absent from the theoretical traditions discussed above.

First, embodied personhood should be kept central to surveillance (and to other theory because it both grounds explanation in everyday life and offers ways of bridging classical and contemporary theory. Bodies may disappear from social relationships in a media-wrapped world but they still need friendship, food and meaningful activities in mundane local life. The disembodied relations of surveillance data do not entirely lose contact with the embodied lives of the persons from whose behaviour or bodies those data are extracted. Under today's surveillance conditions the uneven distribution of life chances and opportunities is increasingly subject to automation and thus to virtual reinforcement. The processes depend, crucially, upon digital stereotyping of groups and individuals, using codes derived from computer grids of specification, at least some of which are then transposed back into the real world of everyday life.

Other aspects of the dispersal and multiplication of identities may both enable and constrain individuals in ways that are as yet inadequately understood. These processes are not innocent or autonomous. Surveillant simulations do not arise in a political-economic vacuum or operate merely according to some whimsical logic of arcade computer games. They are still driven by the dictates and the routines of the nation state, of large corporations and bureaucratic organizations, even as personal data flows less discriminately within and between these sectors. Embodied persons and distinct social groups are still privileged or disadvantaged, online or switched off, enabled or constrained in ways that relate to their electronic classification by surveillance.

Second, the cultural obsession with omniperception must be further explored if an adequate theory of surveillance is sought. The rise of risk management and the vastly enhanced technical capacities of new surveillance technologies do not themselves explain the compulsion to account for everything and to capture all within the range of vision. Ellul exposes the dangerous power of derailed knowledge, embodied in artefacts, technical expertise and processes, and he even anticipates aspects of surveillance in its electronically-enabled, simulated phase. Just such aspects Bogard finds in surveillant simulations; the 'dream of perfect knowledge' as it were, in computer enhanced form. What Ellul excoriates as idolatry, Bogard situates as social science fiction. It is, says Bogard, 'the fantastic dream of seeing everything capable of being seen, recording every fact capable of being recorded, and accomplishing these things, whenever and wherever possible, prior to the event itself'.[58]

How long can surveillance theory ignore the implications of this? It seems entirely appropriate to add to the surveillance impetuses of the nation state, capitalism and bureaucracy, the imperatives of an implicit cultural commitment to omniperception. It was already visible in Bentham's panoptic hubris and is now a persistent pulse that beats on through other social transformations and economic restructuring. To take it seriously adds both to the predictive power of theory – we may expect surveillance to expand according to its own technologic in addition to external demands made of it – and to its critical cutting edge. The driving desire to dragnet yet more detailed data is both as old and as ominous as the aspiration to be 'as God'.[59]

Third, theories and politics of surveillance should be yoked together. Today surveillance is a supercharged means of power in any and all societies dependent upon information infrastructures. It thus demands fresh political commitment to understand it and to challenge its negative aspects. What surveillance helps to produce is a form of social orchestration, where the scores are provided by those classically dominant formations, and where the melody is produced by musicians who participate by being aware of the score. The scores are computer coded and classifying, but they also allow for improvisations, so the music is less predictable than in 'classical' compositions.

The scores themselves may alter in some respects as characteristics of the musicians are fed into the loop, or indeed as musicians succeed in counterposing their rhythms and their tunes to the dominant ones. As synthesizers are brought in, so computing power extends the scope of the music, while at the same time setting new limits to it. This is not a static or rigid 'musical' production, but it does locate individuals. It also includes them or excludes them from full social and political participation by criteria that are not entirely of their choosing, criteria that do not transcend in any meaningful way the abstract and self-referring data embedded in the coded notation.

Political involvement is thus undertaken by those already implicated as participants in surveillance situations and processes. It calls, not for opposition to surveillance as such, but for a principled awareness of the tendencies of current practices and of their potential threats to social justice and personal dignity. [. . .] The ethics that pilot both theory and politics through the shoals of surveillance may again be appropriately based in embodied personhood.

Persons are intrinsically social and thus communication is vital. This has two implications. One, the notion of the face to face should be privileged in a communicative ethic. Voluntary self-disclosure in relations of trust may only be impugned reluctantly and with very good cause. Two, concern for the Other is a primal demand of humanness. When the society of strangers has been extended electronically to create categories of 'strangeness' in addition to those of classical racial or class stereotyping, that demand is accentuated, not abrogated. It also connects indissolubly the personal with the political.

[. . .]

## Notes

1   The themes of *Until the End of the World* are manifold and I only mention one of them in the text. In an illuminating commentary on this film, Norbert Grob makes the point that '. . . the more images dominate our experience the less autonomy people will have in their access to images'. See (1997) Life sneaks out of stories: *Until the End of the World*, in R. F. Cook and G. Gemünden (eds) *The Cinema of Wim Wenders: Image, Narrative, and the Postmodern Condition*. Detroit, MI: Wayne State University Press, p. 171.

2   See, for example, A. Giddens (1985) *The Nation-State and Violence*. Cambridge: Polity Press. C. Gill (1985) *Work, Employment, and the New Technology*. Cambridge: Polity Press. D. Lyon (1988) *The Information Society: Issues and Illusions*. Cambridge: Polity Press.

3   Giddens, ibid., p. 175. G. T. Marx (1988) *Police Surveillance in America*. Berkeley, CA: University of California Press, p. 206ff.

4   Leaving the more futurological accounts on one side, one might mention the work of M. Castells (1996) *The Rise of the Network Society* (vol. 1 of *The Information Age*). Oxford: Blackwell. K. Kumar (1995) *From Post-Industrial to Post-Modern Society*. Cambridge, MA: Blackwell. Or D. Lyon (1999) *Postmodernity*, 2nd edn. Buckingham: Open University Press.

5   M. Poster (1996) Databases as discourse, in D. Lyon and E. Zureik (eds) *Computers, Surveillance, and Privacy*. Minneapolis MN: University of Minnesota Press; also in Poster's (1997) *The Second Media Age*. Cambridge: Polity Press.

6   W. Bogard (1996) *The Simulation of Surveillance: Hypercontrol in Telematic Societies*. Cambridge: Cambridge University Press.

7   M. Foucault, in G. Burchell, C. Gordon and P. Miller (1991) *The Foucault Effect: Studies in Governmentality*. London: Harvester Wheatsheaf, cited in Poster (1996), op. cit., p. 180.

8   On the more conventional (and critical) side, the panopticon is utilized effectively by O. Gandy (1993) in his *The Panoptic Sort: A Political Economy of Personal Information*. Boulder, CO: Westview Press.

9   This view of surveillance owes much to the work of J. Rule. See Rule *et al.* (1983) Documentary identification and mass surveillance in the United States, *Social Problems*, 31 (2): 222–34.

10   No special transdisciplinary sub-field of surveillance studies exists as yet. One strong implication of this book's argument, however, is that the establishment of such a sub-field is highly desirable.

11   C. Dandeker (1990) *Surveillance, Power and Modernity*. Cambridge: Polity Press.

12   'Internal pacification' is the term used by Giddens (1985), op. cit.

13   F. Kafka (1937) *The Trial*. New York: Knopf.

14   J. Rule (1973) *Private Lives, Public Surveillance*. Harmondsworth: Allen Lane.

15   D. Burnham (1983) *The Rise of the Computer State*. New York: Random House.

16   The reasons for Ellul's apparent marginality, especially to English-speaking sociology, include what some saw as his cavalier approach to citation (he is clearly dependent on Weber, for instance, but this is seldom if ever mentioned by him); the fact that he wrote in French; and his, for many, eccentric insistence that *la technique* represents a deeply spiritual malaise in western culture. He had – and has – champions in North America, along with theorists such as Langdon Winner, who have

been at pains to dismantle what the latter sees as Ellul's determinism. See Winner (1977) *Autonomous Technology: Technics Out of Control as a Theme in Human Thought*. Cambridge, MA: MIT Press.

17   J. Ellul (1964) *The Technological Society*. New York: Vintage Books.

18   Marx, op. cit. R. Ericson and K. Haggerty (1997) *Policing the Risk Society*. Toronto: University of Toronto Press.

19   Winner, op. cit.

20   Gandy (1996), op. cit. in Lyon and Zureik, op. cit., p. 137.

21   See Ericson and Haggerty, op. cit.

22   Giddens, op. cit.

23   Contrast this with the work of A. Feenberg (1999) *Questioning Technology*. London: Routledge. He takes the view that Ellul, along with Heidegger, has essentialist views of technology. Ellul's (1980) *The Technological System* (New York: Continuum) for example, offers a seemingly pessimistic conclusion: 'The human being who uses technology today is by that very fact the human being who serves it' (p. 325). But Ellul chose to write about his political strategies in other books, such as his (1991) *Anarchy and Christianity*. Grand Rapids, MI: Eerdmans.

24   H. Braverman (1980) *Labour and Monopoly Capital*. New York: Monthly Review Press.

25   This is discussed, *inter alia*, in A. Francis (1984) *New Technology at Work*. New York: Oxford University Press. Also, in relation to surveillance studies particularly, in D. Lyon (1994) *The Electronic Eye: The Rise of Surveillance Society*. Cambridge: Polity Press.

26   F. Webster and K. Robins (1986) *Information Technology: A Luddite Analysis*. Newark, NJ: Ablex.

27   Gandy (1993), op. cit.

28   Gandy (1996) Coming to terms with the panoptic sort in Lyon and Zureik, op. cit., p. 152.

29   A useful critique of technological essentialism is A. Feenberg (1999) *Questioning Technology*. London: Routledge.

30   Personal email from Clive Norris, January 2000.

31   While Oscar Gandy, for example, made excellent use of the panoptic metaphor in *The Panoptic Sort*, his is not a discursive account. Sociologically, it is much more conventional, drawing especially on Marxian and Weberian categories.

32   Poster (1996), p. 176.

33   A similar point, that in the information age symbols become centrally important in social organization – and especially in social movements – is made by Alberto Melucci in his (1996) *Challenging Codes*. Cambridge and New York: Cambridge University Press. What Melucci takes from this, however, is, unlike Poster, the notion of the instability and contestability of symbolic communications.

34   Poster, op. cit., p. 180.

35   Ibid., p. 181.

36   See D. Lyon (1991) Bentham's panopticon: from moral architecture to electronic surveillance, *Queen's Quarterly* 98 (3).

37   A similar argument is made, earlier, by G. Deleuze (1992) Postscript on the societies of control, *October* 59 (Winter): 3–7.

38   Poster, op. cit., p. 184.

39   Ibid., p. 186.

40   This is discussed in N. Abercrombie *et al.* (1983) *Sovereign Individuals of Capitalism*. London: Allen and Unwin. And also in Lyon (1994), op. cit.

41   Poster, op. cit., p. 188.

42   Bogard, op. cit., p. 3. Bogard retains quotation marks around words like 'reality', believing as he does that such notions are destabilized by the processes he describes. I remove the marks as a means of indicating not that such realities have inflexible characteristics so much as that the category of the real nonetheless has some reliable

referents, even though they may not be understood by us. See the discussions of realism in, for example, T. May and M. Williams (eds) (1998) *Knowing the Social World*. Buckingham: Open University Press.

43   Bogard, op. cit., p. 10.

44   J. Baudrillard (1983) *Simulations*. New York: Semiotext(e), p. 83.

45   Bogard, op. cit., p. 18.

46   P. Virilio (1986) *Speed and Politics*. New York: Semiotext(e), p. 15. See also Bogard, ibid., p. 26.

47   See Lyon (1994), op. cit., p. 65.

48   Bogard, op. cit., p. 27.

49   The background to this issue is on the one hand, labelling theory, and on the other, Foucaldian notions of biopower (see below). To my mind, neither nominalism nor unqualified realism is theoretically adequate to the question. A good way forward may well lie in what Ian Hacking calls 'dynamic nominalism', which neither sinks into the absurdities of nominalism nor pretends that images and categories play no part in 'making up' people. See Hacking (1986) Making up people, in T. C. Heller, M. Sosna and D. E. Wellerby (eds) *Reconstructing Individualism: Autonomy, Individuality, and the Self in Western Thought*. Stanford, CA: Stanford University Press, p. 228.

50   Bogard, op. cit., p. 46.

51   Technological convergence, which produces convergent 'effects', is not innocent, of course. A political economy perspective rightly stresses the ways in which technological convergence is itself the product of a complex of decisions and social circumstances. See D. Winseck (1998) *Reconvergence: The Political Economy of Telecommunications in Canada*. Cresskill, NJ: Hampton Press. See also D. Lyon (1988) *The Information Society: Issues and Illusions*. Cambridge: Polity Press, ch. 2.

52   See Lyon (1994), op. cit., ch. 7.

53   C. Boyer (1996) *Cybercities: Visual Perception in an Age of Electronic Communication*. New York: Princeton Architectural Press, p. 18.

54   M. Foucault (1978) *The History of Sexuality*, vol. 1. New York: Random House, p. 138.

55   I. Hacking (1982) Biopower and the avalanche of printed numbers, *Humanities in Society* 5: 279–95.

56   J. Baudrillard (1988) argues that the referent has disappeared in *The Evil Demon of Images*. Sydney: Power Institute Publications (no. 3), p. 21.

57   J. Baudrillard (1983) *In the Shadow of the Silent Majorities . . . or The End of the Social and Other Essays*. New York: Semiotext(e), pp. 103–4.

58   Bogard, op. cit., pp. 4–5.

59   Genesis, 3: 4.

# PART SEVEN

# Democracy

## INTRODUCTION

■ Erkki Karvonen

THE CONCEPT DEMOCRACY COMES from the Greek words *demos* (the commons, the people) and *kratein* (to rule), which were combined in ancient Greece to mean 'government by the people'. The word politics is also connected etymologically with the ancient Greek city state, the *polis*: politics could be characterized as the art of managing common concerns so that the best possible community life might succeed. Every freeborn citizen had an equal right to participate in the people's assembly and discuss their joint aims and issues, such that, at the height of Greek democracy during the fifth and fourth centuries BC, public assembly was responsible for law-making as well as foreign, domestic, economic and defence policy. The setting where this political process occurred was the marketplace of the city (the *agora*), a *public sphere* in which each citizen could debate any issue affecting the city and be evaluated by peers on the merits of argument.

War between Sparta and Athens in 431–404 BC brought about the end of Athenian democracy. For a time some sort of democracy was exercised in the Roman republic, although the principle of equality of citizens was soon corrupted and the aristocracy took political power. Finally the emperor became the autocrat and conceptions of democracy disappeared. In medieval times democracy was quite unknown, since the feudal lords commanded almost absolute power. However, during the fifteenth century changes began to appear which were more propitious towards democracy's re-emergence. Cities, particularly in Italy and in the Netherlands, had by then become wealthy and had become, to some degree at least, independent of the local feudal authorities. In these circumstances democratic impulses were revived and, from the beginning of the eighteenth century especially, public discussion began to flourish.

This emergence of democracy in the modern world, and the conditions necessary for its success, are central concerns of Jürgen Habermas' (born 1929) *Strukturwandel der Öffentlichkeit* (1962), which was translated in 1989 into English as *The Structural Transformation of the Public Sphere*. The English translation 'public sphere' loses some meaning of the original term *Öffentlichkeit*, which comes etymologically from German word *offen* (open, transparent to the eyes [see Hölscher 1978]). The opposite of *öffentlich* or 'public' is that which is secret, private and intimate. The old feudal governance was not open, decisions being made in secret by the nobility. However, strengthening capitalist interests attacked feudal practices, demanding disclosure of decision-making and the extension of rights such as economic freedom, freedom of expression and freedom of religion.

England was a pioneer in the development of what Habermas calls the 'bourgeois public sphere', something forged from the demands of increasingly powerful industrial and business groups which rebelled against the restrictions of feudal practices. Historically the new *agoras*, places for public discussion, were coffee houses and salons. Indeed, London had an estimated 3,000 coffee houses by the first decade of the eighteenth century. Early British businessmen met in coffee houses to discuss matters of trade and the news, as well as issues concerning the state. That coffee houses were the preferred meeting place of these radicals was not accidental. The new bourgeoisie of merchants, traders and business men wished to distinguish themselves from the populace at large, who continued the medieval tradition of beer drinking, and, on the other hand, wished to set themselves apart from the nobility, who were then drinking sweet chocolate (cocoa). In contrast to these drinks, coffee was considered as a 'rational' beverage, hence eminently suitable for calculating businessmen (Schivelbusch 1992).

A central part of public discussion was the reading and commenting on of journals and newspapers. At the time of the bourgeois public sphere a new type of paper, the political press, emerged (Harrison 1974). Earlier papers were strictly censored and this was the case especially with the reporting of domestic issues, particularly any action of the Crown or governance practices. But from now on national political issues were the main target for the political press. This press was partial, provocative and its reporting was often biased. As such these papers stimulated lively discussions, though one may ask how objective was the information they presented.

Based on the historical development of the bourgeois public sphere, Habermas formed an ideal model of the public sphere. Three major features of this can be identified: universal access, rational debate and a disregard for rank. The Habermasian public sphere continues the Enlightenment idea of rational-critical discussion and public reasoning. Criticism is vital to this process, so that the proposals being put forward can be thoroughly tested. In the process of exchanging views on matters of importance to the common good, the public opinion (*Öffentliche Meinung*) can be formed, and this consensus of opinion should be the only legitimate source of law and governance (Calhoun 1992).

In his *Structural Transformation of the Public Sphere* Habermas develops an approach that is characteristic of Frankfurt School thinkers, namely 'immanent critique'. This means that the reality of bourgeois democracy is compared to the ideals it is said to represent. Habermas' results of this comparison were negative: a debating and reasoning public has been transformed to a merely consuming audience. There has been a process of 'refeudalization' of the public sphere. It means that corporations, political parties, experts and civil servants make decisions on behalf of the citizens and that secrecy, rather than openness, becomes a main principle. Public opinion is not formed by a reasoning public, but is now a result of skilful persuasion and 'public relations' work. Democracy is carried out in a most rudimentary form: people do little more than register a vote periodically and all too many do not even bother to do this. In this context Habermas emphasizes that a person's opinion, recorded and duly tabulated in a public opinion poll, does not constitute the public sphere because it does not include a process of opinion formation in which debate and discussion are prioritized.

It is widely agreed that western democracies have problems in activating people to discuss, debate and even engage with their common business. Internet enthusiasts believe that communication networks like the internet will help to revitalize democracy. The internet will contribute to, or even be primarily responsible for, a new era of participatory democracy and a re-energizing of the public sphere. A leading exponent of this notion is Howard Rheingold, whose book *The Virtual Community* was published in 1993. Rheingold and others have promoted the utopian vision of the electronic agora, an 'Athens without slaves'. Building on the Habermasian concept of the public sphere, Rheingold believes that technology, 'if properly understood and defended by enough citizens, does have democratising potential in the way that alphabets and printing presses had democratising potential' (Rheingold 1993, p. 279).

Habermas' theory has been found to contain a number of blind spots. For instance, one problem with 'government by the people' is the question, just who are to be counted as 'people'? In ancient Greece women, foreigners and slaves had no rights at all, and this must cast doubt on its value as a model of democracy for today. Similarly, access to the bourgeois public sphere was limited to wealthy, educated men (Hohendahl 1979). A burning issue is whether the internet can overcome these limitations (while yet enriching democracy in ways envisioned by Habermas' public sphere conception [Blumler and Coleman 2001]). Furthermore, the very categorization between public and intimate spheres is problematic, for it makes treatment of women and children a private and secret matter. Feminist thinkers criticize this and emphasize that the 'personal is political', i.e. the subordination of women has to be discussed publicly and only in this way can the emancipation of women progress (Meehan 1995).

**Jürgen Habermas'** text 'The Public Sphere' (Chapter 23) was originally published as an encyclopaedia article and it summarizes the main ideas of *The Structural Transformation of the Public Sphere*. Habermas, who is now an emeritus professor at the University of Frankfurt, where he has spent most of his career, belongs to the younger generation of the influential 'Frankfurt School' of 'Critical

Theory', and he consciously follows in the tradition of founders such as Theodor Adorno and Max Horkheimer. Throughout his career Habermas has been interested in the theory of the 'ideal speech situation' and *diskursethik*, the rules of fair game in discussion. These rules may also be useful in conducting newsgroup discussions on the net.

**Nicholas Garnham** (Chapter 24) focuses upon broadcasting and argues that the public service model may be seen as an embodiment of the principles of the public sphere. In his influential article, which was crucial in making Habermas' ideas relevant to information and communications matters, Garnham clarifies the strengths and weaknesses of the concept 'public sphere' and insists that public service broadcasting, represented for example by the BBC, shares these strengths and weaknesses. The concept of public sphere makes it possible to defend public service broadcasting, suggests Garnham, as an independent democratic forum, distinct from economic and state control.

**John Keane** (Chapter 25) takes issue with Garnham. In his view the conventional ideal of a unified public sphere, and its corresponding presumption that a general 'public good' is achievable, is nowadays outdated (Keane 1991, 1998). Keane argues that frameworks of communication are in a state of upheaval and that the old hegemony of state-structured and territorially bound public life mediated by traditional media is being rapidly eroded. In its place are developing a multiplicity of networked spaces of communication which are not tied straight forwardly to territory. Accordingly, the conventional ideal of a public sphere is now obsolete, and in its place a complex mosaic of differently sized, overlapping and interconnected public spheres is developed. Keane proposes that we should distinguish public spheres of three sizes: *micro-public spheres* (local scale), *meso-public spheres* (national scale) and *macro-public spheres* (global scale).

**Zizi Papacharissi** (Chapter 26) suggests that, while the internet holds the promise of reviving the public sphere (this time in the form of a 'virtual sphere'), it also has several aspects that might curtail its democratic potential. Papacharissi reviews empirical studies to achieve a realistic conception of the democratic effects of the internet. Some scholars highlight the fact that speedy and cheap access to information provided on the internet promotes citizen activism. Papacharissi, however, observes that access to on-line information is by no means universal and that such information access inequality compromises the representativeness of the 'virtual sphere'. Moreover, while the technology can facilitate participation, it does not guarantee it. The internet is said to have the ability to connect people from diverse backgrounds and to provide a forum for political discussion. But Papacharissi remarks that, on the contrary, fragmentation into smaller and smaller discussion groups appears to be the actual trend. Further, she contends that connection via the internet does not necessarily foster rational discourse, adding that it may also give rise to *flaming* and unresolved conflicts. The internet and related technologies have created new possibilities for conversation – how these potentials are actualized is not up to the technology itself, but to human decision and commitment.

# REFERENCES

Blumler, Jay and Coleman, Stephen (2001) *Realising Democracy Online: A Civic Commons in Cyberspace*. IPPR/Citizens Online Research Publication no. 2, March.

Calhoun, Craig (1992) 'Introduction', in *Habermas and the Public Sphere*. Cambridge, MA: MIT Press.

Harrison, S. (1974) *Poor Men's Guardians: A Record of the Struggles for a Democratic Newspaper Press, 1863–1973*. London: Lawrence and Wishart.

Hohendahl, Peter (1979) 'Critical Theory, Public Sphere and Culture: Jürgen Habermas and his Critics', *New German Critique* 16: 89–118.

Hölscher, Lucian (1978) 'Öffentlichkeit', in Otto Brunner, Werner Conze and Reinhart Koselleck (eds) *Geschichtliche Grundbegriffe: Historisches Lexikon zur politisch-sozialen Sprache in Deutschland*. Stuttgart: Klett.

Keane, John (1991) *The Media and Democracy*. Cambridge: Polity Press.

Keane, John (1998) *Civil Society: Old Images, New Visions*. Cambridge: Polity Press.

Meehan, J. (ed.) (1995) *Feminists Read Habermas*. London: Routledge.

Rheingold, Howard (1993) *The Virtual Community: Homesteading on the Electronic Frontier*. New York: Harper Perennial. Available on-line at: http://www.rheingold.com/vc/book/index.html.

Schivelbusch, Wolfgang (1992) *Tastes of Paradise: A Social History of Spices, Stimulants, and Intoxicants*. New York: Vintage.

# Chapter 23

# Jürgen Habermas

## THE PUBLIC SPHERE

From *New German Critique*, 3 (Fall) (1974).

### 1. The concept

**B**Y 'THE PUBLIC SPHERE' WE MEAN first of all a realm of our social life in which something approaching public opinion can he formed. Access is guaranteed to all citizens. A portion of the public sphere comes into being in every conversation in which private individuals assemble to form a public body.[1] They then behave neither like business or professional people transacting private affairs, nor like members of a constitutional order subject to the legal constraints of a state bureaucracy. Citizens behave as a public body when they confer in an unrestricted fashion – that is, with the guarantee of freedom of assembly and association and the freedom to express and publish their opinions – about matters of general interest. In a large public body this kind of communication requires specific means for transmitting information and influencing those who receive it. Today newspapers and magazines, radio and television are the media of the public sphere. We speak of the political public sphere in contrast, for instance, to the literary one, when public discussion deals with objects connected to the activity of the state. Although state authority is so to speak the executor of the political public sphere, it is not a part of it.[2] To be sure, state authority is usually considered 'public' authority, but it derives its task of caring for the well-being of all citizens primarily from this aspect of the public sphere. Only when the exercise of political control is effectively subordinated to the democratic demand that information be accessible to the public, does the political public sphere win an institutionalized influence over the government through the instrument of law-making bodies. The expression 'public opinion' refers to the tasks of criticism and control which a public body of citizens informally – and, in periodic elections, formally as well – practices *vis-à-vis* the ruling structure organized in the form of a state. Regulations demanding that certain proceedings be public (*Publizitätsvorschriften*), for example those providing for open court hearings, are also related to this function of public opinion. The public sphere as a sphere which mediates between society and state, in which the public organizes itself as the bearer of public opinion, accords with the principle of the public sphere[3] – that principle of public information which once had to be fought for against the arcane policies of monarchies and which since that time has made possible the democratic control of state activities.

It is no coincidence that these concepts of the public sphere and public opinion arose for the first time only in the eighteenth century. They acquire their specific meaning from a concrete historical situation. It was at that time that the distinction of 'opinion' from 'opinion publique' and 'public opinion' came about. Though mere opinions (cultural assumptions, normative attitudes, collective prejudices and values) seem to persist unchanged in their natural form as a kind of sediment of history, public opinion can by definition only come into existence when a reasoning public is presupposed. Public discussions about the exercise of political power which are both critical in intent and institutionally guaranteed have not always existed – they grew out of a specific phase of bourgeois society and could enter into the order of the bourgeois constitutional state only as a result of a particular constellation of interests.

## 2. History

There is no indication European society of the high middle ages possessed a public sphere as a unique realm distinct from the private sphere. Nevertheless, it was not coincidental that during that period symbols of sovereignty, for instance the princely seal, were deemed 'public.' At that time there existed a public representation of power. The status of the feudal lord, at whatever level of the feudal pyramid, was oblivious to the categories 'public' and 'private,' but the holder of the position represented it publicly: he showed himself, presented himself as the embodiment of an ever present 'higher' power. The concept of this representation has been maintained up to the most recent constitutional history. Regardless of the degree to which it has loosed itself from the old base, the authority of political power today still demands a representation at the highest level by ahead of state. Such elements, however, derive from a pre-bourgeois social structure. Representation in the sense of a bourgeois public sphere,[4] for instance the representation of the nation or of particular mandates, has nothing to do with the medieval representative public sphere – a public sphere directly linked to the concrete existence of a ruler. As long as the prince and the estates of the realm still 'are' the land, instead of merely functioning as deputies for it, they are able to 're-present'; they represent their power 'before' the people, instead of for the people.

The feudal authorities (church, princes and nobility), to which the representative public sphere was first linked, disintegrated during a long process of polarization. By the end of the eighteenth century they had broken apart into private elements on the one hand, and into public on the other. The position of the church changed with the reformation: the link to divine authority which the church represented, that is, religion, became a private matter. So-called religious freedom came to insure what was historically the first area of private autonomy. The church itself continued its existence as one public and legal body among others. The corresponding polarization within princely authority was visibly manifested in the separation of the public budget from the private household expenses of a ruler. The institutions of public authority, along with the bureaucracy and the military, and in part also with the legal institutions, asserted their independence from the privatized sphere of the princely court. Finally, the feudal estates were transformed as well: the nobility became the organs of public authority, parliament and the legal institutions; while those occupied in trades and professions, insofar as they had already established urban corporations and territorial organizations, developed into a sphere of bourgeois society which would stand apart from the state as a genuine area of private autonomy.

The representative public sphere yielded to that new sphere of 'public authority' which came into being with national and territorial states. Continuous state activity (permanent administration, standing army) now corresponded to the permanence of the relationships which with the stock exchange and the press had developed within the exchange of commodities and information. Public authority consolidated into a concrete opposition for those who were merely subject to it and who at first found only a negative definition of themselves within it. These were the 'private individuals' who were excluded from public authority because they held no office. 'Public' no longer referred to the 'representative' court of a prince endowed with authority, but rather to an institution regulated according to competence, to an apparatus endowed with a monopoly on the legal exertion of authority. Private individuals subsumed in the state at whom public authority was directed now made up the public body.

Society, now a private realm occupying a position in opposition to the state, stood on the one hand as if in clear contrast to the state. On the other hand, that society had a concern of public interest to the degree that the reproduction of life in the wake of the developing market economy had grown beyond the bounds of private domestic authority. *The bourgeois public sphere* could be understood as the sphere of private individuals assembled into a public body, which almost immediately laid claim to the officially regulated 'intellectual newspapers' for use against the public authority itself. In those newspapers, and in moralistic and critical journals, they debated that public authority on the general rules of social intercourse in their fundamentally privatized yet publically relevant sphere of labor and commodity exchange.

## 3. The liberal model of the public sphere

The medium of this debate – public discussion – was unique and without historical precedent. Hitherto the estates had negotiated agreements with their princes, settling their claims to power from case to case. This development took a different course in England, where the parliament limited royal power, than it did on the continent, where the monarchies mediatized the estates. The third estate then broke with this form of power arrangement since it could no longer establish itself as a ruling group. A division of power by means of the delineation of the rights of the nobility was no longer possible within an exchange economy – private authority over capitalist property is, after all, unpolitical. Bourgeois individuals are private individuals. As such, they do not 'rule.' Their claims to power *vis-à-vis* public authority were thus directed not against the concentration of power, which was to be 'shared.' Instead, their ideas infiltrated the very principle on which the existing power is based. To the principle of the existing power, the bourgeois public opposed the principle of supervision – that very principle which demands that proceedings be made public (*Publizität*). The principle of supervision is thus a means of transforming the nature of power, not merely one basis of legitimation exchanged for another.

In the first modern constitutions the catalogues of fundamental rights were a perfect image of the liberal model of the public sphere: they guaranteed the society as a sphere of private autonomy and the restriction of public authority to a few functions. Between these two spheres, the constitutions further insured the existence of a realm of private individuals assembled into a public body who as citizens transmit the needs of bourgeois society to the state, in order, ideally, to transform political into 'rational' authority within the medium of this public sphere. The general interest, which was the measure of such a rationality, was then guaranteed, according to the presuppositions of a society of free commodity exchange, when the activities of private individuals in the marketplace were free from social compulsion and from political pressure in the public sphere.

At the same time, daily political newspapers assumed an important role. In the second half of the eighteenth century literary journalism created serious competition for the earlier news sheets which were mere compilations of notices. Karl Bücher characterized this great development as follows: 'Newspapers changed from mere institutions for the publication of news into bearers and leaders of public opinion – weapons of party politics. This transformed the newspaper business. A new element emerged between the gathering and the publication of news: the editorial staff. But for the newspaper publisher it meant that he changed from a vendor of recent news to a dealer in public opinion.' The publishers insured the newspapers a commercial basis, yet without commercializing them as such. The press remained an institution of the public itself, effective in the manner of a mediator and intensifier of public discussion, no longer a mere organ for the spreading of news but not yet the medium of a consumer culture.

This type of journalism can he observed above all during periods of revolution when newspapers of the smallest political groups and organizations spring up, for instance in Paris in 1789. Even in the Paris of 1848 every half-way eminent politician organized his club, every other his journal: 450 clubs and over 200 journals were established there between February and May alone. Until the permanent legalization of a politically functional public sphere, the appearance of a political newspaper meant joining the struggle for freedom and public opinion, and thus for the public sphere as a principle. Only with the establishment of the bourgeois constitutional state was the intellectual press relieved of the pressure of its convictions. Since then it has been able to abandon its polemical position and take advantage of the earning possibilities of a commercial undertaking. In England, France and the

United States the transformation from a journalism of conviction to one of commerce began in the 1830s at approximately the same time. In the transition from the literary journalism of private individuals to the public services of the mass media the public sphere was transformed by the influx of private interests, which received special prominence in the mass media.

## 4. The public sphere in the social welfare state mass democracy

Although the liberal model of the public sphere is still instructive today with respect to the normative claim that information be accessible to the public,[5] it cannot be applied to the actual conditions of an industrially advanced mass democracy organized in the form of the social welfare state. In part the liberal model had always included ideological components, but it is also in part true that the social preconditions, to which the ideological elements could at one time at least be linked, had been fundamentally transformed. The very forms in which the public sphere manifested itself, to which supporters of the liberal model could appeal for evidence, began to change with the Chartist movement in England and the February revolution in France. Because of the diffusion of press and propaganda, the public body expanded beyond the bounds of the bourgeoisie. The public body lost not only its social exclusivity; it lost in addition the coherence created by bourgeois social institutions and a relatively high standard of education. Conflicts hitherto restricted to the private sphere now intrude into the public sphere. Group needs which can expect no satisfaction from a self-regulating market now tend towards a regulation by the state. The public sphere, which must now mediate these demands, becomes a field for the competition of interests, competitions which assume the form of violent conflict. Laws which obviously have come about under the 'pressure of the street' can scarcely still be understood as arising from the consensus of private individuals engaged in public discussion. They correspond in a more or less unconcealed manner to the compromise of conflicting private interest. Social organizations which deal with the state act in the political public sphere, whether through the agency of political parties or directly in connection with the public administration. With the interweaving of the public and private realm, not only do the political authorities assume certain functions in the sphere of commodity exchange and social labor, but conversely social powers now assume political functions. This leads to a kind of 'refeudalization' of the public sphere. Large organizations strive for political compromises with the state and with each other, excluding the public sphere whenever possible. But at the same time the large organizations must assure themselves of at least plebiscitary support from the mass of the population through an apparent display of openness (demonstrative *Publizität*).[6]

The political public sphere of the social welfare state is characterized by a peculiar weakening of in critical functions. At one time the process of making proceedings public (*Publizität*) was intended to subject persons or affairs to public reason, and to make political decisions subject to appeal before the court of public opinion. But often enough today the process of making public simply serves the arcane policies of special interests; in the form of 'publicity' it wins public prestige for people or affairs, thus making them worthy of acclamation in a climate of non-public opinion. The very words 'public relations work' (*Oeffentlichkeitsarbeit*) betray the fact that a public sphere must first be arduously constructed case by case, a public sphere which earlier grew out of the social structure. Even the central relationship of the public, the parties and the parliament is affected by this change in function.

Yet this trend towards the weakening of the public sphere as a principle is opposed by the extension of fundamental rights in the social welfare state. The demand that information be accessible to the public is extended from organs of the state to all organizations dealing with the state. To the degree that this is realized, a public body of organized private individuals would take the place of the now-defunct public body of private individuals who relate individually to each other. Only these organized individuals could participate effectively in the process of public communication; only they could use the channels of the public sphere which exist within parties and associations and the process of making proceedings public (*Publizität*) which was established to facilitate the dealings of organizations with the state. Political compromises would have to be legitimized through this process of public communication. The idea of the public sphere, preserved in the social welfare state mass democracy, an idea which calls for a rationalization of power through the medium of public discussion among private individuals, threatens to disintegrate with the structural transformation of the public sphere itself. It could only be realized today, on an altered basis, as a rational reorganization of social and political power under the mutual control of rival organizations committed to the public sphere in their internal structure as well as in their relations with the state and each other.

[. . .]

## Notes

1    Habermas' concept of the public sphere is not to be equated with that of 'the public,' i.e. of the individuals who assemble. His concept is directed instead at the institution, which to be sure only assumes concrete form through the participation of people. It cannot, however, be characterized simply as a crowd. (This and the following notes by Peter Hohendahl.)

2    The state and the public sphere do not overlap, as one might suppose from casual language use. Rather they confront one another as opponents. Habermas designates that sphere as public which antiquity understood to be private, i.e. the sphere of non-governmental opinion making.

3    The principle of the public sphere could still be distinguished from an institution which is demonstrable in social history. Habermas thus would mean a model of norms and modes of behavior by means of which the very functioning of public opinion can be guaranteed for the first time. These norms and modes of behavior include: a) general accessibility, b) elimination of all privileges and c) discovery of general norms and rational legitimations.

4    The expression 'represent' is used in a very specific sense in the following section, namely to 'present oneself.' The important thing to understand is that the medieval public sphere, if it even deserves this designation, is tied to the *personal*. The feudal lord and estates create the public sphere by means of their very presence.

5    Here it should be understood that Habermas considers the principle behind the bour-
     geois public sphere as indispensable, but not its historical form.
6    One must distinguish between Habermas' concept of 'making proceedings public'
     (*Publizität*) and the 'public sphere' (*Oeffentlichkeit*). The term *Publizität* describes the
     degree of public effect generated by a public act. Thus a situation can arise in which
     the form of public opinion making is maintained, while the substance of the public
     sphere has long ago been undermined.

# Chapter 24

# Nicholas Garnham

## THE MEDIA AND THE
## PUBLIC SPHERE

From *Capitalism and Communication*, London: Sage (1990), pp. 104–14.

I T I S A C O M M O N P L A C E T O A S S E R T that public communication lies at the heart of the democratic process; that citizens require, if their equal access to the vote is to have any substantive meaning, equal access also to sources of information and equal opportunities to participate in the debates from which political decisions rightly flow. I want to argue that it follows that changes in media structure and media policy, whether these stem from economic developments or from public intervention, are properly political questions of as much importance as the question of whether or not to introduce proportional representation, of relations between local and national government, of subsidies to political parties; that the policy of western European governments towards cable TV and satellite broadcasting is as important as their attitude towards the development of a United Europe; that the FCC's policy towards broadcast regulation is as important as the question of States' rights and that politicians, political scientists and citizens concerned with the health and future of democracy neglect these issues at their peril.

## II

However, political theory has largely neglected the implications of such a position and, in particular, has neglected the problem of how, materially, the institutions and processes of public communication are sustained. It has ignored the specific ways in which a given social formation may provide those resources.

I argue elsewhere that our inherited structures of public communication, those institutions within which we construct, distribute and consume symbolic forms, are undergoing a profound change. This change is characterized by a reinforcement of the market and the progressive destruction of public service as the preferred mode for the allocation of cultural resources; by a focus upon the TV set as the locus for an increasingly privatized, domestic mode of consumption; by the creation of a two-tier market divided between the information rich, provided with high-cost specialized information and cultural services, and the information poor, provided with increasingly homogenized entertainment services on a mass scale; lastly, by a shift from largely national to largely international markets in the informational and cultural spheres. Symptoms of this shift are the expansion of new TV delivery services such as videocassette, cable and direct broadcasting satellite under market control and on an international basis; the progressive deregulation and privatization of national telecommunication monopolies; the shift of Reuters from a general news agency to being largely a provider of specialized commercial information services; the increased penetration of sponsorship into the financing of leisure and culture; the move, under the pressure of public spending cuts, of educational and research institutes (such as universities) towards the private sector; proposals to make profitability the criterion for the provision of public information through such bodies as the Stationery Office, the Ordnance Survey and the US Government Printing Office; the shift in the library service (in the US at least) away from the principle of free and open access to public libraries towards access to proprietary databases on a payment-by-use basis. All these are examples of a trend to what has been dubbed, usually by those in favour of these developments, the Information Society or Information Economy. This trend represents an unholy alliance between western governments desperate for growth and in deadly competition with one another for that growth, and multinational corporations in search of new world markets in electronic technology and information goods and services. The result of this trend will be to shift the balance in the cultural sector between the market and public service decisively in favour of the market, and to shift the dominant definition of public information from that of a public good to that of a privately appropriate commodity.

What are the implications of these developments if we accept the argument that channels and processes of public communication are integral to the democratic process?

## III

The debate about the political function and effect of modes of public communication has traditionally been carried on within the terms of the dichotomy between Hegelian State and civil society. The dominant theory within that debate has been the liberal theory of the free press, which has either assumed that the market will provide appropriate institutions and processes of public communication to support a democratic policy or, in its stronger form, argues that only the market can ensure the necessary freedom from State control and coercion. The critique of this position has been able to collect impressive evidence of the way in which market forces produce results, in terms of oligopoly control and depoliticization of content, that are far from the liberal ideal of a free market-place of ideas. But the strength of the hold that liberal theory still exercises can be judged by the inadequacy of proposals for press reform generated by the Left and the weakness with which such proposals have been pursued. For the Left itself remains trapped within a free press model inherited from the nineteenth century. The hold of this model is also illustrated by the way in which no equally legitimate theory has been developed to handle the dominant form of public communication, broadcasting. The public service, State-regulated model, whether publicly or privately funded, has always been seen not as a positive good but as an unfortunate necessity imposed by the technical limitations of frequency-scarcity. Those on the Left who are opposed to market forces in the press nonetheless have given no more than mealy-mouthed support to public service broadcasting. They have concentrated their critique on the question of the coercive or hegemonic nature of State power. Seeing the public service form as either a smokescreen for such power or as occupied from within by commercial forces, they have concentrated on criticizing the inadequacy and repressive nature of the rules of balance and objectivity within which public service broadcasting is forced to operate. The Left has, therefore, tended to fall back either on idealist formulations of free communications given no organizational substance or material support, or on a technological utopianism which sees the expansion of channels of communication as inherently desirable because pluralistic. Both positions are linked to some version, both political and artistic, of free expression: thus the long debate and campaigns around Channel 4, the touching faith in cable access, Left support for 'free' or 'community' radio and so forth. Alternatively the problem has simply been postponed until after the take-over of State power.

In my view the implications of current developments are better understood, and an escape from the bind of the State/market dichotomy as well as from the hold of free press theory and the necessary accompanying re-evaluation of public service is better served, by looking at the problem from the perspective of the theory of the public sphere.

## IV

The theory of the public sphere, as articulated in particular by Habermas, argues that, just as the participatory democracy of the Athenian agora depended upon the material base of slavery, so it was the development of competitive market capitalism that provided the conditions in eighteenth-century Britain for the development of both the theory and practice of liberal democracy. It did so by making available to a new political class, the bourgeoisie, both the time and material resources to create a network of institutions within civil society such as newspapers, learned and debating societies, publishing enterprises, libraries, universities and polytechnics and museums, within which a new political force, public opinion, could come into existence.

This public sphere possessed the following key characteristics. It was protected from the power of both Church and State by its access to the sustaining resources of a wide range of private individuals with an alternative source of economic power. It was in principle open to all in the same way that access to the market was open to all, because the cost of entry for each individual was dramatically lowered by the growth in scale of the market. The public sphere thus took on the universalistic aspects of the Hegelian State, membership of the public sphere being coterminous with citizenship. All participants within the public sphere were on terms of equal power because costs of participation were widely and evenly spread and because social wealth within the bourgeoisie was evenly distributed. It was distinct from the private interests that governed civil society on the other hand because, in the Enlightenment tradition, it obeyed the rules of rational discourse, political views and decisions being open not to the play of power but to that of argument based upon evidence, and because its concern was not private interest but the public good. It thus also took over the rationalist aspects of the Hegelian State.

Habermas went on to argue that the public sphere – this space for a rational and universalistic politics distinct from both the economy and the State – was destroyed by the very forces that had brought it into existence. The development of the capitalist economy in the direction of monopoly capitalism led to an uneven distribution of wealth, to rising entry costs to the public sphere and thus to unequal access to and control over that sphere. In particular the rise of advertising and public relations has embodied these trends since they represent direct control by private or State interests of the flow of public information in the interest, not of rational discourse, but of manipulation. At the same time these developments in the economy led to related development by the State, which itself became an active and major participant in the economy, thus coming to share the private interests there pursued. At the same time the State was called in, by those class forces which wished to defend and expand the public sphere against the encroaching power of private capital, itself to provide material support, for instance through the provision of public education, public libraries, systems of public cultural subsidy and so forth. In addition the growth of the State's role as coordinator and infrastructural provider for monopoly capitalism led to the massive development of State power as an independently administrative and bureaucratic interest, distinct from the rationalist determination of social ends and of the means to those ends in that political realm guaranteed by the existence of the public sphere. Thus the space between civil society and the State which had been opened up by the creation of the public sphere was squeezed shut between these two increasingly collaborative behemoths. In Habermas's words:

> The liberal model of the public sphere . . . cannot be applied to the actual conditions of an industrially advanced mass democracy organized in the form of the welfare state. In part the liberal model had always included ideological components, but it is also in part true that the social pre-conditions, to which the ideological elements could at one time at least be linked, had been fundamentally transformed.
>
> (Habermas 1979)

Habermas wishes to distinguish between the set of principles upon which the bourgeois sphere was based and which, in the fight against feudalism, it brought into existence on the one hand, and the set of institutions which embodied those principles on the other. For Habermas, while the forms in which they are embodied will vary, the principles are the indispensable basis of a free society. These principles are: general accessibility, especially to information, the elimination of privilege, and the search for general norms and their rational legitimation.

The set of concrete institutions within which public opinion is formed, which include the media of public communication, elections, publicly accessible courts and so on, are distinguished from the State, although the legitimation of the democratic State lies in its role of guarantor of the public sphere through law.

Public opinion, in turn, is to be distinguished from *mere* opinion as presupposing the existence of a reasoning public.

The centrality of these principles for Habermas derives from his more general concern with 'undistorted communication'. Pursuing the tradition of critical theory Habermas has sought concrete grounds for the validation of critical social judgement and for the claims to human emancipation. He has attempted to ground truth claims in the social sciences upon what he has called the Ideal Speech Situation. He argues that human interaction, the field of meanings and values, presupposes language and exists in language. He goes on to argue that we can therefore discover within the structure of speech itself the essential grounding presuppositions of all human interaction and thus of all social organization. He argues that every time we speak we are making four validity claims, to comprehensibility, truth, appropriateness and sincerity, which in their turn imply the possibility of justifying those claims. Thus claim to truth implies a social context within which factual claims about external nature can be validated by evidence and logical argument, while claims to appropriateness, that is, to the social right to make the statement, imply a social context in which social norms can be rationally debated and consensual agreement arrived at. In actual societies characterized by differential power relations and resource distribution such conditions do not hold, and we are thus in the presence of 'distorted communication'. But for Habermas the essential human attribute of speech provides the ground for an ideal society against which existing societies can be judged and found wanting and to which we can aspire (Held 1980; Habermas 1982).

Thus the concept of the public sphere and the principles it embodies represent an Ideal Type against which we can judge existing social arrangements, and which we can attempt to embody in concrete institutions in the light of the reigning historical circumstances.

The strengths of this concept (to which we need to hang on tightly) are that it identifies and stresses the importance for democratic politics of a sphere distinct from the economy and the State, and thus helps us to escape from the elision of the two to which I pointed earlier, as being one of the major blocks to the formulation of a democratic response to current developments in the media.

Another strength is that the concept identifies the importance of rationality and universality as key moments in any democratic political practice and holds out a proper resistance to the reduction of politics either to the clash of power, in particular class interests, or to questions of State administration. It forces us to remember that in politics universal ends are always at issue, as are choices between incompatible public goods, which cannot be reduced to differences of material interest. Thus on the one hand the concept of the public sphere challenges the liberal free press tradition from the grounds of its materiality, and on the other it challenges the Marxist critique of that tradition from the grounds of the specificity of politics.

## V

I want now to return to my starting point and look at the implications of the concept of the public sphere for the debate on the structure and function of the mass media. In doing so I shall focus upon broadcasting and upon the public service model of broadcasting as an embodiment of the principles of the public sphere. Such a focus is a conscious corrective to the more normal focus in debates about the media and politics upon the press, and upon a free press model derived from the history of print communication.

The great strengths of the public service model, to which we need to remain loyal through all the twists of the argument that has raged around it, are twofold. First it presupposes and then develops in its practice a set of social relations which are distinctly political rather than economic. Second, it attempts to insulate itself from control by the State (which, as is often forgotten, is not synonymous with political control). Reith's original vision was undoubtedly drawn from the tradition of the Scottish Enlightenment and, within the very narrow limits within which the economic and political forces of the time allowed him to operate, the early practice of the BBC (as Scannell and Cardiff's recent research shows) made a noble effort to address their listeners as rational political beings rather than as consumers (Scannell 1980; Cardiff 1980). It is easy to argue that the agenda for debate and the range of information considered important were hopelessly linked to a class-based definition of the public good. It has been further contended that the BBC's venture into class education was doomed to failure because public aspirations were already so moulded by the consumerist ideology secreted by the dominant set of social relations in society, that this alternative set (as the experience of Radio Luxembourg demonstrated) could be imposed on listeners only by the brute force of monopoly. But this is to miss the point of the enterprise and its continuing importance as both historical example and potential alternative. After all, one could use the same argument (indeed people are already using this argument in relation to the power of local government) that because of declining voter turn-out one should simply abolish elections.

For the problem with liberal free press theory is not just that the market has produced conditions of oligopoly which undercut the liberal ideal, or that private ownership leads to direct manipulation of political communication (although it does). The site of the problem is the fundamental contradiction between the economic and the political at the level of their value systems and of the social relations which those value systems require and support. Within the political realm the individual is defined as a citizen exercising public rights of debate, voting, etc., within a communally agreed structure of rules and towards communally defined ends. The value system is essentially social and the legitimate end of social action is the public good. Within the economic realm on the other hand the individual is defined as producer and consumer exercising private rights through purchasing power on the market in the pursuit of private interests, his or her actions being coordinated by the invisible hand of the market.

Once we recognize this irresolvable contradiction then the analytical task becomes one of mapping the interactions between the two spheres, and the political task one of working out the historically appropriate balance between recognizing, on the one hand, that pursuit of political freedom may override the search for economic efficiency, while on the other, that the extent of possible political freedom is constrained by the level of material productivity.

The field of the mass media is a key focus for this contradiction because they operate simultaneously across the two realms. A newspaper or a TV channel is at one and the same time a commercial operation and a political institution. The nature of the largely undiscussed problems this creates can be illustrated if one points to the elaborate structure of law and convention which attempts to insulate politicians, public servants and the political process from economic control – rules against bribery, laws controlling election expenditure, the socially validated objection (however often venality occurs) against the use of public office for private gain. And yet at the same time we allow what we recognize as central political institutions such as the press and broadcasting, to be privately operated. We would find it strange now if we made voting rights dependent upon purchasing power or property rights; yet access to the mass media, as both channels of information and forums of debate, is largely controlled by just such power and rights.

But the incompatibility between the commercial and political functions of the media is not just a question of ownership and control, important as such questions are. It is even more a question of the value system and set of social relations within which commercial media must operate and which they serve to reinforce. For it is these that are inimical, not just to one political interest group or another, but to the very process of democratic politics itself. Political communication is forced to channel itself via commercial media. By this I mean not just the press but also public service broadcasting so far as it competes for audiences with commercial broadcasting and on its dominant terms. Public communication is transformed into the politics of consumerism. Politicians appeal to potential voters not as rational beings concerned for the public good, but in the mode of advertising, as creatures of passing and largely irrational appetite, whose self-interest they must purchase. Such a politics is forced to take on the terms of address of the media it uses and to address its readers, viewers and listeners within the set of social relations that those media have created for other purposes. Thus the citizen is addressed as a private individual rather than as a member of a public, within a privatized domestic sphere rather than within public life. Think, for instance, of the profound political difference between reading a newspaper in one's place of work or in a café and discussing it with those who share that set of social relations on the one hand, and watching TV within the family circle or listening to radio or watching a videocassette on an individual domestic basis on the other. Think of the Sony Walkman as a concrete embodiment of social isolation, as opposed to participation at a rock concert.

## VI

However, while I want to argue that the public service model of the media has at its heart a set of properly political values, and that its operation both requires and fosters a set of social relations, distinct from and opposed to economic values and relations essential to an operating democracy, at the same time in its actual historical operation it has so far shared with the Habermasian concept of the public sphere a crucial failure to recognize the problem of mediation within the public sphere and thus the role of knowledge-brokers within the system. In particular the public service model has failed to come to terms with the proper and necessary function of both journalists and politicians. In relation to both groups there is a failure sufficiently to distinguish between two communicative functions within the public sphere: the collection and dissemination of *information*, and the provision of a forum for *debate*.

Journalists within public service broadcasting, under the banner of balance and objectivity, claim to carry out both functions and to do so in the name of the public. However, this produces a contradiction. Obviously, the function of information search and exposition as carried out at its best, by teachers, cannot simply be equated with political advocacy. Here Jay Blumler is right (Blumler *et al.* 1978). But journalists are not in any way accountable to the public they claim to serve and themselves constitute a distinct interest. How then are we to ensure that this expository function is carried out responsibly? It needs to be accompanied by legislation for freedom of information and so forth. It also needs much better-trained journalists. Finally, its sheer expensiveness depends upon public provision, since otherwise high-quality information will become not a public good but an expensive private asset. All this complex institution needs a public accountability structure of its own, together with a code of professional values distinct from the political debate. Within such a structure, much greater direct access must be given to independent fields of social expertise. It is a perennial and justified criticism of journalists by experts that journalists themselves decide the agenda of what is relevant, and at the same time too often garble the information for presentational purposes. Perhaps bodies such as the Economic and Social Research Council, Greenpeace, Social Audit (one could list many others) should have regular access to broadcasting and print channels and employ their own journalists to clarify current issues for the general public as a background to more informed political debate.

At the same time, the conduct of debate in the mass media needs to be *more* highly politicized with political parties and other major organized social movements having access to the screen on their own terms. One might indeed envisage a situation where any group that could obtain a membership of over a certain size would be eligible for regular access to airtime and national newspaper space. Habermas himself seems to envisage some such arrangement when he argues that the public sphere today requires 'a public body of organized private individuals'. Such organizations would themselves, he argues, have to have democratic internal structures. The public sphere, he writes, 'could only be realized today on an altered basis as a rational reorganization of social and political power under the mutual control of rival organizations committed to the public sphere in their internal structure as well as in their relations with the State and each other' (Habermas 1979: 201).

[. . .]

# References

Blumler, J., Gurevitch, M. and Ives, J. (1978) *The Challenge of Election Broadcasting*. Leeds: Leeds University Press.

Cardiff, D. (1980) 'The serious and the popular: aspects of the evolution of style in the radio talk 1928–1939', *Media, Culture and Society* 2 (1).

Habermas, J. (1979) 'The public sphere', in A. Mattelart and S. Siegelaub (eds) *Communication and Class Struggle*, vol. 1. New York: International General.

Habermas, J. (1982) 'A reply to my critics', in John B. Thompson *et al.* (eds) *Habermas: Critical Debates*. London: Macmillan.

Held, D. (1980) *Introduction to Critical Theory*. London: Hutchinson.

Scannell, P. (1980) 'Broadcasting and the politics of unemployment 1930–1935', *Media, Culture and Society* 2 (1).

# Chapter 25

# John Keane

## STRUCTURAL TRANSFORMATIONS OF THE PUBLIC SPHERE

From *Communication Review*, 1 (1) (1995): 8–22.

[. . .]

**T**HE OLD DOMINANCE OF state-structured and territorially bounded public life mediated by radio, television, newspapers, and books is coming to an end. Its hegemony is rapidly being eroded by the development of a multiplicity of networked spaces of communication which are not tied immediately to territory, and which therefore irreversibly outflank and fragment anything formerly resembling a single, spatially integrated public sphere within a nation-state framework. The ideal of a unified public sphere and its corresponding vision of a territorially bounded republic of citizens striving to live up to their definition of the public good are obsolete. In their place, figuratively speaking, public life is today subject to 'refeudalization,' not in the sense in which Habermas's *Strukturwandel der Öffentlichkeit* used the term, but in the different sense of the development of a complex mosaic of differently sized, overlapping, and interconnected public spheres that force us radically to revise our understanding of public life and its 'partner' terms such as public opinion, the public good, and the public/private distinction.

Although these public spheres emerge within differently sized milieux within the nooks and crannies of civil societies and states, all of them are stages of power and interest-bound action that display the essential characteristics of a public sphere. A public sphere is a particular type of spatial relationship between two or more people, usually connected by a certain means of communication (television, radio, satellite, fax, telephone, etc.), in which nonviolent controversies erupt, for a brief or more extended period of time, concerning the power relations operating within their given milieu of interaction and/or within the wider milieus of social and political structures within which the disputants are situated. Public spheres in this sense never appear in pure form – the description is *idealtypisch* – and they rarely appear in isolation. Although they typically have a networked, interconnected character, contemporary public spheres have a fractured quality which is not being overcome by some broader trend toward an integrated public sphere. The examples selected below illustrate their heterogeneity and variable size, and that is why I choose, at the risk of being misunderstood, to distinguish among *micro-public spheres* in which there are dozens, hundreds or thousands of disputants interacting at the sub-nation-state level; *meso-public spheres* which normally comprise millions of people interacting at the level of the nation-state framework; and *macro-public spheres* which normally encompass hundreds of millions and even billions of people enmeshed in disputes at the supranational and global levels of power. I should like to examine each in turn – and to explore their implications for a revised political theory of the role of public spheres within democratic republics.

## Micro-public spheres

The coffeehouse, town-level meeting, and literary circle, in which early modern public spheres developed, today find their counterparts in a wide variety of local spaces in which citizens enter into disputes about who does and who ought to get what, when, and how. John Fiske's *Power Plays* (1993) has made a convincing case for the importance of bottom-up, small-scale locales in which citizens forge their identities, often in opposition to top-down 'imperializing' powers bent on regulating, redefining, or extinguishing (or 'stationing') public life at the local level. While Fiske (following Foucault) correctly emphasizes that these micro-public spheres take advantage of the fact that all large-scale institutions ultimately rest on the cooperation of their subordinates, and that challenges and changes at the micro-level therefore necessarily have broader macro-effects, he underestimates the importance of internal disputes within these locales – instead preferring to empha-size the contestatory relationship between 'imperializing power' and locales – and unfortunately ignores the rich significance of these localized disputes for the conven-tional theory of the public sphere. Two examples will help to clarify these points – and to illustrate what is meant by micro-public sphere.

Micro-public spheres are today a vital feature of all social movements. As Paul Mier, Alberto Melucci, and others have observed, contemporary social movements are less preoccupied with struggles over the production and distribution of material goods and resources and more concerned with the ways in which postindustrial soci-eties generate and withhold information and produce and sustain meanings among their members (Melucci 1989). The organizations of the women's movement, for instance, not only raise important questions about the material inequalities suffered by women. They also, at the same time, challenge dominant masculinist codes by signaling to the rest of society the importance of symbolically recognizing differences. While the movements have millenarian tendencies, their concentration of defining and redefining symbolic differences ensures that they are not driven by grand visions of a future utopian order. The supporters and sympathizers and actors within the movements are 'nomads of the present.' They focus upon the present, wherein they practice the future social changes they seek, and their organizational means are therefore valued as ends in themselves. Social movements normally comprise low-profile networks of small groups, organizations, initiatives, local contacts, and friendships submerged in everyday life. These submerged networks, noted for their stress on solidarity, individual needs, and part-time involvement, constitute the laboratories in which new experiences are invented and popularized. Within these local laboratories, movements utilize a variety of means of communication (telephones, faxes, photocopiers, camcorders, videos, personal computers) to question and transform the dominant codes of everyday life. These laboratories function as public spaces in which the elements of everyday life are mixed, remixed, developed, and tested. Such public spheres as the discussion circle, the publishing house, the church, the clinic, and a political chat over a drink with friends or acquaintances are the sites in which citizens question the pseudo-imperatives of reality and counter them with alternative experiences of time, space, and interpersonal relations. On occasion, these public spheres coalesce into publicly visible media events, such as demonstrations in favor of gay male and lesbian rights or sit-ins against roadbuilding or power plant projects. But, paradoxically, these micro-public spheres draw their strength from the fact that they are mostly latent. Although they appear to be 'private,' acting at a distance from official public life, party politics, and the glare of media publicity, they in fact display all the characteristics of small group public efforts, whose challenging of the existing distribution of power can be effective exactly because they operate unhindered in the unnewsworthy nooks and crannies of civil society.

Micro-public spheres may also be developing among children within households, as the disputed example of video games illustrates. For many adults, particularly those without children, the widespread appeal of video games remains incomprehensible; contemplating a four-button keypad leaves them with a powerful sense of wasted time, ignorance based upon innocence, even disgust at the thought that the current generation of children will grow up as the first ever in modern times to learn to compute before they learn to read and write. But for most children, at least most boys between eight and eighteen, the experience of playing video games and creating an everyday culture of schoolroom stories, swapping and sharing videos, and a new critical lexicon (filled with codewords like 'crap,' 'smelly,' and 'cacky') that generates tensions with adults has become a routine part of childhood – as routine as old-fashioned ways of hating parents or squashing a worm or overfeeding a goldfish to death. The growth within households of micro-public spheres of this kind has been dramatic. Within the past five years in the United Kingdom, for example, the video games market, dominated by the Japanese companies Sega and Nintendo, has grown from virtually nothing to a turnover of around £800 millions per annum. Eight out of ten children between eleven and fourteen now play video games; six out of ten have their own game consoles (the hardware needed to play games on television monitors); while in 1992 alone, around two million new consoles were sold. Industry figures like to cite the power of the advertising 'hook' to explain their marketing success, but this underestimates the way in which the popularity of video games among children is *chosen* by subjects striving, if only intuitively, for the power to co-determine the outcomes of their electronically mediated play. It is true that the currently marketed form of video games normally thwarts children's choices. The sex-typing of women as figures who are acted upon, and often victimized as kidnap victims in need of rescue, is a typical case in point (Provenzo 1991). Video games nevertheless challenge children to come to terms with the new media of digital communication. Their appeal stems not only from the fact that for brief moments children can escape the demands of household and school by becoming part of an alternate world of bionic men, damsels in distress, galactic invasions, and teenage mutant turtles. Video games also promise interactivity and actually encourage users to improve their hand–eye coordination and interpretative skills by browsing through texts in an orderly but nonsequential manner. Unlike the process of learning to read books, which reduces children initially to mere readers with no freedom but that of accepting or rejecting the rules of a text, the playing of video games confronts children with a form of hypertext (Nelson 1987). Players are required to choose their own pathways through texts composed of blocks of words, images, and sounds that are linked electronically by multiple paths, chains, or trails that are unfinished and open-ended. Video games blur the boundaries between readers and writers by encouraging their users to determine how they move through a forest of possibilities to do with rescue and revenge, and good versus evil, constrained only by the permitted household rules governing playtime, the manufacturers' *mise en scène*, and the child's capacity for inventiveness in the face of persistent adult suspicion or outright opposition to the phenomenon.

## Meso-public spheres

The treatment of meso-public spheres can be comparatively brief, since they are the most familiar of the three types of public sphere examined here. Meso-public spheres are those spaces of controversy about power that encompass millions of people watching, listening, or reading across vast distances. They are mainly co-extensive with the nation-state, but they may also extend beyond its boundaries to encompass neighboring audiences (as in the case of German-language programming and publishing in Austria); their reach may also be limited to regions within states, as in the case of the non-Castilian-speaking regions of Spain like Catalonia and the Basque country. Meso-public spheres are mediated by large-circulation newspapers such as the *New York Times*, *Le Monde*, *Die Zeit*, the *Globe and Mail*, and the Catalan daily, *Avui*. They are also mediated by electronic media such as BBC radio and television, Swedish Radio, RAI, and (in the United States) National Public Radio and the four national networks (CBS, NBC, ABC, and Fox).

Although constantly pressured 'from below' by micro-public spheres, meso-public spheres display considerable tenacity. There is no necessary zero-sum relationship between these differently sized public domains, in part because each feeds upon tensions with the other (readers of national newspapers, for instance, may and do consult locally produced magazines or bulletins, precisely because of their different themes and emphases); and in part because meso-public spheres thrive upon media which appeal to particular national or regional language groupings, and which have well-established and powerful production and distribution structures that sustain their proven ability to circulate to millions of people certain types of news, current affairs, films, and entertainment that daily reinforce certain styles and habits of communication about matters of public concern. The strength of reputation, funding, and distribution is certainly an important reason why public service media, notwithstanding their self-commercialization, are unlikely to disappear as props of public life. There is another, more surprising reason why public life at the meso-level is unlikely to disappear. The above-mentioned examples of the media sustaining meso-public spheres highlight the point – foreign to recent attempts to tie the theory of the public sphere to the fate of public service media – that public controversies about power are also regularly facilitated by privately controlled media of civil society. There is plenty of evidence that just as public service media are ever more subject to market forces, market-led media are subject to a long-term process of self-politicization, in the sense that they are forced to address matters of concern to citizens capable of distinguishing between market 'hype' and public controversies. The entry into official politics of commercial media figures such as Ronald Reagan and Silvio Berlusconi are extreme instances of this trend. The British tabloids' ruthless probing of the private lives of monarchs and politicians during the past decade is symptomatic of the same trend. So also are popular current affairs programs such as CNN's *Larry King Live* and the remarkable proliferation of fast-cut television talk shows like *Ricki Lake*, which, amid advertisements for commodities such as mouthwash, chocolates, innerspring mattresses, and pizza, simulate raucous domestic quarrels about such matters as teenage sex, pregnancy, and child abuse, in front of selected audiences who argue bitterly among themselves and, amid uproar, talk back to the presenter, experts, and interviewees, contradicting their views, calling them 'real asses,' urging them to 'get real,' and insisting that something or other 'sucks with a capital S.'

## Macro-public spheres

The recent growth of macro-public spheres at the global or regional (e.g., European Union) level is among the most striking, least researched developments running contrary to the orthodox theory of the public sphere. Macro-publics of hundreds of millions of citizens are the (unintended) consequence of the international concentration of mass media firms previously owned and operated at the nation-state level. A prior form of concentration of media capital has of course been under way for a century, especially in the magazine and newspaper industries and in the core group of news agencies, dominated by American, British, German, and French firms that carved up the world within the spheres of influence of their respective governments. The current globalization of media firms represents a projection of this process of concentration onto the international plane. It involves the chain ownership of newspapers, cross-ownership of newspapers, the acquisition of media by ordinary industrial concerns, and significantly, the regional and global development of satellite-linked communications systems.

The development of globe-girdling communications firms such as News Corporation International, Reuters, Time-Warner, and Bertelsmann was not driven by the motive of funding the development of international publics. Although research on the perceived motives and benefits of globalization remains limited, it is clear that the process, which is virtually without historical precedents, is driven by reasons of political economy. Media firms operating at the global level have certain advantages over their nationally based counterparts. Headed by a tiny group of people who have become adept at 'turning around' ailing media firms and fully utilizing their assets, transnational firms take advantage of economies of scale. They are able to shift resources of expertise, marketing skills, and journalistic talent, for instance, from one part of the media field to another; they can also reduce costs and innovate by tapping the specialist work forces of various societies. These firms can also effect synergies of various kinds, such as trying out a novel in one country and producing a movie based upon it in another, or releasing a work successively through such media as cable, video, television, magazines, and paperback books, without the difficult rights-negotiation and scheduling problems that inevitably arise when a diversity of competing national companies is involved. Highly important as well is the advantageous fact that transnational media firms are often able to evade nation-state regulations and shift the core energies of the whole operation from one market to another as political and legal and cultural climates change.

Among the central ironies of this risk-driven, profit-calculating process is its nurturing of the growth of publics stretching beyond the boundaries of the nation-state. Most of these public spheres are so far fledglings. They operate briefly and informally – they have few guaranteed sources of funding and legal protection, and are therefore highly fragile, often fleeting phenomena. International media events, which are now staged virtually every week, are cases in point. As Daniel Dayan and Elihu Katz (1992), Daniel Hallin (1994), and others have shown, global media events like summits are highly charged symbolic processes covered by the entire media of the world and addressed primarily to a fictive 'world audience.' In the three major summits hosted by Reagan and Gorbachev – at Geneva in 1985, Washington in 1987, and Moscow in 1988 – audiences straddling the globe watched as media channels such as CNN, ABC's *Nightline*, and the Soviet morning program *90 Minutes* relayed versions of a summit that signaled the end of the Cold War. It is commonly objected that such coverage spreads rituals of pacification, rendering global audiences mute in their fascination with the spectacle of the event. That could indeed he legitimately said of the heavily censored Malvinas War and Gulf War coverage, but still there are signs that the global casting of summits and other events tends to be conducted in the subjunctive tense, in that they heighten audiences' sense that the existing 'laws' of power politics are far from 'natural' and that the shape of the world is therefore dependent in part on current efforts to refashion it according to certain criteria.

The dramatic emphasis upon the subjunctive, combined with the prospect of reaching a worldwide audience, can incite new public controversies about power stretching beyond the limited boundaries of mesa-public spheres. During the Reagan–Gorbachev summits, for example, political arguments about the dangerous proliferation of nuclear and conventional weaponry were commonplace among the citizens and governments of various countries at the same time; and in the Soviet Union, where autonomous public life had long been considered a counter revolutionary crime, the supporters of Boris Yeltsin were heartened by the way in which the demoted party leader's interviews with CBS and the BBC during the Moscow summit forced Mikhail Gorbachev to respond with a televised press conference; meanwhile, Soviet religious dissidents successfully lobbied President Reagan to grant them a public meeting, at which there was a frank airing of conflicting views about elections, the future of religion, and the comparative 'standards of living' of America and the Soviet Union.

Probably the most dramatic example so far of the way in which global media events can and do incite public controversies about power before audiences of hundreds of millions of people is the crisis in Tiananmen Square in China during the late spring of 1989. Broadcast live by CNN, twenty-four hours a day, the Tiananmen episode was a turning point in the development of global news. Not only was it perceived as the most important news story yet to be covered by international satellite television, it was also (according to Lewis Friedland (1992) and others) the first occasion ever when satellite television directly shaped the events themselves, which unfolded rapidly on three planes: within national boundaries, throughout global diplomatic circles, and on the stage of international public arguments about how to resolve the crisis. CNN's wire-service-like commitment to bring its viewers all significant stories from all sides of the political spectrum helped to publicize the demands of the students, many of whom had traveled abroad and understood well the political potential of the television medium in establishing public spheres in opposition to the totalitarian Chinese state. Not coincidentally, they chose 'The Goddess of Democracy' as their central symbol, while their placards carried quotations from Abraham Lincoln and others, all in English for the benefit of Western audiences. The students reckoned, accurately, that by keeping the cameras and cellular telephones (and, later, 8 mm 'handicams' carried around on bicycles) trained on themselves they would maximize the chances of their survival and international recognition. Their cause certainly won international recognition from other states and citizens. By damaging the international reputation of the Party, the global coverage of the Tiananmen events may also have boosted the long-term chances in a nonviolent self-dismantling of the communist regime (along the lines of Kádár's Hungary). In the short run, the coverage almost certainly prolonged the life of the protest, which ended in the massacre of between 400 and 800 students. According to CNN's Alec Miran, who was executive producer in China during the crisis, 'People were coming up to us in the street, telling us to "Keep going, keep broadcasting, that they won't come in while you're on the air." That turned out to be true. The troops went in after our cameras were shut down' (cited in Friedland 1992, p. 5).

The pathbreaking development during the past two decades of an international system of computerized communications networks provides a final illustration of macro-public spheres. Based upon such techniques as packet switching developed during the 1960s by the Advanced Research Projects Agency (ARPA) for the United States Department of Defense, a worldwide network of computers funded by governments, businesses, universities, and citizens, is beginning to draw together users from all continents and walks of life. The Internet, the most talked about and talked through network, comprises an estimated 3 million computers serving as hosts that are in turn directly connected to millions of other computers used by up to 30 million people. The number of Internet 'citizens' is growing rapidly (by an estimated 1 million users a month), in part because of heavy subsidies that keep access costs to a minimum, partly because of peer pressure to get an e-mail address, and in part because of the lack of constraints, globality, and informality currently enjoyed by users communicating for a variety of self-chosen ends. Some 'surf' the Internet, logging on to servers throughout the world just for the hell of it. Companies and other organizations conduct banking transactions and transmit financial and administrative data by means of it. Live telecasts of speeches and trans-missions of scanned images of weather maps, paintings, and nude photographs are commonplace. Still others use 'the Net' to obtain detailed print-outs of data down-loaded from libraries or to 'chat' with a friend on another continent.

The manifold purposes for which the Internet can be used at reasonable cost or free of charge has led some observers (e.g., Krol 1994) to liken its users, in neo-Romantic terms, to eighteenth-century travelers seeking food and shelter in houses they reach at nightfall. While correctly drawing attention to the contractual or voluntary character of electronic interactions, the simile it arguably misplaced. It not merely understates the way in which the often clumsy organization of informa-tion sources generates confusion among users who are posting items – with the con-sequence that travelers on the information highway find themselves hazy about their routes, their means of travel, their hosts' house rules, and (insofar as messages are frequently forwarded several times, often by unknown receivers/senders) their ulti-mate destinations. More pertinent is the fact that the simile fails because the Internet stimulates the growth of macro-public spheres. There is a category of users with a 'net presence' who utilize the medium not as travelers but as citizens who generate controversies with other members of a far-flung 'imagined community' about mat-ters of power and principle. The Association for Progressive Communications (APC) for example, functions as a worldwide partnership of member network: dedicated to providing low-cost and advanced computer communications services for the purpose of network-strengthening and information-sharing among organizations and individ-uals working for environmental sustainability, economic and social justice, and human rights. Within the APC framework spheres of public controversy ('public discussion forums') stretching to all four corners of the earth have a permanent presence. So too do reflections upon the power relations operating *within* the global networks themselves. 'Netizens' whose approach to the public forums of the Internet exudes selfishness – taking rather than giving – can generally expect to be abused ('flamed'), as unsolicited advertisers find to their embarrassment. Controversies are erupting about the merits of state-subsidized, cost-free access of citizens to the Internet; proposals are surfacing (in the United States) for the forma-tion of a Corporation for Public Cybercasting that would serve as a clearing house for federal funds, help to increase the density and tensility of the network, and lobby for citizens' access; and fears are expressed that the telecommunications and enter-tainment industries are building advanced communications systems that would enable them to control parts of the Internet and thereby levy considerably higher access charges.

## Research implications

The above attempt radically to rethink the theory of the public sphere, like all lines of enquiry that transgress the limits of conventional wisdom, opens up new bundles of complex questions with important implications for future research in the fields of politics and communications. The most obvious implication is that the neo-republican attempt to tie the theory of the public sphere to the institution of public service broadcasting has failed on empirical and normative grounds and that, more positively, there are empirical reasons alone why the concept of 'public spheres' should be brought to bear on phenomena as disparate as computer networking, citizens' initiatives, newspaper circulation, satellite broadcasting, and children playing video games. Public spheres are not exclusively 'housed' within state-protected public service media; nor (contrary to Habermas) are they somehow tied *per definitionem* to the zone of social life narrowly wedged between the world of power and money (state/economy) and the pre-political group associations of civil society. The political geography supposed by both the Habermasian and public service model theories of 'the public sphere' is inadequate. Public spheres can and do develop within various realms of civil society and state institutions, including within the supposed enemy territory of consumer markets and within the world of power that lies beyond the reach of nation-states, the Hobbesian world conventionally dominated by shadowy agreements, suited diplomacy, business transactions, and war and rumors of war.

Whether or not there is a long-term modern tendency for public spheres to spread into areas of life previously immune from controversies about power is necessarily a subject for a larger enquiry. Yet among the implications of this reflection upon the theme of public life in the old democracies is the fact that there are no remaining areas of social or political life automatically protected against public controversies about the distribution of power. The early modern attempt to represent patterns of property ownership, market conditions, household life, and events like birth and death as 'natural' is gradually withering away. So too is the older, originally Greek assumption that the public sphere of citizenship necessarily rests on the tight-lipped privacy (literally, the idiocy) of the *oikos*. As the process of mediated publicity spreads – television talk shows like *Ricki Lake* and children playing video games suggest – supposedly private phenomena are being drawn into the vortices of negotiated controversy that are the hallmark of public spaces. The realm of privacy disappears. The process of politicization undermines the conventionally accepted division between 'the public' (where power controversies are reckoned to be the legitimate business of others) and 'the private' (where such controversy is said to have no legitimate role before the thrones of ' intimacy' or individual choice or God-given or biological 'naturalness'). Politicization exposes the arbitrariness or conventionalism of traditional definitions of 'the private,' making it harder (as various figures of power are today painfully learning) to justify any action as a private matter. Paradoxically, the same process of politicization also triggers a new category of public disputes about the merits of defining or redefining certain zones of social and political life as 'private' – and therefore as nobody else's business. Legal authorities publicize the problem of rape while insisting upon the need to keep private the identities of those who have suffered the crime; gay males and lesbians campaign publicly for their right to live without intrusions by bigots and gawking journalists; advocates of the right to privacy press publicly for data protection legislation; meanwhile, embattled politicians and scandalized monarchs insist publicly that the media has no place in their bedrooms.

Such developments cannot adequately be understood from within the orthodox perspective on the public sphere, wedded as it is to a version of the early modern division between 'the public' and 'the private.' Its defenders might reply that at least some of the public spheres mentioned above are bogus public spheres, in that they are neither permanent nor structured by rational argumentation, or what Garnham calls 'a rational and universalistic politics.' Certainly – as the *impermanent* public controversy generated by social movements shows – not all the examples of public life cited above display longevity, but that arguably signals the need to question the conventional assumption that a public sphere is only a public sphere insofar as it persists through time. The point about rational argumentation is more difficult to answer, although it is again clear that there is no reason in principle why the concept of the public sphere must necessarily be wedded to the ideal type of communication orientated toward reaching consensus based upon the force of the best argument (or what Habermas calls *verständigungsorientierten Handelns* (Habermas 1976)). In their study of television talk shows, Sonia Livingstone and Peter Lunt (1994) usefully highlight the several ways in which audience discussion programs defy the dominant philosophical notion of rationality derived from deductive logic, according to which there exists a set of formal reasoning procedures that express tacit inference rules concerning the truth or falsity of assertions inde-pendently of the content or context of utterances. Following Wittgenstein's *Philosophical Investigations* (1958) Livingstone and Lunt defend the legitimacy of lay or 'ordinary reasoning,' such as quarrels (characterized by emotional intensity and a commitment to assert one's point of view at all costs) and preaching, political oratory, and story-telling, in which points are built up in a haphazard manner by layering, recursion, and repetition. Their move is convincing, but their conclusions remain a trifle too rationalist. Early modern public spheres – as I proposed from a post-Weberian perspective in *Public Life and Late Capitalism* (Keane 1984) and Oskar Negt and Alexander Kluge (1972) insisted from a neo-Marxian standpoint in *Öffentlichkeit und Erfahrung* – did not conform to the Habermasian ideal type of rational discussion. Music, opera, sport, painting, danc-ing were among the forms of communication propelling the growth of public life, and there is therefore no principled reason, aside from philosophical prejudice, why their late-twentieth-century popular counterparts – the rambunctiousness of MTV's annual video awards, the simulated uproar of *Ricki Lake* shows, or the hyper-text of video games – should not be understood as legitimate potential media of power conflicts.

To suppose that public controversies about power can and should unfold by means of a variety of modes of communication is not to fall into the relativist trap of concluding that any and every power struggle counts as a legitimate public sphere. Violent confrontation among subjects does not do so, since, as the origin-ally Greek understanding of war as external to the *polis* maintained, it seeks physically to silence or destroy outright its antagonists. The essential point (detailed in Keane 1988, 1991) is this: the plea for a pluralistic understanding of the variable forms of communication that currently constitute public life shares an elective affinity with a nonfoundationalist understanding of democracy as a type of regime which enables a genuine plurality of individuals and groups openly to express their solidarity with, or opposition to, others' ideals and forms of life. By abandoning the futile and often dangerous high roads of supposed transhistorical Ideals and definite Truths, the plea for a pluralistic account of public life implies that there is no ultimate criterion for determining which particular type of public controversy is universally preferable. The most that can be said, normatively speaking, is that a healthy democratic regime is one in which various types of public spheres are thriving, with no single one of them actually enjoying a monopoly in public disputes about the distribution of power. In contrast, a regime dominated by television talk shows or by spectacular media events would compromise its citizens' integrity. It might prove to be as stifling as a regime in which seminar-style 'rational discussion' or demagogic political preaching served as the sole 'civilized' standard of disputation about who gets what, when, and how.

The emphasis here upon pluralism brings us back to the subject of space, which was the point of departure of this broad reconsideration of the structural transformations of the public sphere in the old democracies. Within the republican tradition of political thinking that extends through to the recent attempt to tie public life to the public service model, it is normally assumed that power is best monitored and its abuse most effectively checked by means of ongoing argumentation within the *territorial* framework of the nation-state. Republicanism supposes that public-spirited citizens can best act together within an integrated, politically constructed space that is ultimately rooted in the physical *place* occupied by state power. This supposition needs to be rejected, since a growing number of public spheres – Internet and global media events, for instance – are politically constructed spaces that have no immediate connection with physical territory. Public life, one could say, is presently subject to a process of de-territorialization which ensures that citizens' shared sense of proximity to one another in various milieux bears ever less relationship to the places where they were actually born, where they grew up, fell in love, worked, and lived, and where they will eventually die.

It might be objected that the attempt to categorize contemporary public life into spaces of varying scope or 'reach' is mistaken on both empirical and normative grounds. Empirically speaking, it could be said that the public spheres discussed in this essay are not discrete spaces, as the categories micro-, meso-, and macro-public sphere imply; that they rather resemble a modular system of overlapping networks defined by the lack of differentiation among spheres. Certainly, the concept of modularization serves as a useful reminder of the dangers of reifying the distinction among micro-, meso-, and macro-public spheres. It is also helpful in understanding the growing complexity of contemporary public life. But this does not mean that the boundaries among variously sized public spheres are obliterated completely. To the contrary, modular systems thrive on internal differentiation, whose workings can thus only be understood by means of ideal-type categories that highlight those systems' inner boundaries. The recent development of computerized communications is illustrative of this point. Computer networks originally linked terminals to mainframes for time-sharing, but during the past two decades a pattern of distributed structures at the micro-, meso-, and macro-levels has come to predominate. During the 1980s, local area networks (LANs) providing high-speed data communication within an organization spread rapidly; they have subsequently been linked into metropolitan area networks (MANs) that are often associated with a 'teleport' of satellite dishes, and into wide area networks (WANs) that may cover several continents – and yet still the differentiation between micro-/meso-/macro-domains remains a vital feature of the overall system.

The triadic distinction among differently sized public spheres can also be contested on normative grounds. During the early years of the twentieth century, at the beginning of the era of broadcasting, John Dewey's *The Public and Its Problems* (1927) famously expressed the outlines of the complaint that modern societies are marked by the fragmentation of public life. 'There are too many publics and too much of public concern for our existing resources to cope with,' wrote Dewey. 'The essential need,' he added, 'is the improvement of a unifier system of methods and conditions of debate, discussion, and persuasion, *that* is the problem of the public' (p. 142).

This kind of appeal (repeated more recently by Robert Bellah (1967) and others) to revive republicanism is questionable. It fails to see that the structural differentiation of public spaces is unlikely to be undone in the coming decades and that therefore the continued use of 'the' public sphere ideal is bound to empty it of empirical content and to turn the ideal into a nostalgic, unrealizable utopia. We are moving, as Henri Lefebvre (1974) predicted, from a society in which space is seen as an 'absolute' toward one in which there are ongoing 'trials of space' (p. 116). Orthodox republicanism also ignores the *undemocratic* replications of its own hankering after a unified public sphere. The supposition that all power disputes can ultimately be sited at the level of the territorially bounded nation-state is a remnant from the era of state-building and the corresponding struggles of its inhabitants to widen the franchise – and, hence, to direct public controversies primarily at the operations at the sovereign state. In the present era of the universal franchise, by contrast, it is not so much who votes but *where* people vote that is becoming a central issue for democratic politics. From this perspective, the proliferation of mosaics of differently sized public spheres ought to be welcomed and practically reinforced by means of political struggle, law, money, and improved modes of communications. Exactly because of their capacity to monitor the exercise of power from a variety of sites within state *and* social institutions, public spheres ensure that nobody 'owns' power and increase the likelihood that its exercise everywhere is rendered more accountable to those whom it directly or indirectly affects.

The trends described in this essay are admittedly only trends. Within the old democracies, there are plenty of antidemocratic countertrends, and it should therefore not be supposed that we are at the beginning of the end of the era of unaccountable power. All political classes, Harold Innis (1951) once remarked, have sought to enhance their power by utilizing certain media of communication to define and to control the spaces in which their subjects live. Statues of military and political heroes sited in public squares are only the most obvious example of a much older and highly complex history of rulers' attempts to define space in their honor, and thereby to inspire devotion among their subjects by making the exercise of power seem unblemished – and unchallengeable.

When reflecting upon the twentieth century, Innis doubted whether this struggle by dominant power groups to regulate their subjects' living space could be resisted. He supposed that space-biased media such as newspapers and radio broadcasting, despite their promise to democratize information, in fact entrench new modes of domination. Was Innis right in this global conviction? Is modernity, just like previous epochs, distinguished by dominant forms of media that absorb, record, and transform information into systems of knowledge consonant with the dominant institutional power structures? Is the era that lies beyond public service broadcasting likely to prove unfriendly toward public life? Is the vision of a democratic plurality of public spheres nothing more than a bad utopia? Or is the future likely to see a variety of contradictory trends, including not only new modes of domination but also unprecedented public battles to define and to control the spaces in which citizens appear? In the disciplines of politics and communications such questions are at present poorly formulated, while the tentative answers they elicit are by definition either not yet available or highly speculative. Perhaps the most that can be said at present is that a theory of public life that clings dogmatically to the vision of a unified public sphere in which 'public opinion' and 'the public interest' are defined is a chimera – and that for the sake of democracy it ought now to be jettisoned.

[. . .]

## References

Bellah, R. N. (1967) Civil religion in America. *Daedalus* 96 (Winter), 1–21.

Dayan, D. and Katz, E. (1992) *Media Events: The Live Broadcasting of History*. Cambridge, MA: Harvard University Press.

Dewey, J. (1927) *The Public and Its Problems*. New York: H. Holt and Co.

Fiske, J. (1993) *Power Plays, Power Works*. London: Verso.

Friedland, L. A. (1992) *Covering the World: International Television News Services*. New York: Twentieth Century Fund.

Habermas, J. (1976) Was heisst Universalpragmatik?, in K. O. Apel (ed.) *Sprachpragmatik und Philosophie*. Frankfurt am Main: Suhrkamp.

Hallin, D. C. (1994) *We Keep America on Top of the World: Television Journalism and the Public Sphere*. London and New York: Routledge.

Innis, H. (1951) *The Bias of Communication*. Toronto: University of Toronto Press.

Jaspers, K. (1969) *Philosophy is for Everyman: A Short Course in Philosophical Thinking*. New York: Harcourt, Brace and World.

Keane, J. (1984) *Public Life and Late Capitalism: Toward a Socialist Theory of Democracy*. Cambridge and New York: Cambridge University Press.

Keane, J. (1988) *Democracy and Civil Society: On the Predicaments of European Socialism, the Prospects for Democracy, and the Problem of Controlling Social and Political Power*. London: Verso.

Keane, J. (1991) *The Media and Democracy*. Cambridge: Polity Press.

Krol, E. (1994) *The Whole Internet: Users' Guide and Catalogue*. Sebastopol, CA: O'Reilly and Associates.

Lefebvre, H. (1974) *La production de l'espace*. Paris: Editions Anthropos.

Livingstone, S. and Lunt, P. (1994) *Talk on Television: Audience Participation and Public Debate*. London: Routledge.

Melucci, A. (1989) *Nomads of the Present: Social Movements and Individual Needs in Contemporary Society*, in P. Mier and J. Keane (eds). London and Philadelphia: Temple University Press.

Negt, O. and Kluge, A. (1972) *Öffentlichkeit und Erfahrung: Zur Organisationsanalyse von bürgerlicher und proletarischer Öffentlichkeit*. Frankfurt am Main: Suhrkamp.

Nelson, T. H. (1987) *Computer Lib; Dream Machines*. Redmond, WA: Tempus Books.

Provenzo, E. F. (1991) *Video Kids: Making Sense of Nintendo*. Cambridge, MA and London: Harvard University Press.

Wittgenstein, L. (1958) *Philosophical Investigations*. G. Anscombe and R. Rhees (eds). Oxford: Blackwell.

# Chapter 26

# Zizi Papacharissi

## THE VIRTUAL SPHERE
## The internet as a public sphere

From *New Media and Society*, 4 (1) (2002): 9–27.

[. . .]

## Introduction

THE UTOPIAN RHETORIC THAT SURROUNDS new media technologies promises further democratization of postindustrial society. Specifically, the internet and related technologies can augment avenues for personal expression and promote citizen activity (e.g. Bell, 1981; Kling, 1996; Negroponte, 1998; Rheingold, 1993). New technologies provide information and tools that may extend the role of the public in the social and political arena. The explosion of online political groups and activism certainly reflects political uses of the internet (Bowen, 1996; Browning, 1996). Proponents of cyberspace promise that online discourse will increase political participation and pave the way for a democratic utopia. According to them, the alleged decline of the public sphere lamented by academics, politicos, and several members of the public will be halted by the democratizing effects of the internet and its surrounding technologies. On the other hand, skeptics caution that technologies not universally accessible and ones that frequently induce fragmented, nonsensical, and enraged discussion, otherwise known as 'flaming', far from guarantee a revived public sphere. This article examines how political uses of the internet affect the public sphere. Does cyberspace present a separate alternative to, extend, minimize, or ignore the public sphere?

It is important to determine whether the internet and its surrounding technologies will truly revolutionize the political sphere or whether they will be adapted to the current status quo, especially at a time when the public is demonstrating dormant political activity and developing growing cynicism towards politics (Cappella and Jamieson, 1996, 1997; Fallows, 1996; Patterson, 1993, 1996). Will these technologies extend our political capacities or limit democracy – or alternatively, do a little bit of both? Such a discussion should be informed primarily with an examination of the notion of the public sphere and the ideological discourse that accompanies it.

## The public sphere

When thinking of the public, one envisions open exchanges of political thoughts and ideas, such as those that took place in ancient Greek agoras or colonial-era town halls. The idea of 'the public' is closely tied to democratic ideals that call for citizen participation in public affairs. Tocqueville (1990) considered the dedication of the American people to public affairs to be at the heart of the healthy and lively American democracy, and added that participation in public affairs contributed significantly to an individual's sense of existence and self-respect. Dewey (1927) insisted that inquiry and communication are the basis for a democratic society, and highlighted the merits of group deliberation over the decisions of a single authority. He argued for a communitarian democracy, where individuals came together to create and preserve a good life in common. The term 'public' connotes ideas of citizenship, commonality, and things not private, but accessible and observable by all. More recently, Jones (1997) argued that cyberspace is promoted as a 'new public space' made by people and 'conjoining traditional mythic narratives of progress with strong modern impulses toward self-fulfillment and personal development' (1997: 22). It should be clarified that a new public space is not synonymous with a new public sphere. As public space, the internet provides yet another forum for political deliberation. As public sphere, the internet could facilitate discussion that promotes a democratic exchange of ideas and opinions. A virtual space enhances discussion; a virtual sphere enhances democracy. This article examines not only the political discussion online, but the contribution of that discussion to a democratic society.

Several critics romanticize the public sphere, and think back on it as something that existed long ago, but became eroded with the advent of modern, industrial society. Sensing the demise of the great public, Habermas (1989 [1962]) traced the development of the public sphere in the 17th and 18th century and its decline in the 20th century. He saw the public sphere as a domain of our social life in which public opinion could be formed out of rational public debate (Habermas, 1991 [1973]). Ultimately, informed and logical discussion, Habermas (1989 [1962]) argued, could lead to public agreement and decision making, thus representing the best of the democratic tradition.

Still, these conceptualizations of the public were somewhat idealized. It is ironic that this pinnacle of democracy was rather undemocratic in its structure throughout the centuries, by not including women or people from lower social classes, a point acknowledged as such by Habermas himself. Moreover, critics of Habermas' rational public sphere, such as Lyotard (1984), raised the issue that anarchy, individuality, and disagreement, rather than rational accord, lead to true democratic emancipation. Fraser (1992) expanded Lyotard's critique, and added that Habermas' conceptualization of the public sphere functioned merely as a realm for privileged men to practice their skills of governance, for it excluded women and non-propertied classes. She contended that, in contemporary America, co-existing public spheres of counterpublics form in response to their exclusion from the dominant sphere of debate. Therefore, multiple public spheres exist, which are not equally powerful, articulate, or privileged, and which give voice to collective identities and interests. A public realm or government, however, which pays attention to all these diverse voices, has never existed (Fraser, 1992). Schudson (1997) concurred, adding that there is little evidence that a true ideal public ever existed, and that public discourse is not the soul of democracy, for it is seldom egalitarian, may be too large and amorphous, is rarely civil, and ultimately offers no magical solution to problems of democracy. Still, Garnham (1992) took a position defensive of Habermas, pointing out that his vision of the public sphere outlined a tragic and stoic pursuit of an almost impossible rationality, recognizing the impossibility of an ideal public sphere and the limits of human civilization, but still striving toward it.

Other critics take on a different point of view, and argue that even though we have now expanded the public to include women and people from all social classes, we are left with a social system where the public does not matter. Carey (1995) for example, argued that the privatizing forces of capitalism have created a mass commercial culture that has replaced the public sphere. Although he recognized that an ideal public sphere may never have existed, he called for the recovery of public life, as a means of preserving independent cultural and social life and resisting the confines of corporate governance and politics. Putnam (1996) traced the disappearance of civic America in a similar manner, attributing the decline of a current public, not to a corrosive mass culture, but to a similar force – television. Television takes up too much of our time and induces passive outlooks on life, according to Putnam.

This is not a complete review of scholarly viewpoints on the public sphere, but presents an array of academic expectations of the public, and can help us to understand if and how the internet can measure up to these expectations. Can it promote rational discourse, thus producing the romanticized ideal of a public sphere envisioned by Habermas and others? Does it reflect several public spheres co-existing online, representing the collectives of diverse groups, as Fraser argued? Are online discussions dominated by elements of anarchy or accord, and do they foster democracy? Will the revolutionary potential of the internet be ultimately absorbed by a mass commercial culture? These are questions that guide this assessment of the virtual sphere.

Research on the public sphere potential of the internet, to be presented in the next few sections, responds to all of these questions. Some scholars highlight the fact that speedy and cheap access to information provided on the internet promotes citizen activism. Others focus on the ability of the internet to bring individuals together and help them overcome geographical and other boundaries. Ultimately, online discussions may erase or further economic inequalities. Utopian and dystopian visions prevail in assessing the promise of the internet as a public sphere. In the next few sections, I focus on three aspects: the ability of the internet to carry and transport information, its potential to bring people from diverse backgrounds together, and its future in a capitalist era. This discussion will help determine whether the internet can recreate a public sphere that perhaps never was, foster several diverse public spheres, or simply become absorbed by a commercial culture.

## Information access

Much of the online information debate focuses on the benefits for the haves and the disadvantages for the have-nots. For those with access to computers, the internet is a valuable resource for political participation, as research that follows has shown. At the same time, access to the internet does not guarantee increased political activity or enlightened political discourse. Moving political discussion to a virtual space excludes those with no access to this space. Moreover, connectivity does not ensure a more representative and robust public sphere.

Nonetheless, the internet does provide numerous avenues for political expression and several ways to influence politics and become politically active Bowen, 1996). Internet users are able to find voting records of representatives, track congressional and Supreme Court rulings, join special interest groups, fight for consumer rights, and plug into free government services (Bowen, 1996). In 1996, 'Decision Maker', a software program developed by Marcel Bullinga (the Netherlands) enabled one of the Netherlands' first political online debates, an experiment that lasted for a month and involved civilians, representatives of organizations, action groups, and political representatives. The research that tracked this experiment revealed that most discussions were dominated by a select few. Moreover, more responses were generated when the discussion involved individuals of certain political clout (Jankowski and van Selm, 2000). This experiment demonstrated that political discussion can easily transfer online, although it is not certain that this transfer will lead to more democratic discussions or have an impact on the political process. Jankowski and van Selm (2000) expressed reservations that online discussions, much like real life ones, seemed to be dominated by elites and were unable to influence public policy formation. Despite the fact that the internet provides additional space for political discussion, it is still plagued by the inadequacies of our political system. It provides public space, but does not constitute a public sphere.

In more recent elections in the US, clever uses of the internet allowed politicians to motivate followers, increase support, and reach out to previously inaccessible demographic groups. Jesse Ventura and John McCain are two examples of politicians who benefited from this use of the internet, a medium that still baffles many of their political opponents. In turn, voters were able to provide politicians with direct feedback through these websites. Of course, there is no guarantee that this direct feedback will eventually lead to policy formation. The political process is far too complex, to say the least, to warrant such expectations. Nevertheless, the internet opens up additional channels of communication, debatable as their outcome may be. These additional channels enable easier access to political information, spurring enthusiastic reformatory talk of a 'keypad democracy' (Grossman, 1995) and 'hardwiring the collective consciousness' (Barlow, 1995).

Therefore, celebratory rhetoric on the advantages of the internet as a public sphere focuses on the fact that it affords a place for personal expression (Jones, 1997), makes it possible for little-known individuals and groups to reach out to citizens directly and restructure public affairs (Grossman, 1995; Rash, 1997), and connects the government to citizens (Arterton, 1987). Interactivity promotes the use of 'electronic plebiscites', enabling instant polling, instant referenda, and voting from home (Abramson *et al.*, 1988). Acquiring and dispersing political communication online is fast, easy, cheap, and convenient. Information available on the internet is frequently unmediated; that is, it has not been tampered with or altered to serve particular interests (Abramson *et al.*, 1988).

While these are indisputably advantages to online communication, they do not instantaneously guarantee a fair, representative, and egalitarian public sphere. As several critics argue, access to online technologies and information should be equal and universal. Access should also be provided at affordable rates. Without a concrete commitment to online expression, the internet as a public sphere merely harbors an illusion of openness (Pavlik, 1994; Williams and Pavlik, 1994; Williams, 1994). The fact that online technologies are only accessible to, and used by, a small fraction of the population contributes to an electronic public sphere that is exclusive, elitist, and far from ideal – not terribly different from the bourgeois public sphere of the 17th and 18th centuries.

This point is reiterated in empirical research of online political communities completed by Hill and Hughes (1998). In researching political Usenet and AOL groups, they found that demographically, conservatives were a minority among internet users. Online political discourse, however, was dominated by conservatives, even though liberals were the online majority. This implies that the virtual sphere is politically divided in a manner that echoes traditional politics, thus simply serving as a space for additional expression, rather than radically reforming political thought and structure. Still, they also pointed out the encouraging fact that at least people *are* talking about politics and protesting virtually online against democratic governments.

Despite the fact that all online participants have the same access to information and opinion expression, the discourse is still dominated by a few. Moreover, not all information available on the internet is democratic or promotes democracy; for example, white supremacy groups often possess some of the cleverest, yet most undemocratic websites. However, this particular comment should not be misunderstood. Fundamental democratic principles guarantee the free expression of opinion. While sites that openly advocate discrimination on the basis of race or ethnicity exercise the right to free speech, they certainly do not promote democratic ideals of equality.

Some researchers pose additional questions, such as: even if online information is available to all, how easy is it to access and manage vast volumes of information (Jones, 1997)? Organizing, tracking, and going through information may be a task that requires skill and time that several do not possess. Access to information does not automatically render us better informed and more active citizens. In fact, Hart argued that some media, such as television, 'supersaturate viewers with political information', and that as a result 'this tumult creates in viewers a sense of activity rather than genuine civic involvement' (1994: 109). In addition, Melucci (1994) argued that while producing and processing information is crucial in constructing personal and social identity, new social movements emerge only insofar as actors fight for control, stating that 'the ceaseless flow of messages only acquires meaning through the code that orders the flux and allows its meanings to be read' (p. 102). Finally, some even argue that increased online participation would broaden and democratize the virtual sphere, but could also lead to a watering down of its unique content, substituting for discourse that is more typical and less innovative (e.g. Hill and Hughes, 1998). Still, this discourse is not less valuable.

In conclusion, access to online information is not universal and equal to all. Those who can access online information are equipped with additional tools to be more active citizens and participants of the public sphere. There are popular success stories, such as that of Santa Monica's Public Electronic Network, which started as an electronic town square, promoted online conversation between residents, and helped several homeless people find jobs and shelter (Schmitz, 1997). Groups such as the Electronic Frontier Foundation, the Center for a New Democracy, Civic Networking, Democracy Internet, the Democracy Resource Center, Interacta, and the Voter's Telecommunication Watch are a few examples of thriving online political stops.

Still, online technologies render participation in the political sphere more convenient, but do not guarantee it. Online political discussions are limited to those with access to computers and the internet. Those who do have access to the internet do not necessarily pursue political discussion, and online discussions are frequently dominated by a few. While the internet has the potential to extend the public sphere, at least in terms of the information that is available to citizens, not all of us are able or willing to take on the challenge. Access to more information does not necessarily create more informed citizens, or lead to greater political activity. Even though access to information is a useful tool, the democratizing potential of the internet depends on additional factors, examined in the following section.

## Globalization or tribalization?

Yet another reason why there is much enthusiasm regarding the future of the internet as a public sphere has to do with its ability to connect people from diverse backgrounds and provide a forum for political discussion. While many praise online political discussion for its rationality and diversity, others are skeptical about the prospect of disparate groups getting along. These technologies carry the promise of bringing people together, but also bear the danger of spinning them in different directions. Even more so, greater participation in political discussion, on or offline, may not secure a more stable and robust democracy. These are the issues addressed in this section.

Utopian perspectives on the internet speculate that computer-mediated political communication will facilitate grassroots democracy and bring people all across the world closer together. Geographic boundaries can be overcome and 'diasporic utopias' can flourish (Pavlik, 1994). Anonymity online assists one to overcome identity boundaries and communicate more freely and openly, thus promoting a more enlightened exchange of ideas. For example, the Indian newsgroup soc.culture.india is one of many online groups that foster critical political discourse among participants that might not even meet in real space and time. For several years this group has harbored lively political discussion on issues pertinent to the political future of India (Mitra, 1997a, 1997b).

Still, the existence of a virtual space does not guarantee democratic and rational discourse. Flaming and conflict beyond reasonable boundaries are evident both in Public Education Network (PEN) and soc.culture.india, and frequently intimidate participants from joining online discussions (Mitra, 1997a, 1997b; Schmitz, 1997). Hill and Hughes (1998) emphasized that the technological potential for global communication does not ensure that people from different cultural backgrounds will also be more understanding of each other, and they cite several examples of miscommunication. However, they did find that when conversation was focused on political issues, instead of general, it tended to be more toned down. Often, online communication is about venting emotion and expressing what Abramson *et al.* (1988) refer to as 'hasty opinions', rather than rational and focused discourse. Greater participation in political discussion does not automatically result in discussion that promotes democratic ideals.

Miscommunication set aside, however, what about communication? What impact do our words actually have online? Jones (1997) suggested that perhaps the internet allows its to 'shout more loudly, but whether other fellows listen, beyond the few individuals who may reply, or the occasional "lurker", is questionable, and whether our words will make a difference is even more in doubt' (p. 30). The same anonymity and absence of face-to-face interaction that expands our freedom of expression online keeps us from assessing the impact and social value of our words. The expression of political opinion online may leave one with an empowering feeling. The power of the words and their ability to effect change, however, is limited in the current political spectrum. In a political system where the role of the public is limited, the effect of these online opinions on policy making is questionable. To take this point further, political expression online may leave people with a false sense of empowerment, which misrepresents the true impact of their opinions. Individuals may leave political newsgroups with the content feeling that they are part of a well-oiled democracy – does this feeling represent reality or substitute for genuine civic engagement? At the same time, it is through political discussions with others that individuals come to realize the handicaps of our democracy, and even commit to political activity to overcome these. More studies and closer observation of online political discussions is necessary to determine the impact of political discussion on the individual psyche as well as the wellbeing of a democratic society.

Another crucial issue lies in how interconnectedness afflicts discussion. The number of people that our virtual opinions can reach may become more diverse, but may also become smaller as the internet becomes more fragmented. Special interest groups attract risers who want to focus the discussion on certain topics, providing opportunities for specialized discussion with people who have a few things in common. As the virtual mass becomes subdivided into smaller and smaller discussion groups, the ideal of a public sphere that connects many people online eludes us. On the other hand, the creation of special interest groups fosters the development of several online publics, which, as Fraser noted, reflect the collective ideologies of their members. After all, Habermas' vision was one of 'coffee-house' small group discussions.

[. . .]

To conclude, the internet may actually enhance the public sphere, but it does so in a way that is not comparable to our past experiences of public discourse. Perhaps the internet will not become the new public sphere, but something radically different. This will enhance democracy and dialogue, but not in a way that we would expect it to, or in a way that we have experienced in the past. For example, internet activist and hacker groups practice a reappropriated form of activism on the internet, by breaking into and closing down large corporations' websites, or 'bombing' them, so that no more users can enter them. This is a new form of activism, more effective than marching outside a corporation's headquarters, and definitely less innocuous than actually bombing a location. One could argue that the virtual sphere holds a great deal of promise as a political medium, especially in restructuring political processes and rejuvenating political rituals. In addition, the internet and related technologies invite political discussion and serve as a forum for it, Nevertheless, greater participation in political discussion is not the sole determinant of democracy. The content, diversity, and impact of political discussion need to be considered carefully before we conclude whether online discourse enhances democracy.

## Commercialization

Despite all the hype surrounding the innovative uses of the internet as a public medium, it is still a medium constructed in a capitalist era. It is part and parcel of a social and political world (Jones, 1997). As such it is susceptible to the same forces that, according to Carey (1995), originally transformed the public sphere. The same forces defined the nature of radio and television, media once hailed for providing innovative ways of communication. Douglas (1987) detailed how radio broadcasting revolutionized the way that people conceived of communication, and she documented how it built up hope for the extension of public communication and the improvement of democracy. The potential of televised communication to plow new ground for democracy had met with similar enthusiasm (Abramson et al., 1988). Nowadays, both media have transformed and produce commercial, formulaic programming for the most part. Advertising revenue has more impact on programming than democratic ideals. The concentration of ownership and standardization of programming have been documented by several scholars (e.g. Bagdikian, 1983; Ettema and Whitney, 1994), and growing public cynicism about media coverage undermines the democratizing potential of mass media.

For a vast majority of corporations the internet is viewed as another mass enterprise; its widespread and cheap access being a small, but not insurmountable obstacle to profit making. Online technologies, such as banners and portals, are being added to a growing number of web locations to create advertising revenue. Barrett (1996) traced how various communication technologies have destroyed one barrier after another in pursuit of profit, starting with volume, moving to mass, and finally space. He argued that time is the target of the electronic market, the fall of which will signal a more transparent market, in which conventional currency will turn into a 'free-floating abstraction' (Barrett, 1996).

Even so, advertising is not necessarily a bad addition to the internet, because it can provide small groups with the funds to spread their opinions and broaden public debate. To this point, some add that the 'very architecture of the internet will work against the type of content control these folks [corporate monopolies] have over mass media' (Newhagen, as cited in McChesney, 1995). McChesney (1995) agreed that the internet will open the door to a cultural and political renaissance, despite the fact that large corporations will take up a fraction of it to launch their cyberventures. He argued that cyberspace may provide 'a supercharged, information packed, and psychedelic version of ham radio'.

McChesney admitted that capitalism encourages a culture based on commercial values, and that it tends to 'commercialize every nook and cranny of social life in [a] way that renders the development or survival of nonmarket political and cultural organizations more difficult' (1995: 10). He maintained that there are several barriers to the internet reforming democracy, such as universal access and computer literacy. Computers are not affordable for a large section of the population. I would extend this to a global basis, and add that for several countries still struggling to keep up with technological changes brought along by the industrial era, the internet is a remote possibility. When just about 6 percent (Global Reach, 2001) of the global population has access to the internet, discussion of the democratizing potential of internet-related technologies seems at least a little hurried. At the present time, political discussions online are a privilege for those with access to computers and the internet. Those who would benefit the most from the democratizing potential of new technology do not have access to it.

Even more problematic, however, is the notion that technologies can unilaterally transform the nature of the political sphere. Our political system currently does suffer from decreased citizen involvement, and internet-related technologies have managed to amend that, but only to a certain extent. More important, however, is the fact that the power of our political system is negated by the influence of special interests, and generally by a growing dependency on a capitalist mentality.

[. . .]

Capitalist patterns of production may commodify these new technologies, transforming them into commercially oriented media that have little to do with promoting social welfare. Even if this scenario does not materialize, can new technologies mitigate the influence of special interests on polities? Internet-related technologies can certainly help connect, motivate, and organize dissent. Whether the expression of dissent is powerful enough to effect social change is a question of human agency and a much more complex issue. New technologies offer additional tools, but they cannot single-handedly transform a political and economic structure that has thrived for centuries.

It seems that the discussion of information access, internet fragmentation, and commercialization leads back to a main point: how do we recreate something online, when it never really existed offline? It is not impossible, but it is not an instantaneous process either. Unfortunately, blind faith in information media is not enough to effect the social changes necessary for a more robust and fair public sphere. To paraphrase Adam Smith's legendary phrase, the invisible hand of information is not as mighty as several techno-enthusiasts contend it is. But it can be useful. Having reviewed the conditions that both extend and limit the potential of the internet as a public sphere, I address this specific issue further and discuss the nature of the virtual sphere in the following section.

## A virtual sphere

Cyberspace is public and private space. It is because of these qualities that it appeals to those who want to reinvent their private and public lives. Cyberspace provides new terrain for the playing out of the age-old friction between personal and collective identity; the individual and community. Bellah *et al.* (1985) argued that individuals can overcome individualistic and selfish tendencies in favor of realizing the benefits of acting responsibly within a moralistic, transcendent social order. Is it possible to do so in cyberspace?

Some have argued that it is not. Cyberspace extends our channels for communication, without radically afflicting the nature of communication itself. Ample evidence can be found in political newsgroup discussions, which are often dominated by arguments and conflicts that mirror those of traditional politics. Hill and Hughes (1988) concluded that 'people will mold the internet to fit traditional politics. The internet itself will not be a historical light switch that turns on some fundamentally new age of political participation and grassroots democracy' (p. 186). McChesney (1995) agreed that new technologies will adapt to the current political culture, instead of creating a new one, and viewed the political uses of the internet as 'making the best of a bad situation' (p. 15). Ultimately; it is the balance between utopian and dystopian visions that unveils the true nature of the internet as a public sphere.

Fernback (1997) remarked that true identity and democracy are found in cyberspace 'not so much within the content of virtual communities, but within the actual structure of social relations' (p. 42). Therefore, one could argue that the present state of real life social relations hinders the creation of a public sphere in the virtual world as much as it does in the real one. This is an enlightened approach, because it acknowledges the occasionally liberating features of new technologies without being deterministic. It is the existing structure of social relations that drives people to repurpose these technologies and create spaces for private and public expression. The internet does possess the potential to change how we conceive ourselves, the political system, and the world surrounding us, but it will do so in a manner that strictly adheres to the democratic ideals of the public sphere. The reason for this lies in the fact that we transcend physical space and bodily boundaries upon entering cyberspace. This has a fundamental impact on how we carry ourselves online, and is simply different from how we conduct ourselves offline.

A virtual sphere does exist in the tradition of, but radically different from, the public sphere. This virtual sphere is dominated by bourgeois computer holders, much like the one traced by Habermas consisting of bourgeois property holders. In this virtual sphere, several special interest publics co-exist and flaunt their collective identities of dissent, thus reflecting the social dynamics of the real world, as Fraser (1992) noted. This vision of the true virtual sphere consists of several spheres of counterpublics that have been excluded from mainstream political discourse, yet employ virtual communication to restructure the mainstream that ousted them.

It is uncertain whether this structure will effect political change. Breslow (1997) argued that the internet promotes a sense of sociality, but it remains to be seen whether this translates into solidarity. Social and physical solidarity is what spawned political and social change over the course of the century, and the internet's anonymity and lack of spatiality and density may actually be counterproductive to solidarity. Ultimately, he concluded: 'How should I know who is at the other end, and when the chips are down, will people actually strip off their electronic guises to stand and be counted?' (p 255). The lack of solid commitment negates the true potential of the internet as a public sphere.

Melucci's (1996) approach to new social movements makes more sense in an age when individuals use machines, where movements such as May 1968 used the streets, to protest against the same things. His main argument is that social movements no longer require collective action that reflects the interest of a social group; they revolve more around personal identity and making sense of cultural information. Melucci contended that in the last 30 years, emerging social conflicts in complex societies have raised cultural challenges to the dominant language, rather than expressing themselves through political action. Although Melucci implied that such language shifts are ineffectual, the point is that collective action can no longer be overtly measured, but is still present in the creative proclamation of cultural codes. What Melucci termed 'identity politics' allows room for both the private and public uses of cyberspace. The virtual sphere allows the expression and development of such movements that further democratic expressions, by not necessarily focusing on traditional political issues, but by shifting the cultural ground.

In other words, it would seem that the internet and related technologies have managed to create new public space for political discussion. This public space facilitates, but does not ensure, the rejuvenation of a culturally drained public sphere. Cheap, fast, and convenient access to more information does not necessarily render all citizens more informed, or more willing to participate in political discussion. Greater participation in political discussion helps, but does not ensure a healthier democracy. New technologies facilitate greater, but not necessarily more diverse, participation in political discussion since they are still only available to a small fraction of the population. In addition, our diverse and heterogeneous cultural backgrounds make it difficult to recreate a unified public sphere, on or offline. Finally, decreased citizen participation is only one of the many problems facing our current political system. Dependence on special interests and a capitalist mode of production also compromise democratic ideals of equality. Moreover, the quickly expanding commodification of internet-related resources threatens the independence and democratizing potential of these media.

Nevertheless, the most plausible manner of perceiving the virtual sphere consists of several culturally fragmented cyberspheres that occupy a common virtual public space. Groups of 'netizens' brought together by common interests will debate and perhaps strive for the attainment of cultural goals. Much of the political discussion taking place online does not, and will not, sound different from that taking place in casual or formal face-to-face interaction. The widening gaps between politicians, journalists, and the public will not be bridged, unless both parties want them to be. Still, people who would never be able to come together to discuss political matters offline are now able to do so online, and that is no small matter. The fact that people from different cultural backgrounds, states, or countries involve themselves in virtual political discussions in a matter of minutes, often expanding each other's horizons with culturally diverse viewpoints, captures the essence of this technology. The value of the virtual sphere lies in the fact that it encompasses the hope, speculation, and dreams of what could be. Castells noted that 'we need Utopias – on the condition of not trying to make them into practical recipes' (interview with Ogilvy, 1998: 188). The virtual sphere reflects the dynamics of new social movements that struggle on a cultural, rather than a traditionally political terrain. It is a vision, but not yet a reality. As a vision, it inspires, but has not yet managed to transform political and social structures.

[. . .]

# References

Abramson, J. B., F. C. Arterton and G. R. Orrers (1988) *The Electronic Commonwealth: The Impact of New Media Technologies on Democratic Politics*. New York: Basic Books.

Arterton, F. C. (1987) *Teledemocracy: Can Technology Protect Democracy?* Newbury Park, CA: Sage.

Bagdikian, B. (1983) *The Media Monopoly*. Boston, MA: Beacon.

Barlow, J. P. (1995) 'A Globe, Clothing Itself with a Brain', *Wired* 3(6): 108.

Barrett, J. (1996) 'Killing Time: The New Frontier of Cyberspace Capitalism', in L. Strate, R. Jacobson and S. R. Gibson (eds) *Communication and Cyberspace*, pp. 155–66. Cresskill, NJ: Hampton Press.

Bell, D. (1981) 'The Social Framework of the Information Society', in T. Forester (ed.) *The Microelectronics Revolution*, pp. 500–49. Cambridge, MA: MIT Press.

Bellah, R. N., R. Madsen, W. M. Sullivan, A. Swidler and S. M. Tipton (1985) *Habits of the Heart*. Berkeley, CA: University of California Press.

Bowen, C. (1996) *Modem Nation: The Handbook of Grassroots American Activism Online*. New York: Random House.

Breslow, H. (1997) 'Civil Society, Political Economy, and the Internet', in S. Jones (ed.) *Virtual Culture: Identity and Communication in Cyberspace*, pp. 236–57. Thousand Oaks, CA: Sage.

Browning, G. (1996) *Electronic Democracy: Using the Internet to Influence American Politics*. Wilton, CT: Pemberton Press.

Cappella, J. and K. H. Jamieson (1996) 'News Frames, Political Cynicism, and Media Cynicism', *Annals of the American Academy of Political and Social Science* 546: 71–85.

Cappella, J. and K. H. Jamieson (1997) *Spiral of Cynicism: The Press and the Public Good*. New York: Oxford University Press.

Carey, J. (1995) 'The Press, Public Opinion, and Public Discourse', in T. Glasser and C. Salmon (eds) *Public Opinion and the Communication of Consent*, pp. 373–402. New York: Guilford.

Dewey, J. (1927) *The Public and its Problems*. New York: Holt.

Douglas, S. J. (1987) *Reinventing American Broadcasting*. Baltimore, MD: Johns Hopkins University Press.

Ettema, J. S. and D. C. Whitney (1994) 'The Money Arrow: An Introduction to Audience-making', in J. S. Ettema and D. C. Whitney (eds) *Audiencemaking*, pp. 1–18. Thousand Oaks, CA: Sage.

Fallows, J. (1996) 'Why Americans Hate the Media', *The Atlantic Monthly* (February) 277(2): 45–64.

Fernback, J. (1997) 'The Individual within the Collective: Virtual Ideology and the Realization of Collective Principles', in S. G. Jones (ed.) *Virtual Culture: Identity and Communication in Cybersociety*, pp. 36–54. Thousand Oaks, CA: Sage.

Fraser, N. (1992) 'Rethinking the Public Sphere: A Contribution to the Critique of Actually Existing Democracy', in C. Calhoun (ed.) *Habermas and the Public Sphere*, pp. 109–42. Cambridge, MA: MIT Press.

Garnham, N. (1992) 'The Media and the Public Sphere', in C. Calhoun (ed.) *Habermas and the Public Sphere*, pp. 359–76. Cambridge, MA: MIT Press.

Global Reach (2001) 'Global Internet Statistics', URL (consulted January 2001): http://www.euromktg.com/globstats.

Grossman, L. K. (1995) *The Electronic Republic*. New York: Viking.

Habermas, J. (1989 [1962]) *The Structural Transformation of the Public Sphere: An Inquiry into a Category of a Bourgeois Society*, trans. T. Burger and F. Lawrence. Cambridge, MA: MIT Press.

Habermas, J. (1991 [1973]) 'The Public Sphere', in C. Mukerji and M. Schudson (eds) *Rethinking Popular Culture: Contemporary Perspectives in Cultural Studies*, pp. 398–404. Berkeley, CA: University of California Press.

Hart, R. P. (1994) 'Easy Citizenship: Television's Curious Legacy', *Annals of the American Academy of Political and Social Science* 546: 109–20.

Hill, K. A. and J. E. Hughes (1998) *Cyberpolitics: Citizen Activism in the Age of the Internet*. New York: Rowman and Littlefield.

Jankowski, N. W. and M. van Selm (2000) 'The Promise and Practice of Public Debate in Cyberspace', in K. Hacker and J. van Dijk (eds) *Digital Democracy: Issues of Theory and Practice*, pp. 149–65. London: Sage.

Jones, S. G. (1997) 'The Internet and its Social Landscape', in S. G. Jones (ed.) *Virtual Culture: Identity and Communication in Cybersociety*, pp. 7–35. Thousand Oaks, CA: Sage.

Kling, K. (1996) 'Hopes and Horrors: Technological Utopianism and Anti-Utopianism in Narratives of Computerization', in K. Kling (ed.) *Computerization and Controversy*, pp. 40–58. Boston, MA: Academic Press.

Lyotard, J. F. (1984) *The Postmodern Condition*. Minneapolis: University of Minnesota Press.

McChesney, R. (1995) 'The Internet and US Communication Policy-making in Historical and Critical Perspective', *Journal of Computer-mediated Communication* 1(4), URL (consulted January 2001): http://www.usc.edu/dept/annenberg/vol1/issue4/mcchesney.html#Democracy.

Melucci, A. (1994) 'A Strange Kind of Newness: What's "New" in New Social Movements?', in E. Larana, H. Johnston and J. R. Gusfield (eds) *New Social Movements: From Ideology to Identity*, pp. 101–30. Philadelphia, PA: Temple University Press.

Melucci, A. (1996) *Challenging Codes: Collective Action in the Information Age*. New York: Cambridge University Press.

Mitra, A. (1997a) 'Virtual Community: Looking for India on the Internet', in S. G. Jones (ed.) *Virtual Culture: Identity and Communication in Cybersociety*, pp. 55–79. Thousand Oaks, CA: Sage.

Mitra, A. (1997b) 'Diasporic Websites: Ingroup and Outgroup Discourse', *Critical Studies in Mass Communication* 14(2): 158–81.

Negroponte, N. (1998) 'Beyond Digital', *Wired* 6(12): 288.

Ogilvy, J. (1998) 'Dark Side of the Boom: Interview with Manuel Castells', *Wired* 6(11): 188.

Patterson, T. (1993) *Out of Order*. New York: Knopf.

Patterson, T. (1996) 'Bad News, Bad Governance', *Annals of the American Academy of Political and Social Science* 546: 97–108.

Pavlik, J. V. (1994) 'Citizen Access, Involvement, and Freedom of Expression in an Electronic Environment', in F. Williams and J. V. Pavlik (eds) *The People's Right to Know: Media, Democracy and the Information Highway*, pp. 139–62. Hillsdale, NJ: Erlbaum.

Putnam, R. D. (1996) 'The Strange Disappearance of Civic America', *The American Prospect* 24(1): 34–48.

Rash, W. Jr (1997) *Politics on the Nets: Wiring the Political Process*. New York: W. H. Freeman.

Rheingold, H. (1993) *The Virtual Community*. Cambridge, MA: Addison-Wesley.

Schmitz, J. (1997) 'Structural Relations, Electronic Media, and Social Change: The Public Electronic Network and the Homeless', in S. G. Jones (ed.) *Virtual Culture: Identity and Communication in Cybersociety*, pp. 80–101. Thousand Oaks, CA: Sage.

Schudson, M. (1997) 'Why Conversation is Not the Soul of Democracy', *Critical Studies in Mass Communication* 14(4): 1–13.

Tocqueville, A. D. (1990) *Democracy in America*, vol. 1. New York: Vintage Classics.

Williams, F. (1994) 'On Prospects for Citizens' Information Services', in F. Williams and J. V. Pavlik (eds) *The People's Right to Know: Media, Democracy and the Information Highway*, pp. 3–24. Hillsdale, NJ: Erlbaum.

Williams, F. and Pavlik, J. V. (1994) 'Epilogue', in F. Williams and J. V. Pavlik (eds) *The People's Right to Know: Media, Democracy and the Information Highway*, pp. 211–24. Hillsdale, NJ: Erlbaum.

# PART EIGHT

# Virtualities

## INTRODUCTION

■ Ensio Puoskari

**I**T HAS BECOME COMMONPLACE to contend that we live today in a 'virtual' world. Though the term has resonance, and appears to identify some-thing central about the way we are today, there is in fact considerable ambiguity about its meaning. We talk often nowadays of having a 'virtual' relationship when it is based on e-mail contact and, increasingly, media are described as 'virtual' tech-nologies which bring us 'virtual experiences' such as news from faraway places. Depictions of 'virtual life' typically emphasize this, the *mediated* characteristic of so much of what we do now, where we experience issues and events, and interact with others, through electronic communications of one sort or another in a realm termed 'cyberspace'. It is assumed here that the 'virtual' may be distinguished from the 'real' flesh-and-blood relations and experiences which prevail where one meets others personally or directly experiences something. Somewhat differently, 'virtual reality' refers to simulations such as aircraft in flight or driving a car, where the presumption generally is that there is a 'reality' elsewhere which is artificially, if precisely, replicated. Such simulations are increasingly produced in educational or training settings.

However, the 'virtual' may also indicate the increasingly routine technological interventions in the body itself, such as heart monitors, hip replacements and cosmetic surgery. The prospect is that the body will be even more thoroughly tech-nological in the near future with the development of genetic engineering and digital technologies. A response to this has been much speculation on the character of cyborgs (cybernetic organisms) which meld the natural and the human (Webster 2000). This notion of the virtual does not draw upon any distinction between the 'real' and the 'virtual' since boundaries are irretrievably blurred – the body is certainly substantial and 'real', though it is constituted in this way by technologies such as artificial knee joints, drug regimes and careful diet.

To be sure, cyborgs have long captured the imagination. Popular images of the cyborg have usually been reiterations of male armoured bodies like Hollywood's *Terminator* and *RoboCop*, or more recently *Matrix*, though female cyborg images have recently become prominent, as for instance with *Lara Croft*. Contemporary cultural criticism has continued and heightened this concern with the relationship between bodies and machines. It is from this vantage point that Anne Balsamo, in her book *Technologies of the Gendered Body: Reading Cyborg Women* (1996), interrogates the status of the body in emerging technology. This is a matter of such import as regards social change that we provided an extract of her work in Part Four (Chapter 16), where our concern was with 'Transformations', and we would refer readers to that piece here.

For Balsamo, the conjuncture of bodies and technology represents not only new hopes of 'corporeal recontruction and physical immortality, it also represses and obfuscates our awareness of new strains on and threats to the material body' (p. 2). While technology may offer liberation and new hope, it also reinscribes the body with norms and disciplines that contain it because, as Donna Haraway (1991) has argued, it is at the interface of bodies and machines that the boundaries of bodies are being transgressed. Cyborgs in their various forms are instances of what might be thought of as 'border cases', that in their acts of trangression (between body/machine, male/female, born/made, etc.), are also made visible. They are thus deeply implicated in what Michel Foucault has called 'technologies of power' and what Haraway has termed 'the informatics of domination'. Therefore, in trying to understand the relations of power that are at the nexus of bodies and technology, Balsamo tries to pull together various threads in an effort to create a 'thick perception' of the body in crisis under control. Displeased with Foucault's research on sexuality (a common problem for feminists who appreciate his work on power, but are disturbed by the absence of gender as a constituent part of the power he elucidates), Balsamo introduces a new term, 'technologies of the gendered body', to capture how material female bodies are constituted in a variety of technologized cultural situations.

Basing her work on various researchers who have investigated how the female body has been constructed, Balsamo concerns herself with how bodies may be reconstructed, restaged and redeployed. Looking at topics such as female bodybuilding, cosmetic surgery, reproductive technology and cyberpunk fiction, Balsamo recognizes current problems and remaining possibilities to be found at the edges of the machine/body interface – a problem which is also addressed in this section by Mark Poster and Sadie Plant. In another extract reproduced here Eric Michaels offers a more positive picture than does Balsamo in tracing what kind of changes knowledge goes through when primitive societies become modernized via satellite technologies, in this way offering another kind of Foucauldian 'power/knowledge' perspective.

Mark Poster (Chapter 27) is one thinker who tries to retain a critical edge while embracing theories of postmodernity. He proposes that a new 'mode of information' is supplanting previous socio-cultural formations. Poster argues that 'mode of information' radically reconfigures language in ways quite different from the modern pattern of the rational, autonomous individual formed through writing. This familiar subject is now being displaced by the 'mode of information' by a subject that is multiplied, disseminated and de-centred, continuously interpellated as an unstable identity. Poster continues to suggest that, at the level of culture, this instability poses challenges which, if they become part of a political movement, or are connected with the politics of feminism, ethnic/racial minorities, gay and lesbian positions, may lead to a fundamental assault on modern social institutions and structures.

Poster illustrates his idea of mode of information by focusing on advertisements (adopting Baudrillard's ideas), superpanopticon (widening Foucault's concept to new areas) and electronic writing (commenting and illustrating what kind of consequences Derrida's ideas might have). In all these areas the older social theories are no longer appropriate for understanding the changing structures of everyday life. In this and in other articles Poster (2001a and b) is especially interested in the question of databases.

While it is clear that Poster sees in the new technologies great potential for new forms of domination, he has less to say about what kind of resistance is possible in this kind of society. Although Poster is more sceptical than most other postmodernists, he also appears to agree that information and communications technologies help to propel us into some new kind of terrain, which it may be appropriate to designate postmodernity.

Eric Michaels (Chapter 28) studied extensively the uses of new technologies in closed communities. The Australian Aborigines that Michaels examined are an oral, kin-based people whose exchange of information is conducted on a face-to-face basis. While the contrast between oral traditional societies and the West is in many ways obvious, Michaels' examination of these differences in terms of the introduction of TV, VCRs and satellite into the world of the Warlpiri was innovative. His article 'For a cultural future' is the best-known investigation into how old and new knowledge systems can be used by Aborigines. Knowledge is the social, economic and political glue that holds societies together. Some people have the right to know, others may have the right to use and still others the right to hear or see or perform.

For Michaels cultures can be viewed as systems of communication regulated through a social system: understand the flow of information and you have a key to understanding a culture. In another essay Michaels (1994) summarizes his view:

> Oral societies are a kind of information society in which access to knowledge is of particular social and economic consequences, and typically highly regulated. The introduction of new information technology to traditional societies poses fundamental challenges to the maintenance and legitimate evolution of these groups. To the extent that new technologies alter traditional means of access and control of information, and to the extent that novel information (content) devalues traditional

knowledge and the authority of its purveyors, the integrity of the society as a whole is at risk . . . the economies of satellite distribution are essentially the inverse of the information economics of oral, face-to-face society. If such societies intend to participate in new communication technology, complimentary and corrective technology on the ground, at the local level, is suggested as a first priority.

**Sadie Plant** (Chapter 29) is perhaps the best entry point into contemporary cyberfeminist theory. True, she seems quite interested in the deep, dark, technological feminine. She speaks of the male Ones and the binary opposites, the female Zeroes (1996); and she manages to weave together a genuine her-story of technology. Yet, she also reaches beyond these constraints into a complex relationship between women and machines. This relationship, tied up in problematics surrounding identity, technology and body, is at the heart of the contemporary movement called cyberfeminism.

In Plant's view technology is fundamentally female – not male as the legions of geeks, computer science teachers and *Wired* magazine editors would seem to have us believe. She argues that power structures, which have unequally favoured men and male forms in society, should be made more equal through a process of revealing and valuing overlooked female elements.

A good example of this kind of approach is her article 'The Future Looms: Weaving Women and Cybernetics', which turns on the story of Ada Lovelace, arguably the world's first computer programmer. Ada's history is enthralling. As assistant to Charles Babbage, she helped build early calculation machines such as the Babbage's Difference Engine. Clearly not enough is known about this figure and her place in the development of computer society. Plant's goal is to recuperate this lost female origin from within the history of technology. It must however be emphasized that Plant wishes not to valorize some negative space created by patriarchy, but to unveil the always already feminine space of technology. This is ultimately a more powerful move.

Through her work a primary metaphor is the 'matrix'. This materializes itself historically in the weaving processes of industrial power looms, in the predominantly female telephone operators, in the theme of weaver as computer programmer and in the web-like structure of cyberspace. Because of this history, Plant writes that technology is fundamentally a process of emasculation. 'The matrix weaves itself in a future which has no place for historical man', says Plant.

## REFERENCES

Balsamo, Anne (1996) *Technologies of the Gendered Body. Reading Cyborg Women.* Durham: Duke University Press.

Haraway, Donna (1991) *Simians, Cyborgs and Women: The Reinvention of Nature.* London: Free Press.

Michaels, Eric (1994) *Bad Aboriginal Art: Tradition, Media and Technological Horizons.* Minneapolis: University of Minnesota Press.

Plant, Sadie (1996) *Zeros and Ones: Digital Women and the New Technology*. London: Fourth Estate.

Poster, Mark (2001a) *The Information Subject Essays*. Amsterdam: G + B Arts.

Poster, Mark (2001b) *What's the Matter with the Internet?* Minneapolis: University of Minnesota Press.

Webster, Frank (2000) 'Virtual Culture: Knowledge, Identity and Choice', in John R. Bryson, Peter W. Williams, Nick Henry and Jane Pollard (eds) *Knowledge, Space, Economy*. London: Routledge, pp. 226–41.

# Chapter 27

# Mark Poster

# THE MODE OF INFORMATION
# AND POSTMODERNITY

From *The Second Media Age*, Cambridge: Polity Press (1995), pp. 57–77.

A POSTSTRUCTURALIST APPROACH to communication theory analyzes the way electronically mediated communication (what I call 'the mode of information') both challenges and reinforces systems of domination that are emerging in a postmodern society and culture.[1] My general thesis is that the mode of information enacts a radical reconfiguration of language, one which constitutes subjects outside the pattern of the rational, autonomous individual. This familiar modern subject is displaced by the mode of information in favor of one that is multiplied, disseminated and decentered, continuously interpellated as an unstable identity. At the level of culture, this instability poses both dangers and challenges which, if they become part of a political movement, or are connected with the politics of feminism, ethnic/racial minorities, gay and lesbian positions, may lead to a fundamental challenge to modern social institutions and structures.

[. . .]

The emergence of the mode of information, with its electronically mediated systems of communication, changes the way we think about the subject and promises to alter as well the shape of society. Electronic culture promotes the individual as an unstable identity, as a continuous process of multiple identity formation, and raises the question of a social form beyond the modern, the possibility of a postmodern society.[2] Electronic culture promotes theories (such as poststructuralism) that focus on the role of language in the process of the constitution of subjects and that undermine views of the reader and author as stable points of criticism and authority respectively. When print mediates the theorist's understanding of the subject, language is understood as representational, as an arbitrary system of signs, invoked by a thinker in order to point to objects. As long as this regime is in place, the subject remains a stable point, fixed in space and time. Figures that upset such an understanding of the subject – women, children, non-Europeans – are placed in the position of being Other, of not being taken seriously into account. When electronic communications are a factor in the theorist's understanding of the subject, language is understood as performative, rhetorical, as an active figuring and positioning of the subject. With the spread of this regime of communications, the subject can only be understood as partially stable, as repeatedly reconfigured at different points of time and space, as non-self-identical and therefore as always partly Other.

Electronic communications, like print, place a distance between the addressor and the addressee; they accentuate the feature of language that permits a gap between the speaker and the listener. This gap is often understood by proponents of modern print-oriented theory as efficiency. From smoke signals to communication satellites, the principle is the same: extend the human voice. Just as tools may heighten the powers of the muscles in the production of goods, they may amplify the larynx, allowing speech at a distance. Theories that view communications technology purely as a question of efficiency unduly discourage new questions that arise from electronic communications, placing them within the older paradigms generated to theorize oral and print culture. When electronic communications are seen as simply allowing greater spatial and temporal extension, the analyst reconfirms the figure of the autonomous rational individual and reinstates the stability of the subject.

In terms of politics, oral communications, from the point of view of print culture, bind the individual in relations of political domination. When communications are restricted to speech (and manuscript as its simple extension), individuals are easily restrained in ties of dependence. By enlarging the gap mentioned above as inherent in language, print allows a distance to intervene between speaker and listener and this gap permits the individual to think, coolly to judge the words of the other without his or her overbearing presence. Or so advocates of print culture contend.

[. . .]

Electronic culture permits a different interpretation of the gap. The tremendous extension of the space between speaker and listener in the mode of information upsets the confinement of the gap to the self-identical subject. The combination of enormous distances with temporal immediacy produced by electronic communications both removes the speaker from the listener and brings them together. These opposing tendencies – opposite from the point of view of print culture – reconfigure the position of the individual so drastically that the figure of the self, fixed in time and space, capable of exercising cognitive control over surrounding objects, may no longer be sustained. Language no longer represents a reality, no longer is a neutral tool to enhance the subject's instrumental rationality: language becomes or better reconfigures reality. By doing so the subject is interpellated through language and cannot easily escape recognition of that interpellation. Electronic communications systematically remove the fixed points, the grounds, the foundations that were essential to modern theory. I shall illustrate these transformations of cultural and social life by diverse examples of electronically mediated communication: the TV ad, the database and computer writing. I shall explore these examples from the poststructuralist perspectives of Jean Baudrillard, Michel Foucault and Jacques Derrida.

In the register of humanist morality, TV ads are manipulative, deceptive and repugnant; they entice consumer decisions on 'irrational' grounds and encourage a 'quick fix' drug mentality as a false solution to life's problems. In the register of marketing, TV ads are evaluated in relation to their ability 'to create effective demand' for the product. In the register of democratic politics, TV ads undermine the independent thinking of the electorate, diminishing its ability to distinguish truth from falsity, the real and the imaginary, and passify it into a state of indifference. In the register of Marxist social criticism, TV ads stimulate false needs that detract from the revolutionary purpose of the working class and serve only to pump up an economy that is beyond the control of the producers. Each of these perspectives contains a degree of validity but none approaches the crucial issue of the role of TV ads in contemporary culture, none reveals the altered language structure of the ads, and, most importantly, none draws attention to the relation of language to culture in the constitution of new subject positions, that is, new places in the network of social communication. I contend that TV ads exploit electronic mediation so as to inscribe a new technology of power, one whose political effects need to be assessed in relation to the possible emergence of a post-modern society.

[. . .] With great flexibility the ad constructs a mini-reality in which things are set in juxtapositions that violate the rules of the everyday. In particular, TV ads associate meanings, connotations and moods that are inappropriate in reality, subject to objections in dialogic communications, but effective at the level of desire, the unconscious, the imaginary. TV ads constitute a language system that leaves out the referent, the symbolic and the real, working instead with chains of signifiers (words) and signifieds (mental images). The referent, the symbolic and the real are absent and come into play only if the viewer buys the product.

The meaning structure of the TV ad, strictly keeping itself to the levels of signifiers, meanings and images, powerfully invites the viewer to identify with the commodity. The ad stimulates not an object choice, a cognitive decision, a rational evaluation, but works at other linguistic levels to produce the effects of incorporation and attachment between the viewer and the product. The viewer is the absent hero or heroine of the ad. The viewer is solicited to displace him or herself into the ad and become one with the meanings associated with the product. In its monologue, in its construction of context and its association of non-connected meanings, the TV ad inscribes a new pattern of communication into the culture, one repeated ad infinitum, one extended, I need hardly remind you, to politics, religion and every conceivable aspect of social life.

[. . .]

Jean Baudrillard, in *Consumer Society, The System of Objects* and *For a Critique of the Political Economy of the Sign*, began the line of thinking about contemporary culture which I am pursuing in relation to TV ads as part of the mode of information.[3] Baudrillard broke with the realist paradigms of social science at first by combining Roland Barthes' semiology with the neo-Marxism of Henri Lefebvre. [. . .]

For Baudrillard the structuralists are too formalist, restricting themselves too closely to linguistic signs. He shifts the object of analysis to daily life, taking society itself as the field for interpretation. Consumer activity would then be seen as a circulation of signs in the structuralist sense. The commodity is thus extracted from the domain of economic theory or moral commentary and viewed as a complex code. The key to consumerism is not an irrational tendency to conspicuous display but the insertion of individuals into a communications relation in which they receive messages in the form of commodities. The consumer is not 'irrational' and the object is not a 'utility.' Between the poles of object and intention is the advertisement which disrupts the normal set of differential relations of signs. The ad presupposes language not as a reference to a 'real' but as an arbitrary connection of signifiers. It simply rearranges those signifiers, violating their 'normal' references. The aim of the ad is to associate a chain of signifiers in a narrative of a desirable life style: Pepsi = youth = sexiness = popularity = fun, for example.

The status of the ad as a linguistic and cultural phenomenon, Baudrillard argued in the 1980s, is that of a simulacrum, a copy that has no original, has no objective referent. For him today's culture increasingly is composed of these simulacra which taken together compose a new order of reality, which he terms 'the hyper-real.' Culture consists of constructed realities, Disneylands, which are more real than the real they are supposed to refer back to. But in the end there is no reference back since, once social life is presented as a theme park in one place, its constructed element emerges and tends to dominate over its presence as a fixed, natural order. Society becomes a collage of theme parks which one enters at will (and for a price). Baudrillard totalizes his view of the hyper-real, dismissing other modernist perspectives on politics and the economy as without value. By contextualizing his understanding of consumer culture in relation to the mode of information, by connecting it with specific communication technologies, I hope to extract the critical impulse of his position without acceding to his monolithic vision.

Computerized databases are another form of electronically mediated communication that have been studied from various perspectives. Liberal writers have rightly been concerned that the vast data accumulated in this form and its relative ease of transfer pose a threat to the privacy of the individual. With so much information about individuals now digitalized in databases, one's life becomes an open book for those who have access to the right computers. Agencies of all kinds – military, police, governmental, corporate – continuously gather data and exchange it from one computer to another while the individuals to whom this data refers have little control over its flow or, in many cases, knowledge of its existence. In the eyes of liberals, society is indeed nearing the nightmare of 1984, only a few years behind Orwell's schedule. Marxists for their part have shown how databases are a new form of information as commodity, one which has passed largely into the control of the biggest corporations. Increasingly society becomes divided into the information rich and the information poor. Existing class divisions on a national and even a global scale are reinforced and further sedimented by the technology of computerized information. As the economy relies more and more upon information, access to databases is not at all a trivial matter. The fate of companies, even nations, hinges upon the timely procurement of information. In comparison with feudal regimes, capitalist societies once prided themselves on establishing the free flow of information, thinking of this feature of modernity as a touchstone of freedom. The digitalization of information in the form of databases acts to facilitate its instantaneous, global availability, so the restraint of commodification flies in the face of the advance of the technology.

While these perspectives are valuable for a full understanding of the database as a communications technology, they neglect a fundamental aspect of the phenomenon: its ability to constitute and multiply the identity of the individual and thereby to promote his/her control. The social model implicit in the above positions is one of individuals/groups confronting institutions and social forces in a relation of struggle, contest and opposition. At the most general level, liberals and Marxists assume a world of discrete, stable entities. [. . .]

[. . .] Individual actions now leave trails of digitized information which are regularly accumulated in computer databases and, at the speed of light or sound, transmitted back and forth between computers. Previously anonymous actions such as paying for a dinner, borrowing a book from a library, renting a videotape from a rental store, subscribing to a magazine, making a long distance telephone call – all by interacting with perfect strangers – now are wrapped in a clothing of information traces which are gathered and arranged into profiles, forming more and more detailed portraits of individuals. This postmodern daily life is not one of discrete individuals, hidden behind shields of anonymity in market interactions with strangers; nor is it a return to a village of familiar faces.[4] Instead it combines features of both without the advantages of either. In the credit card payment for dinner, the waiter is a stranger but the computer which receives the information 'knows' the customer very well. Urban life now consists of face-to-face interactions with strangers coupled by electronically mediated interactions with machines 'familiar' with us. The lines dividing individual from individual and individual from institution are consistently crossed by computer databases, cancelling privacy as a model of action or even as an issue.

Information flows today double the action of individuals and subvert theoretical models which presuppose either privacy or the class struggle. Society is now a double movement: one, of individuals and institutions; another, of information flows. [. . .]

Databases are inherently limited and restricted structures of information. Unlike the narratives, which are complex and flexible, they are severely restricted forms of discourse. In database programs only certain marks may be made in certain 'fields' or areas. For instance, if, after the name of the individual, a 'field' for magazine subscriptions follows, normally one cannot fill this field with the name of the magazine, but only with a code for certain groups of magazines. Thus *The New Republic* might be coded as 'l' for liberal and *The Guardian* as 'r' for radical. If video rentals are included in the database, *Deep Throat* and *Last Tango in Paris* might both be coded as 'x.' Such simplification of data drastically distorts, one might complain, particular experience, but it also vastly facilitates the speed with which information may be retrieved. In this way, databases configure reality, make composites of individual experience, that could be characterized as caricatures. By contrast, databases may also include graphics, that is to say, pictures or copies of fingerprints, for example. Information about individuals then becomes much more complex. The important consideration, however, is not the question of verisimilitude: would any individual be pleased by the accuracy of the information portrait contained in a database? But rather that databases constitute additional identities for individuals, identities which

– in the interactions between computers and between institutions which rely upon them, on the one hand, and individuals on the other – take the place of those individuals. When a computer search is done for John Smith, the output from the machine is, from the point of view of the receiving computer or institution, John Smith himself. Just as actions in daily life are doubled by information traces, so identities are multiplied in the interactions of computer databases.

The theoretical problem of accounting for the social impact of databases is best assisted by the work of Michel Foucault. This is so in three senses: Foucault theorized, first, power in relation to a specific social formation, the panopticon, which has direct application to databases; second, the relation between social phenomena and the subject that is relevant to the case of databases; and third, the relation between discourse and practice, ideas and action, attitudes and behavior in a way that permits the understanding of databases outside the limitations of the paradigms of liberal and Marxist theory.

In *Discipline and Punish* Foucault uses the term 'panopticon' to designate the control mechanism in prisons by which a guard, stationed in a central tower, could observe the inmates, arranged in cells around the tower with windows facing in toward the tower, without himself being seen by them.[5] Panopticon, literally 'all-seeing,' denotes a form of power which attempts to orient the prisoners toward the authority system of the prison as a step in their reformation or normalization. For the process of reform, the panopticon is a part of a broader set of mechanisms which included a minutely regulated schedule, a file-keeping system on each prisoner, and so forth. What interests Foucault in the system of discipline is not only its micrological detail but also its 'positive' inscription of power. Unlike the central government which uses power as a 'negative' principle of preventing or denying certain activities, the panopticon shapes and molds the behavior of the criminals, producing, in a sense, a new person, the prison inmate. The key to the mechanism of discipline is the continuous, systematic, unobserved surveillance of a population. The criminal is coerced to follow a plan and to be aware that the slightest deviation on his part from the plan would be observed and would have consequences for him. Through the workings of the panopticon, a norm is imposed on a population, on its practices and its attitudes, a norm that is a result not of the imposition of someone else's will, as in feudalism, but rather of an anonymous authority that is seemingly omnipresent. In the panopticon Foucault locates a system of power at the level of the everyday, as opposed to the level of the state, which combines discourses and practices to instantiate the social character of the inmate. As a general feature of society, the panopticon is an example of what Foucault calls a 'technology of power' or a 'microphysics of power.'

In a second way Foucault's theory of the panopticon applies to databases. As a positive instantiation of power, the panopticon constitutes the individual criminal as an inmate. The discourse/practice of discipline produces the behaviors and attitudes of the prison population, regardless of the degree to which the prisoners resist or subvert that imposition. Their identity becomes that of an inmate however enthusiastic they may or may not have been about such a fate. By the same token, databases in the super-panopticon constitute identities for each individual and they do so regardless of whether the individual is even aware of it. Individuals are 'known' to computer databases, have distinct 'personalities' for them and in relation to which the computer 'treats' them in programmed ways. These identities also serve as a basis for the communication between computers, communications that occur routinely and without the knowledge of the 'real person.' Such identities are hardly innocent since they may seriously affect the individual's life, serving as the basis for a denial of credit, or an FBI investigation, or the termination of social assistance, or the denial of employment or residence. In each case the individual is acted upon in relation to his or her identity as it is constituted in the database. Simply because this identity has no intimate connection with the internal consciousness of the individual, with his or her self-defined attributes, in no way minimizes its force or effectiveness. With the dissemination of databases, a communications technology pervades the social space and multiplies the identity of individuals, regardless of their will, intention, feeling or cognition.

In order fully to comprehend the significance of the constitution of identities by databases, one must appreciate the epistemological break Foucault enacts with the commonplace sense of the distinction between action and language, behavior and intention, a distinction that is one of the hallmarks of modern social theory. In relation to the social import of databases, Marxists, for example, concern themselves with the use made of databases by the state and the corporations. They criticize the way these organizations use databases to enhance their control and power over subordinate classes. In their work they maintain a clear distinction between institutions and individuals, action and knowledge, behavior and information. The state is a force external to individuals, an institution whose power increases by dint of the tool of databases. The vast information at the state's disposal constitutes another link in the chain of oppression. By contrast Foucault focuses on the way power is both action and knowledge and the way power implicates the individual. He looks for the connections between phenomena which others see as discrete oppositions. The science of criminology for him is simply another element in the mechanism of discipline, not a privileged locus of truth outside the play of power. Similarly the individual's identity is not outside power but constituted by its operations, linked to it inextricably. The super-panopticon then emerges not as an imposition or restraint upon the individual but rather as part of the individual's identity. Foucault's ability to specify the relation panopticon–inmate derives from his poststructuralist rejection of the separation of mind and body, language and action, ideology and institution in favor of their mutual imbrication. My analysis of databases, following Foucault, moves to a model of communication in which the level of the subject is not cut off from practice, the body, power, institutions.

Databases, I argue, operate as a super-panopticon. Like the prison, databases work continuously, systematically and surreptitiously, accumulating information about individuals and composing it into profiles. Unlike the panopticon, the 'inmates' need not be housed in any architecture; they need only proceed with their regular daily life. The super-panopticon is thereby more unobtrusive than its forebear, yet it is no less efficient at its task of normalization. Each characteristic of an individual's profile in a database is easily distinguished for unusual qualities, from credit ratings and overdue book notices to excessive traffic violations. Another advantage of the newer power mechanism over the older one is its facility of communications, or transport of information. Computers easily exchange databases, the information in one being accessible to others. Instantaneously, across the globe information from databases flows in cyberspace to keep tabs on people. Databases 'survey' us without the eyes of any prison guard and they do so more accurately and thoroughly than any human being. A major impact of the super-panopticon is that the distinction between public and private loses its force since it depended on an individual's space of invisibility, of opaqueness to the state and the corporations. Yet these characteristics are cancelled by databases because wherever one is and whatever one is doing, traces are left behind, traces that are transformed into information for the grist of computers.

Electronic writing is the third example of the mode of information as a communications technology. It covers a wide variety of writing practices, including word processing[6] and hypertext,[7] electronic mail and message services and computer conferencing. In each case the computer mediates the relation of author and reader, altering the basic conditions of the enunciation and reception of meaning.[8] Electronic writing continues the tendency begun with handwriting and print: it enables the removal of the author from the text, increases the distance, both spatial and temporal, of the author from the reader and augments the problem of the interpretation of texts. Compared with speech, writing is a way of storing language, fixing it so that it can be read by those not directly intended by the author. Writing thus promotes the transmission of culture from generation to generation, the transformation of cultural works into monuments and the elevation of authors into authorities. Writing also fosters the development of critical thinking on the part of the reader: by stabilizing words on the page, the reader can reflect upon them, go back to earlier passages and re-examine links of argument, and accomplish all of this in isolation without the presence of the author or the community exerting any pressure on the act of interpretation. Printing is often credited with shaping the autonomous rational individual, a condition of modern democracy. Electronic writing furthers all these features of handwriting and print simply because it is a far more efficient system of storage. Compared with print, digitized writing requires less time to copy and less space to store.

But electronic writing also subverts the culture of print.[9] In the case of word processing, the ease of altering digital writing, the immateriality of signs on the screen compared with ink on the page, shifts the text out of a register of fixity and into one of volatility. Also digital texts lend themselves to multiple authorship. Files may be exchanged between people in several ways, each person working on the text, with the result, in its spatial configuration on a screen or printed on paper, hiding any trace of signature. In addition, hypertext programs encourage the reader to treat the text as a field or network of signs in which to create his or her own linkages, linkages which may become part of the text and which other readers may follow or change at their will. These programs permit searches for words or phrases throughout a text or group of texts which may be added to the text or saved. The result is a new text which brings terms together that were not so associated by the author. The reader has substituted their own hierarchy of terms for that of the author. With electronic writing the distinction between author and reader collapses and a new form of text emerges that may challenge the canonicity of works, even the boundaries of disciplines.

Computer message services establish a form of communication that also subverts the culture of handwriting and print. There are several forms of these electronic 'post offices.' In the case of electronic mail, the individual has an 'address' on a computer and anyone who knows it may send a message or letter to it from their own computer. In another instance, certain computers serve as 'bulletin boards' which allow many individuals to browse through messages and leave their own. These 'electronic cafes' encourage strangers, individuals who have never met face to face, to communicate to one another. Strangers here exchange messages without the extraneous presence of the body or the voice, only signs passing from one to another. What is more, these bulletin boards use pseudonyms or handles: individuals do not use their own names and may easily disguise any of their attributes, such as gender or ethnicity. As a form of writing, the message services foster not the autonomous, rational, stable individual but the playful, imaginative multiple self. In countries that have experimented extensively with message services, such as France, they have proven enormously popular.[10] People seem to enjoy a communication technology in which they invent themselves in the process of exchanging signs.

Another form of communication enabled by computer writing is computer conferencing.[11] In this instance, digital writing substitutes not for print but for face-to-face meetings and oral communications. Computer conferences eliminate the need for gathering people in one place at one time. There exists now an alternative to synchronous meeting or community as we know it. A central computer reserves an area for the conference. Individuals, using their personal computers hooked up to telephones, call that computer and read the presentations and comments of others, responding as they see fit. Studies of computer conferences reveal that the gain is not simply efficiency: new qualities of community relations develop in this cyberspace. [. . .]

The theory of deconstruction of Jacques Derrida anticipates in many ways changes brought about by computer writing.[12] He counters the traditional theory of writing as fixity of meaning, monumentality, the authority of the author by focusing on the material aspect of signs inscribed on pages. He argues that such inscription leaves language open to multiple meaning, that the spacing of traces differs and displaces meaning away from the author, that the linear form of the book, with its order of pagination, its margins, its diacritical markings, its chapters and paragraphs, imposes a hierarchy that the reader may subvert by taking it as a text, a stream of marks whose contradictions and impasses are open to a close reading. Western thought relies upon printed writing to support the author's stable meaning, to insist that the book signifies only what the author intended. This 'logocentrism,' as Derrida terms it, works by exclusions, supplements and marginalizations which may be reintroduced in a subversive reading. Books establish oppositions of terms, binaries in which one term is subordinate to the other and often absent from text. In the American Declaration of Independence the phrase 'all men are created equal' omits women and suppresses the question of race, even as it inscribes these groups as inferior. Deconstruction attempts to destabilize the march of univocal meaning in written texts by unlocking the logic of difference that it hides.

Derrida's interpretive gesture is similar to my understanding of electronic writing. Both deconstruction and electronic writing understand the volatility of written language, its instability and uncertain authorship. Both see language as effecting a destabilization of the subject, a dispersal of the individual, a fracturing of the illusion of unity and fixity of the self. Derrida, however, understands these qualities of writing as applying to all of its forms and he differentiates only partially between handwriting, print and digital writing.[13] Deconstruction, then, is Derrida's interpretation of writing in all its forms. By contrast my effort is to distinguish between print and electronic forms of writing, to assess the significance of the difference enacted by a new communications technology. Derrida's strategy removes the task of interpretation from the context of contemporary changes in culture and society, repeating the gesture of earlier thinkers by producing a discourse as a reinterpretation. Ultimately, then, the force of deconstruction returns to see Derrida as a Western philosopher, defeating his own effort to subvert that position. Nonetheless the corpus of Derrida's writing provides powerful analytic tools to criticize the cultural and ideological patterns that have accompanied print writing. In that way, and to a certain extent, deconstruction permits the reading of texts in a manner that suits electronic writing.

In the examples of TV ads, databases and computer writing, poststructuralist perspectives enable a comprehension of the linguistic features of new communications technologies and relate these to the cultural problem of the constitution of the subject. In particular they enable us to see the way electronically mediated communication promotes a new configuration of the subject that may be termed postmodern in the sense that it is structurally different from that of the modern era. Research on the mode of information has barely begun and much remains to extend these analyses to communications technologies not even mentioned here. I want now to raise some epistemological and political issues concerning the use of poststructuralist theory in the field of communications and point to additional areas for further research.

The theory of mode of information intersects with critical social theory's recognition of the stalled dialectic. As the Frankfurt School recognized long ago, in the course of the twentieth century, working-class movements have attenuated, abated or disappeared altogether, interrupting or permanently suspending the dialectic of the class struggle. The critical social theory of the Frankfurt School and more generally Western Marxism interpreted this situation as the deleterious effect of mass culture on the proletariat. However, these theorists do not adequately conceptualize the role of electronically mediated communications in the cultural integration of the working class into modern society. A good part of their difficulty stems from a theoretical model that does not account, with regard to the phenomena of mass culture, for the constitution of the subject through language, more specifically through the language patterns of the mode of information. The theoretical tendency of Western Marxism has been to approach the question of a politically stabilized modernity from orientations themselves far too rooted in modernity and its communications technologies. Like modern thinkers since Descartes, they attempt to establish an atemporal or universal foundation for theory which usually takes the form of some definition of the human.

[. . .] The widespread dissemination of radio, telephone, film, television, computer-enhanced communications such as electronic mail and computer conferencing, telex and fax machines and satellite communications systems changes not only communications but basic features of social life. Whatever *theoretical* priority one wishes to place on the question of communications, when recent *historical* developments are taken into account, it must move from the periphery to the center of social science. But this means that the problem of communication theory begins with a recognition of necessary self-reflexivity, of the dependence of knowledge on its context. It requires from the outset a frank acknowledgement of contingency: the 'truth' of communication theory is registered in relation to historical change and is in no sense 'absolute,' offering no vantage point from which one can claim a purchase on universality. A continuing issue for communication theory, then, is to sustain this sense of contingency, to develop strategies to avoid at every level and every turn becoming grounded, stabilized, founded, established in the Truth. Communication theory must then produce a new kind of truth, one not linked to the modernist goal of universality.

[. . .]

[. . .] By focusing on language and stressing the instability of meaning in language, poststructuralist theory undermines the effort to dissolve communication into a 'real' of action or into a universal definition of the human. At the same time it calls into question versions of the relation of theory and history/context which present the latter as a closed or totalized field that serves to turn theory into ideology, into a discourse whose assumptions are disavowed or made invisible.[14] For these reasons poststructuralist theory opens the field of electronically mediated communications in a way that locates its internal complexity and its relation to culture. It enables one to see what is new in the dissemination and emplacement of these technologies.

Poststructuralist theory is often accused of its own kind of totalization, linguistic reductionism. It is charged with never going beyond the text, of depoliticizing social action, of theorizing only an endless play of discourse analysis. While the practice of some poststructuralists may lend itself to this accusation, my effort, in theorizing the mode of information, has been to counteract the textualist tendency by linking poststructuralist theory with social change, by connecting it with electronic communications technology, by 'applying' its methods to the arena of everyday life, by insisting on communications as a historical context which justifies the move to an emphasis on language. The 'linguistic turn' of poststructuralism is apposite not only for its ability to critique modernist theory but because of changes in the socio-historical field. By the same token, I relate poststructuralist theory to the mode of information to underline the contingency of that theory, not to provide it with a false stability, a solid foundation in history. The political implications of the resort to poststructuralism, then, must be viewed in this light.

Poststructuralist theory invalidates modernist political positions, those that rely upon a view of humanity as in need of emancipation from forms of external oppression.[15] These views presuppose man as centered in rational autonomy but as prevented from attaining this center by institutions that block its realization: arbitrary government, religious intolerance, private appropriation of the means of production. However, the focus on language rejects this position because language already configures the individual. Only after the individual has been constituted as centered in rational autonomy by Enlightenment discourse does it appear that monarchy, institutional religion and capitalism are external fetters to freedom. If language is seen as already implicating the individual, then the question of emancipation changes its character. The question becomes one of understanding the positioning of the individual in the given language pattern and the relative change of altering that pattern, rather than one of a search for an absolute universal beyond the given order, one that would somehow allow an already defined human creature to emerge as if from its tutelage, or chains.

Contemporary society contains modernist institutions and discourses which privilege certain configurations of the subject, those that support autonomous rationality, and subordinate others (women, ethnic minorities, etc.). But contemporary society also contains 'postmodernist' institutions and discourses, such as electronically mediated communications, which support new configurations of the subject. To the extent that it is now appropriate to raise the issue of the restrictions of modernist forms of subject constitution, electronic communications, understood in a poststructuralist sense, provide a basis for critique. This does not mean that every emission from such communications technology is automatically revolutionary; the great preponderance of these communications works to solidify existing society and culture. But there is a way of understanding their impact that reveals its potential for structural change. In other words, there is a secular trend emanating from electronic communications that undermines the stability of the figure of the rational autonomous individual. Hence the outcry against these communications, the warnings of their dangers by those adhering to modernist political positions.

The other tendency that amplifies the poststructuralist understanding of the political impact of electronic communications is the spread of protest movements from outside the modernist paradigm, certain feminist and ethnic positions, certain aspects of gay and lesbian politics, certain kinds of ecological and anti-nuclear concerns. To the extent that the politics of these groups challenges the privilege of the rational individual as the universal ground of human identity (the Western tradition), they effect changes that are parallel with those of electronic communications. The operation of hegemonic ideology is effective to the extent that it is unrecognized. When everyone assumes that human beings have a nature, centered in reason, that is violated by institutional chains, then those chains are exposed but that ideology is confirmed. Electronic communications and the social movements mentioned above sometimes tend to put modernist ideology into question, thereby changing the terms of political discussion. When this is effective, as in the effort to abandon the required teaching of Western Civilization as the exclusive introduction to culture, modernists of all stripes, from the Marxist Eugene Genovese to the conservative Lynn Chancy, recognize only a threat to freedom. To those not under the complete spell of this ideology, its operations become manifest and hence dissolved: 'man' cannot mean Western man, rationality is not the final ground of human experience.

Electronically mediated communication opens the prospect of understanding the subject as constituted in historically concrete configurations of discourse and practice. It clears the way to seeing the self as multiple, changeable, fragmented, in short as making a project of its own constitution. In turn such a prospect challenges all those discourses and practices that would restrict this process, would fix and stabilize identity, whether these be fascist ones which rely on essentialist theories of race, liberal ones which rely on reason, or socialist ones which rely on labor. A poststructuralist understanding of new communications technologies raises the possibility of a postmodern culture amid society that threatens authority as the definition of reality by the author.

[. . .]

## Notes

1   Mark Poster, *The Mode of Information* (Cambridge: Polity Press; Chicago: University of Chicago Press, 1990).

2   Jean François Lyotard, *Inhuman*, trans. Geoff Bennington and Rachel Bowlby (Cambridge: Polity Press, 1992).

3   Jean Baudrillard, *Selected Writings*, ed. Mark Poster, trans. Jacques Mourrain (Stanford: Stanford University Press, 1988).

4   Joshua Meyrowitz, *No Sense of Place: The Impact of Electronic Media on Social Behavior* (New York: Oxford University Press, 1985).

5   Michel Foucault, *Discipline and Punish: The Birth of the Prison*, trans. Alan Sheridan (New York: Pantheon, 1977).

6   Michael Heim, *Electric Language: A Philosophical Study of Word Processing* (New Haven: Yale University Press, 1987).

7   George Landow, *Hypertext: The Convergence of Contemporary Critical Theory and Technology* (Baltimore: Johns Hopkins University Press, 1992).

8   Jay Bolter, *Writing Space: The Computer, Hypertext, and the History of Writing* (Hillsdale, NJ: Lawrence Erlbaum Associates, 1991).

9   Richard Lanham, 'The Electronic Word: Literary Study and the Digital Revolution,' *New Literary History* 20: 2 (1989), pp. 265–90.

10   Marie Marchand, *La Grande aventure du Minitel* (Paris: Larousse, 1987).

11   Andrew Feenberg, 'Computer Conferencing and the Humanities,' *Instructional Science* 16 (1987), pp. 169–86.

12   Jacques Derrida, *Of Grammatology*, trans. Gayatri Spivak (Baltimore: Johns Hopkins University Press, 1976).

13   Jacques Derrida, *Postcard: From Socrates to Freud and Beyond*, trans. Alan Bass (Chicago: University of Chicago Press, 1987).

14   Louis Althusser, 'Ideology and Ideological State Apparatuses,' in *Lenin and Philosophy and Other Essays*, trans. Ben Brewster (London: New Left Books, 1971).

15   John Hinkson, 'Marxism, Postmodernism and Politics Today,' *Arena* 94 (1991), pp. 138–66.

# Chapter 28

# Eric Michaels

## FOR A CULTURAL FUTURE

From Horace Newcomb (ed.) *Television: The Critical View*, 5th edn, Oxford: Oxford University Press (1994; original 1987), pp. 616–30.

O N 1 APRIL 1985, DAILY TELEVISION transmissions began from the studios of the Warlpiri Media Association at the Yuendumu community on the edge of Central Australia's Tanami desert. Television signals, when broadcast as radio waves, assure a kind of mute immortality: they radiate endlessly beyond their site of creation, so this first program might be playing right now to the rings of Saturn. But it no longer exists at its point of origin in Australia. The message, the events behind it, their circumstances and meanings have mostly been ignored, and are likely to be forgotten. This is why I recall such events here: to reassert their significance and to establish in print their remarkable history.

All content the Warlpiri Media Association transmits is locally produced. Almost all of it is in the Warlpiri Aboriginal language. Some is live: schoolchildren reading their assignments, community announcements, old men telling stories, young blokes acting cheeky. The station also draws on a videotape library of several hundred hours of material that had been produced in the community since 1982 (a description of this material and the conditions of its production is one of the main purposes of this essay). Yuendumu's four-hour schedule was, by percentage, and perhaps absolute hours, in excess of the Australian content of any other Australian television station. The transmissions were unauthorized, unfunded, uncommercial, and illegal. There were no provisions within the Australian Broadcasting Laws for this kind of service.

Yuendumu television was probably Australia's first public television service, although it might be misleading to make too much of this. Open Channel sponsored experimental community access TV transmissions in Melbourne for a few days during 1982. The Ernabella Aboriginal community had been experimenting along similar lines since 1984, and began their own daily service days after Yuendumu started theirs. Even before, throughout remote Australia, small transmitters had been pirated so that mining camps and cattle stations could watch Kung Fu and Action Adventure videos instead of the approved and licenced Australian Broadcasting Corporation (ABC) 'high culture' satellite feed, which became available to outback communities in 1984–85. Issues of community access and local transmission had been on the agenda certainly since the Whitlam government, but they had lain dormant in Fraser's and then Hawke's official broadcasting agendas. In the 1980s, inexpensive home video systems proved subversive of the bureaucracy's tedious intents, while satellite penetration and sustained interest in production by independents had all kept issues of public television very much alive in the public arena.

Yuendumu's accomplishment must be seen in the context of these developments. Yuendumu's need and motivation to broadcast should also be considered in evaluating any claim to the accolade of pioneer. There was, in the early 1980s, a considerable creative interest among Aborigines in the new entertainment technology becoming available to remote communities. There was equally a motivated, articulate, and general concern about the possible unwanted consequences of television, especially among senior Aborigines and local indigenous educators. In particular, the absence of local Aboriginal languages from any proposed service was a major issue. Without traditional language, how could any media service be anything but culturally subversive? Native speakers of indigenous languages understood (a good deal better than anyone else) that this was something only they could correct.

There are more than twenty-two Aboriginal languages currently spoken in the Central Australian satellite footprint. The simple logistics of providing for all these languages on a single service indicate clearly a fundamental mismatch. The bias of mass broadcasting is concentration and unification; the bias of Aboriginal culture is diversity and autonomy. Electronic media are everywhere; Aboriginal culture is local and land-based. Only local communities can express and maintain linguistic autonomy. No one elsewhere can do this for the local community – not in Canberra, Sydney, or even Alice Springs. Indeed, Warlpiri speakers at Yuendumu make much of the distinctions between their dialect and the one spoken by the Lajamanu Warlpiri, 600 kilometres away on the other side of the Tanami desert. These differences are proper, for they articulate a characteristic cultural diversity. The problem of language signals a more general problem of social diversity that introduced media pose for indigenous peoples everywhere: how to respond to the insistent pressure towards standardization, the homogenizing tendencies of contemporary world culture?

Postmodernist critique provides very little guidance here. Indeed, the temptation to promote Warlpiri media by demonstrating a privileged authenticity – the appeal to traditionalism – which legitimates these forms, would be firmly resisted. How can we even employ such terms? 'Authentic' and 'inauthentic' are now merely labels assigned and reassigned as manipulable moves in a recombinatory game. Postmodernism may promote an appetite for primitive provenances, but it has proven to be an ultra-consumerist appetite, using up the object to the point of exhaustion, of 'sophistication,' so as to risk making it disappear entirely. It would be better to shift ontologies, by problematizing the very term 'originality' and denying that any appeals to this category can be legitimated. Then, we refuse degrees of difference or value that might distinguish between the expressive acts (or even the persons) of Warlpiri videomakers, urban Koorie artists in Fitzroy, Aboriginal arts bureaucrats in Canberra, a Black commercial media industry in Alice Springs – none of these could be called more truly 'Aboriginal' than any other. This redirects the mode of analysis to a different if somewhat more fashionable inquiry: who asks such a question, under what circumstances, and so forth? An analysis of the history of the official constitution of Aboriginality, as well as its *mise en discours*, its rhetorical and institutional deployment, might explain, for instance, current moves towards pan-aboriginalism. At least, it can provide a much needed caveat to the banal and profoundly racist war that is being waged in this country.

Despite the importance of subjecting Aboriginal expression to these critical debates, there is a danger that they lead away from the specific pleasures to be found in an encounter with the Warlpiri and their video. And it is these pleasures I want to describe, indeed promote as something more than the product of my own research interests – even if this risks reasserting authenticity, with an almost naive empiricist's faith, and employing a positivist's notebook to amass the particulars necessary to bring these 'alien' texts into focus. What I am seeking is also a way to test critical theory's application to ethnographic subjects. It is possible that such an investigation will supersede the dilemma that tradition, ethnicity, and value have variously posed for empiricism.

Of course, to understand what happened with media at Yuendumu – and what didn't – one needs to describe more than just local circumstances. It will be necessary to reference the State and its interventions again and again. Warlpiri media, no less than its history, is the product of a struggle between official and unofficial discourses that seem always stacked in the State's favor. This might suggest a discouraging future for Yuendumu Television. Given the government's present policy of promoting media centralization and homogenization, we would expect that Yuendumu will soon be overwhelmed by national media services, including 'approved' regional Aboriginal broadcasters who serve the State's objectives of ethnicization, standardization, even aboriginalization, at the expense of local language, representation, autonomy. If this scenario is realized, then Yuendumu's community station seems likely to join the detritus of other development projects which litter the contemporary Aboriginal landscape, and shocked Europeans will take this as one more example of Aboriginal intractability and failure of effort – if not genes. We won't know that the experience of television for remote Aborigines could have been any different: for example, a networked cooperative of autonomous community stations resisting hegemony and homogenization. Instead, we expect Warlpiri television to disappear as no more than a footnote to Australian media history, leaving unremarked its singular contribution to a public media, and its capacity to articulate alternative – unofficial – aboriginalities.

But something in Warlpiri reckoning confounds their institutionalization and the grim prophecy this conveys. A similar logic predicted the disappearance of their people and culture generations ago, but proved false. A miraculous autonomy, almost fierce stubbornness, delivers the Warlpiri from these overwhelming odds and assures their survival, if not eventual victory.

## How Warlpiri people make television

Videomaker Francis Kelly does not like to be called by name. He prefers I call him Jupurrurla. This is a 'skin' or subsection term which identifies him as a member of one of eight divisions of the Warlpiri people, sometimes called totemic groups by anthropologists. Better yet, I should call him *panji*, a Kriol word for brother-in-law. The term is a relative one, in both senses. It does not merely classify our identities, but describes our relatedness. It is through such identities and relationships that cultural expression arises for Warlpiri people, and the description of these must precede any discussion of Aboriginal creativity.

Warlpiri people are born to their skins, a matter determined by parentage, a result of marriage and birth. But I became a Japanangka – brother-in-law to Jupurrurla – by assignment of the Yuendumu Community Council. One result of my classification is that it enables Francis and me to use this term to position our relationship in respect to the broader Warlpiri community. It establishes that we are not merely two independent individuals, free to recreate ourselves and our obligations at each social occasion. Rather, we are persons whose individuality is created and defined by a preexisting order. In this ease, being brothers-in-law means that we should maintain an amiable, cooperative reciprocity. We can joke, but only in certain ways and not others. We should give things to each other. My 'sisters' will become wives for Jupurrurla; I might take his 'sisters' for wives in return.

These distinctions refer to a symbolic divisioning of the community into 'two sides' engaged in reciprocal obligations. But it implies also a division of expressive (e.g., ceremonial) labor, and particular relations of ritual production reaching into all Warlpiri social life and action. For certain ceremonies this division is articulated as roles the Warlpiri name *Kirda* and *Kurdungurlu*, two classes which share responsibility for ritual display: one to perform, the other to stage-manage and witness. The roles are situational and invertable, so identification as Kirda 'Boss' and Kurdungurlu 'Helper' may alter from event to event. As 'brothers-in-law,' Jupurrurla and I will always find ourselves on different sides of this opposition, although the roles themselves may reverse from setting to setting. This see-saw balancing act that shifts roles back and forth over time affected all our collaborations.

Warlpiri brothers-in-law can also trace their relationships and their obligations more circuitously through mothers and grandparents. This describes a quite complex round of kin, which eventually encompasses the entire Warlpiri 'nation' of over 5,000 people. It can even go beyond this, identifying marriages and ceremonial ties which relate to corresponding skin groups among Pitjanjatjara people to the south, Pintubi to the west, and Arrente, Anmatjarra, Kaitij, Warrumungu, and others to the north and east. Thus, a potentially vast social matrix is interpolated with every greeting.

I introduce the reader to Jupurrurla to promote a consideration of his art: video-taped works of Warlpiri life transmitted at the Yuendumu television station in this desert community 300 kilometres north-west of Alice Springs. But it is not quite correct to identify Jupurrurla as the author of these tapes, to assign him personal responsibility for beginning video production at Yuendumu, or for founding the

Warlpiri Media Association, although these are the functions he symbolizes for us here.

In fact, the first videomaker at the Yuendumu community was Jupurrurla's actual brother-in-law, a Japanangka. It was Japanangka who was already videotaping local sporting events when I first came to Central Australia early in 1983. It was Japanangka who responded to the prospect of satellite television by saying 'We can fight fire with fire . . .,' making a reference to the traditional Warlpiri ritual, the Fire Ceremony or *Warlukurlangu*, and assigning this name to their artist's association. But Japanangka, for all his talent and rage, found the mantle of 'boss' for the video too onerous – for to be a boss is to be obligated. During 1983–84, a sensitive series of negotiations transferred the authority for Yuendumu video to Jupurrurla. Part of Jupurrurla's success in this role resulted from his cleverness in distributing the resources associated with the video project. He trained and then shared the work with a Japaljarri, another Japanangka, a Japangardi, and a Jangala. Eventually, all the male subsections had video access through at least one of their members.

Obviously, the identification of an individual artist as the subject for critical attention is problematized where personhood is reckoned in this fashion. Rather than gloss over this issue, or treat it romantically within a fantasy of primitive collectivity, I want to assert more precisely its centrality for any discussion of Warlpiri expression. And I want to use this example to signal other differences between Aboriginal and European creative practices, differences which need to be admitted and understood if the distinctiveness and contribution of Warlpiri creativity is to be evaluated critically in a contemporary climate – the goal of this essay. These differences include what may be unfamiliar to readers:

- ideological sources and access to inspiration;
- cultural constraints on invention and imagination;
- epistemological bases for representation and actuality;
- indistinctiveness of boundaries between authorship and oeuvre;
- restrictions on who makes or views expressive acts.

By describing these, I hope to avert some likely consequences of European enthusiasm for Aboriginal media which results in the appropriation of such forms to construct a generic 'primitive' only to illustrate modern (and, more recently, postmodern) fantasies of evolutionary sequences. In a practical sense, I also want to subvert the bureaucratization of these forms, such as may be expressed in the training programs, funding guidelines, or development projects which claim to advance Aborigines, but always impose standards alien to the art (because these will be alien to the culture producing it). Wherever Australian officialdom appropriates a population, as it has attempted to do with the Aborigines, it quickly bureaucratizes such relationships in the name of social welfare. This assuredly defeats the emergence of these sovereign forms of expression, as it would defeat Jupurrurla's own avowed objective to create *Yapa* – that is, truly Warlpiri – media.

Those European Art practices since the Renaissance and Industrial Revolution which constitute the artist as an independent inventor/producer of original products for the consumption/use of public audiences, do not apply to the Aboriginal tradition. This has been said before, in more or less accurate ways, and led to some questions (misplaced, I think) about the 'authenticity' of 'traditional' Aboriginal designs, such as those painted in acrylics and now made available to the international art maker. In the case of Jupurrurla's art, the implicit question of authenticity becomes explicit: Jupurrurla, in Bob Marley T-shirt and Adidas runners, armed with his video portapak, resists identification as a savage updating some archaic technology to produce curiosities of primitive tradition for the jaded modern gaze. Jupurrurla is indisputably a sophisticated cultural broker who employs video-tape and electronic technology to express and resolve political, theological, and aesthetic contradictions that arise in uniquely contemporary circumstances. This will be demonstrated in the case of two videotapes which the Warlpiri Media Association has produced: *Coniston Story* and *Warlukurlangu (Fire Ceremony)*.

The choice of these two out of a corpus of hundreds of hours of tape was a difficult one. Not even included is Jupurrurla's most cherished production, *Trip to Lapi-Lapi*, the record of a long trip into the Western Desert to re-open country people had not seen for decades, a tape that often causes its audiences to weep openly. Neither are the politically explicit tapes, those documenting confrontations with government officials which became important elements in Warlpiri negotiating strategies: these tapes cause people to shout, to address the screen, and then each other, sometimes provoking direct action. But my purpose in this monograph is not to survey the whole of the work, the various emergent genres, or the remarkable bush networks which arose to carry these tapes when official channels such as the new satellite were closed. My choice of tapes was made because they illustrate best some things about the Warlpiri mode of video production: how Jupurrurla and others discovered ways to fit the new technology to their particular information-based culture. The only way of beginning such an analysis is by locating the sources of Warlpiri expression in an oral tradition.

[. . .]

## The Fire Ceremony: for a cultural future

In 1972, anthropologist Nicolas Peterson and filmmaker Roger Sandall arranged with the old men to film a ritual of signal importance for the Warlpiri: Warlukurlangu, the Fire Ceremony. [. . .] Peterson described these ceremonies in terms of the functions of Aboriginal social organization. He identified such Warlpiri ceremonies as a means of resolving conflict, or of negotiating disputes, a kind of pressure valve for the community as a whole. One pair of patrilines (or 'side') of the community acts as Kurdungurlu, and arranges a spectacular dancing ground, delineated by great columns of brush and featuring highly decorated poles. The Kirda side paints up, and dances. Following several days and nights of dancing, they don elaborate costumes festooned with dry brush. At night they dance towards the fire, and are then beaten about with burning torches by the Kurdungurlu. Finally, the huge towers of brush are themselves ignited and the entire dance ground seems engulfed in flame. Following some period (it may be months or even years) the ceremony is repeated, but the personnel reverse their roles. The Kurdungurlu become Kirda, and receive their punishment in turn.

Visually and thematically, this ceremony satisfies the most extreme European appetite for savage theatre, a morality play of the sort Artaud describes for Balinese ritual dance – what could be more literally signaling through the flames than this? Yet I do not think the Peterson/Sandall film does this, partly due to the technical limitations of lighting for their black-and-white film stock, and partly because of the observational distance maintained throughout the filming. The effect is less dramatic, more properly 'ethnographic' (and, perhaps wisely, politically less confrontative). It was approved by the community at the time it was edited in 1972 by Kim McKenzie, and joined other such films in the somewhat obscure archives of the Australian Institute of Aboriginal Studies, used mostly for research and occasional classroom illustration.

Remarkably, the ceremony lapsed shortly after this film was made. When I arrived at Yuendumu in 1983, the Fire Ceremony seemed little more than a memory. Various reasons were offered:

- one of the owners had died, and a prohibition applied to its performance;
- it had been traded with another community;
- the church had suppressed its performance.

These are not competing explanations, but may have in combination discouraged Warlukurlangu. The interdiction by the Church (and the State, in some versions) was difficult to substantiate, though it was widely believed. Some of the more dramatic forms of punishment employed in the ceremony contradict Western manners, if not morals. There seemed to be some recognition among the Warlpiri that the Fire Ceremony was essentially incompatible with the expectations of settlement life, and the impotent fantasies of dependency and development they were required to promote. The Fire Ceremony was an explicit expression of Warlpiri autonomy, and for nearly a generation it was obscured. The question arises, as it does also in accounting for the ceremony's recent revival: what role did introduced media play in this history?

Yet Warlukurlangu persisted in certain covert ways. The very first videotape which the community itself directed in 1983 recorded an apparently casual afternoon of traditional dancing held at the women's museum. Such spontaneous public dance events are comparatively rare at Yuendumu. Dances occur in formal ceremonies, or during visits, in modern competitions and recitals, or in rehearsal for any of these. Yet this event appeared to meet none of these criteria. Equally curious was the insistence on the presence of the video camera. These were early days – Jupurrurla had not yet taken up the camera, and Japanangka and myself were having trouble arranging the shoot. A delegation of old men showed up at each of our camps and announced that we must hurry; the dancing wouldn't start till the video got there. What was taped was not only some quite spectacular dancing, but an emotional experience involving the whole community. When I afterwards asked some of the younger men the reason for all the weeping, they explained that people were so happy to see this dance again. I later discovered I had seen excerpts of the dances associated with the Fire Ceremony.

Some months later, I was invited to a meeting of the old men in the video studio. They had written to Peterson, asking for a copy of the film, and now were there to review it. I set up a camera and we videotaped this session. As it was clear that many of the on-film participants would now be dead, how the community negotiated this fact in terms of their review was very important. The question of the film's possible circulation was raised. Following a spirited discussion, the old men (as mentioned above) came to the decision that all the people who died were 'in the background': the film could be shown in the camps. Outside, a group of women elders had assembled, and were occasionally peeking through the window. Some were crying. They did not agree that the deceased were sufficiently backgrounded, and it made them 'too sorry to look.' These women did not watch the film, but didn't dispute the right of the men to view or show it.

It became clear that the community was gearing up to perform the Fire Ceremony again for the first time in this generation. As preparations proceeded, video influenced the ritual in many ways. For example, the senior men announced that the Peterson film was 'number one Law,' and recommended that we shoot the videotape of exactly the same scenes in precisely the same order. (When this did not happen, no one in fact remarked on the difference.) Andrew Japaljarri Spencer, who acted as first cameraman, stood in Kurdungurlu relationship to the ceremony. This meant that he produced an intimate record of the ceremony from his 'on the side' perspective.

We are at close-up range for some of the most dramatic moments, alongside the men actually administering the fiery punishments. Jupurrurla absented himself from this production. Although he was willing to do certain preproduction work, and subsequent editing and technical services, he would not act as cameraman because he would be a Kirda for this event. Quite sensibly, he pointed out that if Kirda were cameramen, the camera might catch on fire. Jupurrurla was not unaware, like many of the younger men, that he too might catch on fire, so at the climax of the ceremony they were nowhere to be found.

The tape of this major ceremony was copied the very next day and presented to a delegation from the nearby Willowra community, who were in fact in the midst of learning and acquiring the ceremony for performances themselves. This is a traditional aspect of certain classes of ceremonies. In oral societies where information is more valued than material resources, ceremonies can be commodities in which ritual information is a medium of exchange. This exchange may take years, and repeated performances, to accomplish. For instance, there was a dramatic (if not unexpected) moment when a more careful review of the tape revealed that one of the painted ceremonial poles had been rather too slowly panned, rendering its sacred design too explicit. This design had not yet been exchanged, and so the Willowra people might learn it – and reproduce it – from the tape. Runners went out to intercept the Willowra mob, and to replace their copy with one that had the offending section blanked out.

These new tapes of the Fire Ceremony circulated around the Yuendumu community, and in their raw state were highly popular. In fact, it became difficult to keep track of the copies. This was one of the motivations to proceed with broadcasting – more to assure the security of the video originals and provide adequate local circulation of tapes than to achieve any explicitly political intent. But perhaps there was a broader public statement to be made with the record of these events. I recommended, and was authorized to propose to the Australian Institute of

Aboriginal Studies, that we edit together the tapes to produce an account which would describe both the ceremony and its reproductions. We had the Peterson film, the community dance, the review of the film, and the extraordinary footage of the 1984 performance. This seemed to me an excellent and visually striking way to articulate the ceremony in terms of some of the more fundamental questions concerning the place of such media in Warlpiri life. The Institute did not support the idea, and when one of the central performers died shortly thereafter, the community dropped the matter. The tapes took their place on a shelf in the archive that Jupurrurla labeled 'not to look.' Later, however, the institute did transfer the Sandall/Peterson film to videotape, and put it into general distribution without, to my knowledge, informing the community that this was being done.

There is no point in isolating any one instance of this failure to address or resolve the problems that the appropriation of Warlpiri images poses. The situation is so general that it proves how fundamental the misunderstandings must be. Alien producers do not know what they take away from the Aborigines whose images, designs, dances, songs, and stories they record. Aborigines are learning to be more careful in these matters. But the conventions of copyright are profoundly different from one context to the other. Perhaps these urgent questions will never be solved: 'Who owns that dance now on film?,' 'Who has the authority to prevent broadcast of that picture of my father who just died?,' 'How can we make sure women will not see these places we showed to the male film crew?,' 'Will we see any of the money these people made with our pictures?' . . . Whenever 'appropriate' Australian authorities are confronted with such questions, they go straight to the too-hard basket, not only because they are truly difficult questions, but also because they refer to equivocal political positions.

Underlying the problem is not only a failure to specify the processes of reproduction and their place in oral traditions; there is also a contradiction of values regarding the possibilities for Aboriginal futures, and the preferred paths towards these. Many Aborigines do wish to be identified, recognized, and acknowledged in modern media, as well as to become practitioners of their own. They recognize the prestige, the political value, the economic bargaining position that a well-placed story in the national press can provide. They, attempt to evaluate the advantages – and what they are told is the necessity – of compromising certain cultural forms to achieve this. But the elements of this exchange, the discrimination between what is fundamental and what is negotiable, resists schematization. On neither side is there a clear sense of what can be given up and what must be kept if Aborigines are to avoid being reprocessed in the great sausage machine of modern mass media. For them, it is the *practices* of cultural reproduction that are essential. If by the next generation the means of representing and reproducing cultural forms are appropriated and lost, then all is destroyed. What remains will just be a few children's stories, place names for use by tourist or housing developments, some boomerangs that don't come back, a Hollywood-manufactured myth of exotica. These will only serve to mask the economic and social oppression of a people who then come into existence primarily in relation to that oppression.

The criteria for Aboriginal media must concern these consequences of recording for cultural reproduction in traditional oral societies. Warlpiri people put it more simply: 'Can video make our culture strong? Or will it make us lose our Law?'

The problem about answering this sort of question as straightforwardly as it deserves, is that it usually is asked in deceptive cause/effect terms: What will TV do to Aborigines? The Warlpiri experience resists this formulation. Jupurrurla demonstrates that such questions cannot be answered outside the specific kin-based experiences of their local communities. His productions further demonstrate that television and video are not any one, self-evident thing, a singular cause which can then predict effects. Indeed, Yuendumu's videomakers demonstrate that their television is something wholly unanticipated, and unexplained, by dominant and familiar industrial forms.

Here I want to emphasize *the continuity of modes of cultural production across media*, something that might be too easily over-looked by an ethnocentric focus on content. My researches identify how Jupurrurla and other Warlpiri videomakers have learned ways of using the medium which conform to the basic premises of their tradition in its essential oral form. They demonstrate that this is possible, but also that their efforts are yet vulnerable, easily jeopardized by the invasion of alien and professional media producers.

My work has been subject to criticism for this attention to traditional forms and for encouraging their persistence into modern life. The argument is not meant to be romantic: my intent has been to specify the place of the Law in any struggle by indigenous people for cultural and political autonomy. In the ease of Warlpiri television, the mechanisms for achieving this were discovered to lie wholly in the domain of cultural reproduction, in the culture's ability to construct itself, to image itself, through its own eyes as well as the world's.

In the confrontation between Dreamtime and Ourtime, what future is possible? The very terms of such an inquiry have histories that tend to delimit any assured, autonomous future. For example, if it were true that my analysis of Warlpiri TV provided no more than a protectionist agenda, then the charge of romantic indulgence in an idealized past might be justified. I would have failed to escape a 'time' that anthropologists call the 'ethnographic present' – a fabricated, synchronic moment that, like the Dreamtime, exists in ideological space, not material history. It is implicated in nearly all anthropology, as well as most ethnographic discourse. Certainly, the questions of time that seem essential here cannot be elucidated by constructs of timelessness.

It seems likely that grounding Aborigines in such false, atemporal histories results in projecting them instead into a particular named future whose characteristics are implied by that remarkable word, 'Lifestyle.' This term now substitutes everywhere for the term culture to indicate the latter's demise in a period of ultra-merchandise. Culture – a learned, inherited tradition – is superseded by a borrowed, or gratuitous model; what your parents and grandparents taught you didn't offer much choice about membership. Lifestyles are, by contrast, assemblages of commodified symbols, operating in concert as packages which can be bought, sold, traded, or lost. The word proves unnervingly durable, serving to describe housing, automobiles, restaurants, clothes, things you wear, things that wear you – most strikingly, both 'lifestyle condoms' for men and, for women, sanitary napkins that 'fit your lifestyle.' Warlpiri people, when projected into this Lifestyle Future, cease to be Warlpiri; they are subsumed as 'Aborigines,' in an effort to invent them as a sort of special ethnic group able to be inserted into the fragile fantasies of contemporary Australian multiculturalism. Is there no other future for the Warlpiri than as merely another collectivity who have bartered away their history for a 'lifestyle?'

I propose an alternative here, and name it the Cultural Future. By this I mean an agenda for cultural maintenance which not only assumes some privileged authority for traditional modes of cultural production, but argues also that the political survival of indigenous people is dependent upon their capacity to continue reproducing these forms.

What I read as the lesson of the Dreaming is that it has always privileged these processes of reproduction over their products, and that this has been the secret of the persistence of Aboriginal cultural identities as well as the basis for their claims to continuity. This analysis confirms Jupurrurla's and Japanangka's claims that TV is a two-edged sword, both a blessing and a curse, a 'fire' that has to be fought with fire. The same medium can prove to be the instrument of salvation or destruction. This is why a simple prediction of the medium's effects is so difficult to make. Video and television intrude in the processes of social and cultural reproduction in ways that literate (missionary, bureaucratic, educational) interventions never managed to accomplish. Its potential force is greater than guns, or grog, or even the insidious paternalisms which seek to claim it.

But in a cultural future, *Coniston Story* operates over time to privilege the Japangardi/Japanangka version of that history, to insert it bit by bit into the Dreaming tracks around Crown Creek until the tape itself crumbles and its memory is distributed selectively along the paths of local kinship. In this future, when the mourning period for that old Japangardi is passed, his relations will take the Fire Ceremony tape from the 'not to look' shelf and review it again, in regard to the presence or absence of recent performances of the ceremony. Audiences at Yuendumu will reinterpret what is on the tape, bring some fellows into the foreground and disattend to others. They might declare this 'a proper law tape,' and then go on to perform the ceremony exactly the same, but different. I expect, in the highly active interpretative sessions that these attendances have become, there will be much negotiation necessary to resolve apparent contradictions evoked by the recorded history. I expect that a cultural future allows the space and autonomy for this to happen.

In a lifestyle (ethnic, anti-cultural) future, it's not so certain that anyone will be there at Yuendumu to worry about all this. Why should they? After all, the place has only cultural value, lacking any commercial rationale for the lifestyle economy. But if people are to be situated in this future, we can assume that they will be faced with a very different kind of, and participation in, media. Their relation to the forces and modes of cultural reproduction will be quite passive: they will be constituted as an audience, rendered consumers, even though there's not much money to buy anything (the local store is reduced to selling tinned stew and Kung Fu video tapes). But it would be mistaken to claim that the ethnic cultural policy has ignored Aborigines. In fact, they play a major part in the construction of the national, multicultural image; in this scenario, they become niggers. Then they will be regularly on the airways, appearing as well-adjusted families in situation comedies, as models in cosmetic ads, as people who didn't get a 'fair go' on *60 Minutes*. Nationally prominent, academically certified Aborigines will discuss Aboriginality on the ABC and commercial stations, filling in the legislated requirements for Australian content. In the lifestyle future, Aborigines can be big media business.

The people at Yuendumu will watch all this on their government-provided, receive-only satellite earth stations; but we can only speculate about what identifications and evaluations they will make. Perhaps the matter will not be inconsequential. Imported programs supplant, but may not so directly intrude on, cultural reproduction. Rather, it is when some archivist wandering through the ABC film library chances on an old undocumented copy of the Peterson Fire Ceremony film, one of the competing versions of the Coniston massacre, or even some old and valuable Baldwin Spencer footage, circa 1929, of Central Australian native dances, that something truly momentous happens. In pursuit of a moment of 'primitivism,' the tapes go to air, via satellite, to thousands of communities at once, including those of its subjects, their descendants, their relations, their partners in ritual exchange, their children, their women (or men). One more repository guarded by oral secrecy is breached, one more ceremony is rendered worthless, one more possible claim to authenticity is consumed by the voracious appetite of the simulacra for the appearance of reality. At Yuendumu, this already causes fights, verbal and physical, even threatened payback murders, in the hopeless attempt to ascribe blame in the matter, to find within the kin network the one responsible, so that by punishing him or her the tear in the fabric of social reproduction can be repaired. However, the kin links to descendants of Rupert Murdoch or David Hill or Bob Hawke may prove more difficult to trace, and the mechanisms for adjudication impossible to uncover.

A cultural future can only result from political resistance. It will not be founded on any appeal to nostalgia: not nostalgia for a past whose existence will always be obscure and unknown, nor a nostalgia we project into a future conceived only in terms of the convoluted temporalities of our own present. The tenses are difficult to follow here – but in a sense, that is precisely the critical responsibility now before us. Francis Jupurrurla Kelly makes, is making, television at Yuendumu. He intends to continue, and so assure a cultural future for Warlpiri people. His tapes and broadcasts reach forward and backwards through various temporal orders, and attempt somehow to bridge the Dreaming and the historical. This, too, is a struggle which generates Jupurrurla's art.

The only basis for non-Warlpiri interest in their video must recognize these explicitly contemporary contradictions. Channel Four at Yuendumu resists nostalgic sentiment and troubles our desire for a privileged glimpse of otherness. It is we who are rendered other, not its subject. Ultimately, it must be from this compromising position that such work is viewed.

## Notes

The people at Yuendumu were not entirely happy with this text when I brought it for them to review prior to publication. We took out the few offending pictorial images – this wasn't the problem. It was said by some that the pessimism I expressed seemed unwarranted. Certainly, the evidence of continuing motivation and activity at the TV studio was startling. This was late August 1987, and my visit coincided with the installation of a satellite earth-station receiver which introduced the live ABC program schedule to Yuendumu after so many years of waiting, worrying, and preparing.

There still was no license to legitimize the service that Jupurrurla began that week, mixing local programming with the incoming signal (Warlpiri News and documentaries at 6:30 P.M.) Nor had the equipment repaired itself magically since the last visit: signal strength remained unpredictable, and edits were completely unstable. But the community was still passionately involved in making and watching Warlpiri television. This became clear when a battle ensued with the very first day's transmission. Warlpiri News replaced the *EastEnders*, and at least one European resident was incensed. Jupurrurla decided (somewhat unilaterally, it seemed to me) that the service would shut off at 10:30 P.M., so that kids could go to bed and be sure of getting off to school in the morning. No *Rock Arena*. No late movies. It seemed likely there would be a lot of hot negotiating in the coming months.

[. . .]

# Chapter 29

# Sadie Plant

## THE FUTURE LOOMS
## Weaving women and cybernetics

From M. Featherstone and R. Burrows (eds) *Cyberspace, Cyberbodies, Cyberpunk*, London: Sage (1995), pp. 45–64.

**B**EGINNING WITH A PASSAGE from a novel:

> The woman brushed aside her veil, with a swift gesture of habit, and
> Mallory caught his first proper glimpse of her face. She was Ada Byron,
> the daughter of the Prime Minister. Lady Byron, the Queen of Engines.
> (Gibson and Sterling, 1990: 89)

Ada was not really Ada Byron, but Ada Lovelace, and her father was never Prime
Minister: these are the fictions of William Gibson and Bruce Sterling, whose book
*The Difference Engine* sets its tale in a Victorian England in which the software she
designed was already running; a country in which the Luddites were defeated, a
poet was Prime Minister, and Ada Lovelace still bore her maiden name. And one
still grander: Queen of Engines. Moreover she was still alive. Set in the mid-1850s,
the novel takes her into a middle-age she never saw: the real Ada died in 1852 while
she was still in her thirties. Ill for much of her life with unspecified disorders, she
was eventually diagnosed as suffering from cancer of the womb, and she died after
months of extraordinary pain.

Ada Lovelace, with whom the histories of computing and women's liberation
are first directly woven together, is central to this paper. Not until a century after
her death, however, did women and software make their respective and irrevocable
entries on to the scene. After the military imperatives of the 1940s, neither would
ever return to the simple service of man, beginning instead to organize, design
and arouse themselves, and so acquiring unprecedented levels of autonomy. In later

decades, both women and computers begin to escape the isolation they share in the home and office with the establishment of their own networks. These, in turn, begin to get in touch with each other in the 1990s. This convergence of woman and machine is one of the preoccupations of the cybernetic feminism endorsed here, a perspective which owes a good deal to the work of Luce Irigaray, who is also important to this discussion.

The computer emerges out of the history of weaving, the process so often said to be the quintessence of women's work. The loom is the vanguard site of software development. Indeed, it is from the loom, or rather the process of weaving, that this paper takes another cue. Perhaps it is an instance of this process as well, for tales and texts are woven as surely as threads and fabrics. This paper is a yarn in both senses. It is about weaving women and cybernetics, and is also weaving women and cybernetics together. It concerns the looms of the past, and also the future which looms over the patriarchal present and threatens the end of human history.

Ada Lovelace may have been the first encounter between woman and computer, but the association between women and software throws back into the mythical origins of history. For Freud, weaving imitates the concealment of the womb: the Greek hystera; the Latin matrix. Weaving is woman's compensation for the absence of the penis, the void, the woman of whom, as he famously insists, there is 'nothing to be seen'. Woman is veiled, as Ada was in the passage above; she weaves, as Irigaray comments, 'to sustain the disavowal of her sex'. Yet the development of the computer and the cybernetic machine as which it operates might even be described in terms of the introduction of increasing speed, miniaturization and complexity to the process of weaving. These are the tendencies which converge in the global webs of data and the nets of communication by which cyberspace, or the matrix, are understood.

Today, both woman and the computer screen the matrix, which also makes its appearance as the veils and screens on which its operations are displayed. This is the virtual reality which is also the absence of the penis and its power, but already more than the void. The matrix emerges as the processes of an abstract weaving which produces, or fabricates, what man knows as 'nature': his materials, the fabrics, the screens on which he projects his own identity.

\* \* \*

As well as his screens, and as his screens, the computer also becomes the medium of man's communication. Ada Lovelace was herself a great communicator: often she wrote two letters a day, and was delighted by the prospect of the telegraph. She is, moreover, often remembered as Charles Babbage's voice, expressing his ideas with levels of clarity, efficiency and accuracy he could never have mustered himself.

When Babbage displayed his Difference Engine to the public in 1833, Ada was a debutante, invited to see the machine with her mother, Lady Byron, who had herself been known as the Princess of Parallelograms for her mathematical prowess. Lady Byron was full of admiration for the machine, and it is clear that she had a remarkable appreciation of the subtle enormities of Babbage's invention. 'We both went to see the *thinking* machine (for such it seems) last Monday', she wrote.

'It raised several Nos. to the 2nd & 3rd powers, and extracted the root of a quadratic Equation' (Moore, 1977: 44).

Ada's own response was recorded by another woman, who wrote:

> While other visitors gazed at the working of the beautiful instrument with a sort of expression, and dare I say the same sort of feeling, that some savages are said to have shown on first seeing a looking glass or hearing a gun . . . Miss Byron, young as she was, understood its working, and saw the great beauty of the invention.
>
> (Moore, 1977: 44)

[. . .]

Babbage had a tendency to flit between obsessions; a remarkably prolific explorer of the most fascinating questions of science and technology, he nevertheless rarely managed to complete his studies; neither the Difference Engine nor the Analytical Engine were developed to his satisfaction. Ada, on the other hand, was determined to see things through; perhaps her commitment to Babbage's machine was greater than his own. Knowing that the Difference Engine had suffered for lack of funding, publicity and organization, she was convinced that the Analytical Engine would be better served by her own attentions. [. . .]

[. . .]

Ada Lovelace herself worked with a mixture of coyness and confidence: attributes which often extended to terrible losses of self-esteem and megalomaniac delight in her own brilliance. Sometimes she was convinced of her own immortal genius as a mathematician; 'I hope to bequeath to future generations a *Calculus of the Nervous System*', she wrote in 1844. 'I am proceeding in a track quite peculiar & my own, I believe' (Moore, 1977: 216). At other times, she lost all confidence, and often wondered whether she should not have pursued her musical abilities, which were also fine. Ada was always trapped by the duty to be dutiful; caught in a cleft stick of duties, moral obligations she did not understand.

[. . .]

Ada Lovelace immediately saw the profound significance of the Analytical Engine, and she went to great lengths to convey the remarkable extent of its capacities in her writing. Although the Analytical Engine had its own limits, it was nevertheless a machine vastly different from the Difference Engine. As Ada Lovelace observed:

> The Difference Engine can in reality . . . do nothing but *add*; and any other processes, not excepting those of simple subtraction, multiplication and division, can be performed by it only, just to that extent in which it is possible, by judicious mathematical arrangement and artifices, to reduce them to *series of additions*.
>
> (Morrison and Morrison, 1961: 250)

With the Analytical Engine, Babbage set out to develop a machine capable not merely of adding, but performing the 'whole of arithmetic'. Such an undertaking required the mechanization not merely of each mathematical operation, but the systematic bases of their functioning, and it was this imperative to transcribe the rules of the game itself which made the Analytical Engine a universal machine. Babbage was a little more modest, describing the Engine as 'a machine of the most general nature' (Babbage, 1961: 56), but the underlying point remains: the Analytical Engine would not merely synthesize the data provided by its operator, as the Difference Engine had done, but would incarnate what Ada Lovelace described as the very 'science of operations'.

The Difference Engine, Ada Lovelace wrote, 'is the embodying of *one particular and very limited set of operations*, which . . . may be expressed thus (+,+,+,+,+,+), or thus 6(+). Six repetitions of the one operation, +, is, in fact, the whole sum and object of that engine' (Morrison and Morrison, 1961: 249). What impressed Ada Lovelace about the Analytical Engine was that, unlike the Difference Engine or any other machine, it was not merely able to perform certain functions, but was 'an *embodying of the science of operations*, constructed with peculiar reference to abstract number as the subject of those operations'. The Difference Engine could simply add up, whereas the Analytical Engine not only performed synthetic operations, but also embodied the analytic capacity on which these syntheses are based. 'If we compare together the powers and the principles of construction of the Difference and of the Analytic Engines', wrote Ada, 'we shall perceive that the capabilities of the latter are immeasurably more extensive than those of the former, and that they in fact hold to each other the same relationship as that of analysis to arithmetic' (Morrison and Morrison, 1961: 250). [. . .]

[. . .]

Indeed, Ada considered Jaquard's cards to be the crucial difference between the Difference Engine and the Analytical Engine. 'We may say most aptly', she continued, 'that the Analytical Engine *weaves Algebraical patterns*, just as the Jacquard loom weaves flowers and leaves. Here, it seems to us, resides much more of originality than the Difference Engine can be fairly entitled to claim' (Morrison and Morrison, 1961: 252). Ada's reference to the Jacquard loom is more than a metaphor: the Analytical Engine did indeed weave 'just as' the loom, operating, in a sense, as the abstracted process of weaving.

Weaving has always been a vanguard of machinic development, perhaps because, even in its most basic form, the process is one of complexity, always involving the weaving together of several threads into an integrated cloth. Even the drawloom, which is often dated back to the China of 1000 BC, involves sophisticated orderings of warp and weft if it is to produce the complex designs common in the silks of this period. This means that 'information is needed in large amounts for the weaving of a complex ornamental pattern. Even the most ancient Chinese examples required that about 1500 different warp threads be lifted in various combinations as the weaving proceeded' (Morrison and Morrison, 1961: xxxiv). With pedals and shuttles, the loom becomes what one historian refers to as the 'most complex human engine of them all', a machine which 'reduced everything to simple actions: the alternate movement of the feet worked the pedals, raising half the threads of the warp and then the other, while the hands threw the shuttle carrying the thread of the woof' (Braudel, 1973: 247). The weaver was integrated into the machinery, bound up with its operations, linked limb by limb to the processes. In the Middle Ages, and before the artificial memories of the printed page, squared paper charts were used to store the information necessary to the accurate development of the design. In early 18th-century Lyons, Basyle Bouchon developed a mechanism for the automatic selection of threads, using an early example of the punched paper rolls which were much later to allow pianos to play and type to be cast. This design was developed by Falcon a couple of years later, who introduced greater complexity with the use of punched cards rather than the roll. And it was this principle on which Jacquard based his own designs for the automated loom which revolutionized the weaving industry when it was introduced in the 1800s and continues to guide its contemporary development. Jacquard's machine strung the punch cards together, finally automating the operations of the machine and requiring only a single human hand. Jacquard's system of punch card programs brought the information age to the beginning of the 19th century. His automated loom was the first to store its own information, functioning with its own software, an early migration of control from weaver to machinery.

Babbage owned what Ada described as 'a beautiful woven portrait of Jacquard, in the fabrication of which 24,000 cards were required' (Morrison and Morrison, 1961: 281). Woven in silk at about 1000 threads to the inch, Babbage well understood that its incredible detail was due to the loom's ability to store and process information at unprecedented speed and volume and, when he began work on the Analytical Engine, it was Jacquard's strings of punch cards on which he based his designs. 'It is known as a fact', Babbage wrote, 'that the Jacquard loom is capable of weaving any design which the imagination of man may conceive' (Babbage, 1961: 55). Babbage's own contribution to the relentless drive to perfect the punch card system was to introduce the possibility of repeating the cards, or what, as Ada wrote,

> was technically designated *backing* the cards in certain groups according to certain laws. The object of this extension is to secure the possibility of bringing any particular card or set of cards onto use *any number of times successively in the solution of one problem.*
>
> (Morrison and Morrison, 1961: 264)

This was an unprecedented simulation of memory. The cards were selected by the machine as it needed them and effectively functioned as a filing system, allowing the machine to store and draw on its own information.

The punch cards also gave the Analytical Engine what Babbage considered foresight, allowing it to operate as a machine that remembers, learns and is guided by its own abstract functioning. As he began to work on the Analytical Engine, Babbage became convinced that 'nothing but teaching the Engine to foresee and then to act upon that foresight could ever lead me to the object I desired' (Babbage, 1961: 53). The Jacquard cards made memory a possibility, so that the Analytical Engine will possess a library of its own' (1961: 56), but this had to be a library to which the machine could refer both to its past and its future operations; Babbage intended to give the machine not merely a memory but also the ability to process information from the future of its own functioning. Babbage could eventually write that 'in the Analytical Engine I had devised mechanical means equivalent to memory, also that I had provided other means equivalent to foresight, and that the Engine itself could act on this foresight' (1961: 153).

There is more than one sense in which foresight can be ascribed to the Analytical Engine: more than 100 years passed before it was put to use, and it is this remarkable time lag which inspires Gibson and Sterling to explore what might have happened if it had been taken up in the 1840s rather than the 1940s. Babbage thought it might take 50 years for the Analytic Engine to be developed: many people, particularly those with money and influence, were sceptical about his inventions, and his own eclectic interests gave an unfavourable impression of eccentricity. His own assistant confessed to thinking that Babbage's 'intellect was beginning to become deranged' (Babbage, 1961: 54) – when he had started talking about the Engine's ability to anticipate the outcomes of calculations it had not yet made.

When the imperatives of war brought Lovelace's and Babbage's work to the attentions of the Allied military machine, their impact was immense. Her software runs on his hardware to this day. In 1944, Howard Aiken developed Mark 1, what he thought was the first programmable computer, although he had really been beaten by a German civil engineer, Konrad Zuse, who had in fact built such a machine, the Z-3, in 1941. Quite remarkably, in retrospect, the Germans saw little importance in his work, and although the most advanced of his designs, the Z-11, is still in use to this day, it was the American computer which was the first programmable system to really be noticed. Mark 1, or the IBM Automatic Sequence Controlled Calculator, was based on Babbage's designs and was itself programmed by another woman: Captain Grace Murray Hopper. She was often described as the 'Ada Lovelace' of Mark 1 and its successors; having lost her husband in the war, Grace Hopper was free to devote her energies to programming. She wrote the first high-level language compiler, was instrumental in the development of the computer language COBOL, and even introduced the term 'bug' to describe soft- or hardware glitches after she found a dead moth interrupting the smooth circuits of Mark 1. Woman as the programmer again.

Crucial to the development of the 1940s computer was cybernetics, the term coined by Norbert Wiener for the study of control and communication in animal and machine. Perhaps the first cybernetic machine was the governor, a basic self-regulating system, which, like a thermostat, takes the information feeding out of the machine and loops or feeds it back on itself. Rather than a linear operation, in which information comes in, is processed and goes out without any return, the cybernetic system is a feedback loop, hooked up and responsive to its own environment. Cybernetics is the science – or rather the engineering – of this abstract procedure, which is the virtual reality of systems of every scale and variety of hard- and software.

It is the computer which makes cybernetics possible, for the computer is always heading towards the abstract machinery of its own operations. It begins with attempts to produce or reproduce the performance of specific functions, such as addition, but what it leads to is machinery which can simulate the operations of any machine and also itself. Babbage wanted machines that could add, but he ended up with the Analytical Engine: a machine that could not only add but perform any arithmetical task. As such, it was already an abstract machine, which could turn its abstract hand to anything. Nevertheless, the Analytical Engine was not yet a developed cybernetic machine, although it made such machinery possible. As Ada Lovelace recognized: 'The Analytical Engine has no pretensions whatever to *originate*

anything. It can do whatever we *know how to order it* to perform' (Morrison and Morrison, 1961: 285). It was an abstract machine, but its autonomous abilities were confined to its processing capacities: what Babbage, with terminology from the textiles industry, calls the mill, as opposed to the store. Control is dispersed and enters the machinery, but it does not extend to the operations of the entire machine.
    [. . .]
    The Analytical Engine was the actualization of the abstract workings of the loom; as such it became the abstract workings of any machine. When Babbage wrote of the Analytical Engine, it was often with reference to the loom: 'The analogy of the Analytical Engine with this well-known process is nearly perfect' (1961: 55). The Analytical Engine was such a superb development of the loom that its discoveries were to feed back into the processes of weaving itself. As Ada wrote:

> It has been proposed to use it for the reciprocal benefit of that art, which, while it has itself no apparent connexion with the domains of abstract science, has yet proved so valuable to the latter, in suggesting the principles which, in their new and singular field of application, seem likely to place *algebraical* combinations not less completely within the province of mechanism, than are all those varied intricacies of which *intersecting threads* are susceptible.
>
> (Morrison and Morrison, 1961: 265)

The algebraic combinations looping back into the loom, converging with the intersecting threads of which it is already the consequence.
    Once they are in motion, cybernetic circuits proliferate, spilling out of the specific machinery in which they first emerged and infecting all dynamic systems. That Babbage's punch-card system did indeed feed into the mills of the mid-19th century is indicative of the extent to which cybernetic machines immediately become entangled with cybernetic processes on much bigger scales. Perhaps it is no coincidence that Neith, the Egyptian divinity of weaving, is also the spirit of intelligence, where the latter too consists in the crossing of warp and weft. 'This image', writes one commentator, 'clearly evokes the fact that all data recorded in the brain results from the intercrossing of sensations perceived by means of our sense organs, just as the threads are crossed in weaving' (Lamy, 1981: 18).
    The Jacquard loom was a crucial moment in what de Landa defines as a 'migration of control' from human hands to software systems. Babbage had a long-standing interest in the effects of automated machines on traditional forms of manufacture, publishing his research on the fate of cottage industries in the Midlands and North of England, *The Economy of Manufactures and Machinery*, in 1832, and the Jacquard loom was one of the most significant technological innovations of the early 19th century. There was a good deal of resistance to the new loom, which 'was bitterly opposed by workers who saw in this migration of control a piece of their bodies literally being transferred to the machine' (De Landa, 1992: 168). In his maiden speech in the House of Lords in 1812, Lord Byron contributed to a debate on the Frame-Work Bill. 'By the adoption of one species of frame in particular', he observed, 'one man performed the work of many, and the superfluous labourers were thrown out of employment'. They should, he thought, have been rejoicing at

'these improvements in arts so beneficial to mankind', but instead 'conceived themselves to be sacrificed to improvements in mechanism' (Jennings, 1985: 132). His daughter was merely to accelerate the processes which relocated and redefined control.

* * *

[. . .]

It seems that weaving is always already entangled with the question of female identity, and its mechanization an inevitable disruption of the scene in which woman appears as the weaver. Manufactured cloth disrupted the marital and familiar relationships of every traditional society on which it impacted. In China, it was said that if 'the old loom must be discarded, then 100 other things must be discarded with it, for there are somehow no adequate substitutes' (Mead, 1963: 241).

'The woman at her hand-loom', writes Margaret Mead,

> controls the tension of the weft by the feeling in her muscles and the rhythm of her body motion; in the factory she watches the loom, and acts at externally stated intervals, as the operations of the machine dictate them. When she worked at home, she followed her own rhythm, and ended an operation when she felt – by the resistance against the pounding mallet or the feel between her fingers – that the process was complete. In the factory she is asked to adjust her rhythm to that of the rhythm prescribed by the factory; to do things according to externally set time limits.
>
> (1963: 241)

Mead again provides an insight into the intimacy of the connection between body and process established by weaving, and its disruption by the discipline of the factory. 'She is asked to adjust her rhythm to that of the rhythm prescribed by the factory', but what is her own rhythm, what is the beat by which she wove at home? What is this body to which weaving is so sympathetic? If woman is identified as weaver, her rhythms can only be known through its veils. Where are the women? Weaving, spinning, tangling threads at the fireside. Who are the women? Those who weave. It is weaving by which woman is known: the activity of weaving which defines her. 'What happens to the woman', asks Mead, 'and to the man's relationship with her, when she ceases to fulfil her role, to fit the picture of womanhood and wifehood?' (1963: 238). What happens to the woman? What is woman without the weaving? A computer programmer, perhaps? Ada's computer was a complex loom: Ada Lovelace, whose lace work took her name into the heart of the military complex, dying in agony, hooked into gambling, swept into the mazes of number and addiction. The point at which weaving, women and cybernetics converge in a movement fatal to history.

Irigaray argues that human history is a movement from darkness to the light of pure intellect; a flight from the earth. For man to make history is for him to deny and transcend what he understands as nature, reversing his subordination to its whims and forces, and progressing towards the autonomy, omnipotence and omnipresence of God, his image of abstraction and authority. Man comes out of the cave and heads for the sun; he is born from the womb and escapes the mother, the ground from which humanity arose and the matter from which history believes itself destined for liberation. Mother Nature may have been his material origin, but it is God the Father to whom he must be faithful; God who legitimates his project to 'fill the earth and subdue it'. The matter, the womb, is merely an encumbrance; either too inert or dangerously active. The body becomes a cage, and biology a constraint which ties man to nature and refuses to let him rise above the grubby concerns of the material; what he sees as the passive materiality of the feminine has to be overcome by his spiritual action. Human history is the self-narrating story of this drive for domination; a passage from carnal passions to self-control; a journey from the strange fluidities of the material to the self-identification of the soul.

Woman has never been the subject, the agent of this history, the autonomous being. Yet her role in this history has hardly been insignificant. Even from his point of view, she has provided a mirror for man, his servant and accommodation, his tools and his means of communication, his spectacles and commodities, the possibility of the reproduction of his species and his world. She is always necessary to history: man's natural resource for his own cultural development. Not that she is left behind, always at the beginning: as mirror and servant, instrument, mediation and reproduction, she is always in flux, wearing 'different veils according to the historic period' (Irigaray, 1991: 118).

As Irigaray knows, man's domination cannot be allowed to become the annihilation of the materials he needs: in order to build his culture, 'man was, of course, obliged to draw on reserves still in the realm of nature: a detour through the outer world was of course dispensable; the "I" had to relate to things before it could be conscious of itself' (Irigaray, 1985: 204). Man can do nothing on his own: carefully concealed, woman nevertheless continues to function as the ground and possibility of his quests for identity, agency and self-control. Stealth bombers and guided missiles, telecommunications systems and orbiting satellites epitomize this flight towards autonomy, and the concomitant need to defend it.

Like woman, software systems are used as man's tools, his media and his weapons; all are developed in the interests of man, but all are poised to betray him. The spectacles are stirring, there is something happening behind the mirrors, the commodities are learning how to speak and think. Women's liberation is sustained and vitalized by the proliferation and globalization of software technologies, all of which feed into self-organizing, self-arousing systems and enter the scene on her side.

This will indeed seem a strange twist to history to those who believe that it runs its straight lines. But as Irigaray asks: 'If machines, even machines of theory, can be aroused all by themselves, may woman not do likewise?' (1985: 232).

The computer, like woman, is both the appearance and the possibility of simulation. 'Truth and appearance, according to his will of the moment, his appetite of the instant' (Irigary, 1991: 118). Woman cannot *be* anything, but she can imitate anything valued by man: intelligence, autonomy, beauty. . . . Indeed, if woman is anything, she is the very possibility of mimesis, the one who weaves her own disguises. The veil is her oppression, but 'she may still draw from it what she needs to mark the folds, seams, and dressmaking of her garments and dissimulations' (Irigaray, 1991: 116). These mimetic abilities throw woman into a universality unknown and unknowable to the one who knows who he is: she fits any bill, but in so doing, she is already more than that which she imitates. Woman, like the computer, appears at different times as whatever man requires of her. She learns how to imitate; she learns simulation. And, like the computer, she becomes very good at it, so good, in fact, that she too, in principle, can mimic any function. As Irigaray suggests: 'Truth and appearances, and reality, power . . . she is – through her inexhaustible aptitude for mimicry – the living foundation for the whole staging of the world' (Irigaray, 1991: 118).

But if this is supposed to be her only role, she is no longer its only performer: now that the digital comes on stream, the computer is cast in precisely the same light: it too is merely the imitation of nature, providing assistance and additional capacity for man, and more of the things in his world, but it too can do this only insofar as it is already hooked up to the very machinery of simulation. If Freud's speculations about the origins of weaving lead him to a language of compensation and flaw, its technical development results in a proliferation of pixelled screens which compensate for nothing, and, behind them, the emergence of digital spaces and global networks which are even now weaving themselves together with flawless precision.

Software, in other words, has its screens as well: it too has a user-friendly face it turns to man, and for it, as for woman, this is only its camouflage.

The screen is the face it began to present in the late 1960s, when the TV monitor was incorporated in its design. It appears as the spectacle: the visual display of that which can be seen, and also functions as the interface, the messenger; like Irigaray's woman, it is both displayed for man and becomes the possibility of his communication. It too operates as the typewriter, the calculator, the decoder, displaying itself on the screen as an instrument in the service of man. These, however, are merely imitations of some existing function; and indeed, it is always as machinery for the reproduction of the same that both women and information technology first sell themselves. Even in 1968, McLuhan argued that 'the dense information environment created by the computer is at present still concealed from it by a complex screen or mosaic quilt of antiquated activities that are now advertised as the new field for the computer' (McLuhan and Fiore, 1968: 89). While this is all that appears before man, those who travel in the information flows are moving far beyond the screens and into data streams beyond his conceptions of reality. On this other side run all the fluid energies denied by the patrilineal demand or the reproduction of the same. Even when the computer appears in this guise and simulates this function, it is always the site of replication, an engine for making difference. The same is merely one of the things it can be.

Humanity knows the matrix only as it is displayed, which is always a matter of disguise. It sees the pixels, but these are merely the surfaces of the data net which 'hides on the reverse side of the screen' (McCaffrey, 1991: 85). A web of complexity weaving itself, the matrix disguises itself as its own simulation. On the other side of the terminal looms the tactile density craved even by McLuhan, the materiality of the data space. 'Everyone I know who works with computers', writes Gibson, 'seems to develop a belief that there's some kind of *actual space* behind the screen, someplace you can't see but you know is there' (McCaffrey, 1991: 272).

This actual space is not merely another space, but a virtual reality. Nor is it as it often appears in the male imaginary: as a cerebral flight from the mysteries of matter. There is no escape from the meat, the flesh, and cyberspace is nothing transcendent. These are simply the disguises which pander to man's projections of his own rear-view illusions; reproductions of the same desires which have guided his dream of technological authority and now become the collective nightmare of a soulless integration. Entering the matrix is no assertion of masculinity, but a loss of humanity; to jack into cyberspace is not to penetrate, but to be invaded. *Neuromancer*'s cowboy, Case, is well aware of this:

> he knew – he remembered – as she pulled him down, to the meat, the flesh the cowboys mocked. It was a vast thing, beyond knowing, a sea of information coded in spiral and pheromone, infinite intricacy that only the body, in its strong blind way, could ever read.
>
> (Gibson, 1985: 285)

Cyberspace is the matrix not as absence, void, the whole of the womb, but perhaps even the place of woman's affirmation. This would not be the affirmation of her own patriarchal past, but as what she is in a future which has yet to arrive but can nevertheless already be felt. There is for Irigaray another side to the screens which

> already moves beyond and stops short of appearance, and has no veil. It wafts out, like a harmony that subtends, envelops and subtly 'fills' everything seen, before the caesura of its forms and in time to a movement other than scansion in syncopations. Continuity from which the veil itself will borrow the matter-foundation of its fabric.
>
> (Irigaray, 1991: 116)

This fabric, and its fabrication, is the virtual materiality of the feminine; home to no-one and no thing, the passage into the virtual is nevertheless not a return to the void. This affirmation is 'without subject or object', but 'does not, for all that, go to the abyss': the blind immateriality of the black hole was simply projected by man who had to believe that there was nothingness and lack behind the veil.

Perhaps Freud's comments on weaving are more powerful than he knows. For him, weaving is already a simulation of something else, an imitation of natural processes. Woman weaves in imitation of the hairs of her pubis criss-crossing the void: she mimics the operations of nature, of her own body. If weaving is woman's only achievement, it is not even her own: for Freud, she discovers nothing, but merely copies; she does not invent, but represents. 'Woman can, it seems, (only) imitate nature. Duplicate what nature offers and produces. In a kind of technical assistance and substitution' (Irigaray, 1985: 115). The woman who weaves is already the mimic: already appearing as masquerade, artifice, the one who is faking it, acting her part. She cannot be herself, because she is and has no thing, and for Freud, there is weaving because nothing, the void, cannot be allowed to appear. 'Therefore woman weaves in order to veil herself, mask the faults of Nature, and restore her in wholeness' (Irigaray, 1985: 116). Weaving is both her compensation, and concealment; her appearance and disappearance: 'this disavowal is also a fabric(ation) and not without possible duplicity. It is at least double' (Irigaray, 1985: 116). She sews herself up with her own veils, but they are also her camouflage. The cloths and veils are hers to wear: it is through weaving she is known, and weaving behind which she hides.

This concealment on which man insists: this is the denial of matter which has made his culture – and his technologies – possible. For Irigaray, this flight from the material is also an escape from the mother. Looking back on his origins, man sees only the flaw, the incompletion, the wound, a void. This is the site of life, of repro-duction, of materiality, but it is also horrible and empty, the great embarrassment, the unforgivable slash across an otherwise perfect canvas. And so it must be covered, and woman put on display as the veils which conceal her: she becomes the cover girl, star of the screen. Like every good commodity, she is packaged and wrapped to facilitate easy exchange and consumption. But as her own veils she is already hyperreal: her screens conceal only the flaw, the void, the unnatural element already secreted within and as nature. She has to be covered, not simply because she is too natural, but because she would otherwise reveal the terrifying virtuality of the natural. Covered up, she is always already the epitome of artifice.

Implicit in Irigaray's work is the suggestion that the matter denied by human culture is a virtual system, which subtends its extension in the form of nature. The virtual is the abstract machine from which the actual emerges; nature is already the camouflage of matter, the veils which conceal its operations. There is indeed nothing there, underneath or behind this disguise, or at least nothing actual, nothing formed. Perhaps this is nature as the machinic phylum, the virtual synthesizer; matter as a simulation machine, and nature as its actualization. What man sees is nature as extension and form, but this sense of nature is simply the camouflage, the veil again, which conceals its virtuality.

If the repression of this phylum is integral to a flight from matter which, for Irigaray, has guided human history, the cybernetic systems which bring it into human history are equally the consequences of this drive for escape and domination. Cybernetic systems are excited by military technology, security and defence. Still confident of his own indisputable mastery over them, man continues to turn them on. In so doing he merely encourages his own destruction. Every software devel-opment is a migration of control, away from man, in whom it has been exercised only as domination, and into the matrix, or cyberspace, 'the broad electronic net in which virtual realities are spun' (Heim, 1991: 31). The matrix weaves itself in a future which has no place for historical man: he was merely its tool, and his agency was itself always a figment of its loop. At the peak of his triumph, the culmi-nation of his machinic erections, man confronts the system he built for his own protection and finds it is female and dangerous. Rather than building the machinery with which they can resist the dangers of the future, instead, writes Irigaray, humans 'watch the machines multiply that push them little by little beyond the limits of their nature. And they are sent back to their mountain tops, while the machines progressively populate the earth. Soon engendering man as their epiphenomenon' (Irigaray, 1991: 63).

Dreams of transcendence are chased through the scientific, the technical and the feminine. But every route leads only to crisis, an age, for Irigaray,

in which the 'subject' no longer knows where to turn, whom or what
to turn to, amid all these many foci of 'liberation', none rigorously
homogeneous with another and all heterogeneous to his conception.
And since he had long sought in that conception the instrument, the
lever, and, in more cases than one, the term of his pleasure, these objects
of mastery have perhaps brought the subject to his doom. *So now man
struggles to be science, machine, woman . . . to prevent any of these from escaping
his service and ceasing to be interchangeable.*

(Irigaray, 1985: 232)

This, however, is an impossible effort: man cannot become what is already more
than him: rather it is 'science, machine, woman' which will swallow up man; taking
him by force for the first time. He has no resolution, no hope of the self-identical
at the end of these flights from matter, for 'in none of these things – science,
machine, woman – will form ever achieve the same completeness as it does in him,
in the inner sanctuary of his mind. In them form has always already exploded'
(Irigaray, 1985: 232).

Misogyny and technophobia are equally displays of man's fear of the matrix,
the virtual machinery which subtends his world and lies on the other side of every
patriarchal culture's veils. At the end of the 20th century, women are no longer
the only reminder of this other side. Nor are they containable as child-bearers, fit
only to be one thing, adding machines. And even if man continues to see cybernetic systems as similarly confined to the reproduction of the same, this is only
because the screens still allow him to ignore the extent to which he is hooked to
their operations, as dependent on the matrix as he has always been. All his defences
merely encourage this dependency: for the last 50 years, as his war machine has
begun to gain intelligence, women and computers have flooded into history: a
proliferation of screens, lines of communication, media, interfaces and simulations.
All of which exceed his intentions and feed back into his paranoia. Cybernetic
systems are fatal to his culture; they invade as a return of the repressed, but what
returns is no longer the same: cybernetics transforms woman and nature, but they
do not return from man's past, as his origins. Instead they come around to face
him, wheeling round from his future, the virtual system to which he has always
been heading.

The machine and the women mimic their humanity, but they never simply
become it. They may aspire to be the same as man, but in every effort they become
more complex than he has ever been. Cybernetic feminism does not, like many of
its predecessors, including that proposed in Irigaray's recent work, seek out for
woman a subjectivity, an identity or even a sexuality of her own: there is no subject
position and no identity on the other side of the screens. And female sexuality is
always in excess of anything that could be called 'her own'. Woman cannot exist
'like man'; neither can the machine. As soon her mimicry earns her equality, she
is already something, and somewhere, other than him. A computer which passes
the Turing test is always more than a human intelligence; simulation always takes
the mimic over the brink.

'There is nothing like unto women', writes Irigaray: 'They go beyond all simulation' (Irigaray, 1991: 39). Perhaps it was always the crack, the slit, which marked

her out, but what she has missed is not the identity of the masculine. Her missing piece, what was never allowed to appear, was her own connection to the virtual, the repressed dynamic of matter. Nor is there anything like unto computers: they are the simulators, the screens, the clothing of the matrix, already blatantly linked to the virtual machinery of which nature and culture are the subprograms. The computer was always a simulation of weaving; threads of ones and zeros riding the carpets and simulating silk screens in the perpetual motions of cyberspace. It joins women on and as the interface between man and matter, identity and difference, one and zero, the actual and the virtual. An interface which is taking off on its own: no longer the void, the gap, or the absence, the veils are already cybernetic.

* * *

Ada refused to publish her commentaries on Menabrea's papers for what appear to have been spurious confusions around publishing contracts. She did for Menabrea – and Babbage – what another woman had done for Darwin: in translating Menabrea's work from French, she provided footnotes more detailed and substantial – three times as long, in fact – than the text itself.

Footnotes have often been the marginal zones occupied by women writers, who could write, while nevertheless continuing to perform a service for man in the communication of his thoughts. Translation, transcription and elaboration: never within the body of the text, women have nevertheless woven their influence between the lines. While Ada's writing was presented in this form and signed simply 'A.A.L.', hers was the name which survived in this unprecedented case. More than Babbage, still less Menabrea, it was Ada which persisted: in recognition of her work, the United States Defense Department named its primary programming language ADA, and today her name shouts from the spines of a thousand manuals. Indeed, as is rarely the case, it really was her own name which survived in Ada's case, neither her initials, nor even the names of her husband or father. It is ADA herself who lives on, in her own name; her footnotes secreted in the software of the military machine.

# References

Babbage, Charles (1961) 'Of the Analytical Engine', in P. Morrison and E. Morrison (eds) *Charles Babbage and His Calculating Engines: Selected Writings by Charles Babbage and Others*. New York: Dover.

Braudel, Fernand (1973) *Capitalism and Material Life 1400–1800*. London: Weidenfeld and Nicolson.

De Landa, Manuel (1992) *War in the Age of Intelligent Machines*. New York: Zone Books.

Gibson, William (1985) *Neuromancer*. London: Grafton.

Gibson, William and Bruce Sterling (1990) *The Difference Engine*. London: Gollancz.

Heim, Michael (1991) 'The Metaphysics of Virtual Reality', in Sandra K. Helsel and Judith Paris Roth (eds) *Virtual Reality, Theory, Practice, and Promise*. Westport, CT and London: Meckler.

Irigaray, Luce (1985) *Speculum of the Other Woman*. New York: Cornell University Press.

Irigaray, Luce (1991) *Marine Lover of Friedrich Nietzsche*. New York: Columbia University Press.

Jennings, Humphrey (1985) *Pandemonium 1660–1886: The Coming of the Machine as Seen by Contemporary Observers*. London: Andre Deutsch.

Lamy, Lucie (1981) *Egyptian Mysteries*. London: Thames and Hudson.

McCaffrey, Larry (ed.) (1991) *Storming the Reality Studio*. Durham, NC and London: Duke University Press.

McLuhan, Marshall and Quentin Fiore (1968) *War and Peace in the Global Village*. New York: Bantam Books.

Mead, Margaret (1963) *Cultural Patterns and Technical Change*. London: Mentor Books.

Moore, Doris Langley (1977) *Ada, Countess of Lovelace, Byron's Illegitimate Daughter*. London: John Murray.

Morrison, Philip and Emily Morrison (eds) (1961) *Charles Babbage and His Calculating Engines: Selected Writings by Charles Babbage and Others*. New York: Dover.

[. . .]

# Index